As he died to make men holy,
Let us die to make men free.

JULIA WARD HOWE

A FREE CHURCH, A HOLY NATION

*Abraham Kuyper's
American Public Theology*

John Bolt

WILLIAM B. EERDMANS PUBLISHING COMPANY
GRAND RAPIDS, MICHIGAN / CAMBRIDGE, U.K.

© 2001 Wm. B. Eerdmans Publishing Co.
255 Jefferson Ave. S.E., Grand Rapids, Michigan 49503 /
P.O. Box 163, Cambridge CB3 9PU U.K.

Printed in the United States of America

06 05 04 03 02 01   7 6 5 4 3 2 1

Library of Congress Cataloging-in-Publication Data

Bolt, John, 1948-
A Free Church, A Holy Nation: Abraham Kuyper's American public theology /
John Bolt.
p.   cm.
Includes bibliographical references and index.

ISBN 0-8028-4254-2 (alk. paper)
1. Christianity and politics — United States. 2. Kuyper, Abraham,
1837-1920.   I. Title.
BR115.P7B656   2001
261.8′092 — dc21

00-063607

www.eerdmans.com

To My "Kuyperian" Teachers

Professor H. Evan Runner

In Memory of
My father, Berend Bolt (1922-99)
Professor Gordon J. Spykman (1926-93)

Contents

PART ONE
COMPARATIVE HISTORICAL STUDIES

CONTENTS

CONCLUSION

APPENDICES

Preface

Abraham Kuyper (1837-1920), the multitalented Dutch neo-Calvinist theologian, church reformer, university founder, journalist, and statesman,
may be more appreciated in North America today than he is in his own beloved
Netherlands. While American evangelical leaders such as Charles Colson increasingly appeal to his life and thought as inspiration for distinctively Christian social, cultural, and political action,[1] the influence of Kuyper's legacy in his
homeland has noticeably diminished.[2] The political party he founded and almost single-handedly brought into being and to power is no more.[3] The church

---

1. Charles Colson with Ellen Santilli Vaughn, *The Body: Being Light in Darkness*
(Dallas: Word, 1992), 103-7, 114, 183, 194-99. For a more general overview of Kuyper's rel-
evance for North American evangelicals, see Mark A. Noll, *The Scandal of the Evangelical
Mind* (Grand Rapids: Eerdmans, 1994), 138, 216, 224.

2. These comments about diminished interest in Kuyper in his native Netherlands
must be interpreted as a broad religious, cultural, social, and political generalization and
not in the sense that there is virtually no interest at all in the man, his ideas, or his accomplishments in the Netherlands. The Free University of Amsterdam, in June 1998, sponsored a successful international conference on Kuyper during the centennial commemoration of his 1898 visit to America (Princeton Seminary in February 1998 and Calvin
Seminary in October 1998 sponsored similar conferences), and a number of its faculty
have contributed significantly to a renaissance in Kuyper scholarship during the last decade. See James Bratt's review article on recent Kuyper literature, "In the Shadow of Mt.
Kuyper: A Survey of the Field," *Calvin Theological Journal* 31 (1996): 51-66; also see nn. 26-
31 below.

3. Kuyper was the driving force behind the establishment of the Antirevolutionary
Party (ARP) in 1879, the first modern political party in the Netherlands. He wrote its plat-

communion (eventually becoming *De Gereformeerde Kerken in Nederland*) he led out of the National Reformed Church *(Nederlandse Hervormde Kerk)* because its Reformed orthodoxy was suspect, now harbors its own arguably heterodox theologians.[4] Furthermore, the Reformed Free University of Amsterdam he founded in 1880, and which served for years internationally as an inspirational model for distinctively Christian higher education, has self-consciously become a pluralistic institution.[5] Finally, his beloved Netherlands, with its international notoriety of moral permissiveness, generated in large measure by the sixties' counterculture, seems to many observers more like a pagan Babylon than the biblically shaped, Geneva-inspired Jerusalem that Kuyper dreamed of, in nostalgia and hope.[6] This book is in part a response to American evangelical interest in Abraham Kuyper, an interest heightened by the 1998 centennial commemoration of Kuyper's own onetime visit to this continent to deliver the Stone Lectures at Princeton Theological Seminary in October 1898.[7]

Abraham Kuyper has been the dominant spiritual-intellectual-theological figure in my life. His role as the inspirational leader of a Dutch neo-Calvinist religious revival a century ago created and indelibly shaped the church family into which I was born and baptized *(Gereformeerde Kerken in Nederland)*. He has also been the shaping influence in the Christian Reformed Church in North America, the church in which I was raised, nurtured in the faith, educated, and serve as a minister, and in whose theological seminary I now have the privilege to teach. My spirituality has unconsciously as well as consciously been formed in a Kuyperian-Calvinist fashion. Kuyper's own definition of the dominating principle of Calvinism sums this up neatly: "*the Sovereignty of the Triune God over the whole Cosmos, in all its spheres and kingdoms, visible and invisible.*"[8] Alternatively, in the mem-

---

form (*Ons Program* [Amsterdam: H. J. Kruyt, 1879]), and served as its chairman until just before his death in 1920. Though the ARP had been a key partner in most of the Dutch governments of the twentieth century, it disbanded in 1980 and joined with other Christian political parties, notably the Roman Catholic one, to form a new party, the Christian Democratic Action.

4. See, e.g., the recent volumes by a prominent *Gereformeerde* theologian, Free University professor emeritus Harry Kuitert, *I Have My Doubts: How to Become a Christian without Becoming a Fundamentalist* (Valley Forge, Pa.: Trinity Press International, 1993); *Jezus: Nalatenschap van het Christendom* (Kampen: Kok, 1998); also C. J. De Heyer, *Jesus Matters: 150 Years of Research* (Valley Forge, Pa.: Trinity Press International, 1997).

5. That change is nicely charted in J. Roelink, *Een Blinkend Spoor 1879-1979* (Kampen: Kok, 1979).

6. See, e.g., James C. Kennedy, *Nieuw Babylon in Aanbouw: Nederland in de Jaren Zestig* (Amsterdam: Boom, 1995).

7. Abraham Kuyper, *Lectures on Calvinism* (Grand Rapids: Eerdmans, 1931).

8. Kuyper, *Lectures on Calvinism*, 79.

orable words of Kuyper's most frequently quoted phrase: "There is not a square inch [lit. 'thumb's breadth'] in the whole domain of our human experience over which Christ, who is Sovereign over *all*, does not cry, 'Mine!'"[9]

Autobiographical self-indulgence, however, is hardly sufficient reason for a book of this size and scope. Though Abraham Kuyper is best known and influential primarily in the ethnic-religious community of the Christian Reformed Church in North America (CRCNA),[10] his example of combining orthodox, evangelical, Calvinistic piety with explicitly religious social and political activism has become an attractive and inspiring model for North American Christians.[11] Roman Catholic theologian of public religion Richard John Neuhaus observes that "today some of the most provocative and rigorous thought about religion and society is being done by those who call themselves Calvinists, especially by those who identify with the Calvinist 'revisionism' of Abraham Kuyper (d. 1920), the Dutch theologian and political leader."[12] Why? Why Kuyper?

9. James D. Bratt, ed., *Abraham Kuyper: A Centennial Reader* (Grand Rapids: Eerdmans, 1998), 488; Dutch: Abraham Kuyper, *Souvereiniteit in Eigen Kring* (Kampen: Kok, 1930), 32. This address was delivered on October 20, 1880, at the opening of the Free University of Amsterdam.

10. For Kuyper's shaping role in the life and thought of the Christian Reformed Church, see James D. Bratt, *Dutch Calvinism in Modern America: A History of a Conservative Subculture* (Grand Rapids: Eerdmans, 1984), esp. chap. 2.

11. A recent volume providing biographical sketches of Christians who were active in politics, as a source of encouragement to contemporary political engagement for American Christians, includes a chapter on Abraham Kuyper along with others on Edward VI of England, Pilgrim leader William Bradford, colonial governor John Winthrop, Bill of Rights author Nathaniel Ward, Declaration of Independence signer and Princeton University president John Witherspoon, Delaware governor Richard Bassett, abolitionist William Wilberforce, and Scotland Yard detective Sir Robert Anderson. Kuyper is the only nonnative English-speaking person on the list, and the volume's author speaks of him and his life of Christian public service as "one of Holland's greatest contributions" to America (147); Robert A. Peterson, *In His Majesty's Service: Christians in Politics* (Lafayette, La.: Huntington House, 1995).

12. Richard John Neuhaus, *The Naked Public Square: Religion and Democracy in America* (Grand Rapids: Eerdmans, 1984), 175. Neuhaus's footnote (p. 271) refers specifically to a significant and frequently cited volume arguing for pluralism in American education, R. McCarthy, D. Opperwal, W. Peterson, and G. Spykman, *Society, State, and Schools: A Case for Structural and Confessional Pluralism* (Grand Rapids: Eerdmans, 1981). Perhaps the foremost North American political analyst working self-consciously from a "Kuyperian" perspective is James W. Skillen, director of the Association for Public Justice and the Center for Public Justice in Washington, D.C. See, for example, his edited volume of Abraham Kuyper, *The Problem of Poverty* (Grand Rapids: Baker, 1991), and *The Scattered Voice: Christians at Odds in the Public Square* (Grand Rapids: Zondervan, 1990). Nicholas Wolterstorff (in the Abraham Kuyper [!] lectures for 1981, delivered at the

As we shall see in chapter 2, moving through the later decades of the twentieth century, American evangelicals have increasingly been marginalized from public life by a dominant liberal-secular mind-set. This has not occurred without some complicity on its own part, as evangelical Christianity in its conflicts with modernism retreated into fundamentalism. Along the way, the public identity and character of America, historically seen by many as "Christian America," was fundamentally altered. The process of change, hidden for many years as the nation continued to live under the influence of Christian America's moral capital, became obvious in the countercultural upheavals of the 1960s. In the 1970s and 1980s, shocked to discover that "their" America had been taken from them, conservative American evangelicals reacted by forming political action groups — moral majorities and Christian coalitions. Politically engaged evangelical Christians, particularly in the so-called "Christian Right," have become a significant force in American political life in the last decades of the twentieth century.[13] The boldness of evangelical activism was not always supported by clearly thought out, principled political strategy. In addition to covering too many issues to do any of them full justice, evangelical activists often failed to set political and strategic priorities in their campaigns. It soon became clear that not only were they out of practice for the political battles and culture wars they entered, they were also — by some of their leaders' own admission — theologically and philosophically ill-equipped for the task.[14]

Kuyper-founded Free University of Amsterdam) links what he refers to as "world-transformative" Kuyperian Christianity with the concerns and objectives of liberation theology in his *Until Justice and Peace Embrace* (Grand Rapids: Eerdmans, 1983). Wolterstorff's book is considered in some detail in chap. 6 below, 272-75. What exactly is meant by *neo*-Calvinism is considered in some detail in app. A.

13. Beginning with Baptist pastor Jerry Falwell's Moral Majority movement in the late 1970s through Pat Robertson's run for the Republican Party presidential nomination in 1988 to the formation and political activism of Robertson's Christian Coalition movement in the 1990s.

14. According to Michael Horton, "Modern evangelicals simply do not share with their Puritan forebears a love of learning and of this world and its culture. . . ." For this reason, he judges, it is *dangerous* for American evangelicals to enter the culture wars, "dangerous in the sense that we are unprepared for it" (*Beyond Culture Wars* [Chicago: Moody, 1994], 26-27). In a foreword to Horton's book, Drew University theologian Thomas Oden agrees: Horton "is correct that evangelicals (with few exceptions) are theologically ill-equipped to battle intelligently and constructively to penetrate postmodern culture" (10). Former Christian Coalition director Ralph Reed agreed when he spoke of "the retreat of evangelicals from social and political action" in the twentieth century, with the result that "we have now had two full generations of Bible-believing Christians . . . with virtually no hands-on experience in the political decision-making process" (Ralph Reed, *Politically Incorrect: The Emerging Faith Factor in American Politics* [Dallas: Word, 1994], 3). For an

In that context Abraham Kuyper becomes an attractive model, first of all because his own political activism was directed to cultural and political emancipation for orthodox Calvinists who had been marginalized from public life by the dominant liberal secularism of the late nineteenth-century Netherlands.[15] It is precisely such emancipation that Jerry Falwell, Pat Robertson, and D. James Kennedy plead for American evangelicals one hundred years later. In addition, Kuyper's journalism and his work in establishing the new Free University of Amsterdam, along with his thoughtful sociocultural critique of liberalism, point to essential and as yet unfinished work for American evangelical public theology.

There is another reason why Kuyper may be useful to the current discussion in American evangelical circles. It has proven to be difficult for active participants in current American evangelical debates about Christianity and politics to rise above their own partisanship.[16] Taking a sympathetic figure from the past, and a European at that, at least affords an opportunity for a fresh look at critical issues at some distance from the heat of the present debate. In addition, Kuyper, like Alexis de Tocqueville before him, not only visited America (in 1898)[17] but was knowledgeable about and profoundly appreciative of the American political experiment in ordered liberty. There is thus a natural affinity — rooted in common love for the ideal of America, particularly its promise of liberty — between Kuyper and many of today's politically involved American evangelicals.

---

evangelical historian's passionate exploration of the thesis that American evangelicals lack a public theology equal to their political concern, see Noll, 149-76.

15. The only American orthodox Christian intellectual and culture critic of comparable stature to Kuyper in the last one hundred years who could potentially also be considered a model for contemporary evangelicals is another Calvinist, J. Gresham Machen, of Princeton Seminary and Westminster Seminary. See the superb biography on Machen by Darryl Hart, *Defending the Faith: J. Gresham Machen and the Crisis of Conservative Protestantism in Modern America* (Baltimore: Johns Hopkins University Press, 1994). On Machen as a North American Kuyper, see George Harinck, "Give Us an American Abraham Kuyper: Dutch Calvinist Reformed Responses to the Founding of the Westminster Theological Seminary in Philadelphia," *Calvin Theological Journal* 33 (1998): 299-319.

16. Efforts to find a "third way" beyond the characteristic polarities of "right" and "left" often seem little more than disguised partisan pronouncements masquerading as alternatives to themselves; see discussion on "culture wars" in chap. 8 below, 384-87.

17. See C. A. Admiraal, "De Amerikaanse Reis van Abraham Kuyper," in *Historicus in het Spanningveld van Theorie en Praktijk*, ed. C. A. Admiraal, P. B. M. Blaas, and J. Van der Zande (Leiderdorp: Leidse Onderwijsinstellingen, 1985), 111-66; Dirk Jellema, "Kuyper's Visit to America in 1898," *Michigan History* 42 (1958): 227-36; J. Stellingwerf, *Abraham Kuyper en de Vrije Universiteit* (Kampen: Kok, 1987), 227-52.

Kuyper's rich and subtle thought is not easy to categorize and is thus appealed to by people of diverse political persuasion. Some draw from his emphasis on the *kleine luyden* (small folk) and his stated passion for the poor[18] to generate sympathy for a mild version of Christian socialism or a proto-liberation theology.[19] At the same time, George Grant claims that Kuyper is one of a number of Christians in political life to have "had a profound effect upon the thinking of — Pat Buchanan."[20] Taking a closer look at Kuyper may help discussants in contemporary debates who differ profoundly from each other to at least attempt a second look, to give the opposition an honest consideration. This has the potential of contributing particularly to efforts at overcoming the polarization referred to in the previous paragraph. Finally, all the issues that emerge out of the discussions about evangelical public theology today — theocracy, pluralism, freedom, the critical role of mediating structures and voluntary associations, culture wars, poverty and welfare, the role of the state, coalitions with cobelligerent groups, particularly Roman Catholics — surfaced in Kuyper's own career, and his wrestling with them can be instructive for the present. Above all, as we noted, his context bears an uncanny resemblance to the America of the 1990s: a dominant, liberal-secular elite facing an aroused populist band of highly committed conservative and evangelical *kleine luyden*.

This is not exactly the book I originally had in mind when in 1995 I proposed a research project to the Pew Evangelical Scholars Program to explore the relevance of Kuyper's life and thought for contemporary North American evangelical public theology.[21] With the rise of politically engaged, conservative, evan-

18. Abraham Kuyper, *The Problem of Poverty*, trans. and ed. James W. Skillen (Grand Rapids: Baker, 1991). This address was given to the First Christian Social Congress in the Netherlands, November 9, 1891.

19. Dirk Jellema's translation of Kuyper's *Het Sociale Vraagstuk en de Christelijke Religie* bears the revealing title, *Christianity and the Class Struggle* (Grand Rapids: Piet Hein, 1950). The introduction by John Gritter clearly tilts leftward politically, and claims a definite class-struggle perspective as "in essence also the social philosophy of us Calvinists in America." Nicholas Wolterstorff's 1981 Abraham Kuyper Lectures at the Free University, *Until Justice and Peace Embrace*, include a fascinating comparison between Latin American liberation theology and the neo-Calvinist tradition (chap. 3, "Lima or Amsterdam: Liberation or Disclosure"). For the tensions in Kuyper's understanding and appropriation of the American political tradition that could lead to opposing appropriations of Kuyper's thought, see James D. Bratt, "Abraham Kuyper, American History, and the Tensions of Neo-Calvinism," in *Sharing the Reformed Tradition: The Dutch–North American Exchange, 1846-1996*, ed. George Harinck and Hans Krabbendam (Amsterdam: VU Uitgeverij, 1996), 97-114.

20. George Grant, *Buchanan: Caught in the Crossfire* (Nashville: Nelson, 1996), 122-28.

21. I am deliberately using the term "public theology" rather than the oft-used "political theology" for both negative and positive reasons. Negatively, the latter term is too

gelical Christians as a significant force in American public life since the 1970s, and with the centennial of Kuyper's American visit to deliver the influential Stone Lectures on Calvinism only a few years away, the time seemed propitious for a monograph on Kuyper's public theology, written with contemporary evangelical concerns in mind. As I originally conceived it, the book would be a relatively straightforward, systematic discussion of six or seven key issues facing evangelicals who desired an engagement with contemporary North American political life. I intended to draw heavily from Kuyper's own political career, including his speeches in the Dutch Parliament and his actual legislative accomplishments as well as his journalistic and other written work.[22] The goal was to produce a book on Kuyper that had the potential to serve as a theologically informed practical manual for North American evangelicals involved in politics.

This is not quite how the volume turned out — and not only because the project took eighteen months longer to complete than I had projected. In retrospect I now realize that one of my fundamental premises was off target. On the basis of earlier work, I assumed that the basic interpretation of Kuyper and his sociopolitical vision would be for me relatively straightforward. After all, I was quite familiar with the fundamental Kuyperian themes — antithesis, sphere sovereignty, common grace.[23] I thought that following

---

closely identified with various forms of Marxist theory and, politically, with advocacy of democratic socialism. Political theology is rooted in a universalist kind of ecclesiology where "the church together with other progressive movements becomes the subject of God's transforming work in history" (Arne Rasmussen, *The Church as Polis: From Political Theology to Theological Politics as Exemplified by Jürgen Moltmann and Stanley Hauerwas* [Notre Dame, Ind.: University of Notre Dame Press, 1995], 13). Positively, "public theology" is also more in keeping with the venerable tradition of American "public philosophy," exemplified by Walter Lippman, *The Public Philosophy* (New York: Little, Brown, 1955). My thanks to Princeton Theological Seminary professor Max Stackhouse for this caution and helpful advice about terminology for this study.

22. Making use, therefore, not only of Kuyper's more popular theological works such as *Pro Rege*, 3 vols. (Kampen: Kok, 1911-12), and *Gemeene Gratie*, 3 vols. (Leiden: Donner, 1902); his political platform detailed in *Ons Program* and *Antirevolutionaire Staatkunde*, 2 vols. (Kampen: Kok, 1931); but also Kuyper's political speeches (such as the gathered annual addresses Kuyper gave to the deputies of the *Antirevolutionaire Party* in his capacity as its leader, *Geen Vergeefs Woord: Verzamelde Deputaten-Redevoeringen* [Kampen: Kok, 1951]); and, finally, the massive parliamentary record of Kuyper's lengthy political career in the four volumes of *Parlementaire Redevoeringen* (Amsterdam: Van Holkema & Warendorf, n.d.).

23. The basic outlines of Kuyperian neo-Calvinist social theology are sketched in my Ph.D. dissertation; see John Bolt, "The Imitation of Christ Theme in the Cultural-Ethical Ideal of Herman Bavinck" (Ph.D. diss., University of St. Michael's College, Toronto, 1982), esp. 128-61.

a brief summary of these key ideas, my major task would be a careful review of Kuyper's political praxis in its historical context and framework.[24] As it turned out, however, this latter dimension — Kuyper's political practice — has been underdone in the present work. Instead, this volume has turned out to be a new *interpretation* of Kuyper's public theology, an interpretation that can serve as a basis for the further detailed explication that still begs to be done. As chapters 3 through 5 demonstrate, I became captivated by the intriguing historical comparisons between Kuyper and other key thinkers about America and public theology (Alexis de Tocqueville, Lord John Acton, Jonathan Edwards, Walter Rauschenbusch, and Pope Leo XIII). In addition, as I reviewed Kuyper's own accomplishments, my attention was turned primarily to reframing them on a grander scale by considering him as a movement leader, a "poet" who effectively utilized a "Christian-historical imagination."

As I worked with the large corpus of Kuyper's written work and interacted with the significant body of recent scholarship on him,[25] I became convinced that it was illuminating to see his work in church and nation from a rhetorical and mythopoetic perspective, turning attention away from seeing him *solely* through the more customary lens of philosophical and theological *ideas*. It became necessary then to venture into new areas of broad historical and rhetorical reflection. I was further encouraged to go in this new interpretive direction by the appearance in 1998 of Peter Heslam's helpful, detailed study of Kuyper's *Lectures on Calvinism*.[26] Some of the descriptive work on Kuyper's life and thought that I had originally thought needed to be done for a North American, English-speaking public had been superbly done by Heslam, and I commend his book as an essential companion volume to this one, along with the superbly translated and edited collection of Kuyper essays edited by James Bratt and published during the same year.[27] Papers delivered at the several 1998 Kuyper conferences (Princeton, Amsterdam, Grand Rapids) by James Bratt and Mark Noll that highlighted the horizontal-historical examination of Kuyper especially encouraged me to do the same.

At this point I must also indicate my profound indebtedness to the superb recent historical scholarship on Abraham Kuyper, without which I could never have written this book. In addition to the works of Heslam and Bratt just

24. See n. 22 above.

25. See nn. 26-31 below. Further bibliographic material on Kuyper is given in chap. 1, nn. 8-16.

26. Peter Somers Heslam, *Creating a Christian Worldview: Abraham Kuyper's Lectures on Calvinism* (Grand Rapids: Eerdmans, 1998).

27. Bratt, *Abraham Kuyper.*

mentioned, the following are indispensable and invaluable resources for study-ing Kuyper, his context and his impact: The biography of the early Kuyper by Dr. G. Puchinger;[28] J. Stellingwerf's examination of Kuyper's relation to the Free University of Amsterdam;[29] an entire series of volumes on nineteenth- and twentieth-century Dutch Protestantism published under the auspices of the Historical Documentation Center for Dutch Protestantism (1800-present) at the Free University of Amsterdam, directed by Jan De Bruijn;[30] as well as several important collections of essays from an international group of Kuyper scholars collected by faculty members of the Free University.[31] As the ample footnotes in this volume bear witness, I have also relied heavily on additional secondary scholarship as I ventured into areas outside my own professional, scholarly training, such as literary and rhetorical criticism and American history, includ-ing American art history.

It also became clear to me in the course of this project that it is impossible to treat Kuyper's key ideas and themes in isolation from each other. Thus, in the three "systematic" chapters of this volume focusing on liberty (6), pluralism (7), and culture wars (8), the same cluster of themes gets woven and rewoven back and forth throughout the discussion: the Lordship of Christ, liberty and the need for emancipation, Calvinism, the tyranny of the state, the conflict be-tween the *civitas Dei* and the *civitas mundi* (or *civitas diaboli*), providence and history, boundaries and the blurring of boundaries, and especially the matter of what sort of *language* or *rhetoric* Christians use in the public square. In the course of the book, as I wrestled with understanding and applying to contem-porary life Kuyper's passionate rhetoric and journalistic as well as political strategy, it seems to me that my own writing becomes less descriptively "objec-tive" and perhaps somewhat more engaged. I doubt that this can be avoided in a book that seeks to be true to Abraham Kuyper. Kuyper cannot be presented dis-passionately; his spirit forbids it! Above all else, there is one theme that cannot be stressed too strongly in Kuyper's case: the absolute *imperative* of Christian

28. G. Puchinger, *De Jonge Kuyper (1837-1867)* (Franeker: T. Wever, 1987).

29. Stellingwerf, *Dr. Abraham Kuyper en de Vrije Universiteit.*

30. J. De Bruijn, ed., *Een Land Nog Niet in Kaart Gebracht: Aspecten van het Protes-tants-Christelijk Leven in Nederland in de Jaren 1880-1940* (1987); J. De Bruijn, *Abraham Kuyper — Leven en Werk in Beeld* (Amsterdam: Passage, 1987); J. De Bruijn and G. Abma, eds., *Hoedemaker Herdacht* (1989); J. De Bruijn, ed., *Bepaald Gebied: Aspecten van het Prot-estants-Christelijke Leven in Nederland in de Jaren 1888-1940* (1989).

31. C. Augustijn et al., eds., *Abraham Kuyper: Zijn Volksdeel, Zijn Invloed* (Delft: Meinema, 1987); Harinck and Krabbendam, *Sharing the Reformed Tradition;* C. Augustijn and J. Vree, eds., *Abraham Kuyper: Vast en Veranderlijk — De Ontwikkeling van zijn Denken* (Zoetermeer: Meinema, 1998).

cultural and political engagement. Christ is King! Christians must live *pro rege* also and especially in the *civitas mundi,* also when they write academic tomes on public theology. It is also my profound conviction that passionate engagement can and must be combined with civility; for *free* citizens who prize their liberty and the liberty of those with whom they disagree, opposition in the public square is overcome by *persuasion* and not by coercion. I do indicate my own disagreements at points but have sought diligently throughout to be both fair and civil in disagreement. If at any point I have failed on that score, I ask the reader's forgiveness. With Kuyper I believe that genuine freedom is indissolubly one. Abraham Lincoln was right: "Those who deny freedom to others deserve it not for themselves." The very same is true for civility in public discourse, especially discourse about the character of our public conversation.

This volume is divided into three parts: an introductory section; a horizontal-historical, comparative examination of Kuyper with others; and finally a more analytic, systematic section focusing on the key ideas or themes in Kuyper's public theology. The volume concludes with an extended homily encouraging further reflection and scholarly work on Kuyper as well as Christian sociopolitical action consistent with his vision and true to his memory. The first of the two chapters in the opening section introduces Kuyper as well as the framing categories I will be using in this volume to interpret him, notably, a national mythopoetic Christian-historical imagination. The second introductory chapter sketches the historical and sociocultural context within which contemporary American evangelicals today find themselves drawn to political activism. The underlying concern is to show how Kuyper's thought and practice are particularly appropriate for a contemporary American evangelical public theology.

I need to insert a few parenthetical observations here about the apparently strict American focus of the book's title as well as that of the second chapter. To begin with, my Canadian compatriots would insist that Kuyper's influence has been every bit as significant, especially for Reformed Christians, north of the forty-ninth parallel as below it, and they would be perfectly right. However, that correction does not go nearly far enough. Abraham Kuyper is seriously studied in Africa, Asia, and eastern Europe, and not just in Amsterdam or Grand Rapids, Michigan. There are "Abraham Kuyper Institutes" in Korea, Great Britain, and South Africa, as well as one in the state of Tennessee. Why then a book on Kuyper's public theology that refers to it as an "American" public theology?

Let me intensify the urgency of the question before attempting an answer. In the spring of 1997 Rev. Dr. Kwame Bediako, founder-director of the Akrofi-Kristaller Memorial Center for Mission Research and Applied Theology,

Akropong-Akuapem, Ghana, visited Grand Rapids and spoke to several groups on the Calvin College and Seminary campus and elsewhere. At one such luncheon gathering in the denominational headquarters of the CRCNA, after listening to him describe the chaotic political condition of West Africa and after having just watched two evenings full of a PBS documentary film on Thomas Jefferson, I asked Prof. Bediako if West Africa was not badly in need of its own Thomas Jefferson. He smiled and in his quiet manner responded, "What Africa needs even more today is its own Abraham Kuyper." I was stunned, delighted, and mildly embarrassed as the room broke out in applause. Unlike many others in the room, he did not know that his questioner was in the midst of a sabbatical year, writing a volume on Kuyper's public theology! As I continue to use the word "American" in the book's subtitle as well as the title for the second chapter, I am uncomfortably aware that this has the potential for parochial misunderstanding. I originally had the words "and elsewhere" within parenthesis for the title of chapter 2, and even experimented with adding "and others" to the book's subtitle. Aesthetic and other considerations led me, however, to remove them from the final draft. I judged that "Abraham Kuyper's Poetic Public Theology for Americans (and Others)" and "The Need for an Evangelical Public Theology in America (and Elsewhere)" were, in addition to being cumbersome and ugly, also a misrepresentation of content and could even be taken as a form of imperial hubris and slight. So, though I am not fully satisfied with the outcome, this explanation will have to suffice. I am keenly aware that Kuyper is known, loved, studied, and applied in places other than the United States of America (and Canada), and I trust that some of the ideas, structural analysis, and rhetorical strategies will also be helpful to Christians seeking to be politically obedient to their Lord in other countries.

Finally, however, always keeping in mind the preceding qualifications, I judge that it is fitting to speak of Kuyper's "American" public theology. Kuyper believed deeply in the key role that the American experiment in ordered liberty played in the divine providential unfolding of human liberty. My extended work on this volume has led me to concur with much of that vision, as have the significant geopolitical events of the last two decades — among other things, the fall of the Berlin Wall, Tiananmen Square, and the birth of freedom in eastern Europe and South Africa. At the close of the second millennium, it seems to me beyond debate that as goes the path of *American* liberty, so goes the path of world freedom. My opening narrative in the first chapter, an attempt to provide a contemporary context for Kuyper's public theology, will provide more ample justification for that conclusion than I am able to provide here. It is that conviction, however, a conviction I have come to share with Kuyper, that accounts for the more engaged character of the latter chapters in this volume. What I believe is at stake in the effort to find a legitimate place for an evangelical Christian voice in the American public square is not a trivial matter: it is the very future of American liberty — "whether a nation so conceived and so dedicated can long endure," and even, to once again cite Abraham Lincoln, whether it can so endure as "the last, best hope of mankind."

This book has taken longer to complete than I envisioned. There were numerous times when I wondered whether my reach had exceeded my grasp. I am aware how deeply indebted I am to many others without whom I could never have finished the project. My first word of thanks must go to the Pew Charitable Trusts for awarding me an Evangelical Scholars Program fellowship in 1996-97 that made possible a full sabbatical leave of one year. The administration and Board of Trustees of Calvin Theological Seminary (CTS) facilitated my sabbatical at a difficult juncture in the school's history in terms of faculty staffing, a supportive flexibility for which I am truly grateful. My colleagues at the seminary, especially in the Theological Division, read significant portions of the manuscript and, as usual, offered thoughtful critique and advice. Above all, the administration, faculty, and staff of Calvin Seminary routinely and graciously provide an atmosphere of pleasant working conditions, greater than which can hardly be conceived.

The following have provided encouragement for the project, conversed with me about Abraham Kuyper, read parts of the manuscript and responded with helpful comments, assisted me in translating from Dutch compact poetic or complex legal lines, helped find obscure references, reined in my enthusiasms, prodded me to expand (or, in appropriate cases, contract) my horizons, stimulated my thinking through provocative questions and suggestions, stayed friends, or just kindly put up with an occasionally preoccupied and cranky author of a lengthy work-in-progress. I must also include here the names of staff members at the Hekman Library of Calvin College and Seminary for their professional, courteous, and always kind helpfulness, even under pressure. So, at the risk of inadvertently missing someone, a special THANK YOU to: my family, especially Ruth, Martin Bakker, Randy Blacketer, Clarence Bolt, Harry Boonstra, Carl Bosma, James Bratt, Conrad Bult, Sarah Coakley, John Cooper, James De Jong, Henry De Moor, Richard Eppinga, Edward Ericson, Jr., Ronald Feenstra, Paul Fields, Roger Greenway, Marilyn Grevengoed, George Harinck, Peter Heslam, Paul Kemeny, James Kennedy, David Koyzis, Rev. Tjitze Kuipers, Arie Leder, Walter Lagerwey, Luis Lugo, Marvin Monsma, Richard Mouw, Richard Muller, Mark Noll, Cornelius Plantinga, Jr., James Schaap, Douglas Schuurman, Max Stackhouse, William Stevenson, Kathleen Struck, Henrietta Ten Harmsel, Ann Vander Bijl, Harry Van Dyke, Calvin Van Reken, John Witte, Jr., Nicholas Wolterstorff, and Henry Zwaanstra. CTS doctoral student Stephen

Grabill has been my faculty assistant during the last year of this project. In addition to cheerful, prompt, and competent help in the many tasks he was asked to do, lightening my load considerably, he carefully proofread the final draft, made numerous constructive suggestions, and has been a stimulating conversation partner, earning my sincere gratitude and respect. My thanks also to the committed group of CTS students who took my seminar, Systematic Theology 475: "The Theology of Dutch Neo-Calvinism," in the winter quarter, 1998-99, and whose interest and insight provided the encouragement and energy I needed to complete the last pages of this volume.

Parts of this manuscript also received public scrutiny when presented at seminars and conferences. Prof. Kees Vander Kooi of the Free University Theology Department repeatedly sent me invitations to come and lecture on Abraham Kuyper, and I was able finally to present parts of chapters 1, 2, and 4 to the theology faculty and students in November 1997. My wife and I will not forget our first visit to the Netherlands, and herewith our thanks to Prof. Vander Kooi for the hospitality extended to us. My thanks also to Dr. George Harinck of the Historical Documentation Center for Dutch Protestantism (1800-present)at the Free University for his helpfulness in obtaining archival material on Kuyper during that same visit, and for the ongoing friendship born out of that encounter. My thanks here as well to the faculty and students of the Free University for a stimulating time of conversation about Abraham Kuyper during this memorable visit.

In 1998, the centenary year of Kuyper's visit to Princeton Theological Seminary and his Stone Lectures on Calvinism, I was privileged to attend and present papers at three commemorative conferences, at Princeton Theological Seminary in February, at the Free University of Amsterdam in June, and on the Calvin College and Seminary campus in October. Herewith my thanks to the several organizers and sponsors of the three conferences that together helped generate significant interest in Kuyper scholarship and provide a fitting memorial/testimony to Kuyper's legacy. An abridged version of chapter 5 was presented at the Princeton conference, an abridged version of chapter 2 in Amsterdam, and part of chapter 7 at the Grand Rapids conference. In addition, the core of chapter 4 was presented as an address, "Perhaps, Why Not in America? Jonathan Edwards and Abraham Kuyper and the Millennial Promise of the New World," on November 12, 1998, at Calvin College, cosponsored by the H. Henry Meeter Center for Calvin Studies and the Paul B. Henry Institute for the Study of Christianity and Politics. My thanks to all who conversed with me at the time of these particular events and later about the material I presented, and also to the other conference participants whose presentations inspired and stimulated my work.

Last, but far from least, is a word of thanks to Jon Pott, Editor in Chief at William B. Eerdmans Publishing Company, who believed in this project before I even started, provided much-needed encouragement along the way, and patiently endured my several failures to meet projected deadlines. For the most part I was able to heed his wise counsel to remember that "a good book is never finished, but has to get done." I know very well how much is still unfinished in this study of Abraham Kuyper, but it is finally done!

I am dedicating this volume to three people who have been significant "Kuyperian" influences in my life. Professors H. Evan Runner and Gordon Spykman, each in their own distinct way, were the two great neo-Calvinist formative influences for an entire generation of post–World War II students at Calvin College, and I count it a privilege to have been taught by them. Their enthusiastic proclamation of the neo-Calvinist message continues to have a profound influence on me and many others. To the degree that Abraham Kuyper "lives" at Calvin College and Seminary, their committed, passionate, and above all *persistent* teaching deserves a significant amount of credit.

My father was not an academic but someone who had absorbed Abraham Kuyper's vision of Christian education in every fiber of his being, did pioneer work in starting a new Christian school, and was dedicated to seeing that his children had the educational opportunities he and my mother did not. I miss him, his love, and his encouragement deeply, and my greatest regret about the tardiness of this book is that he did not get to see it in print.

Grand Rapids, Michigan
Ascension Day, *Anno Domini* 1999

JOHN BOLT
Calvin Theological Seminary

List of Figures

INTRODUCTION

CHAPTER ONE

"Let My People Go":
Abraham Kuyper's Christian-Historical
Political Imagination

Poets are the unacknowledged legislators of the world.

Percy Bysshe Shelley

To me there is no past or future in art. If a work of art cannot live always in the present it must not be considered at all.

Pablo Picasso

Time present and time past
And both perhaps present in time future
And time future contained in time past.

If all time is eternally present
All time is unredeemable.

T. S. Eliot, "Burnt Norton"

What we call the beginning is often the end
And to make an end is to make a beginning.
The end is where we start from.

A people without history
Is not redeemed from time, for history is a pattern
Of timeless moments.

T. S. Eliot, "Little Gidding"

The first function of the founders of nations, after the founding itself,
is to devise a set of true falsehoods about origins — a mythology —
that will make it desirable for nationals to continue to live under com-
mon authority, and, indeed, make it impossible for them to entertain
contrary thoughts.

Forrest McDonald

For Abraham Kuyper, the great enemy of the Christian faith in the world of the late nineteenth century was modernism, the powerful, world-shaping vision of human autonomy and scientific reason fashioned by the great thinkers of the eighteenth-century Enlightenment. Whether he described it as a beautiful, powerfully seductive meteorological illusion, a fata morgana,[1] or as a terrifying hurricane-force storm "now arisen with violent intensity," Kuyper judged modernism to be the great "life-system" engaged "in mortal combat" with the Christian faith and described his own life's work as that of a soldier in this battle.[2] In the first of his 1898 Stone Lectures at Princeton Theological Seminary, he spoke of "this struggle . . . in which I myself have been spending all my energy for nearly forty years."[3] Facing the poisonous ideas of the French Revolution in society and politics, or the metastasizing intellectual cancers of pantheism and evolutionism in the academy, Kuyper's vision ranged beyond the immediate horizon to an underlying ultimate spiritual conflict between the *civitas Dei* and the *civitas diaboli*. The "odious shibboleth" of Enlightenment

---

1. Abraham Kuyper, "Modernism: A Fata Morgana in the Christian Domain," in *Abraham Kuyper: A Centennial Reader*, ed. James D. Bratt (Grand Rapids: Eerdmans, 1998), 87-124. On pp. 90-91 of that essay Kuyper explains the meaning of his allusion, evoking Arthurian legend and describing an imaginary aerial specter in southern Italy.

2. Abraham Kuyper, *Lectures on Calvinism* (Grand Rapids: Eerdmans, 1931), 10-11.

3. Kuyper, *Lectures on Calvinism*, 11.

modernism was *ni Dieu, ni maître,* and it had to be opposed manfully with the claims of the Christian faith.[4] But exactly how was this opposition to be motivated and mobilized, and what kinds of weapons did Kuyper himself use in the battle? How do we bring some kind of unity to Kuyper's multifaceted career as minister in the Dutch Reformed Church, university founder, journalist, and politician/statesman? My suggestion in this introductory chapter, and a recurring theme throughout this book, is that the nature of Kuyper's career — as the general of an army engaged in battle against Enlightenment modernism and its manifold pathologies in church, culture, society, and state — is illumined if we think of him as a "poet."[5]

Abraham Kuyper as "Poet"?

It must be acknowledged from the outset that thinking of Kuyper as a poet may not appear initially to be a promising line of inquiry. For one thing, apart from his onetime verse paraphrase of Dutch poet Isaac da Costa at the twenty-fifth anniversary celebration of Kuyper's editorship of *De Standaard,* the daily newspaper he helped found in 1872 — the famous "One passion dominates my life" verse about establishing God's ordinances in all of life[6] — Kuyper left no legacy of poetic verse. Furthermore, when he himself describes the nature of the conflict with modernism as he saw it, he points to a battle of *ideas:*

> From the first, therefore, I have always said to myself, — "If the battle is to be fought with honor and with a hope of victory, then *principle* must be arrayed against *principle:* then it must be felt that in Modernism the vast energy of an all-embracing *life-system* assails us, then also it must be understood that we have to take our stand in a life-system of equally comprehensive and far-reaching power.... When thus taken, I found and confessed, and I still hold, that this manifestation of the Christian principle is given us in *Calvinism.*

4. Kuyper, *Lectures on Calvinism,* 10; an excellent summary of Kuyper's understanding and critique of "modernism" can be found in Peter S. Heslam, *Creating a Christian Worldview: Abraham Kuyper's Lectures on Calvinism* (Grand Rapids: Eerdmans, 1998), 85-112.

5. What exactly I have in mind with the term "poet" will be developed in the course of this chapter; a summary statement can be found in n. 55 below.

6. "Één zucht beheerst mijn leven" (*Gedenkboek: Opgedragen door het festcomité aan Prof. Dr. A. Kuyper, bij zijn vijf en twintigjaren jubileum als hoofdredacteur van "De Standaard"* [Amsterdam: G. J. C. Herdes, 1897], 77). The complete poem and discussion of this celebrative event can be found on 64-68.

From Calvinism have I drawn the inspiration firmly and resolutely to take my stand in the thick of this great conflict of principles."[7]

Life system versus life system, principle against principle — hardly the stuff of *poetic* imagination. Is Kuyper here not speaking like an Enlightenment man himself, reducing immense human spiritual complexities to Cartesian basic, clear and distinct ideas *(beginselen)?* From this it is not surprising that most of Kuyper's interpreters have also seen him primarily as a man of ideas, an intellectual culture critic, a philosopher mightily tilting against the intellectual windmills constructed by the autonomous reason of the Enlightenment. Joris Van Eijnatten, for example, describes Kuyper as "a Dutch social metaphysician of imposing stature."[8] Similarly, James Bratt has observed that "Kuyper's North American followers have largely read him as a theologian and cultural philosopher — that is, as a man of ideas."[9] Thus, we inherit a rich legacy of scholarship about Kuyper the theologian,[10] the church historian,[11] the culture critic,[12] the philosopher of science,[13] the political activist and emancipator,[14] as well as the

7. Kuyper, *Lectures on Calvinism,* 11-12.

8. J. Van Eijnatten, *God, Nederland, en Oranje: Dutch Calvinism and the Search for a Social Centre* (Kok: Kampen, 1993), 10.

9. J. Bratt, "Abraham Kuyper's Public Career," *Reformed Journal* 37, no. 10 (October 1987): 9.

10. E.g., P. A. Van Leeuwen, *Het Kerkbegrip in de Theologie van Abraham Kuyper* (Franeker: T. Wever, 1946); W. H. Velema, *De Leer van De Heilige Geest bij Abraham Kuyper* (The Hague: Van Keulen, 1957); Henry Zwaanstra, "Abraham Kuyper's Conception of the Church," *Calvin Theological Journal* 9 (1974): 149-81.

11. L. Praamsma, *Abraham Kuyper als Kerkhistoricus* (Kampen: Kok, 1946); H. J. Langman, *Kuyper en de Volkskerk* (Kampen: Kok, 1950).

12. A. A. Van Ruler, *Kuypers Idee Eener Christelijke Cultuur* (Nijkerk: Callenbach, 1940); S. J. Ridderbos, *De Theologische Cultuurbeschouwing van Abraham Kuyper* (Kok: Kampen, 1947); Heslam, *Creating a Christian Worldview;* Edward E. Ericson, Jr., "Abraham Kuyper: Cultural Critic," *Calvin Theological Journal* 22 (1987): 210-27.

13. H. Dooyeweerd, "Kuypers Wetenschapsleer," *Philosophia Reformata* 4 (1939): 193-232; Delvin L. Ratzsch, "Abraham Kuyper's Philosophy of Science," *Calvin Theological Journal* 27 (1992): 277-303.

14. On Kuyper the political activist and emancipator, see McKendree Langley, "Emancipation and Apologetics: The Formation of Abraham Kuyper's Anti-Revolutionary Party in the Netherlands, 1872-1880" (Ph.D. diss., Westminster Theological Seminary, 1995); McKendree Langley, *The Practice of Political Spirituality* (Jordan Station, Ont.: Paideia, 1984); J. W. Sap, *Wegberieders der Revolutie: Calvinisme en de Strijd om de Democratische Rechtstaat* (Groningen: Wolters-Noordhoff, 1993), 333-41; C. Augustijn et al., eds. *Abraham Kuyper: Zijn Volksdeel, Zijn Invloed* (Delft: Meinema, 1987); J. Van Weringh, *Het Maatschappijbeeld van Abraham Kuyper* (Assen: Van Gorcum, 1967); Kuyper's biographers also tend to focus on his political career: P. Kasteel, *Abraham Kuyper*

social theorist,[15] but rather little about Kuyper the man of letters, the rhetorician, the poet. Even when reference is made to Kuyper and art, it is primarily Kuyper's *theoretical aesthetic* as articulated, for example, in the fifth Stone Lecture[16] that is discussed, rather than his imaginative, rhetorical, poetic use of language.[17]

Going back to Kuyper's own statement in the Stone Lectures, we are potentially misled by two things. First, though "principle" is obviously appropriate as a translation of Kuyper's famous (*Gereformeerde* or Reformed) *beginselen,* the term "life system" skews our understanding of the Dutch word *wereldbeschouwing* in far too much of an intellectualist direction. The notion of "worldview" (a more literal translation of *wereldbeschouwing*) is not restricted to a set of coherent *ideas* (a *life system*) but can be taken in a metaphorical or

(Kok: Kampen, 1938); H. De Wilde, *Dr. A. Kuyper als Leider van het Volk en als Minister* (The Hague: Nederbragt, 1905); Frank Vanden Berg, *Abraham Kuyper* (Grand Rapids: Eerdmans, 1950); L. Praamsma, *Let Christ Be King: Reflections on the Life and Times of Abraham Kuyper* (Jordan Station, Ont.: Paideia, 1985).

15. D. Th. Kuiper, *De Voormannen: Een Sociaal-Wetenschappelijk Studie over Ideologie, Konflikt en Kerngroepvorming binnen de Gereformeerde Wereld in Nederland tussen 1820 en 1930* (Meppel: Boom; Kampen: Kok, 1972); Wayne A. Kobes, "Sphere Sovereignty and the University: Theological Foundations of Abraham Kuyper's View of the University and Its Role in Society" (Ph.D. diss., Florida State University, 1993); James W. Skillen, "From Covenant of Grace to Equitable Public Pluralism: The Dutch Calvinist Contribution," *Calvin Theological Journal* 31 (1996): 67-96; Mary Stewart Van Leeuwen, "Abraham Kuyper and the Cult of True Womanhood: An Analysis of *De Eerepositie der Vrouw,*" *Calvin Theological Journal* 31 (1996): 97-124. Perhaps the most influential single item of Kuyper's social writing translated into English is his 1891 address to the Dutch Christian Social Congress: *The Problem of Poverty,* trans. and ed. James W. Skillen (Grand Rapids: Baker, 1991).

16. Abraham Kuyper, "Calvinism and Art," in *Lectures on Calvinism,* 142-70; cf. Heslam, 196-223. In addition to Heslam's treatment of Kuyper's fifth Stone Lecture, also see the detailed discussion of Kuyper's theological aesthetics (along with that of his neo-Calvinist successors [Herman Dooyeweerd, Hans R. Rookmaker, and Calvin Seerveld]) by Jeremy Begbie, *Voicing Creation's Praise: Towards a Theology of the Arts* (Edinburgh: T. & T. Clark, 1991), 81-166. Begbie makes the remarkable claim that there are only two significant exceptions to the bleak picture of Protestant theological aesthetics in the twentieth century: "One is the German theologian Paul Tillich, the other is the Dutch Neo-Calvinist tradition stemming from the nineteenth-century scholar Abraham Kuyper. Both . . . make a serious and rigorous attempt to come to terms with the arts theologically" (xvi).

17. Peter Heslam (on 126) also comes close in his discussion of "worldview"; Kuyper's notion of worldview is not primarily a theoretical, scientific one but essentially religious and, formally, rhetorical. Winckel's popular biography of Kuyper also includes concrete examples of Kuyper's style in his discussion of Kuyper's lectures at the Free University on aesthetics; see W. F. A. Winckel, *Leven en Arbeid van Dr. A. Kuyper* (Amsterdam: Ten Have; Grand Rapids: Eerdmans-Sevensma, 1919), 232-39.

mythic-narrative direction, even in experiential and social-practical directions.[18] Kuyper indicates in a footnote of the Stone Lectures that his choice of the term "life system" had been suggested by his "American friends," though he himself preferred the expression "world-and-life-view" as the translation of *wereldbeschouwing* or *Weltanschauung*.[19]

Second, it is fair to ask whether Kuyper's insistent rhetoric about "principles" *(beginselen)* here truly and accurately describes his own actual practice. What we shall attempt to show in this introductory chapter is that Kuyper knew well the sort of claim made by British poet Percy Bysshe Shelley, among others, that "poets are the unacknowledged legislators of the world";[20] furthermore, that he practiced what he preached about the importance of poetry; and finally, that this was recognized by others. But before we consider more closely Kuyper's own "poetic" practice, we shall take a look at two of modernity's defining political moments, provide a general defense of the political importance of poetry, and briefly examine uses of poetic art in political life by Edmund Burke, the American jeremiad sermonic tradition, and Alexis de Tocqueville, respectively. Though this may seem something of an excursus, it will become clear that this discussion of poetry not only provides us with important analytic tools for understanding Kuyper, but also gives us clues for understanding the content of his "American" public theology.

Confronting Modernity's Two Revolutions

In the history of the human quest for liberty, two symbolic events spaced two hundred years apart frame the modern political era. On November 10, 1793, as the Jacobin Reign of Terror was winding down, the Paris Commune of the revolutionary National Convention planned a Festival of Liberty "to celebrate the victory of philosophy over fanaticism."[21] After seizing Notre Dame Cathedral —

18. In a phenomenological analysis of the world's religions, Ninian Smart considers six different worldview dimensions: experiential, mythic, doctrinal, ethical, ritual, and social. See Ninian Smart, *Worldviews: Crosscultural Explorations of Human Beliefs* (New York: Scribner, 1983). See also my comment about Kuyper in the immediately preceding note.

19. Kuyper, *Lectures on Calvinism,* 11 n. 1; cf. Heslam's discussion of this in Heslam, 88-96.

20. P. B. Shelley, *A Defense of Poetry,* ed. Albert C. Cook (Boston: Ginn & Co., 1903), 46; this is the last sentence in Shelley's essay.

21. George Lefebvre, *The French Revolution: From 1793 to 1799,* trans. John Hall Stewart and James Friguglietti (London: Routledge & Kegan Paul; New York: Columbia University Press, 1964), 78.

rebaptized the "Temple of Reason" — the revolutionaries proceeded to "de-Christianize" the former sanctuary by engaging in a public liturgy that celebrated, in the words of Deputy Thuriot de La Rozière, the new "moral order of the Republic, of the Revolution, . . . that will make us a people of brothers, a people of *philosophes*."[22] The cult of "liberty and holy equality" was celebrated thus: "In the interior [of Notre Dame] a gimcrack Greco-Roman structure had been erected beneath the Gothic vaulting. A mountain made of painted linen and papier-mâché was built at the end of the nave where Liberty (played by a singer from the Opéra), dressed in white, wearing the Phrygian bonnet and holding a pike, bowed to the flame of Reason and seated herself on a bank of flowers and plants."[23] Similar cultic festivals of de-Christianization and public affirmation of the new revolutionary civic order took place throughout France. Fueled by the fiery rhetoric of newspaper editor Jacques René Hébert and led by revolutionary enthusiasts such as the former priest Joseph Fouché, a violent iconoclasm erupted, stripping churches, cemeteries, and other public space of all Christian symbols. Liberty trees replaced crucifixes, celebrants engaged in blasphemous parodies of Holy Communion and sang antihymns "to words by Fouché celebrating 'Reason as the Supreme Being.'"[24] With such *fêtes de Raison* — crowned by the exaltation of the goddess Reason/Liberty — becoming the order of the day,[25] the French Revolution at the same time fulfilled Voltaire's wish to *écrasez l' infame* and Rousseau's insistence on a new secular, civil religion.[26]

If 1789 represents the beginning of the modern political era, then, so it has been argued, 1989 may represent its end, since, "within the bounds of these two centuries, an *ideological worldview* has arisen and fallen, come and gone."[27] In ad-

22. Simon Schama, *Citizens: A Chronicle of the French Revolution* (New York: Knopf, 1989), 776.

23. Schama, *Citizens,* 778. Another historian describes the event thus: "Relays of patriotic maidens in virginal white paraded reverently before a temple of philosophy erected where the high altar had stood. From it emerged, at the climax of the ceremony, a red-capped figure representing Liberty. Appreciatively described by an official recorder of the scene as 'a masterpiece of nature,' in daily life she was an actress; but in her symbolic role she led the officials of the commune to the Convention, where she received the fraternal embrace of the president and sectretaries" (William Doyle, *The Oxford History of the French Revolution* [Oxford: Clarendon, 1989], 261).

24. Schama, *Citizens,* 779; for a detailed description of the Reign of Terror, see 126-92.

25. For another detailed account of such a festival, see Philip Dawson, ed., *The French Revolution* (Englewood Cliffs, N.J.: Prentice-Hall, 1967), 119-27.

26. Jean-Jacques Rousseau, *The Social Contract,* trans. Maurice Cranston (Middlesex, U.K., and New York: Penguin Books, 1968), 176-87 (bk. IV, chap. 8, "The Civil Religion").

27. Thomas C. Oden, *Two Worlds: Notes on the Death of Modernity in America and Russia* (Downers Grove, Ill.: InterVarsity, 1992), 32. Oden states his thesis clearly: "The du-

dition to the important symbolic significance of breaching the Berlin Wall, the massive protest of Chinese students in Beijing's Tiananmen Square also qualifies as a premier symbol of the 1989 revolution. Of Tiananmen's important visual symbols, the most pregnant was underreported by the American media. The remarkable photo of the lone protester facing a phalanx of government tanks — advancing on the tragically and ironically named "Avenue of Peace" — on June 5, 1989, is more or less indelibly imprinted on our minds. Yet, as importantly, six days earlier, "just as it looked as if the demonstrations would fade away, to be resumed perhaps only after the summer holidays, the white plaster statue of the Goddess of Democracy was wheeled into the square in three sections and erected, facing the huge portrait of Mao that was hanging over the south gate of the Forbidden City. . . . The statue, 'like the students themselves, seemed immovable, indestructible, and permanent.'"[28] It was at this point, when "it must have looked to [Chinese leader] Deng as if the demonstrations would never stop, . . . [that] it was decided to order the army to clear out the square."[29]

The Chinese students' peaceful protest — symbolized by the thirty-three-foot white Goddess of Democracy statue — was suppressed by brutal state violence against the protesters and the destruction of their symbol. What did the statue represent that precipitated such a major response? The official loudspeaker broadcasts directed at the students in the square called it "a foreign thing" and, "calling attention to the Goddess's resemblance to the Statue of Liberty," proclaimed: "This is China, not America."[30] The significance of the American connection was underscored five years later at the unveiling, in a small park at the edge of San Francisco's Chinatown, of a bronze statue modeled after the original Goddess of Democracy. On that occasion Congresswoman Nancy Pelosi said: "The world witnessed the brutal suppression of individual freedom and liberty in Tiananmen Square. The brave men and women who demonstrated did so in the spirit of our forefathers. They quoted Thomas Jefferson, and built a Goddess of Democracy fashioned after our own Statue of Liberty."[31]

---

ration of the *epoch* of modernity is now clearly identifiable as a precise two-hundred year period between 1789 and 1989, between the French Revolution and the collapse of communism. Such dating of historical periods is always disputable, but this one cries out with clarity, since it was announced with such a dramatic beginning point (the storming of the Bastille), and closed with such a precise moment of collapse (the literal fall of a vast symbolic wall in Berlin). The analogies between the revolutions of 1789 and 1989 will intrigue historians for centuries to come."

28. Jonathan Mirsky, "The Empire Strikes Back," *New York Review of Books* 37 (February 1, 1990): 22-23.

29. Mirsky, 22.

30. Mirsky, 22.

31. *New York Times National,* Sunday, June 5, 1994, L38.

Fig. 1.1. Goddess of Democracy

The temptation to draw universal, metanarrative historical conclusions at this point is almost irresistible. Two revolutions, two hundred years apart, symbolizing a defined era. With 1789 representing the initial triumph of atheistic, secular, totalitarian, and bloody ideology, 1989, then, represents its pathetic end and the ideological, if not yet fully political, triumph of the American experiment. This conclusion in fact has been drawn in the realm of speculative philosophy of history[32] as well as in more sober, empirical, historical accounting of the twentieth century's trajectory.[33] In an example of the latter, political historian David Fromkin summarizes the conclusion of his work as follows, along with appropriate cautionary notes about premature closure on history's end:

> It was a fast and unexpected finish. Coming only a half-century after the United States seemingly solved the problems of German and Japanese expansionism, and less than forty years after America helped to push the countries of Western Europe into releasing their overseas colonies, the sudden and dramatic collapse of the last remaining empire — that of the Soviet Union — was so tidy and satisfying as an ending that it is tempting to think it *was* one; that history is a novel, and this is its last page. For someone trying to make sense of what happened, the challenge is to tell what the plots and subplots were, in other words, that led to the end of empires and the emergence, for the time being, of the United States as the sole global power.[34]

If Abraham Kuyper, a little more than seventy-five years after his death in 1920, were able to read the narrative portrait sketched above of the century's end, he would be pleased. Aside from the tiny reference to Thomas Jefferson in one of the quotations,[35] he would judge the events of recent world history to be a vindication of his own religious sense of world history's providential unfolding. To begin with, Kuyper passionately opposed the spirit of the French Revolution while, of course, fully recognizing its historical importance: "The history of our times," he contended, "starts from the *unbelief* of the French Revolution."[36]

32. Most famously by Francis Fukuyama, *The End of History and the Last Man* (New York: Free Press, 1992).

33. E.g., David Fromkin, *The Time of the Americans: FDR, Eisenhower, Marshall, MacArthur — the Generation That Changed America's Role in the World* (New York: Knopf, 1995).

34. Fromkin, 537.

35. For Kuyper's views on Thomas Jefferson, see his Grand Rapids lecture of October 26, 1898, in app. C of this volume.

36. Kuyper, *Lectures on Calvinism*, 25.

In 1789 the turning point was reached.

Voltaire's mad cry, "Down with the Scoundrel," was aimed at Christ himself, but this cry was merely the expression of the most hidden thought from which the French Revolution sprang. The fanatic cry of another philosopher, "We no more need a God," and the odious shibboleth, "No God, no Master," of the Convention; — these were the sacrilegious watchwords which at that time heralded the liberation of man as an emancipation from all Divine Authority. And if, in His impenetrable wisdom, God employed the Revolution as a means by which to overthrow the tyranny of the Bourbons, and to bring judgement on the princes who abused *His* nations as *their* footstool, nevertheless the principle of that Revolution remains thoroughly *anti-Christian*, and has since spread like a cancer, dissolving and undermining all that stood firm and consistent before our Christian faith.[37]

In sharp contrast, the American Revolution, Kuyper told his American audience at Princeton in 1898, was signally different; its liberty was not grounded in atheistic rebellion against God but in an appropriate, Calvinist-inspired rejection of tyranny. Liberty was a political good, hard-won by Dutch Calvinists in their struggle against Spain as well as by Americans from Great Britain. This liberty and the political experiment that ordered it was a beacon for the future of world history. "America," Kuyper contended that same year in a Grand Rapids, Michigan, address to Dutch-American fellow Calvinists, "is destined in the providence of God to become the most glorious and noble nation the world has ever seen. Some day its renown will eclipse the renown and splendor of Rome, Greece and the old races."[38] Providentially led world history had, in Kuyper's view, a clear and certain telos, and its world stream, for the most part in the modern era fed by the religious springs of Calvinism, was to follow a clearly marked channel:

> There is but one world-stream, broad and fresh, which from the beginning bore the promise of the future. This stream had its rise in Middle Asia and the Levant, and has steadily continued its course from East to West. From Western Europe it has passed on to your Eastern States, and from thence to California. The sources of this stream of development are found in Babylon and in the valley of the Nile. From thence it flowed on to Greece. From Greece it passed on to the Roman Empire. From the Romantic nations it continued its way to the Northwestern parts of Europe, and from Holland and England it reaches at length your continent.[39]

37. Kuyper, *Lectures on Calvinism*, 10.
38. *Grand Rapids Herald*, October 29, 1898; see app. C below.
39. Kuyper, *Lectures on Calvinism*, 32.

What Kuyper adds at this point is particularly striking from our vantage point at the close of the twentieth century (recall that he wrote this in 1898!): "At present that stream [of world history] is at a standstill. *Its Western course through China and Japan is impeded; meanwhile no one can tell what forces for the future may yet lie slumbering in the Slavic races which have thus far failed of progress.* But while this secret of the future is still veiled in mystery, the course of this world stream from East to West can be denied by none."[40] The American experiment in ordered liberty, in other words, is holy, the providentially destined "end of history."

Such unabashed faith in the holy inevitability of the American experiment is hardly the common conviction of Americans themselves today. Rather, the very existence of American civil religion and belief in America's manifest destiny is seen by many as a significant moral and political problem itself. Due to 1960s countercultural attacks on "Amerika," a profoundly anti-American spirit is often expressed in the American academy and the media. Multicultural enthusiasm for "diversity," often arising out of concern that traditional American "founding myths" are exclusionary and oppressive of minorities,[41] has led to the "reinventing of America."[42] For some evangelical Christians this cultural spirit repudiating the "myth" of America's founding as a "Christian nation" and the consequent conviction about providential purpose is reinforced by concerns about the "idolatry" of civil religion.[43] At the same time, it is particularly evangelical Christians — the so-called New Christian Right — who are increasingly becoming the defenders of the idea and ideal of America.[44] It is not necessary at this point to elaborate on the question concerning the health of America's soul except to say that Americans are themselves seriously divided about the present condition and future hope of the American experiment. Stated differently, America is involved in a *Kulturkampf*, a culture war about its very identity as a nation.[45] Public debates about multiculturalism, public education

40. Kuyper, *Lectures on Calvinism*, 33, emphasis added.

41. See, e.g., Leslie Bekowitz et al., eds., *America in Theory* (New York and Oxford: Oxford University Press, 1988).

42. See, e.g., Robert Royal, ed., *Reinventing the American People: Unity and Diversity Today* (Grand Rapids: Eerdmans; Washington, D.C.: Ethics and Public Policy Center, 1995).

43. E.g., Robert D. Linder and Richard V. Pierard, *Twilight of the Saints: Biblical Christianity and Civil Religion* (Downers Grove, Ill.: InterVarsity, 1978).

44. E.g., Pat Robertson, *America's Dates with Destiny* (Nashville: Nelson, 1986); Rus Walton, *One Nation under God* (Nashville: Nelson, 1987).

45. The literature is vast. Among the important titles are James Davison Hunter, *Culture Wars: The Struggle to Define America* (New York: Basic Books, 1991); William J. Bennett, *The Devaluing of America: The Fight for Our Culture and Our Children* (New York:

— particularly the teaching of history and literature — and the role of religion in public life more broadly, not to mention the battles about race, immigration, affirmative action, welfare, abortion, euthanasia, gay rights, and so forth, all point to a crisis of national moral identity. The question we raise here is this: Supposing the claims about a crisis in the American soul[46] to be correct, how does a nation go about repairing its soul? How does one go about healing a national community's wounds? What political actions are required to bring this about? And, recognizing that they faced similar cultural and social ennui, what did earlier Christian social transformers such as Abraham Kuyper do to achieve political and moral change? Or, is politics not the answer? Put differently, how can an unbelieving (secular) civilization be saved? We find a suggestive answer from yet another foreign source, the Russian émigré writer Alexander Solzhenitsyn.

"Beauty Will Save the World"[47]

To transform the world, so modern man believes, one needs the right politics. Politics, in this viewpoint, refers primarily to political platforms, programs, and campaign strategies — in short, political technique.[48] But what about the "vision" that governs the technique? What about the political imagination that provides passion for ideals such as liberty and energy for the hard political work required for success? How is political vision communicated and passed on

Summit Books, 1991); Richard John Neuhaus, *The Naked Public Square: Religion and Democracy in America* (Grand Rapids: Eerdmans, 1984); Richard John Neuhaus, *America against Itself: Moral Vision and the Public Order* (Notre Dame, Ind.: University of Notre Dame Press, 1992); Arthur M. Schlesinger, Jr., *The Disuniting of America: Reflections on a Multicultural Society* (New York and London: Norton, 1992); Robert H. Bork, *Slouching towards Gomorrah: Modern Liberalism and American Decline* (New York: HarperCollins, 1996); Pat Robertson, *The Turning Tide: The Fall of Liberalism and the Rise of Common Sense* (Dallas: Word, 1993). We will be analyzing the current American "culture wars" in greater detail in chap. 8.

46. In addition to the literature cited in the immediately preceding note, see Robert Wuthnow, *The Struggle for America's Soul: Evangelicals, Liberals, and Secularism* (Grand Rapids: Eerdmans, 1989).

47. For this phrase from Dostoyevsky via Solzhenitsyn as well as the inspiration for the following discussion of Solzhenitsyn's moral, artistic vision, I am indebted to Edward E. Ericson, Jr., *Solzhenitsyn: The Moral Vision* (Grand Rapids: Eerdmans, 1980) and *Solzhenitsyn and the Modern World* (Washington, D.C.: Regnery Gateway, 1993); cf. Gregory Wolfe, "Beauty Will Save the World," *Intercollegiate Review* 27, no. 1 (fall 1991): 27-31.

48. For a summary and critique of this view, see Jacques Ellul, *The Political Illusion,* trans. Konrad Kellen (New York: Knopf, 1967).

from generation to generation? Do not iconographic works of art such as the French revolutionaries' Goddess of Reason or the Chinese students' Goddess of Democracy provide us with clues here? Why did these works of art generate such passion in their detractors as well their devotees? Is it not remarkable that a revolution dedicated to reason, to creating a new brotherhood of *philosophes*, judged it necessary to plunder Christian cultic practices and establish an alternative, secular, cultic ritual, even a *civil religion*? Why? Was reason not sufficient to mobilize the revolutionary vanguard and provide the vision for change? Paris and Tiananmen suggest to us that political *imagination* perhaps precedes effective political strategy and that a political *vision*, communicated through symbol, myth, and even ritual, may be necessary to provide the passion for political ideals and the energy required for political success. This leads us to wonder whether art in general (visual or literary) plays a significant *political* role in a nation by imaginatively providing a social vision for its citizens. Is art politically *useful* or — stronger — even *necessary*?

In his Nobel Lecture of 1972 Alexander Solzhenitsyn addresses the political significance of art by calling attention to its dual religious possibilities. There are, he says, two kinds of artists in the world. "One kind of artist imagines himself the creator of an independent spiritual world and shoulders the act of creating that world and the people in it, assuming total responsibility for it — but he collapses, for no mortal genius is able to hold up under such a load. Just as man, who once declared himself the center of existence, has not been able to create a stable spiritual system."[49] In contrast to this Protagorean, if not Promethean, vision of art, Solzhenitsyn sketches a portrait of the artist as servant-apprentice: "Another artist acknowledges a higher power above him and joyfully works as a common apprentice under God's heaven, although his responsibility for all that he writes down or depicts, and for those who understand him, is all the greater. On the other hand, he did not create the world, it is not given direction by him, it is a world about whose foundations he has no doubt" (4-5). Thus, two kinds of people, two kinds of art.[50] Solzhenitsyn probes the spiritual depth of this duality with profound sensitivity by elsewhere pointing to "the line of good and evil" that "cuts through the heart of every human being."[51]

49. Alexander Solzhenitsyn, *Nobel Lecture* (New York: Farrar, Straus & Giroux, 1972), 4; page references that follow in the text are to this work.

50. Kuyper readers will recognize the allusion to his "two kinds of people, two kinds of science" (Abraham Kuyper, *Principles of Sacred Theology*, trans. J. Hendrick de Vries [Grand Rapids: Eerdmans, 1965 (1898)], 150-75).

51. Alexander Solzhenitsyn, *The Gulag Archipelago*, vol. 1 (New York: Harper & Row, 1973), 168.

The religious and political significance of art arises from the recognition that technical reason is insufficient for human life in community. Moral visions precede and serve as a foundation for political strategy and action. The goddess Reason, for example, cannot herself supply the reasons why we should trust her and follow her. "There is no point asserting and reasserting what the heart cannot believe" (7). But art does have the capacity to warm "even an icy and depressed heart, opening it to lofty spiritual experience. By means of art we are sometimes sent — dimly, briefly — revelations unattainable by reason" (6). Why, then, is art needed, especially today? Because in a global village where modern communication systems help us leap over the old barriers of nation and language, we encounter an intense conflict of values. The crisis of our one-world civilization is that there can be no unity when there is a multitude of values. "Given six, four, or even two scales of values, there cannot be one world, one single humanity: the difference in rhythms, in oscillations, will tear mankind asunder. We will not survive together on one Earth, just as a man with two hearts is not meant for this world" (16).

What can be done about this division? Solzhenitsyn asks: "Who will coordinate these scales of values, and how? Who will give mankind one single system for reading its instruments, both for wrongdoing and for doing good, for the intolerable and the tolerable as they are distinguished from each other today? . . . Who is capable of extending such an understanding across the boundaries of his own personal experience? Who has the skill to make a narrow, obstinate human being aware of others' far-off grief and joy, to make him understand dimensions and delusions he himself never lived through?" In other words, how can we get along? How can we together come to a common understanding and vision of our common humanity when the pressures of tribalization are so strong? Is there any way to transcend them? Solzhenitsyn is certain the tactics of the old order will not do it: "Propaganda, coercion, and scientific proofs are all powerless. But, happily, in our world there is a way. It is art, and it is literature" (16-17). Solzhenitsyn shares the judgment that "the decadence of the West" cannot "be turned around through politics and intellectual dialectics . . . [and] that authentic renewal can only emerge out of the imaginative visions of the artist and mystic." This conclusion is rooted in a "conviction that politics and rhetoric are not autonomous forces, but are shaped by the prepolitical roots of culture: myth, metaphor, and spiritual experience as recorded by the artist and the saint."[52]

The reason for Solzhenitsyn's hope in the socially and then politically redeeming value of art is that art has the capacity to "overcome man's unfortu-

52. Wolfe, 27.

nate trait of learning only through his own experience, unaffected by that of others." We learn from mistakes; we repeat disastrous mistakes when we fail to learn from others. "The only substitute for what we ourselves have not experienced is art and literature." Literature in particular also "transmits condensed and irrefutable human experience . . . from generation to generation. It thus becomes the living memory of a nation. . . . Thus literature, together with language, preserves and protects a nation's soul." Solzhenitsyn does not share what he regards as the currently fashionable enthusiasm for the waning of national identities: "Nations are the wealth of humanity, its generalized personalities. The least of them has its own special colors, and harbors within itself a special aspect of God's design." He then issues a stern prophetic warning: "But woe to the nation whose literature is cut off by the interposition of force. That is not simply a violation of 'freedom of the press'; it is stopping up the nation's heart, carving out the nation's memory; it loses its spiritual unity — and despite their supposedly common language, fellow countrymen suddenly cease understanding each other" (17-20).

Even if one grants the noble role of art and literature in promoting human understanding, how do they help resist the forces of violence that stalked the cruelly bloody twentieth century and still stalk the twenty-first century? How can words help "oppose the onslaught of a suddenly resurgent fang-baring barbarism" (24)? What is the role of the artist, the writer? After all, they "send off no rockets, do not push even the lowliest handcart, are scorned by those who respect only material power. Would it not be natural . . . to retreat?" The writer, says Solzhenitsyn, does "not have even this way out. Once pledged to the WORD, there is no getting away from it" (27). How? "What can the writer do against the pitiless onslaught of naked violence?" Answer: Never "forget that violence does not and cannot flourish by itself; it is inevitably intertwined with LYING. Between them there is the closest, the most profound and natural bond: nothing screens violence except lies, and the only way lies can hold out is by violence. Whoever has once announced violence as his METHOD must inexorably choose lying as his PRINCIPLE." The only antidote is the courageous act of not taking part in, of not supporting lies. But "writers and artists can do more: they can VANQUISH LIES! In the struggle against lies, art has always won and always will. Lies can stand up against much in the world, but not against art" (32-33). Dostoyevsky was right: "Beauty will save the world!" Even more direct is the Russian proverb: "ONE WORD OF TRUTH OUTWEIGHS THE WORLD" (34).[53]

53. Cf. the lines from Martin Luther's *Ein Feste Burg*:

And though this world with devils filled,
should threaten to undo us,

Solzhenitsyn's contention that the work of artists saves the world is illustrated by his own example, particularly in *One Day in the Life of Ivan Denisovich* and *The Gulag Archipelago*. He also makes the point explicitly about the Soviet Union in his memoir, *The Oak and the Calf*: "Looking back," he writes, "even a fool would have been able to predict it today: the Soviet regime could certainly have been breached only by literature. The regime has been reinforced with concrete to such an extent that neither a military coup nor a political organization nor a picket line of strikers can knock it over or run through it. Only the solitary writer would be able to do this. And the younger Russian generation would move on into the breach."[54] Solzhenitsyn's claim is echoed by American conservatism's great man of letters, Russell Kirk, who refers to the "armed vision of the poets"[55] as the *sine qua non* for restoring "a living faith to the lonely crowd," for reminding "men that life has ends."[56] Kirk underscores the important caution that "society's regeneration cannot be an undertaking wholly political." In fact, "No less than politicians do, great poets move nations, even though the generality of men may

> we will not fear, for God has willed
> his truth to triumph through us.
> The prince of darkness grim,
> we tremble not for him;
> his rage we can endure,
> for lo! His doom is sure;
> *one little word shall fell him.*

54. Aleksandr Solzhenitsyn, *The Oak and the Calf: Sketches of Literary Life in the Soviet Union*, trans. Harry Willetts (New York: Harper & Row, 1975), 10. In addition to Solzhenitsyn's own political significance as a writer, note should be taken of the significant role played by such twentieth-century writers as South Africans Alan Paton and J. M. Coetzee in inspiring political change. The memoirs of the Cuban prisoner Armanda Valladares, *Against all Hope*, trans. Andrew Hurley (New York: Knopf, 1987), and the Chinese prisoner Nien Ching, *Life and Death in Shanghai* (New York: Grove Press, 1987), also deserve mention here. Among nineteenth-century writers mention needs to made of the Russian Ivan Turgenev (*A Sportsman's Notebook* [1854]) and the important American novel of Harriet Beecher Stowe, *Uncle Tom's Cabin* (1852). On these and the more general role of fiction in inspiring political change, see Michael Hanne, *The Power of the Story: Fiction and Political Change* (Providence, R.I., and Oxford: Berghahn Books, 1994).

55. Here and in what follows, I shall be using the term "poetry" ("poet") as a broad shorthand to refer to those who use words in the service of *imagination* rather than *reason*, *stories* rather than *ideas*, *rhetoric* rather than *dialectic*. The use of "poetry" in this broad sense rather than restricting its use to the literary genre of verse is characteristic of Plato in his *Republic* as well as Philip Sidney, *In Defense of Poetry*, and Percy Bysshe Shelley, *A Defense of Poetry*.

56. Russell Kirk, *The Conservative Mind: From Burke to Eliot*, 7th rev. ed. (Washington, D.C.: Regnery, 1986), 491-92. It is noteworthy that a volume dealing with the "conservative *mind*" nonetheless concludes with the *poetic* testimony of T. S. Eliot, among others.

not know the poets' names." How? "It has been a chief purpose of good poetry to reinterpret and vindicate the norms of human existence." The poet is "no mere defender of the establishments of the hour, the poet is loyal to norms not to factions. . . . Every age is out of joint, in the sense that man and society never are what they ought to be; and the poet senses that he is born to set the time right — not, however, by leading a march to some New Jerusalem, but by allying his art to the permanent things." There is hope, therefore, "if men of affairs can rise to the summons of the poets," for then "the norms of culture and politics may endure despite the follies of the time."[57] It is fitting, therefore, that we conclude this section with the words of America's great twentieth-century poet:

> For, dear me, why abandon a belief
> Merely because it ceases to be true?
> Cling to it long enough, and not a doubt
> It will turn true again, for so it goes.
> Most of the change we think we see in life
> Is due to truths being in and out of favor.
> As I sit here, and oftentimes, I wish
> I could be monarch of a desert land
> I could devote and dedicate forever
> To the truths we keep coming back and back to.
>
> Robert Frost, "The Black Cottage"[58]

But whence does this power of poetry come? Why and how do words change the world?

The Power of Words: *Mythos* and *Logos*

Unlike the weather cliché — everyone talks about it but nobody does anything about it — those who effect significant change in human affairs tend to be both talkers and doers. Perhaps it is more precise to say that talking is one of the most important forms of *political* action. To a large extent historical transformation is accomplished by effective, performative speech.[59] Capturing public imagination

57. Kirk, *The Conservative Mind*, 492-500, passim.
58. Cited by Kirk, *The Conservative Mind*, 492-93.
59. The term "performative" is used here in the more general sense of language that has some action as its goal rather than information or reporting. In a stricter sense "performatives" are words, such as legal acts of a legislature, that actually accomplish an act by their mere utterance. See G. B. Caird, *The Language and Imagery of the Bible* (Philadelphia: Westminster, 1980), 20-25. The pioneer in what has come to be known as "speech-act the-

through persuasive rhetoric is essential for mobilizing movements that bring about significant and lasting change. For great historical change-agents such as John Winthrop, Thomas Jefferson, Abraham Lincoln, Theodore and Franklin D. Roosevelt, Winston Churchill, John F. Kennedy, Martin Luther King, Jr., and Ronald Reagan, their words as much as their deeds live after them. In many cases — "city on a hill," "all men are created equal," "new birth of freedom," "for us the living," "of the people, by the people, for the people," "speak softly, carry a big stick," "nothing to fear but fear itself," "blood, sweat, and tears," "iron curtain," "ask not what your country can do for you," "Ich bin ein Berliner," "I have a dream," "content of character," "evil empire" — the remembered word *is* the deed that lives on and continues to inspire and effect change. To the list here we can add what are likely Abraham Kuyper's own most-quoted words, used time and again by speakers to motivate Christian action: "There is not a square inch [Dutch: *duimbreed* = thumb's breadth] in the whole domain of our human existence over which Christ, who is Sovereign of *all*, does not cry: 'Mine!'"[60]

It is important to reflect on the reason for this. Why do words have such power, and how does the power of words compare with other forms of social power? The Greek orator Isocrates already in the fourth century B.C. recognized that a functioning political society — one that involves its citizens in a deliberative process to establish the laws by which it is governed — requires a healthy level of public discourse. To be opposed to the eloquence of rhetoric, says Isocrates, is to fail to appreciate "that power which of all the faculties that belong to the nature of man is the source of most of our blessings." The use of speech to persuade is precisely the distinguishing mark of our humanity's social capacity. "For in the other powers which we possess we are in no respect superior to other living creatures; nay we are inferior to many in swiftness and strength and in other resources; but, because there has been implanted in us the power to persuade each other and to make clear to each other whatever we desire, not only have we escaped the life of wild beasts, but we have come together and founded cities and made laws and invented arts; and, generally speaking, there is no institution devised by man which the power of speech has not helped us to establish."[61] Words,

---

ory" is the English language philosopher J. L. Austin (*How to Do Things with Words* [Cambridge: Harvard University Press, 1975 (1962)]; cf. Reed Way Dasenbrock, "J. L. Austin," in *Encyclopedia of Rhetoric and Composition*, ed. Theresa Enos [New York and London: Garland, 1996], 53-54).

60. Abraham Kuyper, "Sphere Sovereignty," in *Abraham Kuyper: A Centennial Reader*, 488; Dutch: *Souvereiniteit in Eigen Kring* (Kampen: Kok, 1930), 32. This address was delivered on October 20, 1880, at the opening of the Free University of Amsterdam.

61. Isocrates, *To Nicocles or the Cyprians* 5, 6, trans. George Norlin (London: William Heinemann; New York: Putnam, 1928), 1:79; I am indebted for this citation to Dan-

in other words, create nations. Perhaps nowhere else is that as true as in the United States of America, a nation created in a blaze of words (the sermons of the Revolution) and shaped — legally, institutionally, culturally, and morally — by words.[62] From the Mayflower Compact through the Declaration of Independence and the Bill of Rights and on to Lincoln's Gettysburg Address, America is a nation created, nurtured, renewed, and sustained by words.[63]

Does all speech accomplish this, or only specific kinds of speech? Is verse — for example, the epic poetry of Homer — a suitable and useful vehicle for public, political discourse? According to historian Daniel Boorstin, it was the historical *prose* of Herodotus that signaled the future shape of politics in the West. Rather than a chronicle of heroic and "lonely Solomons keeping their own counsel," politics became "a history of councils, of senates, parlements and parliaments — of men trying to persuade one another, their fellow governors, and the people whom they governed. In politics there was neither time nor opportunity for epics elaborating messages into verse. Prose, the language of everyday life, would be the vehicle of *persuasion*. And the new art of rhetoric would provide the techniques, define the standards, and shape the style of the message." Thus, "the arts of prose became essential to the arts of governing," and derivatively "prose was associated with the earliest hesitant moves toward democracy," because "the rise of prose as an art and rhetoric as a discipline is plainly connected . . . with wider public participation in government."[64]

However, the new emphasis on prose rhetoric also had a shadow side. Rhetoric that persuaded and moved men did not have to be true, and thus Plato, in his *Gorgias,* "denies that rhetoric is an art and defines it as species of flattery, a sham counterpart of justice."[65] Rhetoric, much like advertising in the

---

iel J. Boorstin, *The Creators: A History of Heroes of the Imagination* (New York: Random House, 1992), 220.

62. See Daniel J. Boorstin, *An American Primer* (New York: Penguin Books, 1995 [1966]) for "the 83 most important documents of the American past." On the role of sermons in the American Revolution, see Ellis Sandoz, ed., *Political Sermons of the American Founding Era, 1730-1805* (Indianapolis: Liberty Press, 1991); cf. David W. Hall, ed., *Election Day Sermons* (Oak Ridge, Tenn.: Kuyper Institute, 1996).

63. See Garry Wills, *Lincoln at Gettysburg: The Words That Remade America* (New York: Simon & Schuster, 1992). This observation does not yet take into account the nation-shaping words from preachers, poets, and novelists (Jonathan Edwards, Harriet Beecher Stowe, Nathaniel Hawthorne, Mark Twain, Herman Melville, Walt Whitman, Edward Bellamy, Walter Rauschenbusch, Reinhold Niebuhr, Martin Luther King, Jr.) that indelibly shaped America's conscience and action.

64. Boorstin, *The Creators*, 221, emphasis added.

65. George Kennedy, *The Art of Persuasion in Greece* (Princeton: Princeton University Press, 1963), 15; the reference to the *Gorgias* is 463a6ff.

twenty-first century, is here seen as an "artifice of persuasion," the "shadow of politics."[66] Thus, along with its association "with the earliest hesitant moves toward democracy," the rhetoric of the Greek Sophists in particular also became allied "with opposition to Plato's pursuit of absolutes" and "with appeal to expediency rather than to truth as the guide of political life."[67] In this construction, an antithesis is posited between the poetic/rhetorical use of words — particularly metaphors — to delight and inspire, and the rational, philosophical use of words to determine, define, and display truth.[68] This antithesis between the poetic and rhetorical arts on the one hand and the philosophical methods of searching for truth on the other has been, in a variety of ways, a fixture of the Western intellectual tradition from Plato's *Phaedrus* and *Gorgias* to C. P. Snow's twentieth-century lament about the divide between "the two cultures."[69] In

66. Gary Cronkhite, *Persuasion: Speech and Behavioral Change* (Indianapolis and New York: Bobbs-Merrill, 1969), 19. Increased sophistication in communications technology (and especially in the *control* of such technology) in the twentieth century has also heightened awareness of persuasion through deceit and illusion, and of propaganda. See Jacques Ellul, *Progaganda: The Formation of Men's Attitudes,* trans. Konrad Kellen and Jean Lerner (New York: Knopf, 1965); Ellul, *The Political Illusion.*

67. Boorstin, *The Creators*, 221.

68. In addition to Plato, other characteristic rationalist critiques of rhetoric include those of John Locke and Immanuel Kant:

> Locke: I confess, in discourses where we seek rather pleasure and delight than information and improvement, such ornaments as are borrowed from them can scarce pass for faults. But yet if we would speak of things as they are, we must allow that all the art of rhetoric, besides order and clearness, all the artificial and figurative application of words eloquence hath invented, are for nothing else but to insinuate wrong ideas, move the passions, and thereby mislead the judgment; and so are perfect cheats.

> Kant: Rhetoric, so far as this is taken to mean the art of persuasion, i.e., the art of deluding by means of a fair semblance [as *ars oratoria*], and not merely excellence of speech (eloquence and style), is a dialectic, which borrows from poetry only so much as is necessary to win over men's minds to the side of the speaker before they have weighed the matter, and to rob their verdict of its freedom. . . . Force and elegance of speech (which together constitute rhetoric) belong to fine art; but oratory [*ars oratoria*], being the art of playing for one's own purpose upon the weaknesses of men (let this purpose be ever so good in intention or even in fact) merits no *respect* whatever.

(Cited by Ernesto Grassi, *Rhetoric as Philosophy: The Humanist Tradition* [University Park and London: Pennsylvania State University Press, 1980], 18-19; the citations are from Locke's *Essay concerning Human Understanding,* vol. 2, bk. 3. chap. 10, sec. 34, and Kant's *Critique of Judgment: Part I, Critique of Aesthetic Judgment,* sec. 53.

69. C. P. Snow, *The Two Cultures and the Scientific Revolution* (Cambridge: Cambridge University Press, 1959). For an illuminating account of this conflict in the Renais-

Boorstin's words: "Ever since Plato's time the arts of persuasion have been associated with popular institutions, with the pursuit of compromise and the acceptance of relative and temporary solutions instead of the pursuit of Truth, of the utopian and the ideal."[70]

The general contrast between rhetoric and philosophy should not be exaggerated and must not obscure the important role of rhetoric itself in "the transition from *mythos* to *logos* (i.e., from a mythopoetic theogony to a naturalistic cosmology) as [different] ways of understanding the world. Rhetoric, as both an art of public argument and a theory of civic discourse, was made possible in the fourth century by the development during the Archaic period of rational rather than mythopoetic uses of language. Essential to the theory and technique of rhetoric as these were conceived by Aristotle (whose treatise on the art is the first systematic account and the fullest expression of its Classical theory) are argument, proof, and probability."[71] According to George A. Kennedy, "Aristotle was the first person to recognize clearly that rhetoric as an art of communication was morally neutral, that it could be used either for good or ill." Aristotle's analysis of successful, persuasive rhetoric led to the conclusion that three things were essential: "The truth and logical validity of what is being argued [*logos*]; the speaker's success in conveying to the audience the perception that he or she can be trusted [*ēthos*]; and the emotions that the speaker is able to awaken in an audience to accept the views advanced and act in accordance with them [*pathos*]."[72]

It is necessary, therefore, to draw two important and different contrasts with respect to rhetoric and the rhetorical tradition. On the one hand, in terms of *genre*, rhetorical prose needs to be distinguished from poetry, notably the epic poetry of someone like Homer. On the other hand, since rhetoric depends on *pathos* and effective use of imagery and metaphor as well as *logos* and reason, it can also be distinguished from the rationalist, philosophical tradition that sometimes distrusts the metaphorical use of language.[73] Rhetoric is thus

---

sance humanist tradition, see Grassi, esp. chap. 2, "Rhetoric and Philosophy." How this divide is played out in the arena of higher education is explored by Bruce A. Kimball, *Orators and Philosophers: A History of the Idea of Liberal Education* (New York: Teacher's College, Columbia University, 1986).

70. Boorstin, *The Creators*, 221.

71. Christopher Lyle Johnstone, "Introduction: The Origins of the Rhetorical in Archaic Greece," in *Theory, Text, Context: Issues in Greek Rhetoric and Oratory*, ed. Christopher Lyle Johnstone (Albany: State University of New York Press, 1996), 9.

72. George A. Kennedy, *Aristotle on Rhetoric: A Theory of Civic Discourse* (New York: Oxford University Press, 1991), ix.

73. In addition to n. 67 above, see Janet Martin Soskice, *Metaphor and Religious Language* (Oxford: Clarendon, 1985), 10-14.

sometimes distinguished from poetry and associated with the more logically ordered prose tradition, and at other times it is associated with poetry and contrasted to philosophy and reason. Stated somewhat differently, bearing in mind that Aristotle wrote two classic works on composition, the *Rhetoric* and the *Poetic*,[74] the distinction between those two terms "connoted two fields of composition, two habits of conceiving and ordering, two typical movements. The movement of the one the ancients saw as primarily intellectual, a progress from idea to idea determined logically: that of the other, as primarily imaginative, a progress from image to image determined emotionally."[75] To complicate matters further, there is, in addition, an important distinction between a mythopoetic consciousness that "sees in the world the work of divine personalities whose caprices, contests, and couplings have created the [often unpredictable] history in which human beings are caught up" and a rational, naturalistic worldview "ordered according to an in-dwelling, singular self-consistent [rationally knowable] principle." In the latter, "the *kosmos* is ordered by a *logos*."[76]

For our purposes in this chapter, in order to bring the contrasts sketched above into the orbit of contemporary debates, we shall use a broad brushstroke contrast between two different strategies for arriving at foundational convictions about human life in society — and for resolving the crises facing a given civilization — under the labels of *mythos* and *logos*.[77] It is the former, the broad-ranging category of imaginative, symbolic, metaphorical, and mythical-narrative use of language — in contrast to a more abstract, scientific-descrip-

74. Charles Sears Baldwin, *Ancient Rhetoric and Poetic* (New York: Macmillan, 1924), 1: "On the one hand, the ancients discerned and developed an art of daily communication, especially of public address, τέκνη ῥητορική, *ars oratoria*, rhetoric; on the other hand, an art of imaginative appeal, τέκνη ποιητική, *ars poetica*, poetic."

75. Baldwin, 3.

76. Baldwin, 10. Finally, to complicate matters even more, the Christian philosophical tradition, from the second-century apologists through Thomas Aquinas and John Calvin to Alvin Plantinga, *both* affirms the reality of a personal, providential power upholding the cosmos *and* insists that the cosmos is an ordered cosmos with a discernible natural law. Jesus Christ is the *Logos* by whom all things are created and *in* whom they hang together (John 1; Col. 1). In post-Enlightenment terms this is (confusedly) to join together a mythopoetic consciousness with an ostensibly scientific, rational one.

77. For what follows in this paragraph I am indebted to Stanley Parry, "Reason and the Restoration of Tradition," in *What Is Conservativism?* ed. Frank S. Meyer (New York, Chicago, and San Francisco: Holt, Rinehart & Winston, 1965), 107-32. For a variant on the clash between two worldviews, one rationalist and utopian, the other traditional and realist, see Thomas Sowell, *A Conflict of Visions: Ideological Origins of Political Struggles* (New York: Morrow, 1987). The elitist, gnostic character of contemporary, socially ameliorative utopianism is neatly described in Sowell's *Vision of the Anointed: Self-Congratulation as a Basis for Social Policy* (New York: Basic Books, 1995).

tive, philosophical emphasis on *ideas* — that I have in mind when I use the term "poetry" or "poet." The division between *mythos* and *logos* is significant for the two different ways each fundamental orientation shapes attitudes and practice of social and political life. The former is rooted in a more or less pessimistic view of human nature and man's ability to know and do the good, and thus relies on revelation, on shared human experience, on tradition expressed through myth, narrative, and history to ameliorate the worst in humanity and encourage the best. It is suspicious and even fearful of rationalist, utopian schemes to fix the world. The latter has a more rosy view of human nature and regards whatever intransigencies to human communal progress that still remain after well-intentioned, well-thought-out reforms to be irrational vestiges of flawed structures or institutions (racism, sexism, militarism) and eminently remediable by appropriate (i.e., rational) and concerted education (or therapy).

The rationalist view and strategy is parasitic; it depends on a commonly accepted moral order established by healthy tradition. The difficulty, thus, in a situation of civilizational crisis is that "reason operates effectively in its own right when it moves within the context of a healthy tradition" but "becomes helpless when it has no context of tradition within which to operate."[78] A glaring illustration of this vacuum comes from the writings of University of Virginia pragmatist philosopher Richard Rorty. According to Dean Mark Schwehn of Valparaiso University, Rorty "in a 1983 essay ponders how citizens of a Western democracy would respond to a hypothetical child found wandering in the woods as a sole survivor of a nation whose culture and religion have been destroyed. Such a child would have, Rorty says, 'no share in human dignity,' since the child's moral community no longer exists."[79] Rorty's chilling conclusion is softened somewhat by his claim that "under the ministrations of Westerners, this stranger would surely be 'reclothed with dignity,' because 'the Jewish and Christian element in our tradition' contains certain universalist ideals — ideals that are still 'gratefully invoked,' he admits, 'by free-loading atheists like myself.'"[80]

The reason why reason is utterly unable to solve the problem of a civilizational crisis "rests essentially on the fact that in all moral reason there is a necessary element of subjectivity." Reason only has available the method of persuasion, but "the basic precondition" for effective persuasion "is a com-

78. Parry, 108-9.

79. Mark Schwehn, "A Christian University: Defining the Difference," *First Things*, no. 93 (May 1999): 27.

80. Schwehn, 27; Rorty, it is interesting to note, is a grandson of Social Gospel theologian Walter Rauschenbusch.

monly accepted moral order." Thus, "in a collapse of tradition, i.e. of a commonly accepted moral order, reason becomes helpless."[81] For us moderns specifically, the problem is this: because the Enlightenment sought to solve the problem of moral truth in the same "objective scientific" manner as it pursued data about the natural universe, it deliberately discarded the pattern of traditional moral judgments made in particular, historical communities "as pure pre-rational preferences without foundation in objective reality." The Enlightenment ideal "was to formulate moral principles apart from the insights of moral man,"[82] and its project of justifying morality, according to Alasdair MacIntyre, therefore "had to fail."[83] By itself reason cannot provide the reasons why we should look to reason for the foundation of our moral life. This foundational unity, "the organizing principle of the tradition [of a community], its root perception, is held by way of belief, of faith, rather than by way of a ratiocinative establishment of truth."[84] Poetry, in other words, is seen to trump philosophy.

Where, we now need to ask, does Abraham Kuyper fit in the tradition of word users, orators, rhetoricians, particularly in his own lifelong argument against Enlightenment rationalism? There is little debate about the important role of the early nineteenth-century Dutch spiritual-literary renewal movement, the *Réveil*, on Kuyper and the rise of neo-Calvinism.[85] Included here are two important *literary* figures, the poets Willem Bilderdijk (1756-1831) and Isaac da Costa (1798-1860), both of whom, as we shall see later in this chapter, profoundly influenced Kuyper. For now we simply observe that both were self-consciously *political* poets, calling attention here to Bilderdijk's own understanding of the positive relation between poetry and politics reflected in two of

81. Schwehn, 109-10.
82. Schwehn, 110; for a fuller account of this development and the crisis of Enlightenment morality, see Alasdair MacIntyre, *After Virtue*, 2nd ed. (Notre Dame, Ind.: University of Notre Dame Press, 1984).
83. MacIntyre, chap. 5, "Why the Enlightenment Project of Justifying Morality Had to Fail." Technical reason, MacIntyre observes, "can speak only of means. About ends it must be silent. Reason cannot even, as Descartes believed, refute scepticism; and hence a central achievement of reason according to Pascal, is to recognize that our beliefs are ultimately founded on nature, custom and habit" (54).
84. Parry, 116.
85. All textbook treatments of Kuyper and neo-Calvinism begin with a discussion of the *Réveil*. See H. Algra, *Het Wonder van de Negentiende Eeuw*, 6th ed. (Franeker: T. Wever, 1979 [1966]); A. J. Rasker, *De Nederlandse Hervormde Kerk vanaf 1795*, 2nd rev. ed. (Kampen: Kok, 1981 [1974]). The standard scholarly treatment of the *Réveil* is M. Elisabeth Kluit, *Het Protestantse Réveil in Nederland en Daarbuiten, 1815-1865* (Amsterdam: Paris, 1970).

his written works: a prize essay published in 1783 entitled "Exploration of the Relationship between Poetry and Rhetoric to Philosophy" ("Verhandeling over het verband van de dichtkunst en welsprekendheid met de wijsbegeerte") and another prize work, this time in verse, "The Influence of Poetry on Government" ("De Invloed der Dichtkunst op het Staetsbestuur").[86] To set the stage for considering Kuyper's use of political poetry to create and sustain a new Christian-democratic political movement and party, we shall first consider two illustrative examples of political rhetoric in actual practice — one in the parliamentary career of the British orator and writer Edmund Burke,[87] and the other in the sermonic form, the jeremiad, as used by American preachers.[88] This will be followed by a summary of Alexis de Tocqueville's discussion of the role played by art and literature in a democracy like America.[89] Our consideration of the jeremiad as well as Tocqueville's discussion will help us see significant linkages between Kuyper's vision of liberty and the American experiment.[90]

Political Rhetoric in Action: Edmund Burke; the American Jeremiad

To counter the common charge leveled by contemporary advocates of multicultural ideology that the traditional canon of Western literature reflects an oppressive, hegemonic order, privileging a dominant ruling class of European white males, Daniel Ritchie considers the "India writings" of British statesman and political theorist Edmund Burke (1729-97). Ritchie judges that these writings serve as a clear literary counterexample to an ideological multicultural approach. Best known for his writings on the French Revolution,[91] Burke's parlia-

86. The former was republished in Amsterdam, 1836; the latter appears in Willem Bilderdijk, *De Dichtwerken van Bilderdijk*, 16 vols. (Haarlem: A. C. Kruseman, 1858), 8:3-20.

87. For this example of Burke I am especially indebted to Daniel E. Ritchie, "From Babel to Pentecost: Burke's India, Ideological Multiculturalism, and a Christian Poetics," *Christianity and Literature* 43, nos. 3-4 (spring-summer 1994): 393-414.

88. My primary source here is Sacvan Bercovitch, *The American Jeremiad* (Madison: University of Wisconsin Press, 1978).

89. Tocqueville discusses this in the second volume of *Democracy in America*, pt. I, chaps. 9-21. Citations given in the text are to the translation by George Lawrence, edited by J. P. Mayer (New York: Harper & Row, 1966).

90. The place of Kuyper's own work in the long tradition of Dutch Calvinist jeremiads is considered in Eijnatten, esp. 258-95.

91. Edmund Burke, *Reflections on the Revolution in France*, ed. Conor Cruise O'Brien (London and New York: Penguin Books, 1982 [1790]).

mentary career was distinguished particularly by his opposition to what he regarded as the tyrannical behavior of India's British governor-general, Warren Hastings, finally leading up to the ultimately unsuccessful impeachment proceedings against Hastings in 1786-87. Ritchie suggests that a *literary* study of Burke's India writings opens new vistas into their *political* significance, specifically that "a literary analysis of structure (the structure of 'sympathy') and of allusion (classical allusion) will produce new knowledge of Burke's achievement."[92] Ritchie's concern is to show, via Burke's India writings, "that traditional literary study can deal with the very real existence of political oppression without adopting current ideological criticism."[93]

In the thousands of pages Burke wrote, along with the numerous speeches he gave, on Britain's colonial involvement in India, "Burke realized that his main difficulty . . . was to create sympathy in his audience for a different culture."[94] It was here that Burke's own earlier work on aesthetics helped him.[95] "In his early *Enquiry into the Origins of Our Ideas of the Sublime and Beautiful,* Burke noted the empirical fact that human beings enjoy viewing the calamities of others as long as their terrors are somewhat removed. But the great speaker does not want painful descriptions to arouse enjoyment but rather sympathy in his audience."[96] According to Burke, human beings are created so that "we should be united by the bond of sympathy, [and the Creator] has strengthened that bond by a proportionable delight; and there most where our sympathy is most wanted — in the distress of others." Thus, "the sympathetic pain one feels in 'real calamities prompts us to relieve ourselves in relieving those who suffer.'" "Sympathy is therefore a bridge between the pains of others, fictional or real, and oneself: the words of poetry and 'eloquence' succeed (where simple verbal descriptions fail) in raising sympathy for the sufferer by placing the 'sublime' and terrible possibilities of suffering before the listener or reader." And from this follows social obligation and political action: "The sublime, in Burke's theory, was always associated with the possibility of pain, but in the case of real as opposed to fictional pain the listener's pleasure in the sublime comes in sympathetic identification with the sufferer and in providing relief from that suffering."[97]

According to Ritchie, Burke put this theory into good practice in his India

92. Ritchie, 401.
93. Ritchie, 399.
94. Ritchie, 401.
95. Edmund Burke, *A Philosophical Enquiry into the Origins of Our Ideas of the Sublime and Beautiful,* ed. J. T. Bolton (London: Routledge & Kegan Paul, 1958 [1757]).
96. Ritchie, 401.
97. Ritchie, 401. Burke citations are from *Enquiry* 1.14, 15.

speeches and writings. "The word 'sympathy' occurs frequently in the Indian speeches, particularly where Burke's rhetoric is most urgent."[98] Burke shows himself to be committed to the rhetorical tradition (in distinction from the philosophical/rational tradition) when he indicates his preference for descriptions that "affect rather by sympathy than imitation, [those that] display rather the effect of things on the mind of the speaker, or of others, than to present a clear idea of the things themselves" (*Enquiry* 5.5). It needs to be noted that Burke thus links the aesthetic with the political. In Ritchie's words: "It is highly significant, and rarely noted at present, that the *Enquiry* joins the work of *speakers* — presumably including Parliamentary orators — with that of poets; he unites the appeal of political rhetoric with that of tragedy. Burke's theory connects the literary, historical, and political aspects of the objects of sympathy. He believed that God had created humanity for the exercise of sympathy, but that the works of human art had to elicit sympathy for its proper use."[99] In his appeals for sympathy, for the British to act more justly in India (and — in other speeches — in Ireland), Burke recounted stories of oppression and drew significant historical parallels that would affect his English audience, such as referring to an important India bill before Parliament as the "*Magna Charta* of Hindostan."[100] Ritchie also notes that Burke used numerous classic allusions (Roman Senate, Cicero) as "a key resource to arouse his audience's horror at the structure of British imperialism." Such allusions work on the presumption of "a universal human nature, stretching from Rome through Britain to India, and provides [for Burke] a means for judging contemporary British politics against its own literary inheritance."[101] It is here that the tradition of Western literature makes possible the West's own self-criticism.[102]

The use of rhetoric and poetic imagination to nurture social and political transformation can also be seen in the sermonic form of the jeremiad, "or the *political sermon,* as the New England Puritans sometimes called this genre,"[103] a prominent perennial in American life from the colonial days to the present. The

---

98. Ritchie, 402.

99. Ritchie, 402.

100. Edmund Burke, "Speech on Mr. Fox's East India Bill," in *The Writings and Speeches of Edmund Burke in Twelve Volumes* (Boston: Little, Brown, 1901), 2:441. This lengthy speech (pp. 431-536) is also remarkable for its many stories of injustice and its eloquent descriptions and numerous allusions that evoke sympathy.

101. Ritchie, 404.

102. A possibility closed off to ideology, according to Ritchie: "Ideological multiculturalism lacks the inner resources to restrain its own cultural power and criticize its own excesses, for it cuts off the tradition of self-criticism, founded on the presupposition of moral and religious duty, that western literature often displays" (412).

103. Bercovitch, xiv.

jeremiad is a clear example of the function of rhetoric in a culture to "both reflect and affect a set of particular psychic, social, and historical needs."[104] According to Bercovitch, the American jeremiad was "a mode of public exhortation that originated in the European pulpit, was transformed in both form and content by the New England Puritans, persisted through the eighteenth century, and helped sustain a national dream through two hundred years of turbulence and change." He adds that it "was a ritual designed to join social criticism to spiritual renewal, public to private identity, the shifting 'signs of the times' to certain traditional metaphors, themes and symbols." Finally, he argues "that the jeremiad has played a major role in fashioning the myth of America," and that this identity must therefore be seen "in literary and historical terms. Myth may clothe history as fiction, but it persuades in proportion to its capacity to help men act in history." Total fictional myth is inadequate for shaping public, social identity. "Ultimately, [a myth's] effectiveness derives from its functional relationship to facts."[105]

The jeremiad is addressed to a covenant people who are favored by God and for that reason have special obligations. John Winthrop, on the *Arbella*, told the first shipload of emigrants in the exodus from England that they were to be "a city on a hill; the eyes of all peoples are upon us," and in his 1630 sermon "A Modell of Christian Charity" spelled out the covenantal consequences of being called to be the "New Israel" with an "Errand into the Wilderness":

> Thus stands the cause between God and us: we are entered into Covenant with him for this work, we have taken out a Commission. The Lord hath given us leave to draw our own articles. We have professed to enterprise these Actions upon these and these ends [and] we have hereupon besought him of favor and blessing. Now if the Lord shall please to hear us, and bring us in peace to the place we desire, then hath he ratified this Covenant and sealed our Commission [and] will expect a strict performance of the Articles contained in it. But if we neglect the observance of these Articles which are the ends we have propounded, and dissembling with our God, shall fall to embrace this present world and prosecute our carnal intentions, seeking great things for ourselves and our posterity, the Lord will surely break out in wrath against us [and] be revenged of such a perjured people and make us know the price of the breach of such a covenant.[106]

104. Bercovitch, xi.
105. Bercovitch, xi.
106. In Edwin S. Gaustad, *A Documentary History of Religion in America to the Civil War*, 2nd ed. (Grand Rapids: Eerdmans, 1993), 107.

The covenantal understanding and the jeremiad sermon form came from Europe but, according to Bercovitch, had in America from the beginning its own different content. The European jeremiad was a "lament over the ways of the world" and "decried the sins of 'the people' — a community, a nation, a civilization, mankind in general — and warned of God's wrath to follow."[107] It was different for the American Puritans. Believing that theirs was a special mission from God, that they had been chosen "not only for heaven but as instruments of a sacred historical design," their theocratic community was not only "a model to the world of Reformed Christianity" but also "a prefiguration of New Jerusalem to come." For this reason, though "they asserted [the threat of divine judgment] with a ferocity unparalleled in the European pulpit," they also "qualified it by considering God's judgments as corrective rather than destructive."[108] The laments about community sin, the threats of judgment, the calls for repentance were framed in the basic conviction that America's history was prophetically destined for greatness; the errand into the wilderness by the New Israel would eventually lead to Canaan, to the New Jerusalem.[109]

It was this conviction that accounts for the persistence of the Puritan jeremiad through the transformations effected in it by the First and Second Great Awakenings, the westward expansion and visions of imperial Manifest Destiny, right through the civil rights movement and the rise of the Religious Right in the second half of the twentieth century. America, Bercovitch notes, was

> a country that, despite its arbitrary territorial limits, could read its destiny in its landscape, and a population that, despite its bewildering mixture of race and creed, could believe in something called an American mission, and could invest that patent fiction with all the emotional, spiritual, and intellectual appeal of a religious quest. Here was the anarchist Thoreau condemning his backsliding neighbors by referring to the Westward errand; here the solitary singer Walt Whitman, claiming to be the American way; here, the civil rights leader Martin Luther King, Jr., descendent of slaves, denouncing segregation as a violation of the American dream; here an endless debate about national identity, full of rage and faith; Jeffersonians claiming that they, and not the priggish heirs of Calvin, really represented the errand; conservative politicians hunting out socialists as conspirators against the dream; left-wing polemics proving that capitalism was a betrayal of the country's sacred origins.

107. Bercovitch, 7.
108. Bercovitch, 8.
109. The classic treatment of the "errand" metaphor is Perry Miller's much-discussed essay "Errand into the Wilderness," in *Errand into the Wilderness* (Cambridge, Mass., and London: Harvard University Press, Belknap Press, 1956), 1-15.

The prophetic question is: "'When is our errand to be fulfilled?' 'How long, O Lord, how long?' And the answers, again as in the Puritan jeremiads, invariably joined lament and celebration in reaffirming America's mission."[110]

In the many mutations and permutations of the American ideal, it was the activity of the poets and preachers (and, as we shall see, landscape painters), using the old and powerful (mostly biblical) metaphors (exodus, errand into the wilderness, New Israel, frontier, providential destiny), that shaped and sustained the national identity and vision. The French nineteenth-century visitor to America Alexis de Tocqueville, mostly celebrated for his insights into American *political* values and practice, also knew that the American democratic experiment in ordered liberty needed literature to fuel the required democratic imagination.

Alexis de Tocqueville on the Democratic Imagination

Tocqueville begins the second volume of *Democracy in America* with the observation that though Americans pay little attention to the formal study of philosophy, there does exist "a uniform method and rule for the conduct of intellectual inquiries." This universal method Tocqueville judges as Cartesian: "each American relies on individual effort and judgment." However, the Cartesian method is followed by Americans with singular lack of self-consciousness; Cartesian intellectual self-reliance is habitual, not reflective. "Of all the countries in the world, America is the one in which the precepts of Descartes are the least studied and best followed" (429). The pedigree of this attitude, according to Tocqueville, goes back to the Protestant Reformation's emphasis on the priesthood of all believers: "Luther, Descartes, and Voltaire all used the same method, and they differed only in the greater or lesser extent to which they held it should be applied" (431). The extension of the Reformation principle to more radical questioning of everything became possible only when the conditions of equality for all people increased. More thorough independence of mind requires conditions of general equality (432-33).

At the same time, however, the independence of mind and intellectual liberty that Tocqueville considers a defining characteristic of the American mental habit has not led to anarchy. In fact, in seeming contradiction to it, intellectual self-reliance is accompanied by strongly held communal religious convictions that are also relatively unexamined; they are "believed in without discussion."[111]

110. Bercovitch, 11.
111. For a more contemporary interpretation on this phenomenon, see Richard Hofstadter, *Anti-intellectualism in American Life* (New York: Vintage Books, 1963 [1962]).

The strength of America's spiritual heritage is the crucial factor here. "In the United States religion is mingled with all the national customs and all those feelings which the word fatherland evokes. For that reason it has peculiar power." Thus, while there are "an infinite variety of ceaselessly changing Christian sects" in America, "Christianity itself is an established and irresistible fact which no one seeks to attack or to defend." This has had a profound effect on the moral character of American society, on its habits of the heart. "Since the Americans have accepted the main dogmas of the Christian religion without examination, they are bound to receive in like manner a great number of moral truths derived therefrom and attached thereto" (432). The end result of this is a growing readiness to trust and live by mass public opinion, which "becomes more and more mistress of the world." The shadow side is that a different kind of tyranny then becomes possible, a "despotism of the majority": "So, in democracies public opinion has a strange power of which aristocratic nations can form no conception. It uses no persuasion to forward its beliefs, but by some mighty pressure of the mind of all upon the intelligence of each it imposes its ideas and makes them penetrate men's very souls" (435). In this way, Tocqueville fears that "democracy might extinguish that freedom of the mind which a democratic social condition favors" and "the human spirit might bind itself in tight fetters to the general will of the greatest number" (436).

Religious beliefs are thus in many respects the exception to Tocqueville's observations about the American pattern of independence and Cartesian intellectual habits of self-reliance. Instead, a generalized public opinion prevails as an unexamined habit under conditions of equality. Tocqueville judges this to be a good thing. For while it is true that all societies require "dogmatic beliefs, that is to say, opinions which men take on trust without discussion" (433), it is even more true for democratic and equal societies that encourage independence and individualism. "In times of enlightenment and democracy the human spirit is loath to accept dogmatic ideas and has no lively sense of the need for them, *except in the matter of religion*" (445, emphasis added). A free and open inquiring mind can only be free to roam intellectually if the most fundamental questions about human life are settled. As Tocqueville concludes: "It is therefore of immense importance to men to have fixed ideas about God, their souls, and their duties toward their Creator and their fellows, for doubt about these first principles would leave all their actions to chance and condemn them, more or less, to anarchy and impotence" (443). These fundamental beliefs "are therefore the ideas above all others which ought to be withdrawn from the habitual action of private judgment and in which there is most to gain and least to lose by recognizing an authority" (443). This point is so crucial in Tocqueville's judgment that he summarizes it with one of his famous either-or epigrammatic phrases:

"For my part, I doubt whether man can support complete religious independence and entire political liberty at the same time. I am led to think that if he has no faith he must obey, and if he is free he must believe" (444).[112] From a purely human point of view, religion is useful for societal well-being, and "the great usefulness of religion is even more apparent among egalitarian peoples than elsewhere" (444). This utility of religion is recognized even by the unbeliever, according to Tocqueville: "The unbeliever, no longer thinking religion true, still considers it useful. Paying attention to the human side of religious beliefs, he recognizes their sway over mores and their influence over laws. He understands their power to lead men to live in peace and gently to prepare them for death. Therefore he regrets his faith after losing it, and deprived of a blessing whose value he fully appreciates, he fears to take it away from those who still have it" (299).[113]

However, aside from brief comments about the importance of few external ceremonies and the need for religions to limit themselves to their "proper" spiritual sphere, Tocqueville does not give many clues about *how* these fundamental and essential basic beliefs are to be passed on and nurtured. He does suggest that the most successful religions will be those that clearly distinguish central doctrines from secondary ones and hold them firmly (447), those that best respect majority public opinion and encourage the democratic instincts that are not hostile to particular religious beliefs, as well as those that concern themselves for this life as well as the life to come (449). In terms of content, Tocqueville also judges that conditions of equality tend to foster religious conceptions of "a single God who imposes the same laws on each man and grants him future happiness at the same price." In other words, "the conception of the unity of mankind ever brings them back to the idea of the unity of the Creator" (445). Because under conditions of equality "the concept of unity becomes an obsession," Tocqueville thinks that democratic societies incline toward pantheism and notions of the indefinite perfectibility of man (451-53).

But hints about the *content* of religions that are friendly to freedom and democracy do not answer the *how* question. If we take a point of departure from our earlier consideration of Solzhenitsyn's argument that "beauty saves the world," we could expect Tocqueville to appeal to the role of art and literature as the proper means by which a democratic people transmit and nurture their ideals. If art more broadly points to the permanent things, to the basic

112. Earlier in the first volume Tocqueville made a similar point: "Despotisms may be able to do without faith, but freedom cannot" (294).

113. For an eloquent statement of the same sentiment by a contemporary atheist (and socialist!), see Michael Harrington, *The Politics at God's Funeral: The Spiritual Crisis of Western Civilization* (New York: Holt, Rinehart & Winston, 1983).

transcendent points of reference for human life in society, then the human quest for beauty (and, through it, truth) is a crucial component in maintaining the habits of the heart necessary for life in a democratic community. When we add to this Tocqueville's concern about the social utility of religion, we are led to some notion of civil religion supported by salutary "social myths" which could then be propagated by civic art and literature as well as civic pageantry and ritual.[114]

Tocqueville does make an appeal to art (though not civic art to serve social myths), but in an indirect manner. He defines poetry as "the search for and representation of the ideal" and, like Solzhenitsyn,[115] contends that it is "not the poet's function to portray reality but to beautify it and offer the mind some loftier image" (483). But before he comes to that point, he makes a number of telling observations about the possibility of art and literature in a democracy. He notes that there is a paucity of intellectual and artistic activity in the United States, "that few of the civilized nations of our times have made less progress than the United States in the higher sciences or had so few great artists, distinguished poets, or celebrated artists" (454). However, Tocqueville judges this to be an accident of exceptional historical circumstance rather than a necessary consequence of the democratic situation. Though Americans have a greater taste for the useful than they have love for beauty because "democratic peoples . . . cultivate those arts which help to make life comfortable rather than those which adorn it" (465), the artistic impulse is not dead in America. Conditions lead to the expansion of artistic quantity while quality declines (468). "Democracy not only encourages the making of a lot of trivial things but also inspires

114. This claim about salutary social myths (minus the reference to art) is in fact made by Jack Lively, *The Social Thought of Alexis de Tocqueville* (Oxford: Clarendon, 1962), 196-97, and Marvin Zetterman, *Tocqueville and the Problem of Democracy* (Stanford, Calif.: Stanford University Press, 1967), 120-24. Catherine Zuckert's critique of Lively and Zetterman is persuasive, since both rely on phrases such as "is a little more than . . ." (Zetterman) and "it is only a short move from . . ." (Lively) and neither cites passages from Tocqueville that come close to a notion of "salutary social myth." See Catherine Zuckert, "Not by Preaching: Tocqueville on the Role of Religion in American Democracy," *Review of Politics* 43, no. 2 (April 1981): 259-80; I am indebted to Zuckert's article for the references to Lively and Zetterman.

115. For a significant comparison between Tocqueville and Solzhenitsyn, see Stephen Baron, "Morality and Politics in Public Life: Tocqueville and Solzhenitsyn on the Importance of Religion to Liberty," *Polity* 14, no. 3 (spring 1982): 395-413. Though Baron's key contrast between Tocqueville's instrumental/utilitarian understanding of religion as a limiter for democratic man and Solzhenitsyn's notion of religion's role in spiritually and morally transforming the person is clearly spelled out, he, like most interpreters of Tocqueville, overlooks the role of art and the artist.

the erection of a few very large monuments" with "nothing at all between these two extremes" (469). Lacking the leisurely opportunities of aristocratic classes, a democratic people "with but short time to spend on books [will] want it all to be profitable. They like books which are easily got and quickly read, requiring no learned researches to understand them. They like facile forms of beauty, self-explanatory and immediately enjoyable; above all they like things unexpected and new" (474).

Tocqueville is not reluctant to be specific about the range of subjects that serve a democratic imagination. Whereas aristocratic climates encourage poetic inspiration to range into the transcendent and supernatural, to celebrate what is old and fixed and dwell on gods and heroes, "the spread of equality over the earth dries up the old springs of poetry." With the loss of the great themes and subjects, "poets first turned their eyes to inanimate nature. Gods and heroes gone, they began by painting rivers and mountains." Tocqueville disagrees with those who judge that "this poetry embellishing the physical and inanimate things that cover the earth is the true poetry of democracy," and instead regards "it only as a transitional phenomenon." He concludes: "In the long run I am sure that democracy turns man's imagination away from externals to concentrate it on himself alone. Democratic peoples may amuse themselves momentarily by looking at nature, but it is about themselves that they are really excited. Here, and here alone, are the true springs of poetry among them" (484).[116] In addition, the democratic imagination is future rather than past oriented, and is likely to celebrate the nation as a whole more than individual subjects, and link the nation's destiny to "include the destiny of the whole human race" in its scope. If poets "strive to connect the events they commemorate with the general designs of God for the universe, and without showing the hand of the Supreme Governor, reveal His thought, they will be admired and understood, for the imagination of their contemporaries is following the same road" (486). In Tocqueville's own summary:

> Among a democratic people poetry will not feed on legends or on traditions and memories of old days. The poet will not try to people the universe again with supernatural beings in whom neither his readers nor he himself any longer believes, nor will he coldly personify virtues and vices better seen in their natural state. All these resources fail him, but man remains and the poet needs no more. Human destiny, man himself, not tied to time or place, but *face to face with nature and with God*, with his passions, his doubts, his unexpected good fortune, and his incomprehensible miseries, will for these peo-

116. Is Tocqueville predicting the inevitability of a poet like Walt Whitman?

ples be the chief and almost sole subject of poetry. . . . Equality, then, does not destroy all the subjects of poetry. It makes them fewer but more vast. (487)

Tocqueville's observations were prescient. The landscape art of Hudson Valley painters such as Thomas Cole and his pupil Frederick Church celebrated nature and nature's God. In fact, art historian Barbara Novak notes, "by the time Emerson wrote *Nature* in 1836, the terms 'God' and 'nature' were often the same thing and could be used interchangeably. . . . If Nature was God's Holy book, it *was* God."[117] Nineteenth-century landscape art had mass appeal and served religiously and metaphorically to place America in the broader narrative of universal providential history. As art critic Robert Hughes notes, "The wilderness, for nineteenth-century American artists, is mostly stress-free. Its God is an American God whose gospel is Manifest Destiny. It is pious and full of uplift. No wonder it was so quickly absorbed as a metaphor of religious experience by the first mass audience American art was to reach. It dovetailed so well with the pieties of its time."[118] The painters became the new priests of a national nature religion nurturing a new spiritual community. "In painting the face of God in the landscape so that the less gifted might recognize and share in that benevolent spirituality, they were among the spiritual leaders of America's flock."[119] One nineteenth-century writer, linking the sublimity of nature with the providential errand that was so foundational to the jeremiad, described the new nationalist iconographic spirituality this way:

> God has promised us a renowned existence, if we will but deserve it. He speaks this promise in the sublimity of Nature. It resounds all along the crags of the Alleghanies. It is uttered in the thunder of Niagara. It is heard in the roar of two oceans, from the great Pacific to the rocky ramparts of the bay of Fundy. His finger has written it in the broad expanse of our Inland Seas, and traced it out by the mighty Father of Waters! The august TEMPLE in which we dwell was built for lofty purposes. Oh! that we may consecrate it to LIBERTY and CONCORD, and be found fit worshippers within its holy wall![120]

117. Barbara Novak, *Nature and Culture: American Landscape and Painting, 1825-1875* (New York: Oxford University Press, 1980), 3.

118. Robert Hughes, *American Visions: The Epic History of Art in America* (New York: Knopf, 1997), 140-41.

119. Novak, 15.

120. James Brooks, *The Knickerbocker* (1835); quoted by Novak, 15.

Fig. 1.2. Frederick Church's *Niagara*

From this it can be seen how the artistic representations of America's natural riches — viewed as God's blessings on his chosen people — served the needs of national identity and purpose for the new country. In Novak's judgment: "Perhaps it is safe to say that despite its international complexion, nineteenth-century nature worship was more strongly nationalistic in America than elsewhere. For nature was tied to the group destiny of Americans united within a still-new nation, 'one nation, under God.' This is perhaps a key explanation for the acceptance of immanence by the religious orthodoxy." In sum, "Christianity and nationalism, two forms of hope, two imprimaturs of destiny, continually emerged from the face of American nature."[121]

Others saw the American march westward over nature and native in a more historically grounded biblical-metaphorical light: as an exodus into the promised land. George Caleb Bingham's *Daniel Boone Escorting Settlers through the Cumberland Gap*, joining the exodus motif with the flight into Egypt, re-

---

121. Novak, 16-17. The intense focus on nature did mean that the greatest of the early nineteenth-century landscape painters also worried about the impending shadow of industrialization. Thomas Cole's nature nostalgia, reflected in his *Falls of Kaaterskill*, also led him to express artistically his anxiety about impending storms of doom as human culture, technological domination, and the general human lust for power and wealth threaten the idyllic harmony of nature. In his five-painting *Course of Empire Series*, Cole metaphorically traces the cyclical pattern of decline from wilderness to garden to imperial consummation to destruction, and finally, to desolation. See, e.g., Hughes, 147-50; Novak, 10-13; cf. William H. Turner and Alan Wallach, eds., *Thomas Cole: Landscape into History* (New Haven and London: Yale University Press; Washington, D.C.: National Museum of American Art, 1994).

Fig. 1.3. George Caleb Bingham's *Daniel Boone Escorting Settlers
through the Cumberland Gap*

Fig. 1.4. Albert Bierstadt's *Lander's Peak*

Fig. 1.5. Emanuel Leutze's *Westward the Course of Empire Takes Its Way*
(Westward Ho!)

flected a more widespread image of Daniel Boone as a Moses figure and a warrior against savage Indians.

The culmination of this vision of American expansionism as providentially inevitable is artistically portrayed in such works as Albert Bierstadt's *The Rocky Mountains, Lander's Peak* and with spectacular obviousness by Emanuel Leutze's visual representation of the heliotropic myth, *Westward the Course of Empire Takes Its Way (Westward Ho!)*.

It also needs to be noted that the shadow side of this manifest destiny doctrine was not ignored by painters. Bierstadt's and Leutze's vision must be set next to the more somber look out over the Pacific in Tompkins Harrison Matteson's haunting work *The Last of the Race.*

Fig. 1.6. Tompkins Harrison Matteson, *The Last of the Race*

Abraham Kuyper the Poet

We took note earlier in this chapter of Kuyper's clear affirmation of faith in America's providential destiny. When, in October 1898, Kuyper told his Grand Rapids Dutch-American audience that "America is destined in the providence of God to become the most glorious and noble nation the world has ever seen ... [its eventual] renown will eclipse the renown and splendor of Rome, Greece and the old races,"122 he was mouthing conventional late nineteenth-century American platitudes. But how, we now ask, does his passion for the cause of Calvinist cultural and political revival in order to achieve liberty in his own beloved Netherlands tie in with this vision and with the thread we have been exploring about the role of art and literature in national, cultural, and social renewal? Does Kuyper conceive of art as an essential ingredient in his programmatic strategy to emancipate the marginalized orthodox Dutch Cal-

122. *Grand Rapids Herald,* October 29, 1898; see app. C.

vinists of the latter nineteenth century? Or, considered from another perspective, where does one place Kuyper on the continuum of rhetorical versus philosophical critique? Does his passionate opposition to the French Revolution translate into partisanship for the rhetorical and poetic tradition *against* the *philosophes?*

In short, my answer to this question is yes. The explication of a more complete answer will be developed in three stages. First, we need to show that Kuyper was aware of the importance of "poetry" in the religious-national renewal and accompanying liberty he sought for his own nation. Second, we shall illustrate from Kuyper's work that he practiced what he preached, that he acted as a poet. Thirdly, we shall summarize the judgment of other interpreters of Kuyper's career who also saw him as a poet.

Let us recall the purpose of this discussion. We are considering the category of "poet" as a way of helping us understand Kuyper's success as a movement leader, especially his efforts to emancipate the marginalized Dutch orthodox Reformed masses *(Gereformeerde kleine luyden)* and mobilize them into an effective political force for change.[123] Specifically, this involves a consideration of how Kuyper revived and used a Dutch, Christian-historical imagination[124] — including biblical and national metaphors, symbols, narratives, and myths — to accomplish this goal. He did not, in the first place, mobilize a people by positing reasonable, abstract "Reformed principles" *(Gereformeerde beginselen),* therewith *intellectually* besting the principles and setting aside the arguments of Enlightenment *philosophes.* Rather — as journalist, churchman, political leader of the Antirevolutionary Party, and public speaker extraordinaire — he effectively captured the political *imagination* of the Dutch *Gereformeerde volk* with powerful rhetoric, well-chosen biblical images, and national mythology, and in this way moved them to action. That is the essence of the claim made in this introduction that it is helpful to think of Kuyper as a "poet": Kuyper as a man of *rhetoric* and *mythos* more than[125] Kuyper as a man of *logos* and *wetenschap.* It is in the realm of poetic imagination, in other words, that we can discern a certain unity to Kuyper's multifaceted career. The roles of Kuyper the

123. In addition to the literature cited in n. 14 above, see Jan Hendriks, *De Emancipatie van de Gereformeerden* (Alphen aan den Rijn: Samsom, 1971).

124. For a more complete treatment of what is meant by the term "Christian-historical," see the last section of this chapter.

125. The comparative ("more than") is deliberately chosen over any adversative ("rather than," "instead of"). The point here is not that Kuyper should be seen as a romantic opponent of all *logos,* but that viewing him primarily in terms of *mythos* is helpful in accounting for the shape and tenor of his career as a neo-Calvinist visionary and leader of a sociopolitical movement.

emancipator of a marginalized national minority; Kuyper the church reformer, university builder, and professor;[126] Kuyper the theologian, the politician, and party leader; and Kuyper the journalist acquire a significant unity when we think of him in this very broad sense as a "poet" with a remarkable imaginative facility to use and apply scriptural imagery, Dutch national history and mythology, and a grand historical sense of providential purpose to move and persuade his audience.

Kuyper and the Poetic Tradition: The *Réveil*

As we now examine Kuyper's place in and use of the poetic/rhetorical tradition, let us first consider a few superficial points of comparison between Kuyper and other figures we discussed earlier in this chapter. In his Stone Lectures on Calvinism, Kuyper devoted one complete lecture to Calvinism and art.[127] It is worth noting that, in line with Tocquevillian appreciation, Kuyper does not disparage the democratizing of art in the nineteenth century. Though he "admits" that "the homage of art by the profanum vulgus must necessarily lead to art corruption," nonetheless, he adds, "in this cold, irreligious and practical age the warmth of this devotion to art has kept alive many higher aspirations of our soul, which otherwise might readily have died, as they did in the middle of the last century" (142-43). In keeping with his general purpose in the Stone Lectures, namely, to celebrate the contributions of Calvinism as well as encourage its further development, Kuyper points to the role that Calvinism played in the advancement of three areas, poetry, painting, and music. Concerning poetry, he notes with regret that he can say no more because he would "have to disclose to you the treasures of our own Dutch literature," and that is impossible because "the narrow bounds within which our Netherland language is confined have excluded our poetry from the world at large" (164). However, in words that are similar to those we encountered earlier from Solzhenitsyn, Kuyper notes that, unlike the limitations of language, "the *eye* is international, and," he adds, "music heard by the ear is understood in every heart" (165).

In terms of content, Kuyper points to the democratic character of the great seventeenth-century Dutch Masters like Rembrandt who "no longer considered worthy of notice [only those] who were superior to the common man, *viz.*, the

126. See J. Stellingwerf, *Dr. Abraham Kuyper en de Vrije Universiteit* (Kampen: Kok, 1987).

127. "Calvinism and Art." Kuyper, *Lectures on Calvinism*, 142-70; page references that follow in the text are to the Stone Lectures. For a helpful critical interpretation of this lecture, see Heslam, 196-223; also see n. 16 above.

high world of the Church and of the priest, of knights and princes.[128] But," says Kuyper, "since then, the people had come of age, and under the auspices of Calvinism, the art of painting, prophetic of a democratic life of later times, was the first to proclaim the people's maturity" (165). In all of this "it was seen that non-churchly life was also possessed of high importance and of an all-sided art motive." It was not only in aristocratic societies that art could flourish. In fact, the newfound liberty born out of Calvinism created "a field on which free art could flourish," and "Calvinism alone was able to plough that field." Kuyper allows his democratic sympathies full rein at this point: "Having been overshadowed for many centuries by class-distinctions, the common life of many came out of its hiding-place like a new world, in all its sober reality. It was the broad emancipation of our ordinary earthly life, and the instinct for liberty, which thereby captured the heart of the nations and inspired them with delight in the enjoyment of treasures so long blindly neglected" (166). The elevation of the ordinary was rooted in the theological conviction that the world was the theater of God's glory; that creation bears the image of divinity (θειότης).[129] It is here that Kuyper's views again approach the description of art in a democratic society given by Tocqueville and the practice of American nineteenth-century landscape artists whose work, in the judgment of art historians such as Barbara Novak, is not unrelated to that of seventeenth-century Dutch landscape artists.[130] Also, as we shall explore more fully in the fourth chapter, Kuyper's reflections provide an interesting comparison with the theological understanding of beauty in America's great Calvinist theologian, Jonathan Edwards. We now turn to a more general consideration of Kuyper's political and social imagination.

To begin with, much in our earlier discussion of Solzhenitsyn and the role of beauty in saving the world would resonate well with Kuyper. Both the appeal to "permanent things"[131] and the Augustine-like description of the spir-

128. On Kuyper's understanding of the democratic character of Calvinism's influence on art, also see Abraham Kuyper, *Het Calvinisme en de Kunst* (Amsterdam: Höveker & Wormser, 1888), 24-25.

129. Kuyper, *Het Calvinisme en de Kunst*, 11.

130. Novak speaks of certain works offering "such conclusive visual evidence that it is hard to believe that they do not result from a direct (Holland) or indirect (Holland via England) cause and effect." Novak also observes that "the social similarities between the Dutch republic of the seventeenth century — with its Protestantism, its respect for humble things, its middle-class citizens — and the American republic of the nineteenth century indicate basic affinities that require further study" (233-34).

131. Kuyper unceasingly spoke of "divine ordinances," simply a more theologically framed way of referring to the permanent things. For a helpful anthology of essays inspired by T. S. Eliot's (via Russell Kirk) concern about art and the permanent things, see Andrew A. Tade and Michael H. McDonald, eds., *The Permanent Things: Toward the Re-*

itual conflict dividing humanity into two that Solzhenitsyn describes in his No-bel Lecture would have struck a deeply sympathetic chord with Kuyper and his profound sense of divine law and the *antithesis* in human experience.[132] When describing the spiritual battle "in which I myself have been spending all my en-ergy for nearly forty years," Kuyper speaks of Christianity and modernism as "two *life-systems* wrestling with one another in mortal combat." Furthermore, his characterization of the two combatants is almost identical to Solzhenitsyn's: "Modernism is bound to build a world of its own from the data of the natural man, and to construct man himself from the data of nature while, on the other hand, all those who reverently bend the knee to Christ and worship Him as the Son of the living God, and God himself, are bent upon saving the 'Christian Heritage.'"[133] Modern man is Promethean man, and the Christian servant-ap-prentice artist is his mortal enemy. Finally, Kuyper the nineteenth-century ro-mantic and believer in the distinct spiritual character and vocation of different nations[134] would heartily agree with Solzhenitsyn's appeal to literature as the "living memory of the nation," and he would echo Solzhenitsyn's warning: "But woe to the nation whose literature is cut off by the interposition of force. That is not simply a violation of 'freedom of the press'; it is stopping up the nation's heart, carving out the nation's memory; it loses its spiritual unity. . . ."[135]

---

covery of a More Human Scale at the End of the Twentieth Century (Grand Rapids: Eerd-mans, 1995).

132. It should be noted that Peter Heslam, who contends that "in the realm of art Kuyper spoke as one not directly involved, and as one who showed little sign of artistic cre-ativity," pointedly observes that Kuyper's sense of the antithesis seems not to have affected his understanding of art to the degree it did his view of science. Heslam notes that Kuyper does not speak of human consciousness as the starting point for art as it is for science, and that Kuyper does not antithetically speak of "two kinds of people, two kinds of art" to complement his notion of "two kinds of science." Furthermore, in a stance that is quite uncharacteristic of his general position in the Stone Lectures, Kuyper fails to plead for a specifically Christian art. Heslam concludes from this that "Kuyper clearly felt that, in terms of effecting social change, politics and science [topics of two other Stone Lectures] were more important than the arts . . . [and] no-one [in the nineteenth century] proposed that the arts could provide a radically new order and a means of solving all manner of problems in human society, as was thought to be the vocation of science" (Heslam, 217). In my judgment, Heslam is largely correct about Kuyper's *theory*, but I believe his observa-tions are less true for Kuyper's *practice*. Kuyper, I am arguing here — as rhetorician, as preacher, as journalist, as parliamentarian, as political poet — was a creative artist and used his word-artistry self-consciously to effect significant social and political change.

133. Kuyper, *Lectures on Calvinism*, 11.

134. See Abraham Kuyper, *Ons Program*, 4th ed. (Amsterdam and Pretoria: Höveker & Wormser, n.d.), par. 8-10.

135. Solzhenitsyn, *Nobel Lecture*, 20.

The issue of the *nation's* soul and its health brings us to the place where all discussions about the revival of nineteenth-century Dutch Calvinism begin, with the international literary-spiritual renewal movement known as the *Réveil*.[136] Its two most important *literary* figures, the poets Willem Bilderdijk (1756-1831) and Isaac da Costa (1798-1860), we must remember, were self-consciously *political poets,*[137] and the major literary work of Kuyper's own immediate mentor, Guillaume Groen van Prinsterer (1801-76), was a political-historical tract on the French Revolution rivaling that of Edmund Burke.[138]

The governing passion of all three of these men of the *Réveil* was the spiritual restoration of the Dutch *national* soul, the recovery of a sense of providential purpose for the Dutch nation as a New Israel, a model for all nations.[139] Furthermore — and this was the abiding lesson that Kuyper and his neo-Calvinist movement[140] learned from the *Réveil* men — the spiritual core of

136. See n. 85 above.

137. See the collection *Politieke Poëzy van Mr. Isaac da Costa* (Haarlem: A. C. Kruseman, 1854). This includes da Costa's famous prescient observations about the revolutionary mood that eventually led to the revolutions of 1848, "Wachter! Wat is er van den Nacht?" Da Costa's own *Voorafsprak* to the "Hollandsche Maatschappij van Fraaie Kunsten en Wetenschappen," on December 13, 1847, prior to his premier public reading of *Wachter!* (pp. 41-43), is also very illuminating as an expression of his political views. As noted earlier, Bilderdijk's understanding of the positive relation between poetry and politics is reflected in two of his written works: "Exploration of the Relationship between Poetry and Rhetoric to Philosophy" ("Verhandeling over het verband van de dichtkunst en welsprekendheid met de wijsbegeerte," 1783) and "The Influence of Poetry on Government" ("De Invloed der Dichtkunst op het Staetsbestuur"). See above, 27-28.

138. Groen van Prinsterer, *Ongeloof en Revolutie* (Leiden, 1847); English translation with significant background introduction and annotation: Harry Van Dyke, *Groen Van Prinsterer's Lectures on Unbelief and Revolution* (Jordan Station, Ont.: Wedge, 1989). Cf. Burke, *Reflections on the Revolution in France.*

139. On the Netherlands as "New Israel," see G. Groenhuis, *De Predikanten,* Historische Studien 23 (Groningen: Wolters-Noordhof, 1976); G. Groenhuis, "Calvinism and National Consciousness: The Dutch Republic as the New Israel," in *Britain and the Netherlands* (The Hague, 1981), 118-33; G. J. Schutte, *Het Calvinistisch Nederland* (Utrecht: Erven J. Bijleveld, 1988).

140. Both Kuyper and his neo-Calvinist co-laborer Herman Bavinck produced works on Willem Bilderdijk: Abraham Kuyper, *Bilderdijk in zijne Nationale Beteekenis* (Amsterdam and Pretoria: Höveker & Wormser, 1906); Herman Bavinck, *Bilderdijk als Denker en Dichter* (Kok: Kampen, 1906). Kuyper, it should be noted, in addition to his *theological* lectures at the Free University, also gave lectures on linguistics and aesthetics in the faculty of letters (J. De Bruijn, *Abraham Kuyper — Leven en Werk in Beeld* [Amsterdam: Passage, 1987]). A helpful study of Bilderdijk's relation to international literary and intellectual currents of the late eighteenth and early nineteenth centuries is Walter

Dutch national life was believed to be the Reformed or Calvinist religion. To see this in a clear fashion we turn to Kuyper's own reflections on poetry's national significance in an address he gave in 1906 at the Concertgebouw in Amsterdam on the occasion of the unveiling of a commemorative bust of poet Willem Bilderdijk to be placed in the Rijksmuseum.[141]

Kuyper begins by pointing to Bilderdijk's role in restoring the Dutch national soul at a time of major decline. Maintaining the vitality of distinct and independent nations, Kuyper adds, is necessary for the well-being of humanity as a whole. The Dutch nation's past is honored for its sense of liberty, its artistic genius, its intellectual prowess, and its moral health (6). Yet, it is a mark of national decline that the Dutch failed adequately to honor its artistic noble spirits. Even Rembrandt's glory had diminished to the point that it was Bilderdijk in 1806 who cried out: "Raise Rembrandt from his ashes before my adoring eyes" (7). What changed this situation, and rescued Rembrandt from undeserved obscurity, was international recognition and, above all, international *money*. But, while "the palette speaks an international language," poets sing to a narrow audience and do not get a listening ear beyond narrow national boundaries. Kuyper cites British poet Robert Southey, who noted the same in his "Epistle to Cunninghame":

> "And who is Bilderdijk?" me think thou sayest
> A ready question; yet which, trust me, Allan,
> Would not be asked, had not the curse that came
> From Babel, clipt the wings of Poetry.
> Napoleon asked him once, with cold fixed look,
> "Art thou then in the world of letters known?"
> And meeting his imperial look with eye
> As little wont to turn away before
> The face of man, the Hollander replied:
> "At least I have done that whereby I have
> There to be known deserved." . . .
> True lover of his country and his kind;
> In knowledge and in inexhaustible stores
> Of native genius rich; philosopher,
> Poet and sage. The language of a state

Lagerwey, "Bilderdijk and the German Enlightenment" (Ph.D. diss., University of Michigan, 1958).

141. Kuyper, *Bilderdijk in zijne Nationale Beteekenis*. This was also the 150th anniversary of Bilderdijk's birth. What follows is taken from this address; page references to direct quotations are cited in the text.

Inferior in illustrious deeds to none
But circumscribed by narrow bounds, and now
Sinking in irrecoverable decline
Hath pent within its sphere a name, with which
Europe should else have rung from side to side.[142]

This international as well as national neglect notwithstanding, Kuyper insists that "it is nonetheless the case that gifted poets are of much higher importance [than visual artists] for elevating a nation spiritually." Even when poetry is not popular, the glow of rich poetry touches the heart, the poet's genius is a spark from above, "from the Father of lights,"[143] and the appropriate memorial for great poets is not *dead* marble but ongoing memory of the poet's genius affecting the nation's *life* (7).

What is ignited by the spark of poetic genius? Feeling? Emotion? Imagination? Language? Rhythm? Rhyme? Of course, all of these, says Kuyper. Who could be a poet without them? "But the poet still reaches deeper; through the rough, tough, superficial externality of things to a world that lurks beneath, behind, beyond it, to the ideal world that sheds light upon and provides fresh air for our anxious reality. The poet conjures up a unity in the midst of brokenness, profusely spreads rays of sunshine to warm the chills of our fear. We become reconciled with our hard and harsh reality by having it placed in the framework of a higher, eternally beautiful necessity" (12). It was this inspired sense of divine purpose that characterized the heroic Dutch Sea Beggars in their revolt against Spain in the sixteenth century, and continued into the seventeenth-century period of Dutch national greatness. The success of the Dutch nation in its golden age was rooted in the conviction of divine providential purpose and was propagated as well as celebrated by *poetry*. "Then," says Kuyper, "there *was* poetry in our [national] song of deliverance, but there was also poetry in our navy captains, in the priests of our art, extending even to our merchant marine and to the skill[144] of our merchants." In the eighteenth century this glorious national vocation was corrupted, by epigones of the descendents of epigones, who frittered away their time and energy in hairsplit-

142. The full English citation is given by Kuyper in an endnote, pp. 55-57; the main, delivered text (p. 9) has eleven lines translated into Dutch.

143. The biblical reference is to James 1:17, a favorite — perhaps the most often quoted — text of Kuyper's fellow Dutch neo-Calvinist, Herman Bavinck; see, *inter alia*, Herman Bavinck, "Common Grace," trans. Raymond C. Van Leeuwen, *Calvin Theological Journal* 24 (1989): 41; Herman Bavinck, *Our Reasonable Faith*, trans. Henry Zylstra (Grand Rapids: Eerdmans, 1956), 19.

144. Kuyper plays on the Dutch word *kunst*, which can mean art in the more formal sense as well as ability, talent, or skill.

ting and magpie-chattering pamphleteering, into a spirit-less Calvinist sense of duty and guilt. "Concerned only with winning pamphlet wars they buried high principle in a mountain of gray, dead ash" (12). By Bilderdijk's day, the nation's soul was directionless and despondent and easily taken captive by a vacuous and conceited Enlightenment, resulting in a life characterized by "mechanical conventionality, teary sentimentality, if not by epicurean lewdness" (13). "There was," observes Kuyper, "too much money. . . . Weakened by luxury, the floodgates could not hold. . . . The ocean's waters sought out Holland's flag" (13).[145]

Kuyper continues, demonstrating mastery of the Dutch language and its history, by heaping scorn on the effort to rescue the nation through artificial cultural refinement. A new and, according to Kuyper, nonsensical word entered the Dutch national vocabulary: *beschaving*, from the root *schaaf*, a (wood) plane. "Unlike organic words such as *Bildung*, *Kultur*, or *Civilisation*, [this meant that] everything had to be planed smooth." But surely, adds Kuyper, a plane is only put to work on a *dead* plank and not on the core of a living tree. The eighteenth-century Enlightenment ran roughshod over the living national branch, planing away the concrete and organic particularities of Dutch life. The result was a barren chaos, "a chaos over which rationalism spun its web of ideas, and in the center of that web sat the proud rationalist on his trembling throne" (14).

It was in opposition to that evil spirit and its consequent atomism and individualism that Bilderdijk invested his heart, soul, and mind and reminded the nation of the holy, organic, and permanent things. Unity was to be found in

> The holy order of this world
> Through the scepter that holds sway
> In each turn from night to day.[146]

What is crucial here is that Kuyper calls attention to Bilderdijk deliberately not turning the tactics of the Enlightenment — i.e., theoretical, rational, scientific argumentation — against itself. Rather he took his stand in his *feeling* of primordial

145. See Simon Schama's lavishly illustrated overview of the Dutch seventeenth century: *The Embarrassment of Riches: An Interpretation of Dutch Culture in the Golden Age* (New York: Knopf, 1987).

146. Kuyper, *Bilderdijk*, 18:

> Het was al saâmgevat in
> De heil'ge orde dezer wereld
> Die den scepter van 't gezag
> Over nachbeurt voert en dag.

being, in the reality of his own heart, in his *sensus divinitatis* (15-16). "Only God *is,* and *his* word, *his* will created all that exists in an organic whole." One does not grasp that unity by deduction from its component atoms; only by instinct or intuition, by artistic imagination, can one approach the "one incredible work of art produced in an unfathomable unity" (17). In fact, Kuyper avers, had Bilderdijk indeed written a theoretical-philosophical treatise against the Enlightenment, "preferably in German — *'eine Philosophie des organisch Einen'"* — no firestorm would have come down on his head. "The public generally allows philosophers their idiosyncrasies" (19). Instead he fought with all his prophetic, *poetic* might against that which was foreign and for that which was authentically, traditionally, historically Dutch. Thanks to Bilderdijk the poet — poetry being the highest form of art (31) — Dutch language, history, and the national (Calvinist) soul were restored and renewed. Bilderdijk, in other words, according to Kuyper, represented "an individual embodiment of the nation's true spirit."[147]

Bilderdijk's appeal to the sense of obligation that arises from the heart was a direct repudiation of eighteenth-century Enlightenment rationalism and the accompanying revolutionary spirit that helped produce the Dutch "patriot" movement in the 1780s and the much-despised Batavian Republic from 1795 to 1805,[148] and influenced the Belgian revolution of 1830 as well as the more general outbreaks of European revolution in 1848. It was in opposition to this "spirit" that Bilderdijk, da Costa, and van Prinsterer exercised their literary genius to set forth an alternative Christian-historical, antirevolutionary vision. The poetic attack was directed at reason because reason itself cannot provide the reasons for moral obligation:

> No, the law that governs us
> In this imperfect life,
> Does not depend on reason's light.
> I feel it speaking in my bosom,
> Seeking vengeance on my neglect;
> It is God who is in command.

The attack on reason, it must be noted, is not a repudiation of all rationality and thought or even of philosophy,[149] but a repudiation of *autonomous* reason that defies God and his Word:

---

147. Eijnatten, 261.

148. See Simon Schama, *Patriots and Liberators: Revolution in the Netherlands, 1780-1813* (New York: Vintage Books, 1992 [1977]).

149. On Bilderdijk's philosophical allegiances, see Bavinck, *Bilderdijk als Denker en Dichter.*

Only a treacherous Reason
That, dissatisfied with God's command,
Thus combats his inspired direction,
And because of this delusion,
Imagines it can suppress
That which The Almighty
Has indelibly engraved on us mortals.[150]

Over against the fragmentation, disorder, and social anarchy resulting from rationalist individualism and revolutionary ideology, Bilderdijk passionately craved and promoted unity, order, harmony, along with creational diversity. Unity was the key feature of his worldview, according to Bavinck. The goal of all understanding, he claimed, was "always unity, unity that is found in God and unity that he has imprinted on creation. Unity in the moral, the natural, the spiritual realms; and from this unity spreading out to all spheres and orders."[151] Yet Bilderdijk clearly distances himself from romantic pantheism, as the following (didactic!) verse makes clear as it mockingly takes the monistic standpoint:

Yes, everything is indeed one;
    But reality diversifies as it approaches perfection.
Even pagans distinguish stones from shrubs;
    One is more complete, the other less;
Such distinctions are hidden in all that is.
    We are a little more complete,
Garlic cloves a bit less;
    And mushrooms still a little more less;
With ginger snaps even more less.

---

150. Bavinck, *Bilderdijk als Denker en Dichter*, 34-35:

Neen, de wet ons voorgeschreven
In dit onvolkomen leven,
    Hangt aan redens inzicht niet.
'k Voel haar in mijn boezem spreken,
Haar verzuiming op mij wreken;
    God is 't, die in haar gebiedt.
't Is alleen de valsche Reden
Die, met God's bestel t' onvreden,
    Dus Zijne inspraak wederstreeft,
En in de oorzaak waant te dringen
Van het geen ons, stervelingen,
    De Almacht ingegriffeld heeft.

151. Bavinck, *Bilderdijk als Denker en Dichter*, 42.

52

All this in a descending slope
But we, we are the most
With nothing higher,
No God nor Spirit.
Yet our exaltation must strive for yet greater loftiness;
Just read Kant and Fichte,
They will prove it to you.[152]

By contrast, Bilderdijk's own cosmology is clearly theistic, rooted in a Creator/creature distinction that acknowledges the creature's utter dependence.

Thou, one, eternal *being*
Origin of all that is and appears to be;
Whose power we read in the universe, in our existence,
In night and daylight!
Almighty, Eternal, Incomprehensible, Worldfounder,
Who embraces all, fills all. . . .
If you should cease to shine your will on our existence
We would be as if we never had been;
Your creating is our being,
Your Spirit alone gives us breath.[153]

152. Bavinck, *Bilderdijk als Denker en Dichter,* 56:

Ja, alles is wel één; maar 't stof is onderscheiden,
Naar 't meer volmaakt is. Steen of heesters aan de heiden
Verschillen; 't een is meer volkomen, 't andere min;
Daar schuilt dit onderscheid van wat bestaan heeft, in.
Wij zijn wat meer volmaakt; wat minder knofleekscheuten;
Iets minder, champignons; nog minder, peperneuten.
Dat gaat zoo dalende af; doch wij, wij zijn het meest;
En hooger is er niet, geen Godheid en geen Geest.
Maar onze hoogheid moet gestaâg nog hooger stijgen;
Lees Kant en Fichte slechts, die zullen 't u bewijzen.

Bilderdijk's use of the French *champignon* here might be doubly ironic in view of his intense opposition to the Gallicanization of the Dutch language (see Bavinck, 145, for Bilderdijk's passion about the independence and purity of the Dutch language).

153. Bavinck, *Bilderdijk als Denker en Dichter,* 53:

Gij, oorsprong van wat is, van alwat schijnt te wezen,
Maar eening, eeuwig *zijn;*
Wiens almacht we in 't heelal, in heel ons aanzijn lezen,
In nacht en zonneschijn!

This religious sense of unity is apprehended only by the heart — not reason — and language, particularly the language of poetry, gives expression to it. "In the same way that God's thoughts are expressed in the created reality he fashioned after his own image, so the human being reveals his or her inner soul in the works of human hands, particularly in the words expressed in human language. As all creation is a mirror of the spiritual, so human language is a parable, an impression, a revelation of the human spirit. Language is born from the human soul . . . and a nation's language an expression of a national soul,"[154] to be treasured as a spiritual gift. Poetry expresses the unity of the soul better than any other form of language; it is a divine gift, lit by a divine spark that reveals a higher and better world.[155]

Bilderdijk's passion was the Dutch *national* soul; his poetic imagination was rooted in Dutch national history, particularly the religious and political emancipation struggle of Dutch Calvinists to obtain freedom from Roman Catholic Spain during the Eighty Years' War. A profoundly committed monarchist, Bilderdijk's ideal was a "government led by a regent who passed beneficial laws, held the reins of power with a firm hand, so that citizens could lead a peaceful and pious life as in the days of Israel when every man lived under his vine and fig tree."[156] Such a ruler governs the nation like a father rules his household, not directed by the sovereign will of the people but by a conscience subject to God's will.[157] Bilderdijk's love of the Netherlands is inseparable from his devotion to the House of Orange.[158] This love was, however, not fully reciprocated by the new monarch, and the failure of the post-1813 Restoration of the Dutch monarchy to live up to his ideal was a profound disappointment to Bilderdijk.[159] Bilderdijk served as a literary John the Baptist, preparing the way

Almachte, Oneindige, Onbegripjpbre, Warelstichter,
   Die 't al omvat, vervult. . . .
Houdt Ge op, ons door Uw wil het aanzijn toe te stralen,
   Wij zijn also nooit geweest;
Uw scheppen is ons zijn, en, zoo wij ademhalen,
   't is werking van Uw geest.

154. Bavinck, *Bilderdijk als Denker en Dichter*, 138, 144.
155. Bavinck, *Bilderdijk als Denker en Dichter*, 158-68.
156. J. C. Van der Does, *Bijdrage tot de Geschiedenis der wording van de Anti-Revolutionaire of Christelijk-Historische Staatspartij* (Amsterdam: W. Ten Have, 1925), 27.
157. Rasker, 78.
158. When the French liberators overran the Netherlands in 1795, Stadtholder Willem V was forced into exile in England and Bilderdijk, upon his refusal to take an oath of loyalty to the new regime (his conscience forbade him to subscribe to the included "Rights of Man"), also fled to London (Lagerwey, 7).
159. Rasker, 76-78.

for the work of his pupils Isaac da Costa and Groen van Prinsterer and the flowering of the Dutch literary-spiritual renewal movement known as the *Réveil*.[160]

The *Réveil* was an international, evangelical, literary-spiritual, aristocratic-nationalist movement, deeply influenced by romanticism and its passionate historical interest and consciousness as well as its emphasis on feeling and religious experience.[161] The strong literary character of the movement was reflected in a devotion to national literature and culture as well as the study of the Bible.[162] Both interests come together in the person of the Amsterdam Portuguese Sephardic Jew Isaac da Costa. Having enjoyed a high degree of religious freedom in seventeenth-century Netherlands, the Jewish community achieved full civil emancipation on condition of their successful assimilation into Dutch life during the Napoleonic era. This enabled the young Isaac to receive a superb education, achieve a solid reputation as a poet, and become part of a select group of students (along with Groen van Prinsterer) privately being tutored in law, language, and Dutch history (*Vaderlandsgeschiedenis*) by Willem Bilderdijk. This encounter brought about a spiritual crisis in da Costa as he wavered between his Jewish past and Christian claims. With the benefit of twenty-five years' hindsight, he described this crisis as follows: "At that time I still remained (rather, I first truly became) an Israelite; and then, thanks to the grace of the God of my fathers and Savior, I confessed Christ."[163] He was baptized in the Reformed Pieterskerk of Leiden on October 20, 1822.

Thanks in part to his identity struggle between Judaism and Dutch Calvinism and a desire to be at home in two worlds, da Costa began to develop bold analogies between Israel and the Netherlands, King David and the House of Orange. One commentator described it thus: "Da Costa remained as much a Jew as a Christian; the chosen people moved from the Jordan to the Amstel River, and the God of Abraham, Isaac, and Jacob, became the God of the Netherlands."[164] That this was no exaggeration is clear from one of da Costa's poems:

O Netherlands, once again you shall
Become the Israel of the West!

160. On the *Réveil* see Kluit, *Het Protestantse Réveil in Nederland en Daarbuiten, 1815-1865*; Rasker, chaps. 6, 7; H. Algra, *Het Wonder van de Negentiende Eeuw: Van Vrije Kerken en Kleine Luyden*, 6th ed. (Franeker: T. Wever, 1979), chap. 7.
161. Rasker, 71.
162. M. Elisabeth Kluit, *Nader over het Réveil* (Kampen: Kok, 1977), 134.
163. Cited by Rasker, 79.
164. Cited by Rasker, 80.

God will encircle your church with light,
Your Kings with David's glory.[165]

"This analogy, full of eschatological expectation with messianic perspectives, also included a look backwards, a longing for an idealized past that needed to be restored."[166]

The attention given to Israel was a characteristic of the international *Réveil*,[167] and this specific analogy between Israel and the Netherlands was not new. During the Eighty Years' War the Calvinist preachers of the so-called Second Reformation[168] were responsible for creating this national mythology, drawing parallels between the bondage of Pharaoh's Egypt and that of Catholic Spain. As historian Pieter Geyl has noted, "Calvinism undoubtedly ranked among the principal cultural forces in the North. With its conception of a 'chosen people,' of the Netherlands as a second Israel, whose history embodied the profoundest sense of the grace of God, it gave style to a larger body of opinion than that of its professed adherents."[169] What was remarkable is the revival of the Israel/Netherlands-as-God's-people analogy in the second decade of the nineteenth century; nothing could be further from the spirit of Enlightenment rationalism and political secularist individualism. Da Costa's vision was a direct protest against the spirit of the age, and half a year after his baptism he published his controversial and influential countercultural tract, *Bezwaren tegen den Geest der Eeuw (Grievances against the Spirit of the Age)*.[170]

For our purposes, we need to take note of da Costa's fourth brief chapter,

165. Cited by Rasker, 80:

> O Nederland, gij zult eens weer
> het Israël van het Westen worden!
> God zal uw Kerk met licht omgorden,
> Uw Koningen met Davids eer.

166. Rasker, 80.

167. Kluit, "Israel: Knooppunt van het Internationale Réveil," in *Nader over het Réveil*, 134-63.

168. The "Second Reformation" refers to a seventeenth- and eighteenth-century flowering of Reformed spirituality and theology in the Netherlands, in many respects analogous to English Puritanism. See Joel R. Beeke, "The Dutch Second Reformation (*Nadere Reformatie*)," *Calvin Theological Journal* 28 (1993): 298-327.

169. Pieter Geyl, *The Netherlands in the Seventeenth Century, Part One, 1609-49* (New York: Barnes & Noble, 1961), 209. A thorough description of the role of Calvinist preachers in shaping this Israel-Netherlands mythology can be found in Groenhuis, *De Predikanten*.

170. Leiden: L. Herdingh en Zoon, 1823; page references in the following paragraph are to this work.

"Schoone Kunst" ("Beautiful Art"). According to da Costa, Enlightenment rationalism demonstrates its poverty particularly in its strikingly impoverished art. Art can flourish only when the spark of native genius is lit by God's spirit (32). Europe's great art — poetry, painting, architecture — was produced before the age of science, before the onslaught of French materialism and German neologism. Since then — a major artistic disaster (33)! This consequence does not surprise da Costa. All art — even that of the pagans — is the fruit of divine inspiration; it cries out: "There is a God in us! See it in our artistic ability!" (33). But the Enlightenment banished God, shut him out. "In the past, poets, painters, architects and builders worked out of faith and to praise [God]; today, to indulge their own luxury and create reputations for themselves. In the past [art pointed us] to a holy heaven; today [it celebrates] a fallen world" (34). Da Costa ends by pointing to the arrival of a new spirit in Dutch poetry, "a spirit of worship, of dependence on a higher reality that alone can provide art with true beauty. As such, poetry is part of a heavenly-led army that will soon restore everything and whose approach is already announced from many different angles. Yet, is this advance of poetry valued by our age? I think not. Nonetheless, this poetry challenges all the fundamental assumptions of the age and has placed before it an entirely different vision. It does not belong to the spirit of the nineteenth century in which it has historically appeared" (35).

Though da Costa's poetic protest was accompanied with specific political proposals,[171] it was his contemporary and fellow student of Bilderdijk, Groen van Prinsterer, who, through his influential *Lectures on Unbelief and Revolution*[172] as well as his political activity in the antirevolutionary movement, began to translate the Dutch political poetry of the early nineteenth century into concrete political and social change. And finally, it was Kuyper who inherited Groen's political mantle and turned the antirevolutionary movement into the Netherlands' first modern political party in 1879. Yet, da Costa's poetic-eschatological, Christian-historical imagination was essential to the eventual success of the Calvinist political program.[173]

171. In a famous letter to the leadership of the Dutch Reformed Church, da Costa answered the oft-repeated "what do you Christians want?" question in this way: "That the king — in the fear of God and according to his Word — acts as a king. However, we also think that it is possible, desirable, even necessary, that this take place in a constitutional form that is contemporary. We absolutely do not want an absolute monarchy. . . . We want a constitution, but one that is grounded on the principles of faith and history" (cited in Van der Does, 61-62).

172. English translation: Van Dyke, 293-540.

173. On this score, da Costa's own preference for the term "Christian-historical" over "antirevolutionary" is worth noting. In an 1854 open letter to Groen, da Costa stated

We are, recall, attempting to establish a case for "poet" as the functional mantle for Abraham Kuyper's many-sided career. The first point of this argument is the contention that Kuyper was fully aware that, to use Shelley's phrase, "poets are the unacknowledged legislators of the world." The preceding overview of Kuyper's profound appreciation for the poetic and historical legacy he inherited from Bilderdijk, da Costa, and Groen[174] may be sufficient evidence for a convincing case, but one more small bit of evidence is worth noting. Shortly after Kuyper founded the Free University of Amsterdam in 1886, he became embroiled in a controversy with his colleague in both politics and the academy, Jhr. A. F. De Savornin Lohman (1837-1924), about the exact meaning of the phrase "Reformed principles" *(Gereformeerde beginselen)* in the crucial founding statute of the university. Lohman's desire to keep the university's basis reduced to a simple affirmation about Scripture was judged by Kuyper — and eventually, the Free University senate — to be inadequate, and an elaborately crafted statement explicating the meaning of the phrase was put in place. In this statement, the *fourth* source for Reformed or Calvinistic principles (after Scripture as interpreted by the Reformed confessions, polemical writings, the history of Calvinism) was put forth as "that which in the realms of scientific and aesthetic activity (in the case of the latter, especially in *poetry*), has been articulated throughout history by Calvinists, on a whole range of topics and in diverse forms."[175] There can be no doubt about it: Abraham Kuyper truly believed in the political importance of poetry!

Kuyper's Poetic Practice: Champion of Liberty

Now we must consider Kuyper's practice. Kuyper, no less than da Costa and Bilderdijk, saw it as his life's mission to restore the Dutch national soul, the Dutch *Christian* national soul, yea, the *Calvinist* national soul. To accomplish

---

that "the name 'Christian-historical' characterizes our party better than the name 'anti-revolutionary.' The hallmark of our party is not found in the repudiation of *all* revolution (i.e. reversal of affairs in church and state); there are good revolutions. Even if we limit our rejection of revolutions to that of 1789, even then we are not consistently anti-revolutionary. We would not want to return to the pre-1795 or pre-1848 conditions. We don't want to go backwards, but forwards" (cited by Van der Does, 72-73).

174. To pick but one additional example: Kuyper's "Maranatha" address to the Antirevolutionary Party Convention in 1891, where he hails the trio for their prophetic insight into the anti-Christian character of the revolutionary spirit (in Bratt, *Abraham Kuyper*, 211-12).

175. J. C. Rullmann, *De Vrije Universiteit: Haar Ontstaan en Haar Bestaan* (Amsterdam: De Standaard, 1930), 191, emphasis added.

this Kuyper knew he had to motivate and mobilize the Dutch Reformed masses (*Gereformeerde kleine luyden*) into Christian political action. We gain insight into Kuyper's strategy for accomplishing this goal with a sneak preview of our fuller discussion in chapter 3 of his 1898 visit to America to deliver the Stone Lectures at Princeton University. Kuyper began his first lecture by describing himself as "a traveller from the old European Continent" overwhelmed by the New World. Drawing a contrast between "the almost frostbound and dull" old stream of Europe and "the eddying waters of your new stream of life," Kuyper spoke grandly about the possibilities of the New World with its rich "store of surprises for the future."[176] Kuyper's focus in the first Stone Lecture was on a favorite theme: the place of liberty in America and America's place in the providential ordering of freedom in history. "America," Kuyper had said already two decades earlier, "lacks no single liberty for which in Europe we struggle."[177] This freedom is historically the fruit of Calvinism; particularly Dutch Calvinism which "liberated Switzerland, the Netherlands, and England, and in the Pilgrim Fathers has provided the impulse to the prosperity of the United States."[178] "The 'free life of free citizens' appeared to [Kuyper] as the fruit of Calvinism."[179] Like many present-day advocates of a "Christian America,"[180] Kuyper was also certain that America would continue to play an important providential role as a beacon of liberty in world history.[181]

But, if the now full-grown plant of American liberty had originally been transplanted from Europe — from Calvinistic Holland, to be specific — what was the situation in Kuyper's own homeland in the nineteenth century? What was the status of liberty for Dutch citizens? Simply, it had been significantly curtailed thanks to the inroads of Enlightenment secularism and the spirit of the French Revolution that acknowledged *ni Dieu, ni maître* (no God, no master). To once again transform the Netherlands into a free and prosperous na-

176. Kuyper, *Lectures on Calvinism*, 9.

177. Abraham Kuyper, "Calvinism: The Origin and Safeguard of Our Constitutional Liberties," *Bibliotheca Sacra* 52 (1895): 391; the original Dutch address was delivered in 1872.

178. Kuyper, *Lectures on Calvinism*, 14-15.

179. Kasteel, 289.

180. See Mark A. Noll, Nathan O. Hatch, and George M. Marsden, *The Search for Christian America*, rev. ed. (Colorado Springs: Helmers & Howard, 1989 [1983]); Robert T. Handy, *A Christian America: Protestant Hopes and Historical Realities*, 2nd ed. (New York: Oxford University Press, 1984).

181. Recall his Grand Rapids statement that "America is destined in the providence of God to become the most glorious and noble nation the world has ever seen. Some day its renown will eclipse the renown and splendor of Rome, Greece and the old races" (*Grand Rapids Herald*, October 29, 1898; cf. app. C below).

tion, the spirit of the age had to be opposed with the spirit of the gospel, with biblical truth and morality. The glorious past of Calvinist Holland had to be reappropriated by recapturing the imagination of the Dutch people for the gospel, with Dutch history *(Vaderlandsgeschiedenis)* and biblical imagery as the chief vehicles. Furthermore, the appeal of a better future had to be *historically realistic* (rather than mere utopian fantasy).[182] Kuyper's visit to America and his report back home[183] about the American experiment were a crucial component of his efforts to revitalize a politically active, culture-transforming Calvinism in the Netherlands. He had to have a living, working model of the civic order he was proposing for his own nation. Kuyper's political agenda for the Netherlands needed a Calvinist-inspired, free and healthy America. His strategy for capturing the imagination of his fellow Dutch citizens, however, was most decidedly a *Dutch* Christian-historical strategy.

Kuyper realized early on that a new, antirevolutionary political movement could not succeed without an effective organ of mass communication. And so the path was cleared for a newspaper that would not only encourage party members but also interpret the world and national news from an antirevolutionary point of view. In later reflections on this, Kuyper noted that since the Dutch press of the late nineteenth century was openly hostile to the Christian faith, a weapon used against the gospel and the Christian nation, he became convinced that the same weapon had to be used *for* the gospel and the Christian nation.[184] "And so," said Kuyper, "the conviction grew in me that the Christian people in the Netherlands had to have their own daily newspaper, a paper that articulated what was in their heart."[185] Building on previous smaller efforts by others such as Groen van Prinsterer, a society was formed in 1870 to publish a paper with its explicit goal stated in the corporation's statutes as "the cultivation of a public mind *(volksgeest)* in a Christian-national direction."[186] Supporting members of the corporation were expected "to acknowledge the

182. As Bercovitch, xi, has noted, effective national mythology cannot be purely fictional: "Myth may clothe history as fiction, but it persuades in proportion to its capacity to help men act in history." Total fictional myth is inadequate for shaping public, social identity. "Ultimately, [a myth's] effectiveness derives from its functional relationship to facts." On the repudiation of a "Calvinist utopia," see Kuyper, *Ons Program*, 477-78.

183. Abraham Kuyper, *Varia Americana* (Amsterdam and Pretoria: Höveker & Wormser, n.d.).

184. Allegations of media bias and efforts by marginalized Christians to establish alternative avenues of communication are not new to the twentieth century nor restricted to the United States alone.

185. *Gedenkboek* (1897), 66.

186. "De bewerking van den volksgeest in Christelijk nationalen zin" (*Gedenkboek* [1897], 9).

Word of God as the foundation for life in the church and the nation." A weekly paper, *De Heraut* (Herald), was published with the following motto on its masthead: "The Herald for a free church and a free school in a free Netherlands."[187]

And then, on April 1, 1872, a new *daily* newspaper, *De Standaard*, was launched. It is here that we see Kuyper's poetic-political genius in full action. He knew exactly what he was doing! The deliberately chosen, symbolically important date was the 300th anniversary of the Sea Beggars' successful capture of the Dutch port of Brill (Briel).[188] The entire country was poised to celebrate the day, the "day of Dutch liberation, a day that represented the breakthrough of the Calvinist spirit."[189] The opening lines of Kuyper's lead editorial in that first issue quoted William of Orange's address to the Sea Beggars: "Because the first concern is the glory of God and the poor believers in the Netherlands, let each of you set aside all personal ambition and egoism." Kuyper added that this "noble advice from the father of our nation should also govern our Christian nation in its national celebration."[190] What was missing from the current festivities, according to Kuyper, was William of Orange's profound conviction that "this work was from God, not from man." He missed, in the festivities, "the honor, praise, thanksgiving, and humility before God."

Furthermore, with that important foundation missing, the national spirit, "breathed into the nation's heart and conscience by God," also deteriorates. Among the casualties: "freedom of conscience, the freedom to serve the God of the Fathers in church and school," as well as the crucial "moral vocation of the nation, the sense that the Netherlands is chosen by God to be the standard-bearer of freedom of conscience." Yet, Kuyper's editorial encouraged: "A remnant that retains this historical treasure remains. Though a small band,[191] remember, 'The fleet of the Sea Beggars was also small!' The calling of this [small band] is so glorious! To engage in battle, not only for oneself and one's children, but also for one's fellow citizens, even for Europe, for humanity — so that *Justice* remains, *freedom of conscience* is not smothered, and the Prince's

187. *Gedenkboek* (1897), 9.
188. "On 1 April 1572, six hundred Gueuz, recently expelled from the English channel ports . . . seized the small port of Brill which had been temporarily left without a Spanish garrison." The Great Revolt, "triggered by the Sea Beggars," was under way. (Jonathan I. Israel, *The Dutch Republic: Its Rise, Greatness, and Fall, 1477-1806* [New York: Oxford University Press, 1995], 170.)
189. *Gedenkboek* (1897), 13.
190. *Gedenkboek* (1897), 28-29.
191. Kuyper was fond of referring to himself and his band of marginalized nineteenth-century Dutch orthodox Calvinists as a remnant, a "Gideon's band." See Van Weringh, 38, 40, 75.

rallying cry once again rings true: 'for the glory of our God!'" Kuyper concluded with a prayer that the God of history might use the commemorative occasion to renew the Dutch nation. It was the privilege of this new venture in journalism, he added, "to once again raise the standard of his Word for Dutch Christians," and it was his prayer that this would be done in full dependence on the God "who had created and saved our Fatherland."[192] That became Kuyper's mission: to appeal to biblical imagery familiar to generations of Netherlanders (Dutch Israel, bondage house, Gideon's band), weave it together with Dutch history (*Vaderlandsgeschiedenis*), and then, with remarkably energetic journalistic and organizational skill, create an orthodox Dutch Reformed people's movement and political party.[193] Kuyper's politics was poetry in action.

Kuyper the Poet Recognized by Others

The final bit of evidence in our case for thinking of Kuyper as a poet comes from the fact that his rhetorical-poetic ability and role was recognized by others, by his contemporaries as well as by more recent Kuyper interpreters. Perhaps we should note in the first place that some of Kuyper's critics judged him to be excessively self-conscious about his own poetic role as a restorer of the Dutch national soul. In a famous cartoon, Albert Hahn portrays a Kuyper whose praise of Bilderdijk's national significance as a poetic genius in the 1906 address at the Concertgebouw in Amsterdam is seen as essentially autobiographical. The caption in the following cartoon, where a triumphant Kuyper is hoisted on the shoulders of his followers, reads: "How (Bilderdijk) was paid homage in the Concertgebouw."

Van Weringh concurs with cartoonist Hahn's point of view, observing that since the address came after the disappointing election of 1905,[194] an election whose chief issue was Kuyper himself, "the role that Kuyper ascribes to Bilderdijk, is undoubtedly in part the role Kuyper had assigned to himself but which, thanks to his election defeat, was impossible for him to play."[195]

It would have been difficult for Kuyper's contemporaries not to link his many accomplishments with artistic creativity thanks to the numerous public celebrations of his work, celebrations noteworthy for their artistic dimensions. A recent commemorative visual biography of Kuyper's life and work supports

192. Van Weringh, 14-15.
193. On Kuyper's place within the long tradition of Dutch Christian-national mythology, see Eijnatten, *God, Nederland, en Oranje*.
194. It was Kuyper's first significant public appearance after his return from abroad following the election defeat. See De Bruijn, 275.
195. Van Weringh, 54.

Fig. 1.7. "Bilderdijk in Concertgebouw"

this impression.[196] The numerous Kuyper fetes — and the Festschrift volumes commemorating them — are striking in the significant role played in them by creative visual and written art (poetry).[197] These occasions were opportunities to honor Kuyper with commemorative artwork[198] as well as for Kuyper to wax poetic.

One example of such an event — the public celebration of Kuyper's seventieth birthday on October 29, 1907 — illustrates this last point well. Kuyper responded to the gifts and well-wishings offered to him on this occasion with this revealing wordplay on his own name (*kuiper* = cooper): "I know how the cooper creates his barrels. The art is to bow the individual staves to one side. He achieves that by putting them in a circle and subjecting them to a small inside fire. The heat pulls the drying wood inward and when all the staves are bowed it is easy to place them inside the band and unite them into a barrel."[199] The es-

196. De Bruijn, *Abraham Kuyper*.

197. See, e.g., the commemorative volume of Kuyper's seventieth birthday celebration: *Kuyper-Gedenkboek 1907* (The Hague: n.p., 1908).

198. See figure 7.2 on p. 316.

199. Cited by Jan Romeyn at the beginning of his essay "Abraham Kuyper: De Klokkenist der Kleine Luyden," in Jan Romeyn and Annie Romeyn, *Erflaters van Onze Beschaving*, vol. 4, *Negentiende Eeuw* (Amsterdam: Em Querido, 1947), 145. I have not been able to confirm this quotation in an original source.

sayist — Marxist Dutch historian Jan Romeyn — who cites this passage as an example of Kuyper's self-consciousness as a national poetic figure, explains it as follows: "The fire was the spirit of Abraham Kuyper, the staves were the orthodox [Reformed] little folk [*kleine luyden*], the barrel became the Anti-Revolutionary Party." Romeyn cites this passage not only to indicate a key characteristic of Kuyper as an important "testator of [Dutch] civilization" but also as a specimen of what he calls Kuyper's "seldom equalled literary ability," an ability so intensely urgent *(dringend)* that it "traced symbols — the underlying unity of things — everywhere, even in places where others hardly saw the individual things."[200] In short, a poetic imagination. Romeyn also ascribes to Kuyper the poetic role that Kuyper himself saw in Bilderdijk.

It was not only admiring critics such as Hahn and Romeyn who saw him as a poet, but also Kuyper's closest allies. We consider one more occasion in which Kuyper was celebrated, the twenty-fifth anniversary of his editorship of the antirevolutionary daily newspaper, *De Standaard,* in 1897. Kuyper concluded his response to the tributes received on this occasion with a rare (for him)[201] verse paraphrase of the Dutch poet Isaac da Costa:

> My life is ruled by but one passion,
> One higher urge drives will and soul.
> May breath fail me before I ever
> allow that sacred urge to fall.
> 'Tis to affirm God's holy statutes
> In church and state, in home and school,
> despite the world's strong remonstrations,
> to bless our people with His rule.
> 'Tis to engrave God's holy order,
> heard in Creation and the Word,
> upon the nation's public conscience,
> till God is once again its Lord.[202]

200. Romeyn, 145.

201. According to De Bruijn (214), this was one of the few poems written by Kuyper and was later put to music by P. Anders.

202. *Gedenkboek* (1897), 77:

> Voor mij, één zucht beheerscht mijn leven,
> Één hooger drang drijft zin en ziel.
> En moog' mij d'adem eer begeven,
> Eer ik aan dien heil'gen drang ontviel,
> 't Is om Gods heil'ge ordonnantiën,
> In huis en kerk, in school en staat,
> Ten spijt van 's werelds remonstrantiën,

It was on that same occasion that Kuyper's fellow neo-Calvinist titan, the great Reformed theologian Herman Bavinck,[203] provided a perspective on Kuyper the poet as seen by sympathetic fellow Calvinists.[204] Bavinck praises Kuyper in the same breath as the Dutch poets Willem Bilderdijk and Isaac da Costa, as well as statesman Guillaume Groen van Prinsterer, as opponents of the "spirit of the age"[205] and standard-bearers of Calvinism and liberty inextricably joined together. Such opposition, Bavinck notes, naturally fosters resistance, and *De Standaard,* like the three *literateurs* it emulates, also received its fair share — a *Kulturkampf* became inevitable. But, he adds, all these men had and used only one weapon in the battle: the power of the *word.* "The depth and strength of their conviction made them all eloquent" in a rich diversity of style. Bilderdijk's "vigorous verses" brought to light the "muscular power" and "inexhaustible riches" of the Dutch language. Da Costa "wreathed [words] with an Oriental hue, with the glow of Old Testament prophecy." Groen van Prinsterer "fashioned images of his ideas in the style of marble block, independent and solid as a rock."

Nonetheless, the language of *De Standaard,* Bavinck judges, surpassed each of these predecessors in "range of emotion, vividness of representation, richness of imagery, in dramatic action, in the power to stir and carry along [the reader]." Bavinck describes Kuyper's style in detail: "It is built up of sentences that are armed with light and approach the foe deftly and movingly,

---

Weervast te setten, 't volk ten baat.
't Is om die ord'ningen des Heeren
Waar Woord èn Schepping van getuigt,
In 't volk zóó helder te graveeren,
Tot weer dat volk voor God zich buigt.

For this new translation of Kuyper's poem I am indebted to my former Redeemer College colleague and friend Harry Van Dyke. Other versions can be found in J. Hendrik De Vries, introduction to Abraham Kuyper, *To Be Near unto God* (Grand Rapids: Eerdmans, 1925), 7, and Heslam, 54-55.

203. Herman Bavinck (1854-1921) was born into a leading family of the Secession Christian Reformed Church *(Christelijke Gereformeerde Kerk)* that split from the Dutch National Reformed Church in 1834, and taught in its seminary at Kampen from 1883 to 1902. After Kuyper's own break from the national church in 1886, Bavinck became the prime force in the secessionist community for union with the Kuyper faction, a union that was accomplished in 1892. Bavinck succeeded Kuyper as professor of theology at the Free University of Amsterdam in 1902 when Kuyper had become the Dutch prime minister. His major work is the four-volume *Gereformeerde Dogmatiek,* first published in the 1890s with a revised version complete by 1911.

204. What follows is taken from *Gedenkboek* (1872), 44-47.

205. Noteworthy is da Costa's tract, *Bezwaren tegen der Geest der Eeuw* (1823), a vigorous critique of the principles of the French Revolution.

joyfully and courageously, with song and music, either to attack or defend, advancing or retreating, but always alert, preferring to be found at the center of the heat of battle." *De Standaard* articles, according to Bavinck, were "often scintillating improvisations on paper, gems of thought and language. With one image, one sentence, a portrait was drawn of the character of a foe, the nature of the battle, the position of the parties. A single expression — suddenly a word that takes flight on every lip — was sufficient; the matter became transparent to everyone's eye. *De Standaard* never provided arid argumentation or lengthy deductive reasoning; the heart and soul of a *man* was always in the word." And then Bavinck makes this judgment about Kuyper the *rhetorician*: "And that man did not *write* to us on paper, he *spoke* to us and reached out through that word to our understanding and will, our heart and conscience, not satisfied until he knew what he had in us." Lest one conclude that Bavinck was a mere Kuyper sycophant, it is important to include here his open acknowledgment of Kuyper's lapses. "I do not want to deny," Bavinck says, "that in the heat of battle the blows on occasion fell too sharply and that in the haze of gunpowder a clear distinction between friend and foe was not always made."

The character of celebrations such as this helped to confirm the very emancipatory-historical imagination — the God-Israel-Netherlands-Orange linkage — that had launched *De Standaard* in 1872 and was a key component of Kuyper's political rhetoric. On the twenty-fifth anniversary celebrations of Kuyper's editorship, along with open references to the symbolic significance of the newspaper's launch date, as the guest of honor and his wife were escorted into the banquet hall, the assembled five thousand sang verses from the Dutch versification of Psalm 68 with its vigorous martial imagery:[206]

> O God, in virtue of thy power —
>   that godlike power which has acted for us —
> command kings to bring gifts to thee
>   for the honour of thy temple in Jerusalem.
> Rebuke those wild beasts of the reeds, that herd of bulls,
>   the bull-calf warriors of the nations;
> scatter these nations which revel in war;
>   make them bring tribute from Egypt,

---

206. Verses 14 and 17 from the Dutch Psalter, corresponding to Ps. 68:28-31, 34-35. I have cited the entire passage, Ps. 68:28-35, since the metrical version in the Dutch Psalter rather loosely translates and incorporates paraphrase summaries of key ideas in neighboring verses. The NEB captures the tone best in superb poetic form. *Gedenkboek* (1897), 27.

precious stones and silver from Pathros;
let Nubia stretch out her hands to God.

All you kingdoms of the world, sing praises to God, sing Psalms
     to the Lord,
    to him who rides on the heavens, the ancient heavens.
Hark! he speaks in the mighty thunder.
Ascribe all might to God, Israel's High God,
    Israel's pride and might throned in the skies.
    Terrible is God as he comes from his sanctuary;
    he is Israel's own God,
who gives to his people might and abundant power.
    Blessed be God. (Ps. 68:28-35, NEB)

Later that same evening, after Herman Bavinck's tribute to Kuyper was concluded with spirited and extended applause (so the official record pointedly notes!), the guests sang a well-known religious-patriotic song composed by Isaac da Costa and laden with martial if not crusading imagery:

They shall not get it,
    Our old Netherlands!
Through all the trials [of the just],
    It remains our father's trust.

They shall not get it,
    The gods of this age!
God has not liberated it for us,
    To provide a legacy for *them*. (Repeat last two lines.)

Or is there a different age,
    God is reserving for us?
A darker destiny,
    From which we shall be saved?
Still, you shall not have us,
    You gods of this age!
Even in decline, we remain
    Devoted to our father's God.[207]

In the same spirit, the first article of the newly founded Antirevolutionary Party program (1879) makes this Dutch Calvinist mythopoetic, reli-

207. *Gedenkboek* (1897), 51.

gious-national consciousness the very basis for its political vision. "The anti-revolutionary or Christian-historical movement embodies, so far as our nation is concerned, the key-note of our national identity, as this received its imprint around 1572, under the leadership of Orange and under the influence of the Reformation. [We] desire to develop this, with all due consideration of the nation's circumstances, in a manner that does justice to the needs of our age."[208]

Kuyper's historical imagination, however, as we have noticed, was not limited to the Netherlands and the House of Orange. Not only did he repeatedly claim, during his 1898 visit to the United States, that the future of Calvinism (and the political liberty inextricably linked to it) was in America,[209] he also subscribed to the "heliotropic myth" that the entire course of human civilization follows the movement of the sun from east to west.[210] "This belief, present in our world for centuries as almost self-evident, reached its zenith in the nineteenth century," had a significant following in the Netherlands, "and it became a factor in the nineteenth-century immigration to America" led by Dutch Reformed Separatist preachers Albertus Van Raalte and Hendrik P. Scholte.[211] Once again it was a poet — well known to Van Raalte, Scholte, and Kuyper alike — who had given the myth a popular force by putting it into verse. Isaac da Costa's poem *Wachter, wat is er van den Nacht? (Watchman, What of the Night?)* included in its description of the world's political situation a lengthy reflection on America, and the notion of a westward journey for human civilization to and then from America, eventually to Russia, was central to it:

> The world was turned around, the west became the East
> Of a new era, which would comfort all our woes.
> The son of Western shores will meet the Easterner
> And free America encounter Russia's powers.[212]

208. Kuyper, *Ons Program,* xv.
209. In his address at Holland, Mich., on October 27, 1898 (on his sixty-second birthday), he explicitly linked America's future to Calvinism, and vice versa: "America looks forward toward a great future but it needs the principles of Calvinism to strengthen its backbone. . . . The future of the development of Calvinistic principles is no longer in Europe but in America." *Holland Daily Sentinel,* October 28, 1898.
210. See Jan Willem Schulte Nordholt, *The Myth of the West: America as the Last Empire,* trans. Herbert H. Rowen (Grand Rapids: Eerdmans, 1995).
211. Schulte Nordholt, *Myth of the West,* x, 90.
212. Des werelds loop keerde om. Dat Westen werd ons 't Oosten
Eens heilstijds, die onze aard van al de smart moet troosten.

For Kuyper the "stream of civilization" in its three successive pre-Calvinist formations — paganism, Islamism, and Romanism — had followed and would follow a clear course westward. Though the Calvinist phase "is now denied [a] leading influence by Modernism, the daughter of the French Revolution," and the "secret of the future is still veiled in mystery," he contended that "the course of this world-stream from East to West can be denied by none."[213] Providentially led world history is of one piece:

> There is but one world-stream, broad and fresh, which from the beginning bore the promise of the future. This stream had its rise in Middle Asia and the Levant, and has steadily continued its course from East to West. From Western Europe it has passed on to your Eastern States, and from thence to California. The sources of this stream of development are found in Babylon and in the valley of the Nile. From thence it flowed on to Greece. From Greece it passed on to the Roman Empire. From the Romantic nations it continued its way to the Northwestern parts of Europe, and from Holland and England it reaches at length your continent.[214]

As one commentator has observed: "In a Kuyperian view of cosmic East-West progress from Sumeria to Silicon Valley, the Spirit follows predetermined channels in the material fabric of culture. In such views of the universe, common to much nineteenth- and twentieth-century apologetics — in that grand mixture of religion, materiality and myth called *God, Nederland en Oranje* — it was generally claimed that God operates via such national channels."[215] The stream of Kuyper's own poetic mythmaking thus followed channels dug by others.

One final illustration of how his contemporaries viewed Kuyper can be seen in the printed program of Kuyper's visit, during his 1898 American tour, to Cleveland, where "Cleveland's Welcome to Holland's Foremost Citizen" describes him as "Statesman, Theologian," and *nota bene! "Literateur."*[216]

De Zoon der Westerkust den Oosterling ontmoet,
En 't vrije America 't vrijmachtig Rusland groet?

(Cited with translation by Schulte Nordholt, *Myth of the West*, 90-91.)

213. Kuyper, *Lectures on Calvinism*, 33.
214. Kuyper, *Lectures on Calvinism*, 32.
215. Eijnatten, 265.
216. Reprinted as plate 14 in George Harinck and Hans Krabbendam, eds., *Sharing the Reformed Tradition: The Dutch-North American Exchange, 1846-1996* (Amsterdam: VU Uitgeverij, 1996), 109, emphasis added.

Dossier
Amerika
1898

Cleveland's Welcome to ❧ ❧ ❧
HOLLAND'S FOREMOST CITIZEN.

PROFESSOR ABRAHAM KUYPER, D. D., LL.D.

STATESMAN, THEOLOGIAN, LITERATEUR,

AT THE

Old Stone Church, Tuesday, November 15, 1898,

7:30 P. M.

Fig. 1.8. Cleveland Program

Thus we see that not all interpreters of Kuyper regard him purely as a man of ideas. His literary legacy has also been noticed by more recent observers. The great contemporary Dutch historian and Americanist[217] Jan Willem Schulte Nordholt, no mean poet himself,[218] finds the poetic *(dichterlijke)* dimension of Kuyper to be the redeeming and humanizing element in the great man's often irritating eccentricities. Though Kuyper's language was often bombastic, Schulte Nordholt contends, he nonetheless had a wonderful capacity to bring images together.[219] Dr. George Puchinger, in his recent reflections on Kuyper's religious life, states the following: "Kuyper had the soul of an artist, with all the accompanying great qualities and flaws. Even in his seriousness he was often playful; he was not only changeable, but even whimsical; not just highly imaginative, but fanciful as well. When he made up a theory, right or wrong, he could elaborate on it endlessly. Moreover, he was not only hurried most of the time, he was also sloppy — and this was made worse by the myriad of daily tasks he had to complete. But with all this he possessed a large measure of something we usually lack: visual imagination."[220]

James Bratt comes to a similar conclusion when he notes that "Kuyper never let himself be a man of pure ideas," adding significantly, "not that he lacked the ability." Rather, "it was as a newspaper editor that Kuyper burst onto the national scene, and by his newspapers that he forged a constituency that remained undyingly loyal to him." Bratt characterizes Kuyper as a "movement leader, an institution builder, as well as an intellectual. Better, he was an intellectual *as* movement leader. . . . Put simply, Kuyper's ideas emerged in the process of identifying, organizing, and pushing a grass-roots constituency to action." Bratt compares Kuyper to Moral Majority leader Jerry Falwell in this regard: Both "undertook the same twofold mission: to awaken a culturally disinherited and despised constituency from its pietistic slumbers and to turn its power against liberal, secularistic, or humanistic hegemony in church and state. Both promised that the venture would return their nations to godly foundations and vanished glory. . . . Both began with local congregational renewal and ended up trying to transform the nation; and both built the same steps in between — Christian lower education, grass-roots political networking, a Christian University."[221]

217. See, for example, Schulte Nordholt, *Myth of the West.*

218. See, for example, Jan Willem Schulte Nordholt, *So Much Sky,* trans. Henrietta Ten Harmsel (Grand Rapids: Eerdmans, 1994).

219. "Interview with J. W. Schulte Nordholt," in G. Puchinger, *Gesprekken over Hondred Jaar Vrije Universiteit* (Delft: Meinema, 1980), 68.

220. George Puchinger, *Abraham Kuyper: His Early Journey of Faith,* ed. George Harinck, trans. Simone Kennedy (Amsterdam: VU Uitgeverij, 1998), 8.

221. Bratt, "Abraham Kuyper's Public Career," 9-10.

Bratt also draws another interesting comparison, especially for Americans: Kuyper and Martin Luther King, Jr. Both were charismatic national leaders, personally and permanently identified with the emancipatory movements they started, with similar goals for their groups: "Full voting rights, equitable schooling, and an end to slurs and prejudice." Kuyper and King also "shared commonalities of biography and style," and "both had first-rate minds which they subordinated to a popular cause." Their legacy? Among other things, a literary one: "Their books survive them." Bratt notes that, for King, what may seem in written form "to be a rhetoric of banality . . . was something else when originally *spoken* to a packed house in the deep South." Similarly, "by all accounts Kuyper was at his best as an orator, which requires that we read him with the memory of a King speech in mind." "It is striking in this connection," Bratt adds, "that King's final address followed Kuyper's favorite strategy. Recounting the history of the West in bold, symbolic strokes, King led his audience to see that they, Memphis garbage workers, stood at the cutting edge of time, agents called of God to lead the redemption of the nation. Rarely did either of these Samsons fail to bring the house down."[222]

Abraham Kuyper's Christian-Historical Imagination

How does this description and interpretation of Kuyper as a poet, as well as Bratt's suggestive comparison of Kuyper and King, square with Kuyper's own understanding of rhetoric, poetry, and art? It is worth noting here that Kuyper, notwithstanding his own commitment to principles and ideas, was sensitive to the problem of ideological rationalism, the attempt to squeeze all reality into the straitjacket of an a priori idea. In fact, he judges this ideological thinking to be the fundamental problem of modernism; history is suppressed for the sake of a dominating idea. In his famous "modernism as fata morgana" address, he contends that the modernist idea "must clash with the *present* as it asserts itself in heart and conscience and with the *past* as it speaks in history." This clash is an "all-or-nothing" battle to the end:

> One or the other has to yield — either Modernism to the facts, or the facts to the modernist idea. If I do not want the former, if the life of my mind has become too closely bound up with Modernism and I therefore believe that above all else that modernist principle is sacred, then of course what history says cannot be valid, nor can what Scripture says of Jesus be true. The whole

222. Bratt, "Abraham Kuyper's Public Career," 11-12.

of the past simply has to be modified, tinted, and transposed until that history, in spite of itself, supports my Modernism. But then, understandably, there can be no talk of the historical sense, for the nerve of that sense has been deadened by my apriorism.[223]

No rationalist, Kuyper explicitly affirmed the value of art. Though he acknowledges in part the validity of the reputation Calvinism bears as an iconoclastic religion,[224] and even downgrades aesthetic, symbolically rich *religious* life as inferior — "a lower level" — he also lauds art as a distinct and fully legitimate "sphere" of human activity along with the "intellectual, ethical, [and] religious."[225] Furthermore, utilizing one of his favorite — i.e., organic — metaphors, he contends that "art also is no side-shoot on a principal branch, but an independent branch that grows from the trunk of our life itself, even though it is far more nearly allied to Religion than to our thinking or to our ethical being."[226] Kuyper's concluding challenge: "Understand that art is no fringe that is attached to the garment, and no amusement that is added to life, but a most serious power in our present existence, and therefore its principal variations must

---

223. Bratt, *Abraham Kuyper*, 114.

224. Two interesting anecdotes are appropriate here. In recognition of his twenty-five-year editorship of *De Standaard*, Kuyper was presented with an elaborately sculpted silver statue, rich in national-historical significance (see *Gedenkboek* [1872], 53; De Bruijn, 217). In his response Kuyper said that his first reaction at the unveiling of this gift was: "Well, it appears that the Calvinists have once again learned to appreciate and value art." Charmingly, the text of Kuyper's speech includes the parenthesis that this remark generated applause. Furthermore, "the elegant form and the purity of the imagery chosen demonstrates that the days are behind us when many among us despised outward form and had no feeling or appreciation for how an aesthetically sensitive eye elevates" (*Gedenkboek*, 62). A second anecdote: When the Free University was officially opened on October 20, 1880, the ceremonial mace of the new university had at its head a silver statue of Minerva, the Roman goddess of wisdom/reason. The Secessionist weekly journal, *De Bazuin*, sharply criticized this, calling it "heathen." Kuyper responded by calling this reaction "iconoclastic fanaticism" and noting that major seventeenth-century Dutch Reformed theologians such as Gisbert Voetius (1589-1676) had also used Minerva as a symbol of scholarship (De Bruijn, 142). On a less aesthetically elevated topic, the same article criticized the opening celebrations of the Free University because wine was served at the banquet. Kuyper responded by citing another who insisted that "Calvinists were not the sort of people who put water in their wine," and added, "one does not nurture a generation of hardy Calvinists with milk chocolate and water" (De Bruijn, 142).

225. Kuyper, *Lectures on Calvinism*, 144-50; cf. Abraham Kuyper, *The Antithesis between Symbolism and Revelation* (Amsterdam and Pretoria: Höveker and Wormser; Edinburgh: T. & T. Clark, n.d.).

226. Kuyper, *Lectures on Calvinism*, 150.

73

maintain, in their artistic expression, a close relation with the principal variations of our entire life."[227]

We shall conclude this introduction with some general observations
about imagination and suggest some categories that will help us map Kuyper's
specific poetic-political contribution.

The nature of imagination is not altogether a mystery, and a basic definition is not impossibly difficult.[228] Philosopher Immanuel Kant's definition is as
good as any with which to begin: "*Imagination* is the faculty of representing in
intuition an object that is *not itself present*."[229] What imagination does, therefore, is to take whatever is not temporally or spatially present to a person and
make it present through images. Imagination is thus tied to the metaphorical
use of language whereby we creatively transfer words from one context to another or, in Nelson Goodman's delightful metaphor, "teach an old word new
tricks."[230] In itself that makes imagination a neutral human faculty, capable of
use for good or ill. Kuyper himself, in fact, made that very point in his Stone
Lectures in a discussion about the theater. "In itself," he noted, "there is nothing
sinful in fiction — the power of the imagination is a precious gift of God himself. Neither," he added, "is there any special evil in *dramatic* imagination."[231]
Thus, neither rationalism's congenital suspicion of imagination in favor of
concepts[232] nor the anxiety in North American evangelical Christianity about
the "pagan" practice of New Age visualization[233] should be permitted to deter

227. Kuyper, *Lectures on Calvinism,* 151.

228. Volumes on imagination are increasing in our postmodern world. The most
thorough and balanced treatment of the subject, in my judgment, remains Eva T. H.
Brann, *The World of the Imagination: Sum and Substance* (Savage, Md.: Rowman &
Littlefield, 1991).

229. Immanuel Kant, *Critique of Pure Reason,* trans. Norman Kemp Smith (New
York: St. Martin's Press, 1968), B 151; cited by Garrett Green, *Imagining God: Theology and
the Religious Imagination* (San Francisco: Harper & Row, 1989), 62.

230. Cited by Colin E. Gunton, *The Actuality of Atonement: A Study of Metaphor,
Rationality, and the Christian Tradition* (Grand Rapids: Eerdmans, 1989), 28.

231. Kuyper, *Lectures on Calvinism,* 74. Nonetheless, Kuyper judged "the *moral sacrifice* demanded of actors and actresses for the amusement of the public" to be sufficient
reason for abstinence by Christians. "The prosperity of Theaters is purchased at the cost of
manly character, and of female purity," he judged (74-75).

232. Gunton, 39; also see n. 72 above.

233. See, among others, Dave Hunt and T. A. McMahon, *The Seduction of Christian-
ity: Spiritual Discernment in the Last Days* (Eugene, Ore.: Harvest House, 1985); Constance
Cumbey, *The Hidden Dangers of the Rainbow* (Shreveport, La.: Huntington House, 1983);
Tex Marrs, *Dark Secrets of the New Age* (Westchester, Ill.: Crossway, 1987). For helpful cri-
tiques of excessive "New Age conspiracy" theories among American evangelicals, see
Douglas R. Groothuis, *Confronting the New Age* (Downers Grove, Ill.: InterVarsity, 1988);

Christians from a proper understanding, appreciation, and use of human imagination. Imagination is no more or less tainted than any other human faculty. As Colin Gunton has noted: "There is nothing godlike about the reason that elevates it above other human faculties, for it is the source of demonic pride as much as of illumination. All our intellectual, aesthetic and moral endeavors fail unless they take place in due repentance and subordination to the truth."[234] A Christian imagination should not be an oxymoron.

What, then, is a Christian imagination? One attempt to define it links it directly to the notion of promise. "The Christian imagination is essentially an imagination of promise, an openness to the present because of the possibilities that it unfolds, a refusal to seek escape from the ravages of time through any subterfuge — either through nostalgia for the past or by flight into the timeless world of aesthetic or 'religious' experience. The Christian imagination is grounded in history, aware of the irreversibility of time, anxious for the fulfillment of its dreams."[235] This is a helpful definition also for the fences it puts up as protection against the possibilities of a corrupt imagination. Imagination that seeks escape into fantasy, that seeks to evade the realism taught by history, is not a Christian imagination but — likely — a gnostic one. It is this emphasis on historical awareness that helps resist the temptation nostalgically to imagine past golden ages or, in revolutionary fashion, to imagine creating future utopias. It is possible to specify this more clearly.

William Kilpatrick, borrowing from earlier treatments by Irving Babbitt and Edmund Burke, distinguishes a *moral* imagination from an *idyllic* one. Simply put, "the moral imagination works within the limits of reality and the idyllic imagination does not. The moral imagination holds up an ideal that is attainable, although only through hard work; the idyllic imagination holds up an ideal that can never be attained in reality, but can easily be attained in fantasy or feeling."[236] Concerning the latter, one recent critic of contemporary culture in fact contends that at the heart of modernity's *rationalism* is the powerful "imaginative dynamic" of escape and liberation.[237] Modernity is really about "a

---

Bob Passantino and Gretchen Passantino, *Witch Hunt* (Nashville: Nelson, 1990); Wolfe, "Beauty Will Save the World."

234. Gunton, 39.

235. John R. May, *Toward a New Earth: Apocalypse in the American Novel* (Notre Dame, Ind., and London: University of Notre Dame Press, 1972), 1.

236. William Kilpatrick, *Why Johnny Can't Tell Right from Wrong: Moral Illiteracy and the Case for Character Education* (New York: Simon and Schuster, 1992), 208.

237. Claes Ryn, "Cultural Origins of Politics: The Modern Imagination of Escape," in *Toward the Renewal of Civilization: Political Order and Culture*, ed. T. William Boxx and Gary Quinlivan (Grand Rapids: Eerdmans, 1998), 17-19.

new way of imagining the world," and that new way is the way of daydreaming about a new order in which humanity is liberated from all the oppressive social institutions that stand in the way of personal freedom.[238] "The world would be a wonderful place if only. . . ."[239] The path from imagination, to scapegoating the villains who stand in the way of my liberation, to eliminating them in revolutionary violence is a short one, as we saw in the twentieth century. By contrast, "the moral imagination takes guidance from external reference points which are considered binding: either God, natural law, or tradition."[240] The moral imagination thus respects and takes its rootage in some form of revelation. Kilpatrick's distinction here is reminiscent of Solzhenitsyn's "two kinds of people, two kinds of art."[241]

What Kilpatrick calls the idyllic imagination can be broken down into two related but nonetheless distinguishable forms: the utopian imagination and the ideological imagination. Utopian dreams, according to a recent, thorough study, are rooted in "two ancient beliefs — the Judeo-Christian faith in a paradise created with the world and destined to endure beyond it, and the Hellenic myth of an ideal, beautiful city built by men for men with the assistance and often in defiance of the gods."[242] Simply put, "utopian thought [is] belief in an unspoiled beginning and attainable perfection."[243] Utopian thought is the dream of an improved, more just society that "seems to haunt the human imagination ineradicably and in all ages."[244] Historically, utopian imaginations have not been satisfied with literary achievement or future heavenly fulfillment; they seek actualization on earth and often become embodiments of ideological imaginations. It is best not to use the term "ideology" in "its widest sense to denote any complex of ideas whatsoever," but to restrict it "to bodies of doctrine that present them-

---

238. Ryn, 11.

239. Ryn, 22; we discuss the constructive aspects of Ryn's essay further in chap. 8, 401-2.

240. Kilpatrick, 208-9; cf. Irving Babbitt, *Rousseau and Romanticism* (Boston: Houghton Mifflin, 1919); Edmund Burke, *Reflections on the Revolution in France,* in *The Portable Conservative Reader,* ed. Russell Kirk (New York: Penguin Books, 1982), 22.

241. See above, 16.

242. Frank E. Manuel and Fritzie P. Manuel, *Utopian Thought in the Western World* (Cambridge: Harvard University Press, Belknap Press, 1979), 1; see further the discussion of utopian literature in relation to the "new world," chap. 2 below.

243. Thomas Molnar, *Utopia: The Perennial Heresy* (New York: Sheed & Ward, 1967; reprint, Lanham, Md.: University Press of America, 1990), 6.

244. George Orwell, "Arthur Koestler," in *The Collected Essays: Journalism and Letters of George Orwell,* ed. Sonia Orwell and Ian Angus, 4 vols. (Harmondsworth: Penguin Books, 1979), 3:274; cited by Krishan Kumar, *Utopia and Anti-Utopia in Modern Times* (Oxford and New York: Basil Blackwell, 1987), 2.

selves as affording systems of belief so complete that whole populations may live by them alone, that are made known and interpreted by leaders ostensibly possessed of special genius or by organized elites not unlike priesthoods, that claim exclusive authority as representing something like revealed truth, and that consequently require the suppression of whatever does not conform."[245] The ideological imagination, in other words, is the same as the revolutionary imagination, and the triumph of the French Revolution is the real beginning of ideology.[246]

The smoke of fury and war thus usually accompanies ideologies, described by Russell Kirk as "fanatic political creeds, often advanced by violence." "By definition," observes Kirk, "'ideology' means servitude to political dogmas, abstract ideas not founded upon historical experience. Ideology is inverted religion, and the ideologue is the sort of person whom the historian Jacob Burckhardt called 'the terrible simplifier.'"[247] The utopian imagination is riddled with contradictions. It is both pessimistic and optimistic at the same time: "pessimistic about individual human nature, but optimistic about the ability of man's social nature, as embodied in society, to overcome the recalcitrance of the individual." Since overcoming that recalcitrance may require considerable coercion, utopians paradoxically also combine a belief in "unconstrained freedom" with a passion to "so thoroughly organize freedom that they turn it into slavery."[248] Focused on destruction of the present evil order and fixated on "constructing an imaginary community and world order," the utopian, "as thinker, is irrational and logical at the same time. Once he constructs his imaginary commonwealth (sometimes even an imaginary world with laws of physics different from ours), once he takes the big leap into another system of thought, he proceeds with strict logic, leaving nothing to chance. His human beings behave, or are made to behave, like automata; the organization of their lives never changes as they perform with clocklike precision the tasks assigned by the central authority." Often borrowing their philosophical anthropology from mechanistic models of science, utopian planners seek to create a people who "are no longer bound by human nature and its rich variations." The citizens of utopias are people who have had "their umbilical cord with mother earth and ordinary humanity severed"; they have become "puppets, quasi-zombies, lacking historical dimension, bereft of freedom and choice."[249] The utopian-ideological imag-

245. Louis J. Halle, *The Ideological Imagination* (Chicago: Quadrangle Books, 1972), 5-6.

246. Halle, 7.

247. Russell Kirk, *The Roots of American Order* (Washington, D.C.: Regnery Gateway, 1991), 9.

248. Molnar, 7-8.

249. Molnar, 8-9.

ination is thus fittingly described by T. S. Eliot as the "diabolical imagination."[250]

By contrast, a Christian moral imagination, even in visionary form, is determinedly historical. Historical consciousness "is the cultivation of an attitude of respect and reverence towards what cannot be seen, towards the invisible sources of meaning and authority in our lives — towards the formative agents and foundational principles that, although no longer tangible, have made possible most of what is worthy of honor and esteem in our day. . . . The tutelage of historical consciousness teaches us what it means to walk by faith, and not only by sight."[251] Historical consciousness is not the same as the academic study of history. "Historical consciousness means learning to appropriate into one's own moral imagination, and learning to be guided by, the memories of discerning others, memories of things one never experienced firsthand."[252] Historical consciousness is a prime example of the "sword of imagination" that alone can give the lie to the modern, positivistic belief "that we live in a world of inert facts to which we impute values." Rather, as historical, remembering creatures we participate in shared memories, we are members of a "community of memory" connected "to all who are bound together by remembrance of, and involvement in," the same story. "Indeed, communities, and nation-states, are ultimately constituted and sustained by shared memories, narratives of foundation, conflict, and perseverance." In sum, "historical consciousness draws us out of a narrow preoccupation with the present and with our 'selves,' and ushers us into another, larger world — a public world that 'cultures' us."[253] This sense of "meaning" is not arrived at through deduction and ratiocination; it comes through apprehension, "a mysterious form of participation that is . . . something very different from mere subjectivity."

It is this historical consciousness, combined with a Christian providential conviction, that was the basis for the political poetry that shaped Abraham Kuyper's public theology and characterized the three nineteenth-century Dutch literary figures who influenced him. The Calvinist political movement of the nineteenth century self-consciously described itself as "Christian-historical," or "antirevolutionary."[254] The background for this terminology is twofold:

250. T. S. Eliot, *After Strange Gods: A Primer of Modern Heresy* (New York: Harcourt, Brace and Co., 1934), 61.

251. Wilfred M. McClay, "History and Memory," *University Bookman* 35, no. 4 (winter 1995): 19.

252. Cf. Solzhenitsyn's observations about the essential role of literature in helping us learn from the experience of others (see above, 17-18).

253. See McClay, 21, for this and quote following.

254. The two terms were used interchangeably. Groen van Prinsterer explained this as

the intellectual revolution brought about by the eighteenth-century Enlighten-ment with its emphasis on the autonomy of reason, and the political "revolu-tion" during the last decades of the same century that introduced French-in-spired, revolutionary, popular sovereignty into the Netherlands. In sum, by contrast, a Christian-historical imagination is one that is rooted in divine reve-lation, honors the past not by slavishly seeking its repristination but by reappropriating its "truth" through creative application to the present, with the visionary promise of future blessing. And finally, it was just such a Christian-historical imagination that nurtured and shaped Abraham Kuyper's public the-ology and sustained him in his public career as a Dutch Calvinist political poet.

---

follows: "'Christian-historical' denotes our positive program, but 'anti-revolutionary' re-minds us of the polemical stance we must take in our time, out of self defence" (Van Dyke, 192). For the history and use of the terms see, in addition, Van der Does, *Bijdrage tot de Geschiedenis der wording van de Anti-Revolutionaire of Christelijk-Historische Staatspartij;* I. A. Diepenhorst, *Historisch-Critische Bijdrage tot de Leer van den Christelijken Staat,* 2nd ed. (Amsterdam: Noord-Hollandsche Uitgevers Maatschappij, 1943).

CHAPTER TWO

The Need for an Evangelical Public Theology in America

America! America!
God shed his grace on thee
And crown thy good with brotherhood
From sea to shining sea!

Katharine Lee Bates (1893)

There is no country in the world where the Christian religion retains a
greater influence over the souls of men than in America.

Alexis de Tocqueville

The Sea of Faith
Was once, too, at the full. . . .
But now I only hear
Its melancholy, long, withdrawing roar,
Retreating. . . .
And we are here as on a darkling plain
Swept with confused alarms of struggle and flight
Where ignorant armies clash by night.

Matthew Arnold, "Dover Beach"

From the perspective of human spirituality, the most extraordinary thing about the twentieth century was the failure of God to die.

Paul Johnson

I t was not supposed to happen this way. American public life in the late twentieth century turned out quite different from what the experts expected. As that century's seventh decade began, the cultural hegemony of evangelical Protestantism that had held sway over American public life well into the century's first decades was believed over for good. Intellèctually buffeted by the twin storms of Darwinist evolutionism and modernist, scriptural higher criticism, American evangelical Christianity in the 1920s and 1930s retreated into fundamentalism. This retreat surrendered the nation's universities, higher education, and culture formation to the aggressive proponents of secularization, neatly defined by Peter Berger as the "process by which sectors of society and culture are removed from the domination of religious institutions and symbols."[1] The emblematic event symbolizing this retreat was, of course, the Pyrrhic victory of evangelical creationism at the famous Scopes monkey trial of 1925.[2] Here evangelicals won the skirmish but "lost the broader public and the larger battle" for the heart of American culture.[3] Historian George Marsden described the con-

---

1. Peter L. Berger, *The Sacred Canopy: Elements of a Sociological Theory of Religion* (Garden City, N.Y.: Doubleday Anchor, 1967), 106. For a description and analysis of the evangelical intellectual retreat, see Mark A. Noll, *The Scandal of the Evangelical Mind* (Grand Rapids: Eerdmans, 1994). On the specific matter of the American university's secularization, see George M. Marsden, *The Soul of the University: From Protestant Establishment to Established Nonbelief* (New York: Oxford University Press, 1994).

2. For a remarkably sympathetic account of the Scopes trial and the "case" presented by William Jennings Bryan, see Gary Wills, *Under God: Religion and American Politics* (New York: Simon & Schuster, 1990), 95-124. Wills contends that Bryan's populist opposition was not to the teaching of evolutionary scientific *theories,* but to the Nietzschean *social* Darwinism that his opponents, notably Clarence Darrow and H. L. Mencken, enthusiastically endorsed. "Nothing," Wills writes, "could be more opposed to Bryan's populist belief that progress will come only from the moral support of the weaker" (102). Wills notes that "thanks to Mencken and to *Inherit the Wind,* a 1950s play that continually re-creates (quite inaccurately) the famous trial on stage and on the screen," the American public's impression of both the trial and Bryan's career as a populist reformer has been indelibly distorted. On the distortions of the Scopes trial perpetuated by *Inherit the Wind,* see also Carol Iannone, "The Truth about *Inherit the Wind,"* *First Things* 70 (February 1997): 28-33.

3. José Casanova, *Public Religions in the Modern World* (Chicago and London: University of Chicago Press, 1996), 143.

sequences of the Scopes trial this way: "In the trial by public opinion and the press, it was clear that the twentieth century, the cities, and the universities had won a resounding victory, and that the country, the South, and the fundamentalists were guilty as charged."[4] What was left of publicly visible evangelicalism after the intellectual battle, was effectively marginalized by the ridicule of writers such as H. L. Mencken. Consequently, "following the trial, the fundamentalist movement collapsed and, once banished from public view, most intellectuals assumed that it had been relegated to the dustbin of history. . . . Along with Pentecostalism and other evangelical sects, fundamentalism became the religion of the disinherited."[5] It needs to be added here that this is a characteristically Northern (perhaps even East Coast) American perspective. As evangelicalism was "dramatically displaced from the center to the fringes of American religious and intellectual life" and "the battle was lost in the North and in establishments of higher learning, the movement's center of gravity shifted. Fundamentalism became a more rural, southern, and anti-intellectual movement."[6] The marginalization of evangelicals had a significant geographical component, which became a crucial factor in the later story.

Evangelical Eclipse

At the same time, evangelicals more broadly, and evangelical eschatology particularly, failed to come to terms adequately with the new industrial, urban world of the postbellum era in America. Progressive Social Gospel Christianity effectively adapted postmillennial optimism to the new realities.[7] Northern Protestantism, in particular, "became ever more committed to the postmillennial faith in the progressive realization of the millennium and in the manifest destiny of Christian America."[8] A *Christian century* was believed to be dawning.[9] In this vein, a writer in the *Methodist Review* in 1914 eloquently

4. George M. Marsden, *Fundamentalism and American Culture: The Shaping of Twentieth-Century Evangelicalism, 1870-1925* (New York: Oxford University Press, 1980), 186; cited by Casanova, 143.

5. Casanova, 143.

6. Duane M. Oldfield, *The Right and the Righteous: The Christian Right Confronts the Republican Party* (Lanham, Md.: Rowman & Littlefield, 1996), 17.

7. For a succinct overview of the change in eschatological conviction around the turn of the century, see James H. Moorhead, "The Erosion of Postmillenialism in American Religious Thought, 1865-1925," *Church History* 53, no. 1 (1984): 61-77.

8. Casanova, 139.

9. The change in name of the Disciples of Christ journal from the *Oracle* to the

summarized the new mood of efficient kingdom building on earth: "Ah! The city which John saw! . . . It will take considerable engineering as well as preaching to get the whole world there. Hail, Engineer, coagent of the millennium."[10] Evangelicals, by contrast, for the most part embraced a defeatist, otherworldly premillennialism.[11] Dwight L. Moody's oft-cited passage from his sermon "The Second Coming of Christ" captures this paradigmatically: "I look on this world as a wrecked vessel. God has given me a lifeboat and said to me, 'Moody, save all you can.'"[12] The combination of intellectual defeat and eschatological retreat effectively led to the "second disestablishment" in America: "Evangelical Protestantism had ceased being the public civil religion of American society."[13]

However, according to one sociologist, "one element from this era survived the disestablishment from the cognitive sphere and from public opinion. The most endearing and enduring inheritance from Puritanism, the Protestant ethic, continued to dominate public morality, the American way of life, and, one could add, 'the American self.'"[14] Though this Puritan legacy survived into the 1950s, the countercultural upheavals of the next decade brought into being the forces leading to what could be called the "third American disestablishment," the pervasive secularization and pluralization of American culture and

---

Christian Century in 1900 is described by its future publisher and editor, Charles Clayton Morrison, in these words: "As the nineteenth century passed into the twentieth, the whole Christian world was in a mood of expectant optimism. The press was full of discussion and prediction of the wonders that would take place in the new era which the new century was ushering in. Dr. George A. Campbell, a Chicago pastor, was at that time editor of *The Oracle*. None of us liked that name. Campbell suggested that this new century must be made a *Christian* century. He accordingly proposed that *The Oracle* be re-Christened with that name. His friends . . . heartily agreed. And so in 1900 it was done. No name could have better symbolized the optimistic outlook of the period" (cited in Linda-Marie Delloff et al., *A Century of "The Century"* [Grand Rapids: Eerdmans, 1984], 4).

10. R. O. Everhart, "Engineering and the Millennium," *Methodist Review* 96 (1914): 44; cited by Moorhead, "Erosion of Postmillennialism," 76.

11. Among the exceptions here would be the tiny tradition of continuing Princeton Presbyterianism represented by J. Gresham Machen and Westminster Theological Seminary as well ethnically based confessional traditions such as the Christian Reformed Church and the Lutheran Church–Missouri Synod.

12. Cited, among others, by Mark A. Noll, *A History of Christianity in the United States and Canada* (Grand Rapids: Eerdmans, 1992), 289.

13. Casanova, 143. For the full story on these seismic shifts in American religious and public life, see Martin E. Marty, *Modern American Religion*, vol. 1, *The Irony of It All, 1893-1919* (Chicago and London: University of Chicago Press, 1986); vol. 2, *The Noise of Conflict, 1919-1941* (Chicago and London: University of Chicago Press, 1991); vol. 3, *Under God, Indivisible, 1941-1960* (Chicago and London: University of Chicago Press, 1996).

14. Casanova, 143-44. Casanova's reference here is to Sacvan Bercovitch, *The Puritan Origins of the American Self* (New Haven: Yale University Press, 1975).

society. "By the mid-1960s there were numerous indications that a 'third disestablishment,' the disestablishment of Protestantism from the American way of life, was under way. From now on, 'the American way of life' would be characterized by the plurality of ways of life, by what could be called moral denominationalism. The disestablishment of the Protestant ethic brought about the secularization of public morality and the emergence of a pluralistic system of norms and forms of life."[15] This disestablishment was both cultural and legal. The reigning secular mood was enshrined in legal code by a series of Supreme Court decisions limiting and even prohibiting religious symbolism and practice in the public square.[16]

The consequences of this redirection were profound for life in America. The city could now be celebrated for its very secularity;[17] the public square was to be naked by design,[18] liberated from the tyranny of oppressive (i.e., Protestant, Puritan) religion. No longer would the village atheist or practitioner of any religion other than Christianity need to feel publicly uncomfortable. Religious practice was to be relegated to the private, personal sphere where it belonged.

But that is not the way it turned out in the America of the twentieth century's final decades. To the surprise — a surprise due in part to deliberate ignoring of the ongoing vitality of Northern, urban evangelical Christianity from 1930 to 1960[19] — and consternation of the nation's cultural elites, public and politically resourceful evangelical Christianity is alive and well in America in the twenty-first century. Only a decade after Harvey Cox's popular manifesto *The Secular City* celebrated the secularized "world come of age" and reiterated Dietrich Bonhoeffer's call for a "religionless Christianity," the influential weekly *Newsweek* proclaimed 1976 "The Year of the Evangelical." An avowedly evangelical, "born-again" Southern Baptist had just been elected president of the United States, sending puzzled pundits to libraries in order to understand a religious reality about which they seemed clueless. A bemused John Chancellor,

15. Casanova, 145.

16. "Specifically, *Engel* v. *Vitale* (1962) and *Abington School District* v. *Schempp* (1963), in which the Court held that voluntary recitation of a nondenominational prayer and devotional Bible reading in the public schools, respectively, were unconstitutional; *Epperson* v. *Arkansas* (1968), where the Court contended that an Arkansas statute forbidding the teaching of evolution was unconstitutional" (Matthew C. Moen, *The Christian Right and Congress* [Tuscaloosa and London: University of Alabama Press, 1989], 12).

17. Harvey Cox, *The Secular City* (New York: Macmillan, 1965).

18. The phrase is from Richard John Neuhaus, *The Naked Public Square: Religion and Democracy in America* (Grand Rapids: Eerdmans, 1984).

19. See Joel A. Carpenter, *Revive Us Again: The Reawakening of American Fundamentalism* (New York and Oxford: Oxford University Press, 1997).

anchoring the *NBC Evening News,* likely revealed broader media ignorance when, in a somewhat condescending tone, he told his viewers: "We have checked on the religious meaning of Carter's profound [born again] experience. It is described by other Baptists as quite a common experience, not something out of the ordinary."[20] Ex-fundamentalist Carol Flake, in her exposé of what she calls "Redemptorama, the fantasy world of evangelical culture," describes a similar reaction from "a stringer from a national newsweekly . . . glancing nervously around at the cheerful multitude applauding Pat Boone during a Jesus Festival" and querying, "'Who *are* these people?'"[21] Equally interesting was the open battle in American public education about "creation science" engaged by evangelical Christians opposed to the evolution dogma of "secular humanism" — more than a half-century after the Scopes trial. In his 1980 campaign President Ronald Reagan told a gathering of evangelicals: "[Evolution] is a theory; it is a scientific theory only, and it has in recent years been challenged in the world of science and it is not yet believed in the scientific community to be as infallible as it was once believed. But if it was going to be taught in the schools then I think that also the biblical theory of creation, which is not a theory but the biblical story of creation, should also be taught."[22]

Reflecting on this, one had to wonder: Had William Jennings Bryan been reincarnated? In 1896 Bryan delivered his famous "gold cross" speech to the Democratic National Convention in Chicago, concluding with these words: "You shall not press down upon the brow of labor this crown of thorns. You shall not crucify mankind upon a cross of gold."[23] Exactly 100 years later another populist presidential candidate (this time a Republican) took up the cause of America's workers against free trade with similar-sounding words: "Rather than making global free trade a golden calf which we all bow down to and worship, . . . [w]e must stop sacrificing American jobs on the altars of trans-national corporations whose sole loyalty is to the bottom line."[24] This same candidate, when asked on national television about the teaching of creationism in public schools, mocked his interrogator (ABC's Sam

20. Cited in William Martin, *With God on Our Side: The Rise of the Religious Right in America* (New York: Broadway, 1996), 150.

21. Carol Flake, *Redemptorama: Culture, Politics, and the New Evangelicalism* (Garden City, N.Y.: Doubleday, 1984), 18, 3.

22. Cited in Wills, 120. Wills is citing Michael Ruse, *Darwinism Defended: A Guide to the Evolution Controversies* (Reading, Mass.: Addison-Wesley, 1982), 292.

23. Cited in Robert W. Cherny, *A Righteous Cause: The Life of William Jennings Bryan* (Boston and Toronto: Little, Brown, 1985), 60.

24. Cited in George Grant, *Buchanan: Caught in the Crossfire* (Nashville: Nelson, 1996), 103.

Donaldson) by quipping that Donaldson was perfectly free to believe that his ancestors were monkeys, but he (Pat Buchanan) believed human beings had been created by a God whose image they bore.[25] All this, we note, is not the way it was supposed to happen. As George Marsden observes:

> Certainly one of the most remarkable developments in American religion since 1930 has been the resurgence of evangelicalism as a force in American culture. Probably it is the one least likely to have been predicted in 1930. Fundamentalism appeared to have been defeated in those major northern denominations in which it had raised serious challenges during the 1920s, and progressives were in control. All that remained to be carried out, according to prevailing sociological theories, were mopping-up operations. Conservative religion would die out as modernity advanced. The backward South would become more like the industrialized North.[26]

Help! The Evangelicals Are Coming (Again)!

Confounding the predictions of pundits, therefore, public evangelical Christianity is actively present if not flourishing in America in the first decade of this new millennium. Politically active evangelicals have made a noticeable comeback and are, to cite the title of a recent collection of essays on the topic, "no longer exiles."[27] Or are they?[28] Judging from the attention paid to the revitalized, politically active evangelicalism, it is hard to tell. Yes, they are back, and even their most bitter opponents pay them the compliment of taking them seriously. In addition to the voluminous writing devoted to it in recent years,[29] the

25. Thus recalling the debate at Oxford in 1860 between Thomas Huxley and Anglican bishop Samuel ("Soapy") Wilberforce over Darwin's *Origin of Species*.

26. George M. Marsden, *Understanding Fundamentalism and Evangelicalism* (Grand Rapids: Eerdmans, 1991), 63.

27. Michael Cromartie, ed., *No Longer Exiles: The Religious New Right in American Politics* (Washington, D.C.: Ethics and Public Policy Center, 1993).

28. Judgments on the place and significance of conservative evangelicals in American public life are, in part, a matter of timing. This chapter was originally conceived in the fall on 1996 and drafted in the spring of 1997. The entire volume was submitted to the publisher in the spring of 1999. Much political and cultural water flowed under the bridge during that interval. For a fuller examination of the implications of this time lag, see chap. 9.

29. The literature on the Religious Right is becoming a growth industry. Included are Chip Berlet, ed., *Eyes Right: Challenging the Right Wing Backlash* (Boston: South End Press, 1995); Robert Boston, *The Most Dangerous Man in America: Pat Robertson and the Rise of the Christian Coalition* (Amherst, N.Y.: Prometheus Books, 1996); David G. Bromley and Anson Shupe, *New Christian Politics* (Macon, Ga.: Mercer University Press,

Public Broadcasting System devoted two quality series to contemporary religion in America and its growing popularity.[30] This observation obviously does

1984); Steve Bruce, *The Rise and Fall of the New Christian Right: Conservative Protestant Politics in America, 1978-1988* (Oxford: Clarendon, 1988); Steve Bruce, Peter Kivisto, and William H. Swatos, Jr., eds., *The Rapture of Politics: The Christian Right as the United States Approaches the Year 2000* (New Brunswick, N.J., and London: Transaction, 1995); Walter H. Capps, *The New Religious Right: Piety, Patriotism, and Politics* (Columbia: University of South Carolina Press, 1990); Jackson Carroll and Wade Clark Roof, *Beyond Establishment: Protestant Identity in a Post-Protestant Age* (Louisville: Westminster/John Knox, 1993); Michael Cromartie, *Disciples and Democracy: Religious Conservatives and the Future of American Politics* (Washington, D.C.: Ethics and Public Policy Center; Grand Rapids: Eerdmans, 1994); Sara Diamond, *Facing the Wrath: Confronting the Right in Dangerous Times* (Monroe, Maine: Common Courage Press, 1996); Dinesh D'Souza, *Falwell, before the Millennium* (Chicago: Regnery Gateway, 1984); Flake, *Redemptorama;* Alec Foege, *The Empire God Built: Inside Pat Robertson's Media Machine* (New York: Wiley, 1996); John George and Laird Wilcox, *American Extremists: Militias, Supremacists, Klansmen, Communists, and Others* (Amherst, N.Y.: Prometheus Books, 1995); James Davison Hunter, *American Evangelicalism: Conservative Religion and the Quandary of Modernity* (New Brunswick, N.J.: Rutgers University Press, 1983); James Davison Hunter, *Evangelicalism: The Coming Generation* (Chicago and London: University of Chicago Press, 1987); Morris A. Inch, *The Evangelical Challenge* (Philadelphia: Westminster, 1978); Robert Kuttner, ed., *Ticking Time Bombs: The New Conservative Assaults on Democracy* (New York: New Press, 1996); Robert C. Liebman and Robert Wuthnow, *The New Christian Right: Mobilization and Legitimation* (New York: Aldine, 1983); Michael Lienesch, *Redeeming America: Piety and Politics in the New Christian Right* (Chapel Hill and London: University of North Carolina Press, 1993); Guenter Lewy, *Why America Needs Religion: Secular Modernity and Its Discontents* (Grand Rapids: Eerdmans, 1996); Gary E. McCuen, *The Religious Right* (Hudson, Wis.: Gary McCuen Publications, 1989); Michael A. Milburn and Sheree D. Conrad, *The Politics of Denial* (Cambridge, Mass., and London: MIT Press, 1996); Richard J. Neuhaus and Michael Cromartie, *Piety and Politics: Evangelicals and Fundamentalists Confront the World* (Washington, D.C.: Ethics and Public Policy Center, 1987); Oldfield, *The Right and the Righteous;* Jeremy Rifkin with Ted Howard, *The Emerging Order: God in the Age of Scarcity* (New York: Putnam, 1979); J. Christopher Soper, *Evangelical Christianity in the United States and Great Britain: Religious Beliefs, Political Choices* (Washington Square, N.Y.: New York University Press, 1994); Ronald E. Thiemann, *Religion in Public Life: A Dilemma for Democracy* (Washington, D.C.: Georgetown University Press, 1996); Robert E. Webber, *The Moral Majority: Right or Wrong ?*(Westchester, Ill.: Crossway, 1981).

30. "Searching for God in America" was produced for Los Angeles PBS affiliate KCET by Hugh Hewitt, and "With God on Our Side" was made by Lumiere Productions for PBS affiliate SCETV (South Carolina). Both series also spun off substantive companion volumes: Hugh Hewitt, *Searching for God in America* (Dallas: Word, 1996); William Martin, *With God on Our Side.* It is worth noting that funding for the "With God on Our Side" project came from a diverse group of foundations, including the evangelical Pew Charitable Trusts as well as "liberal" foundations such as Rockefeller, MacArthur, and Donner.

not include the more ephemeral attention paid to it by the mainstream media, particularly during such times as the anniversary of *Roe* v. *Wade* or during political "hot" seasons such as primaries, conventions, or campaigns.[31] The response to the evangelical resurgence varies from restrained, academic curiosity that over time turns to better understanding, if not sympathy,[32] to what can only be described as outright hostility, even paranoia. What most observers share in common is an initial amazement about the phenomenon, a general bafflement about the resurgence of evangelicalism. Why, they wonder, have the

31. The 1996 Republican Convention, for example, regularly featured TV reporters seeking out women delegates to quiz them about the "abortion plank" and the threat to the GOP of "religious fundamentalists."

32. University of Massachusetts political science professor Guenter Lewy is refreshingly candid about his change of heart. In the preface to his *Why America Needs Religion,* he observes that he started writing the book "with the intention of refuting" the thesis that the crisis of belief caused by aggressive secularism ("the severance of morality from fixed values and standards, the discarding of theological sanctions") was the real reason for America's social pathology. His own conviction was that since knowledge of moral truth was not attainable anyway, it was necessary to accept "the idea of ethical and cultural relativism"; it was simply impossible to adjudicate between diverse and competing moral beliefs and practices. He notes that he "scoffed at the arguments made by religious thinkers such as Richard John Neuhaus, Carl F. H. Henry, and Francis A. Schaeffer that this approach led necessarily to an abdication of moral judgment and nihilism." Furthermore, noting that some religious people were immoral bigots and many humanists morally exemplary human beings, he worried about the danger posed by such critics of secular America to "the cherished American ideal of the separation of church and state. In short, I considered the attack on secular modernity to be a danger to individual liberty as well as an affront to people of goodwill who happened to be agnostics or atheists." But then "A funny thing, if one can call it that, happened on the way to the completion of this book, which I envisaged as a defense of secular humanism and ethical relativism. Positions that I had always supported and taken for granted turned out to be, on new reflection, far less convincing than I had assumed. This change in my outlook began with the realization that with regard to certain moral issues concerning the meaning of life and death, I had more in common with religious moralists such as James A. Gustafson, Paul Ramsey, and Richard McCormick than with most secular humanists." Lewy describes the conclusion of his pilgrimage with characteristic honesty: "I end this intellectual journey with some of my previously held ideas intact and many others discarded. I remain a religious agnostic, but, unlike most atheists, I not only am not hostile to traditional religion, but consider it a highly valuable, not to say essential, social institution. I am convinced that the moral regeneration and repair of a frayed social fabric that this country so badly needs will not take place unless more people take their religion seriously. . . . The urgent task for believers and nonbelievers alike, I submit, is to replenish the moral capital that was accumulated over many centuries from a unique stock of religious and ethical teachings, a fund of treasure that we have been depleting of late at an alarming rate." More restrained but still honest in its fair address to the concerns of the Religious Right is Capps, *The New Religious Right.*

secularizing forces of modernity not killed "fundamentalism"? What occasioned the rise of Rip Van Winkle evangelicals from their political slumbers? In other words, why and why now, here in America?

The assumption behind this incredulity is, of course, the classic Enlightenment sociological modernization theory that the modern world is by nature inimical to religion. As Peter Berger summarizes this theory: "Modernization necessarily leads to a decline of religion, both in society and in the minds of individuals."[33] The survival, not to mention revival, of traditional and publicly aggressive religion begs for explanation; it is "a strange, difficult-to-understand phenomenon."[34] Reflecting on the massive Fundamentalism Project, funded by the progressive MacArthur Foundation and chaired by University of Chicago church historian Martin Marty,[35] Berger asks this question: "*Who* finds this world [of fundamentalism] strange, and to *whom* must it be made understandable?" Berger's answer to his own question — "professors at American elite universities" — led him, he says, to an *Aha!* experience: "The concern that must have led to this Project was based on an upside-down perception of the world. The notion here was that so-called fundamentalism (which, when all is said and done, usually refers to any sort of passionate religious movement) is a rare, hard-to-explain thing. But in fact, it is not rare at all, neither if one looks at history, nor if one looks around the contemporary world. On the contrary, what is rare is people who think otherwise." Berger concludes: "The point of this little story is that the assumption that we live in a secularized world is false."[36]

The concern to find "causes" and explanations for the strange if not inexplicable rise of the Religious Right, nonetheless, remains a preoccupation of observers. A serious candidate for explaining the phenomenon was the "politics of status" theory "pioneered by theorists such as Richard Hofstadter, Daniel Bell, and Seymour Martin Lipset."[37] Though subjected to serious critique "both

33. Peter L. Berger, "Secularism in Retreat," *National Interest* 46 (winter 1996/97): 4.
34. Berger, "Secularism in Retreat," 3.
35. Martin E. Marty and R. Scott Appleby, eds., *The Fundamentalism Project*, vol. 1, *Fundamentalisms Observed* (Chicago: University of Chicago Press, 1991); vol. 2, *Fundamentalisms and Society: Reclaiming the Sciences, Family, and Education* (Chicago: University of Chicago Press, 1993); vol. 3, *Fundamentalisms and the State: Remaking Polities, Economies, and Militance* (Chicago: University of Chicago Press, 1993); vol. 4, *Accounting for Fundamentalisms: The Dynamic Character of Movements* (Chicago: University of Chicago Press, 1994).
36. Berger, "Secularism in Retreat," 3.
37. Oldfield, 36. Oldfield cites the following works (236 n. 1): Daniel Bell, ed., *The New American Right* (New York: Criterion Books, 1955); Daniel Bell, ed., *The Radical Right* (Garden City, N.Y.: Anchor Books, 1963); Seymour Martin Lipset and Earl Raab, *The Politics of Unreason* (Chicago: University of Chicago Press, 1978).

in its original formulation and in its application to the Christian Right," it has nonetheless retained its hold on scholars: "In one form or another, the concept of 'status politics' remains at the heart of scholarly efforts to account for mass-based moral reform movements."[38] This model for understanding social movements has as its premise, thanks to modernizing industrialization, the inevitable displacement and "dispossession" of existing dominant groups by new "elites," thus instigating anxious, reactionary, but ultimately ineffective rearguard actions against the modern world. Daniel Bell describes it as follows:

> What the right as a whole fears is the erosion of its own social position, the collapse of its power, the increasing incomprehensibility of a world — now overwhelmingly technical and complex — that has changed so drastically within a lifetime.
>
> The right, thus, fights a rear guard action. But its very anxieties illustrate the deep fissures which have opened in American society as a whole, as a result of the complex structural strains that have been taking place in the last thirty years or so.[39]

The key to understanding this "status politics" interpretation of the Religious Right is that its proponents make "a fundamental distinction between interest and status politics. The former is characterized by 'the clash of material aims and needs among various groups and blocs,' while the latter deals with 'projective aspirations arising from status aspirations and other personal motives.'" Importantly, while "material interests are held to be rational" and "can be discussed and compromises about them . . . reached," the concerns of participants in any "status movement" are irrational.[40] "The stated goals of status-based movements, it is argued, should not be taken at face value. Demands that flow from personal insecurities often bear little relation to the social problems that spawned dissent. Status-based movements often target the socially prominent, for by tearing down prominent individuals their own status may be reaffirmed."[41]

It is also worth noting that status movements are said to be characterized by a "paranoid style."

38. Oldfield, 36. Oldfield is citing Kenneth D. Wald, Dennis E. Owen, and Samuel Hill, Jr., "Evangelical Politics and Status Issues," *Journal for the Scientific Study of Religion* 28, no. 1 (1989): 1-16.

39. Daniel Bell, "The Dispossessed," in *The Radical Right*, 2-3; cited by Oldfield, 36.

40. Oldfield observes (37, 237 n. 8) that Lipset and Raab's book on status-based movements is titled *The Politics of Unreason*.

41. Oldfield, 37.

Marked by political moralism these movements view politics as a straightforward battle between good and evil. The moral and practical complexities of issues are denied as groups espouse simple solutions to national problems. These simple solutions generally involve the uncovering of conspiracies. The virtuous people can follow the wrong path only if deceived by the machinations of the few. For the Populists, the villains are the international money changers. McCarthyism focuses on international Communist subversion. The John Birch Society revives the conspiracy of the Illuminati. The Christian Right puts forward conspiratorial accounts of the doings of secular humanists.[42]

These movements are thus viewed as threats to democratic, pluralistic societies that operate with the necessary give-and-take of interest politics. Furthermore, "the psychological characteristics of status-anxious individuals are held to be unpleasant; Adorno's *Authoritarian Personality* is cited. A status-based mobilization of these individuals is therefore believed to threaten the stability of democratic norms and the autonomy of elites who defend them."[43]

One of the problems with the status framework approach that treats all concerns of the Religious Right as irrational but symbolically significant reactions against modernizing societal change effected by powerful new elites, is that, like most forms of gnosticism, it is self-justifying and even patronizing. It neither takes expressed cultural or social concerns seriously in their own right nor allows for honest debate about them but trivializes them.[44] "It reduces cultural concerns to surrogates for discontent with one's ranking in a hierarchical social order."[45] Historians of the 1950s and 1960s, according to David Horowitz, "have compounded these problems by showing little sensitivity to democratic and indigenous opponents of modern rationalism, urban liberalism, and cultural pluralism. The spread of European fascism and communism in the 1930s and 1940s convinced many intellectuals inside the United States of the dangers of grass-roots movements fueled by passion or ideology. Much of the work of the 1950s and

42. Oldfield, 38.
43. Oldfield, 38.
44. A striking example of such analysis (by two social psychologists) is Michael A. Milburn and Sherree D. Conrad, *The Politics of Denial* (Cambridge, Mass., and London: MIT Press, 1996). According to the authors, empirical study of the neoconservative, radical Religious Right shows that behind the rage of America's angry white males is rigid, harsh, punitive, authoritarian child-rearing practices. It is these practices that lead to authoritarian, punitive political attitudes in adults. If the authors truly believe this, one could ask why a "to explain all is to forgive all" approach then does not characterize the general attitude of the secular therapeutic community or the media to the Religious Right.
45. Oldfield, 39.

1960s portrayed critics of elite institutions and values as marginal agitators characterized by irrational anxieties, prejudices, ignorance and bigotry."[46] It is surely the case that a fair treatment of movements such as the Religious Right must honestly face the question whether "social trends are moving in destructive directions. Is 'rear-guard' action then necessarily irrational? Shouldn't any reasonable political actors be upset if 'relevant social questions' are being resolved by others who do not share their values?" Are matters such as sexual morality, abortion, and euthanasia — especially in the sensitive area of teaching moral rules and values to children — not of supreme importance? "Those not working from within a status politics framework," notes Oldfield, "might question whether control of hearth, home, and culture is really a 'fringe' issue." Even if it is the case that evangelicals, "acutely aware that they [are] objects of ridicule in the broader society," are thus dismayed by their lack of status, "the movement's opposition to abortion, homosexuality, and 'secular humanism' is genuine and not simply a means for its members to tear down elites and regain lost status." The main concern of the evangelicals he interviewed, notes Oldfield, "was that their *values and culture* were being ridiculed."[47]

Oldfield finally raises what he judges to be the most significant and fundamental objection to the status framework approach. The simple dichotomy between the "increasingly complex and cosmopolitan industrial (or, as is now common, post-industrial) society" and the evangelical community "left behind by the forces of modernity" does not square with demographic facts. In fact, evangelical denominations and congregations that resist key elements of modernity are thriving, while "the mainline Protestant churches, with their active efforts to remain 'relevant' in the face of intellectual trends . . . appear headed for extinction."[48] Furthermore, evangelicals are hardly inflexibly opposed to modernity but have in fact adapted their message to many of its pressures. "Evangelicals have pioneered new methods of appealing to mass publics, utilizing the latest media techniques in their efforts.[49] Even their moral doctrines, the

---

46. David A. Horowitz, *Beyond Left and Right: Insurgency and the Establishment* (Urbana and Chicago: University of Illinois Press, 1997), xi.

47. Oldfield, 39.

48. Oldfield, 40-41. For an analysis of the decline of American mainline, liberal Christianity, accompanied by a passionate critique, see Thomas C. Reeves, *The Empty Church: The Suicide of Liberal Christianity* (New York: Free Press, 1996); a more optimistic outlook is given by Anthony Campolo, *Can Mainline Denominations Make a Comeback?* (Valley Forge, Pa.: Judson, 1995).

49. In fact, it is precisely the remarkable success of Pat Robertson's media "empire" that is cause for concern among his critics. See Foege, *The Empire God Built*. Foege speaks in strikingly modern terms of "the brave new world [Robertson] has created" (8).

'traditional' values many evangelicals so ardently defend, have been adapted to better fit a contemporary ethos of self fulfillment."[50] Another crucial piece of evidence offered by those who insist that evangelical Christianity is not simply antithetically opposed to modernity is the interesting linkage between the growth of evangelical Christianity and explicit modernizing tendencies in such "developing areas" as Latin America.[51] All this is then said to be "evidence of the movement's ability to function, even thrive in a supposedly hostile world."[52]

An intriguing alternative to the "status discontent" theory is offered by University of North Carolina sociologist Christian Smith and his associates in their study *American Evangelicalism: Embattled and Thriving*. Smith explores the status explanation along with other efforts such as the one he calls "sheltered enclave" theory — evangelical religion survives because it is protected from the corrosive acids of modernity — and finds them wanting. "Evangelicalism appears to be thriving despite — or, . . . perhaps precisely *because of* — the fact that it is very much engaged in struggle with the institutions, values, and thought processes of the pluralistic modern world."[53] Since American religious life is highly voluntaristic, Smith notes that what he calls the "competitive marketing theory" — "religious regulation and monopolies create lethargic religions . . . [while] capable religions thrive in pluralistic, competitive environments"[54] — adds another factor to the vitality of modern American evangeli-

50. Oldfield, 42.

51. "The evangelical resurgence is positively modernizing in most places where it occurs, clearly so in Latin America." Opposed to hierarchical models of authority, heavily invested in literacy (to read the Bible) and lay leadership (including women), "it is not fanciful to suggest that in this way Evangelical congregations serve (inadvertently, to be sure) as schools for democracy and social mobility" (Berger, "Secularism in Retreat," 10). See also Lawrence E. Harrison, *The Pan-American Dream: Do Latin America's Cultural Values Discourage True Partnership with the United States and Canada?* (New York: Basic Books, 1996); Michael Novak, *The Spirit of Democratic Capitalism* (New York: Simon & Schuster, 1982).

52. Oldfield, 42. Cf. the judgment of Gordon-Conwell's David Wells that "evangelicalism has become modern," deriving "its power not from its theology but from its culture" (*God in the Wasteland: The Reality of Truth in a World of Fading Dreams* [Grand Rapids: Eerdmans, 1994]). It needs to be noted here that there is a significant and growing body of literature written by evangelicals themselves (including the Wells volume mentioned above) that is critical of what is judged to be excessive evangelical accommodation to modernity.

53. Christian Smith et al., *American Evangelicalism: Embattled and Thriving* (Chicago and London: University of Chicago Press, 1998), 75.

54. Smith, 73; Smith appeals here to the work of Roger Finke and Rodney Starke, "Religious Economies and Sacred Canopies: Religious Mobilization in American Cities, 1906," *American Sociological Review* 53, no. 1 (February 1988): 41-50.

calism. Smith calls his own interpretive framework a "subcultural identity theory of religious strength."[55] Smith's argument is that "evangelicalism is thriving, not because it has built a protective subcultural shield against modernity, but — to the contrary — precisely because it is passionately engaged in direct struggle with pluralistic modernity." In addition, the two critical components of the contemporary world — cultural pluralism and religious competition — have "not damaged evangelicalism, but [have] been the condition[s] in which it has thrived."[56]

Smith's argument can be summarized briefly as follows: By nature human beings long for meaning and a sense of belonging and form themselves in distinctive groups that establish their identities by "drawing symbolic boundaries that create distinction between themselves and relevant outgroups."[57] Under the pressures of tremendous historical change, "modern religious believers can establish stronger religious identities and commitments on the basis of individual choice than through ascription."[58] A group's strength of identity is then also directly related to its being able to position itself over against competing group claims. What this finally means, according to Smith, is that the fragmenting pressures of modernity are actually conducive to strong group identity formation as a counterweight.

Smith formulates his theory in terms of both religious *persistence* and religious *strength*:[59]

Persistence

Religion survives and can thrive in pluralistic, modern society by embedding itself in subcultures that offer satisfying, morally orienting collective identities which provide adherents with meaning and belonging.

Strength

In a pluralistic society, those religious groups will be relatively stronger which better possess and employ the cultural tools needed to create both clear distinction from and significant engagement and tension with other relevant outgroups, short of becoming genuinely countercultural.

---

55. Smith, chap. 4, pp. 89-119.
56. Smith, 88.
57. Smith, 90-91.
58. Smith, 102.
59. The following two theses are found on 118-19.

Conspiracy Left, Conspiracy Right

Problems with the status framework notwithstanding, critics within and outside the church continue to think of the Religious Right in terms of ousted aggrieved "outsiders" wanting to return to the citadels of influence.[60] Thus the results of the 1994 American congressional election were almost universally judged by an unsympathetic mass media as the temper tantrum of "angry white males."[61] Often appearing to project their own fears onto the Christian Right that played no small role in the results of the 1994 election, many observers speculate wildly about the long-range goals of the movement as well as the prospects for its future success. Included here is musing about deep, dark, theocratic plots to deprive Americans of their secular freedoms and to impose a divinely ordered political model on American citizens. For many avowedly secular Americans, the resurgence of evangelical Christians in politics is their worst nightmare come to reality.[62] Since its critics use the status framework to explain the rise of the Religious Right, it is tempting to turn the same analysis on them. We would then need to argue that political leftists are irrationally reacting to what they perceive as their own growing loss of influence and power. This path of mutual accusation and recrimination is not helpful, however, and we shall simply try to describe the rhetoric of conspiracy that is used by both camps to demonize the other. We enter now the murky world of conspiracy thinking and theorizing.

Conspiracy theories are the final refuge of the apocalyptic-sectarian mind-set ("the world is ending; we alone of God's true prophets are left"). Prominent Religious Right leaders such as Pat Robertson have not helped their own campaigns to be taken seriously as responsible public figures by their frequent appeal to conspiratorial explanations of world events and the fear-mongering associated with conspiracy theorizing. Robertson, for example, sets

60. The second chapter of Richard G. Hutcheson's *Mainline Churches and the Evangelicals: A Challenging Crisis* (Atlanta: John Knox, 1981) is entitled "The Outs Move In: A Mainline View of the Evangelical Renascence," while the third introduces martial imagery: "The Target: Mainline Churches."

61. The expression "temper tantrum" (as in, "today the American electorate threw a temper tantrum") was coined by ABC television news anchor Peter Jennings on election night, 1994.

62. A graphic fictional account of these anxieties can be seen in Canadian author Margaret Atwood's work *A Handmaid's Tale* (Toronto: McClelland & Stewart, 1985). Atwood's novel, made into a film, was, if anything, even more frightening. Another film of the 1990s, *Escape from L.A.,* clearly — without any attempt at disguise — portrays former Moral Majority leader Jerry Falwell as its theocratic, hypocritical villain who utilizes all the coercive military power of the state to suppress freedom, especially sexual license.

his book *The New World Order: It Will Change the Way You Live*[63] in the context of the failed "coup" against Soviet president Mikhail Gorbachev.[64] Robertson portrays the attempted coup as a mere stage show, designed only to fool the world into believing that the Soviet Union was liberalizing and democratizing. The revealing moment came to him, he says, when a CNN reporter, on August 21, 1991, when the coup's failure was clear, made the "startling observation . . . [that President Bush's] *new world order* is back on track, now stronger than ever" (ix). Robertson then refers to a section in the book which, he says, "gives a startling and detailed account of the KGB plan that was actually played out in 1989 to lull the West with false 'liberalization'" (x). In addition, this was an old strategy, a parallel to "a virtually identical program carried out by Nicolai Lenin in 1921, a program he called *glasnost*" (x).

Robertson judges American political leaders, including President Bush, who used the term "new world order" repeatedly after the momentous geopolitical changes of 1989, as actively complicit in a dark, secret, utopian plot to establish one world government tyranny, all, of course, in the name of peace, stability, and order. The vision Robertson fears is summarized in his citation from Brock Chisholm, director of the United Nations World Health Organization: "To achieve world government, it is necessary to remove from the minds of men their individualism, loyalty to family traditions, national patriotism, and religious dogmas" (7). What most disturbs Robertson's critics is his linkage of "new world order" rhetoric to a deliberate evil plot for world domination by a small, secret, conspiratorial society called the "Order of the Illuminati" (67). This society, established by "a Bavarian professor named Adam Weishaupt, . . . [was formed] to establish a new world order based on the overthrow of civil governments, the church, and private property and elevation to world leadership of a group of hand-picked 'adepts' or 'illumined ones'" (67). Robertson holds this group, working through the society of Freemasons, responsible for the terrors of the French Revolution, Marxism and the Bolshevik Revolution, and the post–World War II American compromises with world communism,

63. Dallas: Word, 1991; page references that follow in the text are to this work.

64. The foreword of this volume is revealing. Robertson sets up a scenario where his "prophetic" understanding of the "world conspiracy" is confirmed by the events surrounding the failed Soviet coup. According to Robertson, "the manuscript of *The New World Order* was complete, the final proofs had been checked, and the book was essentially on the presses" when the news of the coup broke. The events that followed confirmed the very schemes for a "new world order" that Robertson contends had been outlined in its pages even before the events happened. A similar pattern, though in a very different context, occurs in the narrative of Robertson's apocalyptic novel *The End of the Age*, which will be discussed later in this section.

including the ABM, SALT, and INF treaties with the Soviet Union as well as the general policy of *detente* (68-81). To catch a flavor of Robertson's perspective, here is a citation he uses from British author Nesta Webster:[65]

[T]he same secret ring of Illuminati is believed to have been intimately connected with the organization of the Bolshevik revolution. . . . None of the leading Bolsheviks are said to have been members of the innermost circle, which is understood to consist of men belonging to the highest intellectual and financial classes, whose names remain absolutely unknown. Outside this absolutely secret ring there existed, however, a semi-secret circle of initiates of subversive societies drawn from all over the world and belonging to various nationalities.

Robertson alleges that it is, in fact, such a "secret cabal," what he calls "the Establishment," that is the real power in the United States:

Rest assured, there is a behind-the-scenes Establishment in this nation, as in every other. It has enormous power. It has controlled the economic and foreign policy objectives of the United States for the past seventy years, whether the man sitting in the White House is a Democrat or a Republican, a liberal or a conservative, a moderate or an extremist. This power is above elections, but it has been able to control the results of elections. Beyond the control of wealth, its principal goal is the establishment of a one-world government where the control of money is in the hands of one or more privately owned but government chartered central banks. (96)

When Robertson actually names names (institutions and organizations as well as individual persons), it is no small wonder that the opposition gets nervous. Serious conspiratorial thinking coming from influential people *is* scary. What makes Robertson's conspiracy theorizing even more frightening for many is his explicit tie between these conspiracies and the fulfillment of biblical prophecy. Here is Robertson's own description of that link, as he summarizes the purpose of his book: "This book will place the origin, meaning, and ultimate destiny of the new world order within the clear purview of Bible prophecy, so that you can understand what God has to say about the one-world government that from 1990 onward may trace its public and official debut back to the Tigris-Euphrates Valley, where the first known civilization was born and from whence mankind was scat-

65. One of the infuriating features of Robertson's writing is his failure to provide specific footnote references for the quotations he uses. The author he is apparently citing is listed only in the general bibliography and is thus likely Nesta Webster, *Secret Societies* (New York: Dutton, 1924).

tered because it had rebelled against God, and into which was born Abraham — the man whose seed was appointed by God to redeem the world" (14). *The New World Order,* so Robertson tells us in his foreword, was "updated" to take into account developments in geopolitics in the same way that his earlier book *The New Millennium: Ten Trends That Will Impact You and Your Family by the Year 2000*[66] was updated by breaking events during the Gulf War crisis (xii). *The New World Order* "is actually a continuation of the last [book]" (xiii). In a subsequent book, a novel, *The End of the Age,*[67] Robertson spells out a scenario of world history that follows, in scrupulous fidelity to each detail, the premillennial dispensation scheme developed in the Scofield Bible. While, as we shall see, there have been unfair critiques leveled against Robertson by secularist opponents, Robertson himself has given those critics plenty of ammunition. An unsympathetic reading of his writings *is* in many respects a frightening experience for those who love liberty and fear its suppression by those with theocratic inclinations who speak on behalf of God. But now we must also consider the rhetorical excesses on the other side.

It is a favorite rhetorical move by opponents of the Religious Right to draw explicit links between Christian warfare imagery, wherever and however it is used, and specific acts of public violence. The logic of this critique goes something like this: evangelicals who sing "Onward, Christian Soldiers" and "Stand Up, Stand Up for Jesus, Ye Soldiers of the Cross" in church, or at Billy Graham or Christian Coalition rallies, are the sorts who are likely to join Idaho Christian militia groups, bomb abortuaries, and assassinate abortionists. The martial rhetoric of the Christian Right also, so its critics allege, in good measure contributed to the climate that led to the bombing of the Alfred P. Murrah Federal Building in Oklahoma City on April 19, 1995.[68] It is this event (along with the Branch Davidian disaster in Waco, Texas) that has become iconographic for opponents of the Christian Right. Since then, conspiracy theorists have run wild. The worst instance of domestic terrorism in the history of the United States also led to an excess of journalistic hysteria. Extreme judgment rained down on the "extremists" in the militia movement, the Christian Coalition, the

66. Dallas: Word, 1990.

67. Dallas: Word, 1995.

68. The growing body of literature on "right-wing extremists" regularly takes the Oklahoma City bombing as its point of departure. See, in addition to the literature cited in n. 29: Richard Abanes, *American Militias: Rebellion, Racism, and Religion* (Downers Grove, Ill.: InterVarsity, 1996); James A. Aho, *The Politics of Righteousness: Idaho Christian Patriotism* (Seattle and London: University of Washington Press, 1995); James A. Aho, *This Thing of Darkness: A Sociology of the Enemy* (Seattle and London: University of Washington Press, 1994).

Republican Party — all considered bound together as interlocking parts of a concerted campaign, a conspiratorial "call for revolution by the far right wing of this country."[69] In the words of one commentator: "It has taken the tragedy of Oklahoma City to understand that 'The Aryan Nation' is not the name of an organization of some sort. 'The Aryan Nation' is the goal of the Christian Coalition and the Patriot Militias and the Contract with America and Governor Pete Wilson."[70]

Others were equally indiscriminate in making blanket judgments of their "enemy on the right." Robert Boston, a staff member of Americans United for Separation of Church and State who describes himself as "a leading voice of opposition to the Religious Right," considers 1988 Republican presidential candidate and Christian Coalition founder Pat Robertson "the most dangerous man in America"[71] and pleads for a confrontation: "Let's stand up to the radical forces that would trash our secular democracy and knock down the wall of separation of church and state wherever they operate."[72] The reason for this much-needed confrontation is that, though Americans are unaware of it, "Robertson has a master plan for the nation that he has outlined in books [which] is dangerous to the personal freedom and religious liberty of every American."[73] Boston then lumps together Robertson (and Ralph Reed of the Christian Coalition) with D. James Kennedy (Coral Ridge Ministries), Beverly La Haye (Concerned Women of America), Gary Bauer (Family Research Council), John Whitehead (Rutherford Institute), Kevin Hasson (Beckett Fund), and Paul Weyrich (Free Congress Foundation) with this judgment: "All of these groups espouse theocracy or church-state union to some degree, and all pose a grave threat to our freedoms."[74] Boston is particularly worried that gullible American

69. Cited by George and Wilcox, 247.

70. June Jordan, "In the Land of White Supremacy," *Progressive* (June 1995): 21; cited by George and Wilcox, 247. Others who make direct links between the Religious Right in general (notably Pat Robertson's Christian Coalition and James Dobson's Focus on the Family) and the violence advocacy of militia groups, Klansmen, the Jewish Defense League, the Nation of Islam, and assorted neo-Nazi groups are George and Wilcox (see chapter headings); the essayists in Berlet, *Eyes Right;* and Diamond, *Facing the Wrath.*

71. Ironically, Boston may not be aware that this is the exact language used by hyper-fundamentalist Bob Jones, Jr., concerning Moral Majority founder Jerry Falwell's political activity. See Oldfield, 31.

72. Boston, 20.

73. Boston, 16.

74. Boston, 21. Sara Diamond casts an even more inclusive net by aggregating Focus on the Family; Promise Keepers; Operation Rescue; abortuary bombers and abortion-doctor killers Paul Hill, John Salvi, and Michael Griffin; Francis Schaeffer; R. J. Rushdoony, Gary North, and other theonomists ("Calvinist Reconstructionists"); homeschoolers; the

citizens might be lulled into complacency by the explicit public denials given by Robertson and Reed of their real theocratic ambitions. After all, the denial by conspirators of their conspiracy is itself *prima facie* proof of their conspiratorial cleverness. Reed in particular, he notes, had the "gall" to say, "We believe in a separation between church and state that is complete and inviolable."[75] According to Boston, this "lie" should not fool us because Reed is only the smiling, "good cop" public face of the Christian Coalition; Robertson remains the "bad cop" who is plotting to take away the *secular* freedoms of American citizens: "The [public] shift of focus from Robertson to Reed is part of a careful strategy by the Christian Coalition to make itself appear moderate and nonthreatening to the average American. . . . So Reed is the smiling, nicely groomed young man who stands before the cameras while just behind the curtain lurks the sinister persona of Pat Robertson."[76]

Boston's attack on Robertson demonstrates how difficult it is to discuss the merits and problems with conspiracy believers.[77] Openness and detached reportorial objectivity are also absent in Boston's account of the 1995 Christian Coalition "Road to Victory" rally in Washington, D.C., where he reported that "much of what I saw and heard, sickened, angered, or just plain disgusted me," including "its overwhelming atmosphere of paranoia and siege mentality; its naked partisan overtones; and its utter lack of compassion, charity, and decency." He pillories speakers such as Judge Robert Bork[78] and concludes his

American Center for Law and Justice; the ministry to homosexuals, Exodus International; David Duke; Justice Clarence Thomas; the National Association of Scholars; the U.S. Taxpayers Party; Christian Patriots; and the Rand Corporation. All, she contends, are part of one grand and angry right-wing conspiracy. According to Diamond, there was a "silver lining to the Oklahoma City bombing: the opportunity the incident afforded for public education and dialogue about the growth of right-wing organizations" (Diamond, 205). Apparently oblivious to any sense of the ironic, Diamond makes this claim in the opening sentence of a chapter entitled "Shifting the Blame."

75. Boston, 72.

76. Boston, 32.

77. The logic of Boston's attack on Robertson boils down to this:

- Robertson is a dangerous threat to freedom-loving Americans; he is a conspirator.
- Proof of his evil, conspiratorial intentions is obvious from his repeated accusations that others are conspirators.

Remarkably, Boston does not draw the obvious conclusion from his own wild accusations.

78. "In a weary, pedantic tone, Bork ridiculed Supreme Court justices who dare disagree with his bizarre and rigid interpretation of the Constitution, insisting that they are part of a plot by 'liberal elites' to subvert American culture and instill moral relativism" (115). Boston also refers to Supreme Court associate justice Clarence Thomas as "a Religious Right operative." It must be noted, with gratitude, that Boston reacts viscerally (he is

screed thus: "But perhaps the ugliest feature of the Road to Victory was that, in its haste to embrace every far-right Republican proposal to come down the pike, no matter how paleolithic, the group jettisoned its very last shred of moral compassion — if it ever had any to begin with."[79]

Here we come to the real reason for Boston's vitriol: "The real threat behind Pat Robertson is the fact that he currently holds the Republican Party in a headlock and is making great progress toward his theocratic goals."[80] Boston, like many others on the political left, is fearful for his very political life; after all the progressive successes of the sixties' counterculture, the tide seems to be turning and the prospect of political marginalization seems to him real and awful. Running scared when one's power, influence, and status are threatened does not make for cool, detached, careful analysis. Here, from an anthology of critical essays on the Religious Right, is another voice singing the same song, now with intensified character assassination: "Today, the right has a virtual lock on U.S. politics. It has the momentum, the money, the new ideas, and the votes. Worse still, this is not a 'New Right,' as its architects would have us believe, but the old right in new clothing. That old segregationist army of vengeful reactionaries is now a slick, media-savvy, professional marching troop, bent on the same agenda of retribution against liberalism and deliverance from reform. They are directing a populist revolt against taxes, government, and secularism under the banner of family values and a narrow, rigid, brand of Christianity." Calling readers of the anthology to a "deeper understanding of the current resurgence of the right," the author of the preface insists that this is a "political necessity" rather than a mere "intellectual exercise": "The right's agenda — the complete defeat of liberalism and the left, the silencing of progressive opinions, the restoration of Christian hegemony, and the re-marginalization of all cultures other than that of European Americans — cannot be fought without a thorough understanding of it." After this outburst, the author, in a remarkably self-congratulatory mode, breezily assures the reader that "the collection [of essays] is markedly free of rhetoric, oversimplification, or demonization."[81]

Even treatments of the Religious Right by "academics" are often little more than ill-disguised rallying cries for strategic political activism directed against religious conservatives and for progressive causes. In this vein Sara Dia-

---

"angered and disgusted") to all that evidences an "overwhelming atmosphere of paranoia and siege mentality."

79. Boston, 115. The reader cannot help but marvel at the ironic and unintentionally self-incriminating opening line of Boston's conclusion: "Many foolish things have been written about the Religious Right and the Christian Coalition over the years" (235).

80. Boston, 15.

81. Jean Hardisty, preface to Berlet, 13.

mond (doctorate in sociology, University of California at Berkeley), after revealing her own political stripes by a lament blaming the Christian Right, among others, "for the tens of thousands of civilians who were killed in the name of anti-communism in recent years [in Central America]," wonders out loud about "what might have been." "In most cases, the influence of the Right can be considered in light of what has not happened, as much as in terms of what has." What are the many wonderful improvements that could have made America a better society? Diamond's list is revealing.

> What if the Right had not opposed public funding for AIDS education, and had not continuously stigmatized homosexual people? How many lives might have been saved? What if anti-abortion vigilantes had not terrorized clinics, and feminist activists had not had to spend most of their resources in defense of reproductive choice? Absent the continuous threat to earlier gains, a women's movement might have forged ahead on policies for pay equity and federally funded childcare and health care.
>
> On race matters, the organized Right has kept the civil rights movement stalled at the point of defending the gains of the 1960s. What if civil rights activists had been free to pursue more equitable representation for voters of color in the 1990s? What might have been some of the ripple effects of economic progress for persons of color — in lowering rates of teen delinquency, in easing hostile attitudes toward new immigrants, in countless other aspects of life for millions of people?
>
> We can only imagine where our society would be headed now absent the power of right-wing movements, working in sync with corrupt and entrenched political elites.[82]

What we are being asked to imagine, of course, is the unfettered triumph of political leftism. The anger is directed here at the mere *fact* of opposition. That point is worth highlighting. The political Left wants no opposition! Diamond is frustrated not only by the roadblocks conservatives have erected to slow down or even stop the leftward journey to a progressive society, but also by what she judges to be the inequity of resources for the political battle. "The sheer scope of right-wing movement activity appears overwhelming and, in many respects, it is. The Left has nothing to compete with the Right's multibillion dollar organizational infrastructure."[83] However, though the situation "sounds dismal now" because "at present one cannot see on the horizon a progressive movement massive enough to stop the current onslaught from the Right," this is

82. Diamond, 13-14.
83. Diamond, 17.

"great opportunity, not defeat." "There is growth potential for the Left to learn more about how our system works, including the role of right-wing movements. Every action taken now to blunt the power of the Right and to press for humane policies is a stepping stone on the path toward an eventual respite, and a redirection of the course our country is on."[84]

There is a basic pattern found in critiques of the Right (be it religious or secular) even when the assessment of its future role and success in American politics is quite different. One of American conservatism's prominent public apostates, former William F. Buckley protégé Michael Lind, now a senior editor for the *New Yorker,* begins his recent book, *Up from Conservativism,* with this unambiguous prognosis: "American conservativism is dead."[85] While its influence may still be with us for some time, "even as the Republicans came to power in Congress for the first time in nearly half a century, the mainstream conservative movement in the United States was cracking up," according to Lind. His prognosis: "For the foreseeable future, as for the past half century, the honorable name of conservativism is likely to remain the property, in the United States, of shifting coalitions of libertarians, racists, medievalists, Protestant fundamentalists, supply-siders, flat-taxers, isolationists, gun fanatics, anti-Semites, and eugenics theorists."[86] These together can be held accountable for what Lind describes as the "fact" that the "United States for more than a decade, has been suffering from wave after wave of right-wing terrorism."[87] How did this collapse of conservatism and lapse into terrorism take place? "The conservative intellectual movement was the first element of mainstream conservativism to fail. Intellectual conservativism fell apart beginning in 1992, as a result of the rise of the far right of Pat Robertson, Pat Buchanan, and antigovernment militias."[88] Lind consequently argues that the Republican capture of Congress in 1994 does not represent a conversion to conservatism by Americans but simply the success of a "southern strategy" started for the Republican Party by Barry Goldwater and Richard Nixon. Though conservative intellectuals have tried manfully to effect a conversion to their ideology, the end result has been a disastrous confusion of conservatism with populism.

---

84. Diamond, 17-18. For a different "read" on the actual resources available to the cultural and political Left or Right, respectively, see David Horowitz, "*National Review* Promotes a Rogue and Fouls Its Nest, Part I," *Frontpagemag.com.,* May 3, 1999. The bulk of this first part was a reprise of Horowitz's review of Michael Lind's book *Up from Conservativism: Why the Right Is Wrong for America* (New York: Free Press, 1996).

85. Lind, 1.

86. Lind, 70.

87. Lind, 8.

88. Lind, 1.

In almost half a century, then, the conservative movement has failed to create a conservative majority in the United States. But its effect has been profound and destructive nonetheless. . . . Today the right is defined by Robertson, Buchanan, and the militia movement.

The only movement on the right in the United States that has any significant political influence is the far Right. In the manner of the southern Right from the Civil War until the civil rights revolution, which operated both through the Democratic party and the Ku Klux Klan, or the modern Irish Republican movement, with its party (Sinn Fein) and its terrorist branch (the IRA), the contemporary American far right has both public, political wings (the Christian Coalition, the National Rifle Association, Project Rescue) and its covert, paramilitary, terrorist factions. Although the Christian Coalition and Operation Rescue officially denounce violence, the fact remains that a common worldview animates both the followers of Pat Robertson and Pat Buchanan and the far-right extremists who bomb abortion clinics, murder federal marshals and county sheriffs, and blow up buildings and trains.

That worldview is summed up by three letters, ZOG. ZOG stands for "Zionist-occupied government," the phrase used by far-right white supremacists, anti-Semites, and militia members for the federal government.[89]

Lind concludes with a chilling allusion to Nazi Germany: "The main forces on the right in the 1990s, then, have more in common with the far right of the 1930s than with the mainstream right of the 1980s."[90]

As if he were eager to demonstrate that the editorial offices of establishment media are up to the task of concocting conspiracy theories rivaling those produced in the fever swamps of America's left and right fringes, Lind offers us a portent of America's collapse, since "the United States, on the verge of the twenty-first century, [is] in the control of a Washington cabal of reactionary white politicians from the South and West and their corporate sponsors."[91] Directed by a "conservative brain trust [that] originated in a scheme hatched in the 1970s by William Simon, Irving Kristol, and others" and that "bears a striking resemblance to the CIA-backed network of cultural fronts in the United States and Europe of the early years of the cold war," this cabal operates by stealth and insists on a rigid "party line" where all dissent is punished by the monied interests who cut off foundation grants. These neoconservative foundations, along with "the little magazines, the little institutes and think tanks — all represent the application, in U.S. domestic policies, on behalf of big business and international finance, of

89. Lind, 7-8.
90. Lind, 9.
91. Lind, 23.

techniques earlier used by the CIA to influence opinion abroad."[92] In other words, "a vast right-wing conspiracy." This accusation, notes reviewer Joshua Muravchik, ironically comes from the man who schoolmasters Pat Robertson for his obsession with "the nefarious schemes of international high finance."[93]

Of course, not all treatments of the Religious Right are this fevered, and we shall consider some of the more thoughtful ones later in this chapter. But the fundamental question about whether the religious neutrality of the American Constitution is compatible with even very mild notions of a "Christian America" or whether it demands a thoroughgoing secularism will not go away. It is hard to tell whether it is out of genuine conviction or merely a sign of desperation among critics of the Religious Right that they trot out the old canards of racism and (increasingly) anti-Semitism in the appeal of the Christian Right for "traditional values."[94] The race card, of course, remains a powerful one in American politics, and evoking memories of racist patterns in the southern part of the United States is an important part of the strategy to discredit conservatism in general. Linkage between racism and all forms of Southern conservatism is almost irresistible for political and social analysts.[95] Similarly, the

---

92. Lind, 80-81. The phrase "party line" is found on 86, where Lind alludes to right-wing "plotting" in these groups in the following vague and unprovable as well as irrefutable terms: "The party line tended to be adopted at periodic 'conservative summits,' private meetings once a year or so between conservative editors like Kristol, Podhoretz, and Buckley, occasional journalists like Charles Krauthammer, Republican politicians, and foundation executives. It is as though George McGovern, Dan Rather, and Jesse Jackson met periodically to decide what the party line of 'liberalism' would be and then issued marching orders to their subalterns in the Democratic party and the media."

93. In *Commentary* (September 1996): 88. Once again, as with our earlier analysis of Robert Boston's attack on Pat Robertson's theocratic "conspiracy" (see n. 77 above), the logic of Lind's exposé is most revealing. Here's his judgment on the demagoguery of the Right: "The grass-roots activists are demagogues, of the worst sort. They are demagogues, not only by choice but by necessity. They make their living by frightening the wits out of gullible people" (78). To which the minimal response at least should be: *Tu quoque!*

94. See the discussion of the culture wars in chap. 8, particularly the response of Orthodox Jews such as Rabbi Daniel Lapin to the use of anti-Semitism as a weapon in the culture wars (372-73).

95. Thus, contemporary historical scholarship, as well as much of the political journalism that depends on it, tends readily to dismiss Southern conservatism as a genuine protest against and alternative to Northern, liberal, secular modernism and treats it rather as a mere epiphenomenal excuse for deep-seeded nativism and racism. For a revisionist critique of this historical scholarship, see Eugene Genovese, *The Southern Tradition: The Achievement and Limitations of an American Conservativism* (Cambridge: Harvard University Press, 1995). Genovese insists that there is a genuine Southern conservative tradition, including John Randolph and John Calhoun, characterized by belief in a transcendent order in society as well as in nature, and that today's American religious conservatives are

penumbras of the Holocaust serve opponents of the Religious Right well by raising the specter of "terrors of the Right," but not even all Jews are swayed by it. The response of Jewish medical educator David Stolinsky in his lament about the loss of Christian values may be the best way to respond to the feverish outburst summarized above. "The reason we fear to go out after dark is not that we may be set upon by bands of evangelicals and forced to read the New Testament, but that we may be set upon by gangs of feral young people who have been taught that nothing is superior to their own needs or feelings."[96]

Still, the implicit issue of anti-Semitism in articulated concerns about "theocracy" and the dangerous potential for subverting America's traditional constitutional religious neutrality in order to impose a Christian version of God's law on all her citizens have turned up in the strangest place — in heated debates among political conservatives themselves. The November 1996 issue of *First Things* (a conservative "Journal of Religion and Public Life" edited by one of America's premier interpreters of the American religious scene, Fr. Richard John Neuhaus) featured a symposium titled "The End of Democracy? The Ju-

---

honest heirs to this tradition. Cf. Russell Kirk, *The Conservative Tradition* (Chicago: Regnery, 1953) and *Randolph of Roanoke* (Chicago: University of Chicago Press, 1951).

96. David C. Stolinsky, "America: A Christian Country," *New Oxford Review* (July/August 1994): 21. I am indebted for this reference to Reeves, 55. For another vigorous reaction by a self-proclaimed "conservative Jew," see Don Feder, *A Jewish Conservative Looks at Pagan America* (Lafayette, La.: Huntington House, 1993) and *Who's Afraid of the Religious Right?* (Washington, D.C.: Regnery, 1996). Feder sums up his position this way: "As a religious Jew (a Jew by conviction as well as by birth), I've felt kinship with those the establishment scorns as fundamentalists and incipient theocrats. While I don't share the theology of a Ralph Reed or a D. James Kennedy, I identify completely with their morality. How could it be otherwise. Our values derive from the same source" (*Who's Afraid,* xii). Feder's answer to the reason for the searing searchlight of mainstream media attention on the Religious Right is also worth pondering: "Why all the fuss? Why this intense media focus on the religious right? Why all the wild accusations, distortions, fear-mongering, and hysteria? The answer: to deflect public attention from the ongoing social revolution in this country. So people won't ask why eight out of every ten Americans can expect to be a victim of violent crime at least once in their lives. Or . . . [why illegitimacy and divorce rates are soaring while SAT scores are dropping]. Incredible as it may seem, none of this is attributable to school prayer proposals, public display of religious symbols, or opposition to condom distribution in schools" (11-12). Jewish intellectual Norman Podhoretz, while acknowledging questionable sources for Robertson's conspiracy theories in his book *The New World Order,* also defended him against Michael Lind's accusations of anti-Semitism in view of Robertson's consistent and long-standing support of Israel. See Norman Podhoretz, "In the Matter of Pat Robertson," *Commentary* (August 1995): 27-32; cf. the exchange between Podhoretz, Lind, and others in *Commentary* (January 1996). I am indebted to Joshua Muravchik's review of Lind's *Up from Conservatism* (*Commentary* [September 1996]: 86-88) for this point and these references.

dicial Usurpation of Politics."[97] The symposium participants, including Judge Robert Bork, Prison Fellowship founder and evangelical leader Charles Colson, and academics Russell Hittinger (University of Tulsa), Hadley Arkes (Amherst College), and Robert George (Princeton University), raised serious questions about whether the judicial usurpation of political power might eventually call Christians to civil disobedience. It is worth highlighting the two passages in the editors' introduction, in particular, that caused consternation among some fellow conservatives:

> The question here explored, in full awareness of its far-reaching consequences, is whether we have reached or are reaching the point where conscientious citizens can no longer give moral assent to the existing regime.
>
> America is not and, please God, will never become Nazi Germany, but it is only blind hubris that denies it can happen here and, in peculiarly American ways, may be happening here.[98]

The symposium created no small fuss in the conservative intellectual world. "Two of the seven members of *First Things*' editorial board, the neoconservative scholars Peter Berger and Gertrude Himmelfarb, . . . resigned in protest. Fellow conservatives at *The Weekly Standard* denounced the magazine for succumbing to the 'anti-American Temptation.'"[99] It was Jacob Heilbrunn who, in a cleverly titled article in the *New Republic,* "Neocon *v.* Theocon," set up the conflict between "Jewish neoconservatives" and a group he called "theocons — mostly Catholic intellectuals who are attempting to construct a Christian theory of politics that directly threatens the entire neoconservative philosophy. This attempt, in the eyes of at least some of the neocons, also directly threatens Jews."[100] The culprit, according to Heilbrunn, is none other than Thomas Aquinas: "The theocrats . . . are Thomists, would-be prophets of a new Age of Aquinas; their properly constructed America would . . . be based on the idea [of] the

97. The entire debate is now available in a book-length format; Mitchell S. Muncy, ed., *The End of Democracy?* (Dallas: Spence, 1997).

98. "Introduction," "The End of Democracy? The Judicial Usurpation of Politics," 18, 19. It may be helpful to put the implied question of the second paragraph in perspective with a reminder that noted American novelist Sinclair Lewis asked the same question in his 1935 novel, *It Can't Happen Here.*

99. David Glenn, "The Schism," *Lingua Franca* (February 1997): 24. Also see the responses in the January 1997 issue of *First Things;* the symposium "On the Future of Conservatism," in *Commentary* 103 (February 1997): 14-43; Jacob Heilbrunn, "Neocon *v.* Theocon," *New Republic,* December 30, 1996, 20-24; Ramesh Ponnuru, "Con Job," *National Review,* January 27, 1997, 36-39.

100. Heilbrunn, 21.

natural law of Thomas Aquinas. . . . Their solution [for moral relativism and cultural decadence] is to embrace explicitly the notion of a Christian nation: a nation that accepts the idea of a transcendent divine law that carries universal obligations even for nonbelievers."[101] Heilbrunn judges particularly ominous in this regard the May 1994 declaration published in *First Things*, "Evangelicals and Catholics Together," and notes that "As the neocons provided the intellectual muscle for Reagan conservativism, so now the Catholic Thomists are providing the brainpower for the Christian Coalition."[102]

We shall consider the issue of "theocracy" more thoroughly in chapter 7, but simply observe here that a forced choice between two bigotries — the ugliness of perceived anti-Semitism on the one hand and blatant anti-Catholicism on the other — hardly advances what is an important discussion in American public life. Perhaps at this point it is worth simply noting that an appeal to Aquinas and natural law as justification for civil disobedience is not an exclusive prerogative of Roman Catholic "theocrats." Here's an excerpt from Dr. Martin Luther King, Jr.'s, "Letter from Birmingham City Jail":

> I would be the first to advocate obeying just laws. One has not only a legal but moral responsibility to disobey unjust laws. I would agree with St. Augustine that "an unjust law is no law at all." Now what is the difference between the two? How does one determine whether a law is just or unjust? A just law is a man-made code that squares with the moral law or the law of God. An unjust law is a code that is out of harmony with the moral law. To put it in the terms of St. Thomas Aquinas: an unjust law is a human law that is not rooted in eternal law and natural law.[103]

At this point a brief consideration of the relation between the Religious Right and the Republican Party is in order. The specter of theocratic governance of America is directly linked to the perception that the Republican Party is unduly under the sway of the Religious Right.[104] To paraphrase the frequently cited observation about the Anglican Church in Great Britain as "the Tory Party at prayer": Has the resurgent evangelical political piety merely become a reflection of the Republican Party at prayer? Is God a Republican?

101. Heilbrunn, 22.
102. Heilbrunn, 23.
103. Cited in William J. Bennett, *The Book of Virtues* (New York: Simon & Schuster, 1993), 260.
104. It is interesting to note that this anxiety reflects an assumption that the Republican Party will be the dominant party in America in the foreseeable future.

Republicans Can't Stand Pat

That Pat Robertson "currently holds the Republican Party in a headlock,"[105] or that today he is "the single most important kingmaker in the Republican party,"[106] or even that "the right has a virtual lock on U.S. politics"[107] are eminently debatable political propositions,[108] particularly after the 1988 Republican Party primaries,[109] and for sure after the 1998 congressional elections and the failure of the impeachment process to remove President Clinton from office in the first months of 1999.[110] At the same time, it is undoubtedly the case that though both political parties in the United States have been profoundly affected by the evangelical political resurgence, the Republican Party has been its beneficiary and the Democratic Party the loser.[111] Here too the

105. Boston, 15.

106. Lind, 98.

107. Hardisty, 13.

108. For a careful analysis of voting patterns in the 1992 election that suggest a significant role for the Religious Right but that its ideology has not captured the core of the Republican Party, see Phillip E. Hammond, Mark A. Shibley, and Peter M. Solow, "Religion and Family Values in Presidential Voting," in *The Rapture of Politics*, 55-68.

109. In spite of his high media profile thanks to the Christian Broadcasting Network (CBN), an effective grassroots organization, successful fund-raising, early caucus successes in Michigan and Iowa, and above all his stated conviction that "God was on his side" (even helping avert hurricanes on the eve of important primaries!), Robertson failed to win any of the Southern states on Super Tuesday (March 8, 1988), and finished third in the race for the Republican nomination. For a helpful overview of the Robertson campaign, see Oldfield, 125-82. Oldfield judges that since "a critical factor in Robertson's defeat was the fact that his Republican rivals adopted positions advocated by the Christian Right . . . [and] actively courted Christian Right leaders and their constituency," Robertson's *personal* defeat did not detract from "the attention and respect Republicans were giving the Christian Right as a movement. The nominating battle over, the party adopted and George Bush ran on a platform the Christian Right could enthusiastically endorse. . . . The fact that the GOP had taken up the social issue causes that Robertson's supporters so fervently espoused did limit the candidate's maneuvering room, but it was also a sign that the Christian Right movement had become an established part of the Republican coalition" (181).

110. David Horowitz, in his review of Lind's *Up from Conservativism* (see n. 84 above), points out that Robertson and Buchanan have significantly different political views in many instances, and that if the "far right . . . [was really] the only significant political influence on the Republican Party, why didn't Robertson engineer his own nomination, or at least give it to a soulmate like Phil Gramm or Bob Dornan?"

111. In spite of his contentions that his organization is nonpartisan, the Republican cast of its vision becomes clear when one reads Christian Coalition executive director Ralph Reed's two political "credos," *Politically Incorrect: The Emerging Faith Factor in American Politics* (Dallas: Word, 1994); *Active Faith: How Christians Are Changing the Soul

evangelical/Roman Catholic rapprochement, on right-to-life issues particularly, profoundly realigned American politics. "Northern Catholics and Southern Baptists — two powerful blocs that had traditionally shared an allegiance to the Democratic Party but had also traditionally viewed one another with cultural suspicion — had joined hands in cultural conservatism."[112] The success of the Republicans in capturing Congress in the 1994 election is largely attributed, by foe and friend alike, to the efforts of the Religious Right in general and the Christian Coalition in particular.[113] The galvanizing event for media preoccupation with the role of the Religious Right in the Republican Party, however, was not Pat Robertson's flawed and failed run for the Republican presidential nomination in 1988 but the 1992 Republican Convention in Houston.

> From its "family values" rhetoric to Pat Buchanan's declaration of "cultural war," the 1992 Republican convention provided a national showcase for the Christian Right. The convention illustrated the powerful role the Christian Right plays within the Republican party and laid to rest rumors that the movement was dead. The defeat of George Bush, the candidate that that convention nominated, did little to slow the movement's momentum. Membership in movement organizations skyrocketed and the Christian Right was soon able to claim credit for the sweeping Republican congressional victories of 1994. Major candidates for the 1996 presidential nomination vied with each other to demonstrate their fealty. The Christian Right may or may not help the Republicans, but there is little doubt that the movement is a force to contend with.[114]

This observer holds out little hope for opponents of the Christian Right that it is only a "transitory phenomenon." Putting that judgment to rest, he notes, "is a central theme of this book." "In short," he contends, "the Christian Right will not go away." And furthermore, "Nor will the Christian Right leave the Repub-

---

of American Politics (New York: Free Press, 1996). That Reed's second book was published by a mainline, "secular" publishing house rather than one of the large evangelical houses (Word, Eerdmans, InterVarsity, Zondervan) is itself a significant indicator of public acknowledgment if not acceptance of the Christian Right.

112. Heilbrunn, 23.

113. See, in addition to Oldfield, *The Right and the Righteous,* and Moen, *The Christian Right and Congress,* Mark J. Rozell and Clyde Wilcox, eds., *God at the Grass Roots: The Christian Right in the 1994 Elections* (Lanham, Md.: Rowman & Littlefield, 1995).

114. Oldfield, 1. A copy of Buchanan's address to the Houston convention as well as his response to the furor about it in his speech, "The Cultural War for the Soul of America," are available from "Buchanan 2000," at http://www.buchanan.org/soul.html.

lican party. The movement has already played a key role in a process that, over the last few decades, has redefined both the Democratic and Republican parties."[115] Oldfield contends that the Christian Right, having invested heavily in the Republican Party, "now controls an estimated eighteen state Republican parties and is a significant force in thirteen more."[116]

Others are less sure about the future of the New Christian Right (NCR). Sociologist Steve Bruce reminds us to be wary of the profound bias in reports issued by anti-NCR campaigning organizations such as the People for the American Way who have "an obvious interest in making the wolf at the door seem as fierce as possible."[117] Bruce points to what he regards as a notable lack of success for the NCR in actual legislative achievement on the federal level. It is not helpful, he notes, to debate whether President Bush's 1992 electoral defeat was caused by the "religious right hijacking the Republican platform" or, alternatively and as plausibly, "because he [President Bush] showed insufficient commitment to that platform."[118]

The difficulty in making confident judgments about the electoral success of the NCR is reflected in the contradictory claims made by analysts opposed to its agenda. If it is true, as was widely claimed, that the public face of the NCR, particularly reflected in Pat Buchanan's Houston convention speech, cost the Republicans the White House in 1992,[119] how did it pull off the major victory of 1994? "In 1994, the news media rediscovered the Christian Right, and came away perplexed. The movement seemed to contradict conventional wisdom at every turn. First, many observers were surprised that it was still strong and active, given the responsibility assigned to it for past Republican failures, including the presidential race of 1992." But, as important, notes this writer, is the dominant assumption of analysts and the media that, because "religion is on the wane in modern societies . . . repeated expressions in public affairs, such as the Christian Right . . . are temporary aberrations that will quickly fade away. In fact, the Christian Right has been discovered and dismissed in the press at least

---

115. Oldfield, 1.

116. Oldfield, 2. Oldfield cites as source for this data John Persinos, "Has the Christian Right Taken Over the Republican Party?" *Campaigns and Elections* 15 (September 1994): 20-24.

117. Steve Bruce, "The Inevitable Failure of the New Christian Right," in *The Rapture of Politics*, 7.

118. Bruce, "Inevitable Failure," 10.

119. See James M. Penning, "Pat Robertson and the GOP: 1988 and Beyond," in *The Rapture of Politics*, 105-22, for a good discussion of the praise/blame debate about the role and effect of the Christian Right on the Republican Party and its electoral successes and failures.

four times since it emerged on the national scene with the Moral Majority in 1979."[120]

Whatever the political future holds for the Religious Right, either within the Republican Party or not, it is apparent that it has made an important difference in American politics and cannot be ignored. As Matthew Moen summarizes the thesis of his book *The Christian Right and Congress:* "The thesis undergirding this study is that the movement has been quite successful in influencing the agenda [of Congress]. It has taken numerous issues that were lying virtually dormant on the agenda, redefined and enlarged their appeal, and then placed them on both the systematic and congressional agendas. Moreover, it has obtained action on many of those issues, which is no small accomplishment."[121] Furthermore, there is solid evidence that the Religious Right has profoundly shaped the two American political parties. In fact, one group of political scientists argue that the 1992 election was "potentially a watershed event, marking the beginning of a new set of political alliances and a dramatic new cleavage in the two-party system. Billing the election as both the 'Year of the Evangelical' and the 'Year of the Secular,' they claim that seculars have moved ever more firmly into the Democratic party, and now can be seen as defining that party's cultural core. At the same time, the disaffection of many mainline Protestants from the Republican party has occurred simultaneously with the binding of evangelicals to that party in a manner that puts them now in a position to define the party's cultural core."[122]

What, then, is the prognosis for the Christian Right in general, and in the Republican Party more particularly? Perhaps a somewhat tentative answer such as the following is all that can be ventured.

In general, the 1994 elections were a success for the Christian Right, comparable in many respects to the boost the civil rights movement received in 1964 and the gains made by the labor movement in 1948. Will this situation persist in the future, particularly when the political environment is less conducive to the movement's activities? The answer is unclear. The case studies [of key states] reveal that both the bleak and rosy scenarios can obtain, depending on the interplay of national trends, local circumstances, and move-

120. John C. Green, "The Christian Right and the 1994 Elections: An Overview," in *God at the Grass Roots,* 1.

121. Moen, *Christian Right and Congress,* 1-2.

122. Peter Kivisto, "The Rise or Fall of the Christian Right? Conflicting Reports from the Frontline," in *The Rapture of Politics,* 4. The essay Kivisto refers to is Lyman A. Kellstedt, John C. Green, James L. Guth, and Corwin E. Smidt, "Religious Voting Blocs in the 1992 Election: The Year of the Evangelical?" in *The Rapture of Politics,* 85-104.

ment activities. Given its many strengths, the Christian Right can be a major player in electoral politics and a cornerstone of a resurgent Republican Party. At the same time, the movement's many weaknesses may impose stern limits on its influence and complicate Republican fortunes.[123]

One clear advantage of such predictive modesty is that it promotes efforts to understand the phenomenon rather than contribute to the shrill and polarizing rhetoric of far too many of its opponents and social analysts.[124] It not only takes the issues raised by the Religious Right seriously, but also does not subject conservative Christians to the standard sort of snobbish media ridicule that characterizes them, for example, as "[wearing] white socks and unnatural fibers. In a study by one sociologist, they were even shown to have different (lower) IQs."[125] A more fair-minded observer than many notes (accurately) that "the rapid rise of the Christian Right spawned a potent and sometimes mean-spirited counter attack from those far removed from the conservative Christian culture."[126]

Perhaps more important than political punditry about the future of the Republican Party and the role of the Religious Right in it is the question about the likely future role of religion more generally in American public, political life. Will the New Christian Right and its concerns go away, or does its emergence underscore a persistent and profoundly American pattern of religious life

123. Green, 16-17.

124. John Green follows his comments (n. 106) with this laudable wish: "With any luck, however, the Christian Right will cease to be misunderstood by observers of politics; the essays in this volume represent a step in that direction." The negative formulation ("cease to be misunderstood") is noteworthy in itself, and it needs to be reported that the volume is a rarity among the genre in that it succeeds in this goal.

125. Flake, 3.

126. Matthew C. Moen, "From Revolution to Evolution: The Changing Nature of the Christian Right," in *The Rapture of Politics,* 124. Moen notes the formation of specific anti-NCR groups such as People for the American Way; Rev. William Sloane Coffin's calling NCR leaders "jackasses"; comparisons between Jerry Falwell and the Ayatollah Khomeini; and comparisons of the NCR of the 1970s with the Eurofascism of the 1930s and 1940s. Moen points to the hyperbole in J. K. Hadden and C. E. Swann's classic study of the televangelists (*Prime Time Preachers* [Reading, Mass.: Addison-Wesley, 1981]) when it explains the rise of the Christian Right simply as "a technologically driven monster spawned by master manipulators" and thus "implicitly trivialized the concerns of social conservatives, by casting those concerns as the baggage of unsophisticated followers being duped by clever elites" (125). Moen's review essay is one of the most useful compact surveys of "serious" literature on the NCR. It is also interesting to note that some of the most virulent anti-NCR writing comes from ex-fundamentalists such as Carol Flake. The same is often true for American conservativism in general (Michael Lind, Gary Wills). This deserves further sociology-of-knowledge examination.

that was ignored or denied by secularization theorists? Perhaps it was not at all reasonable for the secularly minded to be so surprised about the recent evangelical political resurgence. In fact, perhaps amazement about the amazement is more appropriate. To understand why this is a real possibility, we need to consider American exceptionalism with respect to religion and modernity.

American Exceptionalism: Evangelicals and the "Almost Chosen People"

Whatever the validity of applying the secularization thesis in its broad outline to the societies of European Christendom after the Enlightenment, social historians, it is now being increasingly acknowledged, should have at least paused before applying it to America. Sociologists Rodney Stark and Roger Finke have carefully analyzed church membership patterns from the colonial period to the present and conclude that, contrary to what would be expected if the secularization model were true, "Rather than declining, the proportion of the churched showed rapid growth from 1776 to 1890 and has shown exceptional stability from 1926 to the present. Rather than decaying, religious institutions have shown a remarkable capacity for mobilizing people into the pew." In sum, "The vibrancy and growth of American religious institutions presents the most open defiance of the secularization model."[127]

Even with respect to Europe, however, it is now being argued by sociologists that the notion of unilinear secularization directly linked to progressive modernization reflects ideology more than empirical social reality. As British sociologist David Martin observes: "I do not regard secularization as involving a more or less unified syndrome of characteristics subject to an irreversible master-trend. And I see the formation of such master trends as often rooted in ideological views of history."[128] Martin insists that "there is no unitary process called 'secularization' arising in reaction to a set of characteristics labelled 'religious.'" In fact, the whole notion of inevitable secularization is rooted in an aggressive, antireligious, utopian goal of "scientific messianism" prominent in such early social theorists as Saint-Simon and Comte: "The whole concept ap-

127. Roger Finke, "An Unsecular America," in *Religion and Modernization: Sociologists and Historians Debate the Secularization Thesis,* ed. Steve Bruce (Oxford: Clarendon, 1992), 148.

128. David Martin, *The Religious and the Secular: Studies in Secularization* (New York: Schocken Books, 1969), 3. On the pervasiveness of and problems created by an idolatry of progress ideology, see Christopher Lasch, *The True and Only Heaven: Progress and Its Critics* (New York and London: Norton, 1991).

pears as a tool of counter-religious ideologies which identify the 'real' element in religion for polemical purposes and then arbitrarily relate it to the notion of a unitary and irreversible process, partly for the aesthetic satisfactions found in such notions and partly as a psychological boost to the movements with which they are associated."[129]

According to Peter Berger, though the data suggest "a massively secular Euro-Culture," they essentially point to "a shift in the institutional location of religion, rather than secularization," thanks to "strong survivals of religion, most of it generally Christian." Berger then observes that, however the data are interpreted, "Europe stands out as quite different from other parts of the world" and "certainly differs sharply from the religious situation in the United States. *One of the most interesting puzzles in the sociology of religion is why Americans are so much more religious as well as more churchly than Europeans.*"[130] If the secularization thesis is discredited more broadly, it is thus clearly problematic as a description of religious life in America. Poll after poll suggests that Americans not only have profound, and fairly traditional, religious *convictions* but also display a remarkable vitality in their religious *practice.*[131] This has been a rather consistent pattern of American life from the days of the Pilgrims to the present. The formation of American national identity was decisively shaped by a sense of religious mission. In the oft-quoted words of Governor John Winthrop on the *Arabella:* "We shall be as a city upon a hill, the eyes of all people are upon us." The Puritan "errand into the wilderness"[132] presupposed a covenantal understanding of the new nation, also articulated with clarity by John Winthrop in his 1630 sermon, "A Modell of Christian Charity":

> Thus stands the cause between God and us: we are entered into Covenant with him for this work, we have taken out a Commission. The Lord hath given us leave to draw our own articles. We have professed to enterprise these Actions upon these and these ends [and] we have hereupon besought him of favor and blessing. Now if the Lord shall please to hear us, and bring us in peace to the place we desire, then hath he ratified this Covenant and sealed our Commission [and] will expect a strict performance of the Articles con-

129. David Martin, 16.

130. Berger, "Secularism in Retreat," 8, emphasis added.

131. For a recent review see George Barna, *The Index of Leading Spiritual Indicators* (Dallas: Word, 1996). A helpful, well-rounded discussion of this issue by essayists such as Paul Johnson and George Marsden, along with a distinguished panel of conversants, can be found in Richard John Neuhaus, ed., *Unsecular America* (Grand Rapids: Eerdmans, 1986).

132. See Perry Miller, *Errand into the Wilderness* (Cambridge, Mass., and London: Harvard University Press, Belknap Press, 1956).

tained in it. But if we neglect the observance of these Articles which are the ends we have propounded, and dissembling with our God, shall fall to embrace this present world and prosecute our carnal intentions, seeking great things for ourselves and our posterity, the Lord will surely break out in wrath against us [and] be revenged of such a perjured people and make us know the price of the breach of such a covenant.[133]

The covenantal errand into the wilderness also presupposed a more democratic civic order. For, "whereas in the old world state authority drew its divine sanction from traditional sacral kingship, in America it took the form of conscious dedication by democratic assemblies expressed in formal documents."[134]

The fascinating combination of deep religious conviction about providential guidance for the American nation with a profoundly voluntary, democratic, populist understanding of religious life remained in place well into the nineteenth century, resulting in what Paul Johnson calls "the most characteristic element in American political philosophy — the belief that the providential plan and the workings of democracy are organically linked." Johnson chooses as his prime exhibit of this conjunction, President Abraham Lincoln. In his first inaugural Lincoln expressed his conviction that the ultimate resolution of the conflict between North and South "would illustrate the way in which the democratic process was divinely inspired": "Why should there not be a patient confidence in the ultimate justice of the people? Is there any better or equal hope in the world? . . . If the Almighty Ruler of nations, with his eternal truth and justice, be on your side of the North, or yours of the South, that truth and that justice will surely prevail by the judgment of this great tribunal of the American people."[135] Johnson observes that no European contemporary of Lincoln's (Napoleon III, Bismarck, Garibaldi, Cavour, Marx, or even Disraeli) would have thought of expressing himself like this or as Lincoln did in his second inaugural when he spoke so eloquently about discerning God's will in the nation's conflict. Nor, he adds, would late nineteenth-century imperialists have dared to justify themselves as President McKinley did at the time of Philippine annexation: "I went down on my knees and prayed Almighty God for light and guidance more than one night. And one night late it came to me this way. . . . There was nothing left for us to do but to take them all and educate the Philippinos and uplift and civilize and Christianize them. And by God's grace do the very best we could

133. In Edwin S. Gaustad, *A Documentary History of Religion in America to the Civil War*, 2nd ed. (Grand Rapids: Eerdmans, 1993), 107.

134. Paul Johnson, "The Almost-Chosen People," in *Unsecular America*, 3.

135. Paul Johnson, 7.

by them, as our fellow men for whom Christ also died."[136] Johnson concludes
that, unlike anything in Europe, "religion and politics are organically linked
in America, movements in one echoing and reinforcing movements in the
other. Just as the strength of religion in America sustains and nurtures democracy, so the vigorous spirit of American democracy continually rein-
forces popular religion. Thus, while America remains the world's most powerful and enthusiastic champion of democracy, it is likely to preserve its
exceptional role as the citadel of voluntary religion."[137]

From Alexis de Tocqueville forward, thoughtful foreign observers of
American life (such as Paul Johnson) have taken note of this American
exceptionalism. Seymour Martin Lipset points to a persistent pattern of an all-
pervasive tenacity that has "always distinguished American religion from religion in other nations." "For almost a century," he adds, "prominent European
visitors who wrote on American life have been unanimous in remarking on the
exceptional religiosity of the society." Lipset then cites Tocqueville's comment
that "there is no country in the world where the Christian religion retains a
greater influence over the souls of men than in America."[138] Tocqueville's explanation for the phenomenon also continues to have its contemporary adherents. Roger Finke concludes his essay "An Unsecular America" by returning "to
the question Tocqueville asked about American religion over 150 years ago: 'I
wondered how it could come about that by diminishing the apparent power of
religion one increased its real strength.'"[139] Finke points out that not only does
the empirical evidence about church life in America contradict the secularization thesis, it is also necessary to "look beyond [the phenomenon of] modernization for the answer" to the question *why*. He points to the role of religious
regulation (i.e., the *lack* of religious regulation) as the important factor: "Without fear of penalty or loss of privileges from the State, sectarian movements
have formed quickly on the American landscape. These movements have served
as a testing ground for religious innovation, have mobilized large segments of

136. Paul Johnson, 8-9.

137. Paul Johnson, 13.

138. Seymour Martin Lipset, *The First New Nation: The United States in Historical
and Comparative Perspective* (New York: Basic Books, 1963), 141. The Tocqueville quote is
taken from *Democracy in America* (New York: Vintage Books, 1954), 1:314. Lipset adds
that "Martineau in 1834, Trollope in 1860, Bryce in 1883, and Weber in 1904, all arrived at
similar conclusions" (141-42). For a discussion of nineteenth-century impressions of
America by European travelers, see Robert B. Downs, *Images of America: Travelers from
Abroad in the New World* (Urbana and Chicago: University of Illinois Press, 1987).

139. Finke, 165; Finke's reference to Tocqueville is *Democracy in America* (New
York: Harper & Row, 1969), 296.

the population, and have held a special appeal to the working classes. Thus, the lack of religious regulation has had a major impact on the expression and organization of religion in the USA."[140]

When Seymour Martin Lipset recently revisited the subject of American exceptionalism, he underscored the same point:

> The emphasis on voluntary associations in America which so impressed Tocqueville, Weber, Gramsci, and other foreign observers as one of the distinctive America traits is linked to the uniquely American system of "voluntary religion." The United States is the first country in which religious groups became voluntary associations. . . . Tocqueville concluded that voluntarism is a large part of the answer to the puzzling strength of organized religion, a phenomenon that impressed most nineteenth-century observers and continues to show up at the end of the twentieth century in cross-national polls taken by Gallup and others. These polls indicate that Americans are the most church going in Protestantism and the most fundamentalist in Christendom.[141]

Lipset also underscores the resultant democratizing tendency of American religion's exceptionalism: "Outside the United States, the historic association of churches with non-democratic forces, especially the aristocracy, meant that the proponents of a newer, freer, more egalitarian and democratic order often had good reason to consider religious *institutions* — and by an understandable if invalid extrapolation, religious *belief* — to be their enemies."[142]

What Lipset's more recent reflections on American exceptionalism emphasize is its moral ambiguity — it is a "two-edged sword." "Exceptional," he observes, does not mean that "America is better than other countries or has a superior culture." Rather, it only suggests "that it is qualitatively different, that it is an outlier. . . . We are the worst as well as the best, depending on which quality is being addressed." What is different is that while "other countries define themselves by a common history as birthright communities,"

140. Finke, 164. This also helps account for the populist, democratic character of religious-political movements such as the New Christian Right. See further, Nathan Hatch, *The Democratization of American Christianity* (New Haven and London: Yale University Press, 1989).

141. Seymour Martin Lipset, *American Exceptionalism: A Double-Edged Sword* (New York and London: Norton, 1996), 61.

142. Lipset, *American Exceptionalism*, 63; this passage is a direct citation from Everett Carl Ladd, *The American Ideology: An Exploration of the Origins, Meaning, and Role of American Political Ideas* (Storrs, Conn.: Roper Center for Public Opinion Research, 1994), 15, emphasis in original.

America "has defined its *raison d'être* ideologically."[143] In G. K. Chesterton's words, "America is the only nation in the world that is founded on a creed."[144] This creed, according to Lipset, "can be described in five terms: liberty, egalitarianism, individualism, populism, and laissez-faire."[145] It is this creedal, quasi-religious character of America as a nation that constitutes its exceptionalism. "Born out of revolution, the United States is a country organized around an ideology which includes a set of dogmas about the nature of a good society."[146]

The churchly language of creed and dogma applied to one's nation brings with it obvious risk. Confusing divine providence with American national interest leads to the idolatry of moral absolutism cloaked in messianic nationalism — America as the "Redeemer Nation."[147] The combination of covenantal self-understanding and eschatological hope, placing "America within an apocalyptic framework of universal history,"[148] could not but lead to utopian notions of American manifest destiny. This utopian orientation, Lipset points out, can be found across the political spectrum, "among liberals and conservatives" as they, each in their own way, "seek to extend the 'good society.'" "Americans are utopian moralists who press hard to institutionalize virtue, to destroy evil people, and eliminate wicked institutions and practices."[149] A good example of such utopian messianism at its worst is the defense of American annexation of the Philippines by Indiana senator Albert J. Beveridge on January 9, 1909:

> We will not renounce our part in the mission of the race, trustee under God, of the civilization of the world. . . . He has made us . . . the master organizers of the world to establish system where chaos reigns. . . . He has made us adept in government that we may administer government among savage and senile peoples. . . . And of all our race, He has marked the American people as His chosen Nation to finally lead in the regeneration of the world. This is the di-

143. Lipset, *American Exceptionalism*, 18.

144. Lipset, *American Exceptionalism*, 31; citation from G. K. Chesterton, *What I Saw in America* (New York: Dodd, Mead, 1922), 7.

145. Lipset, *American Exceptionalism*, 19.

146. Lipset, *American Exceptionalism*, 31.

147. Ernest Lee Tuveson, *Redeemer Nation: The Idea of America's Millennial Role* (Chicago and London: University of Chicago Press, 1968). The epigraph to Tuveson's book is from President Woodrow Wilson: "America had the infinite privilege of fulfilling her destiny and saving the world."

148. James H. Moorhead, *American Apocalypse: Yankee Protestants and the Civil War, 1860-1869* (New Haven and London: Yale University Press, 1978), ix.

149. Lipset, *American Exceptionalism*, 63.

vine mission of America, and it holds for us all the profit, all the glory, all the happiness possible to man. We are trustees of the world's progress, guardians of its righteous peace. The judgment of the Master is upon us: "Ye have been faithful over a few things, I will make you ruler over many things."[150]

However — and thus the aptness of Lipset's "double-edged sword" — an appeal to the same providential purpose and mission for America could be and was used for justice. Reformed pastor Theodore Frelinghuysen's eloquence on behalf of America's aboriginal peoples is the model here: "God, in his providence, planted these tribes on this western continent, so far as we know, before Great Britain herself had a political existence. . . . They have a place in human sympathy, and are just as entitled to a share in the common bounties of a benignant Providence. . . . We have crowded the tribes upon a few miserable acres of our southern frontier; it is all that is left to them of their once boundless forest. . . . I ask, who is the injured, and who is the aggressor?"[151]

Recognizing that there are secular versions of this national millennialism as well as sectarian Protestant ones is an illuminating insight for understanding past and present American culture wars. It is not only politicians who draw on covenant language, and it is not only politicians from the right who do so. Futurologist Jeremy Rifkin exploits evangelical covenantal language to propose what he calls "a steady-state existence" in which society would be guided by a "set of absolute principles or truths that fit the absolute principles and truths of ecology itself." His proposal seems to seek a utilitarian function for an absolutist religious vision whereby people would submit willingly to new absolutes rather than have them imposed on them in a totalitarian fashion. "Whether the Christian renewal movement becomes a pawn in the hands of a fascist regime, or a force for revolutionary change to a steady-state society," he contends, "depends on whether the Christian community embraces the concept of a new covenant vision."[152] President Clinton and Vice President Gore made "new covenant" the foundation of their 1992 campaign. More recently, former Massachusetts Democratic congressman Father Robert Drinan, S.J., did it as well. He concluded a celebratory article on President Clinton's 1996 reelection victory with these words: "Most Americans think of their nation as being on a sacred pilgrimage destined by God's providence to give light and courage to the entire

---

150. Cited by Sidney E. Mead, *The Lively Experiment: The Shaping of Christianity in America* (New York, Evanston, and London: Harper & Row, 1963), 153-54.

151. Cited by Louis Weeks, *A New Christian Nation* (n.p.: McGrath, 1977), 7.

152. Jeremy Rifkin with Ted Howard, *The Emerging Order: God in the Age of Scarcity* (New York: Putnam, 1979), 244, 241.

world," adding the hope that the president, "who is a very intelligent and deeply religious man," will restore that vision.[153]

America's wars receive similar treatment. From the long list of America's wars beginning with the War of 1812 and continuing through the 1991 Gulf War, proponents and opponents usually cast their case in the language of moral crusades having eschatological significance, with their opponents as immoral, anti-American, and even demonic.[154] When a nation thus perceives itself as having "the soul of a church,"[155] it is inevitable that debates about the national creed acquire an ultimacy that politics, at least in a traditional Christian context, does not deserve. Policy differences become heresy, and heretics must be excommunicated even if the result is schisms and the formation of new denominations. A serious public problem arises when, after significant schism, one sect, believing itself to be the true and only representative of the American creed, will not tolerate the heresies and heretics of other sects. The result is political inquisition — neatly identified in America by the anti-Communist crusading of Senator Joe McCarthy — and a tearing of the civic fabric.

Looking for Abraham Kuyper

Reflecting on this reality of American exceptionalism and seeing American cultural disputes largely as denominational squabbles provides a plausible explanation for the rise of the Religious Right in the 1970s. On the one hand, we can see it as a reaction to the 1960s countercultural assault on America and the alliance between religious convictions and national values that characterizes American civil religion. Even when evangelicals were for all intents and purposes languishing in America's cultural, intellectual, and political wasteland, they retained their conviction that the American experiment was providentially ordered and blessed. In the organizational conference for the National Association of Evangelicals (NAE), on the morning of May 4, 1943, Harold John Ockenga delivered the following, familiar-sounding message to the convention delegates:

I believe that the United States of America has been assigned a destiny com-

153. Cited by Richard John Neuhaus, "The Public Square: A Continuing Survey of Religion and Public Life," *First Things* (March 1997): 58.

154. Lipset, *American Exceptionalism*, 65-67.

155. The phrase is originally from G. K. Chesterton. See Sidney E. Mead, *The Nation with the Soul of a Church* (New York, Evanston, San Francisco, and London: Harper & Row, 1975), 48-77.

parable to that of Ancient Israel. God has prepared this nation with a vast and united country, with a population drawn from innumerable blood streams, with a wealth that is unequaled, with an ideological strength drawn from the traditions of classical and radical philosophy, with a government held accountable to law as no other government except Israel has ever been, and with an enlightenment in the minds of the average citizen which is the climax of social development.[156]

Ockenga added that God "has done so for the unquestionable purpose of spreading 'the knowledge of God' and the 'truth [of] the Gospel' throughout the world."[157] Then, in language that sounds familiar to evangelical participants in the culture wars of the 1980s and 1990s, Ockenga directed his hearers' attention to the crisis in America's soul thanks to the rampant secularism of the day. A profound choice lay before them:

> We must examine our direction, our condition and our destiny. We must recognize that we are standing at the crossroads and that there are only two ways that lie open before us. One is the road of the rescue of western civilization by a re-emphasis on and revival of evangelical Christianity. The other is a return to the Dark Ages of heathendom which powerful force is emerging in every phase of world life today. [The world is waiting] for the clear cut, definite, sane and progressive leadership which can inaugurate a new era for Christian influence and effectiveness.[158]

This "new evangelicalism," as Ockenga himself would later call it, above all needed to reengage the world of thought, of the university. "'We have a need of new life from Christ in our nation,' Ockenga was convinced, and 'that need first of all is intellectual.' Unless 'the church can produce some thinkers who will lead us in positive channels our spiral of degradation will continue downward.' Furthermore, he continued, 'there is great need in the field of statesmanship.' Where are the political leaders 'in high places of our nation,' he asked, with a 'knowledge of and regard for the principles of the Word of God?'"[159]

Ockenga's concerns were echoed a few years later by Carl F. H. Henry's el-

156. Harold John Ockenga, "Christ for America," *United Evangelical Action* 2, no. 1 (May 4, 1943): 3-4. I am indebted for this reference to Garth M. Rosell, "Introduction: The Evangelical Vision," in *The Evangelical Landscape: Essays on the American Evangelical Tradition,* ed. Garth M. Rosell (Grand Rapids: Baker, 1996), 7.

157. Rosell, 8.

158. Rosell, 8.

159. Rosell, 9-10.

oquent pleas in his *Uneasy Conscience of Modern Fundamentalism*,[160] but the large mobilization of culturally and politically engaged evangelicals did not take place until the 1970s. Aside from "a small fringe of evangelicals" drawn to the anti-Communist crusades of Carl McIntire and Billy James Hargis (who "failed completely in establishing active political organizations"), evangelicals remained noticeably uninvolved in American politics.[161] After the Second World War, through the Eisenhower decade of the 1950s and until the civic upheavals of the 1960s, American culture Christianity appeared to be flourishing. The phrase "under God" was added to the American Pledge of Allegiance on Flag Day, June 14, 1954, and journalist Claire Cox reported thus on the prosperity of American religion: "Never has religion had it so good . . . never has religion been so institutionalized, so conspicuous, so public. Never has churchgoing been so acceptable, so much 'the thing to do.'"[162]

And then came the sixties! After an unrelenting countercultural assault on "Amerika" as an evil empire, a series of Supreme Court decisions that outlawed prayer in schools and removed barriers to pornography and abortion, and the militancy of a sexual revolution that included compulsory sex education in public schools, evangelicals slowly began to wake from their political slumbers, organize, and fight for the America they believed secular elites had stolen from them.[163] Directing efforts at specific issues such as the Equal Rights Amendment, school prayer, creationism, and attempts to legitimate homosexuality, as well as abortion, evangelicals became significant participants in Ameri-

160. Carl F. H. Henry, *The Uneasy Conscience of Modern Fundamentalism* (Grand Rapids: Eerdmans, 1947).

161. Robert Wuthnow, "Political Rebirth of American Evangelicals," in *The New Christian Right*, 174. Wuthnow overlooks the more successful (and thoughtful) efforts of anti-Communist crusader Fred Schwarz, founder of the United States Christian Anti-Communism Crusade. See Frederick Schwarz, *Beating the Unbeatable Foe: One Man's Victory over Communism, Leviathan, and the Last Enemy* (Washington, D.C.: Regnery, 1996).

162. Cited by Marty, *Under God, Indivisible, 1941-1960*, 293. Reference is to Claire Cox, *The New-Time Religion* (Englewood Cliffs, N.J.: Prentice-Hall, 1961).

163. Sympathy for this basic perspective has come from no less than Christopher Lasch (hardly a fundamentalist!), who argues persuasively in his posthumously published work, *The Revolt of the Elites and the Betrayal of Democracy* (New York and London: Norton, 1995), that the threat to American democracy is not from the masses (as in José Ortega y Gasset's *Revolt of the Masses*) but from "new elites" who are "in revolt against 'Middle America,' as they imagine it: a nation technologically backward, politically reactionary, repressive in its sexual morality, middlebrow in its tastes, smug and complacent, dull and dowdy." Lasch notes that these elites are thoroughgoing internationalists and that "It is a question whether they think of themselves as Americans at all" (5-6). For another version of "elitist power" in America, see Thomas Sowell, *The Vision of the Anointed: Self-Congratulation as a Basis for Social Policy* (New York: Basic Books, 1995).

can politics. At stake were important questions about American cultural and civic identity. Whose America was it — and who decides? And above all, who will teach our children, and what vision of America will they teach?

Once again, the present culture disputes are a denominational squabble. The problem with casting political issues in an ecclesiastical (covenantal, eschatological) frame is that there remains very little room for discussion, much less compromise. A large amount of talk about diversity is often a smoke screen here, as Christopher Lasch has pointed out. "'Diversity' — a slogan that looks attractive on the face of it — has come to mean the opposite of what it appears to mean. In practice diversity turns out to legitimize a new dogmatism, in which rival minorities take shelter behind a set of beliefs impervious to rational discussion."[164] Issues of public significance, and even civic identity, are then determined solely by political will to power. Affirmative action, the "right to choose" an abortion, and the legalization of "gay marriages" — to pick issues of the day — become the new "self-evident truths" that only racist, sexist, and homophobic persons would even ask questions about.[165] Thus one side effectively silences the dissent of civic heresy.

This is a tragic development in American public life, because the issues of concern to the Religious Right are socially momentous and eminently debatable. The "self-evident truths" of the morally smug of one generation are sometimes so obviously refuted by experience that their return to public consciousness requires embarrassing recanting.[166] Perhaps the most-cited example of this is the famous *Atlantic Monthly* cover essay publicly acknowledging that "Dan Quayle Was Right" about media glorification of single parenthood.[167] Less well known is an equally important cover essay by the same author, "The

164. Lasch, *Revolt of the Elites*, 17.

165. The issue of legitimating homosexual practice is a case study of this phenomenon. The decision in 1973 by the board of the American Psychiatric Association to change the designation of homosexuality as a treatable disorder in the *Diagnostic and Statistical Manual of Mental Disorders* was political, the result of aggressive lobbying by homosexuals, and not based on new findings in medical science. The next logical step in this progression is to declare all moral opposition to homosexual practice itself a mental disorder — homophobia. On these issues see Norman Podhoretz, "How the Gay-Rights Movement Won," *Commentary* (November 1996): 32-41; and Elizabeth Moberly's review essay, "Homosexuality and Truth," *First Things* (March 1997): 30-33.

166. Christopher Lasch also points to the political dangers of morally smug secular people when he observes that "self-righteousness, indeed, may well be more prevalent among skeptics than among believers. The spiritual discipline against self-righteousness is the very essence of religion" (*Revolt of the Elites*, 16).

167. Barbara Dafoe Whitehead, "Dan Quayle Was Right," *Atlantic Monthly*, April 1993.

Failure of Sex Education."[168] There is no need for a parallel article with the title "Whittaker Chambers (or Fred Schwarz — even Billy James Hargis?!) Was Right" — the fall of the Berlin Wall settled that question. But other intriguing possibilities offer themselves: In view of the problematic "coeding" of the military — "Phyllis Schlafly Was Right"? Or, in view of increasing acceptance of the legitimacy of homosexual practice and even "gay marriage": "Anita Bryant Was Right"? There is a significant list of intellectual and cultural issues that should remain open to further thoughtful inquiry, and the concerns of the Religious Right are part of that needed discussion.[169]

There are two significant problems facing evangelicals who, out of concern for American civic identity, become politically involved today. The first is a legacy of less-than-helpful allies in some of the causes close to their heart. In the struggle for greater parental choice in the education of their children, they have to contend with the ugliness of "school choice" serving as a rationalizing vehicle for racists who want to maintain educational apartheid. Opposition to abortion becomes more difficult when an abortionist is killed or a clinic bombed. That such events are rare does not diminish the difficulty. But, and this needs to be trumpeted in the public square, though abolitionist John Brown's attack on Harpers Ferry gave good excuse to the defenders of slavery who argued that emancipation would result in anarchy, it was the rightness of his cause, not the means, that keeps his soul "marching on."

The second problem arises from the intellectual retreat of evangelicals after the fundamentalist-modernist wars in the first decades of the twentieth century. Here some balancing perspective is called for, since it is a stereotypical and self-congratulatory put-down of conservatives in general by their opponents on the other side of the political spectrum that they are the "stupid party."[170]

168. Barbara Dafoe Whitehead, "The Failure of Sex Education," *Atlantic Monthly,* October 1994.

169. In addition to the general area of the sexual revolution (including homosexuality), we need to add such scientific issues thought to be settled by secularists as the dogma of Darwinian evolution. See, for example, Michael Behe, *Darwin's Black Box: The Biochemical Challenge to Evolution* (New York: Free Press, 1996); Philip Johnson, *Darwin on Trial* (Downers Grove, Ill.: InterVarsity, 1991); Philip Johnson, *Reason in the Balance: The Case against Naturalism in Science, Law, and Education* (Downers Grove, Ill.: InterVarsity, 1995).

170. Usually attributed to John Stuart Mill. The charge has been repeated recently by Michael Lind, who contends that "In the last fifty years, American intellectual conservativism has been extraordinarily sterile. . . . What is the result of the conservative intellectual renaissance of late twentieth-century America? A few position papers from think tanks subsidized by the aerospace and tobacco industries; a few public-policy pot-boilers slapped together by second-rate social scientists or former student journalists sub-

Yet, the problem is real and cannot be summarily dismissed as only so much hyperbole influenced by ideology. Mark Noll's summary of his exceptional work on the evangelical mind in twentieth-century America acknowledges this pointedly. "From the perspective of 1930, the evangelical mind in America looked dead, dead, dead, as many articulate commentators, including H. Richard Niebuhr, thought it was. Not only were the nation's universities alien territory for evangelicals, but Fundamentalists, the most visible evangelicals, had made a virtue of their alienation from the world of learned culture."[171] What exacerbated this intellectual shortfall, thus, was the fact that strong threads of evangelical theology and practice, including premillennial eschatology and strict separationism, even militated against such political involvement.[172]

As a consequence, when intellectually and politically naive evangelicals entered the political arena, their lack of sophistication was often derided and dismissed. The reality of this obstacle was noted by none other than Ralph Reed in a February 2, 1989, memo to Pat Robertson about the possibility and necessary framework for a new grassroots political organization that eventually became the Christian Coalition: "The half-century of retreat of evangelicals from social and political actions that followed the Scopes Trial of 1925 has had many profound consequences for American Society. Yet surely none is more important than this: we have now had two full generations of Bible-believing Christians . . . with virtually no hands-on experience in the political decision-making process."[173] Where, then, do evangelicals go for political instruction that seeks to be authentically Christian and intellectually responsible and has a demonstrated track record of political success? Mark Noll gives us a clue when he observes that even "at the apparent nadir of evangelical thought in America, new signs of life were stirring, all of which contributed to a more positive approach to Christian thinking and the development of an evangelical mind."[174] Among those signs was the assimilation of ethnic European confessional churches into American church life. In particular, "the Dutch Reformed offered their American counterparts a heritage of serious academic work and experienced philo-

---

sidized by pro-business foundations; a few collections of op-eds by right-wing syndicated columnists. Not one philosopher of world rank, not one great political or constitutional theorist, not one world-class novelist or poet has been enrolled in the ranks of twentieth-century conservative intellectuals, or had anything more than fleeting association with them" (Lind, 88-89).

171. Mark Noll, "The Evangelical Mind," in *The Evangelical Landscape,* 25.

172. See, for example, the tract of Dallas Seminary theologian Robert P. Lightner, *Neo-Evangelicalism,* 4th ed. (Des Plaines, Ill.: Regular Baptist Press, 1971).

173. Reed, *Politically Incorrect,* 3.

174. Noll, "The Evangelical Mind," 25.

sophical reasoning. In their native Holland, these Dutch Reformed had founded at the end of the nineteenth century a major center of higher education, the Free University of Amsterdam; they had made significant contributions to political theory and practice (their leader, Abraham Kuyper, was Prime Minister of the Netherlands from 1900-1905); and they enjoyed a full Christian participation in artistic and cultural life."[175]

Perhaps Noll is being too tentative and modest by only speaking of "signs." We shall not rehearse here the reasons already given in our preface for why Noll's pointing to Abraham Kuyper as an attractive potential model for engaged, evangelical, Christian political activism is on target. Kuyper believed that the American founding and its passion for liberty was fully in line with his own vision, matching positive statements from American historian George Bancroft about Calvinism with those from his own mentor, the nineteenth-century Dutch political thinker and historian Groen van Prinsterer.[176] But above all, Kuyper was committed to an awakened and alert Christian *mind*. Though we noted above that many American evangelical leaders lament what they consider the pitiable condition of evangelical *intellectual* life — "the scandal of the evangelical mind is that there is not much of an evangelical mind"[177] — others paint a more optimistic picture. James C. Turner, director of the Erasmus Institute at the University of Notre Dame, writing in a Roman Catholic monthly, contends that in fact, in addition to the political revival, there *has* been an "equally dramatic turning in evangelical *intellectual* life — though one without the rightward political bent."[178] Turner points to the new bimonthly journal *Books and Culture* that attempts to do for evangelicals what the *New York Review of Books* "has done for secular intellectual life; that is provide a forum in which academic and free-lance intellectuals engage with gusto a general educated public." The appearance of *Books and Culture* is not an accidental fluke according to Turner; rather, it "culminates a kind of evangelical Long

175. Noll, "The Evangelical Mind," 27-28.

176. Abraham Kuyper, *Lectures on Calvinism* (Grand Rapids: Eerdmans, 1931), 78:

Bancroft: "The fanatic for Calvinism was a fanatic for liberty, for in the moral warfare for freedom, his creed was a part of his army, and his most faithful ally in the battle" (from Bancroft's *History of the United States of America,* 15th ed. [Boston, 1853], 1:464).

Groen van Prinsterer: "In Calvinism lies the origin and guarantee of our constitutional liberties."

177. The opening sentence of Noll's *Scandal of the Evangelical Mind,* 3.

178. James C. Turner, "Something to Be Reckoned With: The Evangelical Mind Awakens," *Commonweal* (January 19, 1999). All quotations which follow are taken from this short essay.

March through American intellectual life." Turner refers to individual evangelical scholars such as Mark Noll, Nathan Hatch, George Marsden, Alvin Plantinga, Nicholas Wolterstorff, and Richard Mouw, and singles out two institutions of higher education, Calvin College and Wheaton College, as "seedbeds of an intellectual renaissance within American evangelicalism."

Turner notes that this development is surprising, even puzzling, as he retraces the journey rehearsed earlier in this chapter:

> As recently as 1970, probably no credible prophet would have forecast these developments. The dilapidated state in which evangelical intellectual life found itself during the middle decades of the twentieth century was more than a little ironic. For much of the nineteenth century, an informal evangelical establishment had come close to dominating cultural life in the United States. But in the 1880s and 1890s battles between fundamentalists and modernists . . . effectively destroyed this evangelical near-hegemony. In the 1920s — the decade of the infamous Scopes trial — fundamentalism was decisively defeated within the mainline Protestant churches. Thereafter the fundamentalists withdrew into the periphery of American culture, making scarcely any contribution to the nation's intellectual life.

But then, how did the revival take place? In Turner's words, "given these facts, the evangelical revival seems genuinely puzzling. How did a religious movement that has historically produced preachers rather than professors . . . manage to generate within a couple of decades a distinguished cohort of scholars? How could so sturdy an intellectual life arise on such feeble intellectual traditions?"

The answer, in short, is — Abraham Kuyper! Turner notes that "evangelicals, in fact, did not build, could not have built — on their own intellectual foundations." Here he introduces Calvin College into his story and traces its history and location within the Christian Reformed Church (CRC), described as "a fairly small denomination . . . though weak in numbers . . . sturdy in mind." Most important, the CRC and Calvin College itself are heir to the distinctive Reformed tradition known as "neo-Calvinism," the legacy "of the Dutch politician and theologian Abraham Kuyper." It is through the Calvin College connection, claims Turner, that Kuyperian neo-Calvinism "stamped its decisive impress on many of [the evangelical intellectual leaders]." Kuyperianism is not the only resource on which the revived evangelical intellectual renaissance draws. Others are the Anabaptist tradition; Reinhold Niebuhr; Roman Catholic neoconservatives such as Richard John Neuhaus, Michael Novak, and George Weigel; and especially C. S. Lewis. The evangelical intellectual re-

129

naissance is eclectic and, consequently, supple and adaptable. Nonetheless, Turner concludes: "From my viewpoint, however, the decisive influence on the revival remains neo-Calvinism."

From the preceding we have sufficient warrant to examine specifically Abraham Kuyper's public theology, the structure of his theologically warranted journalistic and political engagement. Before we consider some of Kuyper's key themes in a more systematic manner, we shall attempt to situate Kuyper in a broader, more horizontal/historical context by comparing his impressions of America with two other important nineteenth-century European visitors, Alexis de Tocqueville and Lord John Acton. In the subsequent chapter, Kuyper's vision of America in the divine providential plan will be compared with that of Jonathan Edwards, and in the third historical, orienting chapter, Kuyper's treatment of the "social question" will be compared with that of two contemporaries, American Social Gospel theologian Walter Rauschenbusch and Pope Leo XIII.

PART ONE

COMPARATIVE
HISTORICAL STUDIES

CHAPTER THREE

Liberty's European Pilgrims: Abraham Kuyper, Alexis de Tocqueville, and Lord John Acton

Thanne longen folk to goon on pilgrimages,
And palmeres for to seken straunge strondes,
To ferne halwes, kowthe in sondry londes.

Geoffrey Chaucer

In the beginning, all the world was America.

John Locke

Westward the course of empire takes.
The four first acts already past,
A Fifth shall close the drama with the day:
Time's noblest offspring is the last.

George Berkeley

This new world is probably now discovered, that God might in it begin
a new world in a spiritual respect, when he creates the new heavens
and the new earth.

Jonathan Edwards

The tree of liberty must be refreshed from time to time with the blood
of patriots and tyrants. It is its natural manure.

Thomas Jefferson

In love of liberty and bravery in defense of it, [Holland] has been our great example.

Benjamin Franklin

The purpose of this study is to provide a sketch of Abraham Kuyper's public theology and to explore its contemporary relevance, particularly but not exclusively, for politically involved American evangelical Christians. We begin, in this chapter, with Kuyper's visit to America in 1898[1] and his reflections on the American experiment in ordered liberty. America had a special place in Kuyper's heart, and his vision of America is an important part of his overall public theology. His biographer put it this way: "The new republic of the United States drew Kuyper's heart and head more than old Europe. To a large extent his ecclesiastical and political exertions were even based on what he judged to be the situation in America. He confessed a 'near fanatic sympathy for the life now full-blown in America,' since the 'free life of free citizens' appeared to him as the fruit of Calvinism."[2] In a recent study of Kuyper's Princeton Stone Lectures on Calvinism, the occasion for his visit to the United States, Peter Heslam observes that "primarily in his role as editor of [the daily newspaper] *De Standaard,* Kuyper had demonstrated a sustained and active interest in American affairs and had developed over several decades an image of American history and culture which was inextricably linked to his perception of Calvinism."[3]

1. On Kuyper's visit to the United States, see C. A. Admiraal, "De Amerikanse reis van Abraham Kuyper," in *Historicus in het Spanningsveld van Theorie en Praktijk,* ed. C. A. Admiraal, P. B. M. Blaas, and J. Van der Zande (Leiderdorp: Leidse Onderwijsinstellingen, 1985), 110-65; Dirk Jellema, "Kuyper's Visit to America in 1898," *Michigan History* 42 (1958): 227-36; James D. Bratt, "De erfenis van Kuyper in Noord-Amerika," in *Abraham Kuyper: Zijn Volksdeel, Zijn Invloed,* ed. C. Augustijn et al. (Delft: Meinema, 1987), 203-8; James D. Bratt, "Abraham Kuyper, American History, and the Tensions of Neo-Calvinism," in *Sharing the Tradition: The Dutch–North American Exchanges, 1846-1996,* ed. George Harinck and Hans Krabbendam (Amsterdam: VU Uitgeverij, 1996), 97-114; J. Stellingwerf, *Abraham Kuyper en de Vrije Universiteit* (Kampen: Kok, 1987), chap. 7, "De reis naar America," 227-52; M. L. Mooijweer, "Een voorlijke erfgenaam van Nederland: Abraham en Henriëtte Kuyper over Amerika," in *Amerika in Europese Ogen: Facetten van de Europese beeldvorming van het moderne Amerika,* ed. K. Van Berkel (The Hague: SDU Uitgeverij, 1990), 40-53; Peter S. Heslam, *Creating a Christian Worldview: Abraham Kuyper's Lectures on Calvinism* (Grand Rapids: Eerdmans, 1998).

2. P. Kasteel, *Abraham Kuyper* (Kampen: Kok, 1938), 289. For a lengthy list of places in his writings where Kuyper speaks positively about America, see n. 417.

3. Heslam, 15.

As Kuyper told the story of human liberty in its development, it was Calvinism with its emphasis on divine sovereignty and human dignity that gave birth to political freedom. The Calvinist seed, planted in Switzerland and transplanted to the Netherlands in the sixteenth century, had initially flourished there but then had its growth stunted by compromises forced on the Calvinists, first by Arminian tolerance and finally by the atheistic *ni Dieu, ni maître* worldview of the French Revolution that transformed Dutch life during the French-dominated Batavian Republic from 1795 to 1806.[4] The Calvinist political vision, by contrast, is *antirevolutionary.* For Kuyper the American experiment was Calvinist in its core. In America, a genuine antirevolutionary, truly democratic political vision, brought across the Atlantic by the Pilgrims (after their stay in the Netherlands!), developed into full bloom under the leadership of Washington and the eventual victory of Alexander Hamilton's principles over those of Thomas Jefferson. Kuyper, unafraid to intrude himself into American as well as Dutch national mythology, repeatedly appealed to the important conflict of principles embodied in the clash between these two iconic American founders.[5]

4. This synopsis is taken from the following works of Kuyper: *Lectures on Calvinism* (Grand Rapids: Eerdmans, 1931); "Calvinism: Source and Stronghold of Our Constitutional Liberties" (1874), in *Abraham Kuyper: A Centennial Reader,* ed. James D. Bratt (Grand Rapids: Eerdmans, 1998), 279-320; originally published in English translation as "Calvinism: The Origin and Safeguard of Our Constitutional Liberties," *Bibliotheca Sacra* 52 (1895): 385-410, 646-75; *Antirevolutionaire Staatkunde,* 2 vols. (Kampen: Kok, 1916), passim. For an alternative reading of the history of liberty, see John Emerich Edward Dalberg-Acton, *The History of Freedom* (Grand Rapids: Acton Institute, 1993); a fuller text is in *Selected Writings of Lord Acton,* vol. 1, *Essays in the History of Liberty,* ed. J. Rufus Fears (Indianapolis: Liberty Fund, 1985).

5. Kuyper repeatedly linked Jefferson to atheistic French revolutionary principles and Hamilton to Calvinist, antirevolutionary ones (see *Antirevolutionare Staatkunde,* 1:711); for a thoughtful critique of Kuyper's use of this linkage, see Bratt, "Abraham Kuyper," 100-106. Lord Acton too appealed to the Jefferson versus Hamilton debate (see chapter section below, "Pilgrims to Liberty's Shrine"). For a broad historical perspective on the role of this division in American national mythology, see Claude G. Bowers, *Jefferson and Hamilton: The Struggle for Democracy* (New York: Houghton Mifflin, 1925). Jefferson biographer Alf J. Mapp, Jr. (*Thomas Jefferson: A Strange Case of Mistaken Identity* [New York: Madison Books, 1987], 283), observes that the two men became "the focuses of political polarization.... [P]opular opinion for generations would make them the simplistic symbols of opposing philosophies so that through history they would ride a seesaw of public esteem.... Because many Northerners were wont to blame secession on Jeffersonian democracy, the Virginian's reputation 'merely survived' the Civil War whereas that of Hamilton, the strong advocate of centralized government, 'was remade by it'" (quote from Merrill D. Peterson, *The Jefferson Image in the American Mind* [New York: Oxford University Press, 1962], 222). Kuyper's use of Jefferson as the symbol of the politics of revolution

Even before he came to visit in 1898, Kuyper thus already had definite ideas about America's founding and future.[6] Kuyper shared the view of those visitors described by another important late nineteenth-century visitor, James Bryce, who upon observing the fascination of America's institutions to visitors, called attention to the belief that American political institutions were seen as a "new type, . . . an experiment in the rule of the multitude, tried on a scale unprecedently vast, and the results of which everyone is concerned to watch. And yet they are something more than an experiment, for they are believed to disclose and display the type of institutions toward which, as by a law of fate, the rest of civilized mankind are forced to move."[7] Kuyper, too, left no doubt about his own deep faith in America's providential role as a beacon of liberty in world history. "America," he contended in a Grand Rapids, Michigan, address to Dutch-American fellow Calvinists, "is destined in the providence of God to become the most glorious and noble nation the world has ever seen. Some day its renown will eclipse the renown and splendor of Rome, Greece and the old races."[8]

Kuyper's visit, like that of many other nineteenth-century travelers to America, was thus a pilgrimage[9] to the shrine of liberty, an opportunity to ex-

was not altogether unreasonable, though his sympathies for smaller and local government units places him with respect to this important constitutional/structural question on Jefferson's side against Hamilton's vision of a strong federal government.

6. It is important to note that Kuyper's essay on Calvinism and constitutional liberty was originally published in 1874, long before he became a significant political actor in the Netherlands and prior to any notion of a visit to America in such a capacity. The English translation appeared in 1896.

7. James Bryce, *The American Commonwealth* (New York: Macmillan, 1911), 1:1; Tocqueville also judges the experiment in liberty to be the inevitable wave of the future: "Therefore the gradual progress of equality is fated . . . it is universal and permanent, it is daily passing beyond human control. . . . If patient observation and sincere meditation have led men of the present day to recognize that both the past and the future of their history consist in the gradual and measured advance of equality, that discovery in itself gives this progress the sacred character of the will of the Sovereign Master. In that case effort to halt democracy appears as a fight against God Himself, and nations have no alternative but to acquiesce in the social state imposed by Providence" (quote taken from the Mayer/Lawrence translation of Alexis de Tocqueville, *Democracy in America*, ed. J. P. Mayer, trans. George Lawrence [New York: Harper Perennial, 1988 (1966)], 12, which I will be using throughout).

8. *Grand Rapids Herald*, October 29, 1898; see app. C.

9. I have chosen the term "pilgrim" deliberately, rather than "traveler" or even "tourist," to underscore the religiously committed character of Kuyper's visit. According to J. W. Schulte Nordholt, "The purpose of the tourist is to escape from reality, to find peace in some dreamlike landscape, some Shangri-La. The traveler, on the other hand, is on a voyage of discovery; it is not a dream that he is looking for, but a new reality. The tourist wants to comprehend his world, encompass it, store it somewhere, preferably in his cam-

perience the *novus ordo seclorum* firsthand. To help place Kuyper's visit and his reflections in perspective, they will be compared to those of two other European devotees of liberty, the Frenchman Alexis de Tocqueville, who visited the United States in 1831 and whose *Democracy in America,* in the judgment of many, remains "the most brilliant and searching account of America ever written,"[10] and the great English Victorian-era historian and political thinker Lord John Acton, who crossed the Atlantic in 1853.[11] Tocqueville's framework is central to this discussion since both Acton[12] and Kuyper[13] read and used his interpretation of revolution and of the American experiment.

---

era. The traveler is overwhelmed; he sees only a part, his quest never ends. The tourist wants to recognize, the traveler to discover. The tourist sails on a lake, the traveler on the ocean. The tourist looks for the past, the traveler for the future" ("Dutch Travelers in the United States: A Tale of Energy and Ambivalence," in *A Bilateral Bicentennial: A History of Dutch-American Relations 1782-1982,* ed. J. W. Schulte Nordholt and Robert P. Swierenga (Amsterdam: Meulenhoff; New York: Octagon Books, 1982), 251. In Schulte Nordholt's estimation, "American travelers in Holland were mostly tourists, but Dutch tourists in the United States were travelers. In America there was something to be discovered" (251). Under these terms Kuyper is best considered a "traveler," but the term "pilgrim" suits him still better. Pilgrims are already committed and do not travel so much to discover but to be confirmed and renewed in their larger pilgrimage of life.

10. Sanford Kessler, *Tocqueville's Civil Religion: American Christianity and the Prospects for Freedom* (Albany: State University of New York Press, 1994), xi; the twentieth-century British economist Harold Laski claimed that Tocqueville's *Democracy in America* was "the best book on one country ever written by a citizen of another" (cited by R. Kroes, "Alexis de Tocqueville en James Bryce over de Amerikanse democratie," in *Amerika in Europese Ogen,* 33). According to Kroes, this honor should go to Bryce.

11. See *Acton in America: The American Journal of Sir John Acton,* ed. S. W. Jackman (Shepherdstown, W.Va.: Patmos, 1979). Acton's journal was written when he was only twenty, and is incomplete. His mature reflections on America will thus be more significant in the discussion that follows in this chapter. Though there are other nineteenth-century authors, notably James Bryce, whose travel reflections invite comparisons with those of Kuyper (e.g., Bryce's notes on city politics parallel the concluding section of Kuyper's *Varia Americana* on "Boss Politics"), our concern in this chapter is with the three writers whose interpretive framework is dominated by the notion of liberty; Bryce's treatment is predominantly descriptive and thus dated, while Tocqueville, Acton, and Kuyper remain valuable for contemporary considerations of the *idea* of America. As we shall note later in this chapter, there are also chronological reasons for taking three writers whose visits and reflections arise, respectively, on the three one-third segments of the nineteenth century (1831, 1853, 1898).

12. See David Mathews, *Lord Acton and His Times* (Tuscaloosa: University of Alabama Press, 1968), chap. 7, "Tocqueville."

13. See Kuyper, "Calvinism: Source and Stronghold of Our Constitutional Liberties"; the numerous references to Tocqueville are most clear in the printed Dutch version of this address.

Travelers, Pilgrims, Critics, Utopians

The many nineteenth-century European travelers, including Kuyper, Tocqueville, and Acton, who came to see the new American experiment in liberty and recorded their impressions for posterity were hardly the first chroniclers of travel tales in human history. To place their accounts in perspective, it is helpful to consider the broader phenomenon of travel literature.[14] The appeal of the remote and the exotic has always encouraged the adventurous to travel and stimulated the production of travel tales as well as visual images[15] to satisfy the curiosity of the more timid. "Man has always been an inquisitive animal. Lands beyond the horizon have never ceased to intrigue him. From the days of Herodotus onward, travellers' tales have always found a ready audience."[16] These accounts of faraway places, of course, vary greatly in content and purpose. Some, in the spirit of ancient historians such as Thucydides, Livy, and Tacitus, though hardly without polemical or political interest, purport to be descriptive and historical. Tacitus's own *Germania* and even Marco Polo's travel accounts of Cathay and the imperial glory of Kublai Khan are prime examples of such accounts. Others, including Malory's *Morte d' Arthur,* Chaucer's *Canterbury Tales,* John Mandeville's *Travels,* Cervantes' *Don Quixote,* More's *Utopia,* Shakespeare's *Tempest,* Jonathan Swift's *Gulliver's Travels,* and Coleridge's *Kubla Khan,* are obviously imaginative constructs intended in the first place to entertain as well as provide moral or political instruction, even when their characters have some rootedness in historical reality.[17]

In addition, the travel metaphor serves a more religious, even mythic function in "pilgrim" stories. Pilgrim narratives as old as Homer's *Odyssey* and

14. On the genre of American travel narratives, see Robert B. Downs, *Images of America: Travelers from Abroad in the New World* (Urbana and Chicago: University of Illinois Press, 1987); Van Berkel, *Amerika in Europese Ogen;* Robert Lemelin, *Pathway to the National Character, 1830-1861* (Port Washington, N.Y., and London: Kennikat, 1975); Henry T. Tuckerman, *America and Her Commentators* (New York: Scribner, 1864); Allan Nevins, *America through British Eyes* (New York: Oxford University Press, 1948); Max Berger, *The British Traveller in America, 1836-1860* (Gloucester, Mass.: Peter Smith, 1964). The reverse phenomenon — Americans traveling abroad — should not be overlooked and is discussed by Foster Rhea Dulles, *American Abroad: Two Centuries of European Travel* (Ann Arbor: University of Michigan Press, 1964).

15. For a richly illustrated introduction to the visual portraits of America, see Hugh Honour, *The European Vision of America* (Cleveland: Cleveland Museum of Art, 1975); *The New Golden Land: European Images of America from the Discoveries to the Present Time* (New York: Pantheon Books, 1975).

16. Berger, 6.

17. Finally, in yet another category, are travel accounts written *deliberately* to deceive. See Percy G. Adams, *Travelers and Travel Liars, 1600-1800* (Berkeley and Los Angeles: University of California Press, 1962).

the *Gilgamesh Epic,* as well as more recent ones such as those of Dante and Bunyan, serve as archetypal, sacred journey-and-return myths. Whether taken relatively simply as metaphors for the arduous journey of life with its rewards for heroic triumph over suffering, or more mystically "as a religious allegory of man's renunciation of material pleasures in favour of the transcendent — that sacred 'place from which we came'" — the pilgrimage symbol is profoundly universal among the world's cultures and religions.[18]

> Jews go to Jerusalem and so also Christians. Hindus visit the Ganges; Muslims make their way to Mecca, Buddhists to Sarnath near Benares and members of the Tenri-Kyo sect of Shintoism to Tenri Shi in Japan. When they do so, each and every one is performing an act of practical piety; they are embodying in a journey what is related to the experimental, ritualistic and social dimensions of religion. They are engaged in a search of meaning and for spiritual advancement and their pilgrimage dramatizes their quest for the divine. Indeed a pilgrimage centre is universally regarded as a place of intersection between everyday life and the life of God. It is a geographical location that is worthy of reverence because it has been the scene of a manifestation of divine power or has an association with a holy person.[19]

The tales of pilgrims to antique and exotic lands alternatively provided mythic significance to the destination or sacred place, to the arduous journey to it, or even to the victorious traveler himself. If pilgrimage is a universal religious phenomenon, so is some notion of "sacred space."

> All religious traditions have a "sense" of sacred space — that geographical site at which the human is closest to encountering the sacred, whether the sacred be identified as God, Allah, or Šiva. In most religious traditions, sacred space is distinguished from ordinary space by the construction of a religious building, such as a temple or church. The site of the religious building is predicated on the experience(s) of a miracle, a healing, or a vision by a holy person or religious believer on that exact spot of ground. Thereby the site becomes identified as a sacred place at which the sacred and human beings can interact in a unique but identifiable manner. This place then becomes the "site of the sacred," on which a temple or church will be built and where religious worship, such as the Christian liturgy, will be celebrated.[20]

18. See Simon Coleman and John Elsner, *Pilgrimage Past and Present in the World Religions* (Cambridge: Harvard University Press, 1995); quote on 10.

19. J. G. Davies, *Pilgrimage Yesterday and Today: Why? Where? How?* (London: SCM, 1988), 1-2.

20. Diane Apostolos-Cappadona, "Religion and Sacred Space," in *The Religion Fac-*

The purpose of pilgrimage to sacred places is religious: to pay homage or to worship (Passover in Jerusalem); to honor a vow or fulfill other religious obligation (*hajj* to Mecca, the Crusades); to find illumination (Bodh Gaya, Kyoto); to elicit or renew devotion, including doing penance (Rome, Canterbury, Guadalupe, Fátima, Amritsar); to find cleansing or healing (Benares, Lourdes). But what is the reason for writing *about* pilgrimage?[21]

Undoubtedly, the written accounts are intended in the first place to encourage other pilgrims; the chronicler bears witness to the efficacious power of the pilgrimage. "Diagrams and narratives not only reproduce the topography and experience of the sacred journey, but define and even constitute it. They provide the means for imagining pilgrimage, by shaping the anticipation of a pilgrim before his or her voyage and by guiding experience at the sacred center itself." Representations of the pilgrimage also serve the pilgrim's own quest. "For some pilgrims the construction of a narrative or image after their return provides a means both of reinterpreting and of reliving something of the significance of the trip. It may even represent a sort of personal rite of passage for returning from pilgrimage to one's familiar world."[22] There is a dimension to such accounts, however, that must not be overlooked, namely, social critique.[23]

"Every age," observes the great Dutch historian Johan Huizinga, "yearns for a more beautiful world. The deeper the desperation and the depression about the confusing present, the more intense that yearning."[24] Much of the sociological/anthropological literature on pilgrimage focuses on this disruptive and dissociative dissatisfaction as the transitional context for pilgrimage. Building on the work of Émile Durkheim[25] and Mircea

---

tor: *An Introduction to How Religion Matters,* ed. William Scott Green and Jacob Neusner (Louisville: Westminster/John Knox, 1996), 214.

21. On the varieties of pilgrimage literature, see Davies, 19-41. It needs to be noted that representations of pilgrimage are not limited to word accounts but include images and diagrams as well — maps of the sacred. See, in addition to Davies, Coleman and Elsner, 166-69.

22. Coleman and Elsner, 167.

23. On the social-critical function of pilgrimage and the academic debate about it, see Coleman and Elsner, 198-213; Victor Turner and Edith Turner, *Image and Pilgrimage in Christian Culture: Anthropological Perspectives* (New York: Columbia University Press, 1978); John Eade and Michael J. Sallnow, eds., *Contesting the Sacred: The Anthropology of Christian Pilgrimage* (London and New York: Routledge, 1991); the last volume is a collection of essays from a July 1988 interdisciplinary conference on pilgrimage held in London.

24. Johan Huizinga, *The Autumn of the Middle Ages,* trans. Rodney J. Payton and Ulrich Mammitzsch (Chicago: University of Chicago Press, 1996), 30.

25. Durkheim's influence on this discussion is found in his conviction that "religious belief and practice emerge from, idealize and reinforce human concerns and com-

Eliade,[26] among others, Victor and Edith Turner view pilgrimage as a *liminal* phenomenon, "the state and process of mid-transition in a rite of passage" defined as "the transitional rituals accompanying changes of place, state, social position, and age in a culture." Cultural rites of passage, according to the Turners, "have a basically tripartite processual structure, consisting of three phases: separation, margin or limen, and reaggregation. The first phase detaches the ritual subjects from their old places in society; the last installs them, inwardly transformed and outwardly changed, in a new place in society." The pilgrimage phase is an ambiguous one; the ritual subjects "pass through a cultural realm that has few or none of the attributes of the past or coming state. Liminars are betwixt and between. The liminal state has frequently been likened to death; to being in the womb; to invisibility, darkness, bisexuality and the wilderness."[27]

Though the Turners view pilgrimage as a subverting instrument and more traditional Durkheimian analysts see it as supportive of the established orthodoxies and their social order, what both perspectives have in common is a reductionist, even positivist and generic interpretation of pilgrimage.[28] All pil-

---

munities, so that the sacred exists not as a spiritual reality but rather as the product of social forces" (Coleman and Elsner, 199).

26. Eliade's specific contribution here is his discussion of a "holy place" as the *raison d'être* of pilgrimage. "For Eliade, whose writings heavily influenced Turner's work, every pilgrimage shrine is an archetype of a sacred centre, marked off from the profane space surrounding it, where heaven and earth intersect and where time stands still, where there exists the possibility of breaking through to the realm of the transcendent" (Eade and Sallnow, 6); cf. Mircea Eliade, "Sacred Places: Temple, Palace, 'Centre of the World,'" in *Patterns in Comparative Religion* (New York: World Publishing Co., 1963). It should be noted that, unlike Durkheim, Eliade does not engage in sociological *reduction* of religious experience (of the sacred) to a mere product of social forces.

27. Turner and Turner, 249. It should be noted here that Turner and Turner invert Durkheim's model. Whereas anthropologists who built their analysis on his classic *Elementary Forms of the Religious Life* (1912) understood pilgrimages as "local cults writ large" and as an integrative force contributing to both religious orthodoxy and social cohesion, Turner and Turner consider pilgrimage "so far from reflecting or reinforcing secular social structure, [but as] a liminal phenomenon which betokens the partial, if not complete, abrogation of that structure. Pilgrimage . . . is *anti*-structural: it always tends towards communitas, a state of unmediated and egalitarian association between individuals who are temporarily freed of the hierarchical secular roles and statuses which they bear in everyday life. The achievement of communitas is the pilgrim's fundamental motivation. . . . Pilgrimage, in other words, to the degree that it strips actors of their social personae and restores their essential individuality, is the ritual context *par excellence* in which a world religion strives to realize its defining transcultural universalism; for to reach the individual is to reach the universal" (Eade and Sallnow, 4)

28. Eade and Sallnow, 5. In its most severe Marxist slant, the Durkheimian approach

grimages are viewed as rooted in and serving the same religious impulse. Furthermore, though the Turner thesis receives support from such phenomena as "the location of many sites on the political and economic periphery of societies," the convention of standard clothes "to avoid the overt display of status difference," and the plausible speculation "that pilgrimages resurface at periods of rapid social change and consequent removal from conventional ties,"[29] both theoretical critiques and field studies have challenged it on two counts in particular: its determinism and its homogeneity.[30]

The July 1988 interdisciplinary conference on pilgrimage held in London, which gave rise to the collection of essays edited by Eade and Sallnow,[31] attempted to provide an alternative to the functionalist dichotomy between those who see pilgrimage as supportive of social order and those who regard it as subversive. According to the editors, the conference essayists attempted

> to develop a view of pilgrimage not merely as a field of social relations but also as a *realm of competing discourses.* . . . It is these varied discourses with their multiple meanings and understandings, brought to the shrine by different categories of pilgrims, by residents and by religious specialists, that are constitutive of the cult itself. Equally, a cult might be seen to be constituted by mutual *mis*understandings, as each group attempts to interpret the actions and motives of others in terms of its own specific discourse.[32]

This suggested alternative perhaps reveals more than the editors intend, since, taken to its logical conclusion, of course, this "pilgrim response" approach leaves no room at all for serious scholarly study or reflection on the phenomenon of pilgrimage; it's all in the "eye of the pilgrim."

Others have also noted that this focus on multiple, contesting visions of pilgrimage invokes the idea "only to dismiss it as a meaningful category for study."[33] While they acknowledge that "one cannot avoid the fact that pilgrims, even those visiting the same place, engage in a multiplicity of frequently incompatible interpretations," Coleman and Elsner insist that this approach, which argues for "pilgrimage sites being void of intrinsic meaning," ignores "the con-

implicates pilgrimage as contributing to "the generation and maintenance of ideologies which legitimize domination and oppression" (4).

29. Coleman and Elsner, 201; the speculation is the Turners', who point to "the waning of the Roman Empire, the end of the Middle Ages, and the contemporary era" as times when pilgrimages are popular.

30. Eade and Sallnow, 5; cf. Coleman and Elsner, 200-201.

31. See n. 23 above.

32. Eade and Sallnow, 5.

33. Coleman and Elsner, 202.

siderable *structural* similarities in pilgrimage practices within and between traditions. There are indeed parallels in behaviour to be found across time and culture, even if the implications and meanings of such behaviour vary greatly."[34] According to Coleman and Elsner, one of the key continuities that Eade and Sallnow overlook is the importance of *movement* in pilgrimages, not only in travel to and from shrines but also in ritual circumambulation at the sacred site itself. "Circumambulation . . . both echoes the broader idea of journeying and also demarcates — one can almost say 'encapsulates' — the sacred image or object which has been the goal of the pilgrimage. Even in contemporary pilgrimages, where the traveler may have arrived by bus, car, or even plane, prescribed movement on foot often occurs within the site itself."[35]

It is precisely here — in the focus on movement — that the linkage between the travel accounts and social change is the clearest and most free from ideological contamination. In the first place, "pilgrimage in the world's religions serves to link geographically dispersed peoples by giving travellers the possibility to perceive a common religious identity that transcends parochial assumptions and concerns. As a religious practice, pilgrimage has therefore complemented and incorporated other trans-local activities such as trade, exploration and even scholarly exchange." By directly encountering the diversity of practice in a religion that purports to be universal, the pilgrim experiences the dissonance of "universalizing cultures of 'belief' [being] placed in tension with parochial cultures rooted in 'place.'" The actual experience of travel itself "and the constant possibility of encountering the new . . . makes pilgrimage distinct from other forms of ritual." And finally, "in returning home, the pilgrim can act as an agent of change, by spreading new ideas gleaned on the journey."[36]

What is helpful about editors Eade and Sallnow's introduction to their collection of essays is their analysis of pilgrimage in terms of three distinct coordinates of sacredness: place, person, and text.[37] Of these three, it is the combination of the first (place) and the last (text) that is most fruitful for our understanding of America as the *place* where a new world order is defined by *texts*

34. Coleman and Elsner, 202.
35. Coleman and Elsner, 205.
36. Coleman and Elsner, 205-6.
37. Eade and Sallnow, 9: "The sacred centre, then, can assume many different forms. The thrust of our analytic endeavour should be not towards the formulation of ever more inclusive, and consequently ever more vacuous, generalizations, but instead towards the examination of the specific peculiarities of its construction in each instance. We suggest that the triad of 'person,' 'place,' and 'text' might provide the coordinates for this task as far as Christian pilgrimage is concerned, and perhaps for pilgrimage in other scripturally based religious traditions as well."

(Declaration of Independence, United States Constitution). As Eade and Sallnow describe it, localizing sacredness in a text is the most "abstract and rarified" form of pilgrimage and Jerusalem is "a prime example of what might be called 'textual pilgrimage.' . . . Because of the intimate connection with Christ's biography," pilgrimage to Jerusalem has never been "just, or even primarily, a journey to particular locations, but more importantly a journey through a particular written text, the authorized biblical accounts of Christ's life and death."[38] In the Christian tradition this is also true for Catholic, particularly Ignatian, devotional life centered around the stations of the cross, as well as the piety of personal pilgrimage reflected in Bunyan's famous allegory.

The final step in our consideration of pilgrimage as an analytic tool to understand the function of nineteenth-century liberty visitors to America, is to note the effect of the Protestant Reformation on the notion of pilgrimage and sacredness. In addition to the spiritual critique of pilgrimage abuses (wonderfully catalogued by Chaucer as well as Erasmus in *The Praise of Folly*), the Reformers also criticized the very idea of pilgrimage on theological grounds. The heart of the believer was the sacred place where God's spirit dwelled. "The important thing was not to leave one's country but one's self. Emphasis was laid upon the value of dying with Christ, of undergoing the crucifixion of the self, rather than on actively assuming a cross and travelling to the earthly Jerusalem."[39] Luther's point of view was clearly articulated in his *Letter to the Christian Nobility:* "All pilgrimages should be stopped. There is no good in them: No commandment enjoins them, no obedience attaches to them. Rather do these pilgrimages give countless occasions to commit sin and to despise God's commandments."[40] But, apart from concern about the spiritual abuses in pilgrimage practice, including opportunity for immorality, idolatrous devotion to relics and images, and the general meritoriousness of the act of pilgrimage itself, the Reformation's *indirect* undermining of the very idea of sacred space is equally important. It is not accidental that Luther, in the same address where pilgrimages are denounced, also vigorously opposes the notion of all restricted, sacramentally set-apart sacredness. Priestly or episcopal consecration does not sanctify and set apart — baptism does. "For whoever comes out of the water of baptism can boast that he is already conse-

38. Eade and Sallnow, 8. The essay by Glenn Bowman, "Christian Ideology and the Image of a Holy Land: The Place of Jerusalem Pilgrimage in the Various Christianities" (98-121), is devoted to this topic.

39. Davies, 86.

40. Cited by Davies, 98-99; on the decline of pilgrimage in the Reformation period, see Philip M. Soergel, *Wondrous in His Saints: Counter Propaganda in Bavaria* (Berkeley, Los Angeles, and London: University of California Press, 1993), esp. chap. 2, "The Reformation Decline of Pilgrimage."

crated priest, bishop, and pope, although of course it is not seemly that just anyone should exercise such an office."[41]

The egalitarian implication of this notion of universal priesthood rooted in baptism is transparent; the clergy-laity distinction breaks down because Christian vocation is universal: "It follows from this argument that there is no true, basic difference between laymen and priests, princes and bishops, between religious and secular, except for the sake of office and work, but not for the sake of status. *They are all of the spiritual estate, all are truly priests, bishops and popes.* But they do not all have the same work to do. . . . Christ does not have two bodies, one temporal, the other spiritual. There is but one Head and one body."[42] Similarly, Calvin also desacralizes church buildings while at the same time sanctifying all space devoted to Christ. There is a "lawful use of church buildings" for prayer and worship, Calvin says, but "we in turn must guard against either taking them to be God's proper dwelling places, whence he may more nearly incline his ear to us — as they began to be regarded some centuries ago — or feigning for them some secret holiness or other, which would render prayer more sacred before God. For since we ourselves are God's true temples, if we would call upon God in his holy temple, we must pray within ourselves."[43]

The thoroughness of Calvin's sanctification of this-worldly callings is clear when he refers not to the sacred ministry of the word but to civil magistracy as a "calling, not only holy and lawful before God, but also the most sacred and by far the most honorable of all callings in the whole life of mortal man."[44] When this conviction about the holiness of politics is combined with viewing the public, corporate life of the people as the locus of the sacred, the Calvinist tradition paved the way for *political* pilgrimage, the journey to places where Christ's reign was "enshrined" by means of a text — originally simply scriptural law — effectively governing an earthly polis. Visitors such as John Knox who traveled to Geneva to see Calvin's "school of Christ" are thus (with tragic irony) forerunners of the secularized political pilgrims who in the twentieth century journeyed to Moscow, Beijing, Havana, Hanoi, and Managua to see the latest version of paradise in action.[45]

---

41. Luther, "To the Christian Nobility of the German Nation," in *Luther: Selected Political Writings*, ed. J. M. Porter (Philadelphia: Fortress, 1974), 41.

42. Luther, "To the Christian Nobility," 41, emphasis added.

43. John Calvin, *Institutes of the Christian Religion*, ed. John T. McNeill, trans. Ford Lewis Battles, Library of Christian Classics, vols. 20, 21 (Philadelphia: Westminster, 1960), 3.20.30.

44. Calvin, *Institutes* 4.20.4.

45. On the latter phenomenon see Paul Hollander, *Political Pilgrims: Travels of Western Intellectuals to the Soviet Union, China, and Cuba* (New York and Oxford: Oxford University Press, 1981).

The phenomenon of political pilgrimage, such as the visits of Tocqueville, Acton, and Kuyper to America in the nineteenth century, must also be viewed in light of two related though distinct types in the broader genre of travel literature, namely, "golden age" and utopian works.[46] Alienated human beings living in the midst of oppressive or at least grossly inadequate social and political orders look elsewhere — nostalgically to a golden past or hopefully to an anticipated ideal future — for comfort and redemption.[47] The Manuels begin their extensive survey on seven constellations of utopian expectation and hope with this observation: "Anthropologists tell us that blessed isles and paradises are part of the dream world of savages everywhere."[48] According to the Manuels, there are "two ancient beliefs that molded and nurtured utopia [in the West] — the Judeo-Christian faith in a paradise created with the world and destined to endure beyond it, and the Hellenic myth of an ideal, beautiful city built by men for men with the assistance and often in defiance of the gods," and these two beliefs "were deeply embedded in the consciousness of Europeans."[49] George Orwell suggests that the utopian impulse is deeper and more universal than that of Europeans alone when he writes of "the dream of a just society which seems to haunt the human imagination ineradicably and in all ages, whether it is called the Kingdom of Heaven or the classless society, or whether it is thought of as a Golden Age which once existed in the past and from which we have degenerated."[50]

46. Of the vast literature on utopia and golden age/new world/paradise, the following selection was useful in preparing these paragraphs: Frank E. Manuel and Fritzie P. Manuel, *Utopian Thought in the Western World* (Cambridge: Harvard University Press, Belknap Press, 1979); Antonello Gerbi, *The Dispute of the New World: The History of a Polemic, 1750-1900*, revised and enlarged edition translated by Jeremy Moyle (Pittsburgh: University of Pittsburgh Press, 1973); John Ferguson, *Utopias of the Classical World* (Ithaca, N.Y.: Cornell University Press, 1975); Harry Levin, *The Myth of the Golden Age in the Renaissance* (Bloomington and London: Indiana University Press, 1969); J. C. Davis, *Utopia and the Ideal Society: A Study of English Utopian Writing, 1516-1700* (Cambridge: Cambridge University Press, 1981); Krishan Kumar, *Utopian and Anti-Utopia in Modern Times* (Oxford and New York: Basil Blackwell, 1987); Kenneth M. Roemer, *The Obsolete Necessity: America in Utopian Writings, 1888-1900* (Kent, Ohio: Kent State University Press, 1976); Jeffrey Knapp, *An Empire Nowhere: England, America, and Literature from "Utopia" to "The Tempest"* (Berkeley, Los Angeles, and London: University of California Press, 1992); Krishan Kumar and Stephen Bann, eds., *Utopias and the Millennium* (London: Reaktion, 1993).

47. Recall here our discussion in chap. 1, 72-79.

48. Manuel and Manuel, 1.

49. Manuel and Manuel, 16-17.

50. George Orwell, "Arthur Koestler," in *The Collected Essays, Journalism and Letters of George Orwell*, ed. Sonia Orwell and Ian Angus, 4 vols. (Harmondsworth: Penguin Books, 1970), 3:274; cited by Kumar, 2.

There is an inherent tension in utopian thought, also as it came to explicit Christian expression in millenarian terms:[51] How can the heavenly ideal ever become earthly reality without sacrificing its social and politically critical role as a transcendent goal and norm? "The conception of a heaven on earth that underlies Western utopian thought presupposes an idea of perfection in another sphere and at the same time a measure of confidence in human capacity to fashion on earth what is recognized as a transient mortal state into a simulacrum of the transcendental."[52] Economist Francis Fukuyama recently stated this more crisply in terms of the fundamental problem of all utopian thought and expression: "We cannot picture to ourselves a world that is *essentially* different from the present one, and at the same time better."[53] The desire for a better world thus can never be fully satisfied and cannot be satisfied by imaginative, literary creations alone. The impulse inevitably drives the hopeful utopian to go on pilgrimages to seek examples of newer, better worlds — worlds that inevitably disappoint.[54] It would therefore be reasonable to expect that the discovery of the "new world" would inspire further utopian literature. It did.[55]

New World Mythologies

In many respects America was a myth waiting to be born. "Before America could be discovered, it had to be imagined. Columbus knew what he hoped to

---

51. On the important millenarian developments in the Middle Ages, see Norman Cohn, *The Pursuit of the Millennium: Revolutionary Millenarians and Mystical Anarchists of the Middle Ages,* rev. ed. (New York: Oxford University Press, 1970); also see his *Cosmos, Chaos, and the World to Come: The Ancient Roots of Apocalyptic Faith* (New Haven and London: Yale University Press, 1993); B. McGinn, *Apocalypticism in the Western Tradition* (Brookefield, Vt.: Variorum/Ashgate, 1994); on the important medieval figure Joachim of Fiore, see Marjorie Reeves, *The Influence of Prophecy in the Later Middle Ages: A Study in Joachimism* (Notre Dame, Ind.: University of Notre Dame Press, 1993); Marjorie Reeves, *Joachim of Fiore and the Prophetic Future* (London: SPCK, 1976).

52. Manuel and Manuel, 17.

53. Francis Fukuyama, *The End of History and the Last Man* (New York: Free Press, 1992), 46.

54. For a stirring autobiographical testimony of one pilgrim's disillusion with the long-standing love affair between alienated, leftist American intellectuals and twentieth-century communist experiments in political utopianism, see David Horowitz, *Radical Son: A Journey through Our Times* (New York: Free Press, 1997); an earlier classic in this genre is Richard Crossman, ed., *The God That Failed* (New York: Harper, 1949).

55. In the literature cited in n. 46 above, see especially Knapp, *An Empire Nowhere,* and Davis, *Utopia and the Ideal Society.*

find before he left Europe. Geographically, America was imagined in advance of its discovery as an arboreal paradise, Europe's dream of verdurous luxury."[56] Where did this new world dream come from? Storytellers of the ancient Greek and Roman world had written of a primordial golden age where people — described as δαίμονες ἁγνοι (pure spirits) by Hesiod — "lived like gods without sorrow of heart, remote and free from toil and grief."[57] Few have matched Ovid's eloquence in describing this first age of humanity:

> First flowered the age of gold, which while it knew
> No judge nor law, was freely just and true.
> No penalties were fixed; no threats appeared
> Graven on bronze to make stern edicts feared;
> No judge's words dismayed the suppliant throng;
> Without protectors all were safe from wrong;
> None lusted then for travel: no tall tree,
> Felled on its native hills, then sailed the sea;
> No breakneck trenches ringed the cities round;
> No trumpet straight, no twisted horn gave sound;
> No swords were forged, no soldier plied his trade;
> Men lived at peace, carefree and unafraid;
> Unscarred by plows, and by no contract tied,
> Earth, of her bounty, every need supplied;
> Content with nature's gifts, men plucked the fruit
> Of mountain strawberry and wild arbute;
> Cornels for them and prickly brambles bred.
> For them from Jove's broad tree were acorns shed;
> Spring was eternal, earth a garden blessed
> With blooms unsown, which temperate winds caressed;
> In fields untilled the bursting ears were seen,
> And yellowing harvests where no plows had been;
> And streams of milk and nectar flowing free;
> And gold in green, the honey in the tree.[58]

Wearied by continuing civil strife, the Roman poet Horace "prophesied" a "happy escape" across the ocean to distant shores set apart by Jupiter for the "righteous"

56. Peter Conrad, *Imagining America* (New York: Oxford University Press, 1980), 3.

57. Hesiod, "Works and Days," ll. 111-13, in *The Homeric Hymns and Homerica,* Greek text with English translation by H. G. Evelyn-White (Cambridge: Harvard University Press, 1914), 11.

58. *The Metamorphoses of Ovid,* trans. A. E. Watts (Berkeley and Los Angeles: University of California Press, 1954), 4 (bk. 1, ll. 102-28).

(pius) from the time of the golden age, those "Happy Fields" and "Islands of the Blest" where "every year the land, unploughed, yields corn, and ever blooms the vine unpruned, and buds the shoot of the never-failing olive."[59]

Sixty years after Columbus "discovered" the West Indies for Europeans, Francisco López de Gómara described it as "the greatest event since the creation of the world, excepting the Incarnation and Death of Him who created it."[60] Hugh Honour writes that, by the time of his third voyage, Columbus "had begun to view his discoveries apocalyptically — as offering the possibility of converting all the races of the world, of global Christianity. . . . And it was in a strain of Messianic, almost mystical exaltation that he identified the Orinoco with one of the four rivers which went out of the Garden of Eden, perhaps the Pison, 'which compasseth the whole land of Havilah, where there is gold; and the gold of that land is good: there is bedellium and the onyx stone.'" However, readers of Columbus's account of his journey would have been reminded "not . . . of the Biblical so much as the classical landscape," where "mixed woods, a varied terrain, spontaneous fertility and bird-song, are the essential elements in the ideal poetic landscape from Homer onward."[61] "This classical vision of the Indies was given its definitive form by Peter Martyr, an Italian humanist at the court of Ferdinand and Isabella and a friend of Columbus, in his *Decades de Orbe Novo* . . . (1515). Their inhabitants, he wrote, 'seem to live in that golden world of which old writers speak so much, wherein men lived simply and innocently without enforcement of laws, without quarelling, judges and libels, content only to satisfy nature.' He pictured naked girls dancing 'all so beautiful that one might think he beheld those splendid naiads or nymphs of the fountains, so much celebrated by the ancients.'"[62] Thus began the European fascination with the American "noble savage," a term British poet John Dryden first used for the primitive inhabitants of Europe:

> I am as free as nature first made man,
> Ere the base laws of servitude began,
> When wild in woods the noble savage ran.[63]

---

59. Horace, *The Odes and Epodes*, trans. C. E. Bennett (Cambridge: Harvard University Press, 1934), epode XVI.

60. "López de Gómara's famous remark appeared in the dedication to Charles V of his *Historia de las Indias*, Saragossa, 1552" (Honour, *The New Golden Land*, 272). The sentence is quoted on p. 3 of *The New Golden Land*.

61. Honour, *The New Golden Land*, 5.

62. Honour, *The New Golden Land*, 6.

63. Dryden used the term in his play of 1670, *The Conquest of Granada;* cited by Honour, *The New Golden Land*, 118.

However attractive this vision of the American noble savage was to Europeans of Columbus's and later eras, the realities of native life — including human sacrifice and cannibalism — gave rise to visual and literary images quite the opposite. Columbus's Portuguese contemporary Amerigo Vespucci first published his *Mundus Novus* in 1503 and saw it "translated into five modern languages, and reissued in some thirty editions before 1515, in England, Italy, Germany, the Netherlands, and Portugal."[64] Vespucci's "emphatic, explicit, and salacious" description of uninhibited native American customs and manners included, among other things, gruesome depiction of widespread cannibalism, thus contributing to if not originating the *other* tradition of European reflection on America, the savage as brute beast. Perhaps the most forceful description of this tradition is Thomas Hobbes's portrait of the "'natural condition' of uncivilized mankind as of perpetual war, 'of everyone against everyone,'" in his *Leviathan:* "In such condition, there is no place for industry; because the fruit thereof is uncertain: and consequently no Culture of the Earth; no Navigation, nor use of commodities that may be imported by sea; no commodious buildings; no instruments of moving, and removing things as require much force; no knowledge of the face of the earth; no account of time; no arts; no letters; no society; and which is worst of all, continual fears, and danger of violent death; And the life of man, solitary, poore, nasty, brutish, and short."[65]

The use by Europeans of these conflicting views of the native Americans — noble savage or brute — demonstrates how the portrait "of Americans as a primitive people and the identification of America as the land of the future was more a reflection of the tensions in the life of European culture than objective observation of the New World on the other side of the ocean."[66] "Time and again [the Indians] were dragged into court to give evidence in theological, philosophical, and political disputes, few of which had any direct reference to them. They were cited simply because they were generally believed to preserve intact the most primitive state of human society. As Locke put it: 'In the Beginning all the World was *America.*'"[67] The French *libertin* Louis-Armand de Lahontan published a work in 1703, *Lettres, Voyages, et Dialogues avec un sauvage,* that borrowed heavily from the *Jesuit Relations* and "purports to record his conversations with a Huron chief named Adario."[68] Lahontan's image of the Hurons is the exact counterpoint of his views about his fellow French citizens: "Ils sont libres et nous sommes esclaves." The Huron sage appropriately voices

64. Honour, *The New Golden Land,* 8.
65. Cited by Honour, *The New Golden Land,* 118.
66. Van Berkel, 12.
67. Honour, *The New Golden Land,* 119.
68. Honour, *The New Golden Land,* 122; cf. Van Berkel, 13.

views that are clearly subversive of *French* authority; "the natural freedom enjoyed by the Indians sharply contrasts with the voluntary servitude of Frenchmen to their King, to the laws of the land and the dogmas of the church."[69] Not only does the Indian society treat everyone as equal, with the "poor man [having] right to the superfluity of the rich" sans coercion, but Adario prophesies that in France "at some future date the masses would rise to restore the rights of the nation, destroy the property of individuals, make an equal and just distribution of wealth, in a word establish a form of government so equitable and humane that all members of society would participate in it, each deriving his fortune from the common happiness."[70] Not only was America, in Locke's words, the laboratory for seeing "the beginning," it was also regarded by some as the wave of the egalitarian future. From Lahontan's Adario it was a short step to Rousseau's influential Second Discourse, *On the Origin and the Foundations of Inequality among Men.*[71]

This vision of America, of course, was little more than an extension of Europe and its political conflicts and ideals. Europeans "tended to see in America an idealized or distorted image of their own countries, onto which they could project their own aspirations and fears, their self-confidence and sometimes their guilty despair."[72] The Revolutionary War exemplifies this view that America was an extension of Europe's conflicts, fears, and hopes; Europeans tended to portray it as a struggle between France and Britain. In addition, "some Europeans seem to have read in the Revolution omens for the future of their own countries. A very popular 1778 print, *The Tea Tax Tempest*, likened the colonists' struggle for political independence to that of the Swiss in the thirteenth century and the Dutch in the sixteenth."[73] That same year, Anne Turgot,

69. Van Berkel, 13.

70. Honour, *The New Golden Land*, 122.

71. Van Berkel, 14; cf. Jean-Jacques Rousseau, *The First and Second Discourses Together with the Replies to Critics and Essay on the Origin of Languages*, trans. and ed. Victor Gourevitch (New York: Harper Torchbooks, 1990).

72. Van Berkel, 3.

73. Honour, *European Vision of America*, 9. Honour's commentary alongside the reproduction of the print (#202) reads as follows:

> This famous engraving is an adaptation, in reverse, of a satirical print of 1774 by John Dixon entitled *The Oracle, Representing, Britannia, Hibernia, Scotia, as assembled to consult the Oracle, on the present situation of Public Affairs, Time acting as Priest. Dedicated to Concord.* This expressed the interest in America aroused by news of the Boston Tea Party, which reached England in the *London Evening Post* on January 1774. In the print exhibited, Time, with a magic lantern, shows upon a curtain an allegorical representation of the revolution in America and points this out to four female figures representing the four continents. Eu-

Louis XVI's onetime finance minister, expressed the following wish about America's future: "It is impossible not to hope that this people may attain the prosperity of which they are susceptible. They are the hope of the human race; they may well become its model."[74]

However, as the European settlement of North America increased, the mythical idealization of the Indian "noble savage" declined, eventually displaced by a romantic portrait of European heroes. "Over a period of time, the positive qualities first attributed to the Indians were transferred to white Americans."[75] Though American colonists in the first half of the eighteenth century were portrayed "not unnaturally, just as if they were English country gentlemen, from 1776 onwards . . . there was a growing awareness that the citizen of the United States was different — in Crèvecoeur's famous phrase, 'a new man, who acts upon new principles.'"[76] In the forefront here was "le bon Quaker," celebrated by the French *philosophe* Voltaire "as a kind of noble savage of Christianity."[77] In one of the great iconographic ironies of the eighteenth century, it was Benjamin Franklin who, "with his battered fur hat, long white hair, home-

rope, Asia, and Africa, replace Britannia, Hibernia, and Scotia in Dixon's print. The American Revolution is represented by a tea-pot (like a coffee-pot) over a fire in which stamped documents are blazing. In early impressings, as in that exhibited, a cock, the emblem of France, is blowing at the bellows, but this was removed in later impressions. The contents of the tea-pot are exploding, and a serpent (as used on one of the two American flags at the beginning of the war) and the cap of liberty on its staff are being shot from it into the air — the consequence of the Stamp Act and the tax on tea. Beneath the clouds of smoke a prostrate lion is partly visible, and below lies a flag with three leopards representing the British royal standard, torn, its staff broken. On the left three beasts of prey — a lion, a bear, and a puma or lioness — are fighting. Within the circle, on the right, American soldiers are advancing with a striped flag; before them comes an allegorical figure of America, her upstretched hand about to grasp the cap and staff of liberty from the exploding tea-pot. Behind her is a mounted officer, followed by soldiers with fixed bayonets. On the left British soldiers are fleeing in disorder.

The example of Holland and Switzerland in their contest with tyrants is alluded to, as emblematic of the revolt of the colonies against England, in two medallions in the lower margin. One is inscribed *Auto de fe* and *Holland 1560,* the other *Wilhelm Tell, Switzerland. 1296.*

74. Cited by Honour, *European Vision of America,* 9.

75. Van Berkel, 14.

76. Honour, *European Vision of America,* 9; the reference is of course to the French immigrant farmer Hector St. John de Crèvecoeur, *Letters from an American Farmer,* first published in 1782.

77. Honour, *The New Golden Land,* 142; Van Berkel, 9.

Fig. 3.1. *The Tea Tax Tempest,* by Carl Gutenberg

spun coat, and sparkling white linen, . . . [looking] the very image of 'le bon Quaker,'" became the mythical personification of this new American. In a famous epigram of A. Turgot, captured in Jean Honoré of Fragonard's drawing, Franklin is described as one who "snatched the lightning from heaven and the sceptre from tyranny."[78]

78. Honour, *The New Golden Land,* 149; cf. Honour, *European Vision of America,* #206, where the announcement of the print in the *Journal de Paris* on November 15, 1778, reads as follows:

> *New print, dedicated to the Genius of Franklin.* The ingenious author of this composition, M. Fragonard, Painter to the King, has sought to depict the Latin verse applied to *Franklin, Eripuit coelo fulmen sceptrumque tyrannis,* which one reads at the base of the print.
>
> > Inspired by this verse, which summarizes the spirit and profound understanding of Franklin and his wisdom in the New World revolution, the painter has represented him at once turning aside the lightning with Minerva's shield, as his lightning rods have done, and with the other commanding Mars to attack Avarice and Tyranny; while America, nobly attendant on him and holding a fasces, symbol of

153

Fig. 3.2. Giovanni Battista Nini's *Benjamin Franklin,* 1777

As we now go on to consider three nineteenth-century European pilgrims to the shrine of liberty-in-action, we need to remember that their expectations, concerns, and motivations for writing must be understood in the light of a long

the united provinces, calmly watches the overthrow of her enemies. The drawing depicted in Fig. 3.3 makes use of an alternative version of Turgot's epigram: "Now Lightning seized from heaven, soon the sceptre from tyranny."

Le Docteur Francklin Couronné par la Liberté.

Jam Coelo fulmen rapuit, mox Sceptra Tyrannis.

Fig. 3.3. Jean Honoré of Fragonard's drawing of Benjamin Franklin

tradition of travel and travel literature that definitively shaped the European vision of America. "As a father recognizes both his own past and future in his son,
so Europe was able to see her own past as well as her future in her transatlantic

155

daughter. It is precisely by means of this double perspective that America was able to function again and again as the perfect screen on which could be projected the discussions about European culture."[79]

Pilgrims to Liberty's Shrine

It is clear that Abraham Kuyper thought of himself as a pilgrim to a new and exciting experiment in liberty, the wave of the future. He begins his first Stone Lecture by describing himself as "a traveller from the old European Continent," overwhelmed by having arrived "on the shore of this New World." The contrast felt by such a pilgrim is that between "the eddying waters of your new stream of life" and the "almost frostbound and dull" old stream. The newly arrived pilgrim begins to realize "how so many divine potencies, which were hidden away in the bosom of mankind from our very creation, but which our old world was incapable of developing, are now beginning to disclose their inward splendour, thus developing a still richer store of surprises for the future."[80]

But thinking of Kuyper as a pilgrim is not restricted to his 1898 visit to America. One Kuyper scholar, J. Stellingwerf, has recently suggested, not unreasonably, that he in fact had what could be called a pilgrim temperament or character. He links this to the influence of nineteenth-century romanticism on Kuyper. "The Romantic," he notes, "is characterized above all by escapism from hard reality. Thus one can discern romantic aspects in the flight toward drugs, in its accompanying music, in eroticism, in foreign travel, and in exotic, mysterious religions." With respect to Kuyper, "what we encounter repeatedly are escape in illness, trips to the mountains, to the great city, as well as fantasy by which historical reality is suppressed." The other important typically romantic trait, according to Stellingwerf, is escape to the past. "Catholic longing was directed to the time of an undivided church (neo-gothic) or the triumphant church (neo-baroque). In Kuyper, longing was directed to the Golden Age of Calvin, and he shared the romantic vision of many Netherlanders who romanticized the seventeenth century."[81]

Whatever one might conclude about Kuyper's romanticism more broadly[82] — and Kuyper's vision should not simply be identified with the

79. Van Berkel, 25.

80. Kuyper, *Lectures on Calvinism*, 9.

81. Stellingwerf, 253.

82. In addition to the chapter in Stellingwerf's volume, just cited, also see Edward E. Ericson, Jr., "Abraham Kuyper: Cultural Critic," *Calvin Theological Journal* 22 (1987): 210-

"idyllic imagination" we considered in our first chapter[83] — the opening passage of the Stone Lectures, cited in the first paragraph of this section, warrants the judgment that, in addition to the organic metaphor favored by the romantics, Kuyper had what could possibly be called a romantic or at least an idealized view of America, including its glorious future. America was the home of liberty in a way that Europe had not yet achieved. "America," said Kuyper, "lacks no single liberty for which in Europe we struggle." He then let his enthusiasm run full rein:

> In America there is absolute liberty of conscience; liberty of trade and commerce; free participation by the citizens in all matters of public interest; a government which is responsible in all things; a small army; few onerous taxes; liberty of organization; liberty of the press; liberty of public worship; liberty of thought. The administration of justice is quick and cheap. No such thing as a privileged class is known. There is common equality before the law without reservation. In America modern liberties flourish without limitation.[84]

Kuyper's panegyric is only mildly muted by his accompanying complaint about "too much liberty" as well as the "Yankee spirit in the seaport towns and among the money kings." But even here, he notes, the fact that America "is still very young," has "had to receive within itself the degraded elements of other climes," and has a "vast extent of territory" which exposes it "to a degeneration of its national character"[85] should lead one to be forgiving of these excesses.

These observations of Kuyper are not singular; similar comments and lists of liberties can be found in Tocqueville and Acton. Where Kuyper does stand out, at least in terms of both the degree and intensity of his passion, is in his insistence that American liberty is the fruit of Calvinism, even particularly

---

27; and a response to Ericson, James D. Bratt, "In the Shadow of Mt. Kuyper: A Survey of the Field," *Calvin Theological Journal* 31 (1996): 55-57.

83. See 72-80 above. The key difference is Kuyper's insistence on concrete, historical manifestations of politically or constitutionally guaranteed liberty. How clearly different his view was from that of a Marxist-inspired liberationist imagination will be considered in chap. 6.

84. Kuyper, "Calvinism: The Origin and Safeguard of Our Constitutional Liberties," 391. The Dutch essay was published in 1874.

85. Kuyper, "Calvinism: The Origin and Safeguard of Our Constitutional Liberties," 391. It is fascinating to note that many of the same judgments that Kuyper and others made about nineteenth-century America — the reality of both liberty and license — were made by seventeenth-century visitors to the Netherlands: see Jonathan Israel, *The Dutch Republic: Its Rise, Greatness, and Fall, 1477-1806* (Oxford: Clarendon, 1995), chap. 28, "Freedom and Order," 677-99.

Dutch Calvinism.[86] "As a political name," he contends, "Calvinism indicates that political movement which has guaranteed the liberty of nations in constitutional statesmanship; first in Holland, then in England, and since the close of the last century in the United States."[87] Kuyper appeals to "authorities" who "acknowledge that Calvinism has liberated Switzerland, the Netherlands, and England, and in the Pilgrim Fathers has provided the impulse to the prosperity of the United States."[88] Since, in Kuyper's judgment, "the sun of freedom over

86. Acton takes direct issue with the alleged role of Calvinist Puritanism in shaping the Revolution: "If Calvin prompted the Revolution, it was after he had suffered from contact with Tom Paine; and we must make room for other influences which, in that generation, swayed the world from the rising to the setting sun" (*Selected Writings of Lord Acton,* 1:403). Tocqueville, though he sees the Puritans as the crucial shapers of the American character, lauds the reformer Martin Luther and fails "to recognize the importance of Calvinism in shaping Puritan belief and practice" (Sanford Kessler, "Tocqueville's Puritans: Christianity and the American Founding," *Journal of Politics* 54, no. 3 [1992]: 790). Acton, particularly earlier in his career, had a much more jaundiced view of Luther and his nonlove for liberty: "The notion of liberty, whether civil or religious, was hateful to his despotic nature, and contrary to his interpretation of Scripture" ("The Protestant Theory of Persecution," in *Selected Writings of Lord Acton,* vol. 2, *Essays in the Study and Writing of History,* ed. J. Rufus Fears [Indianapolis: Liberty Fund, 1986], 103). Acton's lectures given at Cambridge, after his appointment as Regius Professor of Modern History in 1895, remain critical of Luther's political conservatism but are also more nuanced and appreciative. See J. E. E. Dalberg-Acton, "Luther," in *Lectures on Modern History,* ed. John Neville Figgis and Reginald Vere Laurence (London: Macmillan, 1952), 90-107. The change in Acton's historiography is highlighted by Norma Marshall, "Lord Acton and the Writing of Religious History," *Journal of Religious History* 10 (1979): 400-415. For a careful historical assessment of the role of American Dutch Reformed clergy in the War of Independence, see James Tanis, "The Dutch Reformed Clergy and the American Revolution," in *Wegen en Gestalten in het Gereformeerd Protestantisme,* ed. W. Balke, C. Graafland, and H. Harkema (Amsterdam: Ton Bolland, 1976), 235-56. The Dutch Reformed of the Middle Colonies were already divided along ecclesiological lines between supporters of the experimental, pietist Calvinism of Theodore Frelinghuysen and his followers *(coetus)* and ecclesiastical traditionalists *(conferentie).* "With the outbreak of the Revolution . . . those committed to experimental religion were numbered among the Whigs; those embracing orderly traditionalism were found among the Tories" (237). For the patriot Whigs, "the Dutch tradition of political and religious struggle [against Spain] was a constantly invigorating factor" (239). Tanis concludes: "Fortunately, for the cause of independence, the preponderance of the Reformed clergy, supported by faithful laymen, were to be found among the Whigs. The Calvinist traditions of individual sacrifice and personal liberty were a major factor in holding the Middle Colonies in the Revolutionary camp and preserving there a bulwark against the British drive to divide the colonies" (255).

87. Kuyper, *Lectures on Calvinism,* 14.

88. Kuyper, *Lectures on Calvinism,* 14-15; Kuyper cites here Conrad Busken Huet,

America first rose over the low countries of the Old Netherlands," he notes with appreciation that the descendants of early Dutch-American immigrants who travel to Europe include the Netherlands on their itinerary. This reverse pilgrimage has as its high point a visit to the Delft harbor, departure point of the Pilgrim Fathers on the *Mayflower*. According to Kuyper, for such visitors Delft is a "sort of Mecca, sanctified by holy tradition."[89]

The superiority of the American project in ordered liberty as well as the uniqueness of America's achievement had been noted earlier in the century by Tocqueville[90] as well as Acton.[91] Both men also emphasized its fragility.[92] Nonetheless, it is important to note key differences in the *context* of the three men's assessment of America. Tocqueville's *Democracy in America* was written only a half-century after America's constitutional settlement, within one generation of the Second Great Awakening — "the most influential revival of Christianity in the history of the United States"[93] — and during the expansionist period of Jacksonian populism. His impressions thus come from what is generally regarded in most respects as the apex of America's dynamic antebellum history.[94] Though he acknowledges that the social habit of Christian moral practice could lead to abundance of hypocrisy, he judges that "nonetheless, America

Het Land van Rembrandt, 2nd ed., 2 vols. (Haarlem: H. D. Tjeenk Willink, 1886), and includes Dutch historians R. Fruin and R. C. Bakhuysen Van Den Brink as well as Americans such as George Bancroft as allies in this claim; cf. Abraham Kuyper, *Varia Americana* (Amsterdam and Pretoria: Höveker & Wormser, n.d.), 61-65, where Kuyper emphasizes the importance of the sixteenth-century Dutch revolt against Spain as the inspirational fountain of modern and American political liberty. For a helpful, balanced treatment of Kuyper's historiography with respect to America, see Bratt, "Abraham Kuyper, American History, and the Tensions of Neo-Calvinism."

89. Kuyper, *Varia Americana*, 63-64. Kuyper does not make the claims about the Dutch factor on his own authority but appeals to such historians as Motley, Campbell, Prescott, and Griffis. For more on the general American late nineteenth-century phenomenon of "Holland mania," see the last section of this chapter, 180-86.

90. Tocqueville, 18, 30, 39, 43, 112-72.

91. See, *inter alia*, John Emerich Edward Dalberg-Acton, "The Civil War in America," in *Selected Writings of Lord Acton*, 1:263-79. Also in *Historical Essays and Studies*, ed. John Neville Figgis and Reginald Vere Laurence (London: Macmillan, 1907), 123-42.

92. See particularly Joshua Mitchell, *The Fragility of Freedom: Tocqueville on Religion, Democracy, and the American Future* (Chicago and London: University of Chicago Press, 1995).

93. Mark A. Noll, *A History of Christianity in the United States and Canada* (Grand Rapids: Eerdmans, 1992), 166.

94. See, e.g., Sidney E. Mead, "When 'Wise Men Hoped': An Examination of the Mind and Spirit of the National Period," in *The Lively Experiment: The Shaping of Christianity in America* (New York, Evanston, and London: Harper & Row, 1963), 90-102.

is still the place where the Christian religion has kept the greatest real power over men's souls; and nothing better demonstrates how useful and natural it is to man, since the country where it now has the widest sway is both the most enlightened and the freest."[95]

What was remarkable about this high level of religious activity, as Tocqueville saw it, was the support the Christian religion provided for liberty. He recalls that the secularizing *philosophes* of the Enlightenment had predicted the inevitable waning of religion. "Religious zeal, they said, was bound to die down as enlightenment and freedom spread." It was precisely this dogma that Tocqueville's American experience contradicted. "The first thing that struck me on arrival in the United States," he says, was "the religious atmosphere of the country. . . . In France, I had seen the spirits of religion and of freedom almost always marching in opposite directions. In America I found them intimately linked together in joint reign over the land."[96] From this Tocqueville concluded that "for Americans the ideas of Christianity and liberty are so completely mingled that it is almost impossible to get them to conceive of the one without the other."[97] Careful examination of this American conviction led him to a more general principle of human affairs. All who "sincerely wish to prepare mankind for liberty" should encourage religious faith among citizens; when instead they "attack religious belief, they obey the dictates of their passions, not their interests. Despotism may be able to do without faith, but freedom cannot. Religion is much more needed in the republic they advocate than in the monarchy they attack, and in democratic republics most of all. How could society escape destruction if, when political ties are relaxed, moral ties are not tightened? And what can be done with a people master of itself if it is not subject to God?"[98]

Apart from his additional, insistent specific reference to Calvinism,[99] Kuyper almost seems to be quoting Tocqueville when he draws the contrast between the European and American approach to liberty: "If with us it has every appearance that the liberty of the people must be purchased at the sacrifice of

95. Tocqueville, 291; this quote is better known in the version of Henry Reeves's translation: "There is no country in the world where the Christian religion retains a greater influence over the souls of men than in America" (New York: Alfred A. Knopf, 1941).

96. Tocqueville, 295.

97. Tocqueville, 293.

98. Tocqueville, 294.

99. Tocqueville's few oblique references to the Calvinist tradition are limited to comments about the Puritans; for a more substantive debate about this issue, see the section later in this chapter, "Tocqueville, Kuyper, and Acton on the Religious Roots of American Liberty."

the faith, there it is Calvinism which, according to the general conviction, offers the surest safeguards for the continued possession of those liberties." Separation of church and state in America, Kuyper concludes, does not come "from the desire to be released from church duties; on the contrary, it starts from the consciousness that the welfare of the church and the progress of Christianity demand this freedom and independence." Christianity's influence in America is potent. "Of the freest country in the world it is asserted by the man who knew it well, 'that the domestic morals there are much stricter than in Europe, and that Christianity reigns without opposition and is the common heritage of all.'"[100]

Liberty's Trial: Lord Acton on the American Civil War

As each of our three pilgrims experienced America in the nineteenth century, to what extent did the experiment in liberty actually measure up to its own ideal? It is here that Lord Acton's observations are the most important for our purposes, because he alone addresses the serious crisis brought about by the Civil War; Tocqueville, of course, could not and Kuyper did not.[101] Acton, however, in an 1866 address, did so directly.[102] Prior to the Civil War, he observes, "the United States had become an object of anxiety or of envy to many, of wonder and curiosity to all mankind" (263). Unlike many other British travelers to America — Frances Trollope and Charles Dickens are good examples — Acton does not snobbishly look down on American cultural accomplishments. "In literature at least," he says, "I entirely dissent from the opinion which denies to Americans an honourable place beside European nations." Though languishing in certain arts such as poetry and painting, Americans are equals to Europeans "in political eloquence and philosophy," and "they surpass us as writers on the

100. Kuyper, "Calvinism: The Origin and Safeguard of Our Constitutional Liberties," 396-97; the quotation is not documented, though since the original Dutch version cites the concluding clause in French, it is likely from Tocqueville. Kuyper cites Toqueville directly eight times in this essay.

101. Though Kuyper did briefly and sympathetically address the sad economic lot of former slaves in America (*Varia Americana*, 9-11), ironically (and even tragically, one might add) his emancipatory sympathies, even in his reflections on the American visit, came to expression in concerns about the Dutch in America and especially in South Africa. For further and more detailed discussion on Kuyper's emancipatory tendencies, see chap. 6 of this volume and the literature cited there.

102. John Emerich Edward Dalberg-Acton, "The Civil War in America: Its Place in History," a lecture to the Literary and Scientific Institution, Bridgnorth, on January 18, 1866, in *Selected Writings of Lord Acton*, 1:263-79; page references which follow in the text are to this essay, which is also found in Acton, *Historical Essays and Studies*, 123-42.

history of the continent and on the art of government" (264). The great American accomplishment is political: "In practical politics they had solved with astonishing and unexampled success two problems which had hitherto baffled the capacity of the most enlightened nations: they had contrived a system of federal government which prodigiously increased the national power and yet respected local liberties and authorities; and they had founded it on the principle of equality, without surrendering the securities for property and freedom" (264). It is this balance of ordered liberty, of equality with security, that, according to Acton, "is necessarily an impressive lesson to England. Our institutions as well as our national character spring from the same roots, and the fortunes they encounter must serve as a beacon to guide us or as a warning to repel" (264-65).

Up to the time of the Civil War, in Acton's judgment, America's example overwhelmingly disproved the prevailing political dogma, reflecting "the verdict of history," namely, "that complete equality is the ruin of liberty, and very prejudicial to the most valued interests of society, civilization, and religion" (265). Thanks to her actual achievement of ordered liberty, America was justifiably the hope of the millions who crossed the ocean as well as additional millions "whose hearts and hopes are in the United States, to whom the rising sun is in the West, and whose movements are controlled by the distant magnet, though it has not drawn them away" (266). But in 1866, this is no longer true. "The time has come," says Acton, "for all men to perceive that these judgments were premature. Five years have wrought so vast a change, that the picture which I have faithfully given of the United States as I found them under President Pierce[103] could not be realized in the awful realities of the present day. . . . The Union which was founded and sustained by the attachment of the people has been restored by force, and the Constitution which was the idol of Americans is obeyed by millions of humbled and indignant men, whose families it has decimated, whose property it has ravaged, and whose prospects it has ruined for ever" (266-67).

The legacy of the Civil War leads Acton to ask Lincoln's question whether "a nation so conceived can long endure," whether the ideal itself as set forth in the Constitution is not flawed. In particular, the question is whether the will of the majority as the absolute and final law — Tocqueville's "tyranny of the majority"[104] — is at odds with the concern to protect the rights of the minority by established law. Acton cites Alexander Hamilton: "There are certain conjunctures when it may be necessary and proper to disregard the opinions which the

103. See Acton's journal of his 1853 visit, *Acton in America* (see n. 11 above).
104. Tocqueville, 246-76.

majority of the people have formed. There ought to be a principle in government capable of resisting the popular current. The principle chiefly intended to be established is this, that there must be a permanent will" (269). Over against this is the Jeffersonian conviction that there is to be no "perpetual Constitution, nor even a perpetual law," since "the earth belongs always to the living generation." Thus, "every people may establish what form of government they please; the will of the nation being the only thing essential" (269). The tension between these two viewpoints came to a head in the struggle between the North and the South, but, according to Acton, it is rooted in a tension built into the very fabric of the American political structure, a tension that he, like Kuyper[105] and many subsequent commentators, views as a straightforward debate between Thomas Jefferson and Alexander Hamilton:

> But it seems clear to me that if slavery had never existed, a community divided by principles so opposite as those of Jefferson and Hamilton will be distracted by their antagonism until one of them shall prevail; and that a theory that defines liberty with a single right, the right of doing all that you have the actual power to do, and a theory which secures liberty by certain unalterable rights, and founds it on truths which men did not invent and may not abjure, cannot both be formative principles in the same Constitution. Absolute power and restrictions on its exercise cannot exist together. (270)

The "one decisive contrast between Europe and America" that exacerbates the problem is that in America "society is cut adrift from the traditions and influence of an ancient civilisation" (272). In America, "nothing is safe that is not supported by popular favour. The ideas of past generations and of civilised contemporaries are not permitted to share or to limit the absolute authority of the present moment. The revolutionary principle which Jefferson introduced cuts them off from one as completely as the Atlantic separates them from the other." While "history is filled with records of resistance provoked by the abuse of power" and in Europe "the people produce the remedy, in America they produce the cause of the disease. There is no appeal from the people to itself" (134).

Acton's prognosis is not a pleasant one. A "degenerate republicanism terminates in the total loss of freedom," and Acton notes that this has been "prophesied" about America (272). The only protection against the tyranny of a centralized federal state is the division of powers into several states and their legal freedom to join in confederacies with other states. The combination of Acton's constitutional sympathies for the Confederacy along with distaste for

105. See n. 5 above.

slavery leads him to this conclusion: "Slavery was not the cause of secession, but the reason of its failure. In almost every nation and every clime the time has come for the extinction of servitude." Acton notes that it would be possible for a historian to show that "the institution of slavery in general . . . has been a mighty instrument not for evil only, but for good in the providential order of the world. Almighty God, in his mysterious ways, has poured down blessings even through servitude itself, by awakening the spirit of sacrifice on the one hand, and the spirit of charity on the other" (273). Nonetheless, no matter how "the voice of nature and of humanity constantly mitigated the law of the land," the end result was that the full human dignity of the slave was denied because "Southern jurisprudence denied that the negro is bound by the same moral code as ourselves" (273-74). The institution of slavery had to be ended; the slave had to be emancipated. However, in Acton's judgment, the Americans failed to carry out the needed emancipation with proper safeguards against "incurable evils of another kind," namely, moderating "the effects of sudden uncondi-tional change," saving "those whom they despoiled from ruin, and those whom they liberated from destitution." The emancipation of the American slave was "an act of war, not of statesmanship or humanity," in which the slave owner was treated as an "enemy" and "the slave [used] as an instrument for his destruc-tion." In sum, "If, then, slavery is to be the criterion which shall determine the significance of the civil war, our verdict ought, I think, to be, that by one part of the nation it was wickedly defended, and by the other as wickedly removed" (277).

In Acton's judgment, something precious in the human quest for liberty was thus lost and replaced by a "spurious liberty . . . that is twice cursed, for it deceives those whom it attracts and those whom it repels. By exhibiting the spectacle of a people claiming to be free, but whose love of freedom means ha-tred of inequality, jealousy of limitations to power, and reliance on the State as an instrument to mould as well as to control society, it calls on its admirers to hate aristocracy and teaches its adversaries to fear the people. The North has used the doctrines of Democracy to destroy self-government. The South ap-plied the principles of conditional federation to cure the evils and correct the errors of a false interpretation of Democracy" (278). His somber analysis not-withstanding, Acton concluded his lecture with a tribute to General Lee and a judgment about the nobility of the Union victors in "staying the hand of ven-geance, remitting punishment and disbanding armies, and treating as an equal the man who had been so lately and so long the most terrible of enemies, and whose splendid talents had inflicted on the people of the Union a gigantic loss in treasure, blood, and fame." This augurs well for the future of America, he concludes: "It is too soon to despair of a community that has among its leading citizens such as these" (279).

Acton's observations about the Civil War raise a question about the very idea of America, about America as the shrine embodying liberty itself. In particular, dealing as they do with the tragic and painful reality of slavery, they raise questions about the religious character of American institutions and their capacity for nurturing and maintaining liberty for all. Exactly what are the roots of America's experiment in ordered liberty? Are they religious at all; and if so, which religion? It is here that we find interesting and instructive contrasts among our three pilgrims.

Tocqueville, Kuyper, and Acton
on the Religious Roots of American Liberty

We have noted Alexis de Tocqueville's initial surprise about the positive role played by active religious faith in nurturing American ideals and practice of liberty. The dogma of the Enlightenment's secularizing *philosophes* predicted the waning of religious enthusiasm as enlightenment and freedom spread. But Tocqueville's American experience contradicted this dogma, suggesting that, contrary to enlightened intuition, religion and freedom were inseparably linked; one could not be conceived without the other. From this he drew his much-cited maxim: "Despotism may be able to do without faith, but freedom cannot."[106]

But now comes the difficult question: *Which* religion helps a people to be free? Is Tocqueville's dictum true for religion in general, or only for a particular religion such as Christianity? Furthermore, if the answer to the last question is affirmative for Christianity (as it seems to have been for Tocqueville), is it a truism for all brands of Christianity or only for some? Does Catholicism nurture liberty as well as Calvinism, for example? A closer look at the views of our three nineteenth-century pilgrims on this question is illuminating. Kuyper's position

---

106. Tocqueville, 294. At the beginning of the twenty-first century, Tocqueville's principle seems in many ways to have been empirically demonstrated, and a growing body of literature is sounding a supportive chorus (see discussion in chap. 2, 89ff.). Dostoyevsky, so it is now often said, was right when he made a similar claim focusing on the shadow side of the dictum: "If God is dead, everything is permitted" (cf. the discussion in chap. 1, "Beauty Will Save the World," 15-20). Stated more positively, history — particularly our experience of totalitarianism in the twentieth century — appears to have verified that it is practically impossible for a people to be both free and good without God (see chap. 2, n. 32).

we have encountered repeatedly in this volume and needs no elaboration here: "Calvinism is the source and only guarantor of religious, constitutionally granted freedom." Tocqueville's position is different; his treatment of the Christianity needed to sustain ordered liberty assumes a more generic version along the lines of C. S. Lewis's *Mere Christianity* with civil religion overtones.[107] Tocqueville refers to the Puritans when he must discuss the founding of New England, and he does call attention to their escape from oppression and their deliberate efforts to establish a godly and free society, to be a "city on a hill."[108] In terms of America's laws, Tocqueville insists that it is necessary to "make careful distinction between elements of Puritan and elements of English origin."[109] Interestingly, the Puritan influence is responsible for the democratic tendency, and the English influence for the aristocratic and antidemocratic.

But is the Puritan/Calvinist spirit the primary resource for America's passion for freedom and equality? Kuyper, of course, thought so. Among his favorite and most-used quotes was one from American historian George Bancroft: "The fanatic for Calvinism was a fanatic for liberty."[110] Kuyper traced the line of political liberty from a seed planted in Calvin's Geneva through its transplantation in the Calvinist Netherlands and Puritan England to its full flowering in New England. As corroboration of this historical scenario, Kuyper cited Bancroft's assessment that America's "enthusiasm for freedom was born from its enthusiasm for Calvinism." In Kuyper's view, America had been providentially blessed as the world's beacon of liberty, and its commitment to Calvinism was responsible for this. Kuyper's explanation for the linkage is important: the Calvinist emphasis on the sovereignty of God is the ground of all liberty. Neither the popular sovereignty of the French Revolution nor the state sovereignty of *ancien régime* absolute monarchism (or modern socialism!) can fulfill the promise of liberty. Individual persons as well as social institutions such as the family do not derive their legitimacy *mediately* from the state but *immediately* from the sovereign God himself. Political freedom is possible when each citizen's clear and final allegiance is to God. This is the genuine equality that in Kuyper's view led to full liberty of conscience and political freedom.[111] In that context, Kuyper came to a conclusion that is very important for our purposes in this chapter. He also judged that the *hierarchically* ordered polity of Rome,

107. See, e.g., Kessler, *Tocqueville's Civil Religion.*

108. Tocqueville, 38, 39.

109. Tocqueville, 48.

110. Kuyper, *Lectures in Calvinism,* 78; the passage is taken from George Bancroft, *History of the United States of America,* 15th ed. (Boston, 1853), 1:319.

111. For Kuyper's mature statement of this position, see *Lectures on Calvinism,* chap. 3, "Calvinism and Politics."

combined with its insistence on sacerdotal mediation, could not bring about full liberty.[112]

On the basis of his observations concerning religion and liberty in America, Tocqueville came to a slightly different conclusion. He notes that "most of English America was peopled by men who, having shaken off the pope's authority, acknowledged no other religion's supremacy, they therefore brought to the New World a Christianity which I can only describe as democratic and republican; this fact favored the establishment of a temporal republic and democracy. From the start politics and religion agreed, and they have not ceased to do so." He then comments on the mass of Irish Catholic immigration and the significant growth of the American Catholic church. He judges them to be "very loyal in the practice of their worship and full of zeal and ardor for their beliefs." Then comes this unexpected, surprising claim: "Nevertheless, they form the most republican and democratic of all classes in the United States. At first glance this is astonishing, but reflection easily indicates the hidden causes thereof." He thinks that "one is wrong in regarding the Catholic religion as a natural enemy of democracy" because the two-level structure of Catholic religious society (priest and people) is hierarchical: "The priest is raised above the faithful; all below him are equal." Tocqueville (the Roman Catholic!) concludes that "Catholicism is like an absolute monarchy" where "the prince apart, conditions are more equal there than in a republic." This means that "Catholicism may dispose the faithful to obedience, but it does not prepare them for inequality. However, I would say," says Tocqueville, "that Protestantism in general orients men much less toward equality than independence."[113]

Lord Acton shared the conviction that religion was essential to freedom. In his *History of Freedom* he observed that among the ancient Greeks the Stoics "made it known that there is a will superior to the collective will of man, and a law that overrules those of Solon and Lycurgus. Their test of good government is its conformity to principles that can be traced to a higher legislator." The conclusion reached by Stoic philosophy, as Acton describes it, sounds remarkably Christian: "That which we must obey, that to which we are bound to reduce all civil authorities, and to sacrifice every earthly interest, is that immutable law which is perfect and eternal as God Himself, which proceeds from His nature, and reigns over heaven and earth and over all the nations." Even rulers must submit to the "voice of God, who comes down to dwell in our souls," and which, rather than any outward authority, is the only "true guide of our con-

112. See, e.g., his address "Maranatha" in Bratt, *Abraham Kuyper: A Centennial Reader*, 205-28.
113. Tocqueville, 288.

duct." In sum: "True freedom, says the most eloquent of the Stoics, consists in obeying God."[114]

Nonetheless, so contends Acton, in all of classical literature, "three things are wanting — representative government, the emancipation of the slaves, and liberty of conscience." These *had* to wait until the fullness of time brought forth the Christian gospel. Though the "wisest of the Gentiles and Jews" grasped most of the essential truths of society and politics, "there was no power in them to avert the doom of that civilisation for which the blood of so many patriots and the genius of such incomparable writers had been wasted in vain. The liberties of the ancient nations were crushed beneath a hopeless and inevitable despotism, and their vitality was spent, when the new power came forth from Galilee, giving what was wanting to the efficacy of human knowledge to redeem societies as well as men."[115]

What "one essential and inevitable transformation in politics" did the Man from Galilee, the Savior of the world, accomplish? The "great problem which philosophy had raised" but "no statesmanship had been able to solve" was *limited government.* "Those who proclaimed the assistance of a higher authority had indeed drawn a metaphysical barrier before the governments, but they had not known how to make it real."[116] This is what was changed by the Christ: divine limits upon governments and freedom for individual persons. "But when Christ said: 'Render unto Caesar the things that are Caesar's, and unto God the things that are God's,' those words, spoken on His last visit to the Temple, three days before His death, gave to the civil power, under the protection of conscience, a sacredness it had never enjoyed, and bounds it had never acknowledged; and they were the repudiation of absolutism and the inauguration of freedom." What Christ did was not only to provide the necessary ideas for limiting state power, the proper understanding of the state's role, but the *ability* to achieve such limitation:

> For our Lord not only delivered the precept, but created the force to execute it. To maintain the necessary immunity in one supreme sphere, to reduce all political authority within defined limits, ceased to be an aspiration of patient reasoners, and was made the perpetual charge and care of the most energetic institution and the most universal association in the world. The new law, the new spirit, the new authority, gave to liberty a meaning and a value it had not possessed in the philosophy or in the constitutions of Greece or Rome before the knowledge of the truth that makes us free.[117]

114. *Selected Writings of Lord Acton*, 1:23-24.
115. *Selected Writings of Lord Acton*, 1:26.
116. *Selected Writings of Lord Acton*, 1:27.
117. *Selected Writings of Lord Acton*, 1:28.

Though Acton traces the foundational roots of political liberty back to the New Testament itself, the full maturation of its concrete application took some time.

Acton concurs with the general sentiment of Tocqueville and Kuyper alike, namely, with "the idea that religious liberty is the generating principle of civil, and that civil liberty is the necessary condition of religious."[118] Though this specific conviction was, in Acton's judgment, "a discovery reserved for the seventeenth century," he traces the notion of "liberty of conscience" back to Thomas Aquinas rather than, as Kuyper did, to John Calvin. It is here, in assessing the thought and legacy of John Calvin, that we see a significant (and perhaps predictable) divergence between the two champions and historians of liberty, the Calvinist Kuyper and the Catholic Acton. Let us first consider Acton's treatment of Calvin in an essay with the provocative title "The Protestant Theory of Persecution."[119]

Acton's basic premise in this essay is that though Catholic persecution in the Middle Ages was "far more sanguinary than any that has been inflicted by Protestants," the Protestant justification for their persecution was new (114). Catholic persecution was rooted in a concern for maintaining social order; Protestant persecution was *required* by a theology that refused to tolerate religious error. This was a major shift. "By placing the necessity of intolerance on the simple ground of religious error, and in directing it against the Church which they themselves had abandoned, they introduced a purely subjective test, and a purely revolutionary system" (115). Calvin in particular is singled out by Acton as the architect of this dogma of intolerance. Calvin, the refugee from France's absolute monarchy, in Acton's view, disregarded all historical and political considerations and was concerned "only how his doctrine could be realised, whether through the instrumentality of existing authorities, or at their expense. In his eyes its interests were paramount, their promotion the supreme duty, opposition to them an unpardonable crime" (122). Acton concludes with

118. *Selected Writings of Lord Acton*, 1:47.
119. In *Selected Writings of Lord Acton*, 2:98-131; page references that follow in the text are to this work. For the discussion that follows in the next paragraphs on Acton's treatment of Calvin, I am profoundly indebted to Marilynne Robinson's intriguing introductory essay in her collection, *The Death of Adam: Essays on Modern Thought* (Boston and New York: Houghton Mifflin, 1998). The comparison between Acton's and Kuyper's interpretation of liberty's roots in America as well as their respective coverage of the Saint Bartholomew's Day Massacre is original. An abbreviated version of this material appeared in the Acton Institute for the Study of Religion and Liberty publication *Religion and Liberty* 9, no. 1 (1999): 8-10, under the title "Whose Liberty? Which Religion? Acton and Kuyper." New in the treatment of this chapter is the critique of Acton's misquotation of Calvin, the point I learned from my reading of Robinson's essay after the shorter essay had been published.

this brutal summary: "There was nothing in the institutions of men, no authority, no right, no liberty, that he cared to preserve, or towards which he entertained any feelings of reverence or obligation" (122).

Calvin's theory, thus, "made the support of religious truth the end and office of the State, . . . the result of this theory is the institution of a pure theocracy" (122-23). In Acton's view, Calvin subordinated the political ends of the state to the religious. The protection of the Calvinist religion was the magistrate's chief task, and a "good" magistrate is not defined in terms of political ends such as equity and justice but in terms of religious commitment. An incompetent, unjust, oppressive prince, by this reckoning, would be considered a "good" ruler and to be obeyed if he were an orthodox Calvinist; an honest, just prince who was a Catholic would be considered a "bad" ruler who could be legitimately resisted. The following lengthy passage summarizes Acton's viewpoint clearly:

> Calvin was as positive as Luther in asserting the duty of obedience to rulers irrespective of their mode of government. He constantly declared that tyranny was not to be resisted on political grounds; that no civil rights could outweigh the divine sanction of government; except in cases where a special office was appointed for the purpose. Where there was no such office — where, for instance, the estates of the realm had lost their independence — there was no protection. This is one of the most important and essential characteristics of the politics of the reformers. By making the protection of their religion the principal business of government, they put out of sight its more immediate and universal duties, and made the political objects of the State disappear behind its religious end. A government was to be judged, in their eyes, only by its fidelity to the Protestant Church. If it fulfilled those requirements, no other complaints against it could be entertained. A tyrannical prince could not be resisted if he was orthodox; a just prince could be dethroned if he failed in the more essential condition of faith. In this way Protestantism became favourable at once to despotism and to revolution, and was ever ready to sacrifice good government to its own interests. (125)

A brief response to Acton's characterization of Calvin is in order here. Marilynne Robinson chose precisely the passage just cited as an example of the sort of unwarranted claims made by altogether too many historians about Calvin.[120] She observes that the passage in Calvin's *Institutes* (4.20.31) that Acton

---

120. Later in the same essay, as further samples of the same genre, she cites Simon Schama, *The Embarrassment of Riches: An Interpretation of Dutch Culture in the Golden Age* (New York: Knopf, 1987); Roland Bainton's 1935 essay, "Protestant Persecutors"; and Israel, *The Dutch Republic*.

cites in his *all-Latin* footnote as evidence for his contention that *religious* rather than *political* reasons govern the right of resistance, in fact proves no such thing at all. Acton omits the immediately preceding introductory paragraph from this section of the *Institutes*: "But however these deeds of men [that is, the overthrow of Old Testament kings] are judged in themselves, still the Lord accomplished his work through them alike when he broke the bloody scepters of arrogant kings and when he overturned intolerable governments. *Audiant principes, et terreantur!* ('Let the princes hear and be afraid')."[121] Acton's footnote citation also excises crucial phrases from the critical third and final paragraph, which follows in its entirety (with passages omitted by Acton shown in italics):

> I am speaking all the while of private individuals. For if there are now any magistrates of the people, appointed to restrain the willfulness of kings (as in ancient times ephors *were set against Spartan kings or the* tribunes *of the people against the Roman consuls or the* demarchs *against the senate of the Athenians* and perhaps, as things now are, such power as the three estates exercise in every realm where they hold their chief assemblies), I am so far from forbidding them to withstand, in accordance with their duty, the fierce licentiousness of kings, *that, if they wink at kings who violently fall upon and assault the lowly common folk, I declare that their dissimulation involves nefarious perfidy, because they dishonestly betray the freedom of the people of which they know that they have been appointed protectors by God's ordinance.*[122]

Robinson notes that "obviously, there is no mention of institutional religion here at all, and certainly not of the Protestant Church."[123] In fact, rather than justifying persecution (which, at any rate, is not exactly the same as "resistance"), Calvin's reasons "for resistance to tyranny are precisely political — defense of 'the freedom of the people.'" It is also worth noting that rather than ap-

---

121. As Robinson does in her essay, I am using the Battles translation of the *Institutes;* this quote from 21:1518-19.

122. The entire footnote (*Selected Writings of Lord Acton,* 2:125 n. 88) reads as follows: "Hoc nobis si assidue ob animos et oculos obverseture, eodem decreto constitui etiam nequissimos reges, quo regum auctoritas statuitur; nunquam in animum nobis seditiosae illae cogitationes venient, tractandum esse pro meritis regem nec aequum esse, ut subditos ei nos praestemus, qui vicissim regem nobis se non praestet. . . . De privatis hominibus semper loquor. Nam si qui nunc sint populares magistratus ad moderandem reum libidinem constituti (quales olim erant . . . ephori . . . tribuni . . . demarchi: et qua etiam forte potestate, ut nunc res habent, funguntur in singulis regnis tres ordines, quum primarios conventus peragunt) . . . illos ferocienti regum licentiae pro officio intercedere non veto."

123. Robinson, 14.

pealing to Christian or ecclesiastically dominated states, Calvin "finds his chief examples of 'magistrates of the people' in pagan governments."[124] Robinson also calls attention to the "rhetorical strategy of emphasis and irony" that Calvin employs with his use of *non veto* at the conclusion of Acton's citation. "*Veto* is the word the Roman tribune of the people spoke to forbid an action of the Senate which he took to be hostile to the interests of the plebeians." In Calvin's use of *non veto* ("I do not forbid"), he "puts himself in the role of a pagan and entirely political 'magistrate of the people.'"[125] Whatever the reason for Acton's lapse from his usual careful and honest historiography here,[126] we must conclude that Acton has not presented a convincing case against Calvin. (Parenthetically, a careful reading of Calvin's dedicatory preface to King Francis I of France would also have led to a different conclusion than the one Acton came to in this essay.) But we must now turn away from Calvin and consider Calvinism and its role in shaping the American experiment in ordered liberty.

Though Acton shares Kuyper's appreciation for America as "the grandest polity in the history of mankind," he takes a different read on the Calvinist/Puritan roots of the American experiment. In a review of James Bryce's famous nineteenth-century study *The American Commonwealth*,[127] the Catholic historian scoffs at the accepted doctrine that Calvinist Puritanism was the inspiration for the American Revolution: "If Calvin prompted the Revolution, it was after he had suffered from contact with Tom Paine; and we must make room for other influences which, in that generation, swayed the world from the rising to the setting sun."[128] Acton concludes the essay we considered earlier in this chapter, "The Protestant Theory of Persecution," with the following fascinating contrast:

> In the same age the Puritans and the Catholics sought a refuge beyond the Atlantic from the persecution which they suffered together under the Stuarts.

124. Robinson, 15.

125. Robinson, 16.

126. Robinson, 17, suggests that Acton, along with his mentor, Johann von Döllinger, both severe critics of their own church, might have been "predisposed to emphasize their ultimate loyalty by engaging in still more vehement criticism of other churches." Perhaps, but, as we shall see in the following section of this chapter on the Saint Bartholomew's Day Massacre, on this same issue in a different context, Acton's honesty as a historian led him to criticism of the very stance toward which he leaned in the essay we have just considered. There are probably no simple explanations here.

127. James Bryce, *The American Commonwealth,* 3 vols. (London: Macmillan, 1888); reprinted as a two-volume set by Liberty Fund, Indianapolis, 1995. Acton's review was initially published in the *English Historical Review* 4 (1889): 388-96; reprinted in *Selected Writings of Lord Acton,* 1:395-405.

128. *Selected Writings of Lord Acton,* 1:403.

Flying for the same reason, and from the same oppression, they were enabled respectively to carry out their own views in the colonies which they founded in Massachusetts and Maryland, and the history of those two States exhibits faithfully the contrast between the two churches. The Catholic emigrants established, for the first time in modern history, a government in which religion was free, and with it the germ of that religious liberty which now prevails in America. The Puritans, on the other hand, revived with greater severity the penal laws of the mother country.[129]

So now we have rival claims for the title "champion of liberty." Like simultaneous claimants to heavyweight boxing titles, each one has some semblance of legitimacy. But it is also important to acknowledge up front that each ecclesiastical tradition also partakes in a history that casts doubt on the claim. Kuyper realized this was true for the Calvinist tradition when he addressed the problem of church and state in his third Stone Lecture:

[The difficulty] lies in the pile and fagots of Servetus. It lies in the attitude of the Presbyterians toward the Independents. It lies in the restrictions of liberty of worship and in the "civil disabilities" under which for centuries even in the Netherlands the Roman Catholics have suffered. The difficulty lies in the fact that an article of our old Calvinistic Confession of Faith [Belgic Confession, art. 36] entrusts to the government the task "of defending against and of extirpating every form of idolatry and false religion and to protect the sacred service of the Church." The difficulty lies in the unanimous and uniform advice of Calvin and his epigones, who demanded intervention of the government in the matter of religion.

Kuyper adds: "The accusation is therefore a natural one that, by choosing in favor of liberty of religion, we do not pick up the gauntlet for Calvinism, but that we directly oppose it." Kuyper then goes on, somewhat defensively, to allege an historical unfairness in highlighting the execution of Michael Servetus "whilst the Calvinists, in the age of Reformation, yielded their victims, by tens of thousands, to the scaffold and the stake." Kuyper's own judgment, however, is unequivocal: "Notwithstanding all this, I not only deplore that one stake [of Servetus], but I unconditionally disapprove of it."[130]

---

129. *Selected Writings of Lord Acton*, 2:131.
130. Kuyper, *Lectures on Calvinism*, 99, 100.

Kuyper and Acton on the
Saint Bartholomew's Day Massacre (1572)

Kuyper's reference to "tens of thousands" of Calvinist victims brings us naturally to the infamous Saint Bartholomew's Day Massacre of 1572. First, a brief history of events.[131] In the ongoing conflict between the Catholic French court and the Calvinist Protestants in the sixteenth century, an uneasy truce had been achieved largely through the mediation of the Huguenot leader, Admiral Gaspard de Coligny, culminating in the religiously "mixed marriage" of Protestant Henry of Navarre and King Charles IX's sister, Marguerite of Valois, on August 18, 1572. Hundreds of Huguenots had come to Paris to participate in the wedding feast, and with the provocation of the keenly Roman Catholic queen mother, Catherine de Médicis, and the apparent acquiescence of Pope Gregory XIII (1502-85; pope from 1572), Admiral Coligny was assassinated on August 24, precipitating a nationwide orgy of Huguenot slaughter by French mobs lasting into the month of October. Estimates indicate a death toll in the neighborhood of 50,000.

While the events of 1572 are in themselves momentous, the "mythological" characterization and propagandist use of them that followed is even more significant.[132] The assassination of Admiral Coligny and the massacre that ensued became one of the chief cornerstones of Protestant martyrology. Thanks to the availability of the printing press and the exodus of Calvinist refugees from France — primarily through Geneva — the memory of the massacre was kept alive throughout Europe and played a significant role in internationalizing the Reformed faith. As the weight of Protestant martyrological interpretation grew, a response from the Catholic side did also. And that brings us back to Kuyper and Lord Acton, both of whom contemporaneously (Acton in 1869 and Kuyper in 1872) wrote substantive essays on the massacre, focusing on the changing Catholic historiography of the late nineteenth century.[133]

Notwithstanding our focus earlier in this chapter on an Acton historiographical misstep, Lord Acton had a well-deserved reputation as a scru-

---

131. On the massacre see Alfred Soman, ed., *The Massacre of St. Bartholomew: Reappraisals and Documents* (The Hague: Martinus Nijhoff, 1974); Philip Erlanger, *St. Bartholomew's Night: The Massacre of Saint Bartholomew*, trans. Patrick O'Brian (New York: Pantheon Books, 1962).

132. See Robert M. Kingdon, *Myths about the St. Bartholomew's Day Massacres, 1572-76* (Cambridge, Mass., and London: Harvard University Press, 1988).

133. John Emerich Edward Dalberg-Acton, "The Massacre of St. Bartholomew," in *Selected Writings of Lord Acton*, 2:198-240 (originally published in 1869); Abraham Kuyper, *De Bartholemeusnacht* (Amsterdam: H. De Hoogh, 1872).

pulous historian whose passion for detailed documentation and honesty in dealing with sources and evidence occasionally got him into trouble with ecclesiastical authorities.[134] Time and again he refused to fudge the historical record even when it portrayed his own church in a negative light. In his Saint Bartholomew's Day essay Acton painstakingly traces Catholic responses to the massacre from an initial posture of defiance to final outright denial. The defiant response alleged Huguenot crimes in plotting against the French court; the massacre was acknowledged but justified as a legitimate reaction to real threats against public order by admitted heretics who deserved no mercy. The culmination of this attitude is reflected in Pope Gregory XIII's commissioning of a commemorative medal and Giorgio Vasari's triumphant painting of the massacre for the Sala Regia of the Vatican palace.[135]

As Acton traces Catholic responses to the massacre, he observes that the posture of defiant acknowledgment ("Yes, we did it; the heretics deserved it!") could not be maintained. The elaborate theories used to validate the slaughter of heretics ("It is part of the punishment of heretics that faith shall not be kept with them. It is even mercy to kill them that they may sin no more")[136] were indefensible. In Acton's judgment, "the theory which was framed to justify these practices has done more than plots and massacres to cast discredit on the Catholics."[137] Furthermore, though there may have been places within Catholicism where "the massacre was welcomed as an act of Christian fortitude," elsewhere, including in France itself, "the great mass of people was struck with consternation," not to mention "horror and compassion."[138] According to Acton, "the majority of the Catholics who were not under the direct influence of Madrid or Rome recognized the inexpiable horror of the crime. But [at the same time] the desire to defend what the Pope approved survived sporadically, when the old fierceness of dogmatic hatred was extinct."[139]

There did, however, come a change in Catholic opinion: "A time came when the Catholics, having long relied on force, were compelled to appeal to

134. An interesting nonbiographical (at least not *directly* autobiographical) reflection by Lord Acton on tensions between Rome and some nineteenth-century Roman Catholic scholars (Acton's examples are the French priest and pioneer of Catholic social "liberalism," Hughes-Félicité-Robert de Lammenais [1792-1854] and the German idealist philosopher Jakob Frohschammer [1821-93]) can be found in *Selected Writings of Lord Acton*, vol. 3, *Essays in Religion, Politics, and Morality*, ed. J. Rufus Fears (Indianapolis: Liberty Fund, 1988), 234-62.

135. A reprint of this painting can be seen in Kingdon, 44.

136. *Selected Writings of Lord Acton*, 2:233.

137. *Selected Writings of Lord Acton*, 2:232.

138. *Selected Writings of Lord Acton*, 2:235.

139. *Selected Writings of Lord Acton*, 2:238.

Fig. 3.4. Giorgio Vasari's painting of the assassination of Coligny for Pope
Gregory XIII for the Sala Regia in the Vatican palace

opinion. That which had been defiantly acknowledged and defended required to be ingeniously explained away. The same motive which had justified the murder now prompted the lie." Fearful of implicating the papacy and thus providing further fuel for the fires of anti-Catholic hatred, apologists for the church simply lied outright: "A swarm of facts were invented to meet the difficulty: The victims were insignificant in number; they were slain for no reason connected with religion; the Pope believed in the existence of the plot; the plot was a reality; the medal is fictitious; the massacre was a feint concerted with the Protestants themselves; the Pope rejoiced only when he heard it was over. These things were repeated so often that they have been sometimes believed." But Acton will have none of it. He concludes his essay with these remarkably honest words: "Such things will cease to be written when men perceive that truth is the only merit that gives dignity and worth to history."[140]

In the summer of 1872, approaching the tricentennial of the massacre, Kuyper also challenged precisely this revisionist Catholic historiography in a series of editorials, later published as a brochure.[141] Using some of the same archival evidence as Acton, though decidedly painting in broader brush strokes, Kuyper called on his fellow Calvinists to revive their martyrology but without continuing hatred for their Catholic compatriots. He also acknowledged Protestant guilt in the wars of religion (though not equally!) and called for genuine freedom of conscience in civic life. It is on this point of freedom for conscience that Acton's and Kuyper's convictions converge, and it is instructive to provide a brief summary of their positions.

The Real Issue: Liberty of Conscience

Even in what may be considered some of Kuyper's most polemical speeches and writings — those in which he invokes dark satanic attacks by his opponents — he nonetheless insists on liberty of conscience for *all* citizens. We shall have opportunity to examine Kuyper's own passionate commitment to this principle in chapter 7 when we consider in greater detail his approach to the "school question," but now we consider only one example, his "Maranatha" address in the city of Utrecht to the annual Antirevolutionary Party (ARP) convention of 1891.[142] Kuyper sets the stage for his comments

140. *Selected Writings of Lord Acton*, 2:240.

141. See n. 133 above.

142. Translation of this address is in Bratt, *Abraham Kuyper: A Centennial Reader*, 205-28; page references which follow in the text are to this work. Further analysis of Kuyper's rhetoric in this address can be found in chap. 7, 319-21 below.

on liberty of conscience by reminding the ARP delegates of Christ's return in judgment "also in the life of *our* nation, to strike his sickle also into the harvest of *our* national life, and *to destroy* the anti-Christian world power with the breath of his mouth (2 Thess. 2:8)" (208). Kuyper observes that their secular opponents — the conservative, the liberal, the radical, and the socialist — "have no inkling" of this reality; "they refuse to acknowledge Jesus' authority in the sphere of politics" (208). Kuyper does point out that this ignorance is not true of their Roman Catholic Dutch compatriots: "Our Roman Catholic countrymen confess with us: 'Whence he will come again to judge the living and the dead.' The Maranatha-event is certainly alive among them" (218). Nonetheless, Kuyper once again appeals to his standard historical mythology about the origins of Dutch liberty and insists: "I reject as firmly as I know how the conclusion that we can therefore stand as one with them. This *cannot* be, due to our glorious history; this *cannot* be, due to the *blood of martyrs* that has been shed: this cannot be *now* or *ever,* due to the shrewd old gentleman at Rome who claims to be the authorized vicar of Christ on earth. . . . I would therefore call it a betrayal of our history and our principles were there ever to be a fusion or even a very close association between our Catholic countrymen and ourselves" (219).

Why? Why this dogged insistence, a determination that Kuyper apparently was willing to modify in order to form a coalition government with the Catholics after the election of 1901? According to Kuyper, one issue and one issue alone: *liberty of conscience:* "What separates us, after all, is the sacred cause of *freedom of conscience* for which we, like our ancestors, would again shed our blood and against which they, however accommodating their practice, remain fundamentally opposed" (219).

As Kuyper brings his address to its climax, he reiterates his appeal to the larger public that "*freedom of conscience,* both direct and indirect, be completely restored. Positive government action in matters pertaining to our *spiritual* life is something we do not desire but fundamentally oppose" (224). What this means is that "in the civil state all citizens of the Netherlands must have equal rights before the law. The time *must* come when it will be considered inconceivable, even ridiculous, to discriminate against or offend anyone, whoever it may be, for his convictions as a Seceder or Doleant,[143] as a Catholic or Jew" (221). This freedom of conscience does not mean an end to all political conflict in the name of tolerance. What it does mean is the mandate to "employ *persuasion* to

---

143. These two terms refer to members of dissenting Reformed churches that were formed after the departures from the National Reformed Church in 1834 (*Afscheiding* or "Secession") and 1886 (*Doleantie*).

the exclusion of all *coercion* in all spiritual matters." Kuyper is a realist about the entailment of such a strategy: his own heavy-duty use of Christian martial imagery notwithstanding, "To us it is only given to fight with spiritual weapons and to bear our cross in joyful discipleship" (219-20). Kuyper does not move from this emphasis on the *imitatio Christi* to political passivity. He insists that "we do not want the government to hand over unbelief handcuffed and chained as though for a spiritual execution. We prefer that the power of the gospel overcome that demon in free combat with comparable weapons." However, the insistence that persuasion replace coercion is a two-way street, and here Kuyper has a major complaint about the failure of secularists to reciprocate in granting Christian believers genuine opportunity for free expression of their religious conscience. His pleas sound remarkably contemporary:

> Only *this* we do not want: that the government arm unbelief to force us, half armed and handicapped by an assortment of laws, into an unequal struggle with so powerful an enemy. Yet that *has* happened and is happening *still*. It happens in all areas of popular education, on the higher as well as the lower levels, by means of the power of money, forced examinations, and official hierarchy. For this reason we may never desist from our protest of resistance until the gospel recover its freedom to circulate, until the performance of his Christian duty will again be possible for every Dutch citizen, whether rich or poor. (224-25)

In chapter 7 we will be exploring in greater detail the question of religious liberty, theocracy, and pluralism and the "baggage" carried into the contemporary debate by Calvinist and Catholic alike, but for now we will close this section by simply citing, without further narrative commentary, a few of Lord Acton's pithy and illuminating aphorisms on freedom of conscience.[144]

> If happiness is the end of society, then liberty is superfluous. It does not make men happy. It depends on the other world. It is the sphere of duty — not of rights. (490-91)

> Liberty is the condition of duty, the guardian of conscience. It grows as conscience grows. The domains of both grow together. (491)

> The center and supreme object of liberty is the reign of conscience. Liberty is the reign of conscience. (491)

144. These are all taken from *Selected Writings of Lord Acton,* 3:489-508; page references will be given parenthetically in the text.

179

All liberty consists in radice in the preservation of an inner sphere exempt from state power. That reverence for conscience is the germ of all civil freedom, and the way in which Christianity served it. That is, liberty has grown out of the distinction (separation is a bad word) of Church and State. (492)

There remained a flaw in [secular] liberalism, for liberty apart from belief is liberty with a good deal of the substance taken out of it. . . . Nations that have not the self-governing force of religion within them are unprepared for freedom. (497)

A final Acton citation that seems prophetically appropriate for the United States in the first decade of the twenty-first century:

Freedom belongs to nations flourishing, not to nations unripe or decaying. How do you determine it? By the presence of moral qualities. A nation that does not respect oaths [is] unfit for juries, without education, that does not condemn dishonesty. Does not all this amount to conscience? Where there is an enlightened conscience, there shall be freedom. Where not, not. Mere enjoyment of material pleasures makes men indifferent. (498)

Postscript: "Holland Mania" in America, 1880-1920[145]

Abraham Kuyper's visit to New Jersey, Michigan, and other eastern parts of the United States in 1898 and his tour of the Dutch settlements to the west coincided with a popular turn-of-the century American craze for all things Dutch. Fascination with Dutch history; Dutch art, architecture, and literature; Dutch furniture, artifacts, and symbols; and genealogy combined with travel to and from the Netherlands to create what art historian Annette Stott has labeled "Holland mania." Edward Bok, editor of the popular *Ladies Home Journal* and of Dutch descent himself, began his October 1903 editorial, "The Mother of America," with this observation about current American interest in matters Dutch:

It is said that twenty thousand more American travelers visited the Netherlands during the past summer than in any previous year. Last winter the li-

145. What follows is inspired by and highly dependent on a volume I chanced upon after I had completed this chapter: Annette Stott, *Holland Mania: The Unknown Dutch Period in American Art and Culture* (Woodstock, N.Y.: Overlook, 1998); parenthetical page references which follow in the text are to this work. Most of the other citations in this section are indebted to Stott.

brarians of the country reported that the study of the history and people of the Netherlands increased to such an extent that several libraries will this year inaugurate separate departments to the literature of the Dutch. The desire for "things Dutch" in the furnishing of American homes has grown with wonderful rapidity. The strong pride in Dutch ancestry is everywhere noticeable where interest in genealogical matters has taken root. Some are inclined to think that this interest in the people of the Netherlands, and in Dutch things generally, is a passing fad. But others who study things more closely lean to the belief that it is based on something more intelligent and permanent: that it rests on a national awakening born of an inherent influence and blood kinship that has too long been lost sight of.[146]

Basing his conclusions largely on the work of historian Douglas Campbell,[147] Bok pointed out to his readers that "the men who founded New York were not Englishmen, but largely Hollanders: that the Puritans who settled Plymouth had lived twelve years in Holland: that the Puritans who settled elsewhere in Massachusetts had all their lives been exposed to a Dutch influence: that New Jersey, as well as New York, was settled by the Dutch West India Company: that Connecticut was given life by Thomas Hooker, who came from a long residence in Holland: that Roger Williams, who founded Rhode Island, was a Dutch scholar: and that William Penn, the founder of Pennsylvania, came of a Dutch mother."[148]

These more or less incidental connections were, however, not as important as the four fundamental institutions of American freedom — education, press, religious worship, suffrage — which did not, so Bok argued, come from England but "directly from Holland." In fact, of the key American founding documents — the Declaration of Independence and the Constitution — one is inspired by, even "based almost entirely upon the Declaration of Independence of the United Republic of the Netherlands; while all through the Constitution its salient points are based upon, and some literally copied from, the Dutch Constitution." Bok's glorious assessment: "In every art which uplifts and adorns human life, in nearly every aspect of human endeavor, Holland has not only added to the moral resources of mankind and contributed more to the fabric of civilization, but has also actually led the way."[149] Bok concludes that

146. Edward Bok, "The Mother of America," *Ladies Home Journal* 20, no. 11 (October 1903): 16.

147. Douglas Campbell, *The Puritan in Holland, England, and America: An Introduction to American History,* 3rd ed., 2 vols. (New York: Harper & Brothers, 1893).

148. Bok, 16.

149. Bok, 16.

most of America's previous history writing — focused too exclusively on her English roots — is being revised by "more enlightened histories." These demonstrate "that most of our previous historical knowledge of our own country stands in need of adjustment, and that it is not at all impossible that our modern growing interest in the people of the Netherlands and its history is a forerunner of our final enlightenment." Though he concludes his editorial with a query about the final verdict concerning "what nation will be given the credit of being 'The Mother of America,'"[150] noting that it is still up for grabs, there is little doubt that Bok considers the Netherlands as the most likely suspect.

According to Stott, Bok's paean about Holland "was one of several competing ethnic claims that emerged at the end of the nineteenth century. Inspired partly by the country's centennial, which focused attention on the colonial era, and partly by the 'new immigration' of Eastern Europeans, which threatened the cultural identity established by the old settlers, these proliferating ethnic studies attempted to anchor American cultural identity in each of the various nations from which the earliest immigrants had come" (Stott, 9). They did have one important thing in common: "Most of them consciously opposed the dominance of England in contemporary theories of American history and culture" (9). As historians called attention to "parallels between the history and culture of the Netherlands and the United States," they lent popular credence to claims promoting "Holland to the position of cradle of American civilization" (10). In searching for "an alternative to Anglo interpretations of American history," the Netherlands had much to offer as a "country that had enjoyed close economic and political ties with the United States, never had engaged in a war against it, and had held a position as an economic and political world leader in the seventeenth century that might have served as a model for the emerging nation. Of all the non-British countries that contributed to the United States, the majority of late-nineteenth-century Americans had perhaps the least accumulated resentment toward the Netherlands and the most in common with it" (10). The attraction that the Netherlands had for Americans was based on familiarity and commonality as well as a parallel promise for a glorious American future:

> Physical appearance, social custom, Protestantism, republicanism, and perceived ideals of democracy and personal freedoms all struck cords of agreement in the two countries. In addition, similarities in the development of the two republics seemed to foretell a dazzling future for the United States. The United Provinces of the Netherlands had risen to economic superiority and

150. Bok, 17.

had ruled the seas and colonized the world after freeing itself from the rule of a foreign monarch. Its successor, the United States of America, expected to do the same in its own bid for world power. (10)

As well as helping fuel a developing American sense of "manifest destiny,"[151] Holland mania was an integral part of the late nineteenth-century American quest for identity, in the midst of waves of new immigrants, an attempt to find "a cultural anchor in the country's diverse ethnic composition" (16). Stott observes that this late nineteenth-century development parallels such contemporary American initiatives in multiculturalism as "Afrocentrism," even claiming that "Afro-centrism is a modern equivalent of Holland Mania" (17).

For our purposes, there are several important points to be noted with respect to Kuyper and his 1898 American visit. When Kuyper arrived on these shores sowing the seed of praise for the Dutch contribution to America and the cause of liberty, the cultural soil had already been generally well tilled. Kuyper's message of spiritual linkage between the Netherlands and the United States in terms of liberty would therefore have been received by friendly, receptive audiences and could potentially have produced a glorious harvest.[152] Kuyper did have at least one significant encounter with the Holland mania phenomenon, a visit to Rochester, New York, where he spoke to what he referred to in his travel journal as a "College Womenclub."[153] In the context of high praise for the "social and moral influence on American life" exercised by "free" women, particularly in their active role as homemakers (huismoeder), Kuyper comments on their intelligent participation in the social and cultural life of the nation as equals of the men. In his visit to the Rochester "College womenclub," he notes that he was struck by their passion for learning, "with none of the pedantry of the 'bluestockings' nor any of the arrogance of the feminists." He then describes the year's activity of this club:

> Both married and unmarried women of this circle consider their ongoing learning so seriously that during this year the object of their study was "The Netherlands." The members had prepared some 50 "papers" [for discussion] and although not one of the 50 writers was of Dutch descent, they plunged much deeper into the history of our Fatherland than the cultured women of our own nation do. And notwithstanding [this accomplishment], they did

151. Note on Manifest Destiny, see discussion in chap. 2, 119-22.
152. For more on Kuyper's American visit, including an itinerary, see app. B.
153. Kuyper reported on this visit in his *Varia Americana*, 40; unless otherwise indicated, quotations that follow are translated from this page.

Fig. 3.5. Robert W. Gibson's 1892 Collegiate Church
and School on West End Avenue in New York City.
Kuyper lectured in this church on December 8, 1898.

not consider it extraordinary, gave themselves no airs because of it, and remained simple and natural in their conversation.

Kuyper concludes with the observation that, for American women, "that which is essentially feminine ['lady-like' is his actual term] is not sacrificed for the sake of intelligence."[154]

One critical difference between Kuyper's message and Holland mania should not be overlooked, however. The broader phenomenon of "Hollandophilia" submerged the *religious* emphasis on the indispensable role of Calvinism as the foundation of all that was *good* as well as Dutch, an emphasis that was at the heart of Kuyper's message. Even the love for the seventeenth-century Dutch art masters, particularly Rembrandt and Vermeer, was rooted more in the perception that their art promoted democratic and republican virtues by its realism, its attention to landscape, still life, portraiture, and the common life of ordinary people rather than wealthy aristocrats (Stott, 24-25). As one American writer (1900) proclaimed in Lincolnesque terms: "Dutch art is of the people and for the people" (25). The religious dimension of the Dutch Masters was not

154. Kuyper, *Varia Americana*, 41.

ignored but subordinated to the political themes of liberty and democracy. Dutch-American art historian Tiemen de Vries put it this way:

> The religious and democratic ideas in which Rembrandt breathed and lived are not more the ideas and feeling only of a poor suffering and struggling people, but they have become the soul and the spirit of the entire great American commonwealth. . . . [N]obody can be surprised that in our days and especially in America Rembrandt is honored with love and sympathy, that his work is the main attraction in every gallery, and that the holy secret of his art is understood and admired by the staunch and sturdy sons of liberty and democracy.[155]

In his fifth Stone Lecture, "Calvinism and Art,"[156] Kuyper indicates that he is aware of the international (including American) traffic in seventeenth-century art of the Dutch Masters as well as the efforts by contemporary artists to "imitate" their motives and style (165).[157] He also emphasizes the democratic and republican character of their art: "Before this period, no account was taken of the people, *they* only were considered worthy of notice who were superior to the common man, *viz.*, the high world of the Church, and of the priests, of knights and princes." Kuyper then calls attention to the "emancipation" of art from its tutelage and dependence on church, court, and wealth thanks to the Reformation. "But, since then, the people had come of age, and *under the auspices of Calvinism*, the art of painting, prophetic of a democratic life of later times, was the first to proclaim the people's maturity" (165). "Calvinism," Kuyper concludes, "alone was able to plough the field on which free art could flourish" (166).[158]

So, having seen both the parallels (democratic character) between Kuyper's reflections on the seventeenth-century art of the Dutch Masters and those of the American Holland mania craze as well as a key difference (the emphasis on Calvinism), we come to what may be the most important aspect of

155. Tiemen de Vries, *Dutch History, Art, and Literature for Americans* (Grand Rapids: Eerdmans-Sevensma, 1912), 114-15; cited by Stott, 26.

156. Kuyper, *Lectures on Calvinism*, 142-70; page references which follow in the text are to this work.

157. See discussion in Stott, chap. 3, "Dutch Art in America," especially the discussion of "The Hague School," 28-34.

158. The idea Kuyper expresses here is not entirely or exclusively his own; he cites as his source, "Carrière." According to Peter Heslam, this is a reference to German philosopher Moriz Carrière, *Die philosophische Weltanschauung der Reformationszeit in ihren Beziehungen zur Gegenwart* (Leipzig: Brockhaus, 1887). Heslam also refers to Kuyper's *Het Calvinisme en de Kunst*, 78 (see n. 87 above). Heslam, 95 n. 35.

our comparison. The key theme of our interpretation of Kuyper's public theology has been the emphasis on Kuyper the poet, the mythmaker, the rhetorician of a movement. The turn-of-the-century Holland mania was part of a broader American cultural effort to remythologize its own origins and reframe its national story in terms of the struggle for liberty. In addition to the travels of American painters to art colonies in the Netherlands,[159] and the products of American artists — original works as well as reproductions[160] — a critical role in this remythologizing of American roots and destiny was played by historians such as John Lothrop Motley,[161] Douglas Campbell,[162] and historical populizer extraordinaire, William Elliot Griffis.[163] Kuyper not only consulted these works, but his portrait of America, the source of its important institutions, and its role in the course of providential history as the vanguard of liberty followed in the riverbed created by the flowing waters of their historiography. Like them, Kuyper the historian was a poet, a rhetorician celebrating in words the myth of America — the "land of the free." To see this same role at work, now also with more profound theological underpinnings, we shall compare in the next chapter Kuyper's vision of America in God's kingdom with that of "America's theologian," Jonathan Edwards.

159. See Stott, chap. 2, "American Artists in Holland."

160. Stott, 34-42; according to Stott, the *Ladies Home Journal*, as part of "a systematic plan for improving the pictures on the walls of the American home," began "printing four-color reproductions of art from American collections. . . . The series of forty masterpieces included only one American artist — Whistler" — and was dominated by Dutch Masters. Apparently, "according the [editor] Bok's autobiography, the *Ladies Home Journal* distributed over 70 million prints from this old master series" (Stott, 36-37).

161. *The Rise of the Dutch Republic* (1855); *History of the United Netherlands* (1867).

162. See n. 147 above.

163. *Brave Little Holland and What She Taught Us* (1894).

CHAPTER FOUR

America as God's Kingdom:
Abraham Kuyper and Jonathan Edwards[1]

We have made such a sure covenant with the King of Kings that we are fully assured that we and all who firmly trust in that covenant will at last be delivered by his strong and mighty hand despite all his and our enemies.

William of Orange (1573)

Thus stands the cause between God and us: we are entered into Covenant with him for this work . . . if the Lord shall please to hear us, and bring us in peace to the place we desire, then hath he ratified this Covenant and . . . will expect a strict performance. . . . But if we neglect the observance of these Articles . . . the Lord will surely break out in wrath against us . . . and make us know the price of the breach of such a Covenant.

John Winthrop, on the *Arabella* (1630)

Of all the dispositions and habits which lead to political prosperity, religion and morality are indispensable supports. . . . Observe good faith and justice toward all nations. . . . Can it be that Providence has not connected the permanent felicity of a nation with its virtue?

George Washington, *Farewell Address* (1796)

1. This chapter title is borrowed in part from M. Darrol Bryant, "America as God's Kingdom," in *Religion and Public Society*, ed. Jürgen Moltmann et al. (New York: Harper & Row, 1970), 49-94.

We Americans are the peculiar, chosen people — the Israel of our time: we bear the ark of the liberties of the world.

Herman Melville, *White Jacket* (1850)

Nowhere is the temptation to idolatry greater than in national life.

Reinhold Niebuhr, *Beyond Tragedy* (1937)

The profoundly pro-American sympathies in Abraham Kuyper's public theology — already noted in earlier chapters — call for a reflective comparison with another "neo-Calvinist,"[2] Jonathan Edwards, "America's theologian."[3] On the face of it, the personal parallels between the two men are striking,[4] not

2. This designation is from Douglas J. Elwood, *The Philosophical Theology of Jonathan Edwards* (New York: Columbia University Press, 1960), 9. For Elwood, the difference between Calvin and Edwards (the reason for the "neo") "appears most prominently in his fundamental conception of God in terms of absolute beauty and not merely absolute power, and in his appeal to immediate experience in our knowledge of God" (9). Roland Andre Delattre (to whom I am indebted for this reference) notes quite correctly that "Elwood's way of drawing attention to this matter is not, however, quite fair to Calvin" (*Beauty and Sensibility ithe Thought of Jonathan Edwards: An Essay in Aesthetics and Theological Ethics* [New Haven and London: Yale University Press, 1968], 121).

3. The designation is from Robert W. Jenson, *America's Theologian: A Recommendation of Jonathan Edwards* (New York and Oxford: Oxford University Press, 1988). Jenson intends this to be more than the obvious "truism that Jonathan Edwards is America's greatest theologian in the sense that his achievement in the discipline of theology is the most weighty to have appeared on this continent." Rather, his book's thesis is "that Edwards' theology meets precisely the problems and opportunities of specifically American theology, and of the nation molded thereby, and that it does so with the profundity and inventive élan that belong to only the very greatest thinkers" (3).

4. It needs to be noted at this point that the scholarship (including recent work) on Kuyper is significant but still manageable, while the field of Edwards scholarship (and Puritan studies in general) has exploded in recent years. Though I shall indicate key points of debate about Edwards interpretation where appropriate, this chapter is not intended so much to shed new light on Edwards as it is on Kuyper through comparison with Edwards, a comparison that to the best of my knowledge has not yet been made. My chief sources for interpreting Edwards's public theology are Bryant, "America as God's Kingdom"; Gerald McDermott, *One Holy and Happy Society: The Public Theology of Jonathan Edwards* (University Park: Pennsylvania State University Press, 1990); Harry Stout, *The New England Soul: Preaching and Religious Culture in Colonial New England* (New York and Oxford: Oxford University Press, 1986), and the helpful collection of essays summarizing the current state of Edwards scholarship, *Jonathan Edwards and the American Experience*, ed.

to mention the interesting possible historical connections in their respective theologies.[5] Even if one discredits some of the legendary material passed on to future generations by their hagiographers, both were indisputably youthful intellectual prodigies,[6] had significant conversion experiences that they chronicled in writing,[7] and thus had a profound sense of and qualified appreciation

---

Nathan O. Hatch and Harry S. Stout (New York and Oxford: Oxford University Press, 1988). On Edwards's view of nature, common grace, and beauty, I am especially indebted to Paula M. Cooey, *Jonathan Edwards on Nature and Destiny* (Lewiston, N.Y., and Queenston, Ont.: Edwin Mellen, 1985); Delattre, *Beauty and Sensibility in the Thought of Jonathan Edwards;* Patricia Wilson-Kastner, *Coherence in a Fragmented World: Jonathan Edwards' Theology of the Holy Spirit* (Washington, D.C.: University Press of America, 1978). My interaction with interpreters of Kuyper will be given in the notes that follow in this and subsequent chapters. For an overview of recent Kuyper scholarship, see James Bratt, "In the Shadow of Mt. Kuyper: A Survey of the Field," *Calvin Theological Journal* 31 (1996): 51-66.

5. McDermott, 79, includes "Dutch Reformed scholasticism, which may have influenced Edwards indirectly through [Moses] Lowman and directly through Petrus van Mastricht," as a key influence on Edwards's eschatology. I have not been able to determine any significant role for van Mastricht in Kuyper's own eschatology. Since Lowman's real teacher in eschatology was Johannes Cocceius, according to McDermott (79), the general antipathy of Dutch neo-Calvinism to Cocceius's dispensational-progressive view of history makes a direct linkage of influences less likely in my judgment, but the question is interesting enough to make further study worth pursuing.

6. "Edwards has been portrayed for two centuries as a prodigy who was well along in Latin studies by the time he was eight years old, and who wrote a fine essay on flying or sailing spiders when only eleven" (David Levin, "Edwards, Franklin and Cotton Mather: A Meditation on Character and Reputation," in *Jonathan Edwards and the American Experience,* 37). Recent scholarship suggests that the spider essay was written when Edwards was in his early twenties (see introduction to *The Works of Jonathan Edwards,* vol. 6, *Scientific and Philosophical Writings,* ed. Wallace E. Anderson [New Haven: Yale University Press, 1980], 6-7). The most famous Kuyper legend arises from his parents' concern about the infant Bram's large head. The German medical professor who was consulted about this reportedly said: "Look out! That's all brain-power!" ("Bewahre, das ist alles Gehirne!") (George Puchinger, *Abraham Kuyper: De Jonge Kuyper [1837-1867]* [Franeker: T. Wever, 1987], 31). The young boy Kuyper is also reported to have "preached" to the sailors in the Maas harbor (Puchinger, 31).

7. Jonathan Edwards, "A Personal Narrative," in *A Jonathan Edwards Reader,* ed. John E. Smith, Harry S. Stout, and Kenneth Minkema (New Haven and London: Yale University Press, 1995), 281-95; also found in Clarence H. Faust and Thomas H. Johnson, eds., *Jonathan Edwards: Selections* (New York: Hill & Wang, 1935), 57-72; Abraham Kuyper, *Confidentie* (Amsterdam: Höveker & Zoon, 1873). Edwards's qualified acceptance of the Great Awakening, including his taking distance from some of its enthusiastic excesses (see his *Religious Affections* treatise), also has an interesting parallel in Kuyper's significant encounter with the nineteenth-century revivalism of Robert Piersall Smith, Ira Sankey, and Dwight L. Moody in 1875 at Brighton, England. Kuyper's reaction initially was "My cup

for experiential Christianity.[8] Both men were remarkably influential and successful churchmen who wrestled with, among other things, the importance of meaningful and committed church membership,[9] and both had their successes crowned with humiliating public repudiation by being "Churchilled" out of power by their own followers.[10] Equipped with impressive intellects and accompanying powerful written and oral rhetorical skills, they were also self-conscious of their own greatness[11] and aroused great opposition as well as undying

runneth over," but within a half-year he also suffered a serious nervous breakdown. See Peter S. Heslam, *Creating a Christian Worldview: Abraham Kuyper's Lectures on Calvinism* (Grand Rapids: Eerdmans, 1998), 40-42.

8. All of Edwards's writing is suffused with his deep "sense of divinity," but perhaps nowhere as profoundly and personally as in his "Sarah Pierrepont" apostrophe and his "Personal Narrative" (in *A Jonathan Edwards Reader,* 281-96; Faust and Johnson, 57-72). Edwards's theological reflections on revival and experiential religion also must be taken into account here. Kuyper's personal piety is clearly expressed in the many volumes of his Scripture meditations, generally regarded as "classic." The following volumes of Kuyper's meditations are available in English translation: *The Practice of Godliness; Women of the Old Testament; His Decease at Jerusalem; When Thou Sittest in Thy House; Keep Thy Solemn Feasts; In the Shadow of Death; Asleep in Jesus; To Be Near unto God; The Death and Resurrection of Christ.* The nuanced appreciation of experiential religion, reflected in Edwards's attitude to the Great Awakening revivals, is found in his 1737 treatise "A Faithful Narrative of Surprising Conversions," in *The Works of Jonathan Edwards,* vol. 4, *Great Awakening,* ed. C. C. Goen (New Haven and London: Yale University Press, 1972), 97-211; his Yale commencement address of 1741, "The Distinguishing Marks of a Work of the Spirit of God" (*Works,* 4:215-88; hereafter *DM*); and particularly in his great treatise *Religious Affections,* vol. 2 of *The Works of Jonathan Edwards,* ed. John E. Smith (New Haven and London: Yale University Press, 1959) (hereafter *RA*).

9. Edwards was dismissed by his congregation in Northampton for challenging the lax church (communion) membership requirements of his grandfather Solomon Stoddard's "halfway covenant"; Kuyper's leadership in the refusal by the Amsterdam consistory of the National Dutch Reformed Church to accept what were judged to be less than authentic applicants for membership led to the second major schism in the Dutch Reformed Church during the nineteenth century, the *Doleantie* of 1886.

10. On Edwards, see immediately preceding note. Kuyper's leadership of the Antirevolutionary Party, which went back to its formation in 1879, was seriously challenged after his term as prime minister from 1901 to 1905. See A. Anema et al., *Leider en Leiding in de Antirevolutionaire Partij* (Amsterdam, 1915).

11. See, e.g., what Perry Miller (*Jonathan Edwards* [New York: William Sloane Associates, 1949], 171) calls Edwards's "assertion of royal prerogative among the Connecticut divines" in DM, 268, where Edwards wraps himself in the ministerial cloak of his grandfather Solomon Stoddard. A similar self-perception may be reflected in Edwards's almost compulsive note taking of every one of his thoughts. Richard Bushman speaks of Edwards's "miserliness" on this matter: "The productions of mind were hoarded and treasured as valued possessions in a vast miser's store of thoughts" (Richard L. Bushman, "Jon-

support well beyond their own lifetimes.[12] Both were unrelenting in opposition,[13] and on occasion used martial imagery to identify their own cause and role in it with the divine plan and purpose.[14] Opposition could then also be regarded as satanic resistance to the kingdom of God.[15] As great men with grand visions of divine purpose and apparently indefatigable energy, they were apparently and not too surprisingly also difficult marriage partners.[16] Perhaps, most

athan Edwards as Great Man: Identity, Conversion, and Leadership in the Great Awakening," in *Critical Essays on Jonathan Edwards,* ed. William J. Scheick [Boston: G. K. Hall, 1980], 46.

12. "Nowhere else did a small band adhering to the protagonist worship him as did the followers of Edwards, the twenty heads of families, 'besides others, women and young people,' who stood by him; but nowhere else did the mass of a town hate a man as the citizenry of Northampton hated Edwards" (Miller, 211).

13. Richard Bushman's assessment of Edwards applies equally well to Kuyper: "Jonathan too [like his father Timothy] refused to give an inch when challenged. In the dismissal controversy at Northampton he would not compromise with his parishioners, nor would he yield a point in the debate with Solomon Williams on admission to communion. In all intellectual disputes Edwards stubbornly beat down his opponents, demolishing even the slightest contradictions. He had to prove himself right in every detail" (Bushman, 45).

14. See Edwards's preface to *Some Thoughts concerning the Present Revival in New England* (hereafter *ST*), in *Works of Jonathan Edwards,* 4:291-92.

15. See, e.g., Abraham Kuyper, "Maranatha (1891)," in *Abraham Kuyper: A Centennial Reader,* ed. James D. Bratt (Grand Rapids: Eerdmans, 1998), 205-29. This tendency is more marked and more problematic in Kuyper than in Edwards and reflects their different roles. Edwards was exclusively a churchman, a preacher of the gospel, a revivalist, for whom opposition (of Charles Chauncy and other opponents of the Great Awakening) meant opposition to the gospel-affirming work of the Holy Spirit in revival. Kuyper, on the other hand, was more a leader of a broad movement, a movement that had social, cultural, and political dimensions that extended far beyond the church. It is one thing to consider opposition to the gospel and Spirit-led revival as originating from the kingdom of darkness (though discerning the authenticity of the Spirit's work is no simple matter, as Edwards knew well); it is another to judge disagreement with one's political judgments as demonic. Edwards comes out better here than Kuyper in two respects. First, he tended to address issues rather than directly name his opponents; throughout the debates about the Great Awakening in the 1740s, Edwards never mentioned Chauncy by name. This may have been, as Perry Miller suggests, deliberate, "a studied insult" (Miller, 177). Kuyper, however, had no such reticence. Second, in his identification with "God's cause," Edwards provided criteria for determining whether a phenomenon was or was not a work of God's Spirit, in many respects leaving the judgment to the reader in a way that Kuyper, who intuited such judgments on behalf of his followers, also did not. In so doing Edwards was also capable of providing a critique of his "friends" (see, e.g., *DM,* 276ff.) in a way that Kuyper — for whom allegiance tended to be an all-or-nothing matter — was not. For a discussion of the Boston "liberal" opposition to Edwards's support of the revival, see Miller, 165-234.

16. For confirmation see Elizabeth D. Dodds, *Marriage to a Difficult Man: The "Un-*

importantly, both were God-intoxicated men, preoccupied with the notion of God's full and complete sovereignty,[17] and in content, both can be said to be theologians of the Holy Spirit.[18] While each of these points warrants further and full exploration, we shall restrict ourselves in this chapter to a comparison of their views on the place of America in the providential history of God's kingdom, their respective interpretations of John's Apocalypse, and the ontological foundation of their public theologies through the categories of trinitarian beauty and common grace.

---

common Union" of Jonathan and Sarah Edwards (Philadelphia: Westminster, 1971), and George Puchinger's treatment of Kuyper's courtship of Johanna Schaay in *De Jonge Kuyper* (chap. 2, "Bram en zijn Jo," 41-90).

17. Edwards describes his spiritual autobiography as a conversion with respect to divine sovereignty:

> From my childhood up, my mind had been full of objections against the doctrine of God's sovereignty, in choosing whom he would to eternal life, and rejecting whom he pleased; leaving them eternally to perish, and be everlastingly tormented in hell. It used to appear like a horrible doctrine to me. But I remember the time very well, when I seemed to be convinced, and fully satisfied, as to this sovereignty of God, and his justice in thus eternally disposing of men, according to his sovereign pleasure. But never could give an account, how, or by what means, I was thus convinced. . . . However, my mind rested in it. . . . And there has been a wonderful alteration in my mind, in respect to the doctrine of God's sovereignty, from that day to this; so that I scarce ever had so much as the rising of an objection against it. . . . But I have often, since that first conviction, had quite another kind of sense of God's sovereignty than I had then. I have often since had not only a conviction, but a delightful conviction. The doctrine has very often appeared exceedingly pleasant, bright and sweet. Absolute sovereignty is what I love to ascribe to God. But my first conviction was not so. ("Personal Narrative," in Faust and Johnson, 58-59; cf. *A Jonathan Edwards Reader*, 283)

Kuyper also defined the essence of his Calvinist faith in terms of divine sovereignty:

> The dominating principle [of Calvinism] was not, soteriologically, justification by faith, but in the widest sense cosmologically, *the Sovereignty of the Triune God over the whole Cosmos*, in all its spheres and kingdoms, visible and invisible. (*Lectures on Calvinism* [Grand Rapids: Eerdmans, 1931], 79)

18. See Wilson-Kastner, *Coherence in a Fragmented World*; W. H. Velema, *De Leer van de Heilige Geest bij Abraham Kuyper* (The Hague: Van Keulen, 1957).

The Kingdom of God in America[19]

In his seminal study *The Kingdom of God in America*, H. Richard Niebuhr has argued rather convincingly that "the meaning and spirit of American Christianity as a movement . . . finds its center in the faith in the kingdom of God."[20] Niebuhr tells us that his original intention in the essay was to show "that the expectation of the kingdom of God on earth was the great common element in our faith and that by reference to it one might be able to understand not only the unity beneath the diversity of American religion but also the effect of Christianity on culture." However, "this attempt to analyze American Christianity by means of this idea of the kingdom on earth failed."[21] Nonetheless, recognizing that American Protestant Christianity "must be understood as a movement rather than as an institution or series of institutions," Niebuhr was led to the conclusion "that the idea of the kingdom of God had indeed been the dominant idea in American Christianity — just as the idea of the vision [of God] had been paramount in medieval faith — but that it had not always meant the same thing. In the early period of American life, when foundations were laid on which we all have to build, 'kingdom of God' meant 'sovereignty of God'; in the creative period of awakening and revival it meant 'reign of Christ'; and only in the most recent period had it come to mean 'kingdom on earth.'" Yet, Niebuhr adds, "it became equally apparent that these were not simply three divergent ideas, but that they were intimately related to one another, and that the idea of the kingdom of God could not be expressed in terms of one of them alone."[22]

The theme of the kingdom of God underscores the role of the Calvinist/Puritan tradition in shaping American Christianity. It is the common (Calvinist!) conviction of the sovereignty of God through the reign of Christ that must be lived *on earth as in heaven* that also links the public theology and practice of Jonathan Edwards and Abraham Kuyper. This linkage between Edwards and Kuyper involves both content and rhetorical application of Christ's kingly reign as a persistent theme used by both men in exhorting the faithful to be true to their calling. Both Edwards and Kuyper refused to restrict the reign of Christ to the "spiritual," to the private rule over the human heart.[23] The biblical-

19. This heading is taken from H. Richard Niebuhr, *The Kingdom of God in America* (New York, Evanston, and London: Harper & Row, 1937).

20. Niebuhr, ix.

21. Niebuhr, xi.

22. Niebuhr, xiii, xiv, xii. The three phases Niebuhr refers to are seventeenth-century Puritanism, eighteenth-century evangelicalism, and the nineteenth-century Social Gospel.

23. For Edwards see especially McDermott, *One Holy and Happy Society;* for Kuyper see his *Pro Rege: Of het Koningschap van Christus,* 3 vols. (Kampen: Kok, 1911-12).

COMPARATIVE HISTORICAL STUDIES

theological move that must be made here to focus on the *diesseitig* dimension of the kingdom is a linkage with the Old Testament this-worldly kingdom of Israel. Put differently, there must be some form of connection between one's contemporary society and the theocratic monarchy of the Old Testament.[24] This is accomplished materially through maintaining the continuity of a *national covenant* between God and the nation and *formally* or *rhetorically* through preaching that regularly calls for *covenant renewal,* as the jeremiad did.[25]

Though Perry Miller, the great reviver of Edwards scholarship in the twentieth century, and his "revisionist" successors claimed that Edwards repudiated the notion of a "national" covenant as articulated by his Puritan predecessors, Harry Stout has convincingly shown through his analysis of Edwards's unpublished "occasional" sermons at "critical" times (disasters, elections, fast days, wars), that Edwards "was every bit the federal theologian that his Puritan ancestors were. Throughout his career as pastor and teacher he adhered exactly to the logic and tenets of the national covenant and reiterated them in exactly the same terms as did his predecessors in the New England pulpit. Nor was he alone among evangelicals . . . [who] generally accepted the federal logic and applied it to their own New England in times of great national trial and stress . . . [especially] when faced with external enemies."[26] In Stout's summary of the role played by these occasional sermons, especially the election sermons, he writes: "In the same way that baptism and communion were 'signs and seals' of the individual covenant of grace, election sermons were a social sacrament signifying that for one more year, New Englanders had kept the faith and were publicly and officially a peculiar people of God."[27]

We shall examine Edwards's considered and careful qualification of the American national covenant later, but now need to explore in greater detail the

---

24. Important overviews of the historic relation between Calvinism and theocratic politics include F. W. Dillistone, *The Structure of the Divine Society* (Philadelphia: Westminster, 1951); David Little, *Religion, Order, and Law: A Study in Pre-Revolutionary England* (New York: Harper & Row, 1969); D. Nobbs, *Theocracy and Toleration: A Study of the Disputes in Dutch Calvinism from 1600-1650* (Cambridge: University Press, 1936); M. Walzer, *The Revolution of the Saints* (Cambridge: Harvard University Press, 1965). For a perspective on the twentieth-century debates on this question in the Dutch Reformed tradition after Abraham Kuyper, see Arnold A. Van Ruler, *Trinitarian Faith and Theocentric Politics,* trans. John Bolt (Lewiston, N.Y., and Queenston, Ont.: Edwin Mellen, 1989).

25. See discussion in chap. 1, 30-33.

26. Harry S. Stout, "The Puritans and Edwards," in *Jonathan Edwards and the American Experience,* 143. Gerald McDermott also concludes that Edwards rather conventionally continued the use of a national covenant in his preaching. See McDermott, chap. 1, "God's Manner with a Covenant People: The National Covenant."

27. Stout, *The New England Soul,* 30.

Dutch-Israel imagery that we introduced in chapter 1.[28] Kuyper himself was not averse to using the Dutch-Israel analogy in his speeches and writing,[29] though he was explicit in his repudiation of a Dutch theocracy.[30] Yet, it was Kuyper's spiritual and intellectual father Groen van Prinsterer who drew the parallels between Israel and the Netherlands more directly in his *Vaderlands-geschiedenis* (history of the fatherland).[31]

Groen traces the history of the Dutch nation from the time of the sixteenth-century Reformation as the history of a Christian people, delivered by God, and called by God to a specific national vocation. "Forty years of martyrdom were followed by eighty years of war. The head is no longer passively placed on the chopping block. The Lord gives deliverance to his people. The Netherlands, reformed by the Gospel, is protected by the hand of the Most High and the sword of the Prince of Orange" (88, §127). According to Groen, the Eighty Years' War (1568-1648) had a "Protestant character" because it flowed out of religious persecution and the triumph of the Reformation. The result was a "religious war" primarily about the principle of "free conscience." Though national independence and liberty were the true goals of the war, Groen acknowledges that less noble self-interest also played a role and that Christians and churches succumbing to a war frenzy tended to lose their spiritual focus and belief that their true strength was in spiritual weapons such as the sword of the Spirit (88).

Groen is firm in his conviction that the "House of Orange is called by

28. See above, 30-33, 38-41, 47, 54-56 .

29. See Abraham Kuyper, *Uit den Diensthuis Uitgeleid* (Kampen: Kok, 1912). In keeping with the spirit of the jeremiad, Kuyper begins his address by acknowledging that the oppression of the orthodox Reformed in the nineteenth century by "liberals" was an act of divine judgment, a "penance for our own and our fathers' guilt" (8). Kuyper also regularly identified himself and his minority neo-Calvinist movement with the core of true Netherlanders, a Gideon's band, the few thousand who had not bowed the knee to Baal, the remnant of God's people. A good example of this is his *Het Beroep op het Volksgeweten* (Amsterdam: B. H. Blankenberg, 1869), where analogies with Israel and the leadership of Moses, Joshua, Elijah, and the prophets Isaiah and Jeremiah are explicitly made. For discussion see J. Van Weringh, *Het Maatschappijbeeld van Abraham Kuyper* (Assen: Van Gorcum, 1967), and J. Van Eijnatten, *God, Nederland, en Oranje: Dutch Calvinism and the Search for a Social Centre* (Kok: Kampen, 1993).

30. Abraham Kuyper, *Antirevolutionaire Staatkunde*, 2 vols. (Kampen: Kok, 1916), 1:273-74; also see the discussion in chap. 7 below on the Kuyper-Hoedemaker debate, 307-31.

31. Mr. Groen van Prinsterer, *Handboek der Geschiedenis van het Vaderland*, 6th ed. (Amsterdam: J. A. Wormser, 1895); citations which follow in the text are to this work; for easier reference the first citation will include the page number of the 1895 edition followed by the paragraph number.

God to a task, a task given to no other.[32] This task, as head of the Republic, for the benefit of all Christendom, is to awaken and strive for the Gospel, liberty, and justice." Orange's success in fulfilling this great calling justifies applying to it the words of Scripture concerning the judges of Israel: "Whenever the Lord raised up a judge for them, he was with the judge and saved them out of the hands of their enemies as long as the judge lived; for the Lord had compassion on them as they groaned under those who oppressed and afflicted them" (66, §104).[33] It is this divine favor alone that gave greatness to the seventeenth-century golden age of the Dutch Republic, according to Groen. "The greatness of the Republic did not consist in a State Administration that [in fact] left most matters unregulated, nor in a freedom that [in fact] existed more in name than in actuality, nor in a national character (volkskarakter) that failed to surpass that of many other nations, but rather in a faith inseparable from God's blessings" (66-67, §105). Staying within the parameters of the classic jeremiad, Groen thus nuances the Dutch-Israel metaphor significantly; it is not the nation per se but the (faithful) church in the nation that comes under divine protection and has a divine calling. "The Lord has planted his church here. He has taken care to maintain her in the face of external and internal assaults. It is for her sake that he favored [us] with a united state and with the choicest abundance of his benefits so that our history, more than that of any other Christian nation, is the story of God's miracles and direction" (67).

This leads Groen to reflect on whether the Netherlands is a "second Israel" (67). He insists that a comparison (vergelijking) is appropriate, though the two nations are not to be judged as equivalent or on the same footing (gelijkstelling). According to Groen, "the blessings of the Gospel" have been given to the Dutch nation "supremely" (uitnemendheid) though not "exclusively" (uitsluiting). Reflecting on the blessings provided the Dutch nation by the Reformation, Groen draws another direct comparison with Israel by paraphrasing and taking the apostle Paul's words in Romans 3:1-2 as his and his nation's own: "What advantage is there then for us? Much in every way! But this is the foremost: to us has been entrusted the words of God" (67). And finally, in a pastiche of texts taken from the Psalms, Groen calls his countrymen to join in Israel's praise for God's deliverance of the nation: "O Lord of Hosts, you brought a vine out of Egypt, you drove out the nations and planted it. You did a

32. On the mythology surrounding the House of Orange, see W. J. C. Buijtendijk et al., Als Eeen Goed Instrument: Werkelijkheid en Mythe ten aanzien van het Oramjehuis (Lochem: De Tijdstroom, [1968?]); Eijnatten, God, Nederland, en Oranje.

33. The Scripture passage is Judg. 2:18. Here, as in the Scripture passages that follow, I am following Groen's free and selective citation of texts using the translation of the New International Version.

mighty work in the days of our fathers, in the days of old. With your hand you drove out the nations and planted our fathers; you crushed the peoples and made our fathers flourish. The Lord gave them the lands of the nations, and they fell heir to what others had toiled for." Groen then emphasizes that the purpose for the inheritance grant that follows in the text is all-important: "That they might keep his precepts and observe his laws. Praise the Lord" (67).[34] Yet, Groen does not step over the salvation-historical boundary between Israel and the Netherlands and propound a straightforward civil religion. God's protection and blessing are upon his *church* and not the nation as such, but that fact is also a benefit to the nation. "Countries and nations *(volken)* are blessed and spared thanks to the faith of some. The Lord would have spared one city destined for destruction for the sake of ten righteous people. 'The Lord blessed the household of the Egyptian because of Joseph. The blessing of the Lord was on everything he [Potiphar] had, both in the house and in the field'" (67).[35]

Again, in keeping with the spirit of the jeremiad, Groen also points to the reality of divine judgment in his Netherlands/Israel parallel. The gospel, he notes, had sufficiently penetrated the life of the Dutch nation to serve as a fence or brake on immorality and "softened the potential problems accompanying an inadequate set of laws along with the powerful seduction provided by wealth." Thanks to the reforming work of the gospel on national life,[36] basic virtues such as "piety, industriousness, trust, modesty, simplicity, humility, patience, and perseverance had become national virtues *(Volksdeugden)*." In an anticipation of the doctrine of common grace that Kuyper would develop so thoroughly that it become a hallmark of Dutch neo-Calvinism,[37] Groen notes that even after evangelical decline, "the influence of Christian practices and of the devout remnant of the population continued to hold back the decline of morals for a long time" (67, §106). Groen then explicitly draws a comparison with Israel under divine judgment, noting that "Our history repeatedly is like *(gelijk)* that of Israel" (68, §107). Here he cites a para-

34. Scripture passages are Pss. 44:1-2; 80:8-9; 105:44.

35. Scripture passage is Gen. 39:5.

36. This theme became a staple of Dutch neo-Calvinism. See Herman Bavinck's address to the 1892 international gathering of Presbyterian and Reformed Churches meeting in Toronto, Canada, "The Influence of the Protestant Reformation on the Moral and Religious Condition of Communities and Nations," in *Alliance of the Reformed Churches Holding the Presbyterian System,* Proceedings of the Fifth General Council, Toronto, 1892 (London: Publication Committee of the Presbyterian Church of England, 1892), 48-55.

37. See Abraham Kuyper, *De Gemeene Gratie,* 3 vols. (Leiden: D. Donner, 1902-5); for a succinct summary of the neo-Calvinist understanding of common grace, see Herman Bavinck, "Common Grace," trans. Raymond C. Van Leeuwen, *Calvin Theological Journal* 24 (1989): 35-65.

phrase of Psalm 106[38] and follows it with a significant list of plagues and disasters that have befallen the Dutch nation and should thus be seen as covenantal judgment.

Walking carefully along the fine edge that separates a proper sensitivity to seeing Christ's reign in history concretely on the one hand, and idolatrous identification of a nation's cause and destiny with the kingdom of God on the other, also characterizes the covenantal jeremiad rhetoric of Jonathan Edwards. In passing we should note that Calvin's followers have not always been as careful as he tried to be to his own caution about not mixing "heaven and earth" and confusing the two kingdoms.[39] According to Sacvan Bercovitch, the late seventeenth-century Puritans with their notion of "national conversion of the Jews" significantly changed the jeremiad tradition's traditional exegesis that viewed "the relation between the old chosen people and the new" as simply "spiritual."[40] By then *figurally* applying Israel's hopes to themselves, believing that "as Israel *redivus* in the type, they could claim all the ancient prerogatives," New Englanders were able rhetorically to fashion a covenantal understanding of their own colonial vocation and destiny. In Bercovitch's words, "It served to establish a distinctive regional tradition for the emigrants and their children, and it provided them with a sense of purpose, direction, and continuity, a mode of social discipline and self-criticism, and an assurance about the future during a troubled time of transition." Stated differently, it functioned as a "process by which the New England clergy tried (rhetorically) to meet the challenges of history"[41] and to maintain the colony's religious conviction about the legitimacy of its divine vocation, its errand into the wilderness. When faced with external threats (the Roman Catholic French, the Indians) or natural disasters such as drought, crop failures, pestilence, disease, fire, and even earthquakes,[42] covenant renewal was called for and accomplished.

38. "Our fathers gave no thought to your miracles; they did not remember your many kindnesses. Yet he saved them for his name's sake. Then they believed his promises and sang his praise. But soon they forgot what he had done and did not wait for his counsel. Therefore the Lord was angry with his people. Many times he delivered them, but they were bent on rebellion. But he took note of their distress when he heard their cry; for their sake he remembered his covenant and out of his great love he relented" (from vv. 7, 8, 12, 13, 40, 43-45). It may or may not be significant that it is *only* here in the passage dealing with covenantal judgment that Groen indicates the actual scriptural source of his words.

39. John Calvin, *Institutes of the Christian Religion* 3.19.15 and 4.20.1, 2.

40. Sacvan Bercovitch, *The American Jeremiad* (London and Madison, Wis.: University of Wisconsin Press, 1978), 75.

41. Bercovitch, 80, 83.

42. New England experienced a "Great Earthquake" in November 1727. For a discussion of Jonathan Edwards's sermonic response to this event, see Stout, "The Puritans and Edwards," 145-47.

We do not need to delve into, much less attempt to settle, the historian's debates about the degree of self-conscious optimism among the New England clergy concerning the final success of the colony's divinely appointed mission.[43] The question we want to consider is whether Edwards's undeniable conviction about and millennial enthusiasm for New England's divine vocation did in fact lead him to conceive of America as a covenantally blessed and destined "redeemer nation," its destiny closely linked to if not virtually identified with the glorious final glory of the New Jerusalem.[44] In other words, did Edwards succumb to a civil religious messianism, a narrow tribalist public theology? There are hints that he did make such an identification.

In a fast-day sermon on 2 Chronicles 23:16 ("And Jehoiada made a covenant between him and between all the people, and between the king that they should be the Lord's people"), delivered in March 1737,[45] Edwards, after explaining the meaning of covenant in the Old Testament, went on to relate the covenantal promise of Exodus 19:6 ("If you keep my covenant ye shall be unto me . . . an holy nation") directly to New England: "We have been greatly distinguished by God as a covenant people. God has distinguished us by making known his covenant to us. We have been in a very [clear] manner a Land of Light. . . . The land of our forefathers has been such a land of such light. . . . You are a people that have been distinguished in the means that God has used with you."

But did such covenantal rhetoric lead to identifying New England's destiny with that of the glorious kingdom of God? Edwards comes close to such identification in the sermons he delivered when the colony was at war with the French. In the sermon just cited Edwards calls his flock to renewed dedication to the Word of God since their future was threatened by "'great numbers of papists' to the North, creating in North America an ominous 'mixture of dark

43. Perry Miller and after him, Sacvan Bercovitch, argue for an "optimistic" interpretation of the jeremiad, a "calculated strategy" in which the "threat" of covenant judgment was only "rhetorical" since God would never forsake his covenant people. See McDermott, esp. 14-36, for a thorough discussion of the broader issue, though not a final word on the jeremiad per se.

44. The conclusion of, among others, C. C. Goen, the editor of Edwards's writings on the Great Awakening in the Yale edition, *Works of Jonathan Edwards*, vol. 4, in his introduction, 71-72. See also his "Jonathan Edwards: A New Departure in Eschatology," *Church History* (March 1959): 25-46; I am persuaded by Gerald McDermott's careful critique of this position in favor of a more universal view of Edwards's millennialism in *One Holy and Happy Society*, chap. 2, "God's Manner with a Covenant People: The National Covenant." A similar critique and conclusion can be found in Bryant, "America as God's Kingdom."

45. The sermon has not yet been published but is carefully analyzed by Stout, "The Puritans and Edwards," 148-49. Quotations which follow are found on these pages.

with light.'" As England and France wrestled for control of the New World, Puritan preachers, Edwards included, sent their men off to war with covenantal blessing and assurance. "If they went to war in dependence on God and honored the terms of his covenant, then they could claim the victory: 'God is ready in such a case to hear the prayer of his People and give them success.'"[46]

The other piece of evidence usually cited by those who argue for seeing Edwards's public theology as a tribal civil religion, a parochially nationalistic messianism, is his description of the Great Awakening as a foretaste of the millennial age which was dawning and to appear in America. In his 1742 treatise *Some Thoughts concerning the Present Revival in New England*,[47] Edwards hints at the dawning of the millennium in America: "The New Jerusalem in this respect (the extraordinary degree of light, love, and spiritual joy) has begun to come down from heaven, and perhaps never were more of the prelibations of heaven's glory given upon earth" (*ST,* 346). He then links the revivals of his day to a hope for America:

> 'Tis not unlikely that this work of God's Spirit, that is so extraordinary and wonderful, is the dawning, or at least a prelude, of that glorious work of God, so often foretold in Scripture, which in the progress and issue of it, shall renew the world of mankind. If we consider how long since the things foretold, as what should precede this great event, have been accomplished; and how long this event has been expected by the church of God, and thought to be nigh by the most eminent men of God in the church; and withal consider what the state of things now is, and has for a considerable time been, in the church of God and world of mankind, we can't reasonably think otherwise, than that the beginning of this great work of God must be near. *And there are many things that make it probable that this work will begin in America.* (*ST,* 353, emphasis added)

In fact, according to Edwards, America was discovered for the millennial age: "This new world is probably now discovered, that the new and most glorious state of God's church might commence there; that God might in it begin a new world in a spiritual respect, when he creates the heavens and new earth" (*ST,* 354). Within the larger context of the new world, Edwards narrows the possible locale even more:

> And if we may suppose that his glorious work of God shall begin in any part

46. Stout, "The Puritans and Edwards," 150; the sermon on 1 Kings 8:44ff. was delivered on April 4, 1745.
47. In *Works of Jonathan Edwards,* 4:289-530.

of America, I think, if we consider the circumstances of the settlement of New England, it must needs appear the most likely of all American colonies, to be the place whence this work shall properly take its rise.

And if these things are so, it gives us more abundant reasons to hope that what is now seen in America, and especially in New England, may prove the dawn of that glorious day: and the very uncommon and wonderful circumstances and events of this work, seem to me strongly to argue that God intends it as the beginning or forerunner of something vastly great. (*ST*, 358)

The possibility of what God is doing also requires that his people actively respond by applying the Lord's work of redemption. Edwards interprets this application in what appears to be a postmillennial perspective.[48]

It is very dangerous for God's professing people to lie still, and not to come to the help of the Lord, whenever he remarkably pours out his Spirit, to carry on the work of redemption in the application of it; but above all, when he comes forth in that last and greatest outpouring of his Spirit, to introduce that happy day of God's power and salvation, so often spoken of. That is especially the appointed season of the application of the redemption of Christ; 'tis the proper time of the kingdom of heaven upon earth, the appointed time of Christ's reign: the reign of Satan as god of this world lasts till then. This is the proper time of actual redemption, or new creation, as is evident by Isa. 65:17-18 and 66:12, and Rev. 21:1. All the outpourings of the Spirit of God that are before this, are as it were by way of anticipation. (*ST*, 258)

But these are not Edwards's only, nor last, reflections on the New England revivals of the 1730s and 1740s. As the criticism of revivalist excesses mounted,[49] Edwards responded with his great work of 1746, *Religious Affections*,[50] in which he judges all experiential religion to be a mixture of true and false affections and calls for spiritual discernment: "'Tis a hard thing to be a hearty zealous friend of what has been *good* and glorious, in the late extraordinary appearances, and to rejoice much in it; and at the same time, to see the evil and pernicious tendency of what has been *bad*, and earnestly to oppose that.

48. According to Bercovitch (chap. 4), Edwards's contribution to the jeremiad tradition and to American millennialism is that he differed from his Puritan *premillennial* forebears by coming to a *postmillennial* view, positing "a golden age within history, and thereby [he] freed humanity, so to speak, to participate in the revolutions of the apocalypse" (94).

49. For example, the charge of Charles Chauncy, in his 1743 treatise, *Seasonable Thoughts on the State of Religion in New England*, that revivalism's raw enthusiasm is subversive of social order.

50. See n. 8 above.

But yet, I am humbly, but fully persuaded, we shall never be in the way of truth, nor go on in a way acceptable to God, and tending to the advancement of Christ's kingdom, till we do so" (*RA*, 85). In a desire to encourage the "good and glorious" in revivals, Edwards joined an initiative begun in Scotland in 1744 that called for

> *united, extraordinary* applications to the God of all grace, suitably acknowledging Him as the fountain of all the spiritual benefits and blessings of His church, and earnestly praying to Him, that He would *appear in his glory,* and favour Zion, and manifest His compassion to *the world of mankind,* by an abundant effusion of His Holy Spirit on *all* the churches, and the *whole inhabitable earth,* to revive true religion 'in *all parts of Christendom,* and to deliver *all nations* from their great and manifold spiritual calamities and miseries, and bless them with unspeakable benefits of His kingdom of our glorious Redeemer, and *fill the whole earth with his glory.*[51]

Edwards publicly joined this call for humility and prayer with his 1747 treatise, *An Humble Attempt to Promote Extraordinary Agreement and Visible Union of God's People in Extraordinary Prayer, for the Revival of Religion and the Advancement of Christ's Kingdom on Earth, Pursuant to Scripture Promises and Prophecies concerning the Last Time.*[52] As Bryant points out,[53] the focus of this treatise is on the church, the *universal* church, rather than America: "As 'tis the glory of the church of Christ, that she, in all her members, however dispersed, is thus *one,* one holy society, one city, one family, one body; so it is very desirable, that this union should be manifested, and become visible; and so, that her distant members should act as one, in those things that concern the common interest of the whole body, and in those duties and exercises wherein they have to do with their common Lord and Head, as seeking of him the common prosperity" (HA, 365).[54] It is also worth noting here how important union, including church union, was for Edwards: "Union is one of the most amiable things, that pertains to human society; yea. 'Tis one of the most beautiful and happy things on earth, which indeed makes earth most like heaven. God has 'made of one

51. The passage was cited by Edwards in his work "An Humble Attempt" (see following note [emphasis is added]); cited by Bryant, 77, who pointed out the universalism in the call by highlighting some of the same phrases.

52. Jonathan Edwards, "An Humble Attempt" (hereafter *HA*), in *The Works of Jonathan Edwards,* vol. 5, *Apocalyptic Writings,* ed. Stephen J. Stein (New Haven and London: Yale University Press, 1977), 307-436.

53. Bryant, 77-79.

54. Cited by Bryant, 78, who observes that "this is a far cry from the parochialism of Edwards' earlier millennial expectations."

blood all nations of men, to dwell on all the face of the earth' [Acts 17:26]; hereby teaching us this moral lesson, that it becomes mankind all to be united as one family" (*HA*, 364-65). A far cry from parochial and idolatrous nationalism indeed!

After his dismissal from Northampton in 1750, Edwards became a missionary to Native Americans at a small outpost on the frontier and, according to Bryant, his post-1750 writings[55] become more critical of actual church and colony life and his eschatology becomes more a transcendent critical principle by which all human actions are judged. Bryant cites the following passages from Edwards's writings of this period as evidence: "In God's sight no man living can be justified; but all are sinners, and exposed to condemnation. This is true of persons of all constitutions, capacities, conditions, manners, opinions, and education; in all countries, climates, nations, and ages; and through all the mighty changes and revolutions, which have come to pass in the habitable world."[56] The eschatological "already/not yet" tension is not broken by a triumphalist millennialism; the "not yet" remains unambiguous:

'Tis no solid objection against God's aiming at an infinitely perfect union of the creature with himself, that the particular time will never come when it can be said, the union is now infinitely perfect.

God in glorifying the saints in heaven with eternal felicity, aims to satisfy his infinite grace or benevolence, by the bestowment of a good infinitely valuable, because eternal: and yet there will never come the moment, when it can be said that now this infinitely valuable good has been actually bestowed.[57]

In Bryant's essay, which we have now considered in some length, it was his concern to show that Edwards at the very least modified his early millennialism in favor of a more universal and transcendent understanding of the kingdom and covenant of God. Gerald McDermott goes further and marshals a significant amount of evidence to show that more generally, even before his exile to

55. *Original Sin, Freedom of the Will, The Nature of True Virtue,* and *Dissertation concerning the End for Which God Created the World.* These treatises are found in the Yale edition of *The Works of Jonathan Edwards,* vols. 3, 1, and 8 (containing both *True Virtue* and *Dissertation*) respectively.

56. *The Works of Jonathan Edwards,* vol. 3, *Original Sin,* ed. Clyde A. Holbrook (New Haven and London: Yale University Press, 1970), 124; cited by Bryant, 83, who adds: "Need we say that this includes millennial America?"

57. Jonathan Edwards, "Dissertation concerning the End for Which God Created the World," in *The Works of Jonathan Edwards,* vol. 8, *Ethical Writings,* ed. Paul Ramsey (New Haven and London: Yale University Press, 1989), 536; cited by Bryant, 85.

Stockton, "Edwards' use of the national covenant was predominantly pessimistic in its treatment of Northampton and New England."[58] The question of change or development in Edwards's views is not as important here as McDermott's agreement with Bryant's conclusion that Edwards's enthusiasm for the approaching millennial age as he saw the unfolding of God's work of redemption in history, was not tribalist but *international*. McDermott concludes that "Edwards must now be added to the distinguished list of American cultural leaders who rejected triumphalist interpretations of American experience."[59] To place that claim into perspective and to continue the comparison with Abraham Kuyper, we shall now consider Edwards's millennialism in general and especially his interpretation of the book of Revelation.

Apocalyptic and Politics

Edwards's millennialism must be seen within his overall vision of the grand sweep of divinely directed redemptive providential history, a vision expressed most explicitly in the thirty sermons — all on Isaiah 51:8 — preached in 1738-39 and posthumously published in 1774 under the title *A History of the Work of Redemption*.[60] "From a literary point of view," notes Darrol Bryant, "*A History of the Work of Redemption* is, to use Northrop Frye's phrase, an encyclopedic myth, or . . . a 'metaphysical vision.' The function of such kinds of literature is to provide orientation; . . . its concern [is] to discern the rhythm of divine activity in history, it creates a 'cosmos' [by which] disorientation is overcome, [and] a people can move confidently into a future secured by a divine promise. The whole historical process is at once ordered and yet opened out. History is, Edwards writes, 'all one work, one design.' And that design is the 'work of Redemption.'"[61]

Here too, many scholars have put forward the claim that "Edwards' millennialism characterized America or New England as a redeemer nation with a mission to save other peoples."[62] In addition to providing a "radical justification

58. McDermott, 17.

59. McDermott, 36.

60. *The Works of Jonathan Edwards*, vol. 9, *A History of the Work of Redemption*, ed. John F. Wilson (New Haven and London: Yale University Press, 1989).

61. Bryant, 62-63.

62. McDermott, 38; for a thorough survey of the literature following this line of thought and a convincing critique of it, see McDermott's second chapter, "The Glorious Work of God and the Beautiful Society: The Premillennial Age and the Millennium," 37-92. Cf. Bryant, "America as God's Kingdom." For what follows in this section I am indebted to McDermott and Bryant.

for early [American] nationalism" and national "self-interest," Edwards's millennialism has also been linked to the "ideal of American progress. Associated with the millennium, American economic and social progress became part of the deity's plan for world redemption."[63] McDermott, however, insists that "in his religious imagination Jonathan Edwards was a world citizen. The parochialism and egoistic nationalism ascribed to him would have struck him as myopic and characteristic only of unregenerate, natural virtue."[64] There is clear evidence for this conclusion in Edwards's treatment of true virtue, which, in distinction from mere natural virtue, does not make affection for any particular being the ultimate goal but always subordinates particular loves (including nations) to what Edwards called "benevolence to *Being in general*" or God.[65] The millennium, in other words, is not ultimate; "it is not being-in-general!"[66] For our purposes in this chapter we shall dwell a little longer on Edwards's interpretation of the Apocalypse of John,[67] comparing it with Abraham Kuyper's.

The Apocalypse was a lifelong obsession of Edwards.[68] He mentioned his preoccupation in his "Personal Narrative,"[69] made entries about the millennium in his private notebooks until the end of his life,[70] and in "a telling sign of the fascination eschatology held for [him], Revelation was the only book of the Bible on which he wrote a separate commentary."[71] Here, incidentally, Abraham Kuyper, who also wrote a full set of meditations on the entire Apocalypse,[72] is closer to his American than his Genevan soul mate. Edwards, it should be noted, also was not reluctant to preach on the last book of the Bible;

63. McDermott, 39.

64. McDermott, 43.

65. Jonathan Edwards, *The Nature of True Virtue* (hereafter *TV*), in *Works of Jonathan Edwards*, 8:554-56, 609-12. Both McDermott and Bryant point this out in their discussion of Edwards's millennialism.

66. Bryant, 84.

67. Jonathan Edwards, "Notes on the Apocalyse," in *The Works of Jonathan Edwards*, vol. 5, *Apocalyptic Writings* (hereafter *AW*), 95-306.

68. "The book of Revelation fascinated Jonathan Edwards, America's premier philosopher-theologian, a fact that has been a source of bewilderment and embarrassment to some students of American thought" (Stephen J. Stein, introduction to *AW*, 1).

69. Faust and Johnson, 65; cited by McDermott, 45.

70. See Stein, introduction to *AW*, 8-29.

71. McDermott, 45. McDermott notes that "in contrast, it was the only book on which Calvin did *not* write a commentary."

72. Abraham Kuyper, *The Revelation of St. John*, trans. John H. De Vries (Grand Rapids: Eerdmans, 1935). This meditational commentary was originally published (as all of Kuyper's meditations were) on a weekly basis (forty-two in total) in *De Heraut* and then posthumously as the last section in a four-volume work, *Van de Voleinding (On the Consummation)*, in 1931 by J. H. Kok, Kampen.

"sixty-six sermons on the Revelation remain among his papers, evidence of a strong homiletic interest in that part of the Bible."[73] A final piece of evidence showing Kuyper's keen interest in Revelation is the remarkably high number of citations of the book in his writings in general, even apart from his meditations on the book. The textual index for Kuyper's works has (by my unofficial count) in the neighborhood of eleven hundred references; by comparison, Paul's letter to the Romans has approximately six hundred.[74]

What joins Edwards's and Kuyper's reflections on Revelation is their common interest in history and the role of specific events in the overall providential divine plan and design. Kuyper's daily editorial reflections in *De Standaard* as well as occasional addresses about such topics as "the crisis in South Africa,"[75] not to mention his parliamentary speeches[76] and addresses to the national meetings of the Antirevolutionary Party,[77] all reflect a thoroughgoing acquaintance with current events in the world and a willingness if not ea-

73. Stein, introduction to *AW*, 15. A list of the extant sermons can be found in *AW*, app. B, 440-43.

74. *Tekstregister op de Werken van Dr. A. Kuyper* (Grand Rapids: B. Sevensma, 1906); this figure is all the more remarkable when one considers that it does not include Kuyper's meditations on the Apocalypse, which were written near the end of his life.

75. Abraham Kuyper, *De Crisis in Zuid-Afrika* (Amsterdam and Pretoria: Höveker & Wormser, 1899); cf. Abraham Kuyper, *Plancius-Rede* (Amsterdam: J. H. Kruyt, 1884). The latter address is a clear example of Kuyper's direct identification of specific military success with divine purpose. At a gathering of the Dutch Reformed labor union *Patrimonium* on March 11, 1884, a delegation of South African dignitaries, including President Paul Kruger and triumphant Transvaal general Nicholaas Smit, were guests of honor. Kuyper's address to the gathering concluded with this battle cry and theatrical gesture as he presented the delegation with a commemorative flag:

> On this flag *Patrimonium* has written this proverb: "In God we shall do brave things!" — You, General with your soldiers, constantly do great things in the Name of your God!
> And now, before this flag is passed into your hands, yet still this one thing: Place your right hand in mine and with that, promise to this people that never, no matter what the future may bring, *may this flag fall into the hands of the British.*

(J. C. Rullmann, *Kuyper-Bibliographie: Deel II (1879-1890)* [Kampen: Kok, 1929], 109)

76. Abraham Kuyper, *Parlementaire Redevoeringen,* 4 vols. (Amsterdam: Van Holkema & Warendorf, 1908-10).

77. Gathered together in a larger collection of keynote addresses to ARP deputies, *Geen Vergeefs Woord: Verzamelde Deputaten-Redevoeringingen* (Kampen: Kok, 1951). Twenty of the first twenty-two main addresses to ARP deputies between April 3, 1879, and May 2, 1918, were delivered by Kuyper in his capacity as chairman of the party. The two exceptions, April 13, 1905, and October 17, 1907, were delivered by Herman Bavinck.

gerness to interpret them in the light of providential purpose. Edwards similarly, while "preoccupied with observing the progress of God's kingdom and praying for its advancement," also carefully monitored "contemporary events for signs of divine activity":[78]

> I had great longings for the advancement of Christ's kingdom in the world. My secret prayer used to be in great part taken up in praying for it. If I heard the least hint of anything that happened in any part of the world, that appeared to me, in some respect or other to have a favorable aspect on the interest of Christ's kingdom, my soul eagerly catched at it; and it would much animate and refresh me. I used to be earnest to read public newspapers, mainly for that end; to see if I could not find some news favorable to the interest of religion in the world.[79]

Yet Edwards and Kuyper were not interested primarily in making historical identifications in order to plot a divine timetable, though neither was reluctant to do some charting.[80] In his "notes" on the Apocalypse, Edwards interpreted the vision concerning the Antichrist as applying to the Roman papacy and calculated on the basis of the forty-two weeks of Revelation 13 and 20 that the papacy would fall "about 1866" (AW, 129).[81] However, in his Humble Attempt Ed-

---

78. Stein, introduction to AW, 10.

79. Jonathan Edwards, "Personal Narrative," in A Jonathan Edwards Reader, 288-89.

80. Though it needs to be noted at this point that Edwards's speculations were in his *private* notebook. Though Edwards did translate his private reflections into sermons, Stephen Stein characterizes the relation between the private and public Edwards this way: "Speculation in private but discretion in public came to be characteristic of him. He kept conjectures to himself in the notebook and in his sermons utilized more conventional and less controversial eschatological ideas — heaven, hell, the blessedness of one and the terror of the other. The millennium, a major subject of Edwards's; private reflections, was noticeably absent as a leading topic in his early sermons, even on occasions when it would have served his announced ends. Sometimes he avoided explicit reference to it, preferring indirect expressions subject to more than one interpretation, perhaps in order to escape the taint of fanaticism and radicalism associated with the idea" (introduction to AW, 19).

81. A striking example is Edwards's careful charting of world events fulfilling the prophecies of the sixth vial in the Apocalypse and the drying up of the Euphrates River (Rev. 16:12). Edwards takes the Euphrates as a metaphor for "the outward carnal supplies of the false antichristian church, in her worldly pomp and vain glory." The prophecy thus means this, according to Edwards: "When the waters that supply this mystical Babylon, come to be dried up in this sense, it will prepare the way for the enemies of antichristian corruption, that seek her overthrow. The wealth of the Church of Rome, and of the powers that support it, is very much its defense. After the streams of her revenues and riches are dried up, or very greatly diminished, her walls will be as it were broken down, and she will become weak and defenseless, and exposed to easy ruin" (HA, 416). In October 1747 Ed-

wards is historically more general. He observes that "it may be many ways for the comfort and benefit of God's church in her afflicted state, to know that the reign of Antichrist is to be no more than 1260 years: and *some things in general* may be argued concerning the approach of it, when it is near. . . . But 'tis not reasonable to expect that God should make known to us beforehand, the precise time of Christ's coming in his kingdom" (*HA*, 395, emphasis added). Kuyper's approach is similar.

While willing to make general summary judgments about broad historical periods[82] and insisting that Revelation does contain predictive, yet-to-be-fulfilled prophecy,[83] Kuyper also insists that our ability to make judgments about current and future historical events is limited and that we should not indulge our speculative curiosity on this matter. To attempt too close a linkage between prophecy and specific current and future events is a form of "pagan soothsaying" rather than biblical prophecy, which, Kuyper insists, provides "general impressions of what is to come, but does so in a fantastic, varying, dioramatic form. [In this way] particulars are hidden in it, but one can only see them in hindsight, *after* the prophecies have been fulfilled." Kuyper sets this forth as a rule: "Prophecy is given to us so that *when it has taken place*, then the church can acknowledge that the Lord has spoken in this way."[84]

Concretely, one can see Kuyper's application of this method in his treatment of the "Babylon" metaphor in Revelation. Babylon must not be taken literally, Kuyper insists, but "must be taken in the figurative sense, as that World Power which *at all times* has been inimical to the Kingdom of God, to Christ

---

wards began a ledger culled from newspapers, magazines, and correspondence of events that indicated to him "the reduction of the revenues and riches of the papacy. Through the next years he watched with delight the misfortunes of the Catholic powers — commercial, political, social, and military — confident that they betokened the approach of better times for the church. In a second list of contemporary events, Edwards tallied evangelical successes throughout the world, entering accounts culled from his reading, his correspondence, and his own experience. He was convinced that the church would begin to prosper while her enemies suffered under the last three vials" (Stein, introduction to *AW*, 46-47). The first list, "An Account of Events Probably Fulfilling the Sixth Vial on the River Euphrates," is published in *AW*, 253-84; the second, "Events of an Hopeful Aspect on the State of Religion," in *AW*, 285-97.

82. See Kuyper, *Revelation of St. John*, 24-25; for Edwards's general framework, see Stein, introduction to *AW*, 12-15.

83. Kuyper considers the first three chapters of the Apocalyse the "historical" part of the book, describing through "ideal types" the condition of the church of all ages. Chapters 4 to the end are "prophecy" concerning the "end times," more specifically the period just prior to the return of Christ (see *Revelation of St. John*, 41-48).

84. Abraham Kuyper, *E Voto Dordraceno*, 4 vols. (Amsterdam: J. A. Wormser, 1893), 2:200 (on Lord's Day 22).

and to His church," a spirit that in the contemporary world "seems to break out in the revolutionary circles of our times in a way that was scarcely deemed possible before."[85] Here we encounter Kuyper's understanding of the nature of apocalyptic literature.

Kuyper's basic distinction or antithesis is between what he calls a "human way of representation" and "the Divine way of viewing things."[86] It is particularly with respect to history that the "human way" is restricted to a mere chronological line of events while the divine eye sees the whole — the end as well as the beginning and the course. "With us beginnings are first and endings later, but with God the result which he plans is first, and from this is inferred what the beginning must be. Thus the reverse order." This is particularly true of salvation history. "We reckon from the Ascension of Christ across a lapse of many centuries until we come to the Consummation, but God considers first the final outcome, and when this has been determined and the process of its unfolding has begun, every requisite to bring about the intended result follows. Note this with special care. With us the outcome of things is the result of preceding data. With God first the end is determined, and only then do the data arise which must eventuate in this outcome of things. . . . The world process, that began with Jesus' Ascension and shall end with the last judgment, forms in the Divine view of things one coherent whole."[87]

But if this is so, how does the divine plan become known to human beings, who are inextricably bound to the finite, historical-causal nexus? Can the divine plan be represented at all to us and, if so, how? The clue here is the nature of apocalyptic language itself. When Kuyper seeks to explain the "Divine way of viewing," he is himself, of course, also restricted to "a human way of representation"; he is forced to use an analogy.[88] "The same principle [from the

85. Kuyper, *Revelation of St. John*, 140, 143, emphasis added.

86. Kuyper, *Revelation of St. John*, 35-36; Dutch: *Van De Voleinding*, 4:81-82. The unequal terms of this antithesis should be carefully noted: "human way of representation" (*menschelijke wijze van voorstelling*) and "Divine way of viewing things" (*Goddelijke beschouwing*).

87. Kuyper, *Revelation of St. John*, 36.

88. It is also noteworthy that Kuyper earlier used an organic/botanical metaphor to establish the difference between the human and divine "ways": "When someone from abroad sends us the seed of a choice plant, which we have never seen and know nothing of, we put it in the ground, and watch the growth of stalk and bud, until we see the flower bloom in all the fulness of its development and enchanting beauty, for then it has come to its Consummation. This is our way of doing things, but this cannot possibly be God's way. God did not somewhere come across the seed of a choice flower, which He planted to see how it would unfold, but His all-seeing eyes saw first the flower that was to be, and from this was inferred what the seed had to be, from which so choice a flower could germinate" (*Revelation of St. John*, 36).

209

end back to the beginning]," he observes, "that operates in art, operates in this [the divine plan and manner]. He who is creative in the world of thought, feels himself suddenly [Dutch has *onmiddelijk*, 'immediately'] apprehended as it were by a striking idea or noble form of art, and only afterwards does he look for the necessary data that will embody the same."[89] Kuyper follows this with a direct rebuke at "members of Reformed churches" who, by "the willful closing of our eyes to what God has given us in art," have engaged in "an entirely unwarranted underestimation of one of the most glorious revelations in God's creation." Then, in a judgment worthy of any of the great romantics,[90] Kuyper notes that "in art there is an inner compulsion that is almost divine. This is especially evident in the spontaneity, the of-itself-ness which in art plays so mighty a role. In our processes of thought idea follows upon idea, as in life event upon event, but in art the things that will presently take shape and form are already beforehand a part as it were of the root of our inner life. The genius, the real artist feels what he shall presently produce take hold of him as an unseen power, and while he does not understand it, it overwhelms him."[91]

Then Kuyper delivers the interpretive payoff for John's Revelation: "And prophecy is part of the world of art, the Apocalypse has its place in it, together with public worship and all the riches of mysticism."[92] As part of the world of art, prophecy and apocalyptic cannot be neatly systematized or lined up to provide an orderly chronology.[93] In fact, Kuyper now pursues a further distinction among the race of humans who make "representations": those Easterners who are accustomed to "mystical representations" and thus, with the Bible, express themselves in the "stylized, symbolic-aesthetic language of the East,"[94] and "we, Westerners, [who] know nothing of these mystical representations which are common in the East and can only faintly visualize

89. Kuyper, *Revelation of St. John*, 36.

90. For a summary of the religious and philosophical patterns of literary romanticism as well as its understanding of poetry as "divinely inspired," see C. De Deugd, *Het Metafysisch Grondpatroon van het Romantische Literaire Denken: De Fenomenologie van een Geestesgesteldheid* (Groningen: J. B. Wolters, 1966).

91. Kuyper, *Revelation of St. John*, 37.

92. Kuyper, *Revelation of St. John*, 37.

93. G. C. Berkouwer, *De Wederkomst van Christus*, vol. 1 (Kampen: Kok, 1961), 274; though see directly below for Kuyper's inconsistency on this matter.

94. Abraham Kuyper, *Encyclopaedie der Heilige Godgeleerdheid*, vol. 3, 2nd ed. (Kampen: Kok, 1909), 168. For this and subsequent references (including translation of some key expressions) to Kuyper's understanding of biblical language, I am indebted to Richard B. Gaffin, Jr., "Geerhardus Vos and the Interpretation of Paul," in *Jerusalem and Athens: Critical Discussions on the Theology and Apologetics of Cornelius Van Til*, ed. E. R. Geehan (n.p. : Presbyterian and Reformed, 1971), 228-37.

them,"[95] thanks to our dominant "penchant for dialectical clarity."[96] It is here, in his understanding of the nature of biblical language and his strong resistance to in any way conceiving of the biblical writers as "theologians," or "systematic thinkers," that Kuyper comes close to positing an antithesis between the aesthetic/literary/rhetorical and the philosophical/scientific mental modes.[97] Yet, even here in his reflection on the Apocalypse, Kuyper is not consistent.[98]

We noted earlier that Kuyper preferred general rather than specific historical identifications of key symbols in the Apocalypse. Thus Babylon is not, as it was for Edwards, the papacy, but "the symbolical name of the earthly power which has established itself among men and set its face against God."[99] Furthermore, particularly over against all forms of chiliastic literalism, Kuyper insists that the millennium is to be understood "symbolically," as is befitting the "peculiar character" of the Apocalypse.[100] And yet, profoundly moved by the devastation of the Great War, Kuyper's rhetoric intensifies in its apocalyptic *fin de siècle* tone and becomes quite specific: "Now that China and Hindustan have entered the arena of the world's life, the prophecy of Rev. 9, 20, 21 is almost *literally* being fulfilled. Heathendom comes more and more to the fore, and in an unprecedented way slaves to idols are participants in the settlement of world problems."[101] Kuyper's interpretive method moves away from the idealist and becomes increasingly historicist:

This is deeply significant to him who accepts the authenticity of the Apocalypse, because even one hundred years ago all this was but cursorily read and no one thought all this could ever be fulfilled; and naturally unbelieving majorities now do not incline to recognize in current events the fulfillment of apocalyptic prophecy. Yet he who accepts that prophecy can not deny that in recent years whole series of phenomena have presented themselves which exactly square with what the Apocalypse foretells; and especially since the world war positive indications are abroad that apocalyptic predictions, whose fulfillment almost no one expected, have now surprisingly and almost literally materialized, and the question is whether the Consummation is not already close at hand. As regards paganism . . . this makes one ask whether this spread of heathen cults among Christian nations does not clearly show

95. Kuyper, *Revelation of St. John*, 34.
96. Kuyper, *Encyclopaedie*, 3:164.
97. See above, 20-28.
98. For what follows in the next paragraph I am indebted to Berkouwer, 1:274 n. 55.
99. Kuyper, *Revelation of St. John*, 106-7.
100. Kuyper, *Revelation of St. John*, 276-77, 271.
101. Kuyper, *Revelation of St. John*, 109, emphasis added.

that even now the closing verses of Revelation 9 are lamentably yet strikingly confirmed by what real life gives one more and more to see and hear.[102]

For Kuyper as well as for Edwards, therefore, the combination of profound conviction about divine redemptive sovereignty *in history* and the need to apply Scripture's promises concretely in the context of history's broken hopes and dashed dreams inevitably results in an ambiguous rather than consistent vision. Maintaining a healthy eschatological balance is not easy when faced with the impossible choice between the Scylla of potentially socially and politically irrelevant transcendence on the one hand and the Charybdis of triumphalist revolutionary millennialism on the other. It is a tribute to Edwards's and Kuyper's spiritual discernment that they were capable of self-correction at critical moments. That they may not have wholly succeeded and that their epigones were less successful in the task is less an occasion to offer critique than it is to learn from them. Perhaps the most significant lesson to be learned here is the caution against basing a public theology too heavily on one's interpretation of how *historical* realities reflect divine providential purpose. Identifying one's public vision and political cause with God's plan makes it unfalsifiable and opens up the real temptation to demagoguery. It is significant that Edwards and Kuyper both did not restrict the foundation of their public theologies to *historical* eschatological readings of divine purpose but also provided other *revelational* and *ontological* grounding for their views.[103]

Trinitarian Beauty and the Order of Common Grace

The profound theocentricity shared by Edwards and Kuyper is a vision in which all creation, humanity included, exists for and reflects God and his glory. God, Kuyper observed, has "impressed a religious expression" on all creation, even "the whole of unconscious nature."[104] The earth, to use Calvin's language, is the "the-

---

102. Kuyper, *Revelation of St. John,* 109-10.

103. This insight is a key contribution of Gerald McDermott's *One Holy and Happy Society.* McDermott also insists that Edwards's "ontology has important implications for social and political theory" (97). We need not explore here whether Edwards's ontology gives rise to a different set of concerns than his historical ones or whether, as Sang Hyun Lee has argued, "Edwards' postmillennialism and the accompanying positive view of history . . . are grounded in, and are properly understood only within, the framework of his dynamic reconception of the divine being" (*The Philosophical Theology of Jonathan Edwards* [Princeton: Princeton University Press, 1988], 215).

104. Kuyper, *Lectures on Calvinism,* 45.

ater of God's glory."[105] This luminescence of nature is a direct consequence of Edwards's and Kuyper's commonly held conviction that the being of the world reflects the very Being of the triune God. To discuss the very inner Being of God, both agree, one must begin with love. For Edwards the essence of the divine being can be expressed in terms of holiness, beauty, or love, and all three are intimately interwoven together.[106] "'Tis in God's infinite love to Himself that His holiness consists. As all creature holiness is to be resolved into love, as the Scripture teaches us, so doth the holiness of God Himself consist in infinite love to Himself. God's holiness is the infinite beauty and excellence of His nature, and God's excellency consists in His love to Himself as we have observed."[107] For Kuyper too, love is the ontological foundation of the triune Godhead. It is "superficial minds," according to Kuyper, who "conceive of the Love of God only as forgiving sin; as too good to tolerate suffering; too peaceable to allow war." But the Christian, rooted in Scripture and knowing that God's love is "*holy* Love," is able to "derive from the Word [a] deeper and richer conception of love" from the triune Being of God himself, for "the Love-life whereby these Three mutually love each other is the Eternal Being Himself. This alone is the true and real life of love."[108] Though Edwards tends to speak more of beauty in relation to the being of the Trinity[109] than Kuyper typically does,[110] the latter shares with his American Puritan counterpart a similar

105. Calvin, *Institutes* 1.5.8; 1.6.2; 1.14.20; 2.6.1; cf. Susan E. Schreiner, *The Theater of His Glory: Nature and the Natural Order in the Thought of John Calvin* (Durham, N.C.: Labyrinth, 1991).

106. See Amy Plantinga Pauw, "'Heaven Is a World of Love': Edwards on Heaven and the Trinity," *Calvin Theological Journal* 30 (1995): 392-401, for a helpful summary of the importance of eschatological love in Edwards's theological and socio-ethical thought.

107. Jonathan Edwards, "An Essay on the Trinity," in *Treatise on Grace and Other Posthumously Published Writings,* ed. Paul Helm (Cambridge and London: James Clarke, 1971), 110. The only other place Edwards systematically explores the doctrine of the Trinity in any sustained way is in his "Miscellanies" (in *The Works of Jonathan Edwards,* vol. 13, ed. Thomas A. Schafer [New Haven and London: Yale University Press, 1994], esp. ##94, 96, 98, 117, 143, 144, 146, 151, 238). For a full listing, see Edwards's own "Table to the 'Miscellanies'" (pp. 113-50) and the editor's "General Index" (pp. 569-79), s.v. "Trinity," but also s.v. "Christ," "Incarnation," and "Spirit." "Miscellanies," #146, is noteworthy as a characteristic statement of Edwards's view that the essence of the divine being is love (and delight): "The word 'spirit,' most commonly in Scripture, is put for affections of the mind; but there is no other affection in God essentially, properly and primarily, but love and delight — and that in himself, for into this is his love and delight in his creatures resolvable" (p. 299).

108. Abraham Kuyper, *The Work of the Holy Spirit,* trans. Henri De Vries (Grand Rapids: Eerdmans, 1941 [1900]), 514-15.

109. Delattre, chap. 7, "Beauty and the Trinity."

110. Though when he speaks of the Holy Spirit's eschatological triumph of love,

conviction about the glorious self-sufficiency of God's love. The following could have been written by Edwards: "Love is not God, but God is love; and he is sufficient to himself to love absolutely and forever. He has no need of the creature, and the exercise of His Love did not begin with the creature whom he could love, but it flows and springs eternally in the Love-life of the Triune God. God is love; its perfection, divine beauty, real dimensions, and holiness are not found in men, not even in the best of God's children, but scintillate only around the Throne of God."[111]

If love is the foundational reality of divine Being, nonetheless there is also a distinction of persons in the Godhead, and Edwards directly, Kuyper indirectly, follow Augustine's trinitarian lead in attributing love in a special way to the third person of the Trinity. "The Holy Spirit," writes Edwards, "is the act of God between the Father and the Son infinitely loving and delighting in each other. . . . And it also appears that the Holy Spirit is this act of the Deity, even love and delight, because from eternity there was no other act in God but thus acting with respect to himself, and delighting perfectly and infinitely in himself, or that infinite delight there is between the Father and the Son; for the object of God's perfect act must necessarily be himself, because there is no other. . . . And as to holiness, 'tis delight in excellency, 'tis God's sweet consent to himself, or in other words, his perfect delight in himself; which we have shown to be the Holy Spirit."[112] Even

Kuyper will also use the word "beauty" along with shining metaphors of luminescence, as in the following passages (all three in less than two full pages!) from his *Work of the Holy Spirit*:

> But even then [when "Love's triumph shall be complete"] the work of the Holy Spirit is not finished, but thenceforth shall continue forever. Then the heavenly felicity will only *begin* to unfold itself in a way wholly divine, and without the slightest impediment the Rose of Love will disclose its brilliant beauty. (545)

> But when the victory is His, and the Sun of Love stands at last in dazzling glory in the cloudless sky, then, and only then, does He begin to show His perfect beauty and to radiate His blessed, cherishing rays. (546)

> But after the judgment, these internal hindrances and external conflicts being ended forever, the Holy Spirit's working shall penetrate from center to circumference and gloriously unfold the inward beauty of the body of Christ. (547)

111. Kuyper, *Holy Spirit*, 515; cf. this passage on the same page: "Before God created heaven and earth with all their inhabitants, the eternal Love of Father, Son, and Holy Spirit shone with unseen splendor in the divine Being. Love exists not for the sake of the world, but for God's sake; and when the world came into existence, Love remained unchanged; and if every creature were to disappear, it would remain just as rich and glorious as ever. Love exists and works in the Eternal Being apart from the creature; and its radiation upon the creature is but a feeble reflection of its being."

112. Edwards, "Miscellanies," #94.

though Kuyper's language is less direct, he is no less passionately eloquent about the Holy Spirit as the Love "which dwells in the heart." "And this is the proper work of the Holy Spirit, that shall remain forever," Kuyper writes. "When there remains no more sin to be atoned for, nor any unholiness to be sanctified, when all the elect shall jubilate before the throne, even then the Holy Spirit shall perform this divine work of keeping the Love of God actively dwelling in their hearts. . . . so long as . . . the Holy Spirit dwells in our hearts . . . even the Love of God dwells in us."[113] It is "the Holy Spirit whom we feel and discover in the soul as Love," because "God is love and through the Holy Spirit Love dwells in all God's children."[114]

What are the social-ethical or public-theological implications of this emphasis on the Holy Spirit, glory, and love?[115] Edwards makes more of this directly than does Kuyper. "For Edwards, Christian love is fundamentally a reaching beyond self to the other. It is a reorientation of concern from self to neighbor."[116] In one of the series of sermons Edwards preached in 1738 on 1 Corinthians 13, "Charity and Its Fruits,"[117] he explained, "They who have a Christian spirit seek not their own things but also the things of others." The "others" here are God and the neighbor; Edwards's two subpoints in the sermon are: "1. A Christian spirit seeks to please and glorify God" and "2. They who have a Christian spirit have a spirit to seek the good of their fellow creatures" (*CF*, 259). This Christian spirit "more particularly," according to Edwards, also is "a merciful spirit" and "a liberal spirit," and "it disposes a person to be public spirited." Edwards spells this out in some detail. "A man of a right spirit is not of a narrow, private spirit; but he is greatly concerned for the good of the public community to which he belongs, and particularly of the town

113. Kuyper, *Holy Spirit,* 520-21.

114. Kuyper, *Holy Spirit,* 521, 526.

115. We leave aside here the important social-ethical implications of Edwards's metaphysics of being and focus on love since our concern is to highlight only those elements in Edwards's thought that have parallels in Kuyper's. For a good summary of the *ontological* dimensions of Edwards's public theology, particularly his understanding of universal benevolence, see McDermott, chap. 3, "Private Affection and Publick Spirit: The Edwardsean Social Ethic," 93-116. We shall, however, consider some of these implications under the category of common grace later in this chapter. For a fascinating and provocative essay exploring the Edwardean (and Puritan) notion of glory as a key to what is distinctive as an American theological theme, see Herbert W. Richardson, "Toward an American Theology," in *Toward an America Theology* (New York: Harper & Row, 1967).

116. McDermott, 107; some of the citations from Edwards that follow are also cited, at least in part, by McDermott.

117. Jonathan Edwards, "Charity and Its Fruits" (hereafter *CF*), in *Works of Jonathan Edwards,* 8:123-397.

where he dwells. . . . A Christian spirited man will also be concerned for the good of his country, and it disposes him to lay out himself for it. . . . They who are of a Christian spirit are of a more enlarged spirit; they are concerned for the good of the church and people of God in general" (*CF*, 259-61). Finally, Edwards speaks directly and pointedly to those who are in positions of public trust in church and state:

> Especially will a Christian spirit dispose those who stand in a public capacity, such as ministers and magistrates and all public officers, to seek the public good. It will dispose magistrates to act as the fathers of the commonwealth with that care and concern for the public good that the father of a family has for the family, watchful against any public dangers, forward to improve their power to promote the public benefit, not being governed by selfish views in their administrations, seeking only or mainly to enrich themselves, or make themselves great, and advance themselves on the spoils of others as wicked rulers very often do. A Christian spirit will dispose ministers not to seek their own, not merely to seek a maintenance, aiming to get whatever they can out of their people to enrich themselves and their families, and to clothe themselves with the fleeces of their flock. But a Christian spirit will dispose them mainly to seek the good of their flock, to feed their souls as a good shepherd feeds his flock, and carefully watches over it, to lead it to good pasture, and defend it from wolves and other beasts of prey. (*CF*, 261-62)

It also needs to be noted that for Edwards the love that reflects a Christian spirit is a universal, *indiscriminate* love as well as a *bodily* love.[118] According to Edwards, "true virtue must chiefly consist in love to God; the Being of beings, infinitely the greatest and best of beings."[119] To distinguish this from inferior, secondary loves, Edwards will also use expressions such as "general benevolence" or "benevolence [consent] to Being in general" (*TV*, 540) to describe the love that is the highest beauty. "But there is another and higher beauty in true virtue, and in all truly virtuous dispositions and exercises, than what consists in any uniformity or similarity of various things; viz. the *union of heart* to *Being in general*, or to God the Being of beings, which appears in these virtues; and which those virtues, when true, are the various expression or effects of. Benevolence to Being in general, or to Being simply considered, is entirely a distinct thing from uniformity in the midst of variety, and is a superior kind of beauty" (*TV*, 571).

118. For both of these points and the Edwards references that follow, I am indebted to McDermott, 107-16.

119. Edwards, *TV*, 8:550.

But that it is secondary does not mean that love for particular beings is unimportant or that it can be neglected: "'Tis true that benevolence to Being in general, when a person hath it, will naturally incline him to justice, or proportion in the exercises of it. He that loves Being, simply considered, will naturally, other things being equal, love particular beings in a proportion compounded of the degree of being, and the degree of virtue, or benevolence to being which they have. And that is to love beings in proportion to their dignity" *(TV,* 571). It is to our fellow human beings, and especially to the poor, that we are duty bound to show love. In a sermon entitled "Christian Charity,"[120] Edwards insists that "this duty is absolutely commanded and much insisted on, in the word of God" ("Charity," 164). The reason Edwards gives is ontological, based on a common created human nature.

> [Charity] is most reasonable, considering the general state and nature of mankind. This is such as renders it most reasonable that we should love our neighbour as ourselves; for men are made in the image of our God, and on this account are worthy of our love. Besides, we are all nearly allied one to another by nature. We have all the same nature . . . God hath made us with such a nature, that we cannot subsist without the help of one another. Mankind in this respect are as the members of the natural body, one cannot subsist alone, without an union and the help of the rest. ("Charity," 164)

Negatively, "he who is all for himself, and none for his neighbours, deserves to be cut off from the benefit of human society, and to be turned out among wild beasts, to subsist by himself as well as he can. A private niggardly spirit is more suitable for wolves, and other beasts of prey, than for human beings" ("Charity," 164-65). Edwards also provides a striking answer to the objection against being charitable to ill-tempered, ungrateful, undeserving, evil people. Since Christ himself loved us "while we were enemies," Edwards reasons, "we are particularly required to be kind to the unthankful and to the evil." Furthermore, in so doing we follow the common grace "example of our heavenly Father, who causes his sun to rise on the evil and on the good, and sendeth rain on the just and on the unjust. We are obliged, not only to be kind to them that are so to us, but to them that hate, and that despitefully use us" ("Charity," 171). Finally, Edwards grounds the obligation to neighbor love in the very created purpose of humanity. Humans are created *by* God and *for* God. In an echo of the opening Lord's Day of the Heidelberg Catechism, Edwards writes:

120. In *The Works of Jonathan Edwards,* ed. Sereno E. Dwight, rev. Edward Hickman, 2 vols. (Edinburgh: Banner of Truth Trust, 1976 [1834]), 2:163-73 (hereafter "Charity").

You should not seek your own things only, for you are not your own. You have not made yourself, nor are you made for yourself; you are neither the author nor end of your being. Nor is it you that uphold yourself in being, nor is it you that provides for yourself; you are not dependent on yourself. But there is another who hath made you, and preserves you, and provides for you. And he who has made you has made you for himself, and for the good of your fellow creatures, and not only for yourself. And besides, you profess yourself to be a Christian; and if you are so, you are not your own, for there is another who has bought you. (*CF*, 268)

The second feature of Edwards's understanding of love that we want to note is its *bodily* character. This is already apparent in his concern for loving the poor and is a key mark of genuine piety. One of the signs of genuine religious affection is its expression in bodily love. Edwards criticizes those who "pretend a great love to men's souls, that are not compassionate and charitable toward their bodies . . . [because] they must part with money out of their pockets. But a true Christian love to our brethren, extends both to their souls and bodies. . . . *And if the compassion of professing Christians towards others don't work in the same ways* [i.e., 'to their bodies'], *it is a sign that it is not true Christian compassion*" (*RA*, 369, emphasis added).[121] Even though sin and the need for charity to the poor will end, love as the gift and task of the Holy Spirit will never end: for Edwards, "Heaven is a world of Love."[122]

In order to explore another dimension of the Holy Spirit's work and its social-ethical, public-theological implication, we need to specify even further the distinctive task of the Holy Spirit. According to Kuyper, the general distinction of the outgoing works of the Godhead is this: "In every work effected by Father, Son, and Holy Ghost in common, the power *to bring forth* proceeds from the Father; the power *to arrange* from the Son; the power *to perfect* from the Holy Spirit."[123] The notion of telos or perfected destiny is the key to the work of the Holy Spirit in Kuyper's judgment: "Thus to lead the creature to its destiny, to cause it to develop according to its nature, to make it perfect, is the proper work of the Holy Spirit."[124] Edwards uses somewhat different language: "'Tis evident that there are no more than these three really distinct in God:

121. Cited, with ellipsis and emphasis, by McDermott, 109.
122. This is the title of the last of Edwards's sermons in the "Charity and Its Fruits" series (*CF*, 366-97); on the progressive nature of heaven's love, also see app. III in the Yale edition of *Works*, vol. 8, *Ethical Writings*, "Heaven Is a Progressive State," 706-38; cf. Pauw, "'Heaven Is a World of Love.'"
123. Kuyper, *Holy Spirit*, 19.
124. Kuyper, *Holy Spirit*, 21.

God, and his idea, and his love or delight. We can't conceive of any further real distinctions."[125] But, as we have already seen, the importance of telos for Edwards too cannot be exaggerated.[126] God created the world for his own glory, but Edwards also describes this in terms of happiness. The end of God's creating "intelligent beings [who] are the consciousness of the universe . . . must necessarily be that they may receive the goodness of God, that is, that they may be happy."[127] "How then," Edwards asks, "can it be said that God has made all things for himself, if it is certain that the highest end of creation was the communication of happiness? I answer, that which is done for the gratifying of a natural inclination of God, may very properly be said to be done for God. God takes complacence in communicating felicity, and he made all things for this complacence. His complacence in this, in making happy was the end of the creation. Rev. 4:11, 'For thy pleasure they are and were created.'"[128] In other words, for Edwards the Spirit's distinctive task can be said to be "to beautify all things."[129] This is nothing other than to say with Kuyper "that the work of the Holy Spirit consists in leading all creation *to its destiny,* the final purpose of which is the glory of God. . . . The glory of God is the ultimate end of every creature."[130]

The tie between eschatology and creation through the perfecting, beautifying work of the Holy Spirit is crucial to the visions of both Edwards and Kuyper. The Spirit which perfects and beautifies through love, which brings creation to its final glory, is the same Spirit directly and intimately involved with creation from the beginning. Kuyper puts it this way: "Wherefore the Spirit's work leading the creature to its destiny includes an influence on all creation from the beginning. And if sin had not come in, we might say that this work is done in three successive steps: first, *impregnating* inanimate matter; second, *animating* the rational soul; third, *taking up his abode* in the elect child of God."[131] Edwards sees it much the same way: "This is very consonant to the of-

125. Edwards, "Miscellanies," #259.

126. See especially Edwards's *Dissertation concerning the End for Which God Created the World.*

127. Edwards, "Miscellanies," #87.

128. Edwards, "Miscellanies," #92.

129. Edwards, "Essay on the Trinity," 111.

130. Kuyper, *Holy Spirit,* 22.

131. Kuyper, *Holy Spirit,* 24; Kuyper's understanding of the threefold task of the Spirit's cosmic work directly parallels that of John Calvin; see John Bolt, "*Spiritus Creator:* The Use and Abuse of Calvin's Cosmic Pneumatology," in P. De Klerk, ed., *Calvin and the Holy Spirit* (papers and responses presented at the Sixth Colloquium on Calvin and Calvin Studies sponsored by the Calvin Studies Society, Calvin Theological Seminary, Grand Rapids, Mich., May 6, 7, 1987), 17-34.

fice of the Holy Spirit," he writes. "His work with respect to creatures, which is threefold, viz. to quicken, enliven and beautify all things, to sanctify intelligent [beings] and to comfort and delight them. He quickens and beautifies all things."[132]

An important part of the Spirit's cosmic work is the universal bestowal of natural, moral, and artistic gifts, a conviction of Calvinist theology generally known as the doctrine of "common grace."[133] "The Spirit of God," notes Edwards, "is supposed sometimes to have some influence upon the minds of men that are not true Christians, and [it is supposed] that those dispositions, frames, and exercises of their minds that are of a good tendency, but are common to them with the saints, are in some respect owing to some influence or assistance of God's Spirit."[134] Edwards's concern here is not in the first place to use the doctrine of common grace as a ground for social ethics and Christian activism, as Kuyper later most surely did, but to emphasize the important difference between saving and common grace, a difference *in kind* and not simply in degree. "And that special or saving grace in this sense is not only different from common grace in degree, but entirely diverse in nature and kind, and that natural men not only have not a sufficient degree of virtue to be saints, but that they have no degree of that grace that is in godly men, is what I have now to shew."[135] Still, his conviction about the commonality of believer and unbeliever in their basic human *nature* and *consciousness* does lead Edwards to the same kind of universal social ethic we have already seen elsewhere in his thought.[136] There is, says Edwards, a universal aesthetic consciousness, constituted by God in nature, with the "tendency to assist those whose hearts are under the influence of a truly virtuous temper, to dispose them to the exercises of divine love, and enliven in them a sense of spiritual beauty" (*TV*, 565). Secondly, there is also a moral sense, a "public conscience," or a "natural conscience," that is "the basis for human concern for justice, duties to family and neighbor, and patriotism."[137] "A third form of consciousness shared by all humans is 'natural pity,'

132. Edwards, "Essay on the Trinity," 111.
133. See H. Kuiper, *Calvin on Common Grace* (Goes: Oosterbaan & Le Cointre, 1928), for an overview of this doctrine in the Reformed tradition; also J. Douma, *Algemene Genade: Uiteenzetting, Vergelijking en Beoordeling van de Opvattingen van A. Kuyper, K. Schilder, en Joh. Calvijn over Algemene Genade* (Goes: Oosterbaan & Le Cointre, 1966).
134. Jonathan Edwards, "Treatise on Grace," in *Treatise on Grace and Other Posthumously Published Writings*, 25.
135. Edwards, "Treatise on Grace," 26.
136. What follows is based substantially on McDermott, 104-6.
137. McDermott, 104; McDermott cites the following passages: Edwards, *TV*, 592-94, 564, 365-66, 596-97, 578, 602-3.

which God has given to humankind for its preservation."[138] Finally, "the fourth form is religious knowledge,"[139] the universal God-consciousness that Calvin called the *sensus divinitatis* or *semen religionis*.[140]

Though Kuyper explores the implications of the doctrine of common grace far more extensively than does Edwards,[141] he is equally insistent on the important difference in kind between particular and common grace. Yet he also wants to do something positive with the doctrine, and his three-volume set of reflections on common grace bear ample testimony to that desire.[142] Kuyper wanted to show that contrary to stereotypical Calvinist expectations about the utter fallenness of the world, "the unbelieving world excels in many things. . . . It is not exclusively the spark of genius or the splendor of talent, which excites your pleasure in the words and actions of unbelievers, but it is often their beauty of character, their zeal, their devotion, their love, their candor, their faithfulness and their sense of honesty." It is the Calvinist doctrine of common grace, Kuyper notes, that alone does justice to radical human sinfulness *and* the arresting of sin and its consequences by divine intervention. "God arrests sin in its course in order to prevent the complete annihilation of His divine handiwork, which naturally would have followed. [Common grace], however, does not kill the core of sin nor does it save unto life eternal, but it arrests the complete effectuation of sin, just as human insight arrests the fury of wild beasts."[143]

We shall not explore the full range of social and political consequences of Kuyper's understanding of common grace but provide a brief general perspective and consider one interesting example, Kuyper's discussion of the apostle Paul's appeal to pagan poetry in his Areopagus address (Acts 17). Kuyper's treatment of the topic of common grace, we need to note, is not without inconsistency and occasional contradiction.[144] At times he speaks of common grace

138. McDermott, 105; Edwards, *TV*, 607.

139. McDermott, 105; Edwards, *TV*, 607.

140. Calvin, *Institutes* 1.3.1.

141. In part this is a direct consequence of the two men living in different historical circumstances. Edwards lived in what was still a predominantly Christian social context in which he was more concerned to proclaim the need for genuine as opposed to false piety than to develop among his hearers an appreciation for the fruits of common grace. Kuyper, on the other hand, needed the doctrine of common grace to help motivate a politically marginalized and culturally antagonistic group of orthodox Reformed Christians toward greater Christian cultural, social, educational, and political activity.

142. Abraham Kuyper, *De Gemeene Gratie*, 2nd ed., 3 vols. (Kampen: Kok, n.d.).

143. Kuyper, *Lectures on Calvinism*, 124-25.

144. According to S. U. Zuidema, "Common Grace and Christian Action in Abraham Kuyper," in *Communication and Confrontation* (Toronto: Wedge, 1972), 52-105.

as independent of special grace, at other times as preparation for special grace and a necessary condition for redemption. The precise relation between special and common grace as the fruit of the redemptive work of Jesus Christ is not clear either, though he does finally achieve a *formal* systematic unity of thought by grounding both special and common grace in the eternal decree of the triune God.[145] Kuyper was less concerned with a systematically worked-out and consistent definition of common grace than with its polemical value in combating the cultural alienation of many orthodox Dutch Reformed people. He thus used the doctrine of common grace "to stimulate, as well as to justify, truly Christian action by God's people from out of the particular grace of regeneration by the light of Holy Scripture. Common grace supplies the believer with the material for fulfilling his calling to be culturally formative and to fight the battle of the Lord in the world of culture. . . . Common grace is *the presupposition of the possibility of* Christian cultural activity."[146]

We conclude our discussion of Kuyper's understanding of common grace by coming full circle back to his place within the broad intellectual tradition, recalling our discussion in chapter 1 about the rhetorical and philosophical traditions.[147] There is one place in Kuyper's writing where he himself makes the marked contrast between the warm heart-passion of poetry and the ice-cold rationalism of a certain type of prose. In one of his meditations in his Heidelberg Catechism commentary on Lord's Day 8 (on the Trinity), Kuyper takes his point of departure from Paul's apologetic Areopagus citation of a Greek poet's claim that "We are also God's offspring" (Acts 17:28).[148] He uses this entry point to denounce pantheism (*Algodendom;* literally, "omnipantheon" — Kuyper is playing on the word *heidendom* [paganism]) but then raises the question of what the possible appeal of pantheism could be for believers. Here Paul's words to the Athenians give us a clue, according to Kuyper. There are, he notes, people who "never drink a drop from the pagan or pantheistic stream" and do not entertain such thoughts in their religious consciousness, but who also "never feel the glow of a single spark of enthusiasm for the Holy Trinity." Though not pantheists, they fall into the opposite deistic error: their image of the divine is a distant, removed, watchmaker god who at creation simply wound up the world machine and lets it run on its own without divine involve-

145. According to S. J. Ridderbos, *De Theologische Cultuurbeschouwing van Abraham Kuyper* (Kampen: Kok, 1947), 94ff.

146. Zuidema, 57.

147. See above, 20-28.

148. Abraham Kuyper, *E Voto Dordraceno: Toelichting op den Heidelbergschen Catechismus,* vol. 1 (Amsterdam: J. A. Wormser, 1892), 151-57; unidentified quotations that follow in this paragraph are found on these pages.

ment until a moment of breakdown when emergency interference is called for. The religious life of such people neither requires nor desires regular communion with God; he is only an emergency measure, called upon in critical moments. Kuyper judges that there are many such "practical deists" in Reformed churches and is not hesitant to call this posture, along with its pantheist counterpart, *sin!* "Anyone who can live ten hours of a day without accounting for God is a practical Deist." Kuyper then turns to Paul's poetic quote, "You are God's offspring," and, noting that Paul emphasizes this as a *poetic* word, concludes that for his audience "here at once a light goes on for you, you understand why so many noble spirits of our time are led astray by the fireworks of Pantheism." In the contrast between the cold, mechanical, artificial soulless intellectualism of deistic *prose* and the warm, passionate, fiery, glowing intensity of pantheism's *poetry*, people who have a heart and are emotional, enthusiastic, and noble in spirit will choose for pantheism. "Pantheism, the omnipantheon, is high poetry." And Paul's response, according to Kuyper, is not simply to denounce the idolatry of the Athenians but to acknowledge the validity of the poetry; not to rebut excessive immanence with excessive transcendence (or vice versa) but to honor both with passionate praise to the fullness of the *triune* God.

> "Concerning God the Father and *our creation*": that is the death knell of all Pantheism since it knows nothing of creation. Then "Concerning God the Son and *our Redemption*": that is the unmasking of all Deism since it has no place for a Word that became flesh. Finally, "Concerning God the Holy Spirit and *our Sanctification*," in order properly to unite immanence and transcendence since *indwelling* of the Holy Spirit precisely tells us that the *temple* in which he dwells is distinguished from the *Indweller*.[149]

Conclusion: An Evangelical American Public Theology?

It is the goal of this study to provide an outline of Abraham Kuyper's public theology in dialogue with a contemporary American evangelical Christianity that is, as we concluded after our survey in chapter 1, searching for more ade-

---

149. This is a direct commentary on Heidelberg Catechism, Lord's Day 8, Question and Answer 24:

> How are these articles [of the Apostles' Creed] divided?

> Into three parts: the first is of God the Father and our creation; the second of God the Son and our redemption; the third of God the Holy Spirit and our sanctification.

quate theological grounding for its social and political activism. The comparisons drawn in this chapter between Kuyper and that other "neo-Calvinist," Jonathan Edwards, provide us with ample evidence of how difficult it is to construct a defensible evangelical Christian public theology for a nation and its Christian citizens, particularly for a nation whose origins and history are so intertwined with religious motives, myths, and ambitions as America is.

The purpose of a public theology is to provide a theological framework within which Christian citizens can conscientiously fashion their political vocation and interpret, evaluate, and transform the civic communities of which they are members. The criteria by which such interpretation and evaluation are made must be carefully chosen and even more carefully applied. The kingdom of God is the biblical reality by which all the kingdoms and republics of this world must be measured. Yet, as we have seen, applying the biblical givens of the kingdom metaphor to any earthly political reality is risky. While indifference to the concrete justice demands of God's kingly rule results in political quietism that leaves civic community to the "prince of this world," linking national destiny too closely to divine providential purpose — even when invoking covenantal judgment — encourages idolatry. When both Bill Clinton and Jerry Falwell — at the close of the secular twentieth century — can use the language of "new covenant" for their quite different political agendas, it is clear that American public life is unavoidably linked to its "city on a hill, almost chosen nation" roots and history. Similarly, when Edwards and Kuyper invoke the historical covenantal link between Israel and America (or the Netherlands in Kuyper's case), they come close to the kind of idolatry mentioned above and provide us with an exemplary caution against facile use of historical and eschatological language for political ends in the New Testament era. The fulfillment of Israel's role and status in the New Testament era is the *church*, the *universal* church and not the Dutch or American Republics. The ontological correctives that both Edwards and Kuyper apply to the historical-eschatological components of their respective public theologies, the universal perspectives of creation and eschaton through the notions of trinitarian beauty and common grace, through the cosmic work of the Holy Spirit, are thus, in my judgment, essential theological building blocks for the project of an American evangelical public theology.[150] Among the benefits of these particular doctrinal foundation

---

150. "Both the evangelicals and the more worldly dominating Americans would have benefitted highly from serious attention to Edwards. They ignored his theology of the Holy Spirit. Both groups believed that America was called to glory, spiritual or worldly, and preferably the two of them together. In Edwards' scheme of things, we are all called to a repentance and service which themselves are God's grace given to us. God's alone is the glory; ours the service, to be carried out as God wills. Edwards' theology of the Holy Spirit

stones is the fact that their pneumatological character is, so it has been eloquently argued, distinctly American. "It has been frequently noted that American Christianity is preoccupied with the Holy Spirit: America is the cradle of
Pentecostalism and the adopted homeland of religious utopianism." Thus any
American evangelical public theology must take its place in the larger conversation about the Holy Spirit's universal work and come to terms with "the American vision of holy worldliness, the sanctification of all things by the Holy
Spirit."[151] Edwards and Kuyper together remain essential guides in this conversation and project.

suffused a profound aura of humility into his appreciation of America's role in history.
One can only lament that his thought was not taken more seriously" (Wilson-Kastner, 71-
72).

151. Richardson, *Toward an American Theology*, 112.

CHAPTER FIVE

The "Social Question" and the Social Gospel: Abraham Kuyper, Walter Rauschenbusch, and Leo XIII

We hold these truths to be self-evident, that all men are endowed by their Creator with certain unalienable Rights, that among these are Life, Liberty, and the pursuit of Happiness.

Thomas Jefferson

The land was ours before we were the land's.
She was our land more than a hundred years
Before we were her people.

Robert Frost

I know no other country where love of money has such a grip on men's hearts or where stronger scorn is expressed for the theory of permanent equality of property.
Alexis de Tocqueville (1831)

You shall not press down upon the brow of labor this crown of thorns, you shall not crucify mankind upon a cross of gold.

William Jennings Bryan (1896)

The chief business of the American people is business.

Calvin Coolidge

In the previous chapter we explored the parallels between the "American" public theologies of Abraham Kuyper and Jonathan Edwards. The comparison, while systematically instructive, was nonetheless historically limited by the large span of time between the two neo-Calvinists. In this chapter we shall compare Kuyper with a socially engaged American theologian who was his contemporary, Walter Rauschenbusch (1861-1918), who, if not "the real founder" of the Social Gospel,[1] was, at least in the considered judgment of Reinhold Niebuhr, its "most brilliant and most generally satisfying exponent."[2] The Social Gospel, writes historian Sidney Ahlstrom, was a "movement widely hailed at home and abroad as the most distinctive contribution of the American churches to world Christianity."[3] This assessment is echoed by the movement's premier historian when he begins his study with this claim: "America's most unique contribution to the great ongoing stream of Christianity is the 'social gospel' . . . [an] indigenous and typically American movement."[4] In this chapter we shall consider (and gently challenge) that judgment by comparing Rauschenbusch's thought with that of Kuyper[5] and another European contemporary, Pope Leo XIII, particularly in his great encyclical of 1891, *Rerum Novarum*.[6] What we are asking, in other words, is whether the claim made by

1. In his *Christianizing the Social Order* (New York: Macmillan, 1919), Rauschenbusch himself pays tribute to "three men who were pioneers of Christian thought in America twenty-five years ago: Washington Gladden, Josiah Strong, and Richard T. Ely" (9).

2. Reinhold Niebuhr, *An Interpretation of Christian Ethics* (New York: Harper & Brothers, 1935), 1.

3. Sidney E. Ahlstrom, *A Religious History of the American People*, 2 vols. (Garden City, N.Y.: Image Books, 1975 [1972]), 2:251. Ahlstrom himself disputes the full indigenity of the Social Gospel (see below, n. 12).

4. Charles Howard Hopkins, *The Rise of the Social Gospel in American Protestantism, 1865-1915* (New Haven: Yale University Press, 1940), 3.

5. When Kuyper visited the United States in 1898 to deliver the Stone Lectures (*Lectures on Calvinism* [Grand Rapids: Eerdmans, 1931]) at Princeton University, he included Rochester, New York — Rauschenbusch's new home of about one year (Rauschenbusch accepted a teaching position at Colgate in 1897) — on his itinerary. See Abraham Kuyper, *Varia Americana* (Amsterdam and Pretoria: Höveker & Wormser, n.d.), 40, 116. Kuyper's visit to Rochester came at the invitation of what he called a "College Womenclub," whom he praised for their interest in pursuing a serious study of Dutch history (to the shame of many Dutch Americans!) and for their profound social influence while avoiding "the pedantry of 'bluestockings' as well as the arrogance of the feminists" (40). Our attention in this chapter will be primarily, though not exclusively, on his 1891 address to the Dutch Christian Social Congress, *The Problem of Poverty*, trans. and ed. James W. Skillen (Grand Rapids: Baker, 1991).

6. Within the confines of this essay it is impossible to do full justice to the full con-

Robert Jenson for Jonathan Edwards, namely, that his "theology meets precisely the problems and opportunities of specifically American Christianity and of the nation molded thereby,"[7] can also be applied to Rauschenbusch and the Social Gospel. The argument that will be advanced here is that the social thought of the two Europeans is in some respects more characteristically "American" than that of Rauschenbusch.

How American Is the Social Gospel?

The issue raised here is not new to the historical discussion about the Social Gospel but a variant of an old debate that has been formulated by two eminent historians of the movement as follows: "Is the social gospel chiefly a response to external events, or is it rather the expression of the internal continuity of aggressive American religion?"[8] Arthur M. Schlesinger's 1931 essay "A Critical Period in American Religion, 1875-1900"[9] argued that the Social Gospel should be considered in terms of a challenge-response framework. "Schlesinger had suggested that American religion in the last quarter of the nineteenth century was reshaped by the way it met the challenge of urbanization and industrialization on the social-political front, and Darwinian thought and German biblical criticism on the intellectual front. Schlesinger's emphasis was on reaction rather than initiative."[10] On the other side, H. Richard Niebuhr — and after

---

tent or consider subtle details of nuance in these three major social theologians. Wide brush strokes will have to suffice along with a more narrow range of texts. In addition to our focus on Kuyper's and Leo's 1891 addresses, we will also concentrate on Rauschenbusch's long-dormant manuscript *The Righteousness of the Kingdom,* edited and introduced by Max L. Stackhouse (Nashville and New York: Abingdon, 1968), written at approximately the same time (see Max L. Stackhouse, "The Continuing Importance of Walter Rauschenbusch," in *The Righteousness of the Kingdom,* 17-18). This limitation is made with full awareness that "Rauschenbusch himself softened his style in his later works" (18). His convictions about Jesus' teaching of the kingdom of God and its implications for economic life, however, remained fundamentally the same.

7. Robert W. Jenson, *America's Theologian: A Recommendation of Jonathan Edwards* (New York and Oxford: Oxford University Press, 1988), 3.

8. Ronald C. White, Jr., and C. Howard Hopkins, *The Social Gospel: Religion and Reform in Changing America* (Philadelphia: Temple University Press, 1976), xiii.

9. Originally published in *Massachusetts Historical Society Proceedings* 64 (October 1930–June 1932): 523-46; republished by Fortress Press, Philadelphia, 1967, as vol. 7 in its Facet Books Historical Series (American Church).

10. White and Hopkins, xiii. According to White and Hopkins, Aaron I. Abell's *Urban Impact on American Protestantism* (1943) and Henry F. May's *Protestant Churches and Industrial America* (1949) also reflect this challenge-response approach.

him, Sidney Mead and Robert T. Handy — stressed the continuity of the Social Gospel with the long tradition of American (Puritan, Protestant) culture-transforming Christianity that sought to Christianize the nation as well as the individual.[11] Perhaps at this point it is best to point to the ambiguities in the evidence, a position to which Sidney Ahlstrom also finally comes.

> Is [the Social Gospel] the most distinctive American contribution as is so often alleged? The facts are confusing. Although its Puritanic concern for the commonwealth is embedded in an indigenous position which is unique, almost every major new element of the Social Gospel betrayed enormous indebtedness to two major foreign influences. From Britain came a legacy of inspiration drawn from the Christian socialism of Charles Kingsley, Frederick D. Maurice, John Ruskin, William H. Fremantle, and the architects of Fabian socialism. From Germany came nearly its entire biblical and theological grounding, as well as the historical view of economic theory by which the social statics of *Manchesterismus* was to be overthrown. The key figure for the Social Gospelers as for many other liberal theologians was Albrecht Ritschl (1822-89), whose Jesus-centered, anti-metaphysical theology of the Kingdom of God provided the movement's chief integrative idea. . . . British and German developments, in short, provided a vital prologue to American Social Gospel history.[12]

A definitive answer to this debate about external forces versus indigenous drive would require, among other things, a careful analysis of the intellectual and religious pedigree of a Social Gospel thinker such as Rauschenbusch, an examination that Donovan Smucker began in his instructive *Origins of Walter Rauschenbusch's Social Ethics*.[13] However, even after one has factored in the role of decidedly American figures such as Washington Gladden, Richard Ely, and Josiah Strong and biblical scholars such as Francis Peabody *(Jesus Christ and the Social Question)* and Shailer Mathews *(The Social Teachings of Jesus)* on Rauschenbusch's social theology, as well as that of tax

---

11. White and Hopkins, xiii-xiv; cf. H. Richard Niebuhr, *The Kingdom of God in America* (New York: Harper & Row, 1937); Robert T. Handy, *The Social Gospel in America, 1870-1920* (New York: Oxford University Press, 1966). Handy observes that "though [the] influences from abroad should not be minimized, the Christian social movement in the United States was fundamentally indigenous. The response to the problems of an urbanized and industrialized society was shaped by the patterns of thought and action that had long been characteristic of American Protestantism" (4).

12. Ahlstrom, 2:254-55.

13. Donovan Smucker, *The Origins of Walter Rauschenbusch's Social Ethics* (Montreal and Kingston: McGill-Queens University Press, 1994).

reformer Henry George and novelist Edward Bellamy *(Looking Backward)* on his socioeconomic views,[14] the basic question is still open. For two reasons: in the first place because the flow of ideas, as Smucker's treatment of Rauschenbusch clearly shows,[15] does not simply begin with American writers writing out of their uniquely American tradition and place. What Smucker says about the appeal of Francis Peabody's *Jesus Christ and the Social Question* to Rauschenbusch could likely be said about other writers and writings that influenced him as well: "The erudition of Peabody's book and its reference to the best in German scholarship no doubt appealed to Rauschenbusch."[16] It is clear from Smucker's study that the specifics of Rauschenbusch's construction of Jesus' social ethics are indeed dependent on the "latest and best" of (German) critical New Testament scholarship as well as recent "discoveries" in the social sciences. Rauschenbusch himself saw the possibility of the new reformation in social Christianity that he believed was taking place in his own day as resting firmly on the foundation of the new social sciences as well as recent "new and improved" portraits of the Old Testament prophets and Jesus uncovered by critical scholarship, and much of this, as Rauschenbusch acknowledged, was foreign in origin.[17]

However, this does not yet settle the matter negatively, since any historical or literary linkage of ideas still leaves aside the most important question: What exactly is the heart of the distinctly American religious experience, if such can even be identified? Though borrowed from abroad, a certain set of ideas could still be true to whatever it is that constitutes the genius of the American religious experience,[18] though it would then be necessary to deny American exceptionalism or to redefine it, as Max Lerner did, in an *inclusive* manner. "The fact is," he writes, "that while American civilization is not immune to the surging beat of world forces, it has developed its own characteristic institutions, traits, and social conditions within the larger frame. . . . What this implies is that exceptionalism *includes* an acceptance of the European ties and does not

14. For a fuller discussion see Smucker, *Origins*, chap. 5, "The Influence of Social and Religious Liberalism," 74-120.

15. Also see Klaus Juergen Jaehn, *Rauschenbusch: The Formative Years* (Valley Forge, Pa.: Judson, 1976); an earlier version of this work appeared as "The Formation of Walter Rauschenbusch's Social Consciousness as Reflected in His Early Life and Writings," *Foundations* 16, no. 4 (October-December 1973) and *Foundations* 17 (January-March 1974).

16. Smucker, *Origins*, 97.

17. See, e.g., Walter Rauschenbusch, *Christianity and the Social Crisis* (Louisville: Westminster/John Knox, 1991 [1907]), 3, 46-47; *Christianizing the Social Order*, 8, 40-68; *A Theology for the Social Gospel* (Nashville and New York: Abingdon, [1917]), 5, 27-29.

18. "America's theologian," Jonathan Edwards, certainly borrowed ideas from abroad.

reject them. The idea of American exceptionalism and the idea of American integration into the broader pattern are not mutually exclusive but are polar facets of the same field of energy. When you speak of American uniqueness, you must speak also in the same framework about the European diversity."[19] Is it then even possible to identify a distinctive American character, spirit, soul, or single set of values? Lerner acknowledges that the temptation is great to find "some single organizing principle in this civilizational pattern, some key that unlocks all the doors," but concludes that "America is a highly polarized field of meaning" and that "the study of American civilization becomes thus the study of the polar pattern itself, not a search for some single key that will unlock causation."[20] Lerner himself attempts to use a "figure-ground perspective," with figure and ground varying "with the purpose on hand" but generally encompassed by the interplay between the broad categories "material" and "moral-psychological." Lerner concludes:

> If there is a figure-ground relation in American civilization it must be sought in the relation between power and ideas, science and conscience, the revolutionary machine and the conservative crust of tradition, mass production and social creativeness, individualist values and collective action, capitalist economics and democratic freedom, class structure and the image of prestige and success in the American mind, elite power and the popular arts, the growth of military power and the persistence of civilian control, the fact of an American imperium and the image of an open constitutional world.

Though this could be interpreted as "proof that American life is deeply split," all these polarities being simply "contradictory parts of a bewildering puzzle," Lerner muses about the possibility that they are rather "signs of an effort, on a grander scale than ever in history, to resolve the conflicting impulses that are to be found in every civilization but each of which occurs here with a strength and tenacity scarcely witnessed elsewhere."[21]

Perry Miller agrees that it is a mistake to attempt "to fix the personality of America in one eternal, unchangeable pattern," since the explanation for America is not to be found in "the conditions of America's existence" but rather "in the existence itself. A man *is* his decisions, and the great uniqueness of this nation is simply that here the record of conscious decision is more precise, more open and explicit than in most countries. . . . Being an American is not some-

19. Max Lerner, *America as a Civilization: Life and Thought in the United States Today* (New York: Simon & Schuster, 1957), 65.
20. Lerner, 71, 73. Lerner supplies a long list on 73.
21. Lerner, 73.

thing inherited but something to be achieved."[22] Stated differently, America is a nation always in the process of further definition, its history, in the words of Max Lerner, "an extended genesis"[23] or, in the terms of Frederick Jackson Turner's famous thesis, an ongoing frontier.[24] This is similar to Miller's conclusion that "generalizations about the American character can amount to no more than a statistical survey of the decisions so far made, and these warrant in the way of hypotheses about those yet to be made only the most tentative estimates." There is a curious irony here, as Miller notes. "However, if my analysis has any truth in it, a back-handed sort of generalization does emerge: he who would fix the pattern of decision by confining the American choice to one and only one mode of response — whether this be in politics, diplomacy, literary form, or morality itself — such a one, in the light of our history, is the truly 'Un-American.'"[25]

Socialism in America: Liberty and Property

The point of this extended consideration of what if anything can be said to constitute the distinctively American genius is that the question is extraordinarily complex, perhaps even condemning Americans to a "complex fate."[26] If so, then a public theology worthy of praise as "authentically American" will have to eschew simple analysis and solutions and give evidence of its sensitivity to the complexity of social, cultural, economic, and political realities. For our purposes in this essay, we shall simplify matters as best we can by directing our attention to one specific and surprisingly neglected[27] feature of the Social Gospel that both defined it and drew the sharpest criticism as well as devoted praise, its kingdom economics, the vision of a cooperative commonwealth — in short, its socialism.[28] There are both

22. Perry Miller, *Nature's Nation* (Cambridge: Harvard University Press, Belknap Press, 1967), 13.

23. Lerner, 35-39.

24. Frederick Jackson Turner, *The Frontier in American History* (New York: H. Holt, 1920).

25. Miller, 13.

26. Miller, 13; Miller is citing an unnamed British observer.

27. "Scholars have investigated Rauschenbusch's theology and ethics rather than his economics" (Rebecca Moore, "Social Redemption and Individual Liberty: Walter Rauschenbusch's Challenge to Henry George," *American Baptist Quarterly* 11, no. 3 [1992]: 259).

28. The term "socialism" is of course both a red flag and susceptible of many meanings. A simple dictionary definition serves the purposes of this essay: "The theory or system of the ownership and operation of the means of production and distribution by soci-

superficial as well as more substantive reasons for this narrow focus on Rauschenbusch's kingdom economics. The superficial connection — almost at the level of linking Kuyper and Rauschenbusch by means of Kuyper's 1898 visit to Rochester only one year after Rauschenbusch began his professorate there[29] — is the way the economic focus links Rauschenbusch with Leo XIII's *Rerum Novarum*. According to Rauschenbusch biographer Dores Sharpe, the American economist Henry George, known for his advocacy of a single tax on land,[30] was a major influence on Rauschenbusch: "To the end of his days Rauschenbusch saw in the George program, with slight modifications to be sure, a fundamental remedy for many of the greatest social evils."[31] Now it just so happens that when *Rerum Novarum* appeared in 1891, Henry George reportedly considered himself to be its chief target. According to his son and biographer, he remarked: "I regard the encyclical letter as aimed at us, and at us alone, almost. And I feel much encouraged by the honor."[32] It is beyond the scope of this essay (not to mention the incli-

---

ety or the community rather than by private individuals, with all members of society or the community sharing in the work and the products" (*Webster's New Twentieth Century Dictionary,* 2nd ed., s.v. "socialism"). On the socialism of the Social Gospel, see Jacob H. Dorn, "The Social Gospel and Socialism: A Comparison of the Thought of Francis Greenwood Peabody, Washington Gladden, and Walter Rauschenbusch," *Church History* 62 (1993): 82-100. (My thanks to Paul Kemeney for this valuable reference.) Dorn shares Rauschenbusch biographer Dores Sharpe's conviction that he was "a convinced socialist" (Dores Robinson Sharpe, *Walter Rauschenbusch* [New York: Macmillan, 1942], 219), contending that Rauschenbusch's engagement with socialism was more intimate and passionate than Gladden's. "He identified more fully with socialist ideals, spoke and wrote under party auspices, and contemplated party membership" (Dorn, 91). Rauschenbusch helped launch the Christian socialist paper *For the Right,* a paper intended to "discuss working class issues 'from the standpoint of Christian socialism'" (91), and, after his visit to Germany in 1891, helped found the Christian socialist fellowship, the "Brotherhood of the Kingdom" (92). Dorn concludes that "Rauschenbusch's socialist connections grew stronger in his last decade" (96).

29. See n. 5 above.

30. Henry George's most important work is *Progress and Poverty* (1879). Recent literature on George includes Robert V. Andelson, "Henry George and Economic Intervention: A Critic Proposes That George's Strictures on Industrial Monopolies Be Revised," *American Journal of Economics and Sociology* 44, no. 4 (1985): 97-105; Robert J. Rafalko, "Was George a Dreamer or a Realist?" *American Journal of Economics and Sociology* 44, no. 4 (1985): 491-95; Jack Schwartzman, "Henry George and the Ethics of Economics," *American Journal of Economics and Sociology* 45, no. 1 (1986): 101-13.

31. Sharpe, 196; cf. the similar judgment of Klaus Jaehn, "Formation," *Foundations* 17 (1974): 78, who notes that Rauschenbusch "was most decisively influenced by Henry George." I am indebted for both citations to Rebecca Moore's helpful essay on both men: "Social Redemption and Individual Liberty," 259.

32. Henry George, Jr., *The Life of Henry George,* Memorial Edition of the Writings of

nation of the writer) to consider this further; I call attention to it here simply to note that the arrows of *Rerum Novarum*, whether intentionally aimed or unintentionally, like the one that killed King Ahab, did hit specific targets, including at least one significant economist influential in the Social Gospel.[33]

Among the more substantive reasons for targeting economics is that the much-discussed "social question" of the late nineteenth century *was* the economic question. From the time that a young Roman Catholic priest, Wilhelm von Ketteler, preached a series of sermons in the Cathedral of Mainz in 1848 entitled "The Social Question"[34] to the year 1891 and Leo's encyclical on "the condition of the workers"[35] and Kuyper's address "The Social Question and the Christian Religion,"[36] the expression "the social question" had a specific, *economic* significance rather than the more general current sociological usage. As the authors of a survey of modern Catholic social teaching observe about the title of their own work: "'Social' here [in the tradition of Catholic social teaching] means all that has to do with those human relationships which grow out of the *economy*: such as come from the system of exchange and the organization of markets, the process of production, the structure of the firm, or the class structure which corresponds to the *economic* situation which itself reflects and is reflected by different types of income and grades of social standing." It is this "restricted use of the word 'social'" that was the "name given to the troubled relations between capitalists and proletarians caused by the industrial revolution of the late eighteenth and early nineteenth centuries. Then one spoke of the 'social question.'"[37]

Henry George, vol. 10 (New York: Doubleday, 1900), 565-66; cited by C. Joseph Neusse, "Henry George and 'Rerum Novarum': Evidence Is Scant That the American Economist Was a Target of Leo XIII's Classic Encyclical," *American Journal of Economics and Sociology* 44, no. 2 (1985): 244; further on the topic of Henry George and *Rerum Novarum*, see J. Brian Benestad, "Henry George and the Catholic View of Morality and the Common Good," pt. I, "George's Overall Critique of Pope Leo XIII's Classic Encyclical, 'Rerum Novarum,'" *American Journal of Economics and Sociology* 44, no. 3 (1985); 365-78; pt. II, "George's Proposals in the Context of Perennial Philosophy," 45, no. 1 (1986): 115-23.

33. It is of historical interest at least to note that Abraham Kuyper was aware of the economic thought of Henry George and mentioned it in his address to the Christian Social Congress in 1891. See Kuyper, *The Problem of Poverty*, 53.

34. Michael Novak, *Freedom with Justice: Catholic Social Thought and Liberal Institutions* (San Francisco: Harper & Row, 1984), 20.

35. *Rerum Novarum*, par. 1.

36. Though its two English translations have been rendered as "Christianity and the Class Struggle" and "The Problem of Poverty," the Dutch title is "Het Sociale Vraagstuk en de Christelijke Religie."

37. Jean-Yves Calvez, S.J., and Jacques Perrin, S.J., *The Church and Social Justice: The Social Teaching of the Popes from Leo XIII to Pius XII* (Chicago: Henry Regnery, 1961), 4,

A second reason for focusing on the economic is that it is precisely here that the pope and the Dutch Calvinist, in my judgment, have a better sense of the American "spirit" than Rauschenbusch and the Social Gospel do. Plainly put, the American spirit is, if not hostile to socialism, at least not enthralled by it. Perhaps there is no one whose academic career has been as dedicated to examining the question of American exceptionalism, with special interest in the relative absence of socialism in America, particularly in comparison with its neighbor to the north, than Seymour Martin Lipset. From his first book, *Agrarian Socialism: The Cooperative Commonwealth Federation in Saskatchewan*,[38] through his comparative study of Canadian and American cultural and political patterns, *Continental Divide: The Values and Institutions of the United States and Canada*[39] and his recent *American Exceptionalism: A Double-Edged Sword*,[40] one of Lipset's preoccupations, in his own words, has been to attempt an answer to the question: "Why is there no effective socialist movement in the United States?"[41] To oversimplify his learned and persuasive argument, Lipset's conclusion is finally to agree with other analysts that "the uniqueness of the historical and cultural factors that have gone into the making of the United States," including "the absence of a European aristocratic or feudal past, a relatively egalitarian-status structure, an achievement-oriented value system, comparative affluence, and a history of political democracy prior to industrialization have all operated to produce a system which remains unreceptive to proposals for class-conscious leftism."[42] What this summary does not include is yet another factor that Lipset does highlight elsewhere, namely, a deeply rooted and profound American antistatism.[43]

American antistatism is clearly linked to the conviction that property

---

emphasis added; for Rauschenbusch's understanding of what was meant by "the social question," see n. 60 below and the citation to which it refers.

38. Seymour Martin Lipset, *Agrarian Socialism: The Cooperative Commonwealth Federation in Saskatchewan*, rev. ed. (Berkeley: University of California Press, 1971 [1950]).

39. Seymour Martin Lipset, *Continental Divide: The Values and Institutions of the United States and Canada* (New York and London: Routledge, 1990).

40. Seymour Martin Lipset, *American Exceptionalism: A Double-Edged Sword* (New York and London: Norton, 1996).

41. Lipset, *Continental Divide*, xvii; cf. Seymour Martin Lipset, "Socialism in America," in *Sidney Hook: Philosopher of Democracy and Humanism*, ed. P. Kurtz (Buffalo: Prometheus Books, 1983), 47-63; Seymour Martin Lipset, "Why No Socialism in the United States," in *Sources of Contemporary Radicalism*, ed. S. Bialer and S. Sluzar, vol. 1 (Boulder, Colo.: Westview, 1977), 30-149, 346-63.

42. Lipset, *American Exceptionalism*, 109.

43. See, e.g., Lipset, *Continental Divide*, 20-24, and the literature cited there.

rights are an essential, if not the primary, protection against tyranny. The Fourteenth Amendment of the United States Constitution makes that point directly: "No State shall make or enforce any law which shall abridge the privileges or immunities of citizens of the United States; nor shall any State deprive any person of life, liberty, *or property,* without due process of law; nor deny to any person within its jurisdiction the equal protection of the laws" (emphasis added). Founders James Madison and Alexander Hamilton explicitly made the point in the *Federalist Papers* that "Government is instituted no less for protection of property than of the persons of individuals" (Madison, *Federalist* #54) and that "protection of property" is part of the "ordinary course of justice" that is the responsibility of "good government" (Hamilton, *Federalist* #70). Alexis de Tocqueville, wondering about the phenomenon that American citizens in general have what he calls "a high idea of political rights" not just for themselves but also for their fellow citizens, links this directly to the universality of property rights. "Why is it," he asks, initiating the question that Lipset was to struggle with a century and a half later, "that in America, the land par excellence of democracy, no one makes that outcry against property in general that often echoes through Europe? Is there any need to explain? It is because there are no proletarians in America. Everyone, having some possession to defend, recognizes the right to property in principle."[44] Tocqueville's comments at the close of this section, "The Idea of Rights in the United States," as in many other places in his classic, provide warning against the willingness to sacrifice liberty on the altar of economic security, a warning heeded by neither the Social Gospel devotees nor their numerous well-intentioned twentieth-century ecclesiastical offspring, a warning, as he himself observed, that bears regular repetition:

> It cannot be repeated too often: nothing is more fertile in marvels than the art of being free, but nothing is harder than freedom's apprenticeship. The same is not true of despotism. Despotism often presents itself as the repairer of all the ills suffered, the support of just rights, defender of the oppressed, and founder of order. Peoples are lulled to sleep by the temporary prosperity it engenders, and when they do wake up, they are wretched. But liberty is generally born in stormy weather, growing with difficulty amid civil discords, and only when it is already old does one see the blessings it has brought.[45]

While Tocqueville judges that the main factor sustaining democratic institutions in the United States is moral — a set of mores born out of and nur-

44. Alexis de Tocqueville, *Democracy in America,* ed. J. P. Mayer, trans. George Lawrence (New York: HarperCollins, 1983 [1966]), 238.
45. Tocqueville, 240.

tured by religion[46] — he places property/land among the highest "accidental" or "providential" causes. "Everything about the Americans, from their social condition to their laws, is extraordinary; but the most extraordinary thing of all is the land that supports them."[47] Though American tradition gave its citizens "a love of equality and liberty, it was God, who, by handing a limitless continent over to them, gave them the means of long remaining equal and free."[48] It is America's openness (the frontier!) and the American spirit of independence and restlessness (even "restless passions," according to Tocqueville) that help ensure liberty and democratic institutions. In a sentence worthy of Adam Smith, Tocqueville observes: "What a happy land the New World is, where man's vices are almost as useful to society as his virtues."[49] Noting that commercial passions stir Americans more deeply than political ones, Tocqueville observes how European émigrés who were "forced to leave their country on account of their political opinions" (i.e., revolutionaries, one of whom Tocqueville calls a "great leveler and an ardent demagogue") become transformed by the American experience of owning property. Tocqueville says he was "astonished" to hear one such person talking "about the rights of property; of the necessary hierarchy that wealth establishes among men, of obedience to the established law, of the influence of good mores in republics, and of the support to order and freedom afforded by religious ideas; and it even happened that he inadvertently quoted the authority of Jesus Christ in support of one of his political opinions."[50] Liberty and democracy, according to the American experience and credo, require prosperity, and prosperity requires property rights as an essential hedge against state tyranny.

46. Tocqueville, 287-301. The following is a summary statement: "I have said before that I regarded the origin of the Americans, what I have called their point of departure, as the first and most effective of all the elements leading to their present prosperity. The chances of birth favored the Americans; their fathers of old brought to the land in which they live that equality both of conditions and of mental endowments from which, as form its natural source, a democratic republic was one day to arise. But that is not all: with a republican social state they bequeathed to their descendants the habits, ideas, and mores best suited to make a republic flourish. When I consider all that has resulted from this first fact, I think I can see the whole destiny of America contained in the first Puritan who landed on those shores, as that of the whole human race in the first man" (279).

47. Tocqueville, 280.

48. Tocqueville, 279.

49. Tocqueville, 284.

50. Tocqueville, 286.

Rauschenbusch's Kingdom Economics

When we now turn to the Social Gospel, we must make allowances for the quite different contexts in which Tocqueville and Rauschenbusch wrote; the Gilded Age highlighted problems of equal opportunity and evidenced greedy rapacity on a scale unprecedented in the Jacksonian era when Tocqueville toured America. Furthermore, the overwhelming realities of rapid-fire industrialization and urbanization not only created misery on a large and visible scale but also highlighted dramatic contrasts between those who had and those who obviously did not. Yet Rauschenbusch's analysis of the problem and his proposed solution do strike the present-day reader as simplistic. His legitimate concern about the practical needs of the poor, in deliberate and self-conscious rejection of "any Christianity so spiritual or other-worldly that it does not change the manner of life of all who accept it,"[51] is in fact itself remarkably otherworldly.

Rauschenbusch believed that "civilization is passing through a great historic transition,"[52] "a social revolution unparalleled in history for scope and power,"[53] the "historic advent of democracy," which presents the Christian church with an unprecedented opportunity for "the spirit of Christianity to form a working partnership with real social and psychological science."[54] The goal is "social salvation," the Christianizing of domestic and international relations,[55] all of which may lead to "a new epoch in the evolution of the race. . . . We now have such scientific knowledge of social laws and forces, of economics, of history that we can intelligently mold and guide the evolution in which we take part." Equipped with the requisite knowledge, all that is required of us, according to Rauschenbusch, is "the will to match our knowledge." Rhetorically, he asks, "Can we marshall the moral forces capable of breaking what must be

51. Rauschenbusch, *Righteousness of the Kingdom,* 179.
52. Rauschenbusch, *Christianizing the Social Order,* 40.
53. Rauschenbusch, *Christianity,* xxxv. It is worth noting here that Rauschenbusch, at the time he wrote *Christianity and the Social Crisis* in 1907, judged that "the social revolution" had not yet reached America. "We have been exempt," he writes, "not because we had solved the problems, but because we had not yet confronted them." Now that the struggle has arrived in America, he judges that it will be "more intense [here] than anywhere else." Why? "The vastness and the free sweep of our concentrated wealth on the one side, the independence, intelligence, moral vigor, and political power of the common people on the other side, promise a long-drawn grapple of contesting forces which may well make the heart of every American patriot sink within him" (xxxv). Already here one wonders if Rauschenbusch was, in fact, reading European realities into the American situation.
54. Rauschenbusch, *A Theology,* 5.
55. Rauschenbusch, *A Theology,* 7, 4.

broken, and then building what must be built? What spiritual hosts can God line up to rout the Devil in the battle of Armageddon?"[56]

Armageddon, in Rauschenbusch's vision, is the class war. "The welfare of the mass," he writes, "is always at odds with the selfish force of the strong."[57] The strong, according to the prophetic tradition of the Old Testament as well as the teaching of Jesus, are the rich, the holders of land and capital who are slaves of Mammon and oppressors of working people: "We have allowed private persons to put their thumb where they can constrict the life blood of the nation at will. The common people have financed the industry of the country with their savings, but the control of industry has passed out of their hands almost completely. The profits of our common work are absorbed by a limited group; the mass of the people are permanently reduced to wage earning positions."[58] The church, in Rauschenbusch's judgment, has far too often taken the path of conservative resistance against the democratic desires of progress for the working class. The weight of institutional tradition pushes the church toward maintaining the status quo or even to reactionary opposition.[59] But the most serious problem is the individualistic character of the church's teaching about salvation.

> The chief purpose of the Christian Church in the past has been the salvation of individuals. But the pressing task of the present is not individualistic. Our business is to make over an antiquated and immoral economic system; to get rid of laws, customs, maxims, and philosophies inherited from an evil and despotic past; to create just and brotherly relations between great groups and classes of society; and thus to lay a social foundation on which modern men individually can live and work in a fashion that will not outrage all the better elements in them. Our inherited Christian faith dealt with individuals; our present task deals with society.[60]

Instead of individualism we need a social Christianity where church and state cooperate (though retaining their separation!) for the sake of humanity, "to transform humanity into the kingdom of God."[61] This was the goal of Jesus.

"Jesus," says Rauschenbusch, "founded a new and higher community on earth, and that implies new and higher laws. His community is revolutionary

56. Rauschenbusch, *Christianizing the Social Order*, 40-41.
57. Rauschenbusch, *Christianity*, 1.
58. Rauschenbusch, *Christianizing the Social Order*, 2.
59. Rauschenbusch, *Christianizing the Social Order*, 30-39.
60. Rauschenbusch, *Christianizing the Social Order*, 41-42.
61. Rauschenbusch, *Christianizing the Social Order*, 380.

and in opposition to the existing order of things; to be in keeping with this character, the new laws must also differ from the existing rules of life." These new laws arise out of Jesus' "central doctrine of the Kingdom of God on earth,"[62] and it is this "Kingdom ideal" that alone has the "spiritual power" to equip the Christian church for "its divine mission to change this sad old earth into the Kingdom of God."[63] The real obstacle is the power of rich classes who are culpable not only for enjoying the fruit of their ill-gotten gain but also for generating covetousness among the poorer classes. Rauschenbusch, in fact, refers to this phenomenon as worthy of millstones.[64] "It behooves Christian people," he writes, "to recognize that Christ is against inequality, and that he denounces the effort to create inequality as hostile to the nature of the Kingdom of God in earth. Therefore they should welcome and foster every effort to abolish the causes of inequality and thus remove the over-powerful temptations from the members of the upper classes and give them a fair chance to become good men and women. A follower of Christ should not wait till the slow change of society rectifies these evils."[65]

At the same time, Rauschenbusch does not repudiate all materiality in his reconstruction of Jesus' vision: "Of course Jesus recognized that we have need of property."[66] And further, "this seems to be Christ's ideal: every man working cheerfully, eating contentedly the fruit of his labor, making the life of the body the foundation for the spiritual life, and sharing with his brother who happens to be in need."[67] Even in what is likely the most "socialist" chapter in Rauschenbusch's corpus, he still insists "that private property is an indispensable basis of civilization and morality" and that "the per capita amount of it . . . ought to increase."[68] At the same time, the strong "public good" qualification of any claims to private property in favor of socializing it makes Rauschenbusch's case for private property sound somewhat hollow. The real point of this chapter is the claim that "the resocializing of property is an essential part of the Christianizing of the social order. . . . If we can resocialize the public property which is now in private possession, we shall democratize industry, secure far greater attention to the problems of public welfare, and win more genuine re-

---

62. Rauschenbusch, *Christianizing the Social Order*, 380.
63. Rauschenbusch, *Christianizing the Social Order*, 20-21.
64. Rauschenbusch, *Righteousness of the Kingdom*, 203.
65. Rauschenbusch, *Righteousness of the Kingdom*, 204.
66. Rauschenbusch, *Righteousness of the Kingdom*, 206.
67. Rauschenbusch, *Righteousness of the Kingdom*, 207.
68. Rauschenbusch, *Christianizing the Social Order*, 426. Rauschenbusch, however, also favorably cites two German authors who insist that "the abolition of private property in land in the interest of society is a necessity" (*Christianity*, 230).

spect for what is truly private property."[69] What Rauschenbusch's real under-standing of "private property" amounts to becomes more clear when we con-sider his interpretation of Jesus' teaching on the matter.

Rauschenbusch insists upon the "radical" and "revolutionary" character of Jesus' teaching and is impatient with any attempt to qualify his "wealth" statements by any distinctions (such as distinguishing personal wealth from in-vestment capital) or by turning them primarily into relative, attitudinal com-mands ("don't acquire *too much* wealth"). What Jesus asks is straightforward: "In short, Christ forbids the citizens of his Kingdom to pile up wealth, and where it is already piled up, he commands them to disperse it. It takes little imagination to picture the changes which obedience to his command would produce in society."[70] Even an appeal to "stewardship" is insufficient: "If that is what we mean when we preach stewardship, we should be denying the private property rights on which capitalism rests and morally expropriating the own-ers." The church is not there yet, Rauschenbusch notes, preferring simply to "appeal to the conscience of powerful individuals to make them realize they are accountable to God." But "the doctrine is not yet based on modern democratic feeling and on economic knowledge about the sources of economic wealth. It calls for no fundamental change in economic distribution, but simply encour-ages faithful distribution of funds. That is not enough for our modern needs."[71]

Rauschenbusch laments the church's failure here to join *the* battle being waged by the world and, in a somewhat uncharacteristically self-congratulatory moral pose, states the issue of the "social question" as forthrightly as any spokesman for the Social Gospel did: "The social question is confessedly the question of our age, and the social question deals primarily with property. If therefore we undertake to set forth the bearing of Christ's teaching more fully, we do so for the sake of the Kingdom, and not because we expect to reap any harvest of love or gain through it."[72]

The central doctrine of the kingdom — "the idea of an ideal human soci-ety, constituted according to divine laws and governed by God"[73] — as taught by Jesus, differed in startling and revolutionary ways from the theocratic messi-anic expectations of his Jewish contemporaries, but its economic doctrine is clear according to Rauschenbusch. "It seems to me," he writes, "that the teach-

69. Rauschenbusch, *Christianizing the Social Order*, 429. This appears to be a claim that all property is public except that which the community through the state permits to be private — hardly in the spirit of American "property rights."

70. Rauschenbusch, *Righteousness of the Kingdom*, 209.

71. Rauschenbusch, *Christianizing the Social Order*, 45.

72. Rauschenbusch, *Christianizing the Social Order*, 211.

73. Rauschenbusch, *Christianizing the Social Order*, 98.

ing of Jesus on property is an entirely plain doctrine, coherent in itself, and well backed by reason, so that there is no excuse for those who make it nebulous. When Jesus says that there is something in wealth which makes the entrance into the Kingdom next to impossible for its possessor, he must mean that the possession of wealth is very closely tied up with injustice and selfishness, which are the contradiction of the justice and love of the Kingdom."[74] Rauschenbusch sets forth the reasons for this in four straightforward propositions, each with extended commentary:[75]

1. It is not possible to get great wealth except by offending against justice.
2. As a man cannot well gain wealth without sacrificing the Christian virtues, so he cannot well possess wealth without damage to his own soul.
3. In the getting and in the having of riches, there is danger to their possessor.
4. Wealth is incompatible with the kingdom.

What, then, must be done? "Every step toward the social equalization of wealth would bring Christ's ethics within the bounds of the possible. If the unrighteous sources of wealth were cut off, there would be no such inequality of possession as there is now. There could not be. Men are by nature unequal, but they are not unequal enough to justify anything like the present inequality of wealth." Rauschenbusch is hopeful. "And when the weakness and inertia of generations of poverty shall have been eliminated by plentiful food and intellectual stimulus (and America has proved that it can be done in two generations), then the inequality will be still more reduced, and we shall have that soundest and most delightful society, the society of intellectual and social equals."[76]

We leave aside here the millennial utopianism of Rauschenbusch's vision and concentrate on the mechanism by which this is to be achieved. Rauschenbusch gives us little help. He encourages Christians "to anticipate the progress of society by private action and, by anticipating it, speed it on," but notes that this "does not exhaust our responsibility."[77] Since Christians "know what kind of society Christ desires, we can further every movement of corporate society in that direction. The abolition of every unjust privilege of wealth-gathering [including private ownership of land?] will tend toward the social equality desired by Jesus. It will make a natural life easier for the poor and remove the tempta-

74. Rauschenbusch, *Christianizing the Social Order*, 212.
75. Rauschenbusch, *Christianizing the Social Order*, 212-36.
76. Rauschenbusch, *Christianizing the Social Order*, 227.
77. Rauschenbusch, *Christianizing the Social Order*, 235-36.

tion from the rich. In addition, every social action tending to fraternal co-operation and unity of interest among men will be an incorporation of Christ's thoughts in the institutions of mankind. Negatively the abolition of injustice, positively fraternal association among equals: these are to be simultaneously the social words of the future."[78] If we persist in asking, "But how shall this be done?" we receive little concrete guidance.[79] Somehow, "society" or the *Weltgeist* will create human solidarity, a kingdom of equality and brotherhood. There are, Rauschenbusch believes, "various forces which cooperate to advance humanity; the dissemination of ideas by idealistic thinkers, the action of individuals strong by hereditary position, personal character or wealth, and the support of enlightened public opinion. History will do the rest."[80]

Rauschenbusch does cite, with apparent approval, a writer who claimed "There is no longer any private morality."[81] He himself also acknowledges the right of private conscience over against the state, pointing to the example of Quakers and Mennonites who refused to swear oaths and serve in the military. But, as the following summary paragraph clearly shows, Rauschenbusch seems blind to the dangers of any state absolutism, indifferent to Tocqueville's concerns about a "tyranny of the majority," and silent about, if not unaware of, the American passion for liberty and the carefully constructed constitutional safeguards against encroachment on individual liberty by such notions as "property rights."

> This is the attitude of the Christian toward government: devoted assistance when government seeks the right, submission to troublesome burdens if they fall on him and do not compel a participation in wrong; passive resistance and public protest against compulsory participation in wrong-doing; and establishment of a new genuine state when the previous one becomes a fraud, a class pretending to be a state. The judgement in every case lies with the individual conscience which, however, is bound before God to have sought all light and wisdom obtainable, and to act in concert with others whenever possible before it sets itself against public action.[82]

The American revolutionary and activist tradition, wary about too much state power and aggressive in asserting its rights, is completely missing here; William

78. Rauschenbusch, *Christianizing the Social Order*, 236.

79. Though we do get some. Rauschenbusch wants land and water rights to be publicly owned and favors a single, direct tax, progressive inheritance taxes, and the total socializing of money (*Christianizing the Social Order*, pt. VI, chap. 3, "The Socializing of Property," 419-29).

80. Rauschenbusch, *Christianity*, 379.

81. Rauschenbusch, *Righteousness of the Kingdom*, 244.

82. Rauschenbusch, *Righteousness of the Kingdom*, 249-50.

Penn rather than Thomas Jefferson seems to be its guiding light. What is also striking, and somewhat remarkable for a Baptist who not only knew but regularly fed himself intellectually and spiritually from the sectarian tradition of Christianity,[83] is that it never seems to have entered Rauschenbusch's mind that such further "Christianizing of America" might be problematic for many American citizens, including the large influx of Jewish immigrants.[84] To raise that question is perhaps anachronistically unfair.

What must never be forgotten in any critique of Rauschenbusch, furthermore, is the genuine, perhaps even evangelical,[85] and courageous character of his Christian passion for the poor. In his pastoral ministry Rauschenbusch practiced what he preached. But what also needs to be noted here is that the way of the Social Gospel was not the only American means by which concern for the poor was expressed. Jonathan Edwards took a backseat to no one in his condemnation of greed, dishonesty, and ill-gotten wealth, and got into trouble with the wealthy and powerful in his Northampton congregation for it. Edwards also set forth a view of human society in light of the heavenly one that relativized the importance of gaining earthly wealth.[86] Yet, Edwards's vision, including his concern about the seduction of wealth and his insistence upon the

83. See Smucker, *Origins*, chap. 4, "The Influence of Anabaptist Sectarianism," 74-120.

84. Though I have not checked the entire Rauschenbusch corpus as thoroughly as I would have liked to, it seems to me that his Social Gospel vision is free from the ugly racist nativism that can be found in such figures as James Shaver Woodsworth, the great Canadian socialist Social Gospeler and founder/leader of Canada's socialist party, the Cooperative Commonwealth Federation. See his *Strangers within Our Gates* (Toronto and Buffalo: University of Toronto Press, 1972 [1909]). Woodsworth, it is worth noting (in 1909!), sees the American example as the one for Canada to avoid: "Very decidedly the social life and ideals of the United States have been affected by alien races." That such mixing of the races is a good thing, "in the highest interest of our country," as apparently claimed by some of his contemporaries, Woodsworth judges to be "unfounded optimism" (182) in spite of his commitment to evolution of the race (183). The fact that Rauschenbusch was the child of German immigrants and served as pastor to Germans undoubtedly accounts in part for this difference.

85. A fair assessment of Rauschenbusch's evangelical piety must take into account his clear call for personal regeneration (see, e.g., *Christianity*, 349); his sermons (see Max Stackhouse, "The Formation of a Prophet: Reflections on the Early Sermons of Walter Rauschenbusch," *Andover Newton Quarterly* 9 [1969]: 137-80); and also his collection of prayers (*Prayers of the Social Awakening* [Boston and Chicago: Pilgrim, 1910]).

86. See, e.g., Gerald R. McDermott, *One Holy and Happy Society: The Public Theology of Jonathan Edwards* (University Park: Pennsylvania State University Press, 1992), 131, 158; cf. Amy Plantinga Pauw, "'Heaven Is a World of Love': Edwards on Heaven and the Trinity," *Calvin Theological Journal* 30 (1995): 392-401.

necessity of compassion and active charity for the poor,[87] is fully consistent with the characteristically American attitude to property sketched above in a way that Rauschenbusch positively fails to match. As Gerald McDermott notes, for Edwards "the first function of government is to secure property and protect citizens' rights: 'The general design of laws is to maintain the rights and secure the properties of mankind.'"[88] This cannot be said about Rauschenbusch's vision, but it can with respect to two of his European contemporaries, Abraham Kuyper and Leo XIII.

The "American" Public Theology
of Two Europeans (1891)

A direct comparison between the origins of Kuyper's and Rauschenbusch's interest in the "social question" is striking. Like Rauschenbusch's pastoral experience in New York's Hell's Kitchen, Kuyper's first pastorate in the small Dutch village of Beesd (Gelderland) is significant not only because it was the place he encountered living examples of orthodox Calvinism which led to his full conversion to it,[89] but also because it introduced the young, academically oriented and gifted pastor to the "social question." According to an early biographer, it was here that Kuyper saw "with his own eyes, that the relationships between the [wealthy] landowner and the peasant day laborer were not as they should be, and so he became a 'democrat.'"[90] As a rural pastor, he saw how the social and legal structures led to a class division in the life of the people that was sinfully unequal rather than the divinely ordained pattern of in-

---

87. See, e.g., Edwards's sermon "Charity," in *The Works of Jonathan Edwards*, ed. Sereno E. Dwight, rev. Edward Hickman, 2 vols. (Edinburgh: Banner of Truth Trust, 1976 [1834]), 2:163-73; cf. his series of sermons "Charity and Its Fruits," in *Works of Jonathan Edwards*, vol. 8, ed. Paul Ramsey (New Haven and London: Yale University Press, 1989), 123-397.

88. McDermott, 131; Edwards's citation is from a sermon, "Dishonesty," *Works of Jonathan Edwards*, ed. Edward Hickman (London, 1834; reprint, Edinburgh: Banner of Truth, 1974), 2:222.

89. See Frank Vanden Berg, *Abraham Kuyper* (Grand Rapids: Eerdmans, 1960), chap. 4, "Village Clergyman"; G. Puchinger, *Abraham Kuyper: De Jonge Kuyper (1837-1867)* (Franeker: T. Wever, 1987), chap. 7, "Beesd."

90. What Kuyper himself understood by "democrat" must be distinguished from its American usage in political terms. It indicates no specific political party allegiance but simply Kuyper's intended populism, his support for the causes of the "ordinary people," *de kleine luyden*. For an illuminating event on the confusion in an American context created by Kuyper's use of the term "democrat," see app. C.

equality.[91] "In this situation of inequality the weaker party was first of all *spiritually* and then *materially* oppressed. This awakened in him a righteous anger to engage in battle against this national sin."[92] The same biographer also calls attention to Kuyper's own practice of charity, actively helping to gather surplus fruit crops from his own orchard for the poor.[93]

The most evident activity of Kuyper as "democrat," however, was his support for and gift of organizational talent to the cause of church reform, specifically the successful establishment of an *elected* local church council against the opposition of the town's wealthy, aristocratic landowner, Count van Bylant of Mariënwaerdt.[94] Kuyper's massive involvement in church reform began with this issue, and in 1867 he wrote a tract on whether it was advisable to push for a more democratic church by establishing such local, elected bodies to govern the church.[95] Kuyper's positive answer to the question he had posed was consistent with his claim to be a "democrat."[96]

This brief sketch is also consistent with another practice, one that neatly parallels Rauschenbusch's.[97] From the time of his first pastorate in Beesd, some

91. This is an important point in Kuyper's social theology. Kuyper did not have a radical egalitarian vision but what he termed an "organic" one which allowed for difference and even economic inequality. Not all difference in economic status is sinful, but some surely is. It is the latter that needs to be addressed by Christians. On Kuyper's firm opposition to radical egalitarianism or, as he liked to call it, "uniformitarianism" (*eenvormigheid*), see Abraham Kuyper, *Eenvormigheid: De Vloek Van Het Moderne Leven* (Uniformitarianism: The curse of modern life) (Amsterdam: H. De Hoogh, 1869).

92. J. C. Rullmann, *Abraham Kuyper: Een Levensschets* (Kampen: Kok, 1928), 34.

93. Rullmann, *Abraham Kuyper*, 34. Rullmann speaks somewhat quaintly about the "dominee himself shaking the trees."

94. Rullmann, *Abraham Kuyper*, 34.

95. Abraham Kuyper, *Wat Moeten Wij Doen, Het Stemrecht aan Onszelven Houden of den Kerkeraad Machtigen? Vraag bij de Uitvoering van Art. 23* (What must we do: Keep voting rights to ourselves or empower the consistory? A question concerning the implementation of Article 23) (Culemborg: A. J. Blom, 1867); see summary description in J. C. Rullmann, *Kuyper-Bibliographie, Deel I (1860-1879)* (The Hague: Bootsma, 1923), 13-23. Article 23 referred to a state regulation governing the churches, passed into law in 1852, that gave opportunity for greater local autonomy for congregations of the Dutch Reformed Church.

96. Kuyper, it should be noted, was careful to distinguish a legitimate democracy in the church, including the right of church members to vote, from notions of radical popular sovereignty; Jesus Christ is the sovereign Lord of the church. He did, it is also interesting to note, raise questions about the new regulation's failure to give women — "the cream, the core, the *aristai* of the congregation" — the right to vote. In *De Heraut* of January 23, 1898 (no. 1048), Kuyper openly advocated the right of women to vote in congregational assemblies (Rullmann, *Kuyper-Bibliographie*, 1:14).

97. For an illuminating treatment of Rauschenbusch's early preaching, see Stackhouse, "Formation of a Prophet," 137-59.

twenty years before Rauschenbusch began his ministry in Hell's Kitchen, New York, Kuyper too preached about individualism, riches, poverty, justice, and injustice — in other words, about "the social question."[98] In the words of his biographer, "Kuyper's social concerns were already apparent in his earliest sermons that are preserved in his archives; these brought him into conflict with the noble landowner of Beesd and that is where he became a democrat."[99] This concern was also reflected in Kuyper's early sermons to the wealthy, urban Amsterdam congregation he served from 1870 on. In his inaugural sermon of August 10, 1870 (on Eph. 3:17, "Rooted and Established"), Kuyper set forth his views — foundational to this public theology — on the church as "institute" and the church as "organism."[100] In this sermon Kuyper pleads for *liberty* for the church; freedom to be a true church in the Dutch Reformed context of the later nineteenth century, he adds, requires a threefold liberation *(vrijmaking)*: liberation from the state, from an oppressive clericalism, and from the power of *money*.[101] Though it is rather lengthy, we shall cite one powerful passage from this sermon that captures Kuyper's passion as well as his eloquence:

> It is not fitting for the church of Christ to bind itself with golden shackles or silver chains to that which conflicts with its nature. The first congregation began with nothing but the Holy Spirit and yet over a long period this treasure became a goldmine. Since then the treasure has been robbed and the Lord put up with the robbery so that eventually his church might demonstrate what it treasured more: the *faith* that had dumped all this gold at her feet, or the *gold* that faith had given her. "Gold and silver are mine," says the Lord, "lasting good and righteousness." But the state also says in its own way: "I have the millions, I have the money that you need for your church." And it is true: the church needs money. Now then, you face two offers. Whose promise, congregation, will you trust? The promise from him who gives you gold as the fruit of faith, or that of the State who binds you with chains to its gold in order to put stumbling blocks in the way of faith's liberty? The choice is yours, but this I must tell you: The treasury of your faith will increasingly become poorer so long as you do not learn to hate the unfree money. Here too,

98. P. Kasteel, *Abraham Kuyper* (Kampen: Kok, 1938), 203; Kasteel (n. 175) refers to sermons in the Kuyper Archive, dossier 1860-1865.

99. Kasteel, 203.

100. Abraham Kuyper, *Predicatiën* (Kampen: Kok, 1913), 327-51; the distinction is basically between the body of Christ gathered around word and sacraments for worship and discipline and the body of Christ in the totality of its multidimensional vocation in the world. Christian political activism, for example, belongs to the responsibility of the church as organism and not to the church as institute.

101. Kuyper, *Predicatiën*, 344-45.

[the saying] holds true: Whoever gains, will lose. Only the one who can be poor will become rich. Whoever is able to despise gold has discovered the goldmine.[102]

When, therefore, we turn to Kuyper's 1891 address to the First Christian Social Congress in the Netherlands on November 9, 1891,[103] we encounter themes that had long been part of his public concern. Kuyper immediately sets out the basic question, "*What should we, as confessors of Christ, do about the social needs of our time?*" and points appreciatively to the example of others such as the British Christian socialists Maurice and Kingsley, Catholic thinkers such as von Ketteler and Le Play, the numerous Catholic social congresses in Europe, and above all to Leo XIII's *Rerum Novarum* (24). Kuyper's appreciation for Catholic social teaching (in a note) is particularly striking: "We must admit, to our shame, that the Roman Catholics are far ahead of us in their study of the social problem. Indeed, very far ahead. The action of the Roman Catholics should spur us to show more dynamism. The encyclical *Rerum Novarum* of Leo XIII states the principles which are common to all Christians, and which we share with our Roman Catholic compatriots" (84). It is worth noting that, like Rauschenbusch, Kuyper wings his first arrows of criticism at the church and its failures. Kuyper contends that "even before a single voice had been heard among Christians outside the Netherlands, our poets Bilderdijk and Da Costa and statesman Groen van Prinsterer had already called our attention to the social need" (24). Kuyper cites Bilderdijk's call to Christians to do penance:

Whenever a people is destined to perish in sin,
It's in the church that the soul leprosy begins. (25)

Kuyper goes on to note that da Costa founded "his Internationale in London in 1864, a quarter of a century before Karl Marx," and that "in 1853, Groen Van Prinsterer frightened the distinguished gentlemen in [Parliament] with his brusque declaration: 'With reference to socialist ideas, one should pay attention to the truly wretched condition of the lower classes, especially to the harm which the higher classes, through their moral corruption and pseudo-science, have brought about among the people.' He declared that in socialism 'there is a measure of truth mingled with error, which gives it its power.' He recognized that 'one should also try to improve material conditions, the injustice of which multiplies the power of the socialist error.'" Now, in 1891, Kuyper adds, "we

102. Kuyper, *Predicatiën*, 345.
103. Page references which follow in the text are to the English translation by James W. Skillen, *The Problem of Poverty* (Grand Rapids: Baker, 1991).

find ourselves fighting a rearguard action . . . [thanks to] our failure to act." It is a shame for Christians when even socialists "so strongly [feel] the bond between social distress and the Christian religion that they have not hesitated to present Christ himself as the great prophet of socialism" (26-27). "We should feel ashamed that the voice of conscience has not spoken more loudly within us before now, or at least that it did not stir us to action. We should feel humiliated that, in the face of so crying a need, we have not long since been acting in the name of Jesus" (28). The appalling physical need pales in significance with the spiritual "demoralization that follows on the heels of material need" and results in raging curses against God and inflames "everything wild and brutish in the human heart" (62). It is especially out of this "abyss of spiritual misery" that Kuyper hears "a cry of accusation against us as Christians. Were not almost all of these who now rage once baptized?" he asks. "And following their baptism, what did we sacrifice for them so that, instead of the caricature of the Christian religion against which they now utter their curses, they might understand something of God's real love in Christ Jesus? What have we Christians in the Netherlands done to stop this ravaging of the social life-blood by the poison of the French Revolution? When the infection became evident on the outside and social sickness took on an epidemic character, what did we on our side do to offer medicine and balm for its cure? . . . There is so much damage to overcome!" (63).

These *mea culpa*s are notably absent in *Rerum Novarum*.[104] Instead, a key reason given for workers being "tossed about helplessly and disastrously in conditions of pitiable and utterly undeserved misery" is that "the old working men's guilds were abolished in the last century and no other means of protection was provided in their place." The deliberate secularization of modern liberal political theory is also scored: "At the same time, all trace of the religion of our fathers was stripped from government and the law. And so it comes about that working men are now left isolated and helpless, betrayed to the inhumanity of employers and the unbridled greed of competitors" (*RN*, §2). The only place in *The Problem of Poverty* where Kuyper voices a similar concern about Christian exclusion from a secularized public square is in his lament about the lack of solid Christian social *thinking*, which he describes as "one of the pitiful fruits of state monopoly, which continues to increase in this country's universities" (23). A clear difference between the encyclical (and this is inherent in the difference in genre, not a reflection of papal lack of compassion) and Kuyper's address to the social congress is that the latter is weighted toward an emotional portrayal of the problem in order to arouse Christian action, while the former

104. Cited in text following as *RN*.

is primarily a thoughtful, analytic setting forth of perennial Christian teaching rooted in Scripture, Christian tradition, experience, and responding to contemporary trends. *Rerum Novarum* weaves compassionate concern unobtrusively through the teaching; Kuyper teaches intermittently in the course of what is essentially an extended jeremiad.

Kuyper and Leo do, however, have a common theological anthropology; they share the same vision of humanity, of human society, and have a common antipathy to socialist/collectivist solutions to the problem of the working poor. The antipathy is rooted in concern about undue state interference in the family, which has "its own rights and duties which depend not at all on the state . . . [and possesses] at least equal rights with the state to choose and employ whatever is necessary for its rightful life and liberty" (*RN*, §§10, 11), and about state assistance destroying personal initiative (72; *RN*, §13). "State and society," Kuyper insists, "each has its own sphere, its own sovereignty, and the social question cannot be resolved rightly unless we respect this duality, . . . thus clearing the way for a free society" (65).[105] The vision of the human condition begins positively with an emphasis on "the primacy of man's *eternal* welfare," a hope cruelly eliminated by the socialist, according to Kuyper, who "for the sake of bettering the lot of humanity in this short span of temporal existence, wildly and recklessly cuts off every prospect of a glory that shall be eternal" (36-37). *Rerum Novarum* states it more positively. It is by relativizing this present material existence that the church offers human beings *more* than economic justice: "But the Church, with Jesus Christ for teacher and guide, seeks persistently far more than justice. She warns men that it is by keeping a more perfect rule that class becomes joined to class in the closest neighborliness and friendship. We cannot understand and value the goods of this mortal life unless we have a clear vision of that other life of immortality. If we lose sight of that, we lose also and at once the true sense of virtue. Everything to do with our material world becomes lost in a mystery which no human mind can fathom" (*RN*, §18).

Relativizing also arises from the conviction that sin is universal; neither are the rich in some sense more perverse than the poor, nor are the poor (even the oppressed poor) privileged in their innocence. Kuyper, while pointing accusingly at the failure of governments to protect the weak but becoming instead "an instrument against them," in Niebuhrian fashion observes that "this was not because the stronger class was more evil at heart than the weaker, for no sooner did a man from the lower class rise to the top than he in his turn took part just as harshly — yes, even more harshly — in the wicked oppression of

105. What we have here *in nuce* is Kuyper's doctrine of sphere sovereignty. For fuller description see Kuyper, *Lectures on Calvinism*, Lecture 3, "Calvinism and Politics," 78-109.

those who were members of his own former class" (33). For this reason Kuyper and Leo both repudiate the notion of class conflict as a means to a more equal society and appeal to an organic idea of society. *Rerum Novarum* states it clearly:

> In the subject under discussion it is a great mistake to imagine that class is spontaneously hostile to class, as if nature had matched together the wealthy owners of the means of production and the unpropertied workers to persist stubbornly in lying wildly about each other. This picture is so far removed from truth and reason as to be directly contrary to both. Just as the different parts of the body unite to form a whole so well proportioned as to be called symmetrical, so also nature has decreed that in the state these twin classes should correspond to each other in concord and create an equilibrium. Each stands entirely in need of the other: there can be no capital without labour, nor labour without capital. Concord begets order and beauty, whereas a continuation of conflict leads inevitably to barbarity and wild confusion. Christian institutions are possessed of marvellous and many-sided strength which enables them to put an end to conflict and to cut away its root. (*RN*, §16)[106]

If statist interference and class conflict alike are repudiated, what alternative strategies for social transformation do Kuyper and Leo suggest? To begin with, neither opposes all government involvement in social and economic matters. It is a "delusion," Kuyper observes, to think "that the intervention of government in social affairs is a novelty of our times" (32). "Government exists to administer [God's] justice on earth, and to uphold that justice. The tasks of family and society therefore lie outside government's jurisdiction. With those it is not to meddle. But as soon as there is a clash among the different spheres of life, where one sphere trespasses on or violates the domain which by divine ordinance belongs to the other, then it is the God-given duty of government to uphold justice before arbitrariness, and withstand by the justice of God, the physical superiority of the stronger" (71). Leo agrees "that the state has no authority to swallow up either the individual or the family," but he also contends that "the public authority must intervene . . . whenever the public interest or that of a particular class is harmed or endangered, provided that this is the only way to prevent or remove the evil" (*RN*, §37).

The appeal to last resort gains credibility when it is accompanied by an equally insistent claim for the right of labor to "organize independently in order to defend its rights" (72). The importance of the "natural right of associa-

106. Cf. Kuyper, *The Problem of Poverty*, 40-41, 44, 52, and 65, for comparable sentiments.

tion," taking up no less than ten paragraphs (§§49-58) of the papal encyclical, may be said to be one of its two chief positive social teachings. The other, fully affirmed by Kuyper, though not emphasized to the same degree, is the vigorous defense of the "natural right of private property" (*RN*, §§3-13). Here too, however, this right is not absolute. The "organic" character of humanity fits with Scripture, excluding not only "an absolute community of goods" but also "just as completely every illusion of a right to dispose of one's property absolutely, as if one were God, without considering the needs of others" (67). Similarly, the papal teaching "can be summarized thus: whoever has been generously supplied by God with either corporal and external goods or those of the spirit, possesses them for this purpose — to apply them equally to his own perfection and, in his role as a steward of divine providence, to the benefit of others" (*RN*, §22). Though the repudiation of an "absolute right of private property" formally brings Rauschenbusch, Kuyper, and Leo together, the emphasis is different. For the Europeans, God's ownership is the essential qualifier leading to stewardship; for Rauschenbusch, the common good exercised through the process of state-guided socializing of property is the real qualifier.

Concluding Observations

Where does this now bring us with respect to our question about a distinctively American public theology that addresses "precisely the problems and opportunities of specifically American Christianity and of the nation molded thereby"?[107] Our conclusion is modest. All three of the men under consideration in this essay share a profound concern for the economic needs of workers, especially those marginalized by big cities and big industry. All three repudiate an individualistic social vision in favor of an "organic," more communitarian model. All three, it must also be said, in some sense affirm private property and repudiate an "absolute" right to its use. And, though we did not consider it here, all three realize the importance of strong families for healthy society in general and economic prosperity in particular.[108] Finally, though also not considered in this chapter, there was among all three a commonality concerning appropriate legislation needed to protect all workers from exploitation and especially women and children from being pressed into serving the industrial machine.[109]

107. See n. 7 above.

108. *RN*, §§10-12; Kuyper, *The Problem of Poverty*, 61, 69; Rauschenbusch, *Righteousness of the Kingdom*, 236-44.

109. Only Kuyper, it should be noted, actually had the opportunity as a legislator to effect such legal change and protection; for details see Kasteel, 202-10.

What, then, is the difference between the Europeans and Rauschenbusch, and whose vision is the more characteristically "American"?

While it is true, as H. Richard Niebuhr's interpretation of Rauschenbusch and the Social Gospel portrays it, that the emphasis on the kingdom of God is an important — perhaps *the* important — theme of continuity in American Christianity,[110] that by itself is not enough to warrant claiming American distinctiveness for the Social Gospel. This is the case, quite apart from the awkward fact that Rauschenbusch's interpretation of the kingdom comes straight from the German liberal theologian Albrecht Ritschl. The key difference between Rauschenbusch and his two European contemporaries Abraham Kuyper and Leo XIII is that they had a clearer eye for the characteristically American *institutional* means of protecting *liberty*. The concerns about state power and intrusion into other social spheres such as the family, the protection against statism through the notion of natural property rights, the recognition of associational freedom and corporate action of free citizens outside of both state and church, all of which make possible and give great *spiritual-moral* power to the church as the *independent* soul and conscience of the body politic — all this, celebrated by Alexis de Tocqueville in *Democracy in America,* was *better* grasped (in principle if not with full clarity)[111] by the two Europeans than by Rauschenbusch.[112] From these observations we raise a few questions.

Does all this perhaps suggest that Rauschenbusch, thoroughly steeped in the Continental theological and sociological currents of his day, interpreted American experience in its light and failed to recognize what was different about the American experiment? For example, did the European phenomenon of class lead him to skew his assessment of the American *social* (not economic!) situation and thus the opportunities available to address economic ills? At the same time, is it possible that the European thinkers we considered in this chapter broke through the class-conflict model in part at least because of the relative success of the American experiment as reported, for example, by Alexis de

110. H. Richard Niebuhr, 161-63.

111. From Kuyper's other writings, notably *Lectures on Calvinism*, it is clear that he did know America and the distinctive character of her institutions. It is also, for example, obvious from his early works such as "Calvinism, the Origin and Guarantee of Our Constitutional Liberties" (*Bibliotheca Sacra* 52 [1895]: 385-410; 646-75) that Kuyper had read *Democracy in America*. To the best of my knowledge (corroborated by personal correspondence with Max Stackhouse), there is no evidence that Rauschenbusch ever did.

112. Rauschenbusch's ecclesiology, however, is clearly voluntarist and thus quite American in character. See Donavan E. Smucker, "Rauschenbusch's View of the Church Dynamic Voluntary Association," in *Voluntary Association: A Study of Groups in Free Societies*, essays in honor of James Luther Adams, ed. D. B. Robertson (Richmond: John Knox, 1966), 159-70.

Tocqueville in his *Democracy in America?* These are tantalizing queries, and if a positive answer to them is correct, it may help account for the fact that after the world-shaking events of 1989, which demonstrated the triumph of the American idea, Kuyper's vision and that of Leo XIII's are still taken seriously as viable options for an American public theology. Can that still be said of Rauschenbusch? One of America's leading commentators on religion in American public life judges that, along with Reinhold Niebuhr, the two leading candidates for helping fashion an American public theology today are Abraham Kuyper and the Catholic social tradition of Leo XIII, especially as applied by Leo's brilliant twentieth-century American Jesuit interpreter, John Courtney Murray.[113] The centenary of *Rerum Novarum*'s publication was celebrated by what may well become an equally historically formative papal encyclical, John Paul II's *Centesimus Annus*. The centennial of Kuyper's Stone Lectures was also remembered on two continents.[114] Will the centenary of Rauschenbusch's *Christianity and the Social Crisis* receive similar attention? Perhaps we gain at least a hint of an answer when we consider in greater detail the place of socialism and liberation in Christian reflection on economic and political life. We go on now to consider liberty's twin stepchildren, liberationism and libertarianism.

---

113. Richard John Neuhaus, "Ralph Reed's Real Agenda," *First Things*, no. 66 (October 1996): 42.

114. For details of the commemorative conferences, see preface.

PART TWO

ISSUES AND OPTIONS
IN AMERICAN EVANGELICAL
PUBLIC THEOLOGY TODAY

CHAPTER SIX

Liberty's Stepchildren:
Liberationists and Libertarians

Proclaim liberty throughout the land unto all the inhabitants thereof.

Leviticus 25:10 (inscribed on the Liberty Bell, 1752)

The Spirit of the Lord is on me,
  because he has anointed me
  to preach good news to the poor.

Luke 4:18 (from Isaiah 61:1)

Those who deny freedom to others deserve it not for themselves.

Abraham Lincoln

Economic and political freedom are inseparable.

F. A. Hayek

Extremism in the defense of liberty is no vice, moderation in the pursuit of justice is no virtue.

Barry Goldwater (1964)

Free at last! Free at last!
Thank God Almighty, we are free at last!

Anonymous, Spiritual, quoted by
Martin Luther King, Jr., at the Lincoln Memorial, 1963

At the heart of liberty is the right to define one's own concept of existence, of meaning, of the universe, and of the mystery of human life.

U.S. Supreme Court, *Planned Parenthood* v. *Casey* (1992)

The historical orientation in the last three chapters was an attempt to place Abraham Kuyper's thought and activity in a context that would highlight his own profound appreciation for the American experiment in ordered liberty. Kuyper's political imagination, we noted in the first chapter, was dominated by the theme of liberty in its historical advance — what we described as a Christian-historical imagination. In the final analysis, so Kuyper believed, liberty was the fruit of the Calvinist religion's fundamental convictions about God's sovereignty and human dignity and had proved to be the leading indicator of the providentially directed world-stream of history as it spread steadily westward from its cradle in the Mediterranean region, through Europe, and then to America.[1] Furthermore, Kuyper was sensitive to the costs historically paid for liberty, the fragility of political liberty, and the profound difficulties involved in maintaining a healthy balance between liberty and order. Liberty did not come easy and was maintained only at considerable cost. When he attempted to rally his troops into battle for their own emancipation, as an integral part of his own rhetorical arsenal he regularly invoked the memory of the sixteenth-century Dutch freedom fighters who defied Spanish tyranny. Kuyper launched his daily newspaper, *De Standaard,* on April 1, 1872, the 300th anniversary of the Sea Beggars' recapture of Brielle, and appealed to this example to motivate his own people to action.[2] There were, Kuyper told his Princeton audience in 1898, three exemplary "historic lands of political freedom": "the Netherlands, England and America."[3] Here too he called attention to the important role of Calvinism in the battles to create and preserve liberty, citing the words of American historian George Bancroft: "The fanatic for Calvinism was a fanatic for liberty, for in the moral warfare for freedom, his creed was a part of his army, and his most faithful ally in the battle."[4] Kuyper had a strong antipathy to polit-

---

1. Abraham Kuyper, *Lectures on Calvinism* (Grand Rapids: Eerdmans, 1931), 32-40; see discussion in chap. 1, 13-14, above.

2. See above, 60-62.

3. Kuyper, *Lectures on Calvinism,* 78.

4. Kuyper, *Lectures on Calvinism,* 78. The citation given in Kuyper's note is Bancroft, *History of the United States of America,* 15th ed. (Boston, 1853), 1:464; (New York, 1891), 1:319.

ical despotism, and since the entry of sin into the world had brought about "the battle of the ages between *Authority* and *Liberty*," he contended that God himself had created human beings with "the very innate thirst for liberty" as "the God-ordained means to bridle the authority wheresoever it degenerated into despotism."[5]

In this tactic Kuyper, the founder and theoretician of the *Antirevolutionary* Party, fierce opponent of the French Revolution, nonetheless built on a tradition of Calvinist-inspired legitimation of revolt against tyranny,[6] providing sanction for what he called "the three great revolutions in the Calvinistic world [that] left untouched the glory of God, nay, they even proceeded from the acknowledgment of his majesty": the sixteenth-century Dutch rebellion led by William the Silent against Spain, the English Glorious Revolution of William and Mary in 1688, and the American Revolution.[7] Apparently, Kuyper's antipathy toward the French Revolution did not transfer to all revolutions; in his view, not all revolutions are created equal. Peter Heslam observes that "for Kuyper the real evil of the French Revolution did not lie in its overthrow of the Bourbon dynasty but in its opposition to divine authority, summed up in the Revolutionaries' slogan *ni Dieu ni maître*. As Kuyper explained in his first Stone Lecture, it was not so much indignation at abuses as the desire to substitute human sovereignty for that of God, that was the principal motive of the Revolutionaries."[8] Kuyper's rhetoric thus can be appealed to with some legitimacy by advocates of an emancipatory or liberationist point of view, and it is not surprising that the turn-of-the-century Boers in South Africa, whose struggle drew Kuyper's attention and profound sympathy,[9] thought of themselves as nineteenth-century "Sea-Beggars."[10]

5. Kuyper, *Lectures on Calvinism*, 80.

6. See J. W. Sap, *Wegbereiders der Revolutie: Calvinisme en de Strijd om de Democratische Rechtstaat* (Groningen: Wolters-Noordhoff, 1993).

7. Kuyper, *Lectures on Calvinism*, 86.

8. Peter Heslam, *Creating a Christian Worldview: Abraham Kuyper's Lectures on Calvinism* (Grand Rapids: Eerdmans, 1998), 148.

9. See Abraham Kuyper, "The South African Crisis," in *Abraham Kuyper: A Centennial Reader*, ed. J. Bratt (Grand Rapids: Eerdmans, 1998), 323-60; on Kuyper and South Africa more broadly, see P. Kasteel, *Abraham Kuyper* (Kampen: Kok, 1938), 273-77, and the literature cited there.

10. See Chris A. J. Van Koppen, *De Geuzen van de Negentiende Eeuw: Abraham Kuyper en Zuid Africa* (Wormer: Inmerc, 1992).

Evangelicals and Liberation[11]

This emancipatory or liberationist emphasis is one of the two main ways that Christian social thought in the second half of the twentieth century developed the idea of liberty. At this point we directly link ourselves to the concerns of the previous chapter — the so-called "social question" of the late nineteenth century and the concern for the poor, particularly those impoverished by the rushing advance of modernization and industrialization. In this chapter we shall bring key themes from Kuyper's sociopolitical vision and practice into conversation with contemporary debates among North American evangelicals about economic issues.[12] Specifically, we shall examine two opposing points of view, namely, a liberationist emphasis[13] and a libertarian

11. This is the title of a significant symposium edited by Carl E. Amerding, *Evangelicals and Liberation* (Phillipsburg, N.J.: Presbyterian and Reformed, 1977).

12. The most helpful overview of the debate that continues among North American evangelicals concerning economics is Craig M. Gay, *With Liberty and Justice for Whom? The Recent Evangelical Debate over Capitalism* (Grand Rapids: Eerdmans, 1991); see also the literature in nn. 13 and 14 below.

13. For a summary of evangelical liberation theologies, see Gay, chap. 1, "Capitalism as Oppression: The Evangelical Left," 22-62. The presentation that follows below must of necessity be summarily brief and representative rather than thorough and detailed. The literature on liberation theology is enormous, and the following volumes are a sample of the literature that has been formative and helpful in shaping the issues explored in this chapter: Gustavo Gutiérrez, *A Theology of Liberation*, trans. and ed. Sister Caridad Inda and John Eagleson, rev. ed. (Maryknoll, N.Y.: Orbis, 1988); Kenneth A. Myers, *Aspiring to Freedom: Commentaries on John Paul II's Encyclical "The Social Concerns of the Church"* (Grand Rapids: Eerdmans, 1988); Ronald H. Nash, ed., *Liberation Theology* (Milford, Mich.: Mott Media, 1984); Ronald H. Nash, *Poverty and Wealth: The Christian Debate over Capitalism* (Westchester, Ill.: Crossway, 1986); Richard J. Neuhaus, ed., *The Preferential Option for the Poor,* Encounter Series, no. 8 (Grand Rapids: Eerdmans, 1988); Richard J. Neuhaus, *Doing Well and Doing Good: The Challenge to the Christian Capitalist* (New York: Doubleday, 1992); Michael Novak, *The Catholic Ethic and the Spirit of Capitalism* (New York: Free Press, 1993); Michael Novak, *Freedom with Justice: Catholic Social Thought and Liberal Institutions* (San Francisco: Harper & Row, 1984); Michael Novak, *This Hemisphere of Liberty: A Philosophy of the Americas* (Washington, D.C.: American Enterprise Institute, 1990); Michael Novak, *The Spirit of Democratic Capitalism* (New York: Simon & Schuster, 1982); Michael Novak, *Will It Liberate? Questions about Liberation Theology* (New York and Mahwah, N.J.: Paulist, 1986); Marvin Olasky, ed., *Freedom, Justice, and Hope: Toward a Strategy for the Poor and Oppressed* (Westchester, Ill.: Crossway, 1988); Marvin Olasky, *The Tragedy of American Compassion* (Washington, D.C.: Regnery, 1992); Amy L. Sherman, *Preferential Option: A Christian and Neoliberal Strategy for Latin America's Poor* (Grand Rapids: Eerdmans; Washington, D.C.: Institute on Religion and Democracy, 1992); George Weigel and Robert Royal, eds., *Building the Free Society: Democracy, Capitalism, and Cath-*

one.[14] Both approaches are rooted in and appeal to the notion of liberty, have ardent defenders in the evangelical world, and have spokespersons who, in varying degrees, appeal to Abraham Kuyper for support.[15] The key difference between them is that liberationists value equality or "social justice" as the highest political good, even at the cost of some freedom, while libertarians give that honor to freedom itself at the cost of equality.

It is worth noting at this point that this polarity was not unknown to the framers of the American Constitution. In *Federalist* #10, James Madison addressed the problem of "factions" or group-interest passion at the expense of the public good.[16] A faction is clearly a "mischief" in the body politic and can be "cured," Madison observed, either "by removing its causes" or "by controlling its effects." He then addresses the first option: "There are again two methods of removing the causes of faction: the one, by destroying the liberty which is essential to its existence; the other, by giving to each citizen the same opin-

---

olic Social Teaching (Grand Rapids: Eerdmans; Washington, D.C.: Ethics and Public Policy Center, 1993); George Weigel, ed., *A New Worldly Order: John Paul II and Human Freedom (A "Centesimus Annus" Reader)* (Washington, D.C.: Ethics and Public Policy Center, 1992).

14. Here too our discussion and bibliography must be abbreviated. Important recent texts include Doug Bandow, *The Politics of Envy: Statism as Theology* (Brunswick, N.J.: Transaction, 1994); David Boaz, *Libertarianism: A Primer* (New York: Free Press, 1997); David Boaz, ed., *The Libertarian Reader* (New York: Free Press, 1997); George Carey, ed., *Freedom and Virtue: The Conservative/Libertarian Debate* (Wilmington, Del.: Intercollegiate Studies Institute, 1998); Lansing Pollock, *The Free Society* (Boulder, Colo.: Westview, 1996). A review of earlier libertarian evangelicals, including P. J. Hill, James D. Gwartney, Ronald Nash, and George Roche, can be found in Gay, 96-99.

15. We will pay special attention to two important works that make significant appeals to the Kuyperian tradition, Nicholas Wolterstorff, *Until Justice and Peace Embrace: The Kuyper Lectures for 1981 Delivered at the Free University of Amsterdam* (Grand Rapids: Eerdmans, 1983), and David Hall, *Savior or Servant? Putting Government in Its Place* (Oak Ridge, Tenn.: Kuyper Institute, 1996). It is apparent that both of these volumes are linked to the Kuyper legacy, but the former displays profound sympathies for key elements of liberation theology while the latter pays the same compliment to libertarianism. It must also be said that neither volume is a pure representative of the respective traditions; both authors nuance their own positions considerably. Furthermore, our discussion will be restricted not only to these two specific texts but also to the one specific issue of economics and liberty/justice. We must bypass the other issues (aesthetics, liturgy, Christian scholarship) included in Wolterstorff's evocative and richly erudite volume as well as the development of his thought reflected, for example, in the as yet unpublished Abraham Kuyper Centennial commemorative Stone Lectures delivered at Princeton Seminary in February 1998.

16. James Madison, Alexander Hamilton, and John Jay, *The Federalist Papers,* ed. Isaac Kramnick (New York: Penguin Books, 1977), 122-28; citations which follow are taken from these pages of this edition.

ions, the same passions, and the same interests." The first of these "solutions" is "folly," a cure worse than the disease: "It could never be more truly said than of the first remedy that it was worse than the disease. Liberty is to faction what air is to fire; an aliment without which it instantly expires. But it could not be less folly to abolish liberty, which is essential to political life, because it nourishes faction than it would be to wish the annihilation of air, which is essential to animal life, because it imparts to fire its destructive agency." The second "solution" — substantive equality — is, according to Madison, "as impracticable as the first would be unwise. As long as the reason of man continues fallible, and he is at liberty to exercise it, different opinions will be formed." Furthermore, "the diversity in the faculties of men, from which the rights of property originate, is not less an obstacle to a uniformity of interests." Thus, "the most common and durable source of factions has been the various and unequal distribution of property." In sum, "the latent causes of faction are thus sown in the nature of man," and rather than attempt to eliminate factions by removing their causes — an impossible task — wise and prudent government will find "relief only . . . in the means of controlling its *effects*." Madison concludes by calling a "rage" for "equal division of property" a "wicked and improper project." For Madison, liberty clearly trumps equality. However, the debate did not stop with the arguments of federalist republicans such as Madison and Hamilton but continues, also among American evangelical social thinkers into the twenty-first century. We shall first attempt a working definition of liberation theology, provide some examples of recent North American evangelical liberation theologies, and then summarize the debate about liberation theology that took place within the evangelical community, especially during the decade of the 1980s.[17] Then we

17. In addition to volumes edited by Carl Amerding *(Evangelicals and Liberation)* and written by Ronald Nash *(Poverty and Wealth)*, see John Bernbaum, ed., *Economic Justice and the State: A Debate between Ronald H. Nash and Eric H. Beversluis* (Grand Rapids: Baker, 1986), and Franky Schaeffer, ed., *Is Capitalism Christian?* (Westchester, Ill.: Crossway, 1985). Much of the intense discussion about liberation theology became moot after the revolutions of 1989 that significantly discredited the Marxist and socialist elements of the liberationist paradigm. It is interesting to note that after 1989 even some influential Latin American liberation theologians such as Leonardo Boff acknowledged the bankruptcy of much liberationist *economic analysis* and turned their attention and political passion to the questions of environment and ecology; see Leonardo Boff, *Ecology and Liberation: A New Paradigm,* trans. John Cumming (Maryknoll, N.Y.: Orbis, 1995). For another "revisioning" of liberation theology, see José Comblin, *Called for Freedom: The Changing Context of Liberation Theology,* trans. Phillip Berryman (Maryknoll, N.Y.: Orbis, 1998). Comblin observes that "the decline and fall of the Soviet Union have also had an impact on Latin America . . . [particularly] . . . on the way that redemocratization has taken place" (xv). He hastens to add, however, that "this does not mean that socialism has no future" (xvi).

shall do the same for libertarian thought, finally using Kuyper's insights on the human quest for liberty to clarify the key issues that are in debate between these two positions.

The term "liberation theology" covers a multitude of revolutionary causes and movements, and the reality referred to by it is better spoken of in the plural: "liberation theologies."[18] Liberation theologies include geographically situated political movements (Latin American, African, or Asian liberation theology), ethnically based liberation movements (Hispanic, black), sex-oriented liberation theologies (feminist, gay, lesbian), and finally ecological theologies advocating the liberation of Mother Earth herself.[19] With this great diversity of "theologies of liberation," it is almost impossible to provide a single or simple definition. Yet there are commonalities that are consistently appealed to in all expressions of liberation theology. The starting point for all is the *experience* of oppression and the conviction that theological reflection must begin with a commitment of *solidarity* with the oppressed and a concomitant active *praxis* of liberation from such oppression. In the words of Latin American Gustavo Gutiérrez, in many respects the "father" of liberation theology: "Theology is a reflection — that is, a second act, a turning back, a reflecting that comes after action. Theology is not first; the commitment is first. Theology is the understanding of the commitment and the commitment is action. The central action is charity, which involves commitment, while theology arrives later on."[20] Gutiérrez elaborates on the nature of the "action" upon which theology must reflect: "The praxis on which liberation theology reflects is a praxis of solidarity in the interests of liberation and is inspired by the gospel."[21] Liberation theology is not seen by its proponents as merely adding "a new theme for reflection" by theologians, but rather "as a *new way* to do theology. Theology as critical reflection on historical praxis is a liberating theology, a theology of the liberating transformation of the history of humankind. . . ."[22]

18. This is also the mode of speech favored by most liberation theologians themselves; see Arthur F. McGovern, *Liberation Theology and Its Critics: Toward an Assessment* (Maryknoll, N.Y.: Orbis, 1989), xv-xviii, "One Liberation Theology or Many?" When the term is used in the singular in this chapter, it will refer for the most part to the specific phenomenon that gave the term its public currency, the Latin American liberation theology represented by such figures as Gustavo Gutiérrez, Juan Luiz Segundo, José Míguez Bonino, Jon Sobrino, Leonardo Boff, and Clovis Boff.

19. For a fairly thorough listing (from which this was taken), see Alfred T. Hennelly, S.J., *Liberation Theologies: The Global Pursuit of Justice* (Mystic, Conn.: Twenty-Third Publications, 1995).

20. Alfred T. Hennelly, ed. and trans., *Liberation Theology: A Documentary History* (Maryknoll, N.Y.: Orbis, 1990), 63.

21. Gutiérrez, xxx.

22. Gutiérrez, 12.

Gutiérrez concludes with a paraphrased theological application of Karl Marx's famous eleventh thesis on Ludwig Feuerbach, "The philosophers have only interpreted the world, in various ways; the point is to change it":[23]

> This is a theology which does not stop with reflecting on the world, but rather tries to be part of the process through which the world is transformed. It is a theology which is open — in the protest against trampled human dignity, in the struggle against the plunder of the vast majority of humankind, in liberating love, and in the building of a new, just, and comradely society — to the gift of the Kingdom of God.[24]

The path toward the transformed world taken by liberation theologians is biblically rooted in the exodus motif, is structured by social analysis borrowed from essentially Marxist categories, and is driven by utopian, eschatological expectation. A few brief comments on each of these.

Israel's exodus from Egyptian bondage and recurring biblical allusions to the exodus in Old Testament sabbath and jubilee legislation; the prophetic critiques of ill-gotten wealth and other injustice by Amos, Isaiah, Jeremiah, and others; as well as Jesus' Luke 4 proclamation of liberty in his Nazareth sermon on Isaiah 61 are the foundational biblical building blocks for all versions of liberation theology. Black theologian James Cone's statement in his *God of the Oppressed* captures neatly the importance of the exodus for liberation theology:

> In God's revelation in Scripture, we come to the recognition that the divine liberation of the oppressed is not determined by our perceptions but by the God of the Exodus, the prophets and Jesus Christ, who calls the oppressed into a liberated existence. Divine revelation *alone* [Cone's emphasis] is the test of the validity of this starting point. And if it can be shown that God as witnessed in the Scriptures is not the Liberator of the oppressed, then Black theology would either have to drop the "Christian" designation or choose another starting point.[25]

Borrowing important categories from the Old Testament theology of Gerhard von Rad,[26] Gutiérrez inverts the narrative order of Scripture and interprets cre-

23. David McLellan, ed., *Karl Marx: Selected Writings* (Oxford: Oxford University Press, 1977), 158.

24. Gutiérrez, 12.

25. James Cone, *The God of the Oppressed* (New York: Seabury Press, 1975), 88; cited by Carl Amerding, "Exodus: The Old Testament Foundation of Liberation," in *Evangelicals and Liberation*, 47-48.

26. See Gerhard von Rad, "The Theological Problem of the Old Testament Doctrine

ation itself as an exodus act of salvation and liberation. "The Bible," he says, "establishes a close link between creation and salvation. But the link is based on the historical and liberating experience of the Exodus. . . . The God of Exodus is the God of history and of political liberation more than the God of nature. Yahweh is the Liberator, the *goel* of Israel. . . . The Covenant and the liberation from Egypt were different aspects of the same movement, a movement which led to encounter with God."[27] Finally, the exodus as liberation is paradigmatic for human action, "for human participation in the building of society. . . . By working, transforming the world, breaking out of servitude, building a just society, and assuming its destiny in history, humanity forges itself."[28] Stated somewhat differently, human activity directed toward political liberation is an act of "human self-creation."[29]

For its starting point in the *experience* of oppression as well as its commitment to the *praxis* of liberation as the basis for reflection, liberation theologies are indebted to Marxist thought. Once again we turn to Gutiérrez, who attributes the Marxist focus on praxis and world transformation as the reason for a theological turn that seeks "to reflect on the meaning of the transformation of this world and human action in history." It is this confrontation with Marxism, he adds, that "helps theology to perceive what its efforts at understanding the faith receive from the historical praxis of humankind in history as well as what its own reflection might mean for the transformation of the world."[30] Specifically, the categories by which liberation theology interprets the world are the basic dualities of oppressor and oppressed, categories which, when translated into more concrete *economic* categories, yield terms such as "dependence," "developed versus undeveloped," or "center/core versus periphery." Whatever the categories used, with varying degrees of intensity and accusation the point is the same: the underdeveloped poor of this world are the dependent, oppressed victims of the powerful and successful developed peoples who have achieved their wealth and power at the expense of the poor and intentionally hold them in a state of dependency in order to maintain their own privilege.[31] This situation of injustice and oppression is then said to cry out to heaven for redress,

---

of Creation," in *The Problem of the Hexateuch and Other Essays,* trans. E. W. Trueman Dicken (New York: McGraw-Hill, 1966), 131-43; on Gutiérrez's dependence on von Rad, see Gutiérrez, 86-90.

27. Gutiérrez, 86, 90.

28. Gutiérrez, 90.

29. Gutiérrez, 87.

30. Gutiérrez, 8.

31. For a useful summary of these categories and the basic liberationist argument, see Novak, *Spirit of Democratic Capitalism,* 272-314.

and the answer of the biblical God of the exodus, the Liberator of the oppressed, is the demand: "Let my people go!" The biblical God is on the side of the poor; he has, in the preferred formulation of liberation theology, "a preferential option for the poor."[32]

And finally, liberation theology is eschatological-utopian in character. To begin with, it seems obvious that any movement-building activity that is committed to world transformation must have some degree of hope that its transformative goals are achievable. As Gutiérrez puts it: "The commitment to the creation of a just society and, ultimately, to a new humanity, presupposes confidence in the future. This commitment is an act open to whatever comes."[33] But what Gutiérrez describes here is much more than merely a preference for persons who temperamentally tend to see half-full cups rather than half-empty ones; he believes that a radically new spirituality is taking shape in the world. "The spiritual condition of today's person is more and more determined by the model of the person of tomorrow. Human self-awareness is heavily affected by the knowledge that humanity is outgrowing its present condition and entering a new era, a world 'to the second power,' fashioned by human hands. We live on the verge of human epiphany, 'anthropophany.'"[34] A new and radically different historical consciousness has developed, one that is future oriented rather than past oriented. "History is no longer, as it was for the Greeks, an *anamnesis,* a remembrance. It is rather a thrust into the future. The contemporary world is full of latent possibilities and expectations. History seems to have quickened its pace."[35]

Gutiérrez acknowledges that this state of affairs has not fully arrived in Latin America. He appeals to the assessment of educator Paulo Freire that there still exists in Latin America a "precritical consciousness, that is, the consciousness of one who has not [yet] taken hold of the reins of one's own destiny." However, Gutiérrez is convinced that "the revolutionary process now under way is generating the kind of person who critically analyzes the present, con-

32. The precise term "preferential option for the poor" comes from a key document with that title of the Third General Conference of the Latin American Bishops, meeting in Puebla de los Angeles, Mexico, January 27–February 13, 1979. See Hennelly, *Liberation Theology,* 253-58. The document's opening paragraph concludes with this sentence: "We affirm the need for conversion on the part of the whole church to a preferential option for the poor, an option aimed at their integral liberation."

33. Gutiérrez, 121.

34. Gutiérrez, 121. Here Gutiérrez cites Karl Rahner, "Christianity and the 'New Man,'" in *Theological Investigations,* trans. Karl-H. Kruger, vol. 5 (Baltimore: Helicon, 1966), 135-53; and Harvey Cox, *On Not Leaving It to the Snake,* (New York: Macmillan, 1967), 91-150.

35. Gutiérrez, 121.

trols personal destiny, and is oriented towards the future . . . [and] whose actions are directed toward a new society yet to be built." In summary: "A profound aspiration for the creation of a new humanity underlies the process of liberation which the [Latin American] continent is undergoing."[36] This is what Gutiérrez and other Latin American liberation theologians mean by utopian and eschatological. The focus on the future, on hope, is said to be the teaching of Jesus about the kingdom of God. In fact, Gutiérrez even contends that there are "many points of agreement between the Zealots and the attitudes and teachings of Jesus, for example, his preaching of the coming of the Kingdom and the role he himself plays in its advent."[37] A utopian vision involves both a "denunciation of the existing order" and "an annunciation of what is not yet, but will be; the forecast of a different order of things, a new society. It is the field of creative imagination which proposes the alternative values to those rejected. . . . Utopia moves forward; it is a pro-jection into the future, a dynamic and mobilizing factor in history."[38]

Finally, Gutiérrez insists that this liberationist utopian vision is *not* an ideology. Ideologies are irrational and dogmatic while utopia "leads to an authentic and scientific knowledge of reality and to a praxis which transforms what exists."[39] It is at this point that we come back to the essential role of Marxist analysis in liberation theology. Like the claims made by old-line Marxists, the oppressor/oppressed class-conflict interpretation of society in general, and economic activity in particular, is insistently referred to as "scientific." Thus, Argentine theologian José Míguez Bonino claims that the choice by liberation theology for Marxist analysis is "an option for structural over against purely individual change, for revolution over against reformism, for socialist over against capitalist development or 'third' solutions, for 'scientific' over against idealistic or utopian socialism."[40] Whatever one may conclude about the scientific character of Marxist analysis, it does appear to an outside observer that liberation theologies are consistently dogmatic in both their fierce repudiation of democratic capitalism as an economic system as well as their warm embrace of

36. Gutiérrez, 121.

37. Gutiérrez, 131. The one key point of difference between Jesus and the Zealots, according to Gutiérrez, is Jesus' "awareness of the universality of his mission [which] did not conform with the somewhat narrow nationalism of the Zealots." This seems a rather remarkable claim for Gutiérrez to make, considering the decided partiality (preferential option for the oppressed) that is at the heart of all liberation theology.

38. Gutiérrez, 136.

39. Gutiérrez, 137.

40. José Míguez Bonino, *Christians and Marxists: The Mutual Challenge to Revolution* (Grand Rapids: Eerdmans, 1976), 19.

socialism. Accompanying this posture is also a unanimously hostile attitude toward the world's lead society of democratic capitalism, the United States of America.

The oppressor/oppressed interpretive framework of economics described above, and the appeal to the biblical theme of exodus/liberation as the answer to the problem of world poverty, was taken up by North American evangelical Ronald Sider in his influential book *Rich Christians in an Age of Hunger*.[41] In the face of appalling poverty and hunger in the world, it is not surprising that this book, with its compassionate spirit and stirring call to share the blessings of our wealth, struck a chord with many North American evangelical Christians. Armed with a barrage of statistics and heart-wrenching anecdotes, Sider attempts to show that the affluence of North America and Europe is the *cause* of third-world poverty, thanks to the structurally evil exploitation of the world's powerless by the powerful. He then claims that the God of the exodus, sabbath, and jubilee is "on the side of the poor," and calls on North American Christians to adopt a simpler lifestyle, including a graduated tithe. Though Sider admits he has "only an incomplete idea of what a modern version of the year of Jubilee would look like," he is convinced that Levitical-jubilee legislation can be directly translated into modern terms as "a divine demand for regular, fundamental redistribution of the means for producing wealth."[42] Sider neither advances an analysis of how wealth is created in the first place nor suggests a specific mechanism for ensuring its redistribution. *Rich Christians,* its concrete statistics and anecdotes notwithstanding, is thus a truly *utopian* work; it stands nowhere but offers a vision of the future in hope. While it is excessive to charge

41. Ronald J. Sider, *Rich Christians in an Age of Hunger* (Downers Grove, Ill.: InterVarsity, 1977). Sider's book received passionate response, both positive and negative. In addition to encouraging considerable literature of a similar genre (such as Stanley Mooneyham's *What Do You Say to a Hungry World?* [Waco, Tex.: Word, 1975]), Sider's analysis was taken over by church task forces on world poverty and hunger such as that of the Christian Reformed Church, which issued a report, "And He Had Compassion on Them: A Christian Response to World Hunger," a report of the Christian Reformed Church's Task Force on World Hunger (Grand Rapids: CRC Publications, 1978). The most critical (and acerbic) response was that of theonomist David Chilton, *Productive Christians in an Age of Guilt-Manipulators: A Biblical Response to Ronald J. Sider* (Tyler, Tex.: Institute for Christian Economics, 1981); a more nuanced and tempered critique is given by John Schneider, *Godly Materialism: Rethinking Money and Possessions* (Downers Grove, Ill.: InterVarsity, 1994).

42. Sider, 223. Interestingly enough, Pat Robertson also advocates a jubilee year when debts are canceled and accumulated property is redistributed; see Pat Robertson, *Answers to 200 of Life's Most Probing Questions* (Nashville: Nelson, 1984), 262-63. I am indebted for this reference to Justin Watson, *The Christian Coalition: Dreams of Restoration, Demands for Recognition* (New York: St. Martin's Press, 1997), 41 n. 100, p. 200.

Sider with holding to a view that is based on "statism, political centralization, and 'theft by majority vote'" (i.e., socialism), as Gary North does in his preface to David Chilton's clever but mean-spirited *Productive Christians in an Age of Guilt-Manipulators*,[43] it is more than fair to chide him for never explaining "how nations might follow suit without granting dictatorial powers over corporations and individuals."[44] Finally, it is also fair to ask whether Sider's approach in fact does any genuine good for the world's poor. Though the call to simplicity and generosity is unquestionably commendable and spiritually desirable, the main effect of *Rich Christians* may be that it only contributes to what Rousas J. Rushdoony has called a "politics of guilt and pity."[45] Of Sider's book, too, it is fair to ask Michael Novak's persistent question: "But will it liberate?"[46]

Sider's is a gentle, pastoral kind of liberation theology that remains evangelical in its understanding of sin and salvation, refusing to reduce liberation to its economic dimension and nuanced in its notion of God's partiality to the poor.[47] Other North American public evangelicals, such as the late William Stringfellow,[48] Tony Campolo,[49] and Jim Wallis of *Sojourners* fellowship,[50] are more radical in their use of liberationist rhetoric and analysis, particularly in their denunciation of democratic capitalism and America as a society and a nation.[51] One of the most sophisticated and eloquent treatments in this genre by a

43. Gary North, preface to Chilton, 14.

44. Schneider, 198 n. 15.

45. Rousas J. Rushdoony, *Politics of Guilt and Pity* (Fairfax, Va.: Thoburn, 1978 [1970]).

46. Novak, *Will It Liberate?*

47. See, for example, Sider's third chapter, "God and the Poor," 59-85; particularly his discussion of the exodus as God's fidelity to his covenant promise to Abraham (61).

48. William Stringfellow, *Conscience and Obedience: The Politics of Romans 13 and Revelation 13 in Light of the Second Coming* (Waco, Tex.: Word, 1977); *Dissenter in a Great Society: A Christian View of America in Crisis* (New York: Holt, Rinehart & Winston, 1966); *An Ethic for Christians and Other Aliens in a Strange Land* (Waco, Tex.: Word, 1973); *My People Is the Enemy: An Autobiographical Polemic* (New York: Holt, Rinehart & Winston, 1964).

49. See Tony Campolo, *Wake Up America! Answering God's Radical Call While Living in the Real World* (New York: HarperCollins, 1991); *Is Jesus a Republican or a Democrat? And Fourteen Other Polarizing Issues* (Dallas: Word, 1995); *We Have Met the Enemy and They Are Partly Right* (Waco, Tex.: Word, 1985).

50. Jim Wallis, *Agenda for a Biblical People* (New York: Harper & Row, 1976); *The Call to Conversion* (San Francisco: Harper & Row, 1981); *Who Speaks for God?* (New York: Delacorte, 1996); "A View from the Evangelical Left," *Christianity Today*, April 19, 1985, 26-27.

51. For a more thorough review of the evangelical Left, see Gay, 22-60.

North American evangelical, however, comes from the hand of a philosopher who openly identifies himself as standing in the neo-Calvinist tradition of Abraham Kuyper.[52] In fact, the lectures that form the basis for Nicholas Wolterstorff's wide-ranging and elegant book *Until Justice and Peace Embrace* were delivered as the first "Abraham Kuyper Lectures" in 1981 at Kuyper's own Free University of Amsterdam.[53] Wolterstorff sets the tone for his volume in the preface where he alludes to the "radical" character of historic Calvinism as set forth by Michael Walzer in his study of the Puritans: "the Calvinist saint [is] the first of those self-disciplined agents of social and political reconstruction who have appeared so frequently in modern history" (ix).[54] Prior to suggesting concrete solutions for world poverty and its related ills, Wolterstorff believes it is necessary to raise consciousness among Christians in the developed and wealthy part of the world. "I am persuaded," he writes, "that the deepest reason for the perpetuation of our predicament is that too few people in our Western society are persuaded that things *ought* to be different and that they are called to work toward a new order" (vii). We are living, he observes, "in dark and dangerous times. Dark, because we in the First World are continuing to refuse to share the wealth of our rich, indulgent societies with those impoverished millions whom we dominate; and dangerous, because in those two great Enlightenment experiments, the United States and the Soviet Union, there is now a deep sense of failed ideas." Wolterstorff concludes: "Today a new order is desperately needed. What it must look like we do not yet know. In the meanwhile, I shall speak of darkness, but also of light; of danger, but also of hope" (x).

Wolterstorff begins *Until Justice and Peace Embrace* by making an important distinction between a "world-avertive" or "other-worldly" form of religion

52. In his treatment of the "equality versus liberty" debate among North American evangelicals, Craig Gay places Wolterstorff's *Until Justice and Peace Embrace* in a middle category he describes as "the evangelical center," a group characterized by "concern about capitalism" but not yet fully in the liberation theology camp. Gay observes that Wolterstorff "suggests that a liberation theology tempered by neo-Calvinism might offer a better model for [the] process of disclosure than the mere attempt [by Free University economist Bob Goudzwaard in his book *Capitalism and Progress*] to disclose capitalism." Where Wolterstorff differs from the evangelical Left, according to Gay, is that "he does not contend that the evangelical failure in this respect has necessarily been due to ideological entanglement" and, finally, "Wolterstorff has not been willing to condemn the market system outright" (Gay, 142-43). Gay's is one of the most nuanced and therefore fair treatments of Wolterstorff's position that I have come across.

53. Published by Eerdmans, Grand Rapids, 1983; page references that follow in the text are to this work.

54. The citation is from Michael Walzer, *The Revolution of the Saints: A Study in the Origins of Radical Politics* (Cambridge: Harvard University Press, 1965), vii.

and a "world-transformative" kind of religion. In the case of the latter — Wolterstorff's own clear preference — of which historic Calvinism is a clear type, there is a conviction that the saints are God's instruments rather than mere vessels and that it is their obligation to change the structures of a fallen world. "The reformation of society according to the Word of God: this was the Calvinist goal" (18). It is the calling of the saints "to struggle to establish a holy commonwealth here on earth." In setting forth this vision of the Calvinist social and political revolutionary, Wolterstorff is not unaware of the shadow side of saints self-consciously taking responsibility for God's world. Calvinists, he notes, "spoke of justice" but "failed to think through how they could live together in a just society with those with whom they disagreed." And second, Calvinism also produced its share of triumphalists, whom Wolterstorff defines as "[some]one who believes that the revolution instituting the holy commonwealth has already occurred and that his or her task is now simply to keep it in place" (22, 21).

When Wolterstorff turns to an analysis of the world's economic realities, he makes use of the "world-system" theory of Immanuel Wallerstein[55] and posits the thesis that the appalling disparity of economic and other benefits in the international capitalist order is due to the domination of the weak and dependent *periphery* by the powerful and wealthy *core* (31). The world economy is a zero-sum game: "it is not possible theoretically for all states to 'develop' simultaneously" (33). Though the modern world system does provide the "fundamental worth" of "expansion of freedom by mastery and expansion of freedom of self-direction," it does so only *for some,* and that is its fundamental flaw: "The expansion of range of choice is distributed with appalling unevenness. Gross inequality of benefits pervades the system. But is it not true that the longing for a measure of equality is just as deep in mankind as the longing for expanded choice? Inequality always has to be justified. Equality speaks for itself." Wolterstorff then adds a comment that suggests a moral equivalence of straight choice between commensurate values in the world's democratic-capitalist societies and totalitarian socialist ones. "The West grasps freedom at the cost of inequality, thereby consigning the economically impoverished to all the constraints of poverty. The East grasps equality at the cost of freedom, thereby consigning the politically powerless to all the inequities of tyranny" (39). Though Wolterstorff does not offer a full program or description of the solution to this state of affairs, he does offer, in the third chapter

---

55. See Immanuel Wallerstein, *The Modern World-System: Capitalist Agriculture and the Origins of the European World Economy in the Sixteenth Century* (New York: Academic Press, 1974); Immanuel Wallerstein, *The Capitalist World Economy* (Cambridge: Cambridge University Press, 1979); cf. Wolterstorff, *Until Justice,* chap. 2, "The Modern World-System."

of *Until Justice and Peace Embrace,* a sympathetic portrait of Latin American liberation theology, agreeing with its explanation of the causes of poverty (domination and exploitation) but raising significant questions about the precise meaning of "liberation." Wolterstorff is at his most perceptive when he focuses his critique on the well-ingrained practice in contemporary biblical theology of reversing the creation-redemption or creation-exodus order of the biblical narrative. As a result, "salvation and history . . . remain unlinked. If we understand liberation in such a way as to make it plausible to read history as the history of liberation, then there is no plausible link between liberation on the one hand and salvation from sin on the other. But if we understand liberation in such a way that it is directly linked to salvation from sin, then it becomes implausible to read history as the history of liberation" (49). These observations are then followed by a crucial question: "After liberation, what?" (51). In other words, what is the nature of the freedom achieved by liberating praxis?

This is a critical question that needs to be asked of all liberation theologies, but unfortunately Wolterstorff himself disappoints us at exactly the same point. He stirs the reader's heart with an eloquent description of the biblical vision of "shalom" without giving so much as a hint *how* this can be achieved in the real world. He simply asserts:

> The situation is not that we in the West (and the East!) want to help the poor but do not know how; the situation is that we know how but do not want to. It is now clear that mass poverty is not the normal situation of mankind. . . . it is in good measure the effect of our world-wide economic system and of the political structures that support it — of the unregulated and unqualified pursuit of profit by enterprises from the core, of systems of land ownership in the Third World that deprive workers of all incentive, of repressive governments in the Third World supported by those of the core, of aid programs designed not to help the poor but to win skirmishes in the contest of the superpowers. (97)

If Wolterstorff is correct that "we know how but do not want to," it is disappointing in a major way that he limits himself to grand, sweeping denunciations of systems without any of the concrete suggestions that Ron Sider, for example, gives in *Rich Christians in an Age of Hunger.*[56] It is worth observing here

---

56. It was exactly this premise ("we know how [to help] but do not want to") that called forth the charge from one of Wolterstorff's reviewers that he was being "coy" on economic specifics. See Richard John Neuhaus, "The Goal Is Not to Describe: A Review of *Until Justice and Peace Embrace,*" in *Is Capitalism Christian?* 449-56. Wolterstorff responded to Neuhaus's review in the *Reformed Journal* 34, no. 12 (December 1984): 23-29.

that someone whose analysis is quite different from Wolterstorff's does in fact agree with the premise that "we do know what to do." According to Michael Novak, the history of twentieth-century economic failures and successes provides incontrovertible proof that the tried and proven route to economic well-being involves a threefold mutually supportive order of religious, political, and economic freedom of morally good people.[57] This means that locating the single source of economic inequality in *systems* of oppression with a free society such as the United States, seen in a morally equivalent sense as an equal opportunity oppressor with totalitarian societies, is not only an intellectual failing but also morally problematic. Wolterstorff's point is correct and well taken: if we know what must be done to raise the world's poor out of their misery and fail to do it (especially by offering wrong solutions), we are indeed morally culpable. On this issue, as Novak indicates, there is formally no disagreement between liberation theologians and advocates of a free-market, democratic capitalist model. Novak cleverly refers to both as "liberation theologies," distinguishing a "Latin American" version from a "North American liberation theology."

> This radical discontinuity between North American liberation theology and Latin American liberation theology — this disparity in the practical judgment rendered upon the free economy — should not blind the unwary to a powerful unity of aim. The aim both of democratic capitalism as the liberal societies of North America conceive of it, and of socialism as the liberation theologians of Latin America conceive of it, is to lift up the poor. The theology of both Americas is "an option for the poor." The radical question is a practical one. Which sorts of economic institutions, in fact, do lift up the poor? On this, persons of good will often disagree. What works in one place, some argue, does not or will not work in another. The principle that all Christians are committed to — *at least now, when the methods of attaining it have become so well known* — is that the condition of the poor must be bettered. *There is today no excuse for the sort of imprisonment inflicted on the poor by material destitution.*[58]

The Libertarian Impulse

The suggestion of moral equivalence between the United States as the bearer of liberty and the former Soviet Union as the representative of an admittedly

57. See especially Novak, *Spirit of Democratic Capitalism.*
58. Novak, *Will It Liberate?* 6, emphasis added.

flawed socialist experiment in equality is a rather consistent theme found in European and North American sympathizers of liberation theologies. The logic of this equivalence pits the value of freedom and strictly instrumental justice against the value of equality or "social justice"[59] and tends to minimize differences in favor of finding fault with both systems and societies for their respective failures. It is here, at the point where most liberationists tend to downplay the importance of freedom for the sake of equality and social justice as a higher good, that libertarianism lodges its vehement protest. For libertarians, freedom is the highest of values. In the words of a recent articulate spokesman for the cause, "libertarianism is the view that each person has the right to live his life in any way he chooses so long as he respects the equal rights of others. . . . Libertarians defend each person's right to life, liberty, and property — rights that people possess naturally, before governments are created."[60]

Key differences notwithstanding, at one level the libertarian and liberationist visions clearly merge: the desire for freedom from external and oppressive domination and regulation. When Gutiérrez describes the process of liberation as activity directed toward "human self-creation"[61] and Wolterstorff speaks favorably of the "expansion of freedom of self-direction,"[62] no libertarian would find fault. The key difference between the two visions is that liberationism focuses on the oppressive, freedom-denying role of "systems" more broadly, including the economic system of markets, while libertarians focus their attention on the individual person and fear the oppressive role of only one system, the state. In so doing, libertarians open themselves up to the charge that they ignore the real power of economic and social systems, including cultural patterns such as religions. Conversely, its sensitivity to oppressive systems notwithstanding, liberationism often seems to have a blind eye to the hegemonic power of the state, provided that those who hold the reins of power are properly motivated and well intentioned with a preferential option for the poor and oppressed and have equality as their political goal. Where the divergence is greatest between the two, and where the dividing line between North American evangelicals of the "left" and "right" has been drawn self-consciously by both

59. It is fair to ask whether the expression "social justice" is a gain over simple "justice." Justice by its very nature is social; it involves giving to different persons that which is properly "due" them. Since "social justice" focuses on the *outcomes* and results of social transactions rather than on the procedural fairness of the transactions themselves, the very notion of "social justice" points to a goal that can never be met on this side of the consummation of Christ's perfect kingdom.

60. Boaz, *Libertarianism*, 2.

61. Gutiérrez, 87.

62. Wolterstorff, *Until Justice*, 39.

groups, is with respect to the value placed on a democratic order, including a free-market economy. Liberation theologians consistently repudiate free-market capitalism and opt for forms of socialism, while libertarians do the exact reverse. Libertarians insist that good social order comes not by the conscious design and plan of some omnicompetent agency such as the state, but by the "spontaneous order" of "a multitude of individuals exercising a set of 'compossible' rights."[63] Social order, in other words, emerges "as an unintended consequence of the actions of many individuals,"[64] and, according to libertarian premises, it is the *sole* task of the state to secure the "imprescriptible" or inalienable rights of individual persons, nothing more. In sum:

> Libertarianism is the view that each man is the absolute owner of his life, to use and dispose of as he sees fit; that all social actions should be voluntary; and respect for every other man's similar and equal ownership of life and, by extension, the property and fruits of that life, is the ethical basis of a humane and open society. In this view, the only function of law or government is to provide the sort of self-defense against violence that an individual, if he were powerful enough, would provide for himself.[65]

"Each man is the absolute owner of his life, to use and dispose of as he sees fit"? With this view, how can a Christian, much less a Reformed Christian who confesses with the Heidelberg Catechism, "I am not my own," possibly be a libertarian?[66]

When evaluating a political position, it makes all the difference what the leading question is. The starting point of the question contains assumptions that govern and frame the answer. Germane to the issues we are considering in this chapter, it makes a world of difference if one asks the question "what causes poverty?" or leads with "how are wealth and prosperity generated?" In the former, inequality and poverty are assumed to be aberrations that demand explanation and solution; in the latter, the ability to overcome the "normal" condi-

---

63. Tom G. Palmer, "The Literature of Liberty," in Boaz, *The Libertarian Reader,* 428.

64. Palmer, 428.

65. Karl Hess, in *The Concise Conservative Encyclopedia,* ed. Brad Miner (New York: Free Press, 1996), s.v. "libertarianism."

66. One issue where there would seem to be irremediable conflict between a Christian and libertarian viewpoint is abortion, where pro-choice defenders of abortion rights insist on the "right to do with my body as I see fit." For a wonderful Christian rebuttal of this posture, see Elizabeth Achtemeier and Terry Schlossberg, *Not My Own: Abortion and the Marks of the Church* (Grand Rapids: Eerdmans, 1995); Doug Bandow also sees abortion as the "irreconcilable conflict" between Christians and libertarians (*The Politics of Envy,* 39-52).

tions of human deprivation and suffering requires attention. Two different visions of humanity are reflected here — one idyllic or utopian and the other "tragic" — and these two distinct anthropologies will result in conflicting political strategies. In the former case one seeks to root out the "causes" of evil, in the latter one searches for the incentives that assist human beings to minimize evil and maximize the good, all the while fully aware that the perfect solution is never realizable,[67] that in fact the perfect might be the enemy of the good.[68] So the question "how can a Christian possibly be a libertarian?" could easily be countered by "how can a Christian possibly be a statist?"[69] Similarly, after hearing a defense of the free market by a libertarian, it is perfectly reasonable for a socially sensitive Christian to respond with some version of "how could a Christian not be in favor of a political strategy that sides with the poor and the oppressed?" From this brief to-and-fro it should be clear that posing the issue in this fashion — "Is it Christian to be x or y?" (where x and y represent an identifiable political ideology or unified constellation of political ideas) — is not the most helpful way of guiding Christians in their responsibilities as citizens.[70]

Perhaps we can make some headway by attempting a more modest evaluation: simply dealing with the fundamental motivating impulse that drives the libertarian vision and considering to what extent it is *compatible* with a biblical or Christian worldview.[71] Whether in an extreme individualist form as summarized above or in a more moderate guise, all libertarians are concerned about the accumulation and concentration of *political* power by the state and its agencies as a threat to personal liberties. For Christian libertarians this fear is rooted in biblical anthropology — the conviction that sinful human beings need to be restrained in the exercise of political power. American Christian libertarians often point to the careful attempt by the Founding Fathers of their nation to provide *institutional* checks and balances on state power as expressions of this in-

---

67. For a helpful overview of these two conflicting visions (to which the preceding brief description is indebted), see Thomas Sowell, *A Conflict of Visions: Ideological Origins of Political Struggles* (New York: Morrow, 1987).

68. See Novak, *Freedom with Justice*, 16-38.

69. The title of chap. 3 in Christian libertarian Doug Bandow's *Politics of Envy* is "Should Christians Be Statists?"

70. This was recognized by Franky Schaeffer when, in his introduction to *Is Capitalism Christian?* (xvi), he reflected on the question raised by the volume's title and observed that capitalism as an economic system "is merely a tool and can therefore be no more 'Christian' than the George Washington Bridge is 'Christian.'"

71. We will return the favor for liberation theologies more fully later in this chapter, though the appreciative comments about Sider's and Wolterstorff's concern and compassion for the poor earlier in this chapter must not be overlooked.

sight. Characteristic is the following statement by James Madison in *The Federalist Papers* #51: "Ambition must be made to counteract ambition. The interest of the man must be connected with the constitutional rights of the place. It may be a reflection on human nature that such devices should be necessary to control the abuses of government. But what is government itself but the greatest of all reflections on human nature? If men were angels, no government would be necessary. If angels were to govern men, neither external not internal controls on government would be necessary."[72] When put in the context of concerns about expansion of state power and increasing intrusion of the state in the life of citizens, the libertarian impulse does resonate with the biblical data. The first item in David Boaz's *Libertarian Reader* is 1 Samuel 8, where the prophet gives Israel God's own warning about the power that the king they desire ("to be like the other nations") will arrogate unto himself. Boaz observes that "this story reminded Europeans for centuries that the state was not divinely inspired. Thomas Paine, Lord Acton, and other liberals cited it frequently."[73]

It is with this more modest question in view — is the libertarian posture of seeking limits on state power *compatible* or *consistent* with a biblical worldview? — that we shall briefly summarize David Hall's mining of the biblical record for Christian political principles in his book *Savior or Servant?*[74] We pay attention to Hall at this point because his obvious debt to Abraham Kuyper[75] raises the question: Can Kuyper in any sense be considered a libertarian?

Hall begins with the biblical record and doctrine of creation in Genesis 1. The dominion mandate in Genesis 1:26-28 reminds us that "governing" and "government" is not "inherently evil or malicious. It is not merely a 'necessary evil.' Ruling or dominion is an activity assigned to humans before the fall, not as a necessary evil resulting from the entrance of sin into the world" (18). At the same time, the doctrine of creation reminds us that human governing is *delegated* by God the Creator. This has two important implications. "Governance, by nature, is delegated from the Creator. The roles within governments, therefore, are not purely human, nor created by the will of man" (17). Human beings therefore owe rulers respect and honor "as unto the Lord." However, "any system which rules

72. Madison, Hamilton, and Jay, 319-20. This is the passage with which David Hall begins the preface to his *Savior or Servant?*

73. Boaz, *The Libertarian Reader*, 5.

74. Page references to this work will be given parenthetically in the text.

75. Not only are there numerous references to and significant block quotations from Kuyper in Hall's book, but the foundation he directs and which published *Savior or Servant?* is named, significantly, the Kuyper Institute.

will do so sensitive to its status as created, and not confuse itself with, nor usurp, the prerogatives of its Creator" (17). The state is not divine!

The bulk of the Bible's teaching on the state, of course, is post-fall. Though "even in a perfect world, government would be needed for order, rank, and efficiency," we live in a fallen world and "the fact of sin insures the need for the state" (25). This requires of Christians a realism about politics and its possibilities. "The OT manifests a realism, a startling absence of utopianism, not expecting that all societal ills will be eradicated by some program, political movement, or institution" (25). The major political principle that Hall draws from this is that human governments require careful checks and balances that "provide for regular and thoughtful means of accountability" (26). It is the Christian theology of sin and humanity that must shape civil government, and the best means for restraint on sinful, arbitrary exercise of power is a well-designed constitution. Here Hall cites Kuyper:

> Calvin's profound conception of sin is likewise the outcome of the recognition of the sovereignty of God. . . . he was republican because he knows that even kings are sinners, who yield to temptation perhaps more readily than their subjects, inasmuch as their temptations are greater. . . . He knows equally well that the self-same sin moves the masses, and that, hence resistance, insurrection, and mutinies will not end, unless a righteous constitution bridles the abuse of authority, marks off its boundaries, and offers the people a natural protection against despotism and ambitious schemes.[76]

The rest of the Old Testament serves as a commentary on these basic insights. The Tower of Babel story in Genesis 11 is a warning against state divinization (and one-world government — "God desired decentralization and effected it by his providence" [31]); the Joseph narrative suggests the importance both of personal and corporate saving for the future as well as a role "in catastrophic times" for a centralized government (34-35); the division of the kingdom under Rehoboam is a reminder that "even the best of earthly pursuits or political organization must rank far below the pursuit of God's everlasting kingdom that will never end" (70). From the monarchic history of Israel and Judah, Hall concludes that "the very

76. Abraham Kuyper, "Calvinism: The Origin and Safeguard of Our Constitutional Liberties," *Bibliotheca Sacra* (October 1895): 665-66; essay reprinted as "Calvinism: Source and Stronghold of Our Constitutional Liberties (1874)," in *Abraham Kuyper: A Centennial Reader,* 279-321. Peter Heslam rightly observes that Kuyper's claims about Calvin being a "republican" are "disingenuous" and, when repeated in his Stone Lectures in 1898, were "colored by his desire to declare the Calvinistic origins of the republican government of the United States and thus to recommend the benefits of Calvinism to an American audience" (Heslam, 144, 145).

best kind of government is the covenantal kind of government — that which is based on constitutional promises that do not change with the caprice of various human administrations" (77). The major point of Old Testament history, prophecy, and poetry, however, is the affirmation that God alone is the sovereign monarch, over all the nations and over world history as well as Israel's. This means that "leaders are under God's wrath as well" (96) when they fail to maintain justice. "No political philosophy is complete, nor rises above the platform as anything other than a humanist manifesto, without including the sovereignty of God" (98). Two final Old Testament points from the book of Daniel: God does work with unbelieving rulers, and second, believers are to serve God above all others. There is an appropriate resistance to wrongful laws. "God was Sovereign over sovereigns and resistance to impious laws was proper under certain conditions" (100).

From the New Testament Hall draws familiar lessons from the standard passages. The episode of Jesus and the Pharisees discussing Caesar's coin reminds us that payment of taxes to civil authorities is proper and that there is a limitation to each sphere (civil and religious duties) and a proper division of labor between them (123). Tithes and taxes are distinct. What is striking is the conclusion of Hall's chapter on the Gospels, where he concludes that the teaching of Jesus does not lead us to renounce the state but to seek to influence it. "Christians should not merely be in favor of limiting government; they should also be engaged in moral reform of the platforms underneath it. . . . Christians must follow the political teachings of Jesus in public policy. Jesus did not call for an abandonment of the public square, but a patient re-clothing. His chosen methods are to use individuals, families, charities and the church to saturate values" (132). Then follows a citation from Abraham Kuyper's 1891 address to the Christian Social Congress:

> Christianity conceals in its womb a much greater treasure of rejuvenation than you surmise. Until now it has exerted its power only on the individual and only indirectly on the state. But anyone who, as believer or as unbeliever, has been able to spy out its secret dynamic, must grant that Christianity has been able to exert a wonderful organizing power on society also; and not till this power breaks through will the religion of the cross shine before the whole world in all the depths of its conception and in all the wealth of the blessings which it brings.[77]

At this point it appears that we have moved some distance from a libertarian point of view to one that almost sounds theocratic, where the church is

---

77. Abraham Kuyper, *Christianity and the Class Struggle* (Grand Rapids: Piet Hein, 1950), 17; reprinted with a new introduction by James Skillen as Abraham Kuyper, *The Problem of Poverty* (Grand Rapids: Baker, 1991).

also seen as "the lasting incarnation of Christ as a transforming agent for society and politics" (132). Yet, in the exegesis Hall provides for his own conclusion here, he cites evangelical libertarian Doug Bandow as a model of the "balance" he is trying to achieve, a balance that avoids political dogmatism and gives *liberty* for divergent Christian political points of view:

> Christians should be politically involved. But as believers enter the policy-making process they must be careful to advance genuine biblical standards when they are claiming to represent a Christian perspective. Believers must be especially careful to eschew the temptation to declare God behind every item on their personal political agenda, using their religious affiliation to advance positions that have little or no spiritual dimension. There are, in fact, political controversies that cannot be decided with reference to specific Scriptures; in such cases, the issue can be framed by biblical principles. . . .[78]

Moving into the remainder of the New Testament (Acts-Revelation), Hall deals with the economic and civil dimensions of the early church's relation to the state. The sharing of goods in the early chapters of Acts mandates not an "enforced communitarianism" (134) but "voluntary charity" (135). Obedience to as well as honor and respect for civil authority are required of Christians, even when governments *permit* conduct among their citizens that Christians judge to be immoral (Hall includes in a list: prostitution, abortion, use of drugs) but do not *compel* it. It is under situations of *compulsion* to do evil that resistance to civil authority is not simply permitted but required of Christians — "We must obey God rather than men" (Acts 5:29) — though resistance should never be violent. Christians must then also be willing to accept punishment for their disobedience (137).[79]

The basic principles that Hall thus emphasizes from the biblical record are: the legitimacy and limitation of government authority under the sovereignty of God, the equal obligation of citizens to honor and obey civil authority in all things lawful and to resist when compelled to disobey the ultimate Sovereign, and the correlative and secondary implication that there is Christian liberty when it comes to the application of biblical principles in the specific *form* a government takes or the *policies* it mandates.[80] One additional theme in Hall's

78. Doug Bandow, *Beyond Good Intentions* (Wheaton, Ill.: Crossway, 1988), 119.

79. What Hall summarizes here is the principled strategy set forth by Martin Luther King, Jr., in his "Letter from Birmingham City Jail." The text can be found in William J. Bennett, *The Book of Virtues* (New York: Simon & Schuster, 1993), 258-62.

80. It is worth noting here that it is precisely this freedom to create civil orders that are not exact replicas of the Old Testament theocracy, that theonomist Rousas J.

book must be noted here: the consistent call in Scripture to have an open heart for and ready hands to help the poor. Whether in the Levitical legislation or in its prophetic application, whether in the instruction and example of our Lord or of his apostles, the picture is consistent according to Hall: the poor and needy, the weak and oppressed demand the attention and care of the believing community. Hall thus shares the passion of liberation theologians for the poor, though — consistent with libertarian presuppositions — he insists that this concern does not necessarily imply state-mandated schemes for redistribution as the remedy, but voluntary charity.[81]

Abraham Kuyper on the Quest for Liberty

In recent years the Kuyperian, neo-Calvinist tradition has been a home for lib-eration-minded and libertarian thinkers alike, though the preponderance of North American neo-Calvinists, according to Craig Gay, are to be found in the first category. Gay observes that "intellectuals in the Christian Reformed Church have played a particularly influential role in shaping contemporary evangelical social and political-economic thought, especially at the progressive end of the evangelical spectrum. . . . Self-consciously Reformed intellectuals . . . have emerged at the forefront of progressive evangelical social thought of late."[82] This leads us to consider Kuyper's views on liberty more closely. Would

---

Rushdoony excoriates as a "deadly and derelict" notion, even "heretical nonsense," in John Calvin's theology. See *The Institutes of Biblical Law* (Nutley, N.J.: Craig Press, 1973), 9. Rushdoony is referring to Calvin's *Institutes of the Christian Religion* 4.20.14.

81. Thus echoing the influential work recently done by evangelical social historian Marvin J. Olasky, *The Tragedy of American Compassion*, and *Renewing American Compassion* (New York: Free Press, 1996).

82. Gay, 131-32. Gay asserts this tendency came about "in large part because of the Reformed tradition of cultural criticism, but it has probably also been due to the difficulties many Reformed scholars have had with American fundamentalism and American cultural conservativism generally" (131). Gay is particularly on target, in my judgment, when he alludes to the importance of H. Richard Niebuhr's fifth model, "Christ Transforming Culture," in his influential *Christ and Culture* (New York: Harper & Row, 1951), linking this model with the Kuyperian and Christian Reformed insistence on the doctrine of "common grace" (132 n. 69; Gay's source here is James Bratt, *Dutch Calvinism in Modern America: A History of a Conservative Subculture* (Grand Rapids: Eerdmans, 1984). What Reformed and Kuyperian devotees of Niebuhr's transformation model tend to overlook is its ethical *and soteriological (!)* universalism. Niebuhr finds fault with Augustine's and Calvin's emphasis on predestination and takes nineteenth-century Christian socialist F. D. Maurice as his prime example of the transformation model.

Kuyper be happy to be considered an honorary member, not to mention patron saint, of either the liberationist or libertarian camp?

We begin with a consideration of the latter, the libertarian position and the concern about state encroachment on personal liberty. The appeal to Kuyper as spokesman for the cause of protecting individual freedom from the growing grasp of the state is well grounded in both Kuyper's rhetoric and practice as a politician. In one of his earliest public political addresses, "Calvinism: Source and Stronghold of Our Constitutional Liberties,"[83] Kuyper begins with a very contemporary-sounding expressed fear that "our civil liberties, though not likely to be lost, may well be restricted." Then he adds the following observation as self-evident to his audience:

> Can it be denied that the centralizing State grows more and more into a gigantic monster over against which every citizen is finally powerless? Have not all independent institutions, whose sovereignty in their own sphere made them a base for resistance, yielded to the magic formula of a single, unitary state? Once there was autonomy in the regions and towns, autonomy for families and different social ranks, autonomy for the courts as well as for the universities, corporations and guilds. And now? The State has annexed all these rights from the provinces, one after another. Then it tells the towns what to do, comes in your front door. Expropriates your property. Commandeers the law, makes trustees and professors its servants, and tolerates no corporation but as its own dependent. (281-82)

Kuyper admits that the "ancient régime" was "rightly cursed" for its violence and oppression of the individual, but also observes that "the sector of our life over which the State spread its net back then had hardly one-tenth the reach of our present government." The telling sign? "Just look at Europe's budgets . . ." (282). Then follows this question: "But is the individual freer now or rather defenseless and helpless when faced with the all-devouring super-corporation of the State? Where will we end if the recent craving for centralization runs its course?" Kuyper then adds a query that sounds eerily prescient of twentieth-century developments. "How will you resist if the deification of the State continues to brand every form of protest a sacrilege from the start? What will re-

83. Originally delivered in 1873 and published as *Het Calvinisme, Oorsprong en Waarborg onzer Constitutioneele Vrijheden* (Amsterdam: B. Van der Land, 1874). For bibliographic information on English translations, see n. 76 above. Though I prefer the title given in the De Vries translation ("Calvinism: The Origin and Safeguard of Our Constitutional Liberties"), the citations that follow (and page references given in the text) are taken from Bratt's *Abraham Kuyper*. See further on the translation of the title, Harry Van Dyke's review of this volume in *Calvin Theological Journal* 33 (1998): 493.

main of your personal freedom if a form of Caesarism eventually develops out of the modern state? If a modern Imperialism, converting its 'panes et circenses' into an economic regime of material well-being, acts as it pleases since no one is able to resist?" Kuyper concludes the opening of his address with a call, borrowed from Alexis de Tocqueville, to citizens to be aroused from their apathy. "Freedom is in danger precisely when citizens lack pride and the state lacks bounds." And then the speech's political payoff: "The goal of the Antirevolutionary party is to avert this danger" (283).

After tracing the history of freedom in reverse chronological order from America through the Puritans and finally back to Theodore Beza and John Calvin in the sixteenth century, Kuyper concludes his defense of the thesis that Calvinism gave birth to and nurtured civil liberty by contrasting his vision with that of nineteenth-century liberalism. Both visions highlight freedom and therefore are not absolute contrasts in terms of their demands or results. With the liberals "we want equal rights for all, whatever their situation or religion. With all our might we will defend freedom of conscience, a free press, freedom of assembly, and freedom of opinion. We desire the liberation of the church by a fair and complete separation from the state, also in financial matters; the liberation of the school, not by giving it back to the church but to the parents under the rules and supervision of the state, since the impersonal state, we believe, cannot be a schoolmaster. . . . We promote decentralization, an organic representation of the people and an ethical colonial policy. We demand more freedom for higher education, more independence for our courts — if necessary by introducing the jury system" (315). Nonetheless, "duo cum faciunt idem, non est idem" [when two do the same thing, it isn't [necessarily] the same thing]. The difference? "We expect everything, and they nothing, from the faith! *From the faith!* That demand we cannot surrender. For we love freedom, and we know from a history of almost three centuries that only faith offers the vital power to guarantee this freedom for ourselves and our children for generations to come" (316).

When Kuyper set forth the platform of the Antirevolutionary Party six years later, he remained true to the principles enunciated in that address. One place where Kuyper's own political understanding and insistence upon a decentralized form of government comes remarkably close to the genius of the American system is in the tenth article of the Antirevolutionary Party Program of 1879, where this particularly strong bias and the call for devolving power to local units is uncannily similar in intent to Article 10 of America's own Bill of Rights.[84]

84. Kuyper's own profound sympathy for regional, local, smaller units of government power and his strong disaffection for centralized government power contradicts one

ARP Platform, art. 10

It is the desire [of the ARP] that local and municipal autonomy be restored by means of decentralization, insofar as this does not conflict with the requirements of national unity nor violate the rights of individual persons.[85]

U.S. Bill of Rights, art. 10

The powers not delegated to the United States by the Constitution, nor prohibited by it to the States, are reserved to the States respectively, or to the people.

Kuyper insisted that freedom from the state's encroachment be *constitutionally* protected. The struggle for freedom in the second half of the nineteenth century, he judged, was precisely here. A few years earlier, in a *De Heraut* article, Kuyper had explained the quest for human liberty as a resistance to two "powers" that tended to become enemies of freedom whenever they strayed beyond their proper boundaries: the church and the state.[86] Though there had been times when *the* struggle had been against the coercive power of church, in the present (1871) it was the state and its transgression of its boundaries that was to be feared. "The battle for freedom of conscience must therefore be directed at the compulsions of the State. That is our struggle."[87] Noting that those who seek to buy and enslave human souls always do it with "songs of freedom" on their lips, Kuyper continues in this article to

---

of his significant (mis)readings of American history. Kuyper repeatedly elevated Alexander Hamilton as his exemplary American antirevolutionary statesman while repudiating Thomas Jefferson because of his sympathies for the French Revolution. At the same time, Kuyper's favoring of local and smaller governmental units made him on this level far more Jeffersonian than Hamiltonian. For a good discussion of Kuyper's misreading of American history, see James D. Bratt, "Abraham Kuyper, American History, and the Tensions of Neo-Calvinism," in *Sharing the Reformed Tradition: The Dutch–North American Exchange, 1846-1996,* ed. George Harinck and Hans Krabbendam (Amsterdam: Vrije Universiteit, 1996), 97-114.

85. Abraham Kuyper, *Ons Program,* 4th ed. (Amsterdam and Pretoria: Höveker & Wormser, 1897), xvii, 158. Kuyper's commentary on the means by which way a revolutionary state-principle denies self-governance and the initiative of the people because of its excessively centralized government (162), is reminiscent of the warnings found in *The Federalist Papers* of James Madison, Alexander Hamilton, and John Jay; see, e.g., *Federalist* #62 (Madison).

86. Kuyper, *Ons Program* (1879), 132; the *Heraut* article was published on June 18, 1871, and appeared (only!) in the original edition of *Ons Program* as an appendix to Kuyper's commentary on the third article of the ARP platform: "[The ARP] acknowledges the eternal ordinances of God's Word, also for the arena of politics; the authority of the state is bound to these ordinances not in a direct manner nor through the pronouncements of a church, but only via the conscience of the magistrates."

87. Kuyper, *Ons Program* (1879), 133.

paint a scenario of falsely proffered "freedom" by "liberals" in one social sphere after another while in fact the state expands its scope of control.[88] The issue he chooses — education — and the conflict he describes have an eerily contemporary ring for North American evangelical Christians in these first years of a new century.[89]

Kuyper begins with the liberal slogans about a free education. "Education is free — provided you send your children to state schools. You are free to start your own schools, at your own expense — provided you continue to pay taxes for state schools. University education is free too — the Netherlands has three State Universities. You don't like the instruction given there or the fact that appointments are strictly controlled by the State? Well, start your own University then; but keep paying your taxes for the others and make sure that you meet the mandatory regulations. And take note! There is freedom of education in our country. You disagree? That's slander!" Kuyper then moves on to the church and the struggle for a church that is financially and politically free from entanglements with the state. "Also, the church is free. Of course, since the State contributes much to its upkeep, it should have the right to regulate certain matters such as who ministers and where, and who is appointed to teach theology at the universities. In this way the State sees to it that a proper submission to the State is taught in the church." Finally, Kuyper links the issues together in terms of the rights and duties of citizens. "You are free as citizens in church and state. To be sure, church consistory members are appointed rather than elected, and only those who have the requisite financial means may elect and be elected." Kuyper reports the scornful challenge he has heard hurled at the orthodox Reformed *kleine luyden* by the Dutch liberal regents. "There may be a few places where 'your people' have both some money and a majority. Elect them!" Kuyper then makes an accusation about the ruthless and unjust tactics of the politically powerful in the Netherlands. When the Christian opposition achieves only modest electoral success, he notes, a gerrymandering of political boundaries takes place, the opposition's potential majority is diffused, and the dominant parties once again win. "But, you have freedom as citizens" is the (empty) slogan. Against this kind of tyranny, Kuyper comments, we are led to do battle with all that we can muster: "The mighty stream of liberty beckons."

Likening liberty's progress to a "mighty flowing stream" is one of

88. What follows is a paraphrase (keeping the direct discourse style used by Kuyper himself) of specific examples in Kuyper's article (*Ons Program* [1879], 133-36).

89. According to James Hunter, education is one of the key areas in today's culture wars. See James Davison Hunter, *Culture Wars: The Struggle to Define America* (New York: Basic Books, 1991), chap. 8.

Kuyper's favorite images.[90] Kuyper begins his first Stone Lecture at Princeton by comparing "the eddying waters" of America's "new stream of life" with the "frostbound and dull" old stream of Europe, and picks up the image later in the same lecture with an all-encompassing vision of the "one world stream, broad and fresh . . . [bearing] the promise of the future."[91] In the essay we are considering here, Kuyper uses the stream image to address the indifference of many of his coreligionists to the danger of growing state power. The modern state, in his view, had removed the orthodox Dutch Reformed from the living stream of liberty and settled them in a quiet pond. From there they would be moved into small wells and finally onto dry ground. "We're not yet on the dry ground," Kuyper observes, "not even yet in the well. But we are no longer in the stream either. . . . and that is where we must be. In the free stream of the spirit that comes down from the mountains and rushes out into the ocean. It is not only that we need water, we need fresh water, that clear, nourishing, flowing water in which life itself is mirrored. Even the most beautiful pond does not have this" (134). And yet, many are satisfied with the little water they get in a mere puddle!

What, then, is freedom, Kuyper asks? His answer, we must note, is not that of the strict libertarian. Freedom is *not* autonomy from every restriction on individual liberty but the "removal of all restrictions and bonds that violate one's true nature" (133). Similarly, it is this effort to ground his understanding of freedom on an *ontological* or *metaphysical* basis that distinguishes Kuyper from the liberationist tradition where the very notion of a *nature* is often seen as a tool of oppression. With that in mind let us take a closer look at Kuyper's liberationist or emancipatory rhetoric.

Abraham Kuyper's Emancipatory Rhetoric

We have already in several places taken note of Kuyper's use of liberation language, particularly in his sketch of the Dutch struggle for freedom from the Spanish (and Roman Catholic) yoke during the Eighty Years' War.[92] Kuyper's application of emancipatory language to the cause he himself headed is indisputable. Choosing to launch the new Calvinist, political daily newspaper on the

90. Unlike the use of this image by Martin Luther King, Jr., I have found no indication that Kuyper rooted his use in the words of the prophet Amos (5:24): "Let justice roll on like a river, righteousness like a never-failing stream." The text register for Kuyper's works, including his devotionals, contains no reference to Amos 5:24.

91. Kuyper, *Lectures on Calvinism*, 9, 32.

92. See above, 60-62.

300th anniversary of the capture of Brielle by the Sea Beggars was no accident. Kuyper's editorial in *De Standaard* on April 1, 1872, began thus:[93]

Freedom
"First of all, since it concerns the *glory of God* and the peace of the poor believers in the Netherlands, let everyone put aside all personal ambition and self-interest." So read the godly decree issued by William of Orange to his Sea Beggars. On this occasion of national rejoicing, may that princely word of the Father of our country also control the minds and hearts of our Christian people today!

Declaring that "it was *the Lord* who did it," so that the Netherlands might be a beacon of liberty to the nations, Kuyper laments the national dementia that resulted in forgetting this wonderful work of God:

What indeed threatens to die out is that distinctive national spirit which the Lord once breathed into our heart and conscience. What is being threatened and violated again is precisely that sacred freedom of conscience: the freedom, in church and school, to serve the God of our fathers in the manner of our fathers. What has almost died out is that sense of our people's moral calling, the conviction that especially the Dutch nation has been chosen to be for itself and for all the peoples of Europe, the standard-bearer not just of freedom but of freedom of conscience.

Kuyper concludes with another favorite image, the small "Gideon's band" of faithful "poor" whose cause is God's and therefore will triumph: "Nevertheless, there still remain people who, in keeping with the demand of history, carry this precious legacy in their heart. It is my prayer that they will not lose heart, though their number is small and their strength is small. 'Small, too, was the fleet of the Beggars!'" If this small band has the courage to fight under the "Standard" of the Word of God[94] and not "despise the voice of history," it will prevail. Kuyper's encouragement to his followers, invoking the privileged status of the small and poor, would stir the heart of any contemporary liberation

93. The entire editorial is available in English translation in Bratt, *Abraham Kuyper*, 317-22; all citations which follow are taken from these pages.

94. Here (on 322) Kuyper cites a stanza from the Dutch national anthem, the "Wilhelmus":

For God's Word ever dear
have I, free, undaunted,
a hero without fear,
risked my noble blood.

theologian: "And if these 'children of history' are found mostly among 'the people of little and average means,' what of it!" The battle must not, says Kuyper, be fought in human strength nor with human arrogance. The oppressed must not in battle (nor in victory!) turn on their foes and become oppressors in turn: "Fight they will if, in conformity to that Word, they do not haughtily scoff at the unfaithfulness of others but, as *children of the people and in solidarity with them, ask their God for forgiveness for the sins of the nation*" (emphasis added). Kuyper concludes his editorial with a prayer that links the destiny of the Dutch fatherland with that of God's people as he invokes the traditional opening *votum* of the Dutch Reformed liturgy, Psalm 124:8: "Our help is in the name of the Lord, the Maker of heaven and earth." "May He, in whose hands lie also the threads of our national life, make our country's celebration [of the liberation from Spain] foster that spirit [of forgiveness]. May He grant us the sacred honor of again raising up the Standard of His Word for our Christian people. So then, may our beginning be His, and may our help in this labor, too, be in the name of the Lord who also created *our* nation and rescued *our* fatherland." It needs to be noted here that, contrary to his expressed views, Kuyper skates close to the edge of a theocratic vision that merges church and state. We shall consider the issue of theocracy in some detail in the next chapter of this volume, but for now we need to consider to what degree Kuyper's emancipatory rhetoric in fact truly supports a liberationist perspective.

There can be no question about Kuyper's commitment to emancipation. His vast rhetorical, journalistic, and organizational political skills were clearly dedicated and directed to the emancipation of the orthodox Dutch Reformed "little folk" *(kleine luyden)*. The overriding theme of all his political activism can be summed up in the Mosaic message of Israel's God to the Egyptian Pharaoh: "Let my people go!" When, in 1912, the seventy-five-year-old Kuyper had opportunity to reflect on the dramatic political success of his Antirevolutionary Party after the century's turn, he explicitly made the connection in a published speech entitled "Delivered from the House of Bondage."[95]

Kuyper's emancipatory rhetoric includes the characteristic themes of contemporary liberation theology: the use of the exodus motif, the elevation and privileged status of the "poor" accompanied by a notion of divine, providential "preferential option for the poor." With history and God on their side, the marginalized and oppressed "people of God" will prevail; their cause —

---

95. Abraham Kuyper, *Uit het Diensthuis Uitgeleid* (Kampen: Kok, 1912). This speech was delivered in Leeuwarden, Groningen, and Rotterdam.

the cause of God's kingdom — will triumph despite overwhelming odds against it!

At the same time, there are notes in Kuyper's rhetoric that are not the mainstay of contemporary liberation theology. Kuyper's preoccupation is liberty, especially liberty of *conscience,* rather than emancipation from oppressive social and political institutions. Kuyper also does not privilege the poor from the reality of their own sin but warns the oppressed not to follow up their liberation by becoming oppressors in turn, a note found wanting in contemporary liberationist rhetoric. In addition, Kuyper would judge the essential role of centralized planning in the socialist models favored by liberation theologians as examples of precisely the sort of *mechanical* imposition on human social spheres favored by gnostic elites that he opposed with all his might. Kuyper's *organic* view of society favors the libertarian notion of "spontaneous order" by also exalting the spontaneous, the instinctive, and the intuitive.

Kuyper clearly was not against intellectual reflection; his rallying cry was against *intellectualism,* which he defined as "the peculiar mentality of those who deny the organic character of life."[96] It was here, from the folk wisdom of the "people," that Kuyper claimed to draw the raw material for the Antirevolutionary political movement. It was here, where faith and "common sense" (or "practical wisdom") are joined in "our instinctive folk-life," that Kuyper draws the line between the Antirevolutionary Party and the Liberal as well as Socialist political parties, both of whom, he contended, "are under the lead of abstract theoreticians."[97] Drawing on important class distinctions, Kuyper observed that "the party organization of the Christian part of the nation had to be very different from that of 'the gentlemen.'" However, the task was difficult because there was no previous model in Dutch life for such a popular political movement: "Since folks had seen no other model of party organization than that of the mandarins, however, they began by copying that — without success. The model fit neither us nor our circumstances. David could not fight Goliath wearing Saul's armour. Only the sling and stone from the creek suited him. And only when this truth sank in did a party organization of our own kind arise among us, one that gave us a chance of mobilizing our forces and leading them to victory."[98]

96. Abraham Kuyper, "Our Instinctive Life," in Bratt, *Abraham Kuyper,* 266.
97. Kuyper, "Our Instinctive Life," 265-73.
98. Kuyper, "Our Instinctive Life," 274-75.

Fig. 6.1. "Pardon me! It was instinctive!" A caricature of Kuyper's retort to the "elite intellectuals" of the Antirevolutionary Party in *Our Instinctive Life.*

Rhetoric and Social Ontology

Kuyper's rhetoric concerning the "poor" and his call for their emancipation from the tyranny of oppressive, moneyed elites are so close to that of liberation theology that we need to specify exactly where the difference, if any, lies. Earlier in this chapter we suggested that Kuyper's attempt to ground his understanding of freedom on an *ontological* or *metaphysical* basis distinguishes his vision from that of liberation theologians. We need to spell this out in greater detail. We shall begin by briefly considering the understanding of emancipation that is found in liberation theology and, ultimately, in Karl Marx himself as a classic exemplar of liberationist views of man and society.[99] We begin with a Marxist-

99. For my summary of Marx's thought I am using the following works: Shlomo Avineri, *The Social and Political Thought of Karl Marx* (London and New York: Cambridge University Press, 1968); Iring Fetscher, *Marx and Marxism* (New York: Herder & Herder, 1971); David Lyon, *Karl Marx: A Christian Assessment of His Life and Thought* (Downers

inspired description of the plight of Latin America's poor as summarized by Argentine theologian José Míguez Bonino.

> *The Latin American revolutionary is confronted with a state of consciousness in the masses in which the slave relationship of traditional society, the cultural alienation imposed by imperialism and the magical forms of folk-religion have produced a lag in the revolutionary consciousness in relation to the demands of the objective situation. In the effort to change this situation, the Marxist revolutionary has found himself side by side with a number of active revolutionary Christians and has discovered, in the new movement within the Christian fold, the potential motivating and mobilizing power of the Christian faith for revolutionary change.[100]*

According to Míguez Bonino, the revolutionary alliance between Christians and Marxists is necessary in Latin America because Christianity was itself a contributor to the "false consciousness" of its "poor." Even in the midst of an objective situation of oppression, "people 'live' their economic and social alienation in a world of mythical representation which political ideology is not able to pierce." Thus, the most powerful spur to genuine consciousness leading to revolutionary action is the Christian faith itself, when "persons and groups" emerge that "seem to be able to break the spell of this alienation *from within the religious consciousness itself*."[101]

What exactly is this "alienation"? On the face of it, there is an interesting parallel between Marx's notion of alienation and Abraham Kuyper's understanding of the conflict between a "mechanical" and an "organic" development of human society. For Kuyper it is artistic life in particular that gives evidence of the organic, spontaneous, instinctive, intuitive expressions of human creative life: "All genuine artistic expression arises spontaneously from the soul of the artist. The impulse is born and imparted in the hidden center of his being and . . . the artistic image as such arises from his hidden self and automatically seeks expression by its own inner drive."[102] For Kuyper the course of human history in its progress shows clearly the universal character of human culturally formative action: "Human knowledge and skill is the common possession of all people collectively, a possession gradually won by

---

Grove, Ill.: InterVarsity, 1979); John McMurty, *The Structure of Marx's World-View* (Princeton: Princeton University Press, 1978); Thomas Sowell, *Marxism: Philosophy and Economics* (New York: Morrow, 1985).

100. Miguez Bonino, 23-24.
101. Miguez Bonino, 26.
102. Kuyper, "Our Instinctive Life," 260.

the effort of succeeding generations and guided in its development by an invisible power."[103]

Marx understood human nature itself in terms of this creative, productive capacity. Man was *homo faber*, which, according to John McMurty, must not be narrowly conceived in terms of toolmaking and productive industry alone, but in the broadest sense as the capacity for all creative work by which a man "raises a structure in his imagination" and then "erects it in reality."[104] McMurty concludes that "for Marx, then, Man the Producer is, in the end, Man the Artist."[105] According to Marx, "as soon as the division of labor and isolation of the means of production from actual work develop in the course of historical progress, it will no longer be possible for men as individuals to appropriate for themselves the whole range of human objectifications; they will be reduced to partial functions and can therefore only partially develop their talents. . . . This is the concept of 'alienation.'"[106] In Marxist terms, alienation is the opposite of development: "Alienation, in Marx's sense is not simply a general malaise but more specifically a misconception of reality growing out of thwarted development — an inversion in which human reality and human needs are made subservient to artificially created things, to the imaginary gods of religion or to the financial institutions of capitalism."[107] In one of his earliest economic writings ("Alienated Labor," 1844), Marx contends that the fundamental alienation in a capitalist society boils down to the categorical division of "the whole of society . . . into the two classes of the property owners and the propertyless workers" (the "proletariat").[108] In this situation the worker's relation to labor, "where he does not belong to himself in his labor but to someone else," parallels his relation to religion: "As in religion the human imagination's own activity, the activity of man's head and his heart, reacts independently on the individual as an alien activity of gods or devils, so the activity of the worker is not his own spontaneous activity. It belongs to another and is the loss of himself."[109] In the same way that religion is a human creation of "an alien, imaginary being which apparently takes on a life of its own,"[110] so too "money debases all the gods of man and turns them into commodities. Money is the universal, self-constituted

---

103. Kuyper, "Our Instinctive Life," 258.

104. McMurty, 22; the terminology is taken directly from the first volume of Marx's *Capital.*

105. McMurty, 26.

106. Fetscher, 313.

107. Sowell, *Marxism,* 34.

108. McLellan, 77.

109. McLellan, 80.

110. Lyon, 48.

value of all things. It has therefore robbed the whole world, human as well as natural, of its own values." Marx concludes: "Money is the alienated essence of man's work and being; this alien essence dominates him; and he adores it."[111]

Since man has thus enslaved himself (Marx speaks of "self-alienation"), he must of course also liberate himself. This is accomplished, in Marx's judgment, by abolishing the class distinction between property owners and the propertyless proletariat; by the abolition of private property itself. It needs to be noted that for Marx the broad rubric of "property" includes the wide array of social institutions including marriage, family, science, and art as well as religion and law. "Religion, family, state, law, morality, science, and art are only particular forms of production [i.e., human creative action] and fall under its general law. The positive abolition of private property and the appropriation of human life is therefore the positive abolition of all alienation, thus the return of man out of religion, family, state, etc. into his human, i.e. social being."[112] We should not become confused by Marx's use of "social" here. The term refers not to our ordinary usage to describe the variety of social relationships in which we humans find ourselves (family, church, neighborhood, nation) but to *universal* humanity, to what Marx calls "species-life." It is to the extent that an individual person becomes free from *particular* social relationships and "relates to himself as to the present living species," that is, to *universal* humanity, that he is truly emancipated, truly free.[113] Marx's view here is neatly captured by the pithy comment of a "Peanuts" cartoon character who summarized her philosophy of life this way: "I love humanity; it's people I can't stand."

How is this universal humanity to be achieved and alienation overcome? In different terms, how can class conflict be transcended *(aufgehoben)?* Marx's answer is found in his endowing the propertyless proletariat with universal "redemptive" significance. In Shlomo Avineri's words, "only because he sees in the proletariat the contemporary and final realization of universality, does Marx endow the proletariat with a historical significance and mission."[114] In Marx's dialectical understanding of history, the transformation of society takes place when the propertyless proletariat becomes self-conscious of its condition and demands that its condition be made universal. When the proletariat "demands the negation of private property it is only laying down as a principle for society what society has laid down as a principle for the proletariat, what has already been incorporated in itself without its consent as the negative result of soci-

111. Cited by Lyon, 48.
112. McLellan, 88.
113. McLellan, 81.
114. Avineri, 59.

ety."[115] An atoning exchange takes place wherein the proletariat as "suffering servant" becomes the prototype of the propertyless and classless society and a new universal humanity is born through emancipation. So how does this take place? Marx spells it out in detail, though the detail is infuriatingly abstract and theoretical:

> [Emancipation takes place] in the formation of a class with radical chains, a class in civil society that is not a class of civil society, of a social group that is the dissolution of all social groups, of a sphere that has a universal character because of its universal sufferings and lays claim to no particular right, because it is the object of no particular injustice but of injustice in general. This class can no longer lay claim to a historical status, but only to a human one. . . . It is, finally, a sphere that cannot emancipate itself without emancipating itself from all other spheres of society and thereby emancipating these other spheres themselves. In a word, it is the complete loss of humanity, and thus can only recover itself by a complete redemption of humanity. This dissolution of society, as a particular class, is the proletariat.[116]

In Christian terminology, the proletariat for Marx is the second Adam, the "new man."

The meaning of emancipation becomes even clearer when we consider Marx's extension of the category "worker" to all persons. What is entailed is opposition to and negation of all forms of "private property," where the term includes marriage and, in fact, "the whole world of culture and civilization."[117]

---

115. McLellan, 73.

116. McLellan, 72-73.

117. McLellan, 87-88. Marx's description in these pages of the place of marriage in communism, where communism is understood as "the positive expression of the overcoming of private property, appearing first of all as generalized private property," is chilling: "[The] process of opposing general private property to private property is expressed in the animal form of opposing to marriage (which is of course a form of exclusive private property) the community of women where the woman becomes the common property of the community." Marx judges this to be first stage of what he calls "crude communism," in which "women pass from marriage to universal prostitution," that needs to be supplanted by a more "natural" communal relationship between men and women. "Communism represents the positive," Marx contends, "in the form of a negation of the negation and thus a phase in human emancipation and rehabilitation, both real and necessary at this juncture of human development. Communism is the necessary form and dynamic principle of the immediate future, but communism is not as such the goal of human development, the form of human society" (96). What the final phase will look like in terms of marriage is not entirely clear, but it is clear that conventional monogamous marriage must be opposed as a form of "private property." It is no accident that marriage is one of the primary targets

For Marx, therefore, emancipation is itself the fundamental, defining, ontological category. Human nature as it ought to be is emancipated human nature; it is *universal* or *social* human nature emancipated from all the oppressive forms of particularity that Marx terms "private property."

When contrasted directly with this Marxist notion of liberation, it is clear that Kuyper's emancipatory rhetoric nonetheless keeps him a long distance from the vision of liberation theology. When one considers the mature expression of Kuyper's sociocultural worldview in the Stone Lectures on Calvinism, it is striking to note where the term "emancipation" appears most frequently. First, it needs to be pointed out that while there is a lecture in this series devoted to politics, there is not one on economics. This is a striking omission, considering the strategic spiritual and sociopolitical importance Kuyper attributed to the "social question" in his 1891 address to the Dutch Christian Social Congress, where he boldly proclaimed: "Standing before the agonizing distress of these times, a distress which at every point is related to the very essence of error and sin, our eye should not be allowed, nor should it be able, to turn away from the *Christus Consolator* [Christ the Consoler], who assuredly addresses our violently disturbed century with the persistent call of his divine compassion: 'Come to *me,* wealthiest century in history, which is so deathly weary and heavy laden, and *I* will give you rest.'"[118] Why did Kuyper not dedicate a lecture to the "social question" in his Princeton series? Perhaps the clue is found in Kuyper's concern in his Princeton lectures to present Calvinism both in its distinctive contribution and in its constructive role for the future of world civilization.[119] With respect to the "social question," Kuyper acknowledges that Calvinists have lagged behind others, including Roman Catholics such as Bishop Wilhelm von Ketteler of Mainz and Pope Leo XIII in his 1891 encyclical, *Rerum Novarum.*[120] Perhaps it is this lag and the appreciation Kuyper has for the more highly developed Roman Catholic tradition of social teaching that led him to exclude the social question in a series of lectures dedicated to setting forth a positive and distinctive Calvinist worldview.

The Stone Lecture where the notion of emancipation appears frequently is "Calvinism and Art."[121] Kuyper begins the lecture by noting the phenome-

---

of all revolutionaries. For more on Marx and marriage, see McMurty, 76-77 n. 8, and the literature cited there.

118. Kuyper, *The Problem of Poverty,* 28.

119. See especially the last of the Stone Lectures on Calvinism, "Calvinism and the Future"; cf. Peter Heslam's helpful commentary on this point in Heslam, 224-50.

120. Kuyper, *The Problem of Poverty,* 24.

121. Kuyper, *Lectures on Calvinism,* 142-70; pages references which follow in the text are to this chapter.

non of art's democratization in the nineteenth century. Freed from the strait-jacket of aristocratic wealth, "artistic refinement, thus far restricted to a few favored circles, now tends to gain ground among broader middle classes, occasionally even betraying its inclination to descend to the widest strata of lower society" (142). While he acknowledges that "the homage of art by the profanum vulgus must lead to art-corruption" (143), Kuyper nonetheless judges this democratization to be a salutary development. Art serves as an important antidote to "the dominating influences of money and barren intellectualism [which] reduce the life of the emotions to the freezing point." He summarizes his point thus: "In this cold, irreligious and practical age the warmth of this devotion to art has kept alive many higher aspirations of the soul, which otherwise might readily have died, as they did in the middle of the last century" (143).

Kuyper continues by observing that "art derived her richest motives from Religion. The religious passion was the gold-mine which financially rendered her boldest conceptions possible." Not only did the church provide the patronage that made it possible for artists to live, she also shaped the *content* of art: "Art-style and the style of worship coincided" (144). Kuyper, however, assesses this state of affairs — "this alliance of religion and art" — as "a *lower* stage of religious and in general of human development" (144). Religion, rather, rises to a "higher plain" when "it graduates from the symbolical into the clearly-conscious life, and thereby necessitates both the division of worship into many forms, and the *emancipation* of matured religion from all sacerdotal and political guardianship" (145, emphasis added). It is Calvinism, so Kuyper argues, that is religiously responsible for encouraging what he calls "a multiformity of life-tendencies" by breaking "the power of the State within the domain of religion" and thus making "an end of sacerdotalism" (145).

The remaining numerous references to "emancipation" in this lecture run in the same vein. Religion "develops into spiritual maturity [as it] extricates itself from art's bandages" because "religion and art have each a life-sphere of their own." When they have "arrived at their highest development, both Religion and Art demand an independent existence, and the two stems which at first were intertwined and seemed to belong to the same plant, now appear to spring from a root of their own" (148). Further in the lecture: "Our intellectual, ethical, religious and aesthetic life each commands a sphere of its own. These spheres run parallel and do not allow the derivation of one from the other" (150). Kuyper sees this diversity as rooted in the very nature of human beings; the diversity is a creational reality that springs from the unity of the human heart. "It is the central emotion, the central impulse, and the central animation, in the mystical root of our being, which seeks to reveal itself to the outer world in this fourfold ramification." Though distinct, these four spheres must not be sundered from one another. "Art is no side-shoot on a principal branch, but an independent branch that grows from the trunk of our life itself, even though it is far more nearly allied to Religion than to our thinking or to our ethical being" (150).

Though Kuyper insists on art's independence from the church and its worship, he does give to art the noble religious calling, "the mystical task of reminding us in its productions of the beautiful that was lost and of anticipating its perfect coming luster." Art has a prophetic task and is a "gift of the Holy Ghost": "Standing by the ruins of this once so wonderfully beautiful creation, art points out to the Calvinist both the still visible lines of the original plan, and what is even more, the splendid restoration by which the Supreme Artist and Master-Builder will one day renew and enhance even the beauty of His original creation" (155). Art, Kuyper insists, "cannot originate from the Evil One; for Satan is destitute of every creative power. All he can do is abuse the good gifts of God." Art can only be what it is supposed to be when it is "in keeping with the [creation] ordinances which God ordained . . . when he called this world into existence" (155). This high calling is best achieved when art is a free, independent, and *mature* sphere of life. Calvinism's contribution, according to Kuyper, consisted in "releasing art from guardianship of the Church" and thus "recognizing its majority" (157). While he acknowledges the role played by the Renaissance and by humanism, Kuyper insists that the "emancipation" and "liberation" (both terms are used promiscuously in the remainder of the lecture) was finally achieved through Calvinism's broad love of liberty in general. "It was the broad emancipation of our ordinary earthly life, and the instinct for liberty, which thereby captured the heart of the nations and inspired them with delight in the enjoyment of treasures so long blindly neglected" (166).

Kuyper adduces two important reasons for Calvinism's strong role in the emancipation of art. First, its strong doctrine of creation, which affirmed the world as "the theater for the mighty works of God" and also emphasized humanity, even after the fall, as the "creation of His hand" placed on earth to "glorify the name of Almighty God" (162). The world and its history continues under divine providential rule, and to the end of God's own glory "He has ordained for this humanity all sorts of life utterances, and among these, art occupies a quite independent place. Art reveals ordinances of creation which neither science, nor politics, nor religious life, nor even revelation can bring to light" (162-63). Using his favorite organic metaphor, Kuyper continues, "[art] is a plant that grows and blossoms upon her own root, and without denying that this plant may have required the help of a temporary support, and that in early times the Church lent this prop in a very excellent way, yet the Calvinistic principle demanded that this plant of earth should at length acquire strength to stand alone and vigorously to extend its branches in every direction" (163). The second positive role of Calvinist teaching on art was "the idea of election by free grace," which "contributed not a little toward interesting art in the hidden importance of what was seemingly small and insignificant." Kuyper draws this contrast: "Thus far the artist had only traced upon his canvas the idealized figures of prophets and apostles, of saints and priests; now, however, when he saw how God had chosen the porter and the wage-earner for Himself, he found interest not only in the head, the figure and the entire personality of the man of the people, but began to reproduce the human expression of every rank and station" (166). Here is Kuyper's summary of the emancipation of art brought about in large measure by the influence of Calvinism: "Ecclesiastical power no longer restrained the artist, and princely gold no longer chained him in its fetters" (167).

From this we can see that Kuyper's understanding of liberation, while it may share some rhetorical cadences with Marxist-inspired liberation theology, rests upon a social ontology that is the exact inverse of Marx's. Marx sees particularity, notably the particularity of concrete social institutions, as oppressive, and emancipation from particularity toward universal humanity as the goal. Marx's vision, philosophically speaking, is monistic in its orientation: *from the many to the One.* It is here that we need to make a critically important distinction between liberation rhetoric and a liberationist social metaphysics. Emancipation is itself the metaphysical principle that shapes Marx's view of human society. Kuyper, by contrast, views the differentiation of society into its particular *spheres* as the "higher" development. For Kuyper, emancipation does not mean dissolving particular and concrete social spheres and institutions but allowing them their independent existence, under the sovereignty of God, to develop and flourish in accord with the normative potential (creation ordinances) given by God in creation itself. Kuyper's sense of emancipation is the liberation from all monistic patterns; he is pluralistic in his social ontology. Kuyper's rhetoric is in some respect formally similar to liberation theology, but his social metaphysic is quite different. Those who appeal to Kuyper's rhetoric in defense of liberation theology, as well as those who appeal to Kuyper's social ontology in critique of liberation theology, need to bear that in mind. Interpreters of Kuyper (and contemporary evangelical social thought) must make a clear distinction between liberation rhetoric and liberationist metaphysics; similar rhetoric can be used with decidedly different social ontologies.

With that final observation about Kuyper's social ontology, we can bring this chapter to a conclusion and go on now to consider the larger question of pluralism in Kuyper's public theology. Pluralism, we should note, has two distinct dimensions. At one level, in distinction from socially and politically *monistic* visions, we can speak of social or *structural* pluralism: public policies that encourage the differentiation of society into strongly independent social spheres. This first understanding of pluralism is what Kuyper was referring to in his characteristic notion of *sphere sovereignty*, which he defined as follows: "In a Calvinistic sense we understand hereby, that the family, the business, science, art, and so forth are all social spheres, which do not owe their existence to the state, and which do not derive the law of their life from the superiority of the state, but obey a high authority within their own bosom; an authority which rules, by the grace of God, just as the sovereignty of the State does."[122] There is, however, another notion of pluralism — *religious* or *confessional* pluralism — which is opposed to *religiously* monistic views of society, to theocracies that seek to impose one state-supported religion on a people.[123]

The issue of pluralism in this second sense — religious pluralism — arises naturally from the discussion in this chapter, since all Christian public theologies are now regularly challenged to defend themselves against the charge that they, no less than the political ideologies arising from Hegel's and Marx's apotheosis of the state, are monistic. More specifically, Christian public theologies are usually charged with secretly harboring *theocratic* impulses. So we need to face the question: Does believing that Jesus Christ is Lord also of one's "secular" nation-state make one a closet theocrat? Are Lordship and liberty intrinsically at odds with each other? Or, more provocatively, conceding the theocratic accusation, can one be both a theocrat *and* a pluralist who believes in religious toleration? Or finally, pushing the envelope to the limit, is the claim of Dutch Reformed theologian Arnold Van Ruler that "toleration can only be maintained on the basis of the theocratic ideal" to be taken seriously?[124] Our next chapter considers the "real agenda"[125] of Dutch neo-Calvinist public theology.

A final postscript to this chapter. From the comparison between Marx's

---

122. Kuyper, *Lectures on Calvinism,* 90.

123. I have taken this distinction from R. McCarthy et al., eds., *Society, State, and Schools: A Case for Structural and Confessional Pluralism* (Grand Rapids: Eerdmans, 1981); a full explanation of the terms can be found on 38ff. The pluralist argument in this volume for greater school choice in America is clearly indebted to the Kuyperian, neo-Calvinist tradition. A more sophisticated set of distinctions between various forms and uses of pluralism is found in a work also coauthored by two neo-Kuyperians, Sander Griffioen and Richard J. Mouw: *Pluralisms and Horizons: An Essay in Christian Public Philosophy* (Grand Rapids: Eerdmans, 1993).

124. Arnold A. Van Ruler, *Calvinist Trinitarianism and Theocentric Politics,* trans. John Bolt (Lewiston, N.Y., and Queenston, Ont.: Edwin Mellen, 1989), 174.

125. This expression is borrowed from Richard John Neuhaus's review of Ralph Reed, *Active Faith* (New York: Free Press, 1996), in *First Things,* no. 66 (October 1966): 42-45.

and Kuyper's quite different social metaphysics, one other issue calls for further examination: theological anthropology. The respective social ontologies of Marxism and neo-Calvinism are ultimately grounded in significantly different views of human nature, human well-being, and human destiny. An adequate discussion of this issue, even if restricted to the sociopolitical implications of the different anthropologies, is beyond the scope of this study and requires a monograph of its own.[126]

---

126. An extensive (1,000 pages of typed manuscript!) overview of Kuyper's anthro-pology has recently been completed by G. Kuijpers, *Abraham Kuyper Over de Mens* (Dordrecht: privately published, 1998).

CHAPTER SEVEN

Tyranny by Another Name?
Theocrats and Pluralists

Give me your tired, your poor,
Your huddled masses yearning to breathe free.

Emma Lazarus, inscription on
the Statue of Liberty, 1883

There is no room in this country for hyphenated Americanism.

Theodore Roosevelt (1915)

The one thing that doesn't abide by majority rule is a person's con-
science. Harper Lee, *To Kill a Mockingbird*, 1960

The test of liberty is the position and security of minorities.

Lord John Acton

Fides suadetur, non cogitur.

Gisbertus Voetius

The Church imposes nothing; she only proposes.

John Paul II

303

Toleration can only be maintained on the basis of a theocratic ideal.

Arnold Van Ruler

Totalitarianism is the possession of reality by a political Idea — the Idea of the socialist kingdom of heaven on earth; the redemption of humanity by political force.

David Horowitz

We are all multiculturalists now.

Nathan Glazer

Perhaps a good place to begin this chapter on theocracy and pluralism is to paraphrase the famous letter of newspaperman Francis Church to a young girl who had lost her faith in Santa Claus: "Yes, Virginia, there are theocrats in America today!"[1] Though the promiscuous accusation of theocracy has become fashionable as a means of silencing any and all religiously framed discourse in the public square,[2] it is important from the outset to take note of the publicly articulated, self-consciously theocratic visions that do exist within the American ecclesiastical and theological world. There are Roman Catholic as well as Protestant versions of theocratic visions, and they come in varying degrees of theocratic intensity. In the case of the former, proponents of a Roman Catholic confessional state line up in opposition to the efforts of Catholic "Americanists," notably Jesuit theologian John Courtney Murray[3] and, more re-

---

1. Francis P. Church, "Is There a Santa Claus?" *New York Sun,* September 21, 1897; in *The Home Book of American Quotations,* selected and arranged by Bruce Bohle (New York: Dodd, Mead, 1967), 82, #16.

2. For a significant catalogue of such (mis)representations, see Ralph Reed, *Politically Incorrect: The Emerging Faith Factor in American Politics* (Dallas: Word, 1994), chap. 4, "The New Amos and Andy: How the Media Portrays People of Faith." A witty, acerbic response to what he judges to be excessive secularist critique of the Religious Right is provided by Jewish syndicated columnist Don Feder, *Who's Afraid of the Religious Right?* (Washington, D.C.: Regnery, 1996). A more serious response, also by an Orthodox Jew and also very sympathetic to the concerns and values of the Religious Right, is Daniel Lapin, *The Real Battle* (Washington, D.C.: Regnery, 1999). This last volume will receive fuller attention in the next chapter dealing with the "culture wars."

3. See John Courtney Murray, S.J., *We Hold These Truths: Catholic Reflections on the American Proposition* (New York: Sheed & Ward, 1960). Murray's legacy is being fiercely debated among American Catholics today; see Donald J. D'Elia and Stephen M. Krason,

304

cently, Richard John Neuhaus,[4] Michael Novak,[5] and George Weigel,[6] all of whom seek support in Catholic social teaching for the values of the American "liberal" democratic experiment. One of the more intriguing of these critiques in recent years is Roman Catholic theologian David Schindler's subtle and profound vision of an ecclesially shaped political *communio, Heart of the World, Center of the Church.*[7] For our purposes in this chapter, the Protestant (and neo-Calvinist!) version is more important. Associated with names such as Rousas J. Rushdoony,[8] Greg Bahnsen,[9] Gary North,[10] and James Jordan,[11] and favoring self-designations such as "theonomy,"[12] "Christian Reconstruction,"[13]

---

eds., *We Hold These Truths and More: Further Catholic Reflections on the American Proposition* (Steubenville, Ohio: Franciscan University Press, 1993).

4. Richard John Neuhaus, *The Naked Public Square: Religion and Democracy in America* (Grand Rapids: Eerdmans, 1984); *The Catholic Moment: The Paradox of the Church in the Postmodern World* (San Francisco: Harper & Row, 1987).

5. Michael Novak, *The Spirit of Democratic Capitalism* (New York: Simon & Schuster, 1982); *The Catholic Ethic and the Spirit of Capitalism* (New York: Free Press, 1993).

6. George Weigel, *Tranquillitas Ordinis: The Present Failure and Future Promise of American Catholic Thought on War and Peace* (New York: Oxford University Press, 1987); *Catholicism and the Renewal of American Democracy* (New York and Mahwah, N.J.: Paulist, 1989); *Freedom and Its Discontents: Catholicism Confronts Modernity* (Washington, D.C.: Ethics and Public Policy Center, 1991).

7. David Schindler, *Heart of the World, Center of the Church:* Communio *Ecclesiology, Liberalism, and Liberation* (Grand Rapids: Eerdmans, 1996).

8. Rousas J. Rushdoony, *The Institutes of Biblical Law* (Nutley, N.J.: Craig Press, 1973); *The Roots of Christian Reconstruction* (Vallecito, Calif.: Ross House Books, 1991).

9. Greg Bahnsen, *No Other Standard* (Tyler, Tex.: Institute for Christian Economics, 1991); also see n. 6 above.

10. See, *inter alia,* Gary North, *The Dominion Covenant: Genesis* (Tyler, Tex.: Institute for Christian Economics, 1982); *Unconditional Surrender: God's Program for Victory* (Tyler, Tex.: Institute for Christian Economics, 1981); *Backward Christian Soldiers? An Action Manual for Christian Reconstruction* (Tyler, Tex.: Institute for Christian Economics, 1984).

11. James B. Jordan, *The Reconstruction of the Church: A Symposium* (Tyler, Tex.: Geneva Ministries, 1985); *The Sociology of the Church: Essays in Reconstruction* (Tyler, Tex.: Geneva Ministries, 1986).

12. See Greg L. Bahnsen, *Theonomy in Christian Ethics* (Nutley, N.J.: Craig Press, 1979).

13. This is the term used by the followers of Rousas J. Rushdoony and their major newsletter, the *Chalcedon Report,* and more academic journal, the *Journal of Christian Reconstruction.* The former has been in existence as a monthly publication since October 1965 (December 1998 was issue no. 401); the latter since the summer of 1974. Both are published by the Chalcedon Foundation, Vallecito, Calif. The Chalcedon Foundation "is a Christian educational organization devoted exclusively to research, publishing, and to co-

and "dominion theology,"[14] this group of thinkers favors a strict application of Old Testament Israelite theocratic law to the United States of America. Rushdoony, for example, contends that Calvin's repudiation of this strict theocratic principle in favor of liberty with respect to concrete national, constitutional law is "heretical nonsense" and a tragic instance where Calvin's "classical humanism gained ascendency" over his biblical vision.[15]

We will be returning to this theocratic viewpoint later in the chapter, but for now we simply take note of it because, though Abraham Kuyper was decidedly not a "theocrat" in this sense, the genealogy of the Christian Reconstruction movement clearly has neo-Kuyperian links.[16] As Richard John Neuhaus accurately observed in a helpful review of this theocratic movement, its selfproclaimed roots are Calvinist and neo-Calvinist:

> The usual appeal [against the charge that theonomy is a novelty in Christian history] is to the American Puritans, to John Calvin, and, frequently, to selected early fathers of the church. Abraham Kuyper (1837-1920), the Dutch theologian and political leader who espoused an intriguing theory of "spheres of sovereignty," is also a considerable influence. [Christian Reconstructionist James] Jordan goes so far as to say that "Christian Reconstruction originally was just Kuyperianism with the Bible." . . . Some

gent communication of a distinctly Christian scholarship to the world at large." Taking its name from the early church Council of Chalcedon (A.D. 451), which affirmed the formula concerning Jesus Christ that he was *vere Deus, vere homo*, the Chalcedon Foundation believes that "this formula directly challenges every false claim of divinity by any human institution" and therefore is "the foundation of Western liberty, for it sets limits on all authoritarian human institutions." (Taken from *Chalcedon Report*, no. 400 [November 1998]).

14. See n. 10 above.

15. Rushdoony, *Institutes of Biblical Law*, 9. Calvin, in turn, (*Institutes* 4.20.14) speaks of the "dangerous and seditious opinion" (as well as "false and foolish") that denies "that a state is well constituted which denies the polity of Moses and is governed by the common laws of nations."

16. One of the defining characteristics of Christian Reconstruction is "presuppositionalism," which Rushdoony himself defines as "a perspective in philosophy and theology whose origins are in several great Dutch thinkers, notably the Dutch-American Cornelius Van Til. Its essential point is that all man's thinking begins with certain axioms of faith, life, and thought which provide him with the essential framework of his world and life view" ("Presuppositionalism," Position Paper no. 230, *Chalcedon Report*, no. 400 [November 1998]: 31). The background for this position can be found in Kuyper's notion of "two kinds of people; two kinds of science" (*Principles of Sacred Theology*, trans. J. Hendrik De Vries [New York: Scribner, 1898], 150-82), and in his description of the conflict between worldviews or "life systems" in his first Stone Lecture (*Lectures on Calvinism* [Grand Rapids: Eerdmans, 1931]).

Reconstructionists describe themselves as neo-Puritans, almost all display Calvinist or neo-Calvinist loyalties, and most evidence sympathy for other experiments in "governance by the saints" such as Oliver Cromwell's reconstruction of Parliament.[17]

Linking this theocratic impulse with the focus of our previous chapter, we also note that Neuhaus follows other commentators in calling Christian Reconstruction a "liberation theology of the right." He notes that though "contemporary theonomists, who wish to think of themselves as conservative, resist the comparison with the liberal Social Gospel and with leftwing evangelicals, not to mention liberation theology," nonetheless they share the latter's theological rationale and a belief "that there is in fact a 'biblical politics' that can and should be implemented now by radically committed Christians."[18] Theonomists and liberation theologians of the Left both believe in the beneficial "rule by saints" on earth, now.[19]

We need therefore to ask: Was Kuyper's neo-Calvinist commitment to and visionary political activity in the name of Christ's Lordship over all of life an instance of theocratic "dominion theology"? Would he, for example, have concurred with Rushdoony's Constantinian insistence that Christians should be preparing "to conquer the world and assert the 'Crown Rights of King Jesus,'" or Gary North's characterization of Jesus' ministry as "a worldwide ministry of conquest, based on the preaching of the gospel of peace"?[20] How do we

---

17. Richard John Neuhaus, "Why Wait for the Kingdom? The Theonomist Temptation," *First Things* 3 (May 1990): 15. The Puritan connection at the conclusion of Neuhaus's observation is intriguing also because the director of the British Kuyper Foundation, Stephen C. Perks, recently published *A Defence of the Christian State* (Taunton, England: Kuyper Foundation, 1998), a sharp critique of the political doctrine of "principled pluralism." The cover of the volume is a portrait of Oliver Cromwell. I obtained a copy of this volume just as I was delivering the manuscript of my book to the publisher, and so a full response to the Perks interpretation of Kuyper will have to be done in a different place than this chapter.

18. Neuhaus, "Why Wait?" 16.

19. See, e.g., Michael Walzer's important study of Puritan politics, *The Revolution of the Saints: A Study in the Origins of Radical Politics* (Cambridge: Harvard University Press, 1965). It is worth noting that Walzer's study is cited by Nicholas Wolterstorff as the premier inspiration for his appreciation of the Calvinist tradition's emphasis on "world-formative" (rather than "world-avertive") Christianity; see *Until Justice and Peace Embrace* (Grand Rapids: Eerdmans, 1983), 3ff.

20. Cited by Neuhaus, "Why Wait?" 16. In an interesting parallel, Lutheran theologian Carl Braaten once characterized the various theologies of revolution and liberation, inspired particularly by the so-called "theology of hope" (Jürgen Moltmann), as a "Constantinianism of the left" (see *The Flaming Center: A Theology of Mission* [Philadelphia: Fortress, 1977]).

understand Kuyper's emphatically Christian political vision in the light of his passion for structural pluralism discussed in the previous chapter?

Abraham Kuyper and the Question of Theocracy

In that chapter we argued that Kuyper's social ontology was formulated in conscious opposition to all monistic visions, whether they be church-controlled societies or state-controlled ones. Kuyper's very definition of liberty was linked to a *structurally pluralistic* social vision that encouraged flourishing *independent* spheres of society. Social spheres and institutions were truly free when, existing *directly* under the sovereign rule of God, they could develop *organically* in accord with their true nature, in accord with the *ordinances* of God's creation. In one of his first editorials as editor of the daily newspaper *De Standaard*, Kuyper stated his principle of the state's independence from any church interference in categorical language: "We absolutely deny the church the right to establish political principles that would bind the state."[21] As Kuyper developed his notion of "sphere sovereignty" further in a fuller definition, he underscored the same right of independent existence for social spheres vis-à-vis the state: "In a Calvinistic sense we understand hereby, that the family, the business, science, art and so forth are all social spheres, which do not owe their existence to the state, and which do not derive the law of their life from the superiority of the state, but obey a high authority within their own bosom; an authority which rules, by the grace of God, just as the sovereignty of the State does."[22] Even stronger, Kuyper explicitly repudiated all theocracies. "We do not desire," he writes in *Ons Program (Our Program)*, the original 1879 platform for the Antirevolutionary Party, "that Reformed Churches receive the power to dictate to the civil authorities how they must apply the Word of God to the political arena." He adds: "In a pluralistic society [lit. 'mixed society'; *'gemengde gemeenschap'*], not only do we not desire such a theocracy but rather we oppose it with all our might."[23] The civil authorities must permit the church an opportunity publicly to express her "feelings" (*gevoelen*) about important civic matters, but this right is a right of *persuasion* only and must never become a legal right (*jure suo*) to dictate public policy. Kuyper adduces two reasons for this position:

21. Cited in James W. Skillen and Rockne M. McCarthy, *Political Order and the Plural Structure of Society*, Emory University Studies in Law and Religion, vol. 2, gen. ed. John Witte, Jr. (Atlanta: Scholars Press, 1991), 237.

22. Kuyper, *Lectures on Calvinism*, 90.

23. Abraham Kuyper, *Ons Program*, 2nd ed. (Amsterdam: J. H. Kruyt, 1880), 46.

1. Theocracy leads to tyranny and national corruption (*volksbederf*).
2. The church lacks the competence to determine specific public policy.[24]

Theocratic visions, in Kuyper's judgment, arise from minimizing the reality of sin and require a level of knowledge that is impossible in this dispensation. Theocracies are impossible because our human insight into God's ordinances as they must be applied to specific, concrete peoples and political situations can never measure up to the level of certainty required to say that a specific public policy or law is indisputably God's will.[25] Kuyper thus fiercely defends the independence of *both* the church and state from improper encroachment by the other on the basis of limited knowledge. The state is not competent to decide which religion, which church, is the true messenger of God on earth, and the church, in turn, is not competent — even with divine revelation in hand — to spell out the details of state policy and law.[26]

Kuyper's argument here is interesting because what he says about theocracy in *Ons Program* is directly relevant to all monistic, totalitarian social visions where gnostic elites, believing they possess universal knowledge, attempt to control, manage, and plan whole societies.[27] Few descriptions of the political future entailed by Karl Marx's monistic vision, for example, match the chilling accuracy of his arch-rival in the First International, the anarchist Mikhail Bakunin:

> This government will not content itself with administering and governing the masses politically, as all governments do today. It will also administer the masses economically, concentrating in the hands of the State the production and division of wealth, the cultivation of land. . . . All that will demand . . . the reign of *scientific intelligence,* the most aristocratic, despotic, arrogant, and elitist of all regimes. There will be a new class, a new hierarchy . . . the world will be divided into a minority ruling in the name of knowledge, and an immense ignorant majority. And then, woe unto the mass of ignorant ones![28]

24. Kuyper, *Ons Program,* 46.

25. Kuyper, *Ons Program,* 49.

26. The few exceptions to this in Kuyper's view will be considered later in this chapter.

27. A penetrating analysis of efforts by contemporary gnostic elites to impose their monistic vision on American society is given by Thomas Sowell, *Vision of the Anointed: Self-Congratulation as a Basis for Social Policy* (New York: Basic Books, 1995).

28. I am indebted for this reference to David Horowitz, *The Politics of Bad Faith: The Radical Assault on America's Future* (New York: Free Press, 1998), 109; the citation is from Sam Dolgoff, ed., *Bakunin on Anarchy* (New York, 1971), 39, emphasis in original.

Long before twentieth-century economists such as Ludwig von Mises and Friedrich Hayek provided detailed arguments why socialism *could not* work because centralized planning required a "knowledge" that could only be provided by the actual market mechanism itself,[29] Kuyper contended that such "divine" comprehensive knowledge is impossible for humans; there is no "organ" by which it could be accessed. Then, in a Bakunin-like prophetic insight, eerily prescient of twentieth-century totalitarian Communist and National Socialist party-controlled regimes, Kuyper adds: "Such an organ [of full and certain knowledge] *must* not be found because it would lead to either a divinization of the State or a secularization of religion."[30] Little did he know that within twenty years of his death in 1920, the twentieth century would witness nations falling prey *at the same time* to the evils of state apotheosis *and* worldly, caesarophilic churches, a combination tragically repeated too many times in the century.[31]

In spite of vigorous protests to the contrary,[32] conservative, evangelical Christian activists[33] regularly draw forth the accusation that their "real agenda"

29. See Ludwig von Mises, *Socialism* (Indianapolis: Liberty Press, 1981); this work was originally published in 1922. Also see Friedrich Hayek, *The Road to Serfdom* (Chicago: University of Chicago Press, 1944).

30. Kuyper, *Ons Program*, 73.

31. For examples of ecclesiastical capitulation to twentieth-century totalitarianism, see Lloyd Billingsley, *The Generation That Knew Not Josef: Marxism and the Religious Left* (Portland, Ore.: Multnomah, 1985); also Edward R. Norman, *Christianity and the World Order* (New York and Oxford: Oxford University Pres, 1979). On the acquiescence of Western intellectuals more generally, including churchmen, see Paul Hollander, *Political Pilgrims: Travels of Western Intellectuals to the Soviet Union, China, and Cuba* (New York: Oxford University Press, 1981). On the evils of the twentieth century in general, see Gerhart Niemeyer, "This Terrible Century," *Intercollegiate Review* 29, no. 1 (fall 1993): 3-10.

32. See, for example, Ralph Reed's insistence that "if religious conservatives took their proper, proportionate place as leaders in the political life of the country . . . civil rights protection would be afforded to all Americans without regard to gender, race, religious beliefs, ethnicity, age, or physical handicap." He observes that in spite of such repeated assurances, "there are still some who believe that the most frightening thing that could happen in America is for people of devout faith to become involved in public life" (*Politically Incorrect*, 10). Orthodox Jewish rabbi Daniel Lapin is even more direct. He is convinced that "all Americans who love freedom, whether or not they are religious, should be reassured, not frightened, by the reawakening of earnest Christianity throughout the land." Furthermore, he judges, the harsh rhetoric directed against public conservative evangelical Christianity, particularly by secular Jews, is a form of "anti-Christian bigotry" (*America's Real War* [Sisters, Ore.: Multnomah, 1999], 12-13).

33. Mainstream secular as well as religious media practically never speak of the "religious left," the media silence implying that such a creature does not even exist. For dissenting voices on this point, see Millard Erickson, *The Evangelical Left* (Grand Rapids:

is nonetheless to establish a theocracy.[34] Kuyper, as well as his antirevolutionary mentor Groen van Prinsterer before him,[35] faced similar characterizations of his own political work, and it is instructive that even *after* his Antirevolutionary Party had obtained and held power in the Netherlands, Kuyper's revised political platform of 1916, the two-volume *Antirevolutionaire Staatkunde,* remained firm in its opposition to "theocracy."[36] The eleventh section of chapter 8 ("Sovereignty") has the subtitle "No Theocracy," and Kuyper begins it with a reference to Léon Duguit's *Traité de Droit Constitutionel,* where Kuyper's own view is characterized as a *"Doctrine théocratique"* and contrasted with Duguit's own liberal view, a *"Doctrine démocratique."*[37]

Kuyper responds to this characterization by acknowledging that on the face of it there is no objection to referring to the neo-Calvinist, antirevolutionary view of authority as "theocratic." After all, Kuyper notes that he and his political movement, along with all Reformed Christians, do believe that "all κράτος, that is all power . . . rests in God and in God alone. In all spheres of life, including politics, all human authority is nothing more than instrumental of divine authority." Nonetheless, Kuyper judges the oft-repeated charge of theocracy against Christian political activism to be an unhistorical anachronism. In a broad sense one could refer to the ancient kingdoms of the East as theocracies where affairs of state were decided by the divine guidance given by priestcraft through signs, oracles, and augury. More precisely, however, Kuyper avers that the term "theocracy" should be reserved

---

Baker, 1997); Ronald H. Nash, *Why the Left Is Not Right: The Religious Left: Who They Are and What They Believe* (Grand Rapids: Zondervan, 1996). Erickson and Nash are both, in differing degrees as well as focusing on different aspects, critics of the evangelical, religious Left. Unusual in its unabashed and self-conscious use of the term "religious left" (or "Protestant left") is the sympathetic portrayal of an important mainline religious publication by Mark Hulsether, *Building a Protestant Left: Christianity and Crisis Magazine, 1941-1993* (Knoxville: University of Tennessee Press, 1999).

34. See Richard John Neuhaus's illuminating review of Ralph Reed, *Active Faith: How Christians Are Changing the Soul of American Politics* (New York: Free Press, 1996), in *First Things* 66 (October 1996): 42-45: "Ralph Reed's Real Agenda." A sympathetic critic of Reed, Neuhaus mentions but does not endorse the accusations of "theocracy" leveled against the Christian Coalition.

35. The modernist theologian Allard Pierson (1831-1896) contended that Groen was a member of the family of famous theocrats that included Plato, Hildebrand, and John Calvin; see his *Oudere Tijdgenooten,* 3rd ed. (Amsterdam, 1922), 120-41 (cited by Rasker, *De Nederlandse Hervormed Kerk vanaf 1795,* 2nd ed. [Kampen: Kok, 1981], 92).

36. What follows in this paragraph is taken directly from Abraham Kuyper, *Antirevolutionaire Staatkunde,* 2 vols. (Kampen: Kok, 1916), 1:273-74.

37. Léon Duguit was a professor of jurisprudence at Bordeaux. *Traité de Droit Constitutionel* was published in Paris, 1913. Kuyper cites from vol. I, pp. 24ff.

Fig. 7.1. This 1874 cartoon of Kuyper's first election to the Dutch Parliament, portraying a pulpiteer schoolmastering his fellow parliamentarians, is titled "A View of the Second Chamber," with the amusing double entendre lowercase elaboration below: "After Dr. Kuyper takes his seat."

for that specific, historical instance of Old Testament Israel and the *direct,* revealed rule of God over his people. That period is over, done: "Even in Israel it no longer exists." Attempts, therefore, to apply Old Testament, Israelite law directly to the rule of modern states are utterly misguided. Kuyper admits here that "unfortunately, many Calvinists have frequently been guilty of precisely such a move," and that is for him only an additional reason why the term "theocracy" is simply unusable for Christian political activism in the modern world.

Calvinism's "Theocracy Problem"

Before we examine Kuyper's own efforts to resolve the tension between acknowledging Christ's full Lordship over political life and preserving liberty of conscience in a pluralistic or "mixed" society, we need to pursue further his suggestion that Calvinists seem particularly prone to the "theocratic tempta-

312

tion."[38] This particular observation may strike the dedicated reader of Kuyper as somewhat odd, since he above all celebrated Calvinism as the foundation of liberty. Specifically, as we have noted several times in this volume, Kuyper saw Puritan Calvinism as the essential spiritual foundation of the American experiment in ordered liberty. Not only did Kuyper make this claim in his 1898 lectures on Calvinism,[39] but the conviction goes back to the very beginning of his public reflections on politics in an 1874 published address, "Calvinism, the Origin and Guarantee of Our Constitutional Liberties."[40] Here, as later in the 1898 Princeton Stone Lectures, Kuyper cites American historian George Bancroft: "My nation's enthusiasm for freedom was born from its enthusiasm for Calvinism."[41] Similarly, another favorite Kuyper quote from Bancroft: "The fanatic for Calvinism was a fanatic for liberty, for in the moral warfare for freedom, his creed was a part of his army, and his most faithful ally in the battle."[42] Kuyper buttressed his argument — that Calvinism was the origin as well as the guarantor of constitutional and civil liberties — with an historical argument: Switzerland, Holland, England, and finally America must be honored as singular examples "with a special certificate of suitability for political freedom. Outside their borders you will look in vain for the origin of our freedom."[43]

The reason is clear according to Kuyper. All four nations represent a developing political vision that reflects a Calvinist conviction about the full and complete sovereignty of God. There are only three possible options for political sovereignty according to Kuyper. The *popular sovereignty* of the Paris Commune in 1789, the Teutonic-inspired notion of *state sovereignty,* or a derived and limited state sovereignty *under divine sovereignty,* a sovereignty that yields further to independent sovereign social spheres.[44] In other words, a commitment to political liberty flows from and rests upon a conviction about the Lordship of Jesus Christ.

Kuyper's case for linking civil liberty with Calvinism and its key doctrine of divine and cosmic Lordship is thus both an historical argument as well as a

---

38. The term is inspired by Neuhaus's essay "Why Wait for the Kingdom? The Theonomist Temptation."

39. Kuyper, *Lectures on Calvinism,* passim.

40. Abraham Kuyper, "Calvinism: The Source and Stronghold of Our Constitutional Liberties (1874)," in *Abraham Kuyper: A Centennial Reader,* ed. J. Bratt (Grand Rapids: Eerdmans, 1998), 279-322; original (and fuller) translation by J. Hendrik De Vries published in *Bibliotheca Sacra* 52 (July and October 1895): 385-410, 646-75.

41. Kuyper, "Calvinism," 283.

42. Kuyper, *Lectures on Calvinism,* 78.

43. Bratt, *Abraham Kuyper,* 283.

44. See n. 10 above.

theologically based social-metaphysical one. Historically, as he saw it, it is the lands where Calvinism flourished that developed polities honoring and protecting liberty. But from the theological root principle of Calvinism — "cosmologically, *the Sovereignty of the Triune God over the whole Cosmos,* in all its spheres and kingdoms, visible and invisible"[45] — Kuyper also, as we noted in the previous chapter,[46] derived a *structurally pluralistic* social ontology with a clearly defined and *derived* sovereignty in the state, society, and church.

It is possible to find fault with details of Kuyper's Calvinistic historical argument, though even that other famous Genevan, Jean-Jacques Rousseau, hardly a card-carrying member of the Christian Coalition, nonetheless praised John Calvin for his contribution to — liberty! Said Rousseau: "Those who consider Calvin only as a theologian fail to recognize the breadth of his genius. The editing of our wise laws, in which he had a large share, does him as much credit as his *Institutes.* . . . [S]o long as the love of country and liberty is not extinct among us, the memory of this great man will be held in reverence."[47] Nonetheless, Kuyper's argument needs qualification and nuance. He overlooks the important historical contribution of the Baptists to religious liberty, for example.[48] And more persuasive than Kuyper's historical restrictions is Jean Bethke Elshtain's argument that the roots of political liberty and democratic polity need to be traced further back beyond the sixteenth-century Reformation to the early church. Her argument is simply that "Christianity introduced a strong principle of universalism into the ancient world even as it proclaimed a vision of the 'exalted individual' brought into being by a loving creator, not, therefore, the mere creature of any government, any polis, any Empire." The end result of this "moral revolution" was the endorsement of an "elemental freedom." "Liberated individuals formed communities to validate their newfound *individualities* and to shore up the transformed, symbolically charged good represented by the new social body, the body is one but has many members."[49] Thus the coming into existence of the Christian church as a many-membered unified body, and as an alternative society with its

45. Kuyper, *Lectures on Calvinism,* 79.

46. See above, 301.

47. For this reference I am indebted to its citation by John Witte, Jr., "Moderate Religious Liberty in the Theology of John Calvin," *Calvin Theological Journal* 31 (1996): 359-60; the reference is to *Du contrat social,* bk. 2, chap. 7, in Jean-Jacques Rousseau, *The Social Contract and the Discourse on the Origin of Inequality,* ed. Lester G. Crocker (1792; reprint, New York: Washington Square Press, 1967), 44 n.

48. See, *inter alia,* Ernst Troeltsch, *The Social Teaching of the Christian Churches,* trans. Olive Wyon, 2 vols. (1931; reprint, Louisville: Westminster/John Knox, 1992), 2:691-729.

49. Jean Bethke Elshtain, "'In Common Together': Christianity and Democracy in America," in *Christianity and Democracy in Global Context,* ed. John Witte, Jr. (Boulder, Colo.: Westview, 1993), 71.

own ultimate allegiance,[50] combined with its anthropology that gave new dignity to man as God's image bearer, can be said to be the main originating contributor to the world's history of lasting ordered liberty.

In fairness to Kuyper, it needs to be noted that though in public addresses as well as on the printed page he consistently and emphatically always traced the origins of a democratic polity back to Calvin, he did on occasion nuance his argument, as when he posed the following rhetorical question to the audience listening to his address "Calvinism: Source and Guarantor of Our Constitutional Liberties":

> Does this imply that I think everything remained dark until Calvin, and that the first light followed his appearance? Ladies and gentlemen, I reject so unhistorical a thought. Even the brightest genius remains a child of his time, and Calvin's majestic edifice was also undergirded by the past. No, the reformer from Geneva was not the first to mix the thirst for freedom, the distaste for tyranny, with the blood of the Germanic people. . . . When Calvin came on the scene the Christian church had existed for fifteen centuries; that she in her true spiritual offspring did not opt for tyranny had been clearly demonstrated by the hero of Tarsus to the Corinthians, by Ambrose in Milan to the Emperor Theodosius, by Wycliffe in his shackles, by Huss at the stake, and by Luther at the Diet of Worms.[51]

Kuyper here finds three sources of liberty — Christianity, the Teutonic spirit ("Arminius in the Teutenburg Forest and Claudius Civilis on our own soil knew how to break the chains of slavery"), and "the influence of the Renaissance, which gave a new voice to the heroes of Marathon and restored the splendor of the glory of Greece and ancient Rome." However, these three, Kuyper contends, worked at odds with each other. What was needed was a combination of forces whereby "the Germans' passion [was] channeled, the church purified, the Renaissance sanctified, and the three rubies strung on one chain." Kuyper's grand conclusion: "This Calvin did! The *power* of the Germanic, the *freedom* of the Christian, and the *nobility* of the classical he smelted in the fire of his spirit into that precious metal from which Holland minted its patroness, with Scripture and liberty cap competing on its legend: 'hac nitimur, hanc tuemur!' [by this we strive, this we guard]."[52]

50. This greater allegiance results in a notion of "dual citizenship" with a genuine concern for the earthly *civitas* checked by an ultimate allegiance to, and hope for (!), the heavenly one. The classic statement of this dual citizenship is found in the early church document, *The Epistle to Diognetus* (found, among other places, in vol. 1 of the Ante-Nicene Fathers).

51. Bratt, *Abraham Kuyper*, 312.

52. Bratt, *Abraham Kuyper*, 312.

Fig. 7.2. Gift presented to Abraham Kuyper by the ARP. Figure on top of pedestal is the Netherlands Maid, holding in her hand a banner on which is engraved Psalm 124:8. The two women on the lower base represent history and religion and hold in their hands respectively, *Ons Program* and the Bible.

There is yet one more mildly dubious Kuyperian historical contention that we need to note at this point. In an illuminating essay, James Bratt has shown that Kuyper misread the roots of the American order because he "magnified New England into the United States as a whole," thereby ignoring the South and, very ironically, marginalizing "the mid-Atlantic region and with it possible Dutch contributions to the United States."[53] Here too the broader judgment of I. A. Diepenhorst concerning Kuyper's use of scholarly arguments to buttress his journalistic and political rhetoric holds true: "Even though a careful researcher may sometimes find Kuyper's scriptural prooftexts a bit forced, even though the [historical] facts may now and then be reshaped to fit a clear and distinct pattern that had been cast from the mold of previously ascertained truths, even though disparate and mutually exclusive images were pressed into a new unity, one cannot deny Kuyper the honor of being a great and original thinker."[54]

Therefore, his small historiographical missteps notwithstanding, let us for the sake of argument grant Kuyper his general portrait of the positive role played by historic Calvinism in the development of liberty. We then need to ask historic Calvinism some tough questions. Let's begin with Calvin.[55]

We need not acquiesce with Roland Bainton's unkind judgment that "if Calvin wrote anything in favor of religious liberty, it was a typographical error,"[56] to grant that Calvin's description of the magistrate's responsibility gives us problems with respect to full religious freedom. The magistrate who, we must not forget, has legitimate coercive sword-power is called upon by God, according to Calvin, to uphold the first (duties to God) as well as the second (duties to neighbor) table of the law. It is therefore the task of magistrates to protect, promote, and nourish true religion as much as it is to punish thieves and murderers and defend the cause of the poor and fatherless.[57] Calvin finds it preposterous to imagine be-

53. James Bratt, "Abraham Kuyper, American History, and the Tensions of Neo-Calvinism," in *Sharing the Reformed Tradition: The Dutch–North American Exchange, 1846-1996,* ed. George Harinck and Hans Krabbendam (Amsterdam: VU Uitgeverij, 1996), 102.

54. I. A. Diepenhorst, *Historisch-Critische Bijdrage tot de Leer van den Christielijken Staat,* 2nd ed. (Amsterdam: Noord-Hollandsche Uitgevers Maatschappij, 1943), 117.

55. For a thorough and balanced treatment of Calvin and religious as well as political liberty, including the significant scholarship on the question, see the essay by John Witte cited in n. 47 above.

56. Roland H. Bainton, *Concerning Heretics. . . . An Anonymous Work Attributed to Sebastian Castellio* (New York: Octagon Books, 1935), 74; cited by Witte, "Moderate Religious Liberty," 361.

57. John Calvin, *Institutes of the Christian Religion,* ed. John T. McNeill, trans. Ford Lewis Battles (Philadelphia: Westminster, 1960), 4.20.9.

ing more concerned for intrahuman justice than for the honor and glory of God related to true worship. "No government can be happily established unless piety is the first concern." Pointing to the time of the judges in Israel, when each man did as he pleased because there was no king, Calvin notes that "holy kings are greatly praised in Scripture because they restored the worship of God when it was corrupted or destroyed, or took care of religion that under them it might flourish pure and unblemished." From this Calvin concludes: "This proves the folly of those who would neglect the concern for God and would give attention only to rendering justice among men. As if God appointed rulers in his name to decide earthly controversies but overlooked what was of far greater importance — that he himself should be purely worshiped according to the prescription of his law."[58]

Similarly the author of the 1563 Belgic Confession — who, significantly, was martyred for his faith — nonetheless penned a theocratic ideal paralleling Calvin's. Article 36 of the Belgic Confession, "The Civil Government," includes the following: "And their office is, not only to have regard unto and watch for the welfare of the civil state, but also that they protect the sacred ministry, and thus may remove and prevent all idolatry and false worship; that the kingdom of the antichrist may be thus destroyed and the kingdom of Christ promoted. They must, therefore, countenance the preaching of the gospel everywhere, that God may be honored and worshiped by every one, as he commands in his Word."[59] Similar passages can be found in other Reformation confessions such as the First and Second Helvetic Confessions, the Scotch Confessions, and the Westminster Confession, all of which attribute the same task to the magistrate.[60] The point here should be obvious: its fabled reputation for liberty notwithstanding, the Reformed confessional and theological world, no less than the Roman Catholic magisterial tradition of social teaching[61] and the oft-quoted statements of Thomas Aquinas on the legitimacy of punishing heretics,[62] must contend with a literary legacy of expressed theocratic desire.[63] The best society is believed to be a

58. Calvin, *Institutes* 4.20.9.

59. In Philip Schaff, *Creeds of Christendom,* 4th ed., 3 vols. (1877; reprint, Grand Rapids: Baker, 1977), 3:432.

60. See Schaff, 3:229, 305-6, 474-76, 485-86, 669-70.

61. A superb overview of Roman Catholic magisterial teaching on this very issue was given by Avery Dulles in a (yet) unpublished paper, "Religious Pluralism," given at a conference, "A Centenary of Christian Social Teaching: The Legacy of Abraham Kuyper and Leo XIII," sponsored by the Acton Institute and Calvin Theological Seminary and held at Calvin College, Grand Rapids, Mich., October 30-31, 1998.

62. On the question of Thomas's understanding of civil punishment of heretics, see Michael Novak, "Thomas Aquinas versus Heretics," in *On Cultivating Liberty: Reflections on Moral Ecology,* ed. Brian C. Anderson (Lanham, Md.: Rowman & Littlefield, 1999), 161-82.

63. One the best surveys of the entire Reformed confessional and theological legacy

Christian one where God's will, supported by the magistrate if necessary, is the rule of life. American evangelicals (along with Calvinists and Roman Catholics) must realize that when they enter the contemporary North American public square *as self-consciously Christian* citizens, they take the baggage of that theological, literary, and confessional/magisterial legacy with them.

Actually, for those who take Abraham Kuyper seriously as a model for contemporary, distinctively Christian social and political thought and action, the problem is even worse than just sketched. Let us open a small window into the world of Kuyperian political rhetoric, a world that has familiar sounds in it for those of us who have more recently heard the "culture wars" language of the contemporary American Religious Right. The date is May 12, 1891. (For orientation purposes, *Rerum Novarum* was released to the public three days later on May 15, and the Dutch Christian Social Congress where Kuyper delivered his rightly famous address, "The Problem of Poverty,"[64] which invites comparison with Pope Leo XIII's encyclical *Rerum Novarum,* was still six months away.) The occasion is the Antirevolutionary Party Convention in the city of Utrecht, where Kuyper's convention address carries the clarion title "Maranatha."[65] Kuyper begins by noting that this Christian cry is the crossroads dividing the ARP delegates from their political opponents. "To them the return of the Lord is an illusion hardly worth the laughter of ridicule; to us it is the glorious end of history — also the history of our national existence — which we invoke with the laughter of a holy joy" (207). Kuyper insists on the *political* significance of the "Maranatha" cry. What does it imply? "Just this: that, when the history of nations will have exhausted itself and cannot continue, the king anointed by God will appear to intervene in the life of *our* nation, to strike his sickle also into the harvest of *our* national life, and *to destroy* the anti-Christian world power with the breath of his mouth (2 Thess. 2:8)" (208). By contrast, "of this reality the Conservative, the Liberal, the Radical, and the Socialist have no inkling. . . . They refuse to acknowledge Jesus' royal authority in the sphere of politics" (208). If one does honor the Lordship of Christ, he to whom has been given all power and authority in heaven and on earth, Kuyper asks, "then obviously it will not do to confess all this of peoples and nations with-

---

of theocratic desire that the magistrate defend and promote true (i.e., Reformed) worship is the study committee of advice to the Synod of the Dutch *Gereformeerde Kerken* about deleting the offending passage on magisterial involvement in worship, chaired by Kuyper's fellow neo-Calvinist, the theologian Herman Bavinck, *Advies in zake het Gravamen tegen Artikel XXXVI der Belijdenis* (Amsterdam: Höveker & Wormser, 1905).

64. Abraham Kuyper, *The Problem of Poverty,* trans. and ed. James Skillen (Grand Rapids: Baker, 1991).

65. Text can be found in Bratt, *Abraham Kuyper,* 205-28; page references to this work will be given in the body of the text.

out applying it to *your own nation,* without taking account of it in the Netherlands *even today*" (211).

This "theocratic" confession with its strong martial-military overtones does not lead Kuyper to postmillennial optimism achieved by a progressive Christianization of the nations; on the contrary, he reminds his listeners of the scriptural teaching that "in the end" matters will get worse, as "an appalling *anti-Christian* world power [will arise] which, if Christ did not break it, would rip this whole world forever out of the hands of its God and away from its own destiny" (211).[66] This anti-Christian power, Kuyper contends, has already gained command in nineteenth-century Holland and Europe. Later in the speech Kuyper notes that a major difference between his audience and their political opponents is that they believe in Satan while their opponents do not. This calls for a *Kulturkampf.* The Maranatha cry means "you may not join them or connive with them. Nor may you abandon the country to them" (213). Heady stuff, and by merely substituting such contemporary villains as "secular humanists," "moral relativists," "liberals," "Democrats," very familiar to American evangelicals in the public square one hundred years later. Marching orders for a crusading army of theocrats!

But here is the remarkable thing: Kuyper, the general, openly admits that he had pitched this heated rhetoric so high to motivate his "troops" lest they get bogged down in the nitty-gritty details of the upcoming political campaign. Kuyper admits he is using fevered rhetoric to mark the enemy clearly, so that "we may experience a holy thrill if our basic drive is love for Christ. Only those who know that they are propelled by that love will be powerful in this campaign" (214). But, one wants to ask Kuyper, does he not know the enormous risks of thus demonizing his political opponents and triumphalistically sacralizing his own cause? Does he really want each election campaign to be a jihad? Well, yes, he knows the risks and, no, he does not want a crusade. In this same speech he pleads for fairness in appreciating the positive notes even in the anti-Christian choruses of the other side: "Nor in our own country," he notes, "would you be entirely fair if you failed to appreciate our Conservatives' *historical bent,* neglected to honor our Liberals' *love of liberty,* overlooked the Radicals' *sense of justice,* and counted as nothing the nobler Socialists' *compassion* with so much indescribable misery" (212). And then, amazingly, in an opposing vein, though he had just cooperated with them in a coalition government, Kuyper contends that the issue that separates Calvinist antirevolutionaries from their Roman Catholic compatriots "is the sacred cause of *freedom of conscience* for which we, like our ancestors, would again shed our blood

---

66. On this point alone Kuyper clearly parts company with contemporary Christian Reconstructionists and their "dominion theology."

Fig. 7.3. Kuyper addressing a crowd of supporters,
most likely a Christian school gathering.

and against which they, however accommodating their practice, remain fundamentally opposed" (219). And finally, once again the "good cop" Kuyper: "*Freedom of conscience* — precisely for that reason we must employ *persuasion* to the exclusion of *coercion* in all spiritual matters. . . . In the civil state all citizens of the Netherlands must have equal rights before the law" (219-21).

Hervormde Theocrats and Article 36:
Kuyper and Hoedemaker

In this vein we need to note that it was largely through Kuyper's initiative that the 1905 Synod of the Dutch *Gereformeerde Kerken,* in a decision paralleling Vatican II's "Declaration on Religious Liberty," *Dignitates Humanae,*[67] excised

67. Text in Austin Flannery, O.P., ed., *Vatican Council II: The Conciliar and Post-Conciliar Documents* (Collegeville, Minn.: Liturgical Press, 1975), 799-812. The key statement in the Declaration is found in the opening of the first chapter: "The Vatican Council declares that the human person has a right to religious freedom. . . . The Council further declares that the right to religious freedom is based on the very dignity of the human per-

from Article 36 of the Belgic Confession the troubling passage about the magistrate's responsibility to protect and promote true worship, destroy the kingdom of anti-Christ and promote the kingdom of Christ.[68] A brief historical overview of the context within and the process by which that decision was reached as well as a short synopsis of its key arguments is instructive for our understanding of Kuyper's views concerning church and state.

On June 17, 1892, after prolonged discussions, a union church came into being, formed from the two major defections suffered by the national *Nederlandse Hervormde Kerk* — the *Afscheiding (Secession)* of 1834[69] and the Kuyper-led *Doleantie* of 1886.[70] The two respective churches, the *Christelijke Gereformeerde Kerk* and the *Nederduitsche Gereformeerde Kerken*, merged into a new body, *De Gereformeerde Kerken in Nederland (GKN)*.[71] At the synodical gathering of the union church in Middelburg on August 11, 1896, eight delegates[72] who had voiced public reservation about Article 36 nonetheless arose to indicate their full acquiescence to the Three Forms of Unity.[73] Subsequently they submitted a *gravamen*, or

---

son as known through the revealed word of God and by reason itself. This right of the human person to religious freedom must be given such recognition in the constitutional order of society as will make it a civil right" (800).

68. See Bavinck, *Advies in zake het Gravamen tegen Artikel XXXVI der Belijdenis*. Page references which follow in the text are to this volume.

69. On the 1834 Secession and its consequences, see W. Bakker et al., eds., *De Afscheiding van 1834 en Haar Geschiedenis* (Kampen: Kok, 1984).

70. On the *Doleantie* see W. Bakker et al., eds., *De Doleantie van 1886 en Haar Geschiedenis* (Kampen: Kok, 1986).

71. See Rasker, 189-90. It needs to be noted that not all members of the *Christelijke Gereformeerde Kerk* joined the union church; some continued with the original church, keeping its name. See W. Van 't Spijker et al., eds., *Een Eeuw Christelijk-Gereformeerde: Aspecten van 100 Jaar Christelijke Gereformeerde Kerken* (Kampen: Kok, 1992).

72. Kuyper was one of the eight delegates to this 1896 synod who together submitted a *gravamen*, or official "objection," to Article 36. Among the others were F. L. Rutgers, M. Noordzij, D. K. Wielenga, P. Biesterveld, H. Bavinck, and J. H. Donner. It is worth noting that the signatories to the *gravamen* came from both groups (the 1834 *Afscheiding* and Kuyper's 1886 *Doleantie*) that joined to form the new united *GKN* in 1892. Only Rutgers, Kuyper's colleague in Church Polity at the Free University, was a *Doleantie* member; all the others were from the *Afscheiding* church. It is also noteworthy that the *Afgescheiden* clergymen were politically active, notably in the significant debates about the school question in the 1870s (see next section in this chapter), a political activity that was noted by Kuyper and Groen van Prinsterer; see H. Algra, *Het Wonder van de Negentiende Eeuw: Over Vrije Kerken en Kleine Luyden*, 6th ed. (Franeker: T. Wever, 1979 [1966]), 165-67.

73. At broader ecclesiastical assemblies (classis, synod) in the Dutch Reformed Church tradition, all delegates publicly indicate their full subscription to the doctrines taught in the Heidelberg Catechism, Belgic Confession, and Canons of Dordt. The wording of the Form of Subscription (taken from the CRCNA) is as follows: "We . . . do hereby,

official objection, against the clauses in Article 36 that called upon the magistrate to use his sword power to remove heresy and promote Christian orthodoxy. The signers of the *gravamen* stated that "believing this obligation to be in conflict with God's word, they were conscience-bound to refuse making this confession and to repudiate it." They called on the church to respond to their objection and indicated their full willingness to be further instructed by the church on the matter.[74] The 1896 synod appointed a study committee to deal with the issue and to consult with non-Dutch Reformed churches about the wisdom of changing a confession that had itself received international approval and acceptance (at the Synod of Dordt, 1618-19). Among the curious appointments to this committee were two of the sponsors of the *gravamen* — Herman Bavinck and Abraham Kuyper. When the commission failed to report to the 1899 General Synod of Groningen as well as the 1902 Synod of Arnhem,[75] new deputies were appointed to the commission and its mandate narrowed. The responsibility for obtaining advice from Reformed churches outside the Netherlands was taken away. The new committee judged that such advice would be neither effective (*doeltreffend*) nor necessary (*noodzakelijk*) because the number of such churches was small and their views on the matter were divided anyway. The committee in its final report also notified the synod that it had taken on itself an additional responsibility for narrowing its mandate to the specifics of Article 36 and that it had declined to set forth a more fully developed, principled, theoretical statement on the proper relation between state and church (3).

The report divides the commission's responsibility into two parts:

1. A determination of the validity of the *gravamen*'s interpretation of Article 36. Do the article's offending clauses really mean what the objectors judge them to mean?
2. If the *gravamen*'s interpretation of Article 36 is correct, does its claim measure up to a proper, biblical understanding of the magistrate's task? Negatively stated, are the objectors correct in their judgment that Article 36 is in fact an unwarranted teaching, "not in conformity with the Word of God, but in conflict with it" (1-2, 25)?

sincerely and in good conscience before the Lord, declare by this our subscription that we heartily believe and are persuaded that all the articles and points of doctrine contained in the Confession and Catechism of the Reformed Churches, together with the explanation of some of the aforesaid doctrine made by the National Synod of Dordrecht, 1618-1619, do fully agree with the Word of God."

74. *Advies in Zake*, 1-2.

75. The final report indicates that "one of the committee members had sought release from his responsibility" (p. 3). This is undoubtedly a reference to Abraham Kuyper, who had been elected prime minister in 1901.

On the first point, the deputies submitting the advice to synod did not take the cheap and easy route of contextually marginalizing the offense of the text. They cite Philip Schaff's discussion (and repudiation) of the tendency among some Scots Presbyterians to interpret similar objectionable clauses in *their* confessions "mildly" so as "to disclaim persecuting sentiments."[76] Instead, the deputies insist that the text be taken seriously, that is to say literally, in its original intent. After an extensive survey of other Reformed confessions, the teaching of Reformed theologians, and the practice of the Dutch Reformed churches, the report concludes that the passages under review in Article 36 intend to say that "it is the calling and duty of civil authority as such — without doing violence to conscience or invading private life — to use all the appropriate means at its disposal (legal stipulations, proscribing public religious observances, punishing sectarians and heretics), to guard the public square entrusted to its care by resisting and suppressing all sects, churches and persons that, in its judgment, are guilty of idolatry, false worship, or cooperation with the kingdom of the anti-Christ" (25).[77] In sum, the deputies conclude that the *gravamen's* reading of Article 36 was correct.

On the second point, the report tips its hand almost immediately when it states as a hermeneutic principle that the theocratic model of Israel's monarchy cannot "simply be set forth as a rule for Christian magistrates in our day," since it would violate the "boundary that divides the Old and New Testaments" (26). The following elaboration of this hermeneutic guideline is then offered:

> Nation and church were one and the same in Israel. God as Israel's King was her lawgiver and the monarchy as well as the cult *(eeredienst)* bore a typical character; civil and ecclesiastical discipline were identical. All this is changed in the New Dispensation: Church and state are independent of each other; spiritual discipline is distinguished from civil punishment; the typical monarchy is fulfilled in Christ's spiritual Kingship; making laws is entrusted to earthly authorities. *Therefore, it is contrary to God's intention that we apply Israel's laws directly to our life in the state.* (26, emphasis added)

What about the New Testament then? According to the deputies, God gave the New Testament church no clear command as to how a Christian magistrate ought to deal with heresy, idolatry, and the kingdom of anti-Christ (27). Paul's

76. Schaff, 1:791.

77. It is also worth noting here that the deputies point out that both the Reformed confessional as well as theological tradition primarily have in mind the Roman Catholic Church (9).

well-known injunctions (Rom. 13; 1 Tim. 2) deal with the response of Christian believers to a *pagan* civil authority; the New Testament is silent on the responsibility of a *Christian* magistrate. We cannot, they conclude, appeal to a *direct* New Testament command from God concerning this matter (27-28).

However, aside from *direct* commands, there is another approach to Scripture that does provide direction for Christian believers, also those with civic responsibility and authority. From the Old Testament theocratic administration, and especially from the New Testament teaching concerning the kingdom of Christ, it is possible to gather key *principles* that remain binding upon the Christian church and also on the Christian magistrate. Since our Lord's kingdom is "spiritual" ("not of this world" — John 18:36), "all attempts to extend his rule or to defend it by external coercion were repudiated by Christ himself as in conflict with the nature of his kingdom" (28). That this principle was to be held valid by his disciples in all ages and not just during his own sojourn on earth is made utterly clear in the parable of the wheat and weeds (Matt. 13:29-31, 36-43; p. 28). Only Christ himself has the right of ultimate judgment on the wicked. Until then human society, even a Christian society, is characterized by *simul iustus et peccator*. The report also adds that God never promised that he would give civil authorities the special guidance of the Holy Spirit so that they would be able to discern the true from the false church. In fact, history teaches (and the Reformed confessions profess)[78] that civil authorities often persecute the true church and protect the false one (29). For these and other reasons the report concludes: "Your deputies can come to no other conclusion than that the *gravamen* submitted [against Article 36] is correct and that the words of our confession to which it is directed are not in agreement with what the Word of God teaches us" (30). Though its task could be said to be finished with this conclusion, the report continued and spelled out what the commission deputies judged to be the two key *Reformed principles (Gereformeerde beginselen)* on church-state matters:

1. Freedom of conscience.
2. Church and state are two independent powers that ought not violate each other's domain.

At the Synod of Utrecht in 1905, the *Gereformeerde Kerken in Nederland* removed the offending phrases from its official text of the Belgic Confession.[79]

---

78. See Belgic Confession, Article 29.
79. See H. C. Endedijk, *De Gereformeerde Kerken in Nederland: Deel I, 1892-1936* (Kampen: Kok, 1990), 105-7.

This step toward acknowledging the legitimacy of what can rightfully be called a confessionally *neutral* state was precisely the bone of contention between Kuyper and significant sympathetic political adversaries in the national *Hervormde Kerk,* including his onetime colleague in the theology faculty at the Free University, Philippus Jacobus Hoedemaker (1839-1910).[80] Hoedemaker was born in Utrecht in a family that was ecclesiastically "mixed"; his father was from Seceder stock, his mother a member of the national *Hervormde Kerk.* The family emigrated to the United States in 1851, settling in Kalamazoo, Michigan. Hoedemaker studied theology at the seminary of the Reformed Church in America in New Brunswick, New Jersey, and later also at a Congregational seminary in Chicago. After serving for one year as minister in the Olivet Church of Chicago, Hoedemaker returned to Europe, in 1862, studying for one year in Germany before returning to the city of his birth. In 1867 he completed his doctoral studies at the University of Utrecht with a dissertation entitled "The Problem of Freedom and the Theistic Idea of God," a critical examination of the modernist, determinist theology represented in the Netherlands by the great University of Leiden theologian J. H. Scholten, one of Abraham Kuyper's influential teachers. Hoedemaker was Kuyper's soul mate as to whether significant reform was needed in the National Reformed Church, but his vision for the method of reform was markedly different. Hoedemaker's sympathies for Kuyper's program were sufficient to enable him to join the Free University theology faculty when the school opened in 1880, but he resigned in 1887 when it became apparent that Kuyper's reform efforts had led to an irrevocable split from the national church.

80. On Hoedemaker and his theology in general, see G. Ph. Scheers, *Philippus Jacobus Hoedemaker* (Wageningen, 1937); R. H. Bremmer, *Kuyper, Hoedemaker en de Doleantie* (Apeldoorn, 1986); G. Abma and J. De Bruijn, eds., *Hoedemaker Herdacht* (Baarn: Ten Have, 1989); L. G. Zwanenburg, "Wormser en Hoedemaker," in *Rondom de Doopvont,* ed. W. Van't Spijker et al. (Kampen: De Groot Goudriaan, 1983), 427-45. More specifically on the political dimensions of Hoedemaker's theology and the critical differences with Kuyper, also on Belgic Confession, Article 36, see Ph. J. Hoedemaker, *Artikel XXXVI onzer Nederduitsche Geloofsbelijdenis tegenover Dr. A Kuijper Gehandhaafd* (Amsterdam: J. H. Van Dam, 1901); G. J. J. A. Delfgaauw, *De Staatsleer van Hodemaker: Een Bijdrage tot de Kennis van de Christelijke-Historische Staatsopvatting* (Kampen: Kok, 1963); Diepenhorst, *Historisch-Critisch Bijdrage tot de Leer van den Christelijken Staat;* J. C. Rullman, "Kuyper — Lohman — Hoedemaker," *Antirevolutionaire Staatkunde* 9 (1933): 39-45; J. Severijn, "Artikel 36 van de Ned. Geloofsbelijdenis. Overheid en Kerkdienst," *Antirevolutionaire Staatkunde* 1 (1924-25): 261-75, 325-33, 369-82. The biographical details that follow are taken from J. De Bruijn's essay, "Philippus Jacobus Hoedemaker: Een Biographische Schets," in *Hoedemaker Herdacht,* 11-30.

The two men were united in their opposition to the reorganization of the Dutch Reformed Church that had been imposed upon it by King William I in 1816 after the restoration of the House of Orange monarchy.[81] This reorganization had established a national synod that functioned as a department of the state; local classes (or presbyteries) had advisory roles but no real governance authority. This development especially made disciplinary action almost impossible, whether for doctrinal heresy or for deviation from the standards of Christian moral conduct. Though Hoedemaker, himself theologically orthodox, shared Kuyper's concerns about the organizational deformities of the national church, he did not join Kuyper's *Doleantie* protest movement of 1886. Whereas Kuyper's ecclesiology[82] was oriented to the autonomy of the local congregation, seeing the national church as a *federation* of churches[83] linked by common allegiance to a written confession, Hoedemaker's vision began with the notion of the church as a *national* entity constituted by *baptism*.[84] All Dutch citizens who are baptized are members of the church, whatever their level of actual participation in its life. Thus, while Kuyper sought to effect church reform through *democratic* polity changes[85] that would empower the local congregation to bring about doctrinal discipline, Hoedemaker sought to maintain the organic, national character of the church and to achieve reform through effective gospel proclamation that called the church *as a whole* to be what it already was thanks to baptism.

Hoedemaker's trademark slogan and the title of a programmatic pamphlet, *Heel de Kerk en Heel het Volk (The Whole Church and the Whole Nation)*,[86] however, does point to another important concern he shared with Kuyper: re-

81. For a succinct summary of events leading up to and including the reorganization of 1816, see Rasker, 19-31.

82. A succinct overview of Kuyper's complex and subtle ecclesiology is given by Henry Zwaanstra, "Abraham Kuyper's Conception of the Church," *Calvin Theological Journal* 9 (1974): 149-81. Book-length treatments can be found in P. A. Van Leeuwen, *Het Kerkbegrip in de Theologie van Abraham Kuyper* (Franeker: T. Wever, 1946); H. J. Langman, *Kuyper en de Volkskerk* (Kampen: Kok, 1950).

83. See discussion below on Kuyper's "associational ecclesiology," 340ff.

84. Here Hoedemaker is an essential link in a series of Dutch Reformed theologians for whom baptism is the act of being incorporated into a national body. This list includes the nineteenth-century lay theologian J. A. Wormser as well as twentieth-century followers of Hoedemaker such as Th. Haitjema and Arnold A. Van Ruler. On Wormser see Zwanenburg, "Wormser en Hoedemaker"; on Wormser's, Haitjema's, and Van Ruler's significance broadly, see Rasker, 253-75, 317-30.

85. See discussion of Kuyper's *democratic* leanings above in chap. 5, 246-47.

86. Ph. J. Hoedemaker, *Aan Jhr. Mr. A. F. de Savornin Lohman. Heel de Kerk en Heel het Volk! Een Protest tegen het Optreden der Gereformeerden als Partij, en een Woord van Afscheid aan de Confessioneele Vereeniging* (Sneek, 1897).

Christianizing the Netherlands; the renewal of a Christian, national culture. As the subtitle of the just-mentioned brochure indicates — "against the rise of Reformed [people] as a party" — Hoedemaker was unwilling to concede any ground to those who sought to secularize the nation by marginalizing its Reformed identity. With respect to our earlier discussion about Article 36 of the Belgic Confession, in a book that appeared the same year that Kuyper became the Dutch prime minister and directly named Kuyper as his opponent, Hoedemaker vigorously and publicly defended the clauses in the confession that the neo-Calvinists found offensive.[87] In this work, with a charge that he must have known would cut Kuyper to the core of his being, Hoedemaker argued that Kuyper's willingness to retreat from the classic Reformed *national* vision to one in which the Reformed were but one "party" in a *confessionally pluralistic* society was, in fact, fruit of the French Revolution.

Kuyper, of course, also wanted a re-Christianized Netherlands, a nation in which God's ordinances were taken seriously by the entire nation. Recall here Kuyper's poetic testimony at the celebration of his twenty-five-year editorship of *De Standaard* in 1897:

> My life is ruled by but one passion,
> One higher urge drives will and soul.
> May breath fail me before I ever
> allow that sacred urge to fall.
> 'Tis to affirm God's holy statutes
> In church and state, in home and school,
> despite the world's strong remonstrations,
> to bless our people with His rule.
> 'Tis to engrave God's holy order,
> heard in Creation and the Word,
> upon the nation's public conscience,
> till God is once again its Lord.[88]

87. Ph. J. Hoedemaker, *Artikel XXXVI onzer Nederduitsche Geloofsbelijdenis tegenover Dr. A Kuijper Gehandhaafd.*

88. *Kuyper Gedenkboek* (Amsterdam: G. J. C. Herdes, 1897), 77:

> Voor mij, één zucht beheerscht mijn leven,
> Één hooger drang drijft zin en ziel.
> En moog' mij d'adem eer begeven,
> Eer ik aan dien heil'gen drang ontviel,
> 't Is om Gods heil'ge ordonnantiën,
> In huis en kerk, in school en staat,
> Ten spijt van 's werelds remonstrantiën,
> Weervast te setten, 't volk ten baat.

Though he shared the passion for the ultimate goal, Kuyper's proposed *method* for national renewal followed a different path than Hoedemaker's. Kuyper's passionate dread of all monistic social visions, a dread he once expressed in an address with the significant title "Uniformity: The Curse of Modern Life,"[89] shaped his understanding of *how* Christian influence should be effected in a modern society and state. In the third article of the Antirevolutionary Party platform, *Ons Program,* he formulated his vision in this way: "[The Antirevolutionary Party] also confesses [that] the eternal principles of God's Word [are applicable] in the realm of the state. [This is true] in the sense that the authority of the state is bound by God's ordinances, not directly, not even by direct proclamations of any church, but only via the consciences of persons in positions of authority."[90] It was this Kuyperian move away from national, institutional, ecclesiastically privileged *direct* influence on the state that Hoedemaker opposed. Hoedemaker insisted that it was not *individual conscience* but the confessing *national* church in its *public* witness to the truth of God's Word that must be the foundation and guarantor of the people's liberty. In his view Kuyper conceded far too much in acknowledging a *neutral* state that could only be influenced through *indirect* means by individual testimony or concerted political action of like-minded Christians. The church as church must have a public role, and the state depends on the church's insight into

---

    't Is om die ord'ningen des Heeren
       Waar Woord èn Schepping van getuigt,
    In 't volk zóó helder te graveeren,
       Tot weer dat volk voor God zich buigt.

For details on the translation given here, see chap. 1, n. 202, above. On another occasion — the "Maranatha" address of May 1891 (see 319-21 above) — Kuyper concluded by directly citing the last stanza from Isaac da Costa's poem "Vrijheid" ("Freedom"):

    For me, *one* goal drives me onward,
       Just one purpose stirs my soul,
    And rather may my life's breath fail me,
       Than I ever lose this goal.
    'Tis this; with holy, joyful heart
    To tear all unbelief apart
       And drive oppression from its throne.
    He who could crush Goliath's power
       Can free this land from evil's hour
    Through one united, heartfelt tone.

(Translated by Henrietta Ten Harmsel; the translation and Dutch original can be found in Bratt, *Abraham Kuyper,* 227-28.)

89. The first essay in Bratt, *Abraham Kuyper,* 19-44.

90. Kuyper, *Ons Program,* 1.

God's will if it is to govern its people well. Kuyper's approach would in effect amputate the ecclesiastical limb from the national torso.[91]

This nineteenth-century Dutch debate about theocracy may seem arcane and of little relevance to our current discussions about American evangelical public theology. However, when we see its direct application to the question of public education (then and now), the picture's focus is much sharper. To lead us into that discussion in the next section of this chapter, a brief summary of Kuyper's own characterization of the debate just narrated is instructive. There is an additional benefit for our purposes since it gives us yet another glimpse into Kuyper's *poetic* use of imagery and metaphor to clarify a point of principle and idea.

In 1885, just prior to his departure for Switzerland on vacation, Kuyper received a copy of a pamphlet written by the "ethical"[92] Dutch Reformed minister, J. H. Gunning, in which he accused Kuyper of labeling ecclesiastical opponents, including Gunning himself,[93] as "belonging to the antiChrist."[94] Kuyper took the charge seriously enough to prepare and complete a counterpamphlet before leaving for his holidays in the mountains.[95] For our purposes we need not examine Kuyper's elaborate defense against Gunning's charge but will consider only Kuyper's summary statement reflecting *his* understanding of the two different approaches to re-Christianizing the Dutch nation that were then present in the Dutch Reformed Church.

Kuyper poses the question directly: "In which manner should the influence of the Christ penetrate the life of the State?" In response to his own question, Kuyper observes that the two distinct directions he will be exploring at least agree on two important points:

---

91. Image used by Zwanenburg, 444.

92. The designation "ethical" (Dutch: *ethische*) is not to be confused with the moralistic approach to the Christian faith that one finds in liberal culture-Protestantism such as that of Albrecht Ritschl, but to a specific school of nineteenth-century Dutch theology that accented the personal and "existential" dimension of the Christian faith. For a discussion of this and other schools of theology in nineteenth-century Netherlands, see James Hutton MacKay, *Religious Thought in Holland during the Nineteenth Century* (London and New York: Hodder & Stoughton, 1911); the most thorough study of this school in comparison with neo-Calvinist theology is Jan Veenhof, *Revelatie en Inspiratie: De Openbarings- en Schriftbeschouwing van Herman Bavinck in Vergelijking met die der Ethische Theologie* (Amsterdam: Buijten & Schipperheijn, 1968).

93. The other two prominent Dutch Reformed pastors opposing Kuyper were Nicolaas Beets (1814-1903) and Daniel Chantepie de la Saussaye (1818-74).

94. J. H. Gunning, *De Heelen en Halven* (The Hague: W. A. Beschoor, 1885).

95. Abraham Kuyper, *Bedoeld noch Gezegd: Schrijven aan Dr. J. H. Gunning Jr.* (Amsterdam: J. H. Kruyt, 1885); citations that follow are to pp. 36-37 of this work.

1. Historically, the Dutch nation is a Christian nation.[96]
2. Christians have an obligation to influence the life of their nation in positive, Christian ways.

The question is not *whether* but *how,* and there are, says Kuyper, two strikingly different ways it can be done. He uses the metaphor of trying to heat a large building with many rooms. One way is to build a fireplace in each room, and the other is to build one large fire and then try to deliver the heat to each room by means of an elaborate system of pipes. In the same manner one can attempt "to warm up the building of State and Society by the Spirit of the Lord" in one of two ways: (1) "Diffuse the Spirit of the Lord through the building by means of invisible pipes and channels" or (2) "Build individual hearths in each room and let the warmth stream out from that which is set apart and distinct." Groen van Prinsterer, according to Kuyper, was committed to the second approach, while the "ethical" theologians in the National Reformed Church opted for the former. Kuyper follows this with another metaphor to reinforce the same point. He refers to phosphorescent paint *(lichtverf)* that absorbs light during daytime hours and then glows in the dark without benefit of a lamp or other source of direct light. "No lamp is visible to observers. The light [source] is unobservable and glows on its own." While the ethical theologians preferred this indirect approach, Groen van Prinsterer, says Kuyper, "insisted upon lighting his own lamp. He did not trust phosphorescent paint."

Lest the point of his metaphors be lost, Kuyper explains himself sans image. "Two systems [for spreading a Christian influence in society] can be imagined. *Either* one goes about *undetected* and [indirectly] seeks to permeate the *entire* building of the state with a Christian atmosphere, *or,* convinced that this is not possible, one *deliberately* and in *specific* areas shines forth the light of its Christian spirit." Kuyper then returns to the metaphoric mode and asks which of two Gospel parables — the parable of the leaven or the parable of the candlestick — is applicable to the life of the state. Once again Kuyper claims to be following Groen in contending that the parable of the leaven is restricted to the individual/personal Christian life of sanctification after conversion and most decidedly *not* applicable to the communal life of society and state. Concretely, this meant opting for separate and distinctly Christian day schools rather than "anemically Christianized public schools. Groen chose the *candlestick,* which in order to be able to provide light *must* be a candlestick set apart." The ethical

96. I am translating Kuyper's *volk* as "nation," though it should be noted here that "nation" should then be understood less in the sense of a legal entity and more in the sense of a "people."

theologians of the national church, in contrast, says Kuyper, chose leaven instead, opting for a christened public school *(volksschool gekerstend),* and spoke of the secularizing (neutralizing, de-Christianizing) of the public school as "demonic." "Which of these two is the true and right approach?" asks Kuyper. "That all depends on what God's Word teaches us about Christendom."

From this debate centering on the issue of education, it is clear that the matter of theocracy as discussed in nineteenth-century Netherlands is not as arcane and irrelevant as it may first have appeared. Social and political strategies about education, for example, are directly impacted by choices made at this level of public theology. Specifically, today, do American evangelicals who are concerned about the education of their children seek to re-Christianize public education — perhaps through a constitutional amendment permitting prayer — or do they acknowledge the appropriate neutrality of state schools in a pluralistic society and seek just means for creating separate and distinctively Christian schools? The precise framing of the issue in all its details is changed somewhat, but the fundamental strategic public-theological choice that must be made is the same. To provide a fuller picture of Kuyper's understanding of the Christian's social and political responsibility in a pluralistic society, we shall now examine the important nineteenth-century Dutch "school question."

The Shape of Confessional Pluralism: The "School Question"

The story of educational conflict in nineteenth-century Netherlands begins in 1806 when the National Reformed Church lost its ownership of elementary education thanks to a new state regulation taking over effective control of the schools.[97] Initially there was no effort to remove or downplay the Christian character of the schools; use of the Bible was not forbidden but even encouraged; and in many places school days were opened and closed with prayer and psalm sing-

97. K. De Jong Ozn, "De Protestanten en het Onderwijs," in *Bepaald Gebied: Aspekten van het Protestants-Christelijk leven in Nederland 1880-1940,* ed. J. De Bruijn (Baarn: Ten Have [Passage], 1989), 167. This essay provides a careful historical-analytic overview of the nineteenth-century debate. Thorough treatments of the struggle for "free schools," as seen from two different points of view within the broader group of orthodox Dutch Calvinists, are provided in two volumes: P. De Zeeuw, *De Worsteling om het Kind: De Strijd voor een Vrije School* (Amsterdam: W. Kirchner, 1925); and P. A. Diepenhorst, *Onze Strijd in de Staten-General,* Deel I, *De Schoolstrijd* (Amsterdam: De Standaard, 1927). For a more succinct summary see entry "De Schoolstrijd," in F. W. Grosheide et al., eds., *Christelijke Encyclopaedie voor het Nederlandsche Volk,* 6 vols. (Kampen: Kok, 1929), 5:107-8.

ing.[98] In addition, clergy of different denominations were given use of school facilities and time for catechetical instruction. The general assumption, however, remained that the state schools were in a significant sense Christian, even Protestant, because the nation itself was predominantly Protestant. It was particularly after the division of 1830, when Belgium became a separate national-legal entity, that a push for greater neutrality in education gained ground, particularly in places where there were sizable pockets of Roman Catholics. Increasingly the schools were pressured into the Enlightenment ideal of a generic religiosity (natural religion) rather than specifically Christian, not to mention Reformed Christian, distinctiveness. Concern about and opposition to this trend came particularly from the 1834 Seceder groups. The Seceders had shown their willingness to suffer significant persecution for their commitment to the Reformed confessions, to a doctrinally orthodox church, and to church discipline in defense of explicitly confessed and practiced holy lives of Christian piety. They were thus also willing, finally, to sacrifice for the education of their children. The greatest difficulty, however, was not financial sacrifice — though this was significant — but legal: the establishment of each separate Christian school required legal permission, and obtaining such licenses involved complicated, time-consuming processing by a government bureaucracy hostile to such schools. And then came the new Dutch Constitution of 1848.

From 1848 on the school question was fundamentally shaped by the "liberal" Dutch Constitution born in that great European revolutionary year.[99] "The main architect of this Constitution was the Liberal statesman Johan Rudolf Thorbecke (1798-1872), who had the English constitutional model in mind as he worked on this project. The Dutch liberals represented the rising bourgeoisie and advocated moderate reform along secular lines."[100] In addition to direct election of delegates to the second chamber as provided for in the new constitution, the government under Premier Thorbecke's leadership also hon-

98. *Christelijke Encyclopaedie,* 5:107.

99. For a general overview of the history leading up to and immediately following the adoption of the 1848 Constitution, see *Algemeene Geschiedenis der Nederlanden* (Utrecht: W. De Haan, 1955), vol. 10 (1840-85), chaps. 1-4; on the specifically constitutional history see W. J. Van Welderen baron Rengers, *Schets eener Parlementaire Geschiedenis van Nederland van 1849 tot 1901,* 3 vols. (The Hague: Martinus Nijhoff, 1948), vol. 1; on the socioreligious context and consequences see the background essays in J. De Bruijn, ed., *Een Land Nog Niet in Kaart Gebracht: Aspekten van het Protestants-Christelijk leven in Nederland 1880-1940* (Amsterdam: Passage, 1987); De Bruijn, *Bepaald Gebied.*

100. McKendree R. Langley, "Emancipation and Apologetics: The Formation of Abraham Kuyper's Anti-Revolutionary Party in the Netherlands, 1872-1880" (Ph.D. diss., Westminster Theological Seminary, 1995), 73-74; on Thorbecke see K. H. Boersema, *Johan Rudolf Thorbecke: Een Historisch-Critische Studie* (Leiden: Brill, 1949).

ored the constitutional provision for the free exercise of religion by approving the restoration of the Dutch Roman Catholic hierarchy in 1853. This move was politically costly for Thorbecke. The announcement from Rome of the hierarchy's restoration was accompanied with rhetoric that generated great anxiety among Protestants. In addition to references about "Calvinist heresy," the papal announcement also referred to "the strength of Dutch Catholicism growing daily."[101] A period of enormous social unrest in the Netherlands followed, the so-called "April movement,"[102] eventually leading to Thorbecke's ouster as the Dutch premier in 1853, an event about which the fifteen-year-old Abraham Kuyper exulted.[103] Nonetheless, in return for Liberal Party support, "the Catholic parliamentary minority tended to support the Liberal policy of the promotion of the secular public school system."[104] Both the character of secularizing "deprotestantization" and the strategy by which orthodox Reformed Christian parents were marginalized have striking parallels with the experiences of Christian parents in American public schools one hundred years later across the Atlantic. Here is an extended passage about the Dutch school situation going back to the 1840s from historian Harry Van Dyke's book on Groen van Prinsterer:

> [During the 1840s] the deprotestantization of the mixed state school was visibly accelerating. Not only was the catechism banned and all doctrinal instruction, however occasional and fragmentary, frowned upon, but in one locality after another, Bible reading was prohibited, often at the request of the Catholic clergy who were offended by nothing so much as the teacher's "protestant" commentary which often accompanied such readings. Lack of trust marked relations between many Catholic parents and non-Catholic teachers, especially in the preponderantly Catholic provinces of the south. North of the rivers, liberal Protestant parents persuaded school superintendents and school boards more and more to muzzle any "religious fanatics" among the teachers; orthodox parents, on the other hand, not blessed with

101. De Zeeuw, 168.

102. See Van Welderen baron Rengers, 1:87-109.

103. In his reflections at the (1897) twenty-fifth anniversary celebrations of *De Standaard*, more than thirty years later, Kuyper reminisces about his reaction to Thorbecke's fall as an indicator of his own political awakening as a youth: "I remember as clearly as though it were yesterday; it was in 1853, the year of Thorbecke's fall. He who stands before you now was at that time the most rabid anti-papist one could imagine and the April movement made me an anti-Thorbeckian of the strongest sort." Kuyper then describes how on April 20 he burst into his father's study, crying out: "Father, father, Thorbecke has fallen!" (*Kuyper Gedenkboek* [1897], 67-68).

104. *Kuyper Gedenkboek* (1897), 67-68. For details see *Algemeene Geschiedenis*, 10:96-112.

the support of the reigning elite, chafed under the growing emphasis in the schools on maintaining "unbiblical" neutrality toward religion and on giving "unprotestant" treatment of the glorious history of the nation. The royal decree of 2 January 1842 provided for one hour of doctrinal instruction a week to be given by a local clergyman acceptable to the majority; it further allowed the religious colour of state schools to reflect local conditions by providing for greater religious pluriformity in the composition of school boards and in the appointment of teachers. In practice, however, one dissenting voice was enough to remove anything "offensive" from curriculum and classroom. On their own accord, or else on strict orders, teachers avoided "controversial" points and retreated to the safety of a bland neutrality.[105]

Reading this, evangelical Christian parents who have in the last twenty-five years seen the elimination of prayer at all public school functions and the systematic removal of all *Christian* religious symbolism from the classroom — all in the name of "religious freedom" — might well wonder if the ACLU had learned its strategy by studying the nineteenth-century Netherlands.

The new Dutch Constitution of 1848 did guarantee religious liberty, also in the area of education. Article 183 stated: "The direction of public education is regulated by the law in order to respect everyone's religious beliefs. Free education will be provided, with the law regulating both the investigation of teachers' competence and the supervision [of the school] by the civil authorities."[106] Supporters of a forthrightly Christian education initially believed that the constitution provided them with legal grounds for establishing *free* local "schools with the Bible."[107] However, this constitutionally guaranteed "freedom" turned out to be much less in reality than it appeared at face value in the legal documents. To begin with, it turned out that such schools would have to be funded completely by parents themselves, in addition to their tax obligations for the general, public schools. Second, the road to establishing such schools, even when paid for completely with parental resources without any state subsidy, was still filled with bureaucratic land mines. The objection to such schools was that they were "sectarian" and therefore divisive, a civil threat. Furthermore, it was argued, "the public schools are Christian enough!" Protests against the injustice of such "double justice" by parliamentarians such as Groen van Prinsterer were dismissed as trivial. Groen reflected on a specific case some thirty years later in a journalistic piece published in 1871.

105. Harry Van Dyke, *Groen Van Prinsterer's Lectures on Unbelief and Revolution* (Jordan Station, Ont.: Wedge, 1989), 36-37.
106. Cited by De Zeeuw, 137.
107. De Zeeuw, 139.

Reformed Christians in the Dutch city of Goes attempted to establish a parentally controlled Christian school in the years immediately after the new constitution was passed into law but ran into one bureaucratic obstacle and legal objection after another. Here are Groen's reflections on this case:

> Thus it was in 1851 in [the city of] Goes. A number of parents *(huisvaders)* who were dissatisfied with the "mixed" public school expressed a desire to educate their children in conformity with the Reformed faith, in the truths common to the doctrinal precepts that all Protestant believers have in common. This they were willing to do at their own expense. Repeatedly this effort was denied. According to the mayor and other civic leaders, the *public* school was *sufficiently Christian.* In those days such folk and the deputized states served as the assayers *(keurmeesters)* of Christianity. My efforts in the Second Chamber [the elected body of the Dutch Parliament] to present the concerns of these fellow believers before the deputies evoked great *hilarity.* An outstanding debater — about whom we later had good reason to say: *quantam mutatis ab illo* [how much is changed from former times] — sought to console me with these words: "you understand the art *de faire montrer les choses* [of making grand display of things], that is to say, taking something of no significance and attaching to it an aura of great meaning."[108]

The strategy described by Groen here was repeated in other locales. "In this way [the authorities] tampered with the freedom extended [to Dutch citizens by legal right]."[109] One of the chapter titles in De Zeeuw's study of the nineteenth-century educational struggle captures the situation precisely: "Freedom without Rights."[110]

The struggle eventually became focused around the revised educational law of 1857 that directed the Dutch public schools to instruct children in "Christian and civic virtues" *(Christelijke en maatschappelijke deugden).* It soon became apparent that the former was understood in terms of the latter and that the two defining adjectives were regarded as functionally equivalent. As "Christian" came to mean nothing more than what is socially and civically important, the schools became effectively de-Christianized. After several decades of struggle trying to resist this trend, Groen finally concluded that Dutch public education was incorrigibly secularized and should be explicitly characterized as such by law. All pretense that the education offered in state

108. Cited by De Zeeuw, 143; Groen wrote this in his "Nederlandsche Gedachten" of September 27, 1871.

109. De Zeeuw, 144.

110. "Vrijheid Zonder Recht," De Zeeuw, chap. 5, pp. 102-32.

schools was somehow "Christian" should be exposed as a sham and its neutrality legally acknowledged. This meant concretely that Christian parents who did not want such an education for their children needed separate, distinctly Christian schools, and Groen not only used his journalistic and parliamentary influence to support that cause but also helped establish several societies for Christian education.[111] It was these efforts on behalf of separate and explicitly Christian schools tied to a repudiation of the Christian character of the state schools that elicited a fierce response among the *Hervormde* clergy who were committed to the notion of the Netherlands as a Reformed Christian nation. Matters came to a head in the election year 1869 when members of the Society for Christian-National School Education *(VCNS)*, in a series of meetings, debated a recommendation, supported by Groen and Kuyper, that the word "Christian" be dropped from the national school law and the state schools' full neutrality be openly and legally acknowledged.[112] It was time, the proponents of the recommendation insisted, to *legally* acknowledge the de facto "reality" of the Dutch public schools' religious neutrality; they were no longer Christian schools.

At the May 18-20, 1869, general meeting of the *VCNS*, Hoedemaker voiced his serious objection to the neutralization proposal. He argued that Reformed Christians could never be at peace with the "reality" of a non-Christian state. A non-Christian state was not only incapable of providing Christian education, morally it could provide no education at all.[113] Kuyper's response to Hoedemaker itself then became a critical issue in the discussion. Kuyper argued that the structure of the present Dutch government — i.e., as framed by the Constitution of 1848 — was deduced from *anti*-Christian principles. Intensifying his rhetoric, Kuyper even claimed that the false state-theory on which the Dutch government was based needed to be "annihilated" *(vernietigd)* because it was "Satanic." According to Kuyper, the goal of the Christian School Society ought to be the wholesale destruction of state-controlled education in favor of parentally guided education.[114]

Kuyper's position was that of a committed pluralist who objected vigorously against any encroachment on the religious liberty of all Dutch citizens. In

111. The *Vereeniging voor Christelijke-Nationaal Schoolonderwijs* (The Society for Christian-National School Education) was established in 1860.

112. For details see A. Goslinga, ed., *Briefwisseling van Mr. G. Groen van Prinsterer met Dr. A. Kuyper, 1864-1876* (Kampen: Kok, 1937), 361-71; meetings were held throughout the year, with the key decisions made in meetings at Utrecht on May 19 and 20 and June 5.

113. Goslinga, 363.

114. Goslinga, 363.

an address entitled "An Appeal to the Conscience of the Nation,"[115] given to the same general meeting of the *VCNS* in Utrecht on May 18, 1869, he made this abundantly clear. Distinguishing his own view from his understanding of Roman Catholic political theory, Kuyper insisted: "By contrast, we desire full liberty for each segment of our society, the unrestricted right to develop its own new national forms in accord with its numbers, its financial resources, its moral strength and spiritual gifts. . . . Precisely because we do not want to be shaped by externally imposed ideas but from those forces that arise from the very life of the nation itself, we oppose any and all coercion that comes from a single quarter of our nation." The crucial *content* issue in the education debate, according to Kuyper, was *history;* more specifically, whether Dutch national history was to be taught from a perspective that honored divine providential guidance in the development of Dutch *liberty!* Kuyper here picked up notes and chords that had been at the heart of Groen's populist, Protestant, Christian chorus: the self-consciousness of the Dutch people is a *Reformed Christian* self-consciousness; the moral conscience of the nation is *Reformed Christian,* and efforts to eradicate this consciousness will erode the liberty of Dutch citizens.[116] In Groen's own phrase: "Calvinism is the origin and guarantor of our constitutional liberties."[117]

Here we need to recall that this Protestant reading of Dutch national history was one of the chief reasons Roman Catholics supported the secular, Liberal political party.[118] Kuyper refers to the taunting suffered by supporters of a distinctly Christian education that their cause was only "the silly obsession of a photophobic sect,"[119] a taunt that Groen later, in general discussion at the same Utrecht meeting, turned on the supporters of the state schools by calling them "sectarian schools of the modernists."[120]

Though this thumbnail historical sketch reveals fascinating parallels with current school debates in the United States — the secular state versus Christian parents; a "Christian" providential interpretation of national (Dutch and

115. Abraham Kuyper, *Het Beroep op het Volksgeweten* (Amsterdam: B. H. Blankenberg, 1869); see, for the citations that follow, 23ff. I am indebted to P. Kasteel, *Abraham Kuyper* (Kampen: Kok, 1937), 81.

116. For a helpful summary of these themes, see J. C. Rullmann, *Kuyper-Bibliographie, Deel I (1860-79)* (The Hague: Bootsma, 1923), 53-57, and the references given there.

117. This phrase from Groen is the title of one of Kuyper's earliest and most famous single public addresses; for English translation see Bratt, *Abraham Kuyper,* 279-322.

118. See above, 334.

119. Cited by Kasteel, 81.

120. Rullmann, 62.

American) history and destiny; a debate about to whom the children belong — we shall leave the nineteenth-century Dutch school debate now and turn to a natural question that arises from it.[121] When a Christian political thinker such as Kuyper, who passionately believed in the providential historical destiny of his nation, nonetheless pleads for religious pluralism in society and for a neutral public school rather than a Christian one, does he then not encourage the secularization process? Are there limits to neutrality, to religious diversity? As we shall now see, Kuyper apparently did think so.

The Limits of Confessional Pluralism: Atheism and Multiculturalism

Kuyper's 1869 appeal to the "conscience of the nation" in his address to the Society for Christian-National Education neatly dovetailed two passions Groen van Prinsterer had brought to the nineteenth-century Dutch Christian-historical consciousness: religious liberty *combined with* national re-Christianization. To the degree that one could speak of this vision as *theocratic*, it was a theocracy to be established by testimony and persuasion rather than coercion. In a February 4, 1874, letter to Groen, Kuyper formulated his convictions thus: "Our foundational principle [*beginsel*] must not be [based on] an effort to [re]impose Christendom by means of direct or indirect coercion. Rather, if Christianity is to regain its free and unfettered territory, it must begin in faith; a faith that appeals to and thus emancipates the conscience of the nation and of individuals. [Only in this way] can the Christian faith rule our social and civic life."[122] Thus, long before obtaining actual political power, five years before the publication of the antirevolutionary platform *Ons Program,* Kuyper clearly articulated a political vision that repudiated theocracy, insisted on freedom of religion and noncoercion, and used a persuasive appeal to conscience, to the *national* conscience. It is here that Kuyper's claim to be a "Christian democrat" or a "Christian liberal" derives its credibility.[123]

121. In addition to the question of religious pluralism and its limits, the Utrecht confrontation also raises the issue of limits on religiously based political rhetoric. One of Kuyper's key opponents in the school struggle, the Dutch Reformed minister Nicolaas Beets, turned on Kuyper at the same meeting and called his use of the term "Satanic" to describe the foundational ideas of the Dutch state "demonic" (Rullmann, 63). The problem of demonizing one's political opponents will be considered in the next chapter, on "culture wars."

122. Goslinga, 279.

123. On the latter term see Goslinga, 280; on the former see app. C below.

For North Americans it may be helpful to interpret Kuyper's vision here briefly from the twofold perspective of Alexis de Tocqueville and Martin Luther King, Jr., perspectives we have considered earlier in this volume. In a nutshell Tocqueville's argument in *Democracy in America* is that religious faith is essential for the self-governing moral disposition and habits required by a democratic society. Furthermore, the health of religion in America depends on the vitality of its *voluntary associational* character; in Ernst Troeltsch's terms, the sort of religion that is needed to sustain democracy must be *sectarian.*[124]

Tocqueville's remarkable insight into the genius of the American experiment was that its liberalism was not, as is often charged, reducible to individualism but to what might be called "associationalism."[125] It is despotism and not liberty that exalts individualism according to Tocqueville: "Despotism, by its very nature suspicious, sees the isolation of men as the best guarantee of its own permanence. So it usually does all it can to isolate them. Of all the vices of the human heart egoism is that which suits it best. A despot will lightly forgive his subjects for not loving him, provided they do not love one another."[126] Conditions of equality, however, do tend to foster individualism, which then, in turn, threatens liberty itself. Tocqueville salutes the wisdom of the American founders who "thought it also right to give each part of the land its own political life so that there should be an infinite number of occasions for the citizens to act together and so that every day they should feel that they depended on one another." Tocqueville concludes: "Local liberties, then, which induce a great number of citizens to value the affection of their kindred and their neighbors, bring men constantly into contact, despite the instincts which separate them, and force them to help one another."[127] Formulated into a social "law," Tocqueville regards the following as "more precise and clearer" than any other: "If men are to remain civilized or to become civilized, the art of association must develop among them at the same speed as equality of conditions spread."[128]

Kuyper understood well this Tocquevillian insight. We have already taken note of his own insistence, formulated in Article 10 of the Antirevolutionary

124. Alexis de Tocqueville, *Democracy in America*, trans. George Lawrence, ed. J. P. Mayer (New York: Harper & Row, 1966), 240-45, 287-301, 442-49, 509-24; Troeltsch, 2:993-94.

125. This insight has recently been "rediscovered" by Barry Alan Shain, *The Myth of American Individualism: The Protestant Origins of American Political Thought* (Princeton: Princeton University Press, 1994).

126. Tocqueville, 509.

127. Tocqueville, 510-11.

128. Tocqueville, 517.

Party's platform, *Ons Program*, on the desirability of shifting political power away from federal to local jurisdictions.[129] The same *associational* bias can be seen in Kuyper's ecclesiology. In keeping with his antitheocratic, anti*volkskerk* perspective, Kuyper pleaded for ecclesial communities characterized by what he called "a free multiformity."[130] Church reform, he insisted, was not to be achieved by repristinating a past ideal national church unity, an approach that was nothing more than an effort "to restore an ecclesiastical form that has already proven unfit. Any new church formation, no matter what, should first of all completely purge away the curse of uniformity, which is the mother of lies." Then follows Kuyper's twofold plea for freedom of conscience and freedom of association; genuine liberty tolerates no coercion:

> Nothing should be forced and nothing united which is not organically one. If there are people of good will who are one in mind and spirit, let them join together and courageously confess the faith of their hearts, but let them not claim any greater unity than that which is really their common possession. Thus, with complete autonomy let groups and circles unite who know what they want, know what they confess, and possess an actual not merely a nominal, unity. If here and there such circles exist which share a common life-trait, let them become conscious of their unity and display it before the eyes of the world, but let it be only that feature and no other bond that unites them.

Kuyper insists he is not advocating congregationalism but, rather, that "true connections between souls" can only manifest themselves "by a voluntary chosen kinship" and "the life of a free church community can manifest itself only where that life finds its own form." Kuyper continues in that same address with a ringing appeal for a recovery of the *national* Dutch soul, a recovery that is essential if the nation is to regain and retain its liberty, a recovery that is impossible without strong religious faith: "So then, people of the Netherlands, if you want to remain a people, let godliness be your primary weapon in the struggle for independence and only secondarily artillery and sidearms. If you love your country, know your calling to become ever more devout, more religious, and believe that the larger the number of children of God who inhabit the land of our fathers, the higher will be the wall which protects its liberty."[131] Tocqueville would have understood.

Kuyper's appeal to conscience, as we also noted earlier, has parallels as

129. See above, 285-86; we noted there the striking parallels with Article 10 of the American Bill of Rights.

130. A. Kuyper, "Uniformity: The Curse of Modern Life," in Bratt, *Abraham Kuyper*, 39; unless otherwise indicated, further citations are from this page.

131. Kuyper, "Uniformity," 43.

well to the civil rights rhetoric of Martin Luther King, Jr.[132] Here it is instructive to consider King's rhetoric paralleling Kuyper's strategy in appealing to *national conscience*. King's call to white America was always a call to the Christian, national American conscience. In addition to the exodus metaphor and Old Testament prophetic passages such as Amos 5:24 ("But let justice roll on like a river, and righteousness like a mighty stream"), King also appealed to America's founding and Constitution as moral grounds for just treatment of his people. Here is a characteristic passage from King's April 3, 1968, sermon to the Memphis sanitation workers:

> All we say to America is, "Be true to what you said on paper." If I lived in China or even Russia, or any totalitarian country, maybe I could understand the denial of certain basic First Amendment privileges, because they hadn't committed themselves to that over there. But somewhere I read of the freedom of assembly. Somewhere I read of the freedom of speech. Somewhere I read of the freedom of the press. Somewhere I read that the greatness of America is the right to protest for right. And so . . . we are going on.

King then joins American conscience with Christian content. "We need all of you. And you know what is beautiful to me, is to see all of these ministers of the Gospel. It's a marvelous picture. Who is it that is supposed to articulate the longings and aspirations of the people more than the preacher?"[133] That combination articulated by King illustrates perfectly what Kuyper meant by a *Christian* and *national* conscience, to which he consistently appealed throughout his journalistic and political career.

But this appeal, arising from and directed to the actual historical-religious life of a people, suggests limits as well as freedom for conscience and expression. In Kuyper's understanding the state is under divine obligation. Article 4 of the Antirevolutionary Party platform puts it this way:

> Civil authority, as God's servant, in a Christian (and thus non-atheistic) nation is obligated to honor God's name, implying the following:
> a. To govern and to pass laws that permit the free influence of the Gospel among our people;
> b. to restrict itself deliberately from any and all direct interference with the spiritual development of the nation;
> c. to treat all church fellowships or religious societies, and thus all citi-

132. See above, 72.
133. In *American Sermons: The Pilgrims to Martin Luther King Jr.*, a volume in The Library of America (New York: Literary Classics of the United States, 1999), 879-80.

zens, with absolute equity, indifferent to what they may believe concerning eternal matters;

d. to recognize the limits of its power with respect to human conscience, insofar as the presumption of respectability is not absent.[134]

The next article (5) sets forth corresponding positive obligations:

> Civil authority rules by the grace of God and derives its legitimacy from God. It thus has the right to ask [citizens] to swear an oath; to set aside the Lord's Day as a day of rest and to pass laws concerning Lord's Day observance that are beneficial to its citizens, to the extent possible refraining from its own activities on the rest day and by means of legal concessions encouraging all commercial enterprises to refrain from activity either partially or completely.[135]

Kuyper acknowledges up front that the antirevolutionary platform at this point clearly distinguishes itself from the "liberal" political vision. The key difference is that the liberal state is "godless," an "atheistic" state *(état athée)*. Specifically, though religion is granted a private, subjective place in the lives of individuals, the public square must be secular, naked of all religious elements.[136]

What Kuyper is arguing for in his exposition of the Antirevolutionary Party platform is a position that is neither theocratic nor radically secularist (liberal). With the tradition of classic liberalism (Locke, Mill), Kuyper wants full freedom of religion; he is opposed to all coercive violations of human conscience. However, he wants full freedom of religious *expression,* also in the public sphere. The difference between him and his liberal opponents, he says later on in *Ons Program,* comes down to this: "Our opponents want religion kept out of public life; they believe mixing religion [with politics] will corrupt government. We argue for non-interference [in religious faith by government] to preserve the holiness of worship." In other words, "the liberal seeks to restrict and enclose the life of faith within the most strictly confined and private limits while we seek exactly the opposite, the expansion of faith's power and influence as far as possible."[137] Kuyper believes that this free *public* exercise is essential for the nation's civic health; in Tocquevillian fashion he insists that failure *publicly* to recognize a higher authority than the state itself will inevitably lead to state apotheosis and tyranny. During and after his visit to America in 1898, he indi-

---

134. Kuyper, *Ons Program*, 2, 71; I am indebted to my colleague Henry De Moor for helpful assistance in translating this syntactically complex legal article.

135. Kuyper, *Ons Program*, 2, 90.

136. Kuyper, *Ons Program*, 72.

137. Kuyper, *Ons Program*, 76.

cated that he thought the American pattern had achieved the difficult balance between free exercise and nonestablishment, and he wistfully reflected on the fact that sessions of Congress and even military campaigns are opened with public prayer.[138] He wished that it were so in his beloved Holland.

As the language in the previous paragraph has suggested, Kuyper's position can be understood by considering the two key clauses in the first article of America's Bill of Rights, the nonestablishment clause and the free exercise clause. The full article reads: "Congress shall make no law respecting an establishment of religion, or prohibiting the free exercise thereof." The intense legal debate in American courts during the second half of the twentieth century was usually framed by pitting the secularist advocates of "nonestablishment" against religious proponents of "free exercise." As Jean Bethke Elshtain and Nicholas Wolterstorff have argued recently, in separate essays, what might be called the "liberal strict separationist" position seems to have gained the legal day in America.[139] This view holds that "it's just too dangerous to let religious people debate political issues outside their own confessional circles, and to act politically, on the basis of their religious views."[140] Elshtain describes this liberal view as "strong separationist," by which is meant the view that "seeks not only a properly secular [i.e., nontheocratic] state — which we have — but also a thoroughly secularized society, one stripped of any and all public markers and reminders of religion." Not only are church and state to be separated, but religion must be similarly separated from all public life. Elshtain observes that implicit in this view is a reluctance to permit "free exercise of religion"; there is a deep hostility to religion. Religion must be privatized so that it will "become invisible to public life" and, hopefully, eventually disappear.

> There is in this position a built-in animus against the determination by religious denominations to sustain their own network of schools, welfare provision, political advocacy, and so on. It presupposes a harsh opposition between Enlightenment values and religious faith. Because there is a wall of separation between religion and society on the level of what holds a democratic society together — a unity that religion always threatens to disrupt — the secular state goes on a rampage and gobbles up society so that it, too,

138. See app. C below, 472.

139. Jean Bethke Elshtain, "The Bright Line: Liberalism and Religion," *New Criterion* (March 1999): 4-13; Nicholas Wolterstorff, "Why We Should Reject What Liberalism Teaches Us about Speaking and Acting in Public for Religious Reasons," in *Religion and Contemporary Liberalism*, ed. Paul J. Weithman (Notre Dame, Ind.: University of Notre Dame Press, 1997), 162-81.

140. Wolterstorff, "Why We Should Reject," 167.

might be thoroughly secularized. That, at least, is the dream outcome for ardent separationists.[141]

In a phrase that Kuyper would heartily approve of since he used a version of it himself, Elshtain refers to this view as "liberal monism," the "view that all institutions internal to a democratic society must conform to a single principle of authority, a single standard of what counts as reason and deliberation."[142]

One of Elshtain's most provocative claims in this essay is that it is precisely where the liberal monist view claims to celebrate pluralism and diversity, thanks to its drive toward privatization, that it in fact "fosters a form of pluralism that requires uniformity and that winds up excluding religion."[143] By excluding public religion *in the name of diversity,* liberal monism not only marginalizes religion but undercuts the very foundations on which genuine pluralism is possible. The proof of this important point can be seen clearly in the currently regnant ideology of multiculturalism.[144]

Multiculturalism is ostensibly and potentially a vehicle for enriching all citizens with the cultural treasures of people other than one's own. However, in the hands of ideologically driven educators it has become yet another tool to marginalize religion, at least the Christian religion held by most of the citizens of the United States. According to one commentator, as practiced in many North American universities "multiculturalism really defends egalitarianism or permissive democracy against the claims of all cultures, even as it empties culture of its content by separating it from intense devotion to a particular country or religion."[145] In the hands of leftist ideologues, what is called multiculturalism is not so much an effort to empathetically enter into the culture of another people as it is a reason to provide critique of Western culture and its Judeo-Christian roots. In Lawler's words, "multiculturalism properly understood is a tool used to devalue one's own culture, meaning one's own religion, with the equal and incompatible claims of others."[146] One of the great ironies

141. Elshtain, "The Bright Line," 8.
142. Elshtain, "The Bright Line," 9.
143. Elshtain, "The Bright Line," 9.
144. A distinction must be made between "multicultural education," which "presents and examines the values and practices of other cultures objectively and critically in a nondoctrinaire manner," and the ideology of multiculturalism "that sees all cultures as essentially equal" except for "Euro-American culture with its Judeo-Christian underpinnings," a culture that is condemned for its "racism, sexism, and classism" (Alvin J. Schmidt, *The Menace of Multiculturalism: Trojan Horse in America* [Westport, Conn: Praeger, 1997], 3).
145. Peter Augustine Lawler, "The Dissident Professor," *Intercollegiate Review* 34, no. 2 (spring 1999): 14.
146. Lawler, 14.

here, according to Lawler and observed by others as well,[147] is that this multicultural critique of Western and American culture and society is itself a thoroughly Western project, cannibalistically feeding off the very cultural capital it seems intent on destroying.[148]

It is beyond the scope of this volume to examine multiculturalism in greater detail. We raise it here as an illustration of an important Kuyperian point. Kuyper's appeal to the "conscience of the nation," to the Christian understanding of providential, national purpose and destiny, has direct parallels with contemporary American conservative Christian political analysts and activists who insist that liberty and genuine diversity can only be maintained by staying true to a national mythology. There are limits to the kind of pluralism that civil authority should encourage. Though freedom of conscience requires that no one be coerced to act contrary to his or her convictions and the very idea of a "thought police" is repugnant to any lover of liberty, the government acts in a self-destructive manner when, in the name of diversity or pluralism or multiculturalism, it actively promotes religious beliefs or ideologies that have as their basic premise the denial of free, public religious exercise, particularly free exercise of the religions that are integral to that nation's very history and character.

In addition, it is apparent that even the most benign forms of multiculturalism[149] — celebrating America because it is now a mosaic, a community of communities or nation of nations[150] — are insufficient as a unifying national vision. As journalist David Brooks has recently observed,

> Multiculturalism, it is now clear, fails as an effective public philosophy. Whatever you may think of its merits as a creed, it indisputably has failed to

147. See Schmidt, *The Menace of Multiculturalism;* John J. Miller, *The Unmaking of Americans: How Multiculturalism Has Undermined America's Assimilation Ethic* (New York: Free Press, 1998).

148. Lawler, 14; cf. John Ellis, *Lost Literature : Social Agendas and the Corruption of the Humanities* (New Haven and London: Yale University Press, 1997).

149. Such as described, for example, by Nathan Glazer, "American Epic: Then and Now," *Public Interest* 130 (1998): 3-20.

150. Interestingly enough, this notion is precisely what Canadian nationalists trumpet *to distinguish* their national identity from the American "melting pot"; see John Porter, *The Vertical Mosaic* (Toronto: University of Toronto Press, 1965); Reginald Bibby, *Mosaic Madness: The Poverty and Potential of Life in Canada* (Toronto: Stoddard, 1990). The precise phrase "community of communities" was coined by former Canadian prime minister Joe Clark. Reginald Bibby is convinced that Canada is becoming a hyper-pluralist country, a situation he describes with a borrowed image from the prophet Ezekiel as "mosaics within mosaics" (Bibby, 8).

achieve what a public philosophy is supposed to achieve. It doesn't lift most people out of themselves and involve them in public life. . . .

Multiculturalism doesn't remind most people of our common bonds or renew pride in country.

Brooks then adds that when multiculturalism is of the ideological sort that nurtures hostility toward America, the problem is exacerbated: "It's simply unrealistic to expect a nation to embrace an ethos that prominently features guilt and self-flagellation. So it's no surprise that faith in public institutions has plummeted as the multicultural ethos has achieved hegemonic control over the schools and public discussion. If multiculturalism is the only public narrative on offer, then most people will cease to identify with public narratives and withdraw from public life."[151] To this we need to add that since the religious dimension of America's national epic is so central to most American conservative evangelicals, ideological multiculturalism marginalizes them from the deepest wellsprings of their patriotism and citizenship. They begin to experience life in their own country as something alien; it seems to them that hostile usurpers have captured the throne. A secular coup has taken place. Kuyper would have understood perfectly; it is exactly how he portrayed the secularizing liberal tendencies in his own country one hundred years ago.

What this all suggests is that the relation between religion and public life, particularly political life, is a delicately balanced one. The ideal of religious liberty itself is threatened no less by an "atheistic" civic polity that deliberately excludes religion and thus encourages an apotheosis of the state than it is by a self-consciously articulated theocratic vision. Kuyper was as rigorous an opponent of theocracy as he was a proponent of self-consciously Christian involvement in political life. He believed that the liberal vision finally would be incapable of sustaining genuine liberty and pleaded simply for the legal right to free exercise, also in the public arena. The civil authorities must permit free exercise, he argued, and while they are therefore not to privilege any particular religion, they also must not, in their zeal to be secular, arm non-Christian citizens who promote a "contra-Gospel."[152] That, for Kuyper, was what the school struggle was finally all about — the state schools were promoting a religion of secular monism that threatened the conscience of Christian believers and their free exercise. As he put it with grace and humor along with passion in his "Maranatha" address of 1891, pleading for "freedom of conscience . . . to be completely restored":

151. David Brooks, "Politics and Patriotism from Teddy Roosevelt to John McCain," *Weekly Standard*, April 26, 1999, 20-21.
152. Kuyper, *Ons Program*, 81-82.

All [the gospel] asks is unlimited freedom to develop in accordance with its own genius in the heart of our national life. We do not want the government to hand over unbelief handcuffed and chained as though for a spiritual execution. We prefer that the power of the gospel overcome that demon in free combat with comparable weapons. Only *this* we do not want: that the government arm unbelief to force us, half-armed and handicapped by an assortment of laws, into an unequal struggle with so powerful an enemy. Yet that *has* happened and is happening *still*. It happens in all areas of popular education, on the higher as well as the lower levels, by means of the power of money, forced examinations, and official hierarchy. For this reason we may never desist from our protest or resistance until the gospel recover its freedom to circulate, until the performance of his Christian duty will again be possible for every Dutch citizen, whether rich or poor.[153]

And, one might ask, why — then, as well as now — why this hostility to the public exercise of religion, particularly the Christian religion, even in politics? As Nicholas Wolterstorff has eloquently queried, why should twentieth-century Americans be so afraid of public religious expression? "So far as I can see," he observes, "the slaughter, torture, and generalized brutality of our century has mainly been conducted in the name of one and another secularism: nationalisms of many sorts, communism, fascism, patriotisms of various sorts, economic hegemony. . . . Liberalism's myopic preoccupation with religious wars is outdated."[154] Perhaps. But as we shall see in our next chapter about the "culture wars," the concern about religion in public life is fierce and opposition to it is mustered in full battle array.

Conclusion: Theocratic Rhetoric and Pluralist Reality

Before we turn to the subject of "culture wars," a final concluding word about the rhetoric and reality of theocracy is in order because it is here that much of the confusion arises. Aside from the basic problem we considered in the previous section — the scaremongering tendency of liberal monists to cast all public religious discourse in the frame of potentially despotic "theocracy" — both the proponents and opponents of self-consciously Christian political activism need to be aware that there are distinct rhetorical levels or audiences involved. It is one thing in the relative privacy of a church basement meeting of a Christian

153. Kuyper, "Maranatha," in Bratt, *Abraham Kuyper*, 224-25.
154. Wolterstorff, "Why We Should Reject," 167.

Coalition chapter to use royal, theocratic rhetoric to motivate the political troops into action: "Jesus is Lord; those who deny him and are hostile to his reign need to be opposed! Let's together sing, 'Onward, Christian soldiers, marching as to war; with the cross of Jesus going on before.' This will be followed by singing, 'Stand up, stand up for Jesus, you soldiers of the cross.'" It is another matter, however, to indiscriminately use similar martial imagery in the public square, knowing full well that skeptical non-Christian fellow citizens and even reporters who may be hostile to the cause are listening. Without capitulating in any way to the radical privatization of religion favored by liberal monists, Christian political activists must be aware of the different arenas in which their speech is heard and reported, and they need to accommodate themselves to this difference.

There is evidence that this awareness is beginning to develop among American evangelical activists. An article in *Focus*, a journal of Pat Robertson's Regent University, recently argued this same point: "To put it bluntly, if the religious right does not want a theocracy in the United States, then its speakers should adopt a rhetorical strategy that does not continue to give people the impression that they do." Noting that too many statements from the Religious Right are identical in form to the classic Puritan jeremiad, the author pleads for evangelical political activists to use another rhetorical form.

> The Puritan jeremiad has led to much confusion. Perhaps it should now be replaced or at least supplemented with approaches that reassure today's diverse audience that the religious right wants to include them in, rather than exclude them from, the community of Americans. Finally it's clear that politically active Christians must struggle to maintain a delicate balance between two difficult and very different duties. They must try to uphold, with their left hand, convictions about what they believe are immutable moral laws, while, with their right hand, they must continue to demonstrate the love of God to those who don't yet believe in him. The religious right might be able to correct some of the popular misconceptions about its goals by leaning its future rhetoric more towards the right.[155]

This is sound advice that also requires a fair turn in response. Surely it is not too much to ask secular journalists to make similar, appropriate rhetorical audience distinctions when commenting on the political activism of conservative evangelical Christians.[156] Contrary to the fevered rhetoric of some fierce oppo-

155. Pamela Robles, *Focus* (summer 1994); cited by Richard John Neuhaus, The Public Square, *First Things*, no. 78 (December 1997): 76.
156. This caution is not necessary for news commentary about the Religious Left.

nents of the Religious Right, singing "Onward, Christian Soldiers" in a church service does not automatically turn evangelical Christians into jihadic crusaders setting out to bomb abortion clinics. Surely this is so obvious as to hardly deserve repeating. However, the problem with any such rhetorical and journalist cease-fire is that the martial imagery is fitting; there *is* a culture *war* going on in America! To that we must now turn.

CHAPTER EIGHT

Ecumenical Jihad:
The Surprising Evangelical-Catholic Culture War Cobelligerency[1]

Onward, Christian soldiers,
Marching as to war,
With the cross of Jesus going on before.

Sabine Baring-Gould

Demonology is the shadow of theology.

Ralph Waldo Emerson

Every difference of opinion is not a difference of principle.

Thomas Jefferson, First Inaugural, 1801

Something there is that doesn't love a wall.

Robert Frost

A House divided against itself cannot stand.

Abraham Lincoln

All your strength is in your union.
All your danger is in discord.

Henry Wadsworth Longfellow

1. This title is inspired by Peter Kreeft, *Ecumenical Jihad: Ecumenism and the Culture War* (San Francisco: Ignatius, 1996).

351

We has met the enemy and it is us.

Pogo (Walt Kelly)

In America today, the only respectable form of bigotry is bigotry directed at religious people.

William Bennett

On a number of occasions in this volume, we have encountered Abraham Kuyper's use of martial, military rhetoric. Kuyper, we noted at the very beginning of the first chapter, believed it was his special calling to enlist the army of God's faithful to do battle against the dark forces of evil modernism that came to full expression in the French Revolution's slogan *ni Dieu, ni maître*. This Augustinian "two cities" spiritual sensitivity, however, so we saw in the previous chapter, did not lead Kuyper to theocratic triumphalism but to a love for liberty and a political commitment to confessional as well as structural pluralism. Though Kuyper's rhetoric often sounded liberationist and theocratic ("Jesus is King . . . let my people go!"), his political practice affirmed freedom of conscience and full civil rights for all Dutch citizens, not just Calvinists. Kuyper demonstrated this concretely when, notwithstanding his fundamental conviction that the Roman Catholic tradition was opposed to full religious and political liberty, he still initiated and brought to fruition a successful political coalition with Roman Catholics as full and equal partners.[2]

Kuyper's action here reflected his profound conviction that "though the history of the reformation has established a fundamental antithesis between Rome and ourselves, it would be narrow-minded and short-sighted to underestimate the real power which even now is manifest in Rome's warfare against Atheism and Pantheism." While Kuyper insists that there remain significant matters of doctrine in which "we are as unflinchingly opposed to Rome as our fathers were," nonetheless it should be immediately obvious, he adds, "that what we have in common with Rome concerns precisely those fundamentals of our Christian creed now most fiercely assaulted by the modern spirit."[3] Against the deconstructive spirit of the French Revolution, Kuyper quite reasonably regarded Roman Catholics as comrades in arms. It is also precisely here that American evangelical leader Charles Colson appeals to Kuyper as a primary inspiration for Colson's own active involvement and leadership in the ecumeni-

2. See P. Kasteel, *Abraham Kuyper* (Kampen: Kok, 1938), 93-151.
3. Abraham Kuyper, *Lectures on Calvinism* (Grand Rapids: Eerdmans, 1931), 183.

cal-cultural alliance Evangelicals and Catholics Together (ECT).[4] Colson had made the appeal for evangelical-Catholic cooperation against the modernist revolutionary culture of death and destruction already in his inspiring and influential book *The Body*,[5] a *cri de coeur* for a deeper, stronger American evangelical ecclesiology. Kuyper would have understood and applauded Colson's explanation for the ECT alliance:

> To bring God's truth about the public good into the public square and to resist the abortionists and mercy-killers, the relativists and the tyrants, Christians must stand together. The controversies that have divided believers for nearly five hundred years are real, to be sure, and none of them is to be minimized. However, the divisions between us are not the battle of the hour, when hosts of secularists and relativists threaten to sweep away the last trace of Christian truth, thought, and influence from our culture. Indeed, the controversies that divide us are far less significant than the common threat that confronts us.[6]

Colson insists that the "call to cooperation [between evangelicals and Catholics] is itself part of our heritage as evangelicals," and he cites two inspirations for such an alliance: American Presbyterian crusader against modernist theology, the Princeton (and later, Westminster) theologian J. Gresham Machen, and Abraham Kuyper. Colson cites the following passage from Kuyper's Princeton Stone Lectures, contending that the situation Kuyper describes for European Christians is "the very situation all Christians now face in America": "Now, in this conflict [against modernist liberalism] Rome is not an antagonist, but stands on our side, inasmuch as she recognizes and maintains the Trinity, the Deity of Christ, the Cross as an atoning sacrifice, the scriptures as the Word of God, and the Ten Commandments. Therefore, let me ask if Romish theologians take up the sword to do valiant and skillful battle against the same tendency that we ourselves mean to fight to the death, is it not the part of wisdom to accept the valuable help of their elucidation?"[7] We see here at the same time Kuyper's use of martial rhetoric and a remarkable transcending of profound and lengthy religious conflict (between Catholics and Protestants) in a cooperative ven-

---

4. See Charles Colson and Richard John Neuhaus, eds., *Evangelicals and Catholics Together: Toward a Common Mission* (Dallas: Word, 1995).

5. Charles Colson with Ellen Santilli Vaughn, *The Body: Being Light in Darkness* (Dallas: Word, 1992), 103-4, 106-7, 114.

6. Colson and Neuhaus, 38.

7. Colson and Neuhaus, 38; citation is from Kuyper's *Lectures on Calvinism*, 183-84.

ture of cobelligerence against a perceived greater threat. Furthermore, committed as Kuyper was to liberty, a liberty he believed was essentially connected to and guaranteed by the religious vision of Calvinism, he nonetheless strove to overcome a significant historical religious division with those whom he regarded as opponents of liberty at a moment when he perceived common cause against an even greater enemy. At all times Kuyper consistently maintained his commitment to full and complete religious and political liberty for all citizens, whatever their religious views. For that reason it is essential, as we concluded at the end of the previous chapter, in the case of both Kuyper and American conservative evangelical Christian political activists today, to look beyond the apparently theocratic rhetoric and grant spokespersons of the Religious Right the benefit of the doubt when they affirm their commitment to the American Constitution and civil rights for all citizens.[8] In both cases (Kuyper and the Religious Right), a willingness to shift allegiances and create new alliances with former religious and political "enemies" signals a greater commitment to freedom, a civic freedom rooted in religious conviction about liberty. This commitment to liberty, demonstrated in a track record of political action, must be acknowledged even by those who are uncomfortable with the martial imagery that fills the rhetoric of conservative, evangelical political activists.

But now we must also consider the flip side of this obligation: Does the use of martial imagery, such as the endorsement of "culture wars" language, by itself contribute to a hostile environment in the public square? Does thinking in battle terms ("under attack or siege," "engaging the enemy"), and using such language in public, unfortunately contribute to what Deborah Tannen has labeled "the argument culture"[9] and thus undermine key goals of the Christian gospel such as reconciliation? More specifically, in view of the growing lament about the increasing lack of civility in American public life,[10] does militancy of

8. Such as Ralph Reed did in his political memoir, *Active Faith: How Christians Are Changing the Soul of American Politics* (New York: Free Press, 1996), 28-29: "The salient question is not whether a religious tradition makes universal claims. . . . The real question is whether a religious tradition (in our case Christianity) attempts to impose its universalist theological claims by force of law. *We do not.* Ours is a public policy agenda, informed by faith but not dictated by any church. It respects the historical and time-honored separation of church and state while affirming the role of faith in politics. . . . Religiously-based activism is neither un-American nor undemocratic."

9. Deborah Tannen, *The Argument Culture: Moving from Debate to Dialogue* (New York: Random House, 1998).

10. Notably, Stephen L. Carter, *Civility: Manners, Morals, and the Etiquette of Democracy* (New York: Basic Books, 1998); cf. Richard J. Mouw, *Uncommon Decency: Christian Civility in an Uncivil World* (Downers Grove, Ill.: InterVarsity, 1992).

any sort — even if only rhetorical — not fuel the fires of uncivility? Is it, in fact, not itself a contributor to uncivility? Should we not call a halt to such rhetoric before the shooting starts?[11] That is the constellation of questions we shall consider in this chapter and, from a different angle, in the next and concluding chapter. Before we consider Kuyper's own example of one hundred years ago, we shall explore in some detail the current "culture wars" phenomenon in American public life, beginning with the question whether it is at all possible to avoid or transcend them.

Is Dissent from the "Culture Wars" Possible?

Gregory Wolfe, editor of *Image: A Journal of the Arts and Religion*, recently voiced his opposition to the use of martial rhetoric by editorially proclaiming that he had become "a conscientious objector in the culture wars." "I have come to the conclusion," he writes, "that these wars are unjust and illegitimate, and I will refuse to fight in them. If necessary, I will move to Canada."[12] Wolfe is not alone in his dissent. Evangelical author Tom Sine is convinced that "culture wars not only precede shooting wars but also provoke them. Growing polarization," he notes, "inevitably raises the stakes, first producing increasingly fiery rhetoric and then including violence. Extreme speech is inextricably bound up with extreme acts." By now, Sine claims, the Holocaust and other examples of twentieth-century genocide should have taught us "that inflamed speech and the demonizing of our enemies will inevitably lead to the shedding of blood."[13]

In somewhat more restrained tones, Richard Mouw has also pleaded for Christian public discourse to be more civil, noting that "when Christians fail to measure up to the standards of kindness and gentleness, we are not the people God meant us to be." At the same time, Mouw also insists that "there are times when it is appropriate to manifest some very uncivil feelings. . . . If I am going to be a more civil person, it cannot be because I have learned to ignore my convictions." He adds, "we need to cultivate a civility that does not play fast and loose with the truth," concluding, "The real challenge is to come up with a *con-*

11. The telltale title of James Davison Hunter's follow-up to his standard study of America's culture wars, *Culture Wars: The Struggle to Define America* (New York: Basic Books, 1991), is *Before the Shooting Begins: The Search for Democracy in America's Culture War* (New York: Free Press, 1994).

12. Gregory Wolfe, "Editorial Statement: Why I Am a Conscientious Objector in the Culture Wars," *Image* 6 (summer 1994): 3-4.

13. Tom Sine, *Cease Fire: Searching for Sanity in America's Culture Wars* (Grand Rapids: Eerdmans, 1995), 2.

victed civility."[14] Michael Horton takes a somewhat different tack in his book *Beyond Culture Wars.* Horton believes that the polarization in the evangelical churches between left and right thanks to the culture wars has derailed the church from its proper task of gospel proclamation; it is "no longer pursuing its authentic mission, broadly speaking." His book, he says, "is a call to the church to reassess its mission, its message, and its agenda." In addition, Horton contends that it is "dangerous" for evangelicals to throw themselves into such a battle; they are unprepared for it, they are theologically and intellectually unarmed.[15] A final example from the Christian academy: a collection of essays that is framed by what one of the editors, David Hoekema of Calvin College, says is a conviction that the common presentation of the culture wars is based on misunderstanding and misrepresentation. "Each side," he suggests, "has misunderstood and misconstrued the other. The conflict between postmodernism and multiculturalism on the one side, and Christian belief on the other, has been waged along the wrong lines of battle. Troops have been massed in defense of positions that have no strategic importance, while possibilities for negotiation and mutually beneficial settlement have repeatedly been spurned."[16]

Before we address the concerns about the cost to civility of using "culture wars" language, a few definitions are needed; we need to sort out what exactly is meant by "culture wars" and related terms such as "polarization," "demonization," and contrasting positives such as "civility" and "toleration/tolerance."[17] The standard work on the morphology of the culture wars remains James Davison Hunter's *Culture Wars: The Struggle to Define America.*[18] Hunter defines "cultural conflict very simply as political and social hostility rooted in different systems of moral understanding." He adds, "the end to which these hostilities tend is the domination of one cultural and moral ethos over all oth-

14. Mouw, 11-12.

15. Michael Horton, *Beyond Culture Wars* (Chicago: Moody, 1994), 10, 11, 27.

16. David Hoekema, introduction in David A. Hoekema and Bobby Fong, eds., *Christianity and Culture in the Crossfire* (Grand Rapids: Eerdmans, 1997), 3.

17. Among the volumes in the vast literature on this topic, I will be relying especially on those listed in the footnotes above and on the following: John C. Green et al., eds., *Religion and the Culture Wars: Dispatches from the Front* (Lanham, Md.: Rowman & Littlefield, 1996); Rabbi Daniel Lapin, *America's Real War* (Sisters, Ore.: Multnomah, 1999); S. D. Gaede, *When Tolerance Is No Virtue* (Downers Grove, Ill.: InterVarsity, 1993).

18. See n. 11 above; the citations that follow are taken from pp. 42-45. Hunter's framing of the issues does have its critics, particularly those scholars who are convinced that the whole "culture wars" phenomenon is a "myth." See Rys H. Williams, ed., *Culture Wars in American Politics: Critical Reviews of a Popular Myth* (New York: Aldine De Gruyter, 1997); also see n. 22 below.

ers." The core of this conflict, according to Hunter, can be traced ultimately and finally to "the matter of moral authority, . . . the basis by which people determine whether something is good or bad, right or wrong, acceptable or unacceptable."

Hunter's analysis is particularly helpful at two important points. He highlights the way the current cultural conflict (hardly the first in American history) differs from previous skirmishes in American religious and cultural life (such as those between Protestants and Catholics as well as those between different varieties of Protestantism). No longer do the key conflicts take place "within the boundaries of a larger biblical culture — among numerous Protestant groups, Catholics, and Jews — over such issues as doctrine, ritual observance, and religious organization." These earlier conflicts were characterized by a common framework in which there "were basic agreements about the order of life in community and nation — agreements forged by biblical symbols and imagery." In other words, previous cultural conflicts took place within an agreed-upon national mythology — a form of civil religion, if you will[19] — and the disagreements had to do with theological and ecclesiastical matters revolving "around specific doctrinal issues or styles of religious practice and organization." That has changed. Today it is the very foundation that is up for debate, "our most fundamental and cherished assumptions about how to order our lives — our own lives and our lives together in this society." Concludes Hunter: "our most fundamental ideas about who we are as Americans are now at odds." What is remarkable is that the new conflict, rooted in commitments "to different and opposing bases of moral authority and the world views that derive from them," has created a cleavage in American life that "is so deep that it cuts across the old lines of conflict, making the distinctions that long divided Americans — those between Protestants, Catholics, and Jews — virtually irrelevant."

This remarkable development in itself will demand our attention in a later section of this chapter, but we need here to note another important point in Hunter's analysis. Hunter emphasizes that "though competing moral visions are at the heart of today's culture war, these do not always take form in coherent, clearly articulated, sharply differentiated world views." Instead, Hunter speaks of two "*polarizing impulses* or *tendencies* in American culture." Coming directly to Hunter's point, he contends that "the cleavages at the heart of the contemporary culture wars are created by . . . *the impulse toward orthodoxy* and *the impulse toward progressivism*." The impulse toward orthodoxy he describes

---

19. See, for example, the classic study by Will Herberg, *Protestant, Catholic, Jew: An Essay in American Religious Sociology,* rev. ed. (New York: Anchor, 1960).

as *"the commitment on the part of adherents to an external, definable, and transcendent authority,"* whereas the progressivist impulse tends to define moral authority "by the spirit of the modern age, a spirit of rationalism and subjectivism." For those progressives that still "identify with a particular religious heritage," this impulse is characterized by *"the tendency to resymbolize historic faiths according to the prevailing assumptions of contemporary life."*

According to Hunter, these conflicting impulses affect the entire range of North American public life — family, education, law, the media, and of course politics. Hunter provides fascinating chapter-length sketches of specific conflicts in each of these areas. Here is a summation of his description of the battle in public education. That the public schools play a significant role in the larger culture war is not a matter of contention; both sides in the dispute agree on this point. On the one side, Hunter cites an opponent of censorship in public education who says, "This country is experiencing a religious crusade as fierce as any out of the Middle Ages. . . . Our children are being sacrificed because of the fanatical zeal of our fundamentalist brothers who claim to be hearing the voice of God. . . . In this religious war, spiced with overtones of race and class, the books are an accessible target." From the opposing point of view, a spokesman for the National Association of Christian Educators claims that "there is a great war waged in America . . . for the heart and mind and soul of every man, woman, and especially child in America. . . . The combatants are 'secular humanism' and 'Christianity.' Atheism, in the cloak of an acceptable 'humanitarian' religious philosophy, has been subtly introduced into the traditional Christian American Culture through the public school system. The battle is for the minds of our youth."[20] Once we stand back from the fierce rhetorical attacks coming from both sides of the conflict in education, perhaps the best vantage point for seeing the educational worldview clash is in the content of the textbooks used in America's public schools. According to Paul Vitz, a close examination reveals a deliberate and systematic rewriting of social studies (history) and literature textbooks to exclude traditional Christian values and even to eliminate direct references to the role of the Christian religion in American public life.[21]

20. Hunter, *Culture Wars,* 201; the second quote is from Robert L. Simonds, *Communicating a Christian World View in the Classroom* (Costa Mesa, Calif.: National Association of Christian Educators, n.d.), 6.

21. Paul Vitz, *Censorship: Evidence of Bias in our Children's Textbooks* (Ann Arbor, Mich.: Servant, 1986). A summary of Vitz's argument can be found in Paul Vitz, "A Study of Religion and Traditional Values in Public School Textbooks," in *Democracy and the Renewal of Public Education,* ed. Richard John Neuhaus (Grand Rapids: Eerdmans, 1987), 116-40.

It seems hard to deny *that* some sort of conflict about the moral foundations of American society and the consequent character of its civic life is taking
place, particularly with respect to the public role of religion in shaping the
moral foundations of American civic life.[22] When we consider the hot-button
political issues that are daily items in the news — abortion, affirmative action,
euthanasia, the family, gay rights, the media and arts — there can be little doubt
that America is embroiled in cultural conflict. Even if we choose not to characterize this conflict in Rabbi Daniel Lapin's terms as "the fiercest internal conflict
in American history since the Abolitionist movement in the 1880s,"[23] its reality
seems incontrovertible. In particular, matters of family life and education are
targeted for the rhetoric of warfare. On the one side are those who speak the
language of "an assault on the family."[24] On the other side is the proliferation of
bumper stickers that specifically target the "family values" language used by
many conservative evangelicals on the religious right: "Hatred is not a family
value." Here, too, spokespersons on both sides of the cultural divide seem to
agree that the issue of "family" and the related issue of education is one of the
key battlefields in the war. It is noteworthy that the debate about the family
does not follow the neat fault lines classically pitting American heartland evan-

22. There are, however, serious deniers (see n. 18 above). The argument of denial
portrays the culture wars as the overheated rhetoric of "extremists" and gives, as the major
reason for referring to the culture wars as a "myth," the evidence that most Americans are
relatively indifferent to the conflict and are reluctant to take stands on either side of the
cultural divide. Polls show that a majority of Americans are not involved and not interested in serving as soldiers in this war; ergo, the culture wars don't exist. It is of course true
that people of good will can read the cultural indicators differently and thus may disagree
about the existence, nature, and extent of the culture wars. However, this must be debated
on the basis of *evidence* — the extent of public square secularization, actual legal hostility
to free exercise of religion, the *tendenz* of American courts and media, and so forth — and
not on what the majority of Americans happen to feel about getting involved. It should
also be noted that *if* there indeed *is* a culture war going on in America, scholarly arguments
denying its existence are a major contributor to one side of the battle. Groups as well as individuals can be in denial.

23. Lapin, 1.

24. See Dana Mack, *The Assault on Parenthood: How Our Culture Undermines the
Family* (New York: Simon & Schuster, 1997); William Gairdner, *The War on the Family*
(Toronto: Stoddard, 1996); George Grant, *The Family under Siege: What the New Social En-
gineers Have in Mind for You and Your Children* (Minneapolis: Bethany House, 1994);
Allan Carlson, *Family Questions: Reflections on the American Social Crisis* (New Brunswick,
N.J.: Transaction, 1988). The role of the popular media in general, but particularly on the
family, is framed in the language of warfare by film critic Michael Medved, *Hollywood vs.
America: Popular Culture and the War on Traditional Values* (New York: HarperCollins,
1992).

gelicalism against the mainstream "Eastern cultural establishment." Books arguing for the reality of an attack on the family are being published by mainstream "secular" publishers as well as the traditional evangelical houses,[25] while books containing varying degrees of critique of evangelical "family values" get published by evangelical publishers.[26] Even self-styled religious and political "liberals" judge that the family is *the* chief arena of culture war conflict, and that many of the conservative critiques of liberal, laissez-faire sexual morality along with the push for legitimacy of "alternative family lifestyles" are valid. Liberals and conservatives are beginning to agree about some of the significant contributors to family breakdown and cultural dissolution.[27] Furthermore, both sides are inclined to see the conflict about the family as a battle for the very soul of American ideals and the future well-being of American society. James Dobson, founder of Focus on the Family, repeatedly speaks of the battle for the family as a battle for the health of the American *res publica,* and his most severe critics in turn have described his work as an attack on America itself.[28] Barry Lynn, executive director of Americans United for Separation of Church and State, contends, "James Dobson and Focus on the Family represent the greatest threat to constitutional liberties in our time."[29] The high-pitched rhetoric is an indication of how high the stakes are regarded by both poles of the cultural divide.[30]

Is it even possible then to dissent from the conflict altogether, to be what Gregory Wolfe calls a "conscientious objector to the culture wars"? Even if we could, would we want to? Is not even the *personal* decision of a man and woman to marry, to have children and homeschool them, a *political* decision, a

25. In addition to Dana Mack's volume (see n. 24 above), published by Simon & Schuster, we could also note Barbara Dafoe Whitehead's expanded version of her *Atlantic Monthy* "Dan Quayle Was Right" essay, *The Divorce Culture,* published by another major "mainstream" nonreligious publisher, Alfred A. Knopf (New York, 1997).

26. E.g., Rodney Clapp, *Families at the Crossroads: Beyond Traditional Roles and Modern Options* (Downers Grove, Ill.: InterVarsity, 1993).

27. See Don S. Browning et al., eds., *From Culture Wars to Common Ground: Religion and the American Family Debate* (Louisville: Westminster/John Knox, 1997). This volume is the first in a projected series, The Family, Religion, and Culture, produced by the "Religion, Culture and Family Project" from the Institute for Advanced Study at the University of Chicago Divinity School.

28. Gil Alexander-Moegerle, *James Dobson's War against America* (Amherst, N.Y.: Prometheus Books, 1997).

29. Alexander-Moegerle, 17.

30. The highly pitched rhetoric also adds credence to those who deny that there really is an important culture war taking place, who point to the rhetorical excesses as "extremists" at work and insist that the battle is not a broad society-wide phenomenon. See nn. 18, 22 above.

volley in the culture wars? Is conscientious objection at all possible? Upon closer inspection it turns out that Wolfe is something less than the total culture war pacifist that the title of his *Image* editorial implies. He observes that his objection "does not mean that I have no principles or refuse to stand up for them: I have strong opinions on most of these conflicts, and am willing to give voice to them when appropriate." What, then, is Wolfe's objection? "What bothers me is *the manner in which these wars are conducted*."[31] More specifically, Wolfe objects to the way "issues that are at root philosophical and theological have been completely politicized. In other words, genuine debate and reflection on the issues has been replaced by the clash of factions fighting for absolutist, ideologically pure visions . . . competing utopian politics that will not rest until there is a complete victory." Wolfe cites a conclusion reached by Hunter that we have reached a point in the cultural conflict where "the only thing left to order public life is power" and insists that, by contrast, "the urgent need at the moment is to recognize that we cannot reduce culture and its various modes of discourse to nothing more than a political battleground. The political institutions of a society grow up out of a rich cultural life, and not the other way around."[32] Furthermore, politicization cripples the formation of healthy cultures because it excludes the most important ingredient, religion: "The process of politicization endangers the ability of religion to permeate and renew the very culture that is being fought over. The culture wars might be likened to two gardeners who spend all their time spraying rival brands of pesticide, while forgetting to water the plants and fertilize the soil. Perhaps the most frightening thing about this syndrome is that it seems to betoken a pervasive despair about the very possibility of cultural renewal."[33] By contrast Wolfe articulates an alternative vision, one he calls "religious humanism": "The new religious humanists know that culture shapes and informs politics far more powerfully than the other way around. They recognize that symbolism, imagery, and language play a crucial role in forming attitudes and prejudices, and they have devoted themselves to nourishing the imaginative life. At a time when the model of Enlightenment rationalism is crumbling under the weight of post-modern cynicism and nihilism, the religious imagination can speak meaningfully into the void."[34]

31. Wolfe, "Conscientious Objector," 3, emphasis added.
32. Wolfe, "Conscientious Objector," 4.
33. Gregory Wolfe, "Editorial Statement: Religious Humanism: A Manifesto," *Image* 16 (summer 1997): 7. The difficulty with this stance can be found in the very first sentence. The very *possibility* of religion influencing culture at all, much less "permeating it," is exactly what is at stake in the culture wars. Radical secularists consider such possibilities themselves to be a violation of strict public-square neutrality.
34. Wolfe, "Religious Humanism," 7.

On closer inspection, then, Wolfe neither denies the reality of significant cultural conflict nor is he truly a conscientious objector in the culture wars; what he objects to is the *manner* in which the battle is being fought. Specifically he objects to *politicizing* the conflict and to the "scorched earth" military strategic goal of "winner takes all." Wolfe judges this to be a serious mistake, because politics does not create culture but the inverse. He thus suggests a different military strategy: not exercise of political will but a persuasive appeal to imagination. Here is Wolfe's summary of the mission for *Image,* the arts journal in which his "conscientious objector" editorial appeared: "*Image* was founded on the premise that Christians have an obligation to nourish the culture of their time, and to enrich their faith by deepening and extending their imagination. *Image* does not speak the language of politics but the language of art inspired by faith. That form of speech lies at the heart of our culture and it must not be allowed to become a dead language."[35] His ultimate desire is to have *Image* "play an important role in restoring a central tradition in art [i.e., the tradition of *Christian* art] to the public square in order to resist the forces that seek to politicize and tribalize civic life." Stated more poetically, the contribution of quality Christian art may help prevent the public square from becoming "like the place in Matthew Arnold's 'Dover Beach,' a country 'where ignorant armies clash by night.'"[36]

Wolfe desires, it seems, not so much to be a "conscientious objector" to the culture wars as to provide an *alternative strategy* to the *manner* in which the culture war is being fought. This is clear from a later *Image* editorial in which he praises the notion of "the artist as prophet." As Wolfe wrestles here with the perennial and thorny question of how the Christian artist, considered *as a prophet,* lives in the real tension — in artistic freedom — of necessarily shocking the sensibilities of the Christian community while at the same time being appropriately dependent upon and responsible to that community, it is striking how he describes the character and telos of public Christian art in his concluding paragraph: "The prophet and the artist may seek to disturb the existing order of things, but they should do so in the name of a deeper order, not in the name of their own genius. The artist will serve the community best not by worrying about either his own autonomy or the community's immediate concerns but by remaining open to transcendent sources of order. By keeping an eye fixed on the distances, the artist will do justice to both art and community."[37]

35. Wolfe, "Conscientious Objector," 4.
36. Wolfe, "Conscientious Objector," 4.
37. Gregory Wolfe, "Editorial: The Artist as Prophet ," *Image* 18 (winter 1997-98): 3-4.

Whether he is aware of it or not, Wolfe has here clearly chosen for and eloquently articulated (for the artistic realm) one of the two poles in the current culture wars. Wolfe's concluding paragraph perfectly restates the core of what Hunter referred to as the *orthodox* impulse or tendency.

We have indulged ourselves this somewhat extended look at Gregory Wolfe's attempt to "dissent" from the culture wars because his position — as an evangelical soldier actively engaged in the battle (in Wolfe's case, with officer rank!) while at the same time pleading for noninvolvement — is not unique. Later in this chapter we shall consider examples of "third way" proponents, political activists who masquerade their political partisanship by posing as alternatives to themselves. There is thus an unintended irony in Wolfe's vigorous expression of cultural pacifism. It would have been more accurate and, in my judgment, more constructive for the editor of *Image* to indicate solidarity with the concerns of the *orthodoxy* army and then engage his compatriots in the cause with a vigorous case for an alternative *strategy*.[38] As it stands, however, by deliberately attempting to set himself above the fray, Wolfe's own efforts to create a "cause" dear to his heart in his *Image* editorial "Religious Humanism: A Manifesto" is likely to fall on deaf evangelical ears. This is particularly true because of the hint of elitism in his accusation that "the majority of conservatives" (that he is acquainted with) are guilty of "cultural Philistinism" as well as despair.[39] This likely consequence is unfortunate because the point Wolfe is making — that the (needed!) renewal of our culture depends more on imagination than on politics — is exactly the point I have been arguing throughout this volume. The irony here is that Wolfe's explicit dissent from the conflict of politicized culture wars ends up itself being a volley in that war, a volley that deserves the tragic military description of "friendly fire."[40]

Nevertheless, Wolfe's point about the dangerous mistake in reducing the cultural conflict of our day to the political realm is well taken and calls us to make some important distinctions among the variety of objections against the

38. From someone such as this author who is a great fan of *Image* magazine, this observation is not intended to cast any aspersions on Gregory Wolfe's motives, only to note the irony in his stated posture.

39. Wolfe, "Religious Humanism," 4.

40. This is the same point made by writer Jack Cashill in his recent essay, "Memo to GOP Moderates: Be Nice to the Right," *Weekly Standard* 4, no. 31 (May 3, 1999): 27-29. Cashill contends that so-called moderates in the Republican Party are hurting their own party's cause by being silent — or worse, following suit — when the political Left in the Democratic Party demonizes the Christian Right. The 1996 election, he observes, exhibited particularly virulent examples of Democratic Party campaign rhetoric that was plainly "anti-Christian demagoguery."

culture wars now taking place. We need to unpack the different senses in which a growing number of commentators today appeal to the notion of "civility" and its political kissing cousin, "tolerance."

The Call for Civility and Tolerance

The reality of American partisan political bickering and posturing, including the regular demonization of one's opponents, has once again brought forth calls for improving national civility. According to Yale University law professor Stephen Carter, this is not a new phenomenon. In fact, he contends, "almost from the nation's inception . . . Americans have held [the attitude] about their own nation: civility is in a decline." "Americans today," he notes, "are like Americans of every era. We think our nation's manners are falling apart." According to Carter, this historical perspective, however, should not make us sanguine about current complaints: "In short, although we Americans have always thought civility is collapsing, I think, this time, we might be right."[41] American concern about the decline of civility and a longing for a recovery of civic virtue may be reflected in the recent revival of interest in the nation's founding and founders. During President Clinton's impeachment trial, news commentators regularly made reference to the *Federalist Papers* and Alexis de Tocqueville's *Democracy in America,* and a noted editor has also recently republished the "rules of civility" written down as a personal guide by America's first president, George Washington.[42]

Stephen Carter's definition of civility is clear and elegant: "I have in mind an attitude of respect, even love, for our fellow citizens, an attitude . . . that has important political and social implications" (xi). Carter does not simply identify civility with manners and proper etiquette, though these are not excluded. Even beyond "a set of standards for conducting public arguments," Carter pushes his readers to the core *moral* conviction that is at the heart of civility: it is what enables us as citizens — in all our diversity and disagreement — to live together. Here is Carter's definition: "Civility, I shall argue, is the sum of the many sacrifices we are called to make for the sake of living together" (11). If civility is indeed in decline — and Carter believes it is — then, while we do need to consider the causes for its decline, we should not dwell on them but focus our efforts on what is needed for renewal. Carter notes that civility "is, and has always been, an idea so

---

41. Carter, xi. Parenthetical page references in next two paragraphs are to this work.
42. Richard Brookhiser, *Rules of Civility: The 110 Precepts That Guided Our First President in War and Peace* (New York: Free Press, 1997).

fragile that, if not carefully nurtured, it will certainly die" and judges that "unfortunately we are not nurturing it at all. We are not preserving the institutions of social life that mediate between politics and the economy on the one hand, and our flimsy moral selves, on the other" (17). We face a disintegration of our social life thanks to the overwhelming "values of the market and of politics — both of which are characterized by an amoral emphasis on *getting* what we want" (16).

At the heart of the problem in public life is the overwhelming pressure of cultural values that encourage us all to seek *our* interests. Even the voluntary associations of our day are dominated by the special interests of particular groups, and they fail to encourage us to seek the *common good*. "They do not call on us, for the sake of our fellow passengers, to control our impulses; instead, they promise to defend our right to exercise them" (17). What associations and organizations, then, do promote civility and make a functioning civil society possible? According to Carter, "the key to reconstructing civility . . . is for all of us to learn anew the virtue of acting with love toward our neighbors." Then comes the problematic suggestion: "Love of neighbor has long been a tenet of Judaism and Christianity, and a revival of civility in America will require a revival of all that is best in religion as a force in our public life. Only religion possesses the majesty, the power, and the sacred language to teach all of us, the religious and the secular, the genuine appreciation for each other on which a successful civility must rest" (18). Carter's response to critics who insist that public expressions of religion are divisive and even potentially explosive is direct and unflinching: "Critics who insist that religion is a danger to civility are misreading both America and religion — and generally have no better idea. The current level of incivility is morally intolerable. And it is getting worse. Without the aid of the nation's religious traditions, we will continue our slide away from a world in which we are able to discipline our desires and toward a world in which the only values that matter are the selfish and acquisitive values of politics and the market" (18-19).

At this fundamental, definitional level, the case for civility seems undeniable and compelling. As Richard Mouw has observed, "kindness and gentleness should be especially characteristic of those of us who are Christians. We were created for kind and gentle living."[43] And further, beyond a *personal* exercise of Paul's "fruit of the Spirit" list in Galatians 5, it is important to extend this vision to civil society. "To be good citizens we must learn to move beyond relationships that are based exclusively on familiarity and intimacy. We must learn how to behave among strangers, to treat people with courtesy not because we know them, but simply because we see them as human beings like ourselves. When we learn the skills of citizenship, Aristotle taught, we have begun to flourish in our human-

43. Mouw, 11.

ness."[44] The key to civility does seem to be, as Carter suggested, a willingness to *sacrifice* for our neighbor's good and for the common civic good.[45] This description and sacrificial posture, we should add, is indeed profoundly Christian, and we must repeat: at this fundamental level the case for full Christian affirmation of an attitude of civility is compelling and obligatory. The call to civility is a genuine, specific derivative of our Lord's command to love our neighbor. Few summaries of that love-command have expressed it as eloquently as Lord's Day 40 of that most beloved of Reformed confessions, the Heidelberg Catechism:

105 Q. *What is God's will for you in the sixth commandment?*
      ("Thou shalt not kill.")

   A. I am not to belittle, insult, hate, or kill my neighbor —
      not by my thoughts, my words, my look, or gesture,
        and certainly not by actual deeds —
   and I am not to be party to this in others;
   rather, I am to put away all desire for revenge.

   I am not to harm or recklessly endanger myself either.

   Prevention of murder is also why
      government is armed with the sword.

106 Q. *Does this commandment refer only to killing?*

   A. By forbidding murder God teaches us
   that he hates the root of murder:
   Envy, hatred, anger, vindictiveness.

   In God's sight all such are murder.

107 Q. *Is it enough then*
      that we do not kill our neighbor
      in any such way?

44. Mouw, 14.

45. With the political sphere especially coming under criticism for its lack of civility, one recent incident in the U.S. Congress that provides a remarkable exception is worth noting, particularly since it took place during the raucously partisan U.S. House of Representatives Judiciary Committee hearings on President Clinton's impeachment. Democrat congresswoman Maxine Waters took her allotted time to engage in a particularly venomous personal attack on committee chairman Henry Hyde. As her time ran out, Hyde struck his gavel and asked, "Would the gentle lady from California like an extension of her time to continue her attack on me?" (David Horowitz, "A Tribute to Henry Hyde," www.frontpagemag.com/dh/david04-22-99.htm).

A. No.
By condemning envy, hatred, and anger
God tells us
   to love our neighbors as ourselves,
   to be patient, peace-loving, gentle,

merciful, and friendly to them,
to protect them from harm as much as we can,
and to do good even to our enemies.[46]

From this we can draw only one conclusion: for Christians the kind of political rhetoric we use is an integral part of our Christian discipleship. Demonizing political opponents and assassinating their character are categorically ruled out for the language Christians use in the public square. Does this mean that conflict itself, including any use of martial imagery, is also ruled out by an appeal to civility?

Carter does address this sort of objection to the notion of civility, the warning that "too much civility might mask deep social conflict," that it might be used by "people in power [to] avoid criticism, or even turn it back on the critic."[47] For example, the call for civility could parallel the exploitative use by advocates of slavery that Scripture enjoins slaves "to obey your masters." This is exactly the parallel Carter cites from an essay by a critic of the notion of civility, Benjamin Mott, who charges that "civility . . . is what slaveholders called for when abolitionists marched."[48] Stated differently, *New York Times* columnist Maureen Dowd, in response to President Clinton's proposal that Americans rid the public square "of this toxic atmosphere of cynicism," insisted that "disagreement, even passionate disagreement, is a noble and necessary condition of democratic life." Dowd concluded, "when political philosophies and political programs collide, civility can be a kind of hypocrisy."[49] All this, Carter observes, is part of a significant current of "anticivility backlash."[50]

In response, Carter points out that the charge of "hypocrisy" leveled by

46. Translation from the Christian Reformed Church, *Psalter Hymnal* (Grand Rapids: CRC Publications, 1987), 911.

47. Carter, 21.

48. Carter, 21; Carter is specifically referring to Benjamin Mott's essay "Seduced by Civility: Political Manners and the Crisis of Democratic Values," *Nation*, December 9, 1996.

49. Carter, 22; the reference is to Maureen Dowd, "Bubba Don't Preach," *New York Times*, February 9, 1997, 15. Dowd is responding to President Clinton's address to the National Prayer Breakfast, February 1997.

50. Carter, 21.

Dowd and others is misplaced. Civility is not an attempt to discourage disagreement. While democracy demands "passionate disagreement," it is not true that "civility in pressing one's passionate cause is ever a form of hypocrisy." On the contrary:

> Civility, as we have already seen, is the set of sacrifices we make for the sake of our common journey with others, and out of love and respect for the very idea that there are others. When we are civil, we are not pretending to like those we actually despise; we are not pretending to hold any attitude toward them, except that we accept and value them as every bit our equals before God. The duty to love our neighbors is a precept of both the Christian and Jewish traditions, and the duty is not lessened because we happen to think our neighbor is wrong about a few things.[51]

It is this moral capacity for civility, for becoming "civilized," that marks our distinct humanity according to Carter. "Our 'form of social life' differentiates us from other animals: we humans, to call ourselves civilized, must have reasons for what we do, reasons apart from mere desire or impulse or even need. Alone of God's creation, we humans are able to apply the test of morality to our actions, and civility calls us to do so." Carter illustrates this point by appealing to the example of Martin Luther King, Jr.,

> whose true genius . . . was not in his ability to articulate the pain of an oppressed people — many other preachers did so, with as much passion and as much power — but in his ability to inspire those very people to be loving and civil in their dissent. This was the antithesis of hypocrisy: it was an act of high principle. The civil rights movement wanted to expand American democracy, not destroy it, and King understood that uncivil dialogue serves no democratic function. Democracy demands dialogue, and dialogue flows from disagreement. But we can, and maybe must, be relentlessly partisan without being actively uncivil. Indeed, the more passionate our certainty that we are right, the more urgent our need to practice the art of civility — otherwise, we make dialogue impossible, and the possibility of dialogue is the reason democracy values disagreement in the first place.[52]

This point is so important that Carter formulates it as one of his essential "rules" of civility: "*Civility assumes that we will disagree; it requires us not to mask our differences but to resolve them respectfully.*"[53]

51. Carter, 23.
52. Carter, 24.
53. Carter, 132.

Yet, the disturbing objection to "civility" will not go away, also as it is used today *against* religious voices in the public square. The public perception seems to be that strongly held religious convictions expressed *publicly* pose grave threats to civility and to civil liberties. Thus the prominent Jewish civil-rights watchdog organization, the Anti-Defamation League (ADL), in 1994 published a 193-page report with the ominous title *The Religious Right: The Assault on Tolerance and Pluralism in America*.[54] The following citations are taken from the ADL's own web-site promotion for *The Religious Right*. According to the ADL, the Religious Right is a theocratic movement seeking to *deny* religious freedom for Americans other than themselves: "During the past 15 years, an exclusionist religious movement in this country has attempted to restore what it perceives as the ruins of a Christian nation by seeking more closely to unite its version of Christianity with state power. Ironically, the groups and activists that have come to be known as the 'religious right' crusade both rhetorically and in their policy aims against the very protection — the separation of church and state — that has secured the vitality of religion throughout American history." A shopping list of debatable political issues from abortion to education vouchers to civil rights are all lumped together into one package with ominous-sounding implications: "This crusade has proceeded in the 1990s through grassroots campaigns to 'return faith to our public schools,' subsidize private religious education, roll back civil rights protections, oppose all abortions, and ensure that 'pro-family Christians' gain control of the Republican Party. National groups with many thousands of members have spurred these efforts, inciting the movement with grim cadences of warfare." At this point, after chastising those who debase "reasonable discourse" with extreme comparisons (abortion paralleling Hitler's "final solution," references to a "homosexual blitzkrieg," public education as "socialist and anti-God"), the ADL promotion ironically engages in its own act of refusal: "The hysteria of this language excites resentment on all sides and degrades or disallows reasonable discourse. It reflects as well a basic rejection of a society that includes dissent and pluralism — the modern democratic state. The political agenda of the religious right movement is, in turn, an attempt to legislate this rejection." The notion that the Religious Right is about the business of establishing a new theocracy is then linked directly with anti-Semitism. "Unsurprisingly, this bitter push to replace the wall of separation with a citadel of Christianity — while suggesting that those who defend the wall are 'enemies of God' — has been abetted, sometimes at the

<hr />

54. Reported by William Norman Grigg, "ADL Campaign against Tolerance," *New American* 10, no. 19 (September 19, 1994): 13-14; the report is still available from the ADL, according to its web site, www.adl.org/publications.

highest levels, by figures who have expressed conspiratorial, anti-Jewish, and extremist sentiments."

In fairness to the ADL, the web-site summary then — rather remarkably in view of its own immediately preceding harsh denunciation — does go on, citing Stephen Carter, to insist that it is the *issues* pushed by the Religious Right and not their *religiosity as such* that is objectionable. "Yet those who object to the religious right movement too often engage the intolerance and stereotyping they purport to decry. As Yale law professor Stephen Carter has suggested recently, critics err when they imply that the religious right poses a concern because of its religiosity rather than its platform. The problems raised by the movement are secular. 'We must be able,' states Carter, 'to distinguish a critique of the content of a belief from a critique of its source.'" In a "what's fair for the goose . . ." argument, the ADL summary insists that evangelical Christians have every right to exercise their civil rights — for example, through concerted activism at the local public school board level.

> The extensive political training and school curricula scrutiny encouraged by religious right groups, for instance, is frequently viewed by critics as a threat to, rather than an exercise of, good citizenship — and a prod for opponents to do likewise. Yet few such concerns regarding church-state separation were sounded by these critics when Christians organized on behalf of civil rights or the nuclear freeze. This is plainly inconsistent and illiberal.
>
> Like anyone else, evangelical Christians have the right to organize, to run for office, to lobby, to boycott, to demonstrate, to attempt to implement their views. More than that, a healthy democracy encourages and depends on their doing so; it depends, that is, on a jumble of voices in the public square. Throughout American history, religion — largely a vigorous, splintery Protestantism — has been at the center of social movements: abolition, temperance, civil rights, opposition to war, abortion. Similarly, contemporary religious right activism has grown out of a widely shared sense of cultural breakdown — buttressed by reams of grievous statistics about crime, health, families — that seems to have exhausted the remedial policies of secular governance.

In fact, the ADL promotion makes a surprising concession to the *necessity* of religious protest in the public square: "Religion has served democracy at such junctures precisely because, separated from the state, it exerts a moral authority that challenges the power of the state. As Carter writes, 'A religion is, at its heart, a way of denying the authority of the rest of the world.' Moreover, it keeps secularists and pluralists honest by asking how pluralism, which entails moral pluralism, is something other than a friendly face of nihilism."

While the ADL's closing concessions about the *rights* and even the *necessity* of religious discourse in the public square is reason for rejoicing, it can hardly escape notice that this *formal* concession fails as an antidote to the previously poisoned well of public, political discourse. While the ADL insists that "religion serves democracy as protest," it is also clear that only certain kinds of protest are acceptable. Mere advocacy of some positions in the public square — opposition to abortion on demand, favoring school vouchers — is *defined* from the outset as illegitimate and uncivil because it is an attack on pluralism and democracy. In fact, mere advocacy of such views is judged as an attempt "to legislate rejection of the modern democratic state" and a "conspiratorial, extremist example of anti-Semitism" to boot. Here, as in some other "liberal" concessions to religious expression in the public square, civility itself is defined in such a way as to automatically exclude certain voices. In his commentary on a recent initiative to "advance the position that religion should not be excluded from the public square," Richard John Neuhaus makes a similar observation about the way parameters for the discussion often exclude voices at the very moment they publicly indicate a desire to include.[55] The particular meeting Neuhaus refers to was held at the Chicago-based Park Ridge Center and was presided over by University of Chicago Divinity School professor Martin Marty. Neuhaus observes that the title of the event, "Dogmatism or Discussion?" and the large preponderance of participants identifiably from the "left" side of the political and religious spectrum, gave "the edge to the dogma of discussionism, with liberal dogma redefined as discussion." The question of truth did not feature prominently in press releases about the event, and Neuhaus concludes that without convictions about truth being openly acknowledged and serious effort given to the process of *persuasion*, "civility is but liberal legerdemain for the sly stifling of those with whom you disagree." Put more bluntly, Neuhaus sums up this approach: "This is civility as in 'Everybody shut up except us!'"

Shortly after the ADL report was filed, on August 2, 1994, seventy-five notable Jewish Americans signed a full-page paid advertisement in the *New York Times* condemning the ADL for "engaging in defamation of its own" in its attack on the Religious Right. The advertisement, which bore the headline "Should Jews Fear the 'Christian Right'?" chastised the ADL for its disreputable tactics: "We are a group of Jews who wish to make it known that we reject the implication of [the ADL] report and deplore its publication. . . . [T]he so-called 'evidence' of a conservative Christian threat to Jewish security is derived from such discreditable techniques as insinuation and guilt by association."

55. What follows is taken from Richard John Neuhaus's regular column, The Public Square: A Continuing Survey of Religion and Public Life, *First Things* 93 (May 1999): 80-81.

Perhaps, for our purposes, the most significant element in this counter-ad was the complaint by the signers that the ADL report erroneously linked liberal ideology and Judaism: "Judaism is not, as the ADL seems to suggest, coextensive with liberalism. Nor, we wish to emphasize, does the Jewish community speak with one voice on the religious and moral — and political — issues of our time. Furthermore, Judaism teaches the principle of Hakarat Hatov, that we have the duty to acknowledge the good done to us. In issuing *The Religious Right* study, the ADL has among other things seriously violated that principle."[56] One of the signatories to the objection, Gary Polland, a Houston attorney who was a member of ADL at the time, protested the linkage between anti-Semitism and opposition to two favored "liberal" causes: abortion on demand and the "radical homosexual agenda." Polland describes the ADL strategy as follows: "While anti-Semitism is rejected by the American populace, public opinion has not yet turned decisively against newly minted sins against political correctness, such as 'homophobia.' In order to poison the public mind against the religious right, the ADL sought to portray 'homophobia' and rejection of feminist demands as morally equivalent to anti-Semitism — and to establish the supposed anti-Jewish sentiments of Evangelicals through insinuation and misrepresentation."[57]

Like a white person denying the charge from an African American that he is a racist, it is difficult for a Gentile to object to Jewish accusations of anti-Semitism since the protest itself then may become part of the evidence for the charge. That strategy itself, of course, is one of the chief ways our public discourse is poisoned. So, here we will give the word to Rabbi Daniel Lapin, an Orthodox Jewish believer and active participant in the current culture wars. Rabbi Lapin is convinced that the ADL concern about the Christian Religious Right is all wrong. He believes that "secularized Americans and many Jews wrongly fear Christianity in America today" and says that he wrote his culture wars book *America's Real War*[58] "to defend American Christian conservatives." He gives three reasons:

> The first is because I desperately want my children, and one day (God willing) my grandchildren and their descendants, to have the option of living peacefully and productively in the United States of America. I am certain this depends upon America regaining its Christian-oriented moral compass.
>
> The second reason is that I am appalled by the great injustice being perpetrated by those Jewish organizations that engage in anti-Christian bigotry. Although many of them were founded explicitly to fight bigotry, and for

56. Grigg, 13.
57. Grigg, 14.
58. See n. 17 above.

many years did just that, today the shrill rhetoric and hate-filled propaganda found in their direct mail is discriminatory and divisive. The very same Jewish organizations would be the loudest protesters were anything even remotely similar being said by non-Jews about Jews. Justice demands that a member of the group doing the defaming also does the defending. God's blueprint clearly included the emergence of Christianity. After all, Christianity has brought monotheism to more people than any other force during the past two millennia. American Jews in particular, owe a debt of gratitude to Christians for the safe haven America has been since its founding.

Third, I wish to counter the *chilul Hashem,* the desecration of God's name, that is caused when His words are misrepresented. Organizations and individuals, many of whom claim to speak in the name of Judaism, are inflicting enormous harm on America by promoting policies that traditional Judaism finds abhorrent. I want to help both Jewish and non-Jewish Americans differentiate between Jewish positions and positions held by some Jews who are more devoted to secularism than Judaism.[59]

Daniel Lapin is a devout Orthodox Jewish rabbi who is convinced that America's Christian religious tradition does not, as secularists so often claim, represent "primitive tribalism and intolerance" but is rather America's only hope for survival. The "tug-of-war going on for the future of our country," he contends, "is whether America is a secular or religious nation." Defending a version of "Christian America" does not mean "that Jews ought to embrace the Christian faith. I believe that all Jews should actively embrace traditional Judaism; I have spent many years of my life helping to bring that about." Nonetheless, he adds, "I am suggesting, at the very least, that Jews should stop speaking and acting as if Christian America is their enemy. I feel that all Americans who love freedom, whether or not they are religious, should be reassured, not frightened, by the reawakening of earnest Christianity throughout the land. I shall try to establish that Jews as well as other minorities have the most to fear from a *post*-Christian America."[60]

Stated differently, the hope for genuine religious tolerance in America, for pluralism, is in recovering a common Christian moral vision. Conversely, contrary to much conventional wisdom, secularism is a *threat* to tolerance and pluralism. In Rabbi Lapin's words, "the choice is between a benign Christian culture and a sinister secular one."[61] We shall see if this formulation has credibility by concluding this section with a few reflections on tolerance.[62]

59. Lapin, 12-13.
60. Lapin, 13.
61. Lapin, 14.
62. My primary resource for the few paragraphs that follow is Daniel Taylor's help-

"Tolerance," writes one recent commentator, may well be the premier virtue in America today; intolerance may be "the only serious sin left." How serious a sin is intolerance? Worse than murder? Perhaps. "Even murder has its mitigating factors, but not this one. It is the pariah sin, the charge that makes you untouchable without need for further explanation. The sin is intolerance, and the greatest sinners in late twentieth-century America are evangelical and fundamentalist Christians. America is sick of intolerant people, and it's not going to tolerate them anymore" (43). What exactly is tolerance, and what does it require of us? In his *Christianity Today* essay, Daniel Taylor provides an important and often ignored "twist" on the matter. Just as Stephen Carter noted that "civility assumes we will disagree" and does not ask us "to mask our differences but to resolve them respectfully,"[63] Taylor prods us to reconsider the nature of tolerance: "First, one is not tolerant of something unless one objects to it. I do not tolerate something I either accept or am indifferent to, because it requires nothing of me. Most social liberals, for instance, cannot rightfully be said to be tolerant regarding homosexual behavior since they have no objection to it. You do not have to tolerate that which you accept or affirm. If you want to know whether a liberal is tolerant, ask what he or she thinks of Jesse Helms or Pat Robertson or Kenneth Starr." Taylor then posits the same counterintuitive proposition that we have already encountered: religious conservatives may be more tolerant than progressive liberals. "If tolerance requires an initial objection, then conservatives, ironically, may be much more tolerant than liberals, because there are so many more things to which they object. The least tolerant person is the person who accepts everything, because such a person is not required to overcome any internal objections. To paraphrase G. K. Chesterton, turnips are singularly tolerant" (43).

Genuine tolerance is not an easygoing laissez-faire indifference; it is not the same as being "interminably open-minded" (44). The subtle dialectic of genuine tolerance requires *sacrifice*; it requires a withholding of coercive power and a willingness to tolerate what one finds objectionable. "If tolerance requires an initial objection, it also implies withheld power. If I would stop something if I could, but am powerless to do so, I am not tolerant, merely impotent. True tolerance means I voluntarily withhold what power I have to coerce someone else's behavior." Once again Taylor turns current conventional wisdom concerning tolerance on its head: the dialectic of tolerance *requires* a certain sense of intolerance, of moral absoluteness and its consequence — moral oppo-

---

ful essay, "Deconstructing the Gospel of Tolerance," *Christianity Today,* January 11, 1999, 43-52; page references that follow in the text are to this essay.

    63. Carter, 132.

sition to certain forms of behavior. "This suggests an interesting paradox within the notion of tolerance. At the core of tolerance is a kind of intolerance. If you can only tolerate that to which you object, then you have already shown yourself somewhat intolerant in making that initial objection" (44).

Taylor goes on to demonstrate how the accusation of intolerance has itself now become a weapon in the arsenal of intolerance. "The charge of intolerance has become a potent weapon in the culture wars, all the more useful because it carries a lot of emotional firepower without requiring a great deal of evidence or logical consistency. People complain about others 'forcing their values' on them, when they are perfectly willing to do the same on many issues" (45).

Religion is regarded by secularists as the great source of intolerance in large measure because the mere fact that religious faith still exists defies the secular conventional wisdom that "enlightened" people will give up their religious superstition with its absolutist, authoritarian claims. What is annoying to secularists is the refusal of religiously orthodox people to give up their "exclusive" dogmas, such as the Christian claim that Jesus Christ is the only Savior for all people. Secularists truly believe that such religious "absolutism" translates *directly* into political absolutes and coercive theocratic ambitions. In this view, someone who believes that Jesus is Lord will be led inexorably to deny the *civil* rights of Muslims and Hindus. While it is tragically true that horrible deeds have been done in the name of the Christian faith (the secular notion of tolerance did, after all, develop in response to the "religious wars" of the seventeenth century), it is still the case that genuine tolerance and respect for the *other*, a tolerance that requires *sacrifice*, does rest on the reality of the *other* being truly an *other*. On this reading, Taylor's observation about liberal versions of religion not really being tolerant seems correct. He observes that

> [A liberal's] religion is ethical humanism — the human quest for being good through human efforts — with a side dish of theism. [Thus] liberal Catholicism and liberal Judaism are not really two different religions getting along with each other, but only different flavors of the same religion. They are much closer to each other in core beliefs than they are to more conservative believers within the religion each espouses. They, in fact, do not really *respect* other religions so much as they try to shame members of other religions to give up their "absolutism" to join them in the progressive club of the open-minded. And they are as absolute in this requirement as any absolutist fundamentalist of any religion. (46)

In the midst of this, Christians who take seriously their civic responsibility must insist upon *civility* and *freedom of religious conscience* (or tolerance) for all citizens. Taylor offers a number of suggestions that would enable Christians to maintain what Richard Mouw called "convicted civility."[64] As Taylor puts the question: "How can we affirm Christian morality, unapologetically rooted in the Bible, without becoming rhetorical bomb throwers?" (52). He gives three sound and concrete suggestions:

> We would do well to tape a verse from James on our foreheads: "Be quick to listen, slow to speak, and slow to get angry." Second, we should listen to the stories of those who oppose us. Everyone has a story to tell, and the surest route to conflict is to suppress the stories of others. A source of frustration for conservative Christians is the feeling that their story is being silenced in the public square. If we want the right to tell our story, however, we must be willing, even eager, to hear the stories of others. And we should listen compassionately, with a bias toward finding common ground rather than listening for an opportunity to attack. (52)

Finally, with special reference to two hot-button issues — abortion and homosexuality — Taylor concludes: "Must Christians be tolerant? Not really — certainly not as our society defines the term. But we must be loving, and that is a far greater challenge, with far greater dangers and rewards. We must find better ways to demonstrate that we do, in fact, love the sinner while we hate the sin" (52).

Sectarian Conflict

One of the striking characteristics of America's current culture wars is the vehemence with which opponents express their disagreement, contempt, hostility, and even hatred for each other. Examples of mutual demonization abound.[65] Evangelical Christians condemn public school education as a "satanically inspired conspiracy of secular humanists." In turn, secularists judge all religious expression in the public square as evil, anti-American bigotry. In fact, even private initiatives to provide alternative educational choices for parents, such as the Children's Scholarship Fund established by Wall Street financier Ted Forstmann and Wal-Mart heir John Walton, receive ultimate malignments from some religious leaders. The April 6, 1999, newsletter of the Baptist Joint

64. Mouw, 12.

65. On the phenomenon of demonization, see Carter, chap. 7, "The Demon on the Other Side."

Committee, a Washington, D.C., lobby group, referred to the "darker dimension" of the "demons that push the drive for vouchers," calling this particular initiative "selfish . . . parochial . . . greedy . . . racist." For good measure a reference to "Hitler's grand schemes" was also thrown in.[66] In such instances, those with whom we disagree are not merely persons with different viewpoints, not even persons with *dumb* views, but *evil* people with *evil* ideas. We demonize the *other.* The logical consequence of such demonization is the desire not simply to cast ideas into disrepute by discrediting them with good arguments and persuasive rhetoric, but ultimately to eliminate the people who hold the views. Thankfully not all who use the rhetoric of demonization follow their beliefs through to the logical end, but there can be little doubt that the rhetoric of demonization thoroughly poisons the public square and makes a civil society practically impossible.

It may be helpful for us to understand this phenomenon in terms of the categories of *sectarian* conflict. America has been described as "the nation with the soul of a church."[67] What needs to be added to that observation is that, speaking more precisely and sociologically in the classic categories developed by Ernst Troeltsch, America is really a "nation with the soul of a sect" (rather than a "church"). What's the difference? Consider how Troeltsch summarizes the key difference between the "church" and the "sect":

> The Church is an institution which has been endowed with grace and salvation as the result of the work of Redemption; because, to a certain extent, it can afford to ignore the need for subjective holiness for the sake of the objective treasures of grace and of redemption.
>
> The sect is a voluntary society, composed of strict and definite Christian believers bound to each other by the fact that all have experienced "the new birth." These "believers" live apart from the world, are limited to small groups, emphasize the law instead of grace, and in varying degrees within their own circle set up the Christian order, based on love; all this is done in preparation for and expectation of the coming Kingdom of God.[68]

With this difference the two types of religious organization also have different social and political concerns and aims. The church is an *inclusive* body, prepared to compromise in order to enfold diverse groups.

66. "The Dark Side of the Religious Left," *Weekly Standard,* May 3, 1999, 3.

67. Sidney E. Mead, *The Nation with the Soul of a Church* (New York, Evanston, San Francisco, and London: Harper & Row, 1975); see n. 155 in chap. 2 above.

68. See E. Troeltsch, *The Social Teaching of the Christian Churches,* trans. Olive Wyon, 2 vols. (1931; reprint, Louisville: Westminster/John Knox, 1992), 2:993-99.

The aim of the Church is to be the Church of the people and of the masses; it therefore transfers all divine and sacred character from individuals to the objective organ of redemption, with its divine endowment of grace and truth. The Church possesses a redeeming energy which is directly miraculous, and in contrast to all other kinds of human power. Thus it possesses an absolute directly divine truth and doctrinal authority over against all human subjectivity. In its very nature such truths must be uniform and universally authoritative. The Church must see to it that the whole nation shall hear the message of salvation, and everyone shall have at least contact with divine salvation. Mercy requires it, and the absolute divine origin of the truth of salvation justifies this procedure.[69]

While the "church" is not altogether averse to coercion (and has, tragically, proved so historically), its sociological premise and purpose logically is *inclusionary* and *universal;* it is represented by Augustine's "Catholic" model of "wheat and tares growing together" rather than by the pure church ideal of the Donatists or Anabaptists. In the same way that the "church" type enfolds dissent into itself by creating new orders, so "churchly" nations can be truly pluralistic. When the fundamental ecclesiastical and political order is stable (Constantinian), it is strong and confident enough to tolerate dissenting groups by enfolding them into its larger whole.

The smaller and elitist "sects," on the other hand, are obsessed with an all-or-nothing compulsion for purity; sects have no space for dissent and therefore must remove it. In Troeltsch's words: "The point of view of the sects, however, is quite different. They do not wish to be popular churches, but Christian denominations composed of 'saints.' The sects are small groups which exist alongside of the State and Society. They also maintain that they possess the absolute truth of the Gospel, but they claim that this truth is far beyond the spiritual grasp of the masses and of the State, and therefore they desire to be free from the State." But here a remarkable irony needs to be noted. The gospel as understood by the sects proscribes violence and coercion. Theoretically, sects emphatically renounce forcing their views on others. However, *internally* the discipline of the sect is legalistic and rigid; sects vigorously practice shunning and excommunication on their members.

Further, since it is precisely this absolute Gospel which forbids them to use force, authority, or law, they also must renounce forcing their opinions upon anyone, either within or without their community. Hence they demand external toleration, the religious neutrality of the State. Within their own bor-

69. Troeltsch, 2:997.

ders, however, they practice a spiritual discipline of doctrine and of morals. Where various sectarian groups exist alongside of each other, they permit the exercise of purely spiritual controversy and merely ethical rivalry without losing faith in the absolute character of the truth they possess. This truth is not meant for the final consummation at the Last Day. Their conception of toleration and freedom of conscience is of a toleration extended to groups like their own by the churches and the ruling powers; within their own borders, however, they had very little idea of toleration, since here Scriptural law prevails.[70]

Now, what happens when the nation as a whole takes on this sectarian character, be it of a religious or a secular sectarian sort? Since the demand of purity dominates sectarian sociology, sectarian governments with coercive sword power *eliminate* their dissenting opposition. The sectarian world brooks no opposition; its view of justice and liberty demands purity. Thus, hard-line theocrats vehemently oppose genuine pluralism; any pluralism that permits "false religions" full opportunity in the public square cannot be tolerated in "Christian America." Similarly, sectarian secularists cannot tolerate even the teeny-tiniest vestige of religious symbolism in the square. The full exercise of the state's coercive power must be used to remove every crèche and menorah from the town squares of America, which are to be kept *purely* and nakedly secular. The NBC television newsmagazine *Dateline* recently aired a story of what seems to be an extreme example of slippery-slope secularist exclusion of religion. Having asked all students in a public school first grade to bring and read their favorite story the next day, the teacher then forbade one boy in the class from reading *his* favorite story about *Jesus!* Remarkably, the school principal defied what most might regard as commonsense fairness by defending the exclusion on grounds of church and state separation.[71] "Can't be too careful; the next thing you know America will be a theocracy!"

The intensity of the culture war rhetoric among the extremists on either side is thus best understood as a conflict between *sectarians* whose ideals of purity claim toleration but who in practice permit toleration only for the likeminded. According to former leftist student radical David Horowitz, one of the major failings among so-called moderates in American public life today is the

70. Troeltsch, 2:998.
71. NBC News, *Dateline*, May 2, 1999. It is the multiplication of events such as these in recent years that makes the denial of culture wars (see nn. 22 and 27 above) not only less plausible but also troubling as a direct suppression of the constitutionally guaranteed free exercise of religion.

failure to acknowledge the radically sectarian character of leftist radicals in their full-blown "assault" on American institutions and ideals. Rather than promoting genuine diversity and pluralism, "the post-Marxian Left has begun its career by launching an all-out assault on the third great achievement of modern history, the liberal community itself. This community, whose paradigm is America, is founded in a universal compact that transcends tribal identities and the multicultural particularism of blood and soil. . . . America is the unique crystallization of an idea of nationality residing in a shared commitment to universal principles and pluralistic values." Horowitz adds that this universal creed, resting on "the truths that are self-evident and on which our freedom finally depends," was "accumulated through practice and acquired by faith — the Judaeo-Christian traditions."[72] Once again the same argument: religion results in freedom; secularism leads to tyranny. There is a critical point here that must not be quickly passed by: the struggle for freedom of religious expression at the heart of the culture wars is the cornerstone of a larger battle for liberty. Deliberately abstaining from the culture wars is thus an abstinence from the battle for liberty.

As an example of religious commitment making a constructive social contribution to the common civic good, the good of liberty — by combining religious passion and civility — we need only recall the American civil rights movement led by Dr. King. Stephen Carter cites it as a prime example of exactly this dual combination — a passionate commitment to moral truth (justice) *and* civility:

> The Civil Rights Movement, of course, had one advantage that today's movements often do not: the religious convictions of the marchers, King often argued, gave them the courage and the power to remain civil, to remain focused, to shun immoral means in the quest for moral ends. Does this mean that faith is necessary to civility? The question may seem a peculiar one in an era when so many prominent intellectuals have concluded that faith is the enemy of civility. For example, the literary theorist Stanley Fish has recently argued that it is the basic feature of religion not to believe in the market place of ideas, but to try to shut it down. The feminist writer Wendy Kaminer, proudly trumpeting her atheism, concludes that religious people consistently "demonize" those who do not believe in God. The silent subtext of such arguments is that we would be a good deal better off — or, at least, a good deal more civil — if religion would simply disappear.

72. David Horowitz, *The Politics of Bad Faith: The Radical Assault on America's Future* (New York: Free Press, 1998), 153-54.

Carter could not disagree more:

> This scary proposition is not only wrong, but dangerous and undemocratic.... Let me stake out a contrarian position: No, faith is not strictly *necessary* to civility: there are plenty of people who lack faith in God who are civil, and there are plenty of people who profess faith in God who are not. At the same time ... I think it likely that only a resurgence in all that is best about religious faith will rescue civility in America, for there is no truer or more profound vision of equality than equality before God.[73]

In sum, civility (and tolerance) requires *sacrifice* and *hope;* religious faith, says Carter, is the *sine qua non* for both:

> A life without faith is a life without the most powerful language of sacrifice and aspiration the human race has ever known. In the absence of God, we cease to understand ourselves, our purposes, our connection to the transcendent. In the Western religious traditions, faith in God provides a *justification* for the equality that liberal philosophy assumes and cherishes but is often unable to defend. In the absence of that language of loving sacrifice, that connection to the transcendent, civility, like any other moral principle, has no firm rock on which to stand. Civility that rests on the shifting sands of secular morality might topple with the next stiff political wind.[74]

To this we would only add that the sort of religious faith that does indeed build civic and civil community must be a confident, *churchly,* inclusive faith rather than a *sectarian* one. What this likely means in practice is that the requisite sort of faith needed to build civic and civil society will need to incorporate some elements of American national, patriotic devotion or civic faith (what has often been referred to as "civil religion").[75] In this instance, what is needed is a nonidolatrous civic faith that clearly and resolutely refuses to be identified with the ultimate beliefs, values, and claims of any particular religion itself — America as such is not and may never be identified with the kingdom of God — but is acknowledged within the working of divine providence as a secondary and penultimate good.

73. Carter, 30.
74. Carter, 31.
75. I am choosing the term "civic faith" (or "patriotic devotion") rather than the more familiar and traditional term "civil religion." Conversations with my friend and Calvin Theological Seminary colleague John Cooper persuaded me that the term "civil religion" may be irredeemably linked with the idolatrous state religion advocated by Rousseau and thus correctly repudiated by many American evangelicals in recent years. See n. 43 in chap. 1 above.

One question arises quite naturally from Stephen Carter's observations about faith and civility: Would faith in the American national creed, a frankly civil faith, be sufficient to sustain the virtue of public civility? Is it possible to move from civility as a generally formal notion governing the style and tone of political discourse to a more profound development of civic virtue? Can Americans, to borrow a phrase used by Michael Sandel and Alan Brinkley, rise above "democracy's discontents"[76] to recover a common national purpose and unified civic virtue?

From Civility to Civic Virtue

The concern about civility in American political life goes deeper than worrying about how politely we express *dis*agreements with one another in the public square. There is in the land a mood of uncertainty about the tenability of the American experiment itself. In a much-discussed[77] and rightly praised book, Michael Sandel, Harvard University professor of law, observes that there is a strange anomaly in the current American discussion about its own national ideals: "At a time when democratic ideals seem ascendant abroad, there is reason to wonder whether we have lost possession of them. Our public life is rife with discontent. . . . Despite the achievements of American life in the last half-century — victory in World War II, unprecedented affluence, greater social justice for women and minorities, the end of the Cold War — our politics is beset with anxiety and frustration."[78]

Sandel suggests, believably, that there are "two concerns that lie at the heart of democracy's discontent": "One is the fear that, individually and collectively, we are losing control of the forces that govern our lives. The other is the sense that, from family to neighborhood to nation, the moral fabric of community is unraveling around us. These two fears — for the loss of self-government and the erosion of community — together define the anxiety of the age. It is an

76. See Michael Sandel, *Democracy's Discontents: America in Search of a Public Philosophy* (Cambridge, Mass., and London: Harvard Univeristy Press, Belknap Press, 1966); Alan Brinkley, *Liberalism and Its Discontents* (Cambridge, Mass., and London: Harvard University Press, 1998).

77. See, e.g., Anita L. Allen and Milton C. Regan, Jr., eds., *Debating Democracy's Discontents: Essays on American Politics, Law, and Public Philosophy* (Oxford and New York: Oxford University Press, 1998). Another collection of essays that is not a direct response to Sandel but treats many of the same issues is Paul Weithman, ed., *Religion and Contemporary Liberalism* (Notre Dame, Ind.: University of Notre Dame Press, 1997).

78. Sandel, 3.

anxiety that the prevailing political agenda has failed to answer or even address."[79] The argument of *Democracy's Discontents* builds upon Sandel's contrast between two rival views of democratic political order. The first is what can be called a "minimalist" as well as a "procedural" liberalism. Here all citizens are seen as strictly autonomous individuals, rationally choosing their own ends, and government is strictly neutral with respect to moral ends. In Sandel's judgment, "the liberalism of the procedural republic provides the public philosophy by which [Americans] live," and its dominance is in good measure the cause of democracy's current discontent: "The procedural republic cannot secure the liberty it promises, because it cannot sustain the kind of political community and civic engagement that liberty requires."[80]

The concluding phrase deserves emphasis: *"liberty requires"* more than *procedural* agreement; even a full commitment to the practice of civility is not enough. *Liberty requires* a certain kind of political *community* and a *civic engagement*. Stated differently, liberty requires a commitment to a national civic community, a civic faith. *Liberty* requires the cultivation of a civic virtue that is characterized by willingness to sacrifice for a *common* good rather than being preoccupied with *individual* rights. Whereas the liberal view sees liberty in terms of freedom from self-government — "a guarantee of my immunity from certain majority decisions" — the contrasting ideal sees liberty "as a consequence of self-government": "I am free insofar as I am a member of a political community that controls its own fate, and a participant in the decisions that govern its affairs." Liberty requires the cultivation of "civic virtues." "Republican freedom requires a certain form of public life, which depends in turn on the cultivation of civic virtue."[81] It is this latter "civic-republican" ideal of self-governing citizens whose identities are shaped by deep patterns of association (in the Tocquevillian sense) that Sandel sees in eclipse today and for which he builds a case in the second half of *Democracy's Discontents*.

We cannot pursue the important discussion of Sandel's proposal further here except as an occasion to summarize some key conclusions about the culture wars, civility, and civic virtue. The culture wars are a reality of American life, and they reflect an important debate about the very nature and future of the American experiment in ordered liberty. Perhaps the question about the culture wars comes down to this: Is this essentially a battle about liberty? The degree to which we are willing to participate in the culture wars may come down to a decision about that question. If the battle is only about differences in

79. Sandel, 3.
80. Sandel, 24.
81. Sandel, 25-26.

politics, about specifics of government policy, it is important for Christians to back off from the fierceness that has characterized much of the culture wars rhetoric in recent years. But what if the culture wars are really about our fundamental liberties? Conflict about liberty cannot be a trifling or indifferent matter for Christians. History shows clearly that genuine liberty is both precious and fragile. The memory of those who died to establish, defend, and preserve the liberty we enjoy must not be dishonored by our unwillingness to engage in cultural and political combat for the same liberty. The fight for liberty is one in which we ought to be willing to engage. It goes without saying that Christians who judge the battle to be one that requires active participation are required to fight in accordance with the appropriate application of Christian "just war" criteria. In the political arena, the rule of civility is at the top of the list.

"Third Ways": A Way to
Transcend the Culture Wars?

At this point in our lengthy chapter, it may be helpful to recap the argument thus far. One of the foundational premises to this volume's study of Abraham Kuyper is the conviction that Christian citizens have both a right and an obligation to be active in the public square *as Christians*. Our discussion in this chapter arose in response to one of the risks inherent in such a project, the danger of scandalizing the gospel itself by use of heavy-duty martial rhetoric that simply and directly identifies cultural and political partisanship with the claims of Christ's kingly rule. When my political opinion is a clear command from Christ, I am tempted to "demonize" my opponent. In this way public discourse is poisoned by sectarian passion, and the political process itself finally breaks down. But what is the alternative? If one rejects the religious politicizing of cultural issues in the current American *Kulturkampf,* what then must one do? Abstain from distinctly Christian political activity altogether? That is a serious proposal we shall consider in the final chapter. However, at this point we shall consider another potentially promising proposal: a self-consciously articulated alternative to the radical polarization between left and right in a concerted effort to find a "third way" that is distinctly Christian. It is fitting to discuss this attempt as an alternative in a book dealing with Abraham Kuyper's public theology, because the search for "third ways" has been a strong suit of Kuyper's North American followers.[82] In this section we shall examine what is arguably

82. See, e.g., G. Spykman et al., *Let My People Live: Faith and Struggle in Central America* (Grand Rapids: Eerdmans, 1988), esp. 14-17, 98-102, 150-52, 196-204; cf.

the most important of such recent attempts, the "Call to Renewal" (CtoR) statement initiated by *Sojourners* fellowship leader Jim Wallis, along with other evangelical social activists such as Tony Campolo and Ron Sider.[83]

CtoR flows from a "commitment to diligently apply spiritual values to the questions of our public life and to offer a Christian alternative to ideological religion." CtoR insists that "there is a Christian alternative that transcends old categories of Right and Left, liberal and conservative," and that its signers are all working to "lift up a clear, visible, and credible alternative to the Religious Right and Left." It rightly insists that what is at stake in the ideological captivity of the Christian faith to a political program "is the meaning of faith itself." "We are dismayed," the authors say, "by those who would undermine the integrity of religious conviction that does not conform to a narrow ideological agenda." An evenhanded critique indicts both the Religious Right (for its virtual identification of Christian politics with the Republican Party platform) and the Religious Left (for the same fault with respect to the Democratic Party platform). Since "neither right-wing religious nationalism nor left-wing religious lobbying will serve us at this critical juncture," they say, "we call ourselves and our churches back to a biblical focus that transcends the Left and the Right." Finally, "politics cannot solve all our problems. Spiritual renewal will be required."

How successful is this Christian "third way" alternative? On closer inspection the formal evenhandedness appears to break down. The cry of dismay about ideological commitments destroying "integrity of religious conviction" is followed immediately with a policy specific that is hardly bipartisan: "And we are deeply concerned about the subversion of prophetic religion when wealth and power are extolled rather than held accountable, and when the gospel message is turned upside down to bring more comfort to those on the top of society than to those at the bottom." Similarly, the call to go beyond politics to "spirituality" is immediately followed by an insistence that "genuine spiritual renewal must not be self-righteous or mean-spirited." That much of this is code language for a generally leftist political tilt becomes even clearer when CtoR's major concern is articulated thus: "we are especially concerned with the harsh rhetoric toward the powerless coming from the nation's capital." Jesus is invoked as the one who "called us to be peacemakers . . . to stop the violence that has overtaken the nation, and address its root causes in the distorted spiritual

' Craig M. Gay, *With Liberty and Justice for Whom? The Recent Evangelical Debate over Capitalism* (Grand Rapids: Eerdmans, 1991), 131-32.

83. See Jim Wallis, *Who Speaks for God? An Alternative to the Religious Right — a New Politics of Compassion, Community, and Civility* (New York: Delacorte Press, 1996); the full "Call to Renewal" statement is given as an appendix, 195-216; citations which follow in the text are taken from these pages.

values and unjust social structures in which we are all complicit." We are called to conversion in which "we must revive the lapsed virtues of personal responsibility and character, and repent for our social sins of racism, sexism, and poverty."

After this rather conventional litany of progressive Christian complaints and commitments, what does CtoR do with the issues at the top of the Christian Right's agenda, namely, life (abortion and euthanasia) and family (education, homosexual activism)? Amazingly, they are not even highlighted in the way that the Christian Left's troika of "racism, sexism, and poverty" are. Instead they are practically eliminated by reducing them to one pole of a set of "false choices": "We refuse the false choices between personal responsibility or social justice, between good values or good jobs, between strong families or strong neighborhoods, between sexual morality or civil rights for homosexuals, between the sacredness of life or the rights of women, between fighting cultural corrosion or battling racism." This remarkable set of polarities is then followed by this somewhat astonishing challenge: "We call ourselves and our churches back to a biblical focus that transcends the Left and Right. We call the Christian community to consider carefully each social and political issue, diligently apply the values of the faith, and be willing to break out of traditional political categories."

There is much in CtoR that all Christians, whatever their political inclination, could heartily affirm. However, in spite of the explicit *claim* to be seeking a "third way," the general orientation of CtoR is clearly leftward. What is troubling is that its authors and signers either do not recognize this or are trying to disguise their own political orientation by posing as alternatives to themselves. In either case, this particular "third way" is not one. In this respect, religiously oriented political movements are much like their fully secular counterparts. It should be added here that though *Sojourners* magazine does try in certain issues to provide additional sides of an issue, the magazine's masthead purpose statement is hardly above the fray: "Sojourners is a progressive Christian voice with an alternative vision for both church and society — beyond both the Religious Right and the secular Left."[84] The Religious Left, in other words, is not equivalent to the Religious Right; it is its "biblical alternative."

In view of the character of the issues that face us in the cultural conflict — notably the matter of who decides about the education of our children — it would seem that on certain issues it is simply impossible to refuse to take sides in the culture wars. It may be that "third ways" are impossible in some instances. Either one is for or against "pro-choice" abortion on demand, for or against state

84. *Sojourners*, January/February 1999, 4.

monopoly of a secular public school system, for or against legitimation of homosexuality as "normal," for or against large state control of business, and industry. While it is possible to nuance each of these either-ors in a significant way, we must come to terms with what James Davison Hunter analyzed as the two competing "tendencies" in the culture wars, the "impulse toward orthodoxy" and the "progressive impulse." In that case, to refuse to choose is also a choice to permit the dominant impulse space and opportunity to overwhelm the weaker one. This is what Kuyper was referring to when, in response to the accusation coming from his liberal critics that the Dutch Calvinist political movement was a theocratic threat to freedom, he protested that freedom was a two-way street:

> All [the gospel] asks is unlimited freedom to develop in accordance with its own genius in the heart of our national life. We do not want the government to hand over unbelief handcuffed and chained as though for a spiritual execution. We prefer that the power of the gospel overcome that demon in free combat with comparable weapons. Only *this* we do not want: that the government arm unbelief to force us, half-armed and handicapped by an assortment of laws, into an unequal struggle with so powerful an enemy. Yet that *has* happened and is happening *still*. It happens in all areas of popular education, on the higher as well as the lower levels, by means of the power of money, forced examinations, and official hierarchy. For this reason we may never desist from our protest or resistance until the gospel recover its freedom to circulate, until the performance of his Christian duty will again be possible for every Dutch citizen, whether rich or poor.[85]

Where do we go from here? Having considered secular alternatives to mere procedural democratic liberalism and the apparent failure of self-styled "third way" approaches, we find a promise for developing civic virtue in a surprising place.

"Ecumenical Jihad"?
Clues from a Surprising Alliance

Earlier in this chapter we encountered a surprising rejoinder to the fears expressed by secular Jews about the successful political resurgence of evangelical Christians: an Orthodox Jewish rabbi defending "Christian America."[86]

85. Abraham Kuyper, "Maranatha," in *Abraham Kuyper: A Centennial Reader,* ed. J. Bratt (Grand Rapids: Eerdmans, 1998), 224-25.
86. For an evangelical or Christian portrayal of this phenomenon, see the article by Bob Jones IV, "Deuteronomy Duo," *World Magazine* (February 15, 1997): 12-15.

The absolutely remarkable character of such an alliance between evangelical Christians and Orthodox Jews must not be overlooked and its significance ignored. The fear of secularists is that public expression of committed religious faith is a danger to civility, to religious freedom and pluralism. The specter of religious warfare, of Belfast and Beirut, is ever on the minds of America's secularists. What is remarkable about developments in American religious life during the last decade is that it has been precisely *committed* religious folk — committed, noncoincidentally, to *public* expression of their faith — who have created alliances of cobelligerence against those who would *secularize* the public square. While the Jewish-evangelical cooperation has been more informal in nature, it has been committed evangelicals and Roman Catholics who formally drafted a cooperative statement of common mission and purpose in March 1994, "Evangelicals and Catholics Together: The Christian Mission in the Third Millennium."[87] In addition, conservative Roman Catholic political activists actually formed Catholic Alliance, a division of the Christian Coalition created by evangelical leader Pat Robertson and with a predominantly evangelical membership.[88]

Considering the long history of Protestant-Catholic tensions in Europe and America as well as the more general ones between Jews and Christians in European history, these developments are directly counterintuitive to the secularist interpretation of modern political history. That reading is rooted in the formulaic conviction: religion equals tyranny and conflict; enlightened secularism equals freedom and tolerance. The remarkable character of this contrary development of committed religious folk rising above historic differences to form cooperative alliances — in the flagship nation of Enlightenment modernism no less — thus serves as an important clue to what is really going on in the culture wars. It is between and among communities that have significant histories of *incivility* and *intolerance* that we have begun to see genuine sacrifice, love of neighbor, civility, and tolerance, and we must ask, "Why?"

The Evangelicals and Catholics Together (ECT) statement is based on a common commitment to the Christian mission: "We enter the twenty-first century without illusions. With Paul and the Christians of the first century, we know that 'we are not contending against flesh and blood, but against the principalities, against the powers, against the world rulers of this present darkness, against the spiritual hosts of wickedness in the heavenly places' (Ephesians 6).

87. See Colson and Neuhaus, *Evangelicals and Catholics Together.* Page references that follow in the text are to this work.
88. See "Truths and Untruths about the Catholic Alliance," *First Things* 60 (February 1996): 7-9.

As Evangelicals and Catholics, we dare not by needless and loveless conflict between ourselves give aid and comfort to the enemies of the cause of Christ" (xvii).

Acknowledging the sins of the past, the ECT statement does not gloss over the question of truth or the reality that there are matters of profound significance that still divide evangelicals and Catholics.

> The love of Christ compels us and we are therefore resolved to avoid such conflict between our communities and, where such conflict exists, to do what we can to reduce and eliminate it. Beyond that, we are called and we are therefore resolved to explore patterns of working and witnessing together in order to advance the one mission of Christ. Our common resolve is not based merely on a desire for harmony. We reject any appearance of harmony that is purchased at the price of truth. Our common resolve is made imperative by obedience to the truth of God revealed in the Word of God, the Holy Scriptures, and by the trust in the promise of the Holy Spirit's guidance until Our Lord returns in glory to judge the living and the dead.
>
> The mission that we embrace together is the necessary consequence of the faith that we affirm together. (xvii)

The church's mission in the world is hampered by division and conflict, and therefore, loving cooperation where possible is essential to the mission of the Christian gospel. "Unity and love among Christians is an integral part of our missionary witness to the Lord whom we serve. 'A new commandment I give to you, that you love one another; even as I have loved you, that you also love one another. By this all men will know that you are my disciples, if you have love for one another' (John 13). If we do not love one another, we disobey his command and contradict the Gospel we declare" (xix). The road to final and full unity in Christ is recognized as an eschatological reality in process, a process that must honor truth and integrity.

> Together we search for a fuller and clearer understanding of God's revelation in Christ and his will for his disciples. Because of the limitations of human reason and language, which limitations are compounded by sin, we cannot understand completely the transcendent reality of God and his ways. Only in the End Time will we see face to face and know as we are known (1 Corinthians 13). We now search together in confident reliance upon God's self-revelation in Jesus Christ, the sure testimony of Holy Scripture, and the promise of the Spirit to his church. In this search to understand the truth more fully and clearly, we need one another. We are both informed and limited by the histories of our communities and by our own experiences. Across the divides of

communities and experiences, we need to challenge one another, always speaking the truth in love, building up the Body (Ephesians 4). (xx)

The distance of the ultimate goal must not, however, stand in the way of that which is realizable now.

As Evangelicals and Catholics, we pray that our unity in the love of Christ will become ever more evident as a sign to the world of God's reconciling power. Our communal and ecclesial separations are deep and long standing. We acknowledge that we do not know the schedule nor do we know the way to the greater visible unity for which we hope. We do know that existing patterns of distrustful polemic and conflict are not the way. We do know that God who has brought us into communion with himself through Christ intends that we also be in communion with one another. We do know that Christ is the way, the truth, and the life (John 14) and as we are drawn closer to him — walking in that way, obeying that truth, living that life — we are drawn closer to one another.

Whatever may be the future form of the relationship between our communities, we can, we must, and we will begin now the work required to remedy what we know to be wrong in that relationship. Such work requires trust and understanding, and trust and understanding require as assiduous attention to truth. We do not deny but clearly assert that there are disagreements between us. Misunderstandings, misrepresentations, and caricatures of one another, however, are not disagreements. These distortions must be cleared away if we are to search through our honest differences in a manner consistent with what we affirm and hope together on the basis of God's Word. (xix)

Common purpose is also found in *public* expression of faith together. Evangelicals and Catholics have found common cause in their concern about America.

Christians individually and the church corporately also have a responsibility for the right ordering of civil society. We embrace this task soberly; knowing the consequences of human sinfulness, we resist the utopian conceit that it is within our powers to build the Kingdom of God on earth. We embrace this task hopefully; knowing that God has called us to love our neighbor, we seek to secure for all a greater measure of civil righteousness and justice, confident that he will crown our efforts when he rightly orders all things in the coming of his Kingdom.

In the exercise of these public responsibilities there has been in recent years a growing convergence and cooperation between Evangelicals and Catholics. We thank God for the discovery of one another in contending for a common cause. Much more important, we thank God for the discovery of one another as brothers and sisters in Christ. Our cooperation as citizens is animated by our convergence as Christians. We promise one another that we will work to deepen, build upon, and expand this pattern of convergence and cooperation.

Together we contend for the truth that politics, law, and culture must be secured by moral truth. With the Founders of the American experiment, we declare, "We hold these truths." With them, we hold that this constitutional order is composed not just of rules and procedures but is most essentially a moral experiment. With them, we hold that only a virtuous people can be free and just, and that virtue is secured by religion. To propose that securing civil virtue is the purpose of religion is blasphemous. To deny that securing civil virtue is a benefit of religion is blindness. (xxiii)

It is in the spirit of *nonsectarian* concern for America's civic life that the ECT signatories affirm their commitment to liberty. All liberty, in the final analysis, depends on full freedom of religion in conscience and expression.

Religious freedom is itself grounded in and is a product of religious faith, as is evident in the history of Baptists and others in this country. Today we rejoice together that the Roman Catholic Church — as affirmed by the Second Vatican Council and boldly exemplified in the ministry of John Paul II — is strongly committed to religious freedom and, consequently, to the defense of all human rights. Where Evangelicals and Catholics are in severe and sometimes violent conflict, such as parts of Latin America, we urge Christians to embrace and act upon the imperative of religious freedom. Religious freedom will not be respected by the state if it is not respected by Christians or, even worse, if Christians attempt to recruit the state in repressing religious freedom.

In this country, too, freedom of religion cannot be taken for granted but requires constant attention. We strongly affirm the separation of church and state, and just as strongly protest the distortion of the principle to mean the separation of religion from public life. We are deeply concerned by the courts' narrowing of the protections provided by the "free exercise" provision of the First Amendment and by an obsession with "no establishment" that stifles the necessary role of religion in American life. As a consequence of such distortions, it is increasingly the case that wherever government goes religion must retreat, and government increasingly goes almost everywhere. Religion, which has been privileged and foundational in our legal order, has in recent years been penalized and made marginal. We contend together for a renewal of the constituting vision of the place of religion in the American experiment.

Religion and religiously grounded moral conviction is not an alien or threatening force in our public life. For the great majority of Americans, morality is derived, however variously and confusedly, from religion. The argument, increasingly voiced in sectors of our political culture, that religion should be excluded from the public square must be recognized as an assault upon the most elementary principles of democratic governance. That argument needs to be exposed and countered by leaders, religious and other, who care about the integrity of our constitutional order. (xxiv)

In terms of practical policies, the ECT statement expresses solidarity of concern about life issues — abortion and euthanasia — and for public policies that encourage the flourishing of mediating institutions as a buffer against state tyranny.

We contend for public policies that demonstrate renewed respect for the irreplaceable role of mediating structures in society — notably the family, churches, and myriad voluntary associations. The state is not the society, and many of the most important functions of society are best addressed in independence from the state. The role of churches in responding to a wide variety of human needs, especially among the poor and marginal, needs to be protected and strengthened. Moreover, society is not the aggregate of isolated individuals bearing rights but is composed of communities that inculcate responsibility, sustain shared memory, provide mutual aid, and nurture the habits that contribute to both personal well-being and the common good. Most basic among such communities is the community of the family. Laws and social policies should be designed with particular care for the stability and flourishing of families. While the crisis of the family in America is by no means limited to the poor or to the underclass, heightened attention must be paid those who have become, as a result of well-intended but misguided statist policies, virtual wards of the government. (xxvii)

This remarkable cooperation, I suggest, is a strikingly *nonsectarian* response to the sectarian conflict of America's culture wars. It clearly takes sides — the *orthodoxy* side of Hunter's typology — but it does so out of clear, articulated concern for the greater, public good. Rather than a movement to be feared for possibly contributing to civil unrest and division, it ought to be welcomed in hope for the recovery and maintenance of American liberty. The final paragraph in the section of the ECT statement dealing with civic responsibility sets forth what I would judge an appropriate (i.e., penultimate, secondary) American civic faith: "We are profoundly aware that the American experiment has been, all in all, a blessing to the world and a blessing to us as Evangelical and Catholic

Christians. We are determined to assume our full share of responsibility for this 'one nation under God,' believing it to be a nation under the judgment, mercy, and providential care of the Lord of the nations to whom alone we render unqualified allegiance" (xxviii). On this level, so it seems to me, it is fair to conclude that Abraham Kuyper would approve of the ECT initiative. For evidence supporting such a claim we turn, once again, to Kuyper's own alliance with Dutch Roman Catholics on the "school question."

Lessons from Abraham Kuyper:
Antithesis and Cobelligerence

Kuyper's public theology is usually described in terms of a dialectic between two important poles or themes in his thought: antithesis and common grace.[89] That conventional portrait goes something like this: Abraham Kuyper was a man committed to the Augustinian antithesis between the City of God and the City of Man, an antithesis he viewed as being reflected in the modern world in the conflict between the Christian gospel and the ideals of the French Revolution. This antithetical Kuyper is the Kuyper of polemics who battled against heresy in the church and secularism in the schools, and for the purity of Reformed principles in the educational creed of the Free University of Amsterdam.[90] "Militant neo-Calvinists" appeal to this antithetical side of Kuyper. What one could call "progressive neo-Calvinists" prefer to appeal to the other pole, the Kuyper of common grace (and social justice) who recognized the abundant gifts given by the Creator Spirit to unbelievers, who insisted that "the unbelieving world excels in many things."[91] This latter Kuyper is the one who gave the stirring address on poverty at the First Dutch Christian Social Congress in 1891.[92] On this reading Kuyper's appreciation for the positive insights of political traditions to which he otherwise and even *in toto* took great exception,[93] as well as his cooperation with the Roman Catholics in government co-

---

89. See, e.g., S. U. Zuidema, "Common Grace and Christian Action in Abraham Kuyper," in *Communication and Confrontation* (Toronto: Wedge, 1972), 52-105.

90. On the antithetical Kuyper see C. Augustijn, "Kuyper en de Antithesis," in *Abraham Kuyper: Vast en Veranderlijk, De Ontwikkeling van zijn Denken*, ed. C. Augustijn and J. Vree (Zoetermeer: Meinema, 1998), 165-82.

91. Kuyper, *Lectures on Calvinism*, 121.

92. Abraham Kuyper, *The Problem of Poverty*, trans. and ed. James Skillen (Grand Rapids: Baker, 1991).

93. See 320 above.

alition, is attributed to his common grace side, at least for the moment, overcoming his antithesis side.

There is much in this conventional portrait that is correct. In fact, it is intriguing to observe that in Kuyper's Stone Lectures, it is in his treatment of "Calvinism and Science" that he provides the most extensive discussion of *both* themes — common grace and the antithesis.[94] However, Kuyper's convictions about common grace are not, in my judgment, the most helpful frame for understanding his political cooperation with Roman Catholics. Instead, this cooperation, I suggest, is more a reflection of Kuyper's antithetical side than the common grace one. The coalition with Roman Catholics was born out of a cultural cobelligerence against the overwhelming and growing pressures of secularism in nineteenth-century Dutch education. What follows is a brief additional discussion of Kuyper's rhetoric and political strategy in this conflict.

Kuyper's actual entry into active parliamentary duty and the extensive political maneuvering on the "schools question" throughout his political career[95] has been covered well by others,[96] and our summary of it in this section will therefore be brief. Thanks to the support of Roman Catholic voters, Kuyper was elected to the Second Chamber of the Dutch Parliament in 1874. He resigned his ministerial office in the Dutch Reformed Church (taking honorable emeritation) and on December 7, 1874, gave his maiden speech in Parliament on the "schools question." Responding to the elementary education bill introduced into the house by Prime Minister Heemskerk, a bill that mandated educational "improvements" in all schools, including private religiously based schools, but provided financial support only for the "neutral" state schools, Kuyper made a plea for free schools. "Education," so Kuyper argued, "should be entirely autonomous, managed by a system of independent provincial and national education boards rather than government agencies. Although the state had the right to legislate on general standards of education, it also had the duty to ensure the right of all parents to send their children to schools of their own

94. Kuyper, *Lectures on Calvinism*, 121-26 (common grace); 130-40 (antithesis).

95. The dominance of the schools question in Kuyper's political career is evident from the fact that in the original 1879 edition of *Ons Program*, Kuyper's discussion of education far exceeds the length devoted to any other topic (465-737). Included here are parliamentary speeches and journalistic pieces from *De Heraut*.

96. See Peter Somers Heslam, *Creating a Christian Worldview: Abraham Kuyper's Lectures on Calvinism* (Grand Rapids: Eerdmans, 1998), 39-46; also Frank Vanden Berg, *Abraham Kuyper* (Grand Rapids: Eerdmans, 1960), 62-90; see also the broader treatment of Kuyper's political vison and practice by McKendree R. Langley, *The Practice of Political Spirituality: Episodes from the Public Career of Abraham Kuyper, 1879-1918* (Jordan Station, Ont.: Paideia, 1984). We have covered key dimension of the school question more extensively in the preceding chapter, 332-39.

choice."[97] Furthermore, educational "choice" must be genuine; the state "must meticulously respect the parents' demand of conscience . . . [and] should, in all fairness and as elemental justice, reimburse the non-state schools for the amount of money which those schools were saving the state."[98]

This particular episode is noteworthy because of what it reveals about the opposition. Kuyper's speech elicited from a rising young star and eventual leader of the Liberal Party, J. Kappeyne van de Coppello, a stinging rejection of the call for educational justice.[99] Kappeyne yielded no quarter on the matter of aid to nonstate schools and concluded his speech with a virtual declaration of war. To those who felt unfairly taken advantage of by the injustice of double taxation for education, Kappeyne simply retorted in effect, "too bad, tough!" Nonetheless, Kappeyne also took up a plea of concern "for the children." After all, "what father among you. . . ."

> Now I ask, can any father assert that it is his duty to withhold elementary education from his child when the school in which that instruction is enjoyed has been opened to the child without cost? If it be said, "if that is what you want, you are oppressing the minority," I would almost say, then that minority had better be oppressed, for in that case it is "the fly which causes the oil of the perfumer to send forth an evil odor" (Eccl. 10:1) and has no right to exist in our society.[100]

The consequences of this response were significant for Dutch politics. Being considered "flies that ruin ointment" and therefore undeserving of a place within Dutch society helped rally together "all those for whom the perpetuation of the non-state schools was a life-and-death-matter, irrespective of their religion or church affiliation."[101] More than anything else, the "schools question" joined Calvinist and Catholic in common cause on the battlefield against the "enemy" of state-mandated secularism.

We do not need to consider the entire history of the Dutch school debate until its resolution granting full legal and financial equality for all parents and children in 1915.[102] What we want to take note of here is Kuyper's rhetorical

97. Heslam, 39-40.

98. Vanden Berg, 73.

99. Johannes Kappeyne van de Coppello (1822-95) was the de facto leader of the liberal faction in the Dutch Parliament after the death of Thorbecke in 1872. He served as prime minister from 1877 to 1879.

100. Vanden Berg, 73-74.

101. Vanden Berg, 74.

102. For bibliography on the school question, see n. 97 in the previous chapter. More specifically on the Antirevolutionary Party's role in the parliamentary debates and

and political-legal strategy in making his appeal for educational freedom of choice. From the beginning of its history, the Antirevolutionary Party was preoccupied with the education issue. A turn-of-the-century expositor of the ARP program observes that "the question has been raised whether the ARP has not been too busy with the school question, giving the appearance that it was an educational party or school party, with no interest in other political issues."[103] Article 12 of its original 1879 party platform stated the matter forthrightly, albeit in somewhat complex fashion:

> [The Antirevolutionary Party] calls for the State:
> 1. To abandon the principle that the government itself should be called to the task of education (except insofar as a lack of resiliency among the citizens makes it necessary).
> 2. [To do] whatever is necessary to prevent government-run schools from [being] misused as instruments of propaganda for or against a particular religion.
>
> And,
> 3. To grant equal rights in education for all citizens regardless of their religious or pedagogical vision.[104]

Kuyper here makes no concession to the state school's claim of general and genial neutrality. The state school has a religious character; it is a "counter-church."[105] In his exposition of this plank in the Antirevolutionary Party platform, Kuyper picks up Groen van Prinsterer's language and refers to the state school as a "sectarian school of Modernism." The character of the school, he notes, is not the real issue; "the state-school is only a means to an end." What end? Imprinting the stamp of revolutionary modernism on the Dutch nation. The strategy by which this was to be accomplished was a step-by-step, deliberate secularization of the home, the church, and the school. Kuyper describes this strategy thus: "[The revolutionaries] attempted to dechristianize the family, then to make the church a laughing-stock, and finally to remove the Bible from the school."[106] However, having underestimated the strength of the Chris-

---

resolution, in addition to Kuyper's *Ons Program* (see n. 95 above), also see H. De Wilde, *De Antirevolutionaire Partij en haar Program van Beginselen* (Wageningen: "Vada," 1902), 204-26.

103. De Wilde, 204.

104. Abraham Kuyper, *Ons Program* (Amsterdam: H. J. Kruyt, 1879), 208; I am indebted to my colleague Henry De Moor for helping me unravel an exceedingly complex article of Dutch legalese.

105. Kuyper, *Ons Program*, 208.

106. Kuyper, *Ons Program*, 214.

tian homes in the Netherlands and their resistance to being emancipated, and finding their way blocked by a resurgent and strengthened Reformed as well as Roman Catholic community, these revolutionaries concentrated all their efforts on the school. In this way, hoping to capture the hearts of the nation's youth for at least six years, they created a "counter-church" out of the state public school. In response, says Kuyper, the movement by Christian believers to establish their own schools came as a shock, and the slogan echoing through the land promoting "schools with the Bible" came across as a war cry.[107] The revolutionaries Kuyper refers to are monists, secular sectarians who tolerate no alternative to their imperialist educational ambitions.

To bring the discussion up to date in a manner that captures Kuyper's polemical passion and sense of religious and cultural urgency, we need only look to current American debates about the family and education. Kuyper's insistence that secular schools were a "counter-church" was echoed by a group of Kuyper-inspired North American Calvinists whose call for greater choice and equal justice in education was a call for a "second disestablishment."[108] Kuyper's battle for educational freedom of choice and his understanding of what was at stake in the "schools question" sounds very similar to the American "culture wars" phenomenon today, as described by former leftist radicals Peter Collier and David Horowitz.[109] According to Collier and Horowitz, too many so-called moderates fail to recognize what is truly at stake in the "assault" on American traditional institutions by the radical political Left. Their description of the "crusade" (note the martial language!) against the family sounds a lot like Kuyper's account of the incrementalist strategy used in the nineteenth-century school debate.

> The crusade [of the Left and its liberal allies to dismantle the nuclear family] does not always take the form of a frontal assault, but pursues many avenues — from no-fault divorce to opposition to parental consent for abortion, to same sex marriage, to rainbow curricula in the schools. It is possible to see all this as an outgrowth of radical individualism[110] — the desire to be free of all restraints. But in fact it has a more powerful impetus — the desire of Leftism

107. Kuyper, *Ons Program*, 214-15.

108. See Rockne McCarthy et al., *Disestablishment a Second Time: Genuine Pluralism for American Schools* (Grand Rapids: Eerdmans, 1982); also see preface, n. 12.

109. Peter Collier and David Horowitz, "It's a War Stupid!" *Heterodoxy* (November 1996); reprinted as a booklet with the same title by the Center for the Study of Popular Culture, Los Angeles, Calif.

110. Collier and Horowitz refer here to the argument in Judge Robert Bork's book *Slouching towards Gomorrah: Modern Liberalism and the American Decline* (New York: HarperCollins, 1996).

to break down all resistance to its totalizing agenda and to deconstruct all social institutions that stand in its way. State power is the messianic force through which the Left intends to implement its social redemption, and the family is the last bulwark against the power of the state. And thus, in the malicious syllogism at the heart of the Left's strategy, the family is the enemy of progress and progressives everywhere.[111]

The reason "why we live in an ideological age and are engaged in an ideological war," according to Collier and Horowitz, is that radical leftists, having engaged in an "audacious political sex-change," appropriated to themselves the label "liberal" and were thus "able to fool others into thinking they shared the same agenda with the liberalism they had displaced." However, there is an enormous difference. "Radicals do not want an equal opportunity society, the hallmark of traditional liberalism. They want socialism — a society of equal results — even if they have to dress it up in the clothing of liberalism to make it palatable."[112] If this analysis by Collier and Horowitz is correct, then our earlier suggestion is confirmed — the culture wars are about liberty!

The Battlefield of the Imagination

We shall now briefly summarize the key general conclusions to which our discussion of Abraham Kuyper and the phenomenon of culture wars has taken us. We shall also summarize a proposal that has the potential for reconciling some of the tensions uncovered in this chapter's discussion. We began by raising some objections to Christian acquiescence in the martial rhetoric of the culture wars. Radical politicization of our social and cultural life, a politicizing that breeds incivility through demonizing the opposition, debases discourse in the public square and thus endangers liberty itself. As *Image* editor Gregory Wolfe observed, we risk turning America's public square into "the place in Matthew Arnold's 'Dover Beach,' a country 'where ignorant armies clash by night.'"[113]

At the same time, we also suggested that cultural pacifism is not really possible. As citizens, Christians *are* in the public square, and while they are obligated by their faith to relate to fellow citizens with respect, civility, and even sacrificial love, the cultural and social decisions they make — notably, how they choose to educate their children — involve them in the culture wars whether they like it or not. Protesting against and self-consciously refusing to contribute

111. Collier and Horowitz, 7-8.
112. Collier and Horowitz, 8.
113. Wolfe, "Conscientious Objector," 4.

to the politicizing of life so that we can bear witness to the conviction that "politics isn't everything," is itself a political act, a volley in the culture wars. Furthermore, if our culture wars are — as Kuyper surely believed about those of his day — in the final analysis a struggle about and for liberty, Christian citizens *ought* not evade their civic duty by avoiding conscription. Like all soldiers in any war, Christians must of course be guided by the gospel-inspired rules of "just war." In the culture wars, one of the primary just-war principles is the requirement of civility.

As an exemplary instance of Christian culture war involvement and appropriate tolerance, we explored in some detail the ECT statement and suggested that the unprecedented, goodwilled, public cooperation of long-standing religious opponents is a noteworthy development in American life. The statement is a response to a perceived public crisis in the American experiment of ordered liberty and at the same time, in its cooperative cobelligerence, a hopeful indicator of a way to restore an appropriate (i.e., nonidolatrous) American civic faith. Finally, we considered the educational battles of Kuyper's day and our own as a case study that illustrates what is at stake in the culture wars — liberty, particularly freedom of conscience and freedom of religious expression.

Now, if the culture wars are indeed about liberty and their intensity is a reflection of their nature as a *sectarian* conflict in which ideological *purity* is seen by both sides as the only final solution, what are Christians who repudiate such politicizing then to do? To paraphrase a popular book by Francis Schaeffer, "How, then, shall we fight?"[114] We come back full circle now to the beginning of this chapter and Gregory Wolfe's suggestion of an alternative to the culture wars from which he claims conscientious objection. Here, again, is Wolfe's summary of the mission for *Image*, the arts journal he edits: "*Image* was founded on the premise that Christians have an obligation to nourish the culture of their time, and to enrich their faith by deepening and extending their imagination. *Image* does not speak the language of politics but the language of art inspired by faith. That form of speech lies at the heart of our culture and it must not be allowed to become a dead language."[115] Wolfe, as we noted above, refers to this vision in which culture shapes politics rather than the reverse, as "religious humanism": "The new religious humanists know that culture shapes and informs politics far more powerfully than the other way around. They rec-

114. For a helpful perspective on a quite different dimension of "spiritual warfare," see John H. Armstrong, "How Shall We Wage Our Warfare," in *The Coming Evangelical Crisis*, ed. John H. Armstrong (Chicago: Moody, 1996), 227-44.

115. Wolfe, "Conscientious Objector," 4.

ognize that symbolism, imagery, and language play a crucial role in forming attitudes and prejudices, and they have devoted themselves to nourishing the imaginative life. At a time when the model of Enlightenment rationalism is crumbling under the weight of post-modern cynicism and nihilism, the religious imagination can speak meaningfully into the void."[116]

Wolfe's proposal, which is fully in line with this volume's sketch of Abraham Kuyper as a "poet,"[117] is a line of thought also pursued by a number of essayists in an instructive as well as inspiring symposium, *Toward the Renewal of Civilization: Political Order and Culture.*[118] Undergirding this collection of essays is the fundamental conviction that Christians must "not give in to the despair and anxiety of our postmodern age" (xiii). According to Archabbot Douglas R. Nowicki, O.S.B., chancellor of Saint Vincent College and author of the volume's foreword, the illustrative parallel to our age is the decaying and anxious world "that Saint Benedict confronted with the collapse of the Roman Empire." As "the Roman Empire was in a state of disintegration" and "optimism gave way to pessimism," Saint Benedict "fled the paganism and pessimism of Rome" and took up a twofold calling: *ora et labora* (xii-xiii).

In our discussion of contemporary culture wars in this chapter, we quickly came to a point of agreement with those who insist that politics cannot save us. In fact, according to Hilton Kramer, not only are our cultural crises not solvable by political solutions, but politics does not even have the capacity to solve merely *political* problems: "the political order is no longer capable of containing the really disruptive political forces that threaten it" (1). The assault by the counterculture on marriage and family, on education, on language itself must be resisted by *cultural* means rather than political ones, according to Kramer. He contends that "what the political Left in this country lost on the field of political battle, it has more than regained in the culture wars." This means that "many of our political battles cannot be won unless we can win back the ground we lost in the culture wars." According to Kramer, "a fundamental retrieval of the intellectual, artistic, and moral territory that has been lost under the assault of the counterculture is now the crucial task." Politics must be renewed by culture, not the other way around: "This is fundamental

116. Wolfe, "Conscientious Objector," 4.

117. See esp. chap. 1 above, 5-8, 42-79.

118. Edited by T. William Boxx and Gary Quinlivan, published by William B. Eerdmans, Grand Rapids, 1998. The symposium was held at Saint Vincent College, Latrobe, Pa., April 10-12, 1997. Our attention here will be focused on the essays by Hilton Kramer ("Institutionalizing the Counterculture," 1-9) and Claes Ryn ("Cultural Origins of Politics: The Modern Imagination of Escape," 10-25). Page references that follow in the text are to these two essays.

not only to a renewal of civilization but to a restoration of the kind of politics that allows us to separate politics from all those other questions we have come to think of as cultural" (9).

Claes Ryn elaborates this line of thought by calling attention to the kind of imagination that is at the heart of modern Enlightenment rationalism. Ryn insists that while the familiar linkage between modernity and rationalism has indeed had profound influence upon the world in which we live, "what needs to be better understood is that we move closer to the heartbeat of modernity if we look behind its *ideas* to the kind of imagination they express" (11).[119] Modernity is really about "a new way of *imagining* the world" (11). Modern people set aside the conviction that the reality of *sin* sets limits on what we can expect from life and not only entertain "great expectations" but regard a "good life" as an *entitlement,* a basic human "right." "For taking the trouble to be born, human beings have rights to food, housing, health care, and so forth." Conversely, following Rousseau's analysis, many see life's trials and disappointments not as a function of flawed human nature but as a consequence of "oppressive, distorting, social institutions and conventions. The remedy, Rousseau argues, is for humanity to cast off the chains that harness its goodness" (13). Having been primed to expect satisfaction and happiness as a fundamental human right, human beings who experience pain and disappointment feel betrayed and begin "to nurse a grudge against life" (14). Soon an ethos of daydreaming takes hold; "in the imagination, as opposed to the historical world in which we act, anything is possible; the dreamer can make for himself an existence according to his own wishes" (15).

From here it is a short step to actual proposals for revolutionary change. "What begins in the imagination of the artistically inclined soon is translated into schemes for transforming society. The imagination having revealed the possibility of a wonderful existence, why put up with life as it is?" (15). Historically, Ryn argues, "in the eighteenth and nineteenth centuries, escape from the present ceases for many to be a brief interlude and becomes a steady accompaniment of daily life. The daydream becomes the vantage point from which to judge existence" (17). As an example of this "modern moral-imaginative dynamic" of escape and liberation, Ryn briefly examines Gustave Flaubert's 1857 novel *Madame Bovary*. The abiding lesson from an analysis of such modern literature is that, having used imagination "to evade the hard and painful task of moral responsibility up close," the modern person "dreams of happiness on entirely different, far easier terms, of a life that can satisfy all of his pent-up desires" (19). For those who are in unhappy mar-

119. This corroborates a point central to this volume; see chap. 1 above, 15-28.

riages, liberative imagination fantasizes a wonderful life with another person. If the social order in which we live does not make all of us equally satisfied, we call for the liberating revolution that will set us all free. The modern world, argues Ryn, is a world filled with romantic-utopian daydreaming: "The world would be such a wonderful place if only . . ." (22). The ugly history of twentieth-century barbarism has clearly shown us that the steps are but few and short in the journey from escapist imagination to concerted efforts to remove the obstacles that are judged to stand in the way of the world becoming such a wonderful place. The path is familiar and well-worn; from dissatisfaction to naming scapegoats and identifying oppressive conspiracies to revolutionary seizure of power. Then comes the elimination of the offending cause of trouble, followed by tyranny. Today *The Protocols of the Elders of Zion;* tomorrow Auschwitz.

Ryn's response to the imagination of escape, revolution, and liberation is not to suppress imagination in favor of reason (the solution of Plato and Locke, to name but two), but to call for a *renewal* of imagination, to "a revitalization of character and a renewed willingness to confront the self and the world as they are" (22). It is important "to expose the modern imagination of daydreaming for what it is. . . . [To show that] the longing for liberation often expresses an ominous drive for uninhibited power." However, intellectual critique is not enough. "It is not possible to defuse escapist imagination with no imagination. . . . Human beings, including self-described rationalists, live in the end according to hopes and anxieties that formed in the imagination. It is their concreteness, their experiential texture that makes them powerful" (23-24). What then? An alternative imagination is needed, a nonescapist, moral imagination: "What we cannot do without, therefore, is the non-escapist imagination, which vividly expressed the actual higher possibilities and the actual dangers of human existence. Truly great art is never didactic, but it attunes us to the real world and to acting within it. Without that kind of imagination, intellectuals claiming to remedy our present difficulties will merely spin abstractions that do little to wean us off our escapism; indeed, their ideas may be only a new version of the problem" (24). The great art of the past can be a help here, but, Ryn contends, it is not enough. We need contemporary great art, and that brings us to a real problem: "Yet our greatest need may be for art from our own time that speaks powerfully to our predicament. There is one problem: great art cannot be ordered up the way think tanks and foundations may order up policy studies, conferences, and research projects. Real art is a miracle, which may appear when and where we least expect it. But we need and wait for such miracles" (25). *Ora et labora!*

We have now returned not just to the beginning of this chapter but to the beginning of our book. The proposal of this concluding section shares Shelley's conviction that "poets are the unacknowledged legislators of the world" and Dostoyevsky's dictum that "Beauty will save the world!"[120] Abraham Kuyper, I think, would agree.

But is that enough? Do we not need at least a little bit of politics to help us along, to make the world a better place? In the next chapter we will consider a remarkable answer to that question from a surprising source.

120. See chap. 1 above, 15-20.

CONCLUSION

CHAPTER NINE

Abraham Kuyper in America Today: Do Evangelicals Really Need a Public Theology?

Any alliance with any political power whatsoever is bound to be burdensome for religion. It does not need their support in order to live, and in serving them it may die.

Alexis de Tocqueville, *Democracy in America*

America is a liberal country that relies on the vitality of conservative institutions to teach the moral habits of democracy that keep us a liberal country.

U.S. Senator Dan Coats, *Mending Fences*

Atheism is a religion; don't try to shove it down our throat!

Mother of first-grade public school child
denied permission to read a Bible story to his class

An Independent is a guy who wants to take the politics out of politics.

Adlai Stevenson, *The Art of Politics*

Politics, as a practice, whatever its professions, has always been the systematic organization of hatreds.

Henry Adams, *The Education of Henry Adams*

Do not suppose that I have come to bring peace to the earth. I did not come to bring peace, but a sword.

Matthew 10:34

What a difference a few years make. What a difference even a single year makes! These concluding pages, written in the spring of 1999, necessarily have a different content and address, a different challenge, than they would have even as few as six months ago. This change is more significant than the obvious, normal, and routine "improvement with age." Had the manuscript for this book been completed on time, it would not have had to address the recently risen challenge to the very heart of its major focus: the relevance of Abraham Kuyper for a much-needed American evangelical theology.[1]

What was the momentous event or cultural challenge involving evangelical public theology that was new in 1999? The rise of the Religious Right as a political force in the 1970s and the barometer of its public influence has always been closely linked to the ebb and flow of American politics, especially federal campaigns. The election of President Jimmy Carter in 1976, the "year of the evangelical," highlighted the entry of Rev. Jerry Falwell's Moral Majority on the American scene. The election of Ronald Reagan in 1980 was attributed in large measure to the New Christian Right's growing influence thanks to its increasingly sophisticated grassroots political organization. Though the flawed and failed presidential campaign of Pat Robertson in 1988, as well as the 1992 electoral victory of the Clinton/Gore ticket, represented setbacks of sorts, the 1994 congressional triumph of the Republican Party, fueled by a conservative "Contract with America," was a moment of euphoria for the Christian as well as the secular American Right. "The tide was turning in America![2] The culture wars were not over but *we* — so the Right believed and its critics feared — are winning crucial skirmishes!" The headline of the neoconservative *Weekly Standard* trumpeted "WE WIN!" after President Clinton, in what the editors referred to

---

1. As it turns out, the author's inability to complete the manuscript by the deadline of the original timetable was, thus, providentially beneficial. Of course! We who are too often "of little faith" need such reminders. The heavenly Father, whose detailed providential care even numbers the hairs on our head and clothes the lilies of the field, would not be indifferent to publishing schedules.

2. The title of a book by Pat Robertson, published one year before the 1994 election: *The Turning Tide: The Fall of Liberalism and the Rise of Common Sense* (Dallas: Word, 1993).

as "the surrender of modern liberalism," announced in his January 23, 1996, State of the Union address that "the era of big government is over."[3]

Leading up to the impeachment of President Clinton and the Senate trial in February 1999, media opponents of the New Christian Right tended to agree with this judgment. The seemingly interminable investigation of President Clinton by Independent Counsel Kenneth Starr underscored a popular public perception gladly encouraged by a liberal media: sex-obsessed religious conservatism was a threat to hard-won freedoms for Americans, particularly the right to an abortion. The fact that Judge Starr was a devout, churchgoing evangelical Christian who — for goodness' sake — actually sang hymns while jogging, along with the focus in his report to Congress on detailed sordid and seamy presidential sexual behavior, fueled a perception that the whole "affair" was, as *New York Times* columnist Anthony Lewis declaimed, an attempted "coup by the Religious Right."[4] Then, in the first months of 1999, the tide was indeed turning. Now, though, it seems to be turning *against* and not *with* the concerns and values of the Religious Right. In fact, after the impeachment trial failed in the U.S. Senate, one of the key architects of the Moral Majority's political strategy, Paul Weyrich, in a public letter to friends, even appeared to raise the white flag of surrender: "The culture war is over," he wrote. "We lost."[5]

The Challenge to *Christian* Politics

This concluding chapter will address that issue directly. Is it indeed over for American conservative, evangelical political activism? Was the idea of an evangelical public theology a bad idea in the first place? As indicated in the preface, from the outset this study was intended to be a book about Abraham Kuyper that would be contemporary, timely, relevant to the current issues and needs of American evangelical Christians in the public square. The author was and remains convinced that Kuyper's life and thought is both an inspiration and an instructive model for self-consciously Christian engagement in the public realms of culture and politics. Though clearly a man bound by his own time and place, Kuyper is still relevant for American evangelicals today, perhaps especially for *American* evangelical political activists. In their newly discovered political zeal, American evangelicals clearly needed theoretical and strategic

3. *Weekly Standard,* February 5, 1996.

4. Printed in the *Grand Rapids Press,* September 29, 1998.

5. Paul Weyrich, "Letter of February 16, 1999," available on-line at http://www.freecongress.org/Libaward/minority.htm.

help in the closing years of the past decade, century, and millennium. Kuyper is an attractive candidate for such a role precisely because of his own awareness of and love for the American experiment, an experiment that was close to his heart because he believed its spirit was Calvinist to the core.

Though my own convictions about the usefulness of the project I envisioned almost five years ago have grown stronger rather than diminished in the interval, it is true that ideas and cultural shifts that appeared to be in the ascendancy then are now under increasingly heavy fire, even from former influential leaders in the Christian Right. In this concluding chapter, we shall specifically engage the challenge to the very project of distinctly *Christian* political engagement. This challenge has been articulated with passion by syndicated journalist Cal Thomas and evangelical pastor Ed Dobson of Calvary Church, Grand Rapids, Michigan, in their recent *mea culpa* on behalf of the Moral Majority organization in which they both once had significant leadership roles.[6] That a book on Abraham Kuyper should conclude with a chapter responding to a direct challenge coming from a successful journalist and an inspirational pastor, both noted for their skill and integrity as effective Christian communicators, seems utterly appropriate. Kuyper's two most important roles as a man gifted in using words in service of the Word were those of church reformer and journalist commenting on culture, society, and politics.

The basic affirmation of *Blinded by Might* is that conservative, evangelical Christians who are concerned about the many social pathologies and moral dysfunctions of American life adopted a strategy that was bound to fail when they embraced a political solution. The authors confess their own "sins" when they acknowledge "once believing that we could make things right through the manipulation of the political system" (8). The biblically directed path to "political and societal restoration" has been "mostly overlooked," the authors charge, in favor of attempts "to achieve success by shortcuts through the dark and deep political jungle" (8). The two reasons for the failure are, first, that when it comes to politics, most evangelicals "are in unfamiliar territory and lack the necessary survival skills," and second, that if we rely "mainly on politics to deliver us, we will never get that right because politics and government cannot reach into the soul. That is something God reserves for himself" (8-9). The authors also find distasteful the arrogance implied in names such as "moral majority" or "Christian coalition," the latter being particularly offensive since it implies "that disagreement with their political positions is, in fact, disagreement with Jesus" (80).

---

6. Cal Thomas and Ed Dobson, *Blinded by Might: Can the Religious Right Save America?* (Grand Rapids: Zondervan, 1999); references to this work will be given in the text.

The authors have not had a theological or political change of heart, they insist. They continue to "support much of what the movement upholds. . . . [They] respect Jerry Falwell for the good he has done as a pastor, a civic leader, a mobilizer of politically docile Christians who had withdrawn from their civic duties, and a man who has the capacity for great kindness and generosity that much of the media has ignored." Furthermore, "politically, we still hold to what are regarded as conservative beliefs [on] . . . abortion . . . pornography . . . drugs" (9). What, then, is the problem? The problem is believing that government could do something about the significant social pathologies that are present in American society. "But we believe that our social maladies are not the cause of our decadence. They are a reflection of it. . . . [They] were not created solely, or even mainly, by government, neither will they be resolved by government." The authors then give the reader a brief civics lesson. "Our founders believed in limited government. Those conservatives who argue that liberals used government to undermine what the Founders began should not now seek to grab the reins of government from liberal hands in order to use government solely to fix problems that are beyond its reach and power to solve" (9-10). It must also be noted in this brief synopsis that Thomas and Dobson "are emphatically not calling for retreat or surrender by conservative Christians, or anyone else on the 'right.'" Rather they are insisting on a reordering of priorities: "What we are calling for is something more powerful and longer-lasting than the endeavor too many of us have devoted too much time to for too long" (10).

The last point is worth reiterating. In Thomas's words, "it isn't that political activism by Christians or anyone else with a religious motivation is, in and of itself, wrong. It is just not the best" (14). Speaking on behalf of both authors, Thomas writes, "Our beliefs about God and the Bible have not changed. Neither has our politics. What has changed is that we no longer believe that our individual or collective problems can be altered exclusively, or even, mainly, through the political process" (15). The broader perspective from twenty years of evangelical activism is that "today very little that we set out to do has gotten done. In fact the moral landscape of America has become worse . . . [our] hopes of transforming the culture through political power, it must now be acknowledged, . . . have failed" (23). Taking abortion as an example, "perhaps the biggest and costliest battle waged by conservative Christians, twenty years of fighting has won nothing" (24). The tragedy of all this effort "was not the failure to succeed, but the waste of spiritual energy that would have been better spent on strategies and methods more likely to succeed than the quest for political power" (27). As Pastor Dobson says later in the book, "the Religious Right has abandoned the greater priority of communicating the gospel for the lesser priority of sanctifying the state. The net result is that they have accomplished neither very well" (109). The authors' "zeal," says Thomas, is "proclaiming a better way to transform society" (117). "[T]oo many religious conservatives have not learned from twenty years of attempts to fit the square peg of the kingdom not of this world into the round hole that is the kingdom of this world" (139).

There is much in this book that is needed, wise counsel for Christian political activists. A triumphalism that puts too much faith in political solutions is no less a Christian eschatological heresy coming from the right of the political spectrum than it is coming from the left. In particular, the warning about preachers actively becoming politically engaged and thereby losing their voice as authentic and credible messengers of Christ is well taken. Politicizing the pulpit is a major mistake. Unlike Moral Majority leader Rev. Jerry Falwell, Pat Robertson, at least, followed the example of Abraham Kuyper in resigning as a minister of the gospel when he founded the Christian Coalition and actively sought the presidential nomination of the Republican Party in 1988. The dangers involved in the explosive mix of religion and politics should never be ignored. Bad politics in the name of Christ is a scandal to the gospel; evangelical zeal mistakenly poured into a political movement rather than the gospel of reconciliation can and has produced apocalyptic zealotry that destroys all hope for a genuinely civil political society. So, the authors conclude quite correctly, "we must not demonize those with whom we disagree" (97). It is, perhaps, this practice of constantly having to find new dragons to slay in order to keep the money flowing into the coffers of political organizations that particularly disturbs the authors. They rightly worry that this fueling of hostility is a serious barrier to the Christian witness that the gospel reconciles rather than divides. Other examples of practical and wise counsel abound in this volume: Before evangelicals tackle the problems of public school education, say the authors, they should look at the state of marriage among evangelicals. "The most important first step in reshaping our nation is that we must keep our marriages together" (132). "The way a culture is reclaimed is through people living by different values" (143). "For a church to get involved in politics runs the risk of implying that there is a proper 'Christian' position on every political issue" (161). The temptation to political influence and power is a seduction for church leaders that takes them away from their real calling. All this and much more is salutary, wise counsel that evangelical political activists ignore at their peril and to which a heartfelt "Amen!" is the only appropriate response.

Now must come the reluctant "however." Notwithstanding the deep respect I have for both authors and their lives of service to God, our Lord's church, and the broader communities they influence with their Christian testimony, I do regret the publication of this particular volume and fear it may do a

412

great deal of unintended harm. *Blinded by Might* troubles and saddens me because I believe the authors have unwittingly provided the enemies of the Christian church and the enemies of liberty (in many cases the same crowd) with high-powered ammunition that will be used against fellow brothers and sisters in the faith. There is a tragic irony about this book; its sometimes harsh and angry tone and its more frequent unfairness and lack of balance in reaction to some of the excesses of the Religious Right symptomatically reflect the very sins it excoriates. What is right about the authors' concerns — and there is much that is right — gets lost in the overkill.

This overkill is reflected especially in the unfair coloring of evangelical political engagement by the repeated rhetorical use of qualifying words such as "only," "totally," and "exclusively."[7] So the authors inform us, "While we believe Christians need to support effective legislation, history has shown that we can't rely *totally* on laws" (65). "*Mere* laws do not change people or culture" (69). "One of the dangers of mixing politics and religion is that you begin to think the *only* way to transform culture is by passing another law" (65). Another rhetorical strategy that achieves the same result is to set certain values or approaches over against each other as either-or polar opposites. "We are not called to change the political beliefs of our opponents, but to announce the good news" (81). "Politics is about power, the Christian faith is about truth" (49). Immediately after this polarity, Thomas observes that "whenever you try to mix the two, power usually wins, at least for the short haul." Furthermore, the mixture of politics and religion is a bad thing because "politics is all about compromise,"[8] while "the church is supposed to be about unchanging standards." Most of the time, so history shows us, says Thomas, the former corrupts the latter much more often than the latter positively influences the former. It is in this section of the book that Thomas also juxtaposes power and love, citing Henri Nouwen: "Maybe it is that power offers an easy substitute for the hard task of love. It seems easier to be God than to love God, easier to control people than to love people, easier to own life than to love life" (53).[9]

In addition, by focusing their criticism on what they refer to as "the quest

7. The emphasis in the citations that follow is added.

8. This observation about compromise needs to be placed in a larger context. All Christian living in the fallen world, especially in the arena of society and politics, involves compromise, as Ernst Troeltsch has so effectively demonstrated in his *Social Teaching of the Christian Churches,* trans. Olive Wyon, 2 vols. (1931; reprint, Louisville: Westminster/John Knox, 1992). For further reflection on the drive for "purity," see the last section of this chapter, "Abraham Kuyper and Saint Benedict."

9. Citation is from Henri J. M. Nouwen, *In the Name of Jesus: Reflections on Christian Leadership* (New York: Crossroad, 1989), 59.

for political power," on efforts by religious conservatives "to use government to fix problems that are beyond its reach and power to solve" (10), Dobson and Thomas perpetuate the popular liberal media perception that conservative, evangelical political activists are closet theocrats who seek to impose their sectarian brand of narrow Christian morality on freedom-loving Americans. Coming from two of Rev. Falwell's earliest and closest associates, this charge and the implied characterization of Falwell's ministry in the previous paragraph gains a credibility it simply does not deserve. Jerry Falwell's ministry at Thomas Road Baptist Church in Lynchburg, Virginia, as both Dobson and Thomas know well, cannot be honestly described with the exclusionary "merely's" and "only's" of the rhetoric the authors use too carelessly.

Dobson and Thomas's book has already become something of a *cause célèbre* in the national media,[10] and the authors run the very risk that their volume warns against, namely, being seduced by powerful interests for political purposes. It is not unreasonable to fear that this volume will continue to be part of the arsenal used by secularist political activists[11] in the war to shut down a Christian presence and voice in the public square. The volume concludes with a series of interviews by Thomas of prominent American public figures, interviews that are intended as testimonies in favor of the authors' position.[12] The interview with television producer Norman Lear, founder of People for the American Way, illustrates how the book might be exploited by those who wish to silence Christian voices. Parenthetically, it is worth noting here that a growing friendship with Lear contributed to one of the defining moments in Thomas's growing disaffection with the Moral Majority. A Moral Majority

10. In addition to local television and radio attention in Dobson's own Grand Rapids, Mich., the king of television newsmagazines, CBS's *60 Minutes*, did a feature on it, May 16, 1999.

11. Such as the American Civil Liberties Union, Americans United for Separation of Church and State, People for the American Way. To refer to these groups as versions of "secularist political activism" does not imply that all members are secular atheists rather than religious people, but only that the goals of each group are singularly devoted to creating and maintaining a secular, religiously naked public square.

12. One of the ten people included in the published interviews that conclude the book is former U.S. senator and 1972 Democratic presidential candidate George McGovern, who says the following: "And we can't transform the moral behavior of any society by doing it through edicts from the top; it has to be a slow progression of moral and spiritual improvement across the society. That's why, for example, I think the concept of what we used to call the Moral Majority comes at it the wrong way. The Moral Majority assumed that the kingdom of God is a Moral Majority. That's neither scripturally nor politically sound." In place of a "moral majority" Senator McGovern says he believes the biblical notion is that of a "saving remnant working within society to bring about the kingdom of God. It is made up of a small number of believers and faithful practitioners of good" (201-2).

414

fund-raising letter had demonized Lear as "the #1 enemy of the American family in our generation," and when asked by an Associated Press reporter whether Thomas agreed with this claim, he responded, "No, I think that's a bunch of crap." Thomas adds this explanation: "Norman Lear was becoming a friend of mine, and I felt it more important to develop a relationship with him than to call him names" (54). We shall return to this matter of Norman Lear and the activist group he founded later, but now we focus on Thomas's interview of his friend in *Blinded by Might.*

Lear responded to Thomas's question about "hostility toward religious faith" in American public life with the claim, "I don't know anybody who feels the [U.S.] courts have shown hostility to faith." On the face of it, that seems remarkable. In view of the numerous concerns expressed by religious people about court-supported secularization — for example, the issue of prayer in public schools — Lear's statement simply indicates that he does not personally know any evangelical Christians.[13] But Lear's point is based less on lack of personal experience with evangelical parents who "feel" such hostility and experience such harassment than it is on his political ideology and ideological definition of religion. How does Lear come to his conclusion that there is no hostility toward religion in America? By defining religion in such strictly personal and private terms that inherently forbid it any public expression: "Religious feeling is personal. It's personal and at its essence it's something that fills the individual soul. I would never understand why it requires public expression if it means the discomfort of somebody else's soul" (244). Does Lear *really* believe that public expressions of religious faith that discomfort somebody else's soul should not be heard in the public square? The answer is found in Lear's own political activism. Surely he must know that People for the American Way, the organization he founded to battle the Moral Majority, makes evangelical Christians very uncomfortable in its relentless pursuit of a secular, religiously neutral and naked public square? If so, by his own principles, he is then under obligation to be silent and not continue pressuring the coercive power of American courts to advance the program of secularization in which he believes so strongly. Yet, while the Moral Majority is no more, People for the American Way remains active and vocal.

Once again, let us not lose track of the key point here. I am in full agreement with Thomas and Dobson that it is an enormous error and scandal to the

13. One is tempted to ask whether Lear has read his friend Cal Thomas's book *The Things That Matter Most* (New York: HarperCollins, 1995), 116-19; Thomas describes the court-created climate of fear ("what *might* the law do?") in public education as "ludicrous" (116).

gospel to politicize the Christian faith and triumphalistically expect political activism and government power to redeem a national society from moral and cultural dysfunctionality. In particular, it is an evangelical disaster for churches and pastors to be distracted from the spiritual obligation they have to disciple people and instead become advocates for particular political agendas. To all that, once again, a hearty "Amen," along with a reminder that this is a message that applies to both the Christian Right and the Christian Left. A direct mixture of politics with the Christian faith in this way is risky, a potential scandal to the gospel itself. "Let the church be the church!" In addition, the political temptation also risks diverting our attention from the only real hope for human individual and social change. It is human hearts transformed by the Holy Spirit's reconciling work that bring about renewal and change. Thomas and Dobson are not the first or only public figures to make this important point,[14] but it needs to be made repeatedly, also specifically for the Religious Right. Why, then, my "however"?

The first reason has already been briefly indicated above. The language used by Thomas and Dobson in places contributes to the impression that the real goal of conservative, evangelical political activism is a theocratic takeover of the American government. That the authors even hint at such a goal is puzzling. Pastor Dobson himself refutes this theocratic premise when he contends that any notion "that the purpose of the Moral Majority was to take over America" is a "false notion." Rather, so he insists, "the Moral Majority was founded as a reaction against a secular society that was increasingly hostile to conservative Christians. Christians believed that they were an oppressed minority and that if they did not stand up, they would be buried by the secularists and humanists." In short, the Moral Majority was a *defensive* organization of Christians: "It was a fortress to protect, not a battleship to attack. We were not interested in taking over America. We were only interested in making sure we did not get overtaken." Dobson then cites directly from a letter by Rev. Falwell: "The government was encroaching upon the sovereignty of both the church and the family. . . . Something had to be done now" (37). Furthermore, the traditional Baptist dogma of "separation of church and state" was expressly affirmed in the original Moral Majority agenda (37).

This important point is confirmed by Thomas's interview in *Blinded by Might* of Pat Robertson, who acknowledges that some of the Christian Coali-

14. See the interview with evangelist Luis Palau, "Changed Hearts, Not Politics, Prompt Social Renewal," *Religion and Liberty: A Publication of the Acton Institute for the Study of Religion and Liberty* 7, no. 1 (January and February 1997): 1-4; also Glenn Loury, "Individualism before Multiculturalism," *Ethics and Public Policy Center "Unum Conversation,"* no. 3.

tion's political rhetoric needed to be toned down, lest the political message get in the way of the matter of first importance — the gospel. "Our first job," says Robertson, "is obviously to serve God and to win people for his kingdom, not to establish the Republicans as the ruling party in America. . . . We should not let anything we do or say having to do with temporal issues turn people away from the gospel" (252-53). If this is so, then the accusation that the Moral Majority wanted to "seek to grab the reins of government from liberal hands in order to use government solely to fix problems that are beyond its reach and power to solve" (10) is a calumny from its secular opponents, a clearly *false* accusation according to Dobson's own testimony about the matter. Why, then, do Thomas and Dobson themselves hint at what their own testimony makes clear is "a false notion"? All this is very confusing.

The authors also send us a mixed message on education. They believe that "many public school children are getting [a] profoundly secularized and politically driven message" at school that, among other things, in its sex education, has as its "goal to strip [children] of their innocence early so that by the time they reach puberty they will be more receptive to what the government educators want to teach them" (134). In fact, many public schools are "education camps" where children "are taught lies" (135). This is a grave charge, and the authors call for a strong response. Practically, they say, this means "we are calling for greater support of private and charter schools that will instill basic Judeo-Christian values in their students" (135). To expect children to be ambassadors for Christ in such a hostile environment is "naive." That accusation against public schools reminds us of Kuyper's charge one hundred years ago that the state schools of the Netherlands were "counter-churches," and the authors' apologia for parental rights and educational justice also has a familiar ring to students of nineteenth-century Dutch history. At stake here is the fundamental freedom of educational choice for parents. Yet, later on in the book they query, "could it be that the moral and educational decline of American public schools is in part due to this exodus of people of faith?" Then comes this proposal that seems to contradict the previous one: "What if we shut down every Christian school in America and the students, teachers, and administrators returned to the public schools — would that have a positive effect? Would it begin to reverse the moral and educational decline in society?" (167-68). At this point we cannot resist raising a question that goes to the heart of the authors' concern: What happened to the insistence that the church is the only agent in society capable of effecting moral renewal? Why does the public school suddenly get included in the group of agencies that are to transform society? More fundamentally, however, is the second proposal not exceedingly unrealistic in light of legal constraints placed on Christian teachers in America's public schools? To paraphrase the authors themselves, to expect that Christian teachers in the public schools are free to be open ambassadors for Christ in such a (legally) hostile environment is *naive.*

The conflicting messages about the education issue illumine one of the troubling things about *Blinded by Might.* The book both acknowledges and then practically seems to deny the culture wars *as a political reality.* Who can quarrel with the proposition that real moral change is effected by God the Holy Spirit in the hearts of individual persons through the means of the gospel testimony? This is a point readily agreed to, for example, by writers as diverse as the liberal Dutch Reformed theologian Harry Kuitert[15] and the dean of American evangelical theologians, Carl F. H. Henry.[16] But the question of who is finally responsible for the moral and other education of America's children — parents or the state? — is one that cannot be settled by appeals to personal regeneration. Not only does it require political *analysis* but it is also clear that, facing a powerful, secular state educational monopoly, it demands political *action.* The question that Thomas and Dobson do not adequately address in their book is whether the situation that American Christian parents face concerning the education of their children warrants *concerted* Christian political action or whether *individual* political action is enough. The authors drop hints that they believe that the critical cultural situation in America that gave rise to the Moral Majority in the first place still obtains. If so, their book is strangely devoid of *cultural* or *political* urgency. What happened to the *cri de coeur* expressed by Thomas in *The Things That Matter Most* only five years ago?

This is a book for those who feel like aliens in their own land. . . .
You are people who already know what you believe, and why. . . .
You go to church on Sunday (or synagogue on Saturday), where you worship an Authority higher than the state or your erogenous zones. You are frustrated that your faith, values, and beliefs seem to be reflected only in your bathroom mirror.

And,

[You] are aware, as perhaps never before, that something has gone wrong in the last three decades, and . . . may at last be ready, under the right leadership, to launch a second American revolution aimed at taking [your] country back

15. Harry Kuitert, *Everything Is Political, but Politics Is Not Everything,* trans. John Bowden (Grand Rapids: Eerdmans, 1986).
16. Carl F. H. Henry, *Aspects of Christian Social Ethics* (Grand Rapids: Eerdmans, 1964), 15-25.

and again creating a government of the people, by the people, and for the people — not government in spite of the people.

Thomas even identifies a culprit — the countercultural values of the sixties generation: "This is a book that recalls the sixties generation's failed promises and how many now leading the country who are from that generation continue to try to implement the philosophy upon which they were based, in spite of the evidence of failure and misery those broken promises created."[17] Thomas's present discomfort with the next-to-last citation above is understandable, but even when we discount the dangerous note of triumphalism in it, there remain valid issues and questions. Whose country is America and whose values govern its major institutions? Is majority opinion reflected in the nation's cultural direction? And, even if majority attitudes are reflected there, are they then true to America's founding ideals and constitutional framework? Alexis de Tocqueville warned against a "tyranny of the majority," a situation in which "habits form[ed] in freedom . . . may one day become fatal to that freedom."[18] At such a time the hope for liberty will reside in a *remnant* of citizens that remains true to liberty's ideals. What must Christians do who are concerned about what they perceive as a drift away from the moral convictions that make a community strong and free; that made America as a nation strong and free? Who will teach our children and who is responsible for appointing the teachers? Parents or the state? If the solution to certain perceived cultural and social problems is not to be found in concerted, explicitly designated *Christian* political action, what then? What do Thomas and Dobson suggest as an alternative?

An Alternative to Christian Political Activism?

If politics cannot save us, what can? Exactly how does preaching and practicing the gospel of reconciliation get translated into concrete transformation of society? Pastor Dobson tells us that early on in his ministry at Calvary Church in Grand Rapids, he "decided that we are to love people unconditionally just as God loved us. I decided that my ministry would not be one of condemnation. . . . I longed to be known as one who preaches a message of love and forgiveness, not a message of hate and condemnation" (152). This statement comes immediately after Pastor Dobson has insisted that "keeping the pulpit free of politics does not mean keeping it free of clear, biblical, moral teaching."

17. Thomas, xv-xvi.
18. Alexis de Tocqueville, *Democracy in America*, ed. J. P. Mayer, trans. George Lawrence (New York: Harper & Row, 1966), 254.

As this is formulated, does Pastor Dobson provide an alternative to the politicizing of the gospel to which he objects so vigorously? Not exactly.

The problem with stating matters in terms of a contrast between "compassionate love" on the one hand and "hateful condemnation" on the other is that this polarity is, as sophisticated observers such as Dobson and Thomas should know well, code language. Forcing a choice between these two is exactly the rhetorical technique used by those who wish to silence a Christian public voice on moral issues, particularly matters of sexual morality. Publicly voiced support for traditional Christian sexual morality is defined as "hateful," and void of all compassion. Opposition to homosexual practice, for example, even when accompanied by clear affirmations favoring full *civil rights* for all persons, including homosexuals, is *defined* by gay activists as "hateful" and "homophobic." Now it is important to be perfectly clear here. It is fitting and necessary to lament the failures of the Christian church to minister appropriately to gay people. It is sad that honest efforts in this ministry, such as those carried out by Pastor Dobson's church (see 160-64), are rewarded with hate mail rather than appreciation and gratitude. Yet, in making this important case one need not, and in fact should not, by using the code language of radical gay activists, concede the terms of the debate to those who would silence Christian freedom of expression in the public square. By defining the traditional Christian moral objection to homosexual behavior as "hate speech," gay activists seek to put it outside the cover of the First Amendment's free speech guarantee. With its lack of clarity on this crucial point, having favorably introduced the very polarity used so effectively by one side in the culture wars, the Thomas/Dobson book thus *itself becomes* a political act; this is an ironic conclusion for a book whose main thesis is that evangelicals should downplay the importance of politics. If the authors really believed their own thesis, they would not have written this book. Dobson and Thomas have not taken us out of the realm of the political, they have simply redefined the political in therapeutic terms, and that redefinition is itself a form of the cultural captivity against which they so rightly warn evangelical political activists.[19]

And here we come to another difficulty with this book, a failure to come to terms adequately with the character and tactics of the opposition. The au-

19. On the therapeutic turn in American culture more broadly, see Philip Rieff, *The Triumph of the Therapeutic: Uses of Faith after Freud* (New York: Harper & Row, 1966); on the same shift in the American evangelical world, see David Wells, *No Place for Truth; or, Whatever Happened to Evangelical Theology?* (Grand Rapids: Eerdmans, 1993); David Wells, *God in the Wasteland: The Reality of Truth in a World of Fading Dreams* (Grand Rapids: Eerdmans, 1994); David Wells, *Losing Our Virtue: Why the Church Must Recover Its Moral Vision* (Grand Rapids: Eerdmans, 1998).

thors state some of their own moral and political convictions openly — they favor educational vouchers, hold traditional Christian moral beliefs about human sexuality, and oppose abortion, euthanasia, drug abuse, and pornography. Here we come back to Cal Thomas's friend Norman Lear, founder of People for the American Way (hereafter PFAW).[20] On each of the issues just indicated, PFAW not only takes the exact opposite view of Dobson and Thomas — opposition to vouchers, in favor of children's rights freely and fully to access the Internet, advocacy for sex education in the public schools, opposition to any religious symbolism or practice in the schools or public square — but frames them all together in terms of a vast theocratic conspiracy by the Religious Right "to impose a set of beliefs and ideas on America's next generation."

The Religious Right, so declares PFAW on its web page, is engaged in a major attack on public education, consisting of "ideological and sectarian demands" that will "coerce religious activity . . . censor entire curricula, including sexuality education, multicultural programs, and guidance and self-esteem programs," and thereby deny children access to quality education. Efforts to prevent children in schools from free access to anything on the Internet, including pornography, are called "attacks on the freedom to learn online," and alternatives to sex education programs such as those that emphasize abstinence are called "fear-based curricula" that prevent the development of "healthy, mature, responsible attitudes about sex and all of its implications, including reproduction and disease prevention." The "fear-based curricula," so we are told, not only are guilty of "promulgating misleading and inaccurate information," they also often use religious motivation, which is "a form of proselytizing that threatens to breach the separation of church and state." The attack on public education by the Religious Right is part of a larger picture according to PFAW: "The growing attack on public education in this country mirrors a troubling trend away from fairness in public policy — welfare laws that punish the poorest citizens; bills to abolish affirmative action and erode religious freedom; misguided tax policies that would hurt cities, children and the poor." So, if one favors educational vouchers as a matter of justice and equity, believes that ending affirmative action is necessary for establishing a truly color-blind society, contends that many current models of sex education are not only ineffective but coarsen children's moral sensitivities, and holds that some control over children's access to the Internet is appropriate — then one is labeled a right-wing fanatic, part of a vast theocratic conspiracy to destroy the American way of freedom and opportunity.

20. Material about the positions held by People for the American Way and the citations that follow were from the organization's web site: http://www.pfaw.org.

It needs to be noted here that the issue about which PFAW, along with kindred organizations such as Americans United for Separation of Church and State,[21] gets so excited is not just state-subsidized voucher plans such as the one recently passed in the Florida legislature.[22] Even privately financed schemes such as that of CEO America, funded by Ted Forstmann and John Walton and channeled through a program called the Children's Scholarship Fund, receive rough treatment. A recent Americans United press release described Forstmann thus: "Ted Forstmann, a Wall Street investment banker and head of the Children's Scholarship fund, helped found and donates generously to Empower America, a right-wing 'think tank' known for its hostility toward public education that employs William Bennett. Bennett, secretary of education under President Ronald Reagan, is perhaps the best-known public school basher in the country. Forstmann is also a board member of the Cato Institute, a libertarian-oriented group that strongly advocates replacing public schools with a voucher system." The press release continues: "CEO America's well heeled backers are free to pursue their agenda of trying to wreck public education, but they shouldn't be held up as heroes for doing it." As committed secularists see it, criticism of public school education is the key strategy of an overall theocratic goal to re-create a Christian America. As a PFAW promotion puts it: "Religious Right leaders have made the campaign to secure *public money for religious schools* with vouchers a keystone of their effort to tear down the wall between church and state."

Now, in the face of this organized effort by secularists, Thomas and Dobson suggest that responding in kind with a well-organized and financed, concerted, and explicitly evangelically grounded political and legal action is a mistake. It has not worked and it will not work. Instead of angry warriors on the warpath for a cause, we need to get rid of our holier-than-thou attitudes, have happier countenances, invest our lives in the needy and hurting, and openly display love for our enemies.[23] "More people can be persuaded through a gentle spirit and consistent living than by condemnation, triumphalism, and judgmentalism (which is not to be confused with legitimate judgments about right and wrong — there is a difference)" (188). While all this is indeed sound *pastoral* advice, does it get at a serious *political* problem that becomes manifest in the concerted opposition to the Religious Right?

21. Information taken from Americans United for Separation of Church and State web site at http://www.au.org.; the press release quoted below in this paragraph is dated April 20, 1999.

22. See the article in the *Weekly Standard,* May 17, 1999, 21-26.

23. Thomas and Dobson, 178-82; page references that follow in the text are to the Dobson/Thomas book.

That is the key issue that Thomas and Dobson do not really face, and, as we shall see in the next section, the failure to address it adequately is more serious than simply an intellectual oversight. It is, rather, a dangerous form of political pacifism that potentially threatens the very liberty of evangelicals in America to express themselves freely in the public square. Dobson and Thomas do not like the rhetoric of "enemies," but they need to face the question whether there really *are* enemies of religious freedom in America today — well-organized and well-financed enemies even. If so, then it is a major mistake for evangelical Christians to lay down their *political* arms. The political arms used by Christians, of course, must not violate Christian faith or love nor in any way compromise the gospel. Yes, the church must be the church and not an arm of a political movement. Yes, Christian conduct in public — including in politics — must measure up to the description of the fruitful, Spirit-governed life described by the apostle Paul in Galatians 5:18ff. Yes, bad politics, especially demonizing one's opponents, risks discrediting the good news of the gospel of God's reconciling love in Christ. So, yes, there is indeed a risk in concerted Christian political activism. The authors hit the target correctly in my judgment when they contend that the name Christian Coalition was poorly chosen because it excludes other religious people, and that the name Moral Majority had about it the sniff of arrogance. Parenthetically, it is only fair to point out that calling one's organization People for the American Way is no less arrogant than the name Moral Majority. It is worth noting here that Abraham Kuyper, who believed passionately in concerted, organized, distinctly Christian political action, nonetheless started a party that did not include "Christian" in its name but focused on a Christian-historical "principle" by calling itself the Antirevolutionary Party. Any number of Christian-based voluntary or educational-political organizations — Center for Public Justice, Institute for Religion and Democracy, Institute on Religion and Public Life, to name but a few — do not explicitly use the name of Christ in their organizational labels. Some even prefer to feature important symbolic ties to the Christian tradition by using historical figures — the Rutherford Institute, the Acton Institute — as identifiers for their organizations. But the issue at stake here is not a name but the very legitimacy of *free* and *organized* Christian public expression. The two authors come at this from different concerns, and each needs to be considered separately.

The formative influence on Pastor Dobson's antipathy to concerted political action in the name of Christ is his personal experience of the tragic religious conflict in Northern Ireland. His personal account of experiences that reflect both the pain of that conflict as well as touching moments of reconciliation in Christ that transcend generations of conflict is moving as well as instructive. Northern Ireland is what Pastor Dobson in greater and lesser ways wants to avoid. So should we all — passionately! But America is not Northern Ireland, and the religious divide in America is not the age-old conflict between the Orange and the Green, but between those who wish to exercise the constitutionally guaranteed freedom of public religious expression and those who seek to denude the public square of any religious presence. For evangelical Christians to engage in self-censorship[24] on this matter may alleviate the problem of potentially scandalizing the faith, but it contributes to the pattern of oppressive secularization, a tendency with serious negative consequences for the civic good.[25] What Dobson and Thomas do not address in their book is the fact that secular resistance to Christian presence in the public square finally applies to individuals as well as groups, and to nonpolitical arenas such as education, the arts, and the media.[26]

Before we consider how that last point potentially affects Thomas's own vocation as an evangelical Christian journalist, we need to elaborate another point made in the previous paragraph: America is not Northern Ireland. What is different about America? Once again, we turn to the perceptive eyes of a European visitor to these shores, Alexis de Tocqueville,[27] and reflect on two of the dominant impressions he had of life in the United States. The first, of course, was the clear separation of ecclesiastical and civil power. Tocqueville was amazed to find that even Catholic priests "all thought that the main reason for the quiet sway of religion over their country was the complete separation of church and state. I have no hesitation in stating that throughout my stay in

24. I am indebted to George Marsden for this term. In dealing with the privatization of faith in the academy, Marsden notes that such privatization is "largely a matter of self-censorship. Younger scholars who are Christian quickly learn that influential professors hold negative attitudes toward open religious expression and that to be accepted they should keep quiet about their faith. So rather than attempting to reflect on the relationship between religious faith and their other beliefs, they learn to hide their religious beliefs in professional settings. Such self-censorship by its very nature proceeds quietly but the attitudes it fosters are pervasive." George Marsden, *The Outrageous Idea of Christian Scholarship* (New York and Oxford: Oxford University Press, 1997), 52. Much has been written about the phenomenon of "political correctness" in the North American academy; an excellent recent introduction is Alan Charles Kors and Harvey A. Silvergate, *The Shadow University: The Betrayal of Liberty on America's Campuses* (New York: Free Press, 1998).

25. The previous note demonstrates the pernicious effects of such self-censorship on truth. The same must be said for justice and, with respect to imagination and the arts, also for beauty. See my earlier discussion of imagination, art, and politics, 15-20, 72-79, 355-364, 398-403.

26. This is, in large measure, due to the deliberate politicizing of nonpolitical spheres of life.

27. The parenthetical page references that follow are to *Democracy in America*.

America I met nobody, lay or cleric, who did not agree about that" (295). What Tocqueville found was that clergy not only were notably absent from political positions, but "most of them seemed voluntarily to steer clear of power and to take a sort of professional pride in claiming that it was no concern of theirs." In addition, he observed that "they were careful to keep clear of all parties, shunning contact with them with all the anxiety attendant upon personal interest" (295). From this, Tocqueville draws an important principle about the relation between politics and religion:

> I know that, apart from influence proper to itself, religion can at times rely on the artificial strength of laws and the support of the material powers that direct society. There have been religions intimately linked to earthly governments, dominating men's souls both by terror and by faith; but when religion makes such an alliance, I am not afraid to say that it makes the same mistake as any man might; it sacrifices the future for the present, and by gaining a power to which it has no claim, it risks its legitimate authority. (297)

By contrast, Tocqueville contends that there was something in European culture and politics that retarded the natural, human development toward liberty. "I am profoundly convinced," he wrote, "that this accidental and particular cause is the close union of politics and religion. Unbelievers in Europe attack Christians more as political than as religious enemies; they hate the faith as the opinion of a party much more than as a mistaken belief, and they reject the clergy less because they are the representatives of God than because they are the friends of authority." Tocqueville concludes: "European Christianity has allowed itself to be intimately united with the powers of this world. Now that the powers are falling, it is as if it were buried under their ruins. A living being has been tied to the dead; cut the cords holding it and it will arise" (301). What Tocqueville observed and concluded is in agreement with one key point made by Dobson and Thomas: the church and its representatives need to be wary about even the mere appearance of coziness with civil power. Not only is it a seduction that compromises the church's vocation and mission, it also sends a message to the broader public that the Christian political vision is restrictively theocratic rather than genuinely pluralistic — a most un-American as well as unchristian message. However, to say this, even to say it emphatically, is not enough. Tocqueville does not conclude from his approval of the *institutional* separation of church and state that public life in a free society can flourish without public religion altogether; that a free society is best nurtured by a naked public square. On the contrary! When those who would prepare a people for liberty, he writes, "attack religious beliefs, they obey the dictates of their passions but not their interests. Despotism may be able to do without faith, but freedom cannot. Religion is much more needed in the republic they advocate than in the monarchy they attack, and in democratic republics most of all." A free society depends on a vital and broad-based religious faith, according to Tocqueville: "How could society escape destruction if, when political ties are relaxed, moral ties are not tightened? And what can be done with a people master of itself if it is not subject to God?" (294).

It is here that Dobson and Thomas fail to provide sufficient distinction and direction. Their objection to direct ecclesiastical and clerical involvement in politics is well taken, and they are correct in insisting that "the church be the church." However, they overstate and undermine something very important when they oppose all forms of political action that are even remotely associated with the name Christian. Here Tocqueville and Abraham Kuyper both provide us with much-needed guidance.

The second of Tocqueville's insightful observations that we need to consider now is his reflection on the highly associational character of American life. "In the United States," he writes, "political associations are only one small part of the immense number of different types of associations found there." Forming associations is a characteristically American phenomenon: "Americans of all ages, all stations in life, and all types of disposition are forever forming associations." Tocqueville lists "commercial and industrial . . . religious, moral, serious, futile, very general and very limited, immensely large and very minute" associations for all sorts of purposes: "to give fêtes, found seminaries, build churches, distribute books, and send missionaries to the antipodes." This is how "hospitals, prisons, and schools" get created. Ideas, too, are communicated through associations, and Tocqueville's contrast with Europe is once again illuminating. "Finally, if [Americans] want to proclaim a truth or propagate some feeling by the encouragement of a great example, they form an association. In every case, at the head of a new undertaking, where in France you would find the government, or in England some territorial magnate, in the United States you are sure to find an association" (513).

For Tocqueville, this associational character of American life is crucial to establishing and maintaining liberty. In what is, in my judgment, one of Tocqueville's most brilliant observations, he takes issue with the oft-repeated contention that America is an individualistic society. It is true, he notes, that while "aristocracy links everybody, from peasant to king, in one long chain, democracy breaks the chain and frees each link" (508). However, a free society does not flourish where isolated individual egos each seek their own selfish interest. And now here is the brilliant insight and principle: "Despotism, by its very nature suspicious, sees the isolation of men as the best guarantee of its own permanence. So it usually does all it can to isolate them. Of all the vices of the human heart, egoism is that which suits it best. *A despot will lightly forgive his subjects for not loving him, provided they do not love one another"* (509, emphasis added). This insight, says Tocqueville, is at the heart of the American political experiment and its emphasis on division and devolution of political power. The natural problem arising from democracy and equality — the anarchy of selfish individual egos in constant conflict — has been solved. "The Americans have used liberty to combat the individualism born of equality, and they have won" (511). How? By devolving political power and encouraging multiple political associations: "The law givers of America did not suppose that a general representation of the whole nation would suffice to ward off a disorder at once so natural to the body social of a democracy and so fatal. They thought it also right to give each part of the land its own political life so that there should be an infinite number of occasions for the citizens to act together and so that every day they should feel that they depended on each other. That was wise conduct" (511). Tocqueville offers us here a litmus test for sniffing out potential tyrants: those who advocate more intrusion into the natural and voluntary associations of our lives, along with the tendency to centralize power, are likely to prove to be tyrants.

To Tocqueville's observations we add a distinction that was a cornerstone of Abraham Kuyper's public theology, the distinction between the church as *institute* and the church as *organism*.[28] Although Kuyper's use of this distinction is not entirely consistent and without ambiguity, the basic idea is clear and serves two distinct purposes. Kuyper understands the institutional church as the body of Christian believers gathered in structured fellowship — pastors, elders, deacons, presbyteries, synods — and regulated by creeds, confessions, and a rule of polity (church order). The purpose of the institution is the evangelizing, gathering, and discipling of a group of believers, who gather for worship, preaching, sacraments, and instruction in the faith. The institutional church's task is limited to her specific sphere;[29] she must not be a direct political agent but must remain true to her own spiritual purpose. This purpose can only be

---

28. Kuyper explicitly considers this distinction in two places: in a sermon, "Geworteld en Gegrond" ("Rooted and Grounded"), in *Predicatiën*, 3rd ed. (Kampen: Kok, 1913), 323-51; and in *De Gemeene Gratie*, 2nd ed., 3 vols. (Kampen: Kok, n.d.), 2:253-60. For a scholarly treatment see P. A. Van Leeuwen, *Het Kerkbegrip in de Theologie van Abraham Kuyper* (Franeker: T. Wever, 1946), 106-21; H. Zwaanstra, "Abraham Kuyper's Conception of the Church," *Calvin Theological Journal* 9 (1974): 149-81.

29. The institute/organism distinction is thus linked to Kuyper's notion of sphere sovereignty. See Abraham Kuyper, *Lectures on Calvinism* (Grand Rapids: Eerdmans, 1931), 59-68, 90-109.

understood when we realize that God is the beginning and end of the church. It is God the Holy Spirit who applies the redemptive work of Christ to believers in regeneration. But regeneration must not be understood narrowly, says Kuyper. "For regeneration does not save a few isolated individuals, finally to be joined together mechanically as an aggregate heap. Regeneration saves the organism itself of our race. And therefore all regenerate human life forms one organic body, of which Christ is the Head, and whose members are bound together by their mystical union with him."[30] This church includes believers of all times and places, the entire *communio sanctorum*, but on earth now is gathered into local congregations of confessing believers. Here is Kuyper's summary of the institutional church's earthly task: "Therefore the Church on earth consists only of those who have been incorporated into Christ, who bow before Him, live in His Word, and adhere to His ordinances; and for this reason the Church on earth has to preach the Word, administer the sacraments, and to exercise discipline, and in everything to stand before the face of God."[31] For Kuyper, the plurality of churches is both the sad consequence of human sin and failing in Christian purity and also the flowering of inevitable and real human diversity, rooted in "differences of climate and of nation, of historical past, and of disposition of mind."[32] Furthermore, the multiformity of churches, he notes, "has been much more favorable to the growth and prosperity of religious life than the compulsory uniformity in which others sought the very basis of its strength." Kuyper's conclusion is similar to Tocqueville's: "That churches flourish most richly when the government allows them to live from their own strength on the voluntary principle; that only the system of a free Church in a free State, may be honored from a Calvinistic standpoint."[33]

However, Kuyper also goes beyond this to insist that the *organic* character of the Christian life must come to expression in the form of *organized* Christian communal activity in areas other than the institutional church. Like Tocqueville, Kuyper valued a society with a highly developed associational life as essential to liberty. From the ecclesiastical inner circle of the believing community, gathered around Word and sacraments, must radiate "beams of faith's light into the realm of common grace,"[34] into the worlds of education, art, science, politics, business, and industry. In Kuyper's view, Christians who go out into their various vocations do so neither as direct emissaries of the institutional church nor as mere individual believers. He is opposed to "church-sponsored" social and political ac-

30. Kuyper, *Lectures on Calvinism*, 59.
31. Kuyper, *Lectures on Calvinism*, 63.
32. Kuyper, *Lectures on Calvinism*, 63.
33. Kuyper, *Lectures on Calvinism*, 65.
34. Kuyper, *De Gemeene Gratie*, 2:350.

tion, and even speaks approvingly of a Calvinist note of "secularization."[35] Christian social, cultural, and political action does not flow *directly* from the structures and authorities of the church, but comes to expression *organically* in the various spheres of life as believers live out the faith and spirituality that develops and is nurtured in the church's worship and discipline. The concrete expression of this life of Christian discipleship is manifested through the rich voluntary associational life of a nation's citizens. Christians, too, can create educational institutions, form trade unions and philanthropic societies and, yes, also political action groups. For Kuyper, this distinctly Christian associational life was, in fact, a mandate of the organic unity of the body of Christ. Christians are not just individual believers; they are a body.

Thomas and Dobson, it seems to me, miss an important opportunity when they fail to consider this alternative. By their strict standard of purity — only the church may be publicly identified as "Christian" — they rule out far too much. The organization that launched the civil rights movement of Dr. King was called the Southern Christian Leadership Conference; a local Grand Rapids, Michigan, organization that provides quality housing opportunities for needy people is called the Inner-City Christian Federation. To this we could add more venerable institutions such as the Young Women's Christian Association and the Young Men's Christian Association. And, today, what about any school, at any level, that declares itself to be decidedly Christian in its orientation and commitment? By Thomas and Dobson's standard, all these designations would be illegitimate. That cure seems worse than the disease. The concern in *Blinded by Might* — scandalizing the gospel with bad politics — is understandable, but the concession that removes the word "Christian" from the civil arena is, if Tocqueville and Kuyper are correct, counterproductive to the cause of liberty itself. Why should Christians voluntarily remove valuable associations from the public square out of squeamishness about offending? For that risk does not go away simply by excising the term "Christian," as Thomas's own situation as a journalist illustrates.

Thomas writes a syndicated column in which he does not disguise his conservative, evangelical Christian bias. His Christian faith and his political conservatism, in other words, are not hidden under a bushel. In a recent column he articulated twenty questions that should be asked of prospective candidates for the American presidency in the election of 2000.[36] Among the questions were:

---

35. Kuyper, *De Gemeene Gratie*, 2:279. Secularization here is understood specifically as being freed from the direct tutelage and patronage of the institutional church.

36. Appeared in the *Grand Rapids Press*, May 14, 1999.

7. Do you favor expanding civil rights legislation to include people on the basis of their sexual preference?

8. Will homosexuals be appointed to positions of trust in your administration?

Now, while Thomas does not represent any organization that publicly identifies itself as "Christian," why is the outrage that could potentially be precipitated by these questions not considered an offense to the Christian gospel in exactly the same way it would be if the Christian Coalition *as a group* had asked the questions?[37] Does Thomas not think that those who seek to silence the Christian Coalition would also want to silence him?[38] That public *individuals* who make known their Christian faith do become targets of secularists is clear from the public demonization of Independent Prosecutor Kenneth Starr, whose evangelical faith became the object of political hatred even though he was not identified with organizations such as the Christian Coalition. It was his *action* that was then attributed to his evangelical faith by his opponents that became the point of contention and rebuke. Furthermore, the fact that neither Promise Keepers nor Focus on the Family actually use the name of Christ in their organizations' identifying name has not prevented them from causing public offense to secularists. The only way to avoid offense is for Christians to avoid the public square altogether — a strategy Thomas and Dobson themselves repudiate.

In view of these realities of American political life today, is the "better way" suggested by Dobson and Thomas — preaching regeneration, practicing reconciliation and love — enough? That politics is not enough is indisputable, and to the degree that evangelicals were seduced into thinking that politics could save American culture, the Thomas/Dobson volume is a salutary reminder that first things must be first. But what about the secondary things? Is individual kindness and gospel testimony sufficient response to *organized* hostility to public expressions of the Christian faith as found in PFAW, the ACLU, the Interfaith Alliance, or Americans United for Separation of Church and State? Advocating school vouchers to facilitate educational freedom of choice

37. When professional football player, linebacker Reggie White of the Green Bay Packers, took part in a newspaper ad urging "hope and healing for homosexuals," black columnist Carl Rowan devoted an entire column to it ("Religious Blacks Adding to Homophobia in America," *Grand Rapids Press,* July 21, 1998). Rowan referred to "supposedly religious black Americans joining in the rabid homophobia of white reactionaries who, if the issue were racial justice, wouldn't give black people the sweat off their toes."

38. The flagship newspaper that carries Thomas's syndicated column *(Los Angeles Times)* has censored cartoonist Johnny Hart ("B.C.") by refusing to print his patented Easter strips that evangelically affirmed the resurrection of Christ.

requires *political* action, and though Dobson and Thomas insist that they want to encourage individual Christians to become politically engaged citizens, not only do they not tell us *how*, but the very structure of their argument discourages such involvement. After all, as they formulate it, politics is about seductive power, not truth or love; politics requires "enemies" while Jesus calls us to love our enemies. Politics is about compromise; the church is about unchanging standards.[39]

What strategy, then, should Christian citizens who seek positively to influence their society use? Curiously, Thomas explicitly suggests a page out of the communist playbook — invisible infiltration. He picks up on the salt metaphor used by Jesus in Matthew 5:13. It is worth paying careful attention to Thomas's precise use of words. "Politically conservative Christians like to use the salt metaphor as the rationalization for their political involvement. They say that political activism is part of the 'salting,' or preserving process. But this is not entirely true, perhaps not even mainly true."[40] Thomas pushes the metaphor to the limit by insisting that in the same way that salt does its work invisibly, Christians should "penetrate" Hollywood, journalism, education, the arts, and so forth, to be an invisible "inside influence" instead of "bashing these institutions from the outside." He then applies yet one more of our Lord's key parabolic metaphors: "So why are religious conservatives devoting so much time, effort, and money to reforming the 'field' (the world) by trying to stop evil (the weeds, which are sown by the devil), instead of sowing more good seed (by bringing more sons and daughters into the greater kingdom)? It is the ultimate temptation." Thomas then adds this "explanation": "Too many Christians today apparently feel a need for government to reflect their values in order for them to feel significant. . . . Why do they seek validation in visibility? Is it because of some deep sense of inferiority? Is their faith so fragile that it is only in seeing it manifested in the corridors of power in Washington that they feel justified?"

With all due respect, this is also the ultimate cheap shot, an astonishingly unfair put-down of fellow believers who struggle for the freedom to bring up their children in the fear of the Lord and are assaulted and harassed for it. Not only that, but Thomas's "invisible penetration" strategy is exactly what secularists and their friends in the media have been exposing and criticizing as the Christian Right's "stealth campaign."[41] Thomas's nonpolitical alternative is it-

39. The posture taken by Dobson and Thomas thus tends in the politically pacifist direction argued for with great eloquence by Anabaptist theologian John Howard Yoder, *The Politics of Jesus* (Grand Rapids: Eerdmans, 1972).

40. Thomas and Dobson, 90. The quotes that follow can be found on pp. 90-91 of *Blinded by Might.*

41. See PFAW publications, "Teaching Fear: The Religious Right's Campaign against

self political and, as deliberately disguised politics, potentially risks creating a scandal for the gospel every bit as serious as the open, explicit, concerted political activism that is the target of *Blinded by Might*.

Where does this extended discussion of the Dobson/Thomas volume now bring us? In sum, a few tentative conclusions:

1. Thomas and Dobson have not, I believe, made a convincing case that all concerted, identifiably religious political activism, rooted in a well-articulated public theology, should be repudiated. Though it is essential that the church restrict its ministry to that spiritual calling given to it by our Lord, refusing to exchange it for political activism, this does not necessitate rejecting other associations of Christian believers acting politically in concert. In fact, there are good civic as well as theological ("one body") reasons in favor of such associations.

2. When Christians become engaged in political activity, either as individuals or in association with other Christians, they need to be sensitive to the seductions and temptations of political power and political gamesmanship. Individuals and groups of Christians in public life risk causing a scandal for the gospel by actions that do not comport with the spirit of the gospel and reflect the fruit of the Holy Spirit.

3. Thomas and Dobson insist that Christian believers are citizens and should be involved in politics but fail to provide an adequate map for the political journey they urge others to take. Evangelicals need a public theology. Our authors make that claim themselves. Dobson notes that in a 1988 book he wrote with Ed Hinson, they "argued that the Moral Majority lacked a long-term vision for its political involvement. . . . We called for a philosophy of political involvement . . . [including] a theological and philosophical basis for our involvement . . . [such as the awareness arising from] a Christian being a citizen of two worlds — one earthly and one heavenly — [and having] an obligation to both."[42] Though Dobson repeats this call in *Blinded by Might*, one wishes that the book had itself made a greater contribution to such an evangelical public theology instead of only serving as yet one more jeremiad.

Why did a book that makes such an important basic point — politics

---

Sexuality Education" and "A Right Wing and a Prayer: The Religious Right in Your Public Schools," both available at PFAW web site http.pfaw.org/issues.

42. Thomas and Dobson, 43-44; the 1988 volume is Ed Dobson and Ed Hinson, *The Seduction of Power* (Old Tappan, N.J.: Revell, 1988).

cannot save us; the church is in trouble if it politicizes the gospel — end up making so many smaller wrong turns? This leads us now to a consideration of a fundamental problem in the premise of some evangelical political activism.

"We Failed!" Great Expectations, Great Illusions, Great Disappointment

When we look closely at the reasons for disillusion among some former leading figures in the Religious Right, prominent is the contention that all the political activism accomplished nothing. Paul Weyrich, in his letter of February 16, 1999, for example, noted that conservatives "assumed that a majority of Americans basically agreed with our point of view . . . so that if we could just elect enough conservatives . . . we could get our agenda implemented."[43] However, notes Weyrich, though "we got our people elected . . . that did not result in the adoption of our agenda." The reason: "Politics itself has failed. And politics has failed because of the collapse of the culture. The culture we are living in becomes an ever-wider sewer. In truth, I think we are caught up in a cultural collapse of historic proportions, a collapse so great that it simply overwhelms politics." What has happened is that "the ideology of Political Correctness, which openly calls for the destruction of our traditional culture . . . now threatens to control literally every aspect of our lives." There is no moral majority in America any longer; Bill Clinton is still in office, we cannot stop partial-birth abortions, and "what Americans would have found absolutely intolerable only a few years ago, a majority now not only tolerates but celebrates." In sum: "We probably have lost the culture war." Dobson and Thomas say much the same thing. "Did the Moral Majority really make a difference?" they ask. "Is the moral condition of America better because of our efforts?" Their answer: "Even a casual observation of the current moral climate suggests that despite all the time, money, and energy — despite the political power — we failed. Things have not gotten better; they have gotten worse."[44] In sum: when it comes to the "hopes of transforming the culture through political power, it must now be acknowledged that we have failed."[45] According to Dobson and Thomas, in terms of legal progress the record is dismal: "On practically every plank of our platform [crime, drugs, abortion, pornography, homosexuality, divorce] we have failed, at least from a legislative and judicial perspective."[46]

43. See n. 5 above.
44. Thomas and Dobson, 42.
45. Thomas and Dobson, 23.
46. Thomas and Dobson, 43.

"We have failed!" In what way and why? What is the failure here? When and how did those who now say "we failed" come to that conclusion? Weyrich's awakening about the failure,[47] as well as the timing of the Dobson/Thomas volume, suggests a link here to the failure to remove President Clinton from office. Weyrich's letter states this openly: "If there really were a moral majority, Bill Clinton would have been driven out of office months ago." President Clinton remains in office because "Americans have adopted, in large measure, the MTV culture that we so valiantly opposed just a few years ago."[48] Dobson and Thomas refer to it more obliquely: "That 70 percent [of Americans] still approved of [President Clinton's] 'job performance' on the day of his impeachment is another indication of the Moral Majority's impotence."[49]

What is happening here is that the political disappointment of some conservative, evangelical political activists is being turned into "an indictment of the character of the American people."[50] But is this accusation anything more than another jeremiad, an Elijah-like protest that projects political-homiletic frustration on its unresponsive congregation? "We preached to you but you would not listen! We tried so hard to awaken Americans, to point out their sins and call them to repentance, but they would not heed us. We have failed!" Richard John Neuhaus observes that it is much too soon to lament the end of politics in America: "To say that politics has failed is to say that the American experiment has definitely failed. There have been and there are today societies in which politics — free deliberation and decision about how to order public life — is precluded. It is the better part of wisdom to know that, in whatever form, it could happen here and may be happening here — as, for instance, in the judicial usurpation of politics. But the claim that it has happened here, that politics has failed, is an apocalyptic excitement to be kept on a tight leash."[51]

Neuhaus's reference to "apocalyptic excitement" helps put this entire discussion in a helpful framework. Classic Christian eschatology is neither optimistically utopian nor given to dark despair. Christians who believe in the reality of Easter and Pentecost affirm in hope the victory of our Lord and the reality of his kingdom as a present as well as future given. Failure to maintain such an "already/not yet" eschatological tension leads to the "all or nothing" thinking reflected in some of the comments we have considered in this chapter.

47. Weyrich was interviewed for the CBS's *60 Minutes* program that aired on May 16, 1999, and what was so striking was his repeated statement that "we failed."

48. Weyrich letter of February 16, 1999.

49. Thomas and Dobson, 42.

50. Richard John Neuhaus, "Bill Clinton and the American Character," The Public Square, *First Things*, no. 94 (June/July 1999): 66.

51. Neuhaus, 66.

Weyrich's letter considers the defeat of the Moral Majority as a signal to Christians that it is time to separate from American culture, "turn off [the television], tune out [popular culture], and drop out [of the dominant institutions]."[52] In a different way, Dobson and Thomas also call evangelicals to "flee for purity" by rediscovering Jesus' way of love and reconciliation and repudiating the politics of power and fear. Dobson and Thomas in their "we have failed" lament also seem to be adopting an "all or nothing" attitude. We did not get our agenda passed — we failed. Neuhaus sums this posture up neatly when he observes, "It expresses a painful deflation of political expectations that can only be explained by a prior and thoroughly unwarranted inflation."[53]

There is one dimension of Weyrich's letter that provides a glimpse into an alternative to apocalyptic withdrawal or retreating into the church as the only vehicle for social and cultural renewal. Weyrich pleads for conservatives to "drop out" and form alternative institutions, to "separate ourselves from the institutions that have been captured by the ideology of Political Correctness, or by other enemies of our traditional culture."[54] Before we consider this "Benedictine" suggestion in the final section of this chapter, we need to address the question of "failure." Have the efforts of the Religious Right been an utter failure? Perhaps even more important, is America in a state of precipitous moral decline and cultural decay?

It is striking that Weyrich, along with former Education Secretary William Bennett, in his book *The Death of Outrage: Bill Clinton and the Assault on American Ideals,* do measure the state of American moral character by the standard of the Clinton presidency and its place in history. Bennett wonders if "the history books will describe the Clinton era as a time during which (to recall the words of John Adams) the President of the United States insidiously betrayed and wantonly trifled away, public trust. The same history books may also describe how a diffident public . . . simply shrugged its shoulders. And finally, that William Jefferson Clinton really was the representative man of our time, when the overwhelming majority of Americans no longer believed that presidential character mattered, and that no man, not even a president, was accountable to the law. . . . Perhaps . . . but we do not yet know."[55]

What we do know is that the debate about President Clinton's impeachment proved the reality of the culture wars. The president's supporters included those who stated the issue in the starkest apocalyptic terms. At a New York Uni-

52. Weyrich letter of February 16, 1999.
53. Neuhaus, 67.
54. Weyrich letter of February 16, 1999.
55. William Bennett, *The Death of Outrage: Bill Clinton and the Assault on American Ideals* (New York: Free Press, 1998), 132-33.

versity rally in December 1998, Harvard law professor Alan Dershowitz threw a shopping basket of high moral principles into the discussion: "A vote against impeachment is not a vote for Bill Clinton. It is a vote against bigotry. It's a vote against fundamentalism. It's a vote against anti-environmentalism. It's a vote against the right-to-life movement. It's a vote against the radical right. This is truly the first battle in a great culture war. And if this President is impeached, it will be a great victory for the forces of evil — genuine evil."[56] At the same rally, "feminist intellectual" Blanche Wiesen Cook invoked the specter of theocracy and called for a remobilization of American leftists: "We are looking at theocrats. We have to mobilize like we mobilized against the war in Vietnam, like we mobilized against slavery. This is about race! This is about crack cocaine in the neighborhoods."[57] Taking these outbursts into consideration, along with Mrs. Clinton's television interview in which she referred to a "vast right-wing conspiracy" that has long been trying to get rid of her and her husband, Richard John Neuhaus speaks of "the never to be underestimated hysteria of the left."[58]

Other observers come to a more measured conclusion. Conservative columnist Paul Gigot of the *Wall Street Journal* does not share the pessimism of Weyrich and others, noting American victory in the Cold War, welfare reform, and the growing popularity of educational choice as positive counterindicators.[59] Gigot also suggests that there may be reasons other than sheer moral relativism for the American public's reluctance to have President Clinton removed from office. But the most forthright repudiation of evangelical gloom comes from Abraham Kuyper's greatest American evangelical fan, Prison Fellowship's Charles Colson.[60] Colson vigorously protests against the talk he says he increasingly hears from "battle-weary evangelicals . . . about abandoning cultural engagement and tending our own backyard instead." Colson not only considers this kind of talk "self-defeating" and "ill-timed," but calls it an example of "unbiblical" and "sinful" despair. He also judges it a matter of deserting the cause at the very moment when "we are on the verge of making a historic breakthrough" and expresses agreement with Pope John Paul II that the year 2000 "will usher in 'a great springtime for Christianity.'" Colson lists as positive signs "the revival of moral discourse," encouraging indications of a decline in

56. *Washington Update,* December 16, 1998; cited by Neuhaus, 72.
57. The description of Cook is Neuhaus's (Neuhaus, 72); the quote is also from Neuhaus, 72.
58. Neuhaus, 71; for a fuller discussion of Mrs. Clinton's remarks on NBC's *Today* show, see Bennett, 55-72.
59. *Wall Street Journal,* February 19, 1999; cited by Neuhaus, 67.
60. Charles Colson, "The Sky Isn't Falling," *Christianity Today,* January 11, 1999, 104. Citations that follow are all taken from this column.

certain social pathologies, the utterly obvious failure of twentieth-century gods and ideologies, and the arrival of "postmodernism," which is nothing more than "a formalized expression of despair." Only Christianity remains on the scene as a testimony to hope. It is time to blow trumpets, not fold up our tents! "To desert the field of battle now would be historical blindness, betraying our heritage just when we have the greatest opportunity of the century. This is the time to make the compelling case that Christianity offers the only rational and realistic hope for both personal redemption and social renewal." Whether or not one reads the signs as positively as Colson does, his point about defeatism and retreat is well taken. What remain unanswered are the specifics of the strategy to be used in the ongoing political witness of Christians in America. For guidance we turn one more time to Abraham Kuyper and what may seem an unlikely partner in mission, Saint Benedict.

Abraham Kuyper and Saint Benedict

In this final section we return to the suggestion made by Paul Weyrich in his now famous letter telling conservatives to acknowledge that they have lost the culture wars. Drop out of popular culture and the dominant institutions of American life, Weyrich pleaded, and establish alternative institutions. Earlier we referred to this as the Benedictine solution, after Saint Benedict of Nursia (ca. 480–ca. 547), the founder of Western monasticism. A similar response was suggested some two decades ago by Alasdair MacIntyre in his academic jeremiad about the state of moral philosophy in the modern Western world.[61] This tack requires in the first place drawing strong parallels between the period in which the Roman Empire declined and our present age. The critical decision that we can call the Benedictine move occurs "when men and women of good will turned aside from the task of shoring up the Roman *Imperium* and ceased to identify the continuation of civility and moral community with the maintenance of that *Imperium*."[62] As the empire collapsed, those with foresight left its institutions and created new ones in which the permanent things of a decaying order were preserved, often unintentionally or simply as a by-product of a higher purpose: "What they set themselves to achieve instead — often not recognizing fully what they were doing — was the construction of new forms of community within which the moral life could be sustained so that both moral-

---

61. Alasdair MacIntyre, *After Virtue: A Study in Moral Theory,* 2nd ed. (Notre Dame, Ind.: University of Notre Dame Press, 1984 [1981]).
62. MacIntyre, 263.

ity and civility might survive the coming ages of barbarism and darkness." Thus, a judgment needs to be made about our culture. Is it going the route of inevitable decline and decay into the oblivion of the Roman imperium? MacIntyre thinks so, and judges that it is likely "that for some time we too have reached that turning point." Then we too need our own Saint Benedict:

> What matters at this stage is the construction of local forms of community within which civility and the intellectual and moral life can be sustained through the new dark ages which are already upon us. And if the tradition of the virtues was able to survive the horrors of the last dark ages, we are not entirely without grounds for hope. This time, however, the barbarians are not waiting beyond the frontiers; they have been governing us for quite some time. And it is our lack of consciousness of this that constitutes part of our predicament. We are waiting not for a Godot, but for another — doubtless very different — Saint Benedict.[63]

Is our situation really that desperate? Here we need to call attention to a very important difference between the fifth- and sixth-century Roman world and our early twenty-first-century situation in North America. In between those two times was the defining moment that created America, the great experiment in ordered liberty where citizens do have political power rooted in liberty and law. That is why we need to bring Saint Benedict together with Abraham Kuyper, who not only knew and valued the importance of alternative cultural institutions but also knew how to utilize the political blessings of liberty in the midst of cultural conflict and marginalization. Synthesizing Benedict and Kuyper is the project of the last paragraphs of this volume, and we do so remembering that both figures were first of all not concerned with saving civilization but with obedience to their Lord. Obedience first; success can then be God's concern.

We suggested earlier that the retreat mentality of some contemporary evangelicals is rooted in an "all or nothing," win grandly or lose dismally approach. That is also the conclusion of columnist Paul Gigot, who notes that the tendency to throw in the towel "always exists on the religious right, which cares more about salvation in the next world than in this one. They tuned out at least

---

63. MacIntyre, 263. Colson comes to an identical conclusion about the "barbarian invaders from within": "We have bred them in our families and trained them in our classrooms. They inhabit our legislatures, our courts, our film studios, and our churches. Most of them are attractive and pleasant; their ideas are persuasive and subtle. Yet these men and women threaten our most cherished institutions and our very character as a people" (Charles Colson with Ellen Santilli Vaughan, *Against the Night: Living in the New Dark Ages* [Ann Arbor, Mich.: Servant, 1989], 23-24).

once earlier this century, after the Scopes trial."[64] Richard John Neuhaus concurs: "There is in fundamentalist-evangelical Christianity, as among some Catholic traditionalists, an apocalyptic temper conducive to hyberbolic renderings of both successes and defeats."[65] A slightly different twist on this is given by the editors of *Public Justice Report*, a publication of the Kuyper-influenced public policy group Center for Public Justice, in a front-page editorial report with the illuminating title, "Driving for Dominance; Fleeing for Purity."[66] The authors of this essay observe that Paul Weyrich's call to flee the corrupt institutions of contemporary American culture is based on a categorical "win or lose" mentality. Since the present majority in America is apparently immoral, the only choice left is to acquiesce or to flee. In the meantime, however, the moral minority needs to recognize its true status as a minority, form a counterculture, and try over time to regain its majority status and its power. "At that time they will be able to give up fleeing for purity and drive again for dominance. Cultural reconstruction [the Benedictine alternative], in other words is a means to the end of saving America." What this framework does is to tie "the success or failure of Judeo-Christian culture to whether the majority of Americans owns that culture."

The authors point to several problems with this approach. To begin with, Weyrich overlooks the fact that many Americans have been building alternative institutions for years:

> Millions of Americans who share [Weyrich's] moral commitments have been building alternative institutions for decades. Long before the growth of the home school movement, which he lauds as a separationist model, there existed Christian and Jewish day schools, CBN, Christian radio stations and burgeoning new churches. If these institutions are what Weyrich has in mind for development during the period of retreat, why does he overlook them in his call for new institutions? If these institutions do *not* represent what he wants and if that is why he believes he must start from scratch to build new ones, how could he have believed that true cultural conservatives ever constituted more than a small minority of America's citizenry?

What is needed, say the authors, is an entirely new strategy, one that repudiates the "'win-everything/lose everything' politics of cultural majoritarianism,

64. Cited by Neuhaus, 67-68.
65. Neuhaus, 68.
66. "Driving for Dominance; Fleeing for Purity," *Public Justice Report* 22, no. 2 (1999); the editor is James Skillen and the associate editor is Michelle N. Voll. All citations that follow are from this essay.

which leads to perpetual oscillation between driving for dominance and fleeing for purity." Instead, Christians ought to seek to make the United States of America "a genuinely pluralist republic." Concretely, this would mean a plurality of educational choices without financial penalty and a proportional representation approach to elections to replace the "winner takes all" practice, which effectively shuts out minority voices. In sum, "rather than driving for dominance or fleeing for purity, every minority and majority should be able to participate steadily in public life all the time on the basis of its own deepest convictions."

This clearly Kuyperian vision presumes the Benedictine practice of creating alternative institutions; it encourages not a retreat from public life but a transforming presence in it through nurturing the very associational life that, according to Tocqueville, was the genius of the American experiment. Kuyper himself helped develop a high level of grassroots associational life among the Dutch Reformed in the late nineteenth and early twentieth century that was the basis of a significant political movement. He established and wrote extensively in newspapers, started a university, established a political party, and pushed, prodded, and cajoled the Dutch government toward establishing a school system that honored a plurality of religious viewpoints without financial penalty to any one view — genuine educational choice. What he accomplished was based on a public theology that moves the Benedictine model into the modern democratic world where Christian citizens need not be passive victims assenting to their marginalization but can take the opportunities to bear witness and to act in ways that are consistent with their deepest convictions.

Evangelical Christians can learn from the writings of John Paul II as he encourages engagement through persuasion, a strategy that he bases clearly on a high Christian anthropology that considers human beings responsive and responsible moral and political agents.[67] A key failing of Weyrich's Moral Majority vision was its *assumption* that Americans shared its vision and that persuasion was thus not needed. The recognition of the need for persuasion alone can provide a model for political discourse that could renew the quality of civility in America's public square. Evangelicals need to learn the art of political persuasion that is true to both Christian conviction and the genius of the American experiment. That is what Kuyper attempted to do in his context; that is what Martin Luther King, Jr., accomplished in his. In addition, the value of a rich and diverse associational, communal life is that it opens up the potential

---

67. For a succinct and clear summary statement of John Paul II's vision of spiritual and cultural renewal, see Rev. Avery Dulles, S.J., "*Centesimus Annus* and the Renewal of Culture," *Journal of Markets and Morality* 2, no. 1 (1999): 1-7.

for ongoing renewal. We must never forget that new, alternative institutions do not guarantee their own future integrity, much less that of the societies they seek to influence. The eventual Benedictine decline gave rise to Cluny in A.D. 909, and in spite of the remarkable accomplishments of the Cluniacs, they were themselves renewed by the Cistercian movement of the twelfth century. In addition, we must also remember that many of America's great universities were originally established as Christian centers of learning, only eventually to slide into the slough of secularization.[68] Even more recently established colleges, including devoutly evangelical ones, are not out of danger of following this route, according to a recent examination by Roman Catholic James Burtchaell.[69] There are no guarantees; only a call for obedience. What Christians should desire is the freedom of opportunity to renew old ideals through new associations and institutions.

As one looks back over the past two decades of American evangelical activism and takes note of new universities, the growth of alternatives to a monopolistic public education, the sophistication of evangelical communications technology, and thriving grassroots political and social organizations, including successful legal and political organizations, one is struck by the parallels with Kuyper's own achievements. In assessing this, prudence and patience are called for rather than celebrative triumphalism; it required forty-five years of hard political work for Kuyper to bring his campaign for educational justice to fruition in Dutch law. Evangelical political activists in the United States have been seriously at work for some twenty-five years now since their awakening in the mid-1970s. Though it is difficult for pragmatic Americans to think in long-range terms, much less to act in accord with them, American Christians need to learn to think in terms of millennia, not in the short-range periods of single presidential or congressional electoral terms. It is here especially that evangelical Christians can learn from the Roman Catholic tradition more generally and from the millennial perspectives of John Paul II particularly. In addition to the works of Abraham Kuyper, my one reading suggestion for evangelical political activists would be John Paul II's Apostolic Letter, *Tertio Millenio Adveniente (On the Coming of the Third Millennium)*. What evangelicals in America need today above all is not more technology for church growth or political activism but the millennial perspective of *hope*. As long as American evangelicals enjoy the opportunities of liberty and the privileges of free citizenship, messages of

68. See George Marsden, *The Soul of the University: From Protestant Establishment to Established Nonbelief* (New York and Oxford: Oxford University Press, 1994).

69. James Tunstead Burtchaell, *The Dying of the Light: The Disengagement of Colleges and Universities from Their Christian Churches* (Grand Rapids: Eerdmans, 1998).

despair and retreat are at the very least inappropriate and may even be sinful expressions of what the classical Christian tradition called *accidie,* or sloth.

Charles Colson is right: "The sky isn't falling."

So was Abraham Kuyper: "There is not a square inch in the whole domain of our human existence over which Christ, who is Sovereign over *all,* does not cry, 'Mine!'"

So was Saint Benedict: *Ora et labora.*

The Debate about Dutch Neo-Calvinism

In Calvinism my heart has found rest.

Abraham Kuyper

Roman Catholic theologian Richard John Neuhaus has argued that "today some of the most provocative and rigorous thought about religion and society is being done by those who call themselves Calvinists, especially by those who identify with the Calvinist 'revisionism' of Abraham Kuyper (d. 1920), the Dutch theologian and political leader."[1] It is Neuhaus's reference to Kuyper's "revisionist" Calvinism that we wish to examine in this appendix. What kind of

1. Richard John Neuhaus, *The Naked Public Square: Religion and Democracy in America* (Grand Rapids: Eerdmans, 1984), 175. Neuhaus's footnote (271) refers specifically to a significant and frequently cited volume arguing for pluralism in American education, R. McCarthy, D. Opperwal, W. Peterson, and G. Spykman, *Society, State, and Schools: A Case for Structural and Confessional Pluralism* (Grand Rapids: Eerdmans, 1981). Perhaps the foremost North American political analyst working self-consciously from a "Kuyperian" perspective is James W. Skillen, director of the Association for Public Justice and the Center for Public Justice in Washington, D.C. See, for example, his edited volume of Abraham Kuyper, *The Problem of Poverty* (Grand Rapids: Baker, 1991), and *The Scattered Voice: Christians at Odds in the Public Square* (Grand Rapids: Zondervan, 1990). Nicholas Wolterstorff (in the Abraham Kuyper lectures for 1981 delivered at the Kuyper-founded Free University of Amsterdam) links what he refers to as "world-transformative" Kuyperian Christianity with the concerns and objectives of liberation theology in his *Until Justice and Peace Embrace* (Grand Rapids: Eerdmans, 1983).

Calvinist was Abraham Kuyper? What in his thought gave rise to the term "neo-Calvinist"? Like its late nineteenth-century analogues, neo-Thomism[2] and neo-Kantianism,[3] Dutch neo-Calvinism represents a revival of interest in and a resurgent influence of the thought of an earlier great thinker, in this case the sixteenth-century reformer John Calvin (1509-64). The term "neo-Calvinism," with emphasis on the "neo," was popularized by Dutch Reformed critics who wished to accent the differences between Calvin and the Calvinism of Abraham Kuyper and his followers.[4] Kuyper, it is worth noting, thought of himself as a Calvinist pure and simple and considered his views to be those of historic Calvinism. As he noted in his famous Princeton Stone Lectures of 1898, the battle

2. On neo-Thomism see Victor B. Brezik, ed., *One Hundred Years of Thomism: Aeterni Patris and Afterwards* (Houston: Center for Thomistic Studies, 1981). Further bibliography, particularly on the Italian revival, is given in Brezik, 22 n. 11.

3. See Thomas E. Wiley, *Back to Kant: The Revival of Kantianism in German Social and Historical Thought, 1860-1914* (Detroit: Wayne State University Press, 1978). This reference is cited by Albert M. Wolters, "The Intellectual Milieu of Herman Dooyeweerd," in *The Legacy of Herman Dooyeweerd: Reflections on Critical Philosophy in the Christian Tradition*, ed. C. T. McIntire (Lanham, Md.: University Press of America, 1985), 1-20. Wolters's essay is interesting for, among other things, its linkage of neo-Calvinism and neo-Kantianism in the thought of the Dutch legal philosopher Herman Dooyeweerd (1894-1977).

4. As far as I am able to determine, the term "neo-Calvinism" was first used in print (in 1897) by a sympathizer of Abraham Kuyper — the Dutch jurist A. Anema. One of Kuyper's sharpest critics, F. M. Ten Hoor — a Christian Reformed pastor and professor of systematic theology at Calvin Theological Seminary from 1900 to 1924 — observed in a footnote to a 1905 essay that the term "neo-Calvinist" was not his invention but a designation given to the new movement by its own adherents. He refers to an untitled "writing" by an unnamed "professor from the Free University" (of Amsterdam): "We did not invent this term, 'neo-Calvinism.' It is regularly used in The Netherlands and we discovered it in a writing from one of the professors at the Free University. The term is thus a self-designation of this new movement itself." ("Het Neo-Calvinisme en de Oude Gereformeerde Belijdenis," *De Gereformeerde Amerikaan* 9 [1905]: 55). In the next issue of the same periodical, Ten Hoor, responding to criticism he had received about his use of the term "neo-Calvinist" in the previous month's issue, reveals his source to be Free University professor of jurisprudence A. Anema, who in his *Calvinisme en Rechtwetenschap* (Amsterdam: W. Kirchner, 1897), on p. 16 of the foreword, acknowledges that his "thinking and willing have found perfect peace in Neo-Calvinism." ("De Docenten aan onze Theologische School in hunne verhouding tot de Kerk," *De Gereformeerde Amerikaan* 9 [1905]: 121). We shall consider Ten Hoor's critique of Kuyper later in this chapter. Substantive and critical discussions of neo-Calvinism can also be found in C. B. Hylkema, *Oud- en Nieuw Calvinisme: Een Vergelijkende Geschiedkundige Studie* (Haarlem: H. D. Willink & Zoon, 1911); Th. L. Haitjema, "Abraham Kuyper und die Theologie des holländischen NeuCalvinismus," *Zwischen den Zeiten* 9 (1931): 331-54; L. J. Hulst and G. K. Hemkes, *Oud- en Nieuw Calvinisme* (Grand Rapids: Eerdmans-Sevensma, 1913).

against "modernism" was a conflict of worldviews or "life-systems," and "this powerful life-system [in which we have to take our stand] is not to be invented nor formulated by ourselves, but is to be taken and applied as it presents itself in history." Furthermore, the true manifestation of the Christian principle is given historically in *Calvinism*. "In Calvinism my heart has found rest. From Calvinism have I drawn the inspiration firmly and resolutely to take my stand in the thick of this great conflict of principles."[5]

A New Calvinism?

This return to Calvinism did not mean slavish imitation of the past, but it did mean a wholehearted affirmation of *the principle of Calvinism*. In Kuyper's own words: "To repristination I am as averse as any man; but in order to place for the defence of Christianity, principle over against principle, the world-view over against world-view, there lies at hand, for him who is a Protestant in bone and marrow, only *the Calvinistic principle* as the sole trustworthy foundation on which to build."[6] Kuyper was thus aware that his version of Calvinism, if it was to be relevant to a new age, had to be a *new* Calvinism. Fidelity to the Calvinist tradition, he contends, "excludes every idea of imitative repristination." Kuyper continues by utilizing one of his favorite — organic — metaphors. "[W]hat the descendents of the Old Dutch Calvinists as well as of the Pilgrim fathers have to do, is not to copy the past, as if Calvinism were a petrifaction, but to go back to the living root of the Calvinist plant, to clean and to water it, and so to cause it to bud and to blossom once more, now fully in accordance with our actual life in these modern times, and with the demands of the times to come."[7] While Kuyper himself seems not to have spoken of "neo-Calvinism" until toward the end of his life,[8] and surely not in the same sense as his critics, it is clear that he was aware that the revived Calvinism of his day was and had to be, in some sense, "new."

The debate about the newness of Kuyper's Calvinism is an important one,

5. Abraham Kuyper, *Lectures on Calvinism* (Grand Rapids: Eerdmans, 1931), 11-12.

6. Kuyper, *Lectures on Calvinism*, 191.

7. Kuyper, *Lectures on Calvinism*, 171.

8. The only reference I have been able to find is in Kuyper's *Antirevolutionaire Staatkunde*, 2 vols. (Kampen: Kok, 1916), 1:626-28. In the three volumes (1,097 pages) of J. C. Rullmann's complete bibliography of Kuyper's writings (*Kuyper-Bibliographie*, I-III [The Hague and Kampen: Js. Bootsma and J. H. Kok, 1923-40]), while there are countless index references to "Calvinisme," "Calvinist (en)," and "Calvinistische," there is not a single one to "neo-Calvinisme" or "nieuw Calvinisme."

particularly as it focuses on the issue of pluralism. Even such an observer as Ernst Troeltsch, who himself was quite uninvolved in the Dutch ecclesiastical and political debates, insists that Kuyper held to a "Liberal-Natural-Law conception of secular affairs," adding somewhat mischievously: "In all these questions, Neo-Calvinism has drifted far away from Calvin — a fact which Kuyper tried in vain to conceal. In the handling of secular questions it has formally come very close to modern Liberalism and Utilitarianism, and the latter finds in it (in Neo-Calvinism) one of the great moral forces which it lacks upon the Continent."[9] Troeltsch, it should be noted, makes this observation with more respect and admiration for modern neo-Calvinism than reproach. In fact, he contends (in 1911) that "actually, Calvinism is the chief force in the Protestant world today," primarily because its vision was the only one "suited to" and "in agreement with the modern democratic and capitalistic development." The Calvinist principle itself is the final or deepest reason for its success in the modern world. "This deeper reason [for Calvinism's success] lies in the active character of Calvinism, in its power for forming churches, in its international contacts, and in its conscious impulse toward expansion, and, most of all, in its capacity to penetrate the political and economic movements of Western nations with its religious ideal, a capacity which Lutheranism lacked from the very beginning."[10] At the same time, however, in a note appended to the very passage we have just cited, Troeltsch indicts Kuyper's Princeton *Lectures on Calvinism* for being historically misleading. This volume, he notes, is "a kind of collective creed of modern orthodox Calvinism" but of dubious historical value. "Otherwise in an absolutely unprecedented degree Neo-Calvinism is here read into the primitive Calvinism of Geneva. It is the book of a dogmatist and a politician, and as such it is extremely instructive; as an historical work, however, it is very misleading."[11] Once again, the later neo-Calvinism is said to be significantly different from Calvin's original Calvinism. "Calvinism has developed into a very widespread movement, which has expanded far beyond its beginnings at Geneva. In order to understand Calvinism, therefore, our primary task is to distinguish the primitive Calvinism of Geneva from its later forms of development. At the outset, however, we must ask the following questions. To what extent are these later developments the logical outcome of primitive Calvinism? How far do they transcend it and what were the causes which led to this development?"[12]

9. Ernst Troeltsch, *The Social Teaching of the Christian Churches*, trans. Olive Wyon, 2 vols. (1931; reprint, Louisville: Westminster/John Knox, 1992), 676.

10. Troeltsch, 576-77.

11. Troeltsch, 879 n. 309. Troeltsch's references are to the German edition, significantly entitled *Reformation wider Revolution*.

12. Troeltsch, 578.

Troeltsch's contention here draws us into a much larger scholarly conversation about the continuity or discontinuity between Calvin and the Calvinism which succeeded him. Troeltsch follows a number of nineteenth-century interpreters in positing a central dogma of predestination in Calvin and in Calvinism.[13] Yet he also anticipates, though in a different way and on different issues, more recent attempts to drive a sharp wedge between Calvin and the Calvinist tradition.[14] For our purposes, we need to consider Troeltsch's interpretation of what he calls "primitive Calvinism" and how, in his judgment, neo-Calvinism departs significantly from it.[15]

To begin with, we must recall Troeltsch's fundamental distinction between the two basic sociological models, the church type and the sect type. According to Troeltsch, the church type is a universal and unifying sociological paradigm. "The Church-type represents the longing for a universal all-embracing ideal, the desire to control great masses of men, and therefore the

13. "The first distinctive feature of Calvinism, and the most important one, is the idea of predestination, the famous central doctrine of Calvinism" (Troeltsch, 581). Troeltsch shares a characteristically nineteenth-century conviction that all concrete historical developments are expressions of "ideas" or single principles. Hence the numerous efforts to determine the essential idea or "essence" of Christianity. For an exploration of Troeltsch's own views of the essence of Christianity, see S. W. Sykes, "Ernst Troeltsch and Christianity's Essence," in *Ernst Troeltsch and the Future of Theology*, ed. John Powell Clayton (Cambridge: Cambridge University Press, 1976), 139-71.

14. See, for example, Basil Hall, "Calvin against the Calvinists," in *John Calvin*, ed. G. E. Duffield (Grand Rapids: Eerdmans, 1968), 19-37; R. T. Kendall, *Calvin and English Calvinism to 1649* (Oxford: Oxford University Press, 1979). The issue here has to do with the alleged discontinuity between Calvin's theology and the "system" of second and following generations of Reformed orthodoxy or scholasticism, a system allegedly dominated by the "central dogma" of predestination in a way that Calvin's was not. Richard Muller has argued vigorously, and perhaps conclusively, that there is considerable continuity between the "systems" of Calvin and Calvinism in his two-part article, "Calvin and the 'Calvinists': Assessing Continuities between the Reformation and Orthodoxy," *Calvin Theological Journal* 30 (1995): 345-75; 31 (1996): 125-60. For a full bibliography and a discussion of the issue, also see Richard A. Muller, *Christ and the Decree: Christology and Predestination in Reformed Theology from Calvin to Perkins* (Grand Rapids: Baker, 1988 [1986]); Richard A. Muller, "Perkins' *A Golden Chaine*: Predestinarian System or Schematized *Ordo Salutis*," *Sixteenth Century Journal* 9, no. 1 (1978): 69-81. A significant critique of the "Kendall thesis" is offered by Joel R. Beeke, "Faith and Assurance in the Heidelberg Catechism and Its Primary Composers: A Fresh Look at the Kendall Thesis," *Calvin Theological Journal* 27 (1992): 39-67.

15. My own reflections on Troeltsch's discussion of Calvinism in *Social Teaching* have been helped considerably by J. Severijn, "Ernst Troeltsch over de Beteekenis van het Calvinisme voor de Cultuurgeschiedenis," *Antirevolutionaire Staatkunde*, Driemaandelijksch, 1 (1927): 1-71.

urge to dominate the world and civilization in general."[16] Accompanying this is an objective view of grace and sacraments along with an incorporation of rational natural law into Christian ethics. To sectarian critics, this latter point in particular was seen to be a compromise with the plain and highly particular law of Christ. The sect type, by contrast, was a particular and voluntary community whose understanding of grace was subjective and whose ethical ideal was radical and rigorously Christian. It should be noted that the sectarian ideal was incorporated into the church type through monastic asceticism, though with a key difference. "The Church ideal of asceticism can never be conceived as a universal ethic; it is essentially unique and heroic. The ascetic ideal of the sect, on the contrary, is, as a matter of course, an ideal which is possible to all, and appointed for all, which, according to its conception, united the fellowship instead of dividing it, and according to its content is also capable of a general realization in so far as the circle of the elect is concerned" (340). The sect type, in other words, also makes its own universal claims. In summary then:

> The Church is that type of organization which is overwhelmingly conservative, which to a certain extent accepts the secular order, and dominates the masses; in principle, therefore, it is universal, i.e. it desires to cover the whole life of humanity. The sects, on the other hand, are comparatively small groups; they aspire after personal inward perfection, and they aim at a direct personal fellowship between the members of each group. From the very beginning, therefore, they are forced to organize themselves in small groups and to renounce the idea of dominating the world. Their attitude towards the world, the State, and Society may be indifferent, tolerant, or hostile, since they have no desire to control and incorporate these forms of social life; on the contrary, they tend to avoid them; their aim is usually either to tolerate their presence alongside of their own body, or even to replace these social institutions by their own society. (331)

Church or Sect?

What is striking about primitive Calvinism, according to Troeltsch, is that "for the first time in the history of the Christian ethic" there arose a corporate "Christian socialism" which fused a church-type ecclesiology with the sect type. Calvin's efforts to create a "Holy Community" in Geneva were in effect "the union of a national Church and a voluntary Church, of the Church as the organ of

16. Troeltsch, 334; parenthetical pages references which follow are to Troeltsch's work.

448

salvation and the sect-ideal, a moulding of the common life on Christian-Socialistic lines which is impossible without the organized rule of Christian thought over Society" (622, 627). It is very clear that Troeltsch considers Calvin's Calvinism to be essentially that of the church type, which also incorporates some elements of the sect type into its ecclesiology. This is apparent from Troeltsch's very "churchly" description of Calvinism:

> The main features of the Calvinistic religious system may then be summed up as follows: a strict insistence upon the Church as the organ which mediates salvation; a very strong and definite emphasis upon the sacraments as objective Divine means of grace; . . . the logical establishment of the Church upon the Bible, as the supernatural element which creates faith, and also proves its supernatural origin by creating fellowship; the catholicity of the Church wherever the Word and the sacraments have been preserved, even under the veil of error and false ceremonies; a universal and uniform dominion of the truth of the Church within the sphere which it can win and control; the theocratic union of Church and State, and the compulsory enforcement of the "pure doctrine," at least externally; the closest union between Church and State, while allowing each to retain its fundamentally distinct character; the acceptance of secular culture and the penetration of the system of "callings" belonging to the realm of Natural Law, with the Christian spirit; the identification of the Decalogue with the Law of Nature and the approximation of positive law to both; and last of all, its conception of the Church itself.

In Troeltsch's judgment, "all these ideas Calvin adopted as finished products . . ." (580-81). Nonetheless, while the Genevan experiment was initiated by the church type and included churchly, Constantinian ideals of universalism, objectivism, and theocracy, it also incorporated key elements of the sect ideal. "Calvinism has, however, incorporated into its idea of the Church so much of the sect-ideal that it was obliged to make the bold attempt (1) of constituting its national church as a church of professing believers, and (2) of constituting its unity of Church and State as a Christian society in the strict sense of the personal Christian faith and character of each individual member." This "concession" to the sectarian ideal did not, however, erase the dominant churchly character of Calvinism. "Calvinism did so far remain a 'Church' that it never questioned the ideal of a unity which included Society and the State, natural life and worship, and the separation of a holy separate community from the ordinary life of humanity always remained a crime." Calvinism achieved this fusion of two seemingly incommensurate ideals by modifying and transforming the "real ideals of the Gospel in order to make them agree with its attachment to the popular morality of the Old Testament. It was by the adaptation of those Gospel ideals to the Old Testament and to the natural-law ethic that Calvinism so far adjusted itself to the practical conditions of life that it became possible to carry them out in practice" (622-23). In short, Calvinism represents a universalizing theocratic vision without the papal, hierarchical institutional frame. It was an attempt "to effect a Christian and ethical transformation of the whole of society and civilization," while at the same time maintaining "a strong independent church." In Troeltsch's own summary:

> In Calvinism the Church is both national and free, a holy community, and an objective institution, a voluntary and a compulsory organization, since it is based on the assumption that all the elect, if they are sufficiently well taught, will open their minds to the Truth, while it is required that all the non-elect must be suppressed, to the glory of God and for the protection of the elect, and must be prevented from expressing both their unbelief and their non-morality in public. *Thus this is the union of the sect and the Church ideal, minus a Royal Head of the Church and patronage.* (653, emphasis added)

Neo-Calvinism is distinguished from primitive Calvinism, in Troeltsch's judgment, by its rejection of this duality, by its repudiation of the church ideal in favor of the sectarian "free church" ideal. The inner tension between the inclusive, universal, national ideal and that of an exclusive holy community, a tension that was resolved in primitive Calvinism by attempting to create holy nations and civilizations, did not, and even perhaps could not, last. The stone of stumbling here was religious toleration, which, according to Troeltsch, "was one logical result of the rise of Congregationalism and of the Free Church movement." The heart of the Free Church ecclesiology "is the destruction of the mediaeval and early Protestant idea of a social order welded together by one uniform State Church, and of one infallible authority with a uniform control of the whole of civilization." The key question here is to what extent this development is "to be attributed to the logical development of Calvinism, and to what extent has this result been affected by external influences of a foreign kind" (656, 658). With this question we come to the heart of the debate about neo-Calvinism.

From Kuyper's neo-Calvinist vantage point, religious toleration or liberty of conscience is a direct result of applying Calvinist principles to public life. Kuyper's observation states the case forthrightly: "And the free churches have exclusively flourished in those countries which were touched by the breath of Calvinism, i.e., in Switzerland, the Netherlands, England, Scotland, and the United States of America." Essential to Calvinism, according to Kuyper, is "a liberty of conscience, which enables every man to serve God *according to his own conviction and the dictates of his own heart*."[17] Kuyper openly acknowledges the historical difficulties of such a claim, the problem "in the pile and faggots of Servetus" and the problem of Article 36 of the Belgic Confession, which "entrusts to the government the task 'of defending against and extirpating every form of idolatry and false religion and to protect the sacred service of the Church.'" Kuyper "deplores" and "unconditionally disapproves" of these elements in the tradition, "yet not as if it were the expression of a special characteristic of Calvinism, but on the contrary as the fatal after-effect of a system, grey with age, which Calvinism found in existence, under which it had grown up, and from which it had not yet been able entirely to liberate itself."[18] Troeltsch's summary of Kuyper's views on this matter are to the point. "Modern Calvinists like Kuyper do not hesitate to ascribe the existence of the Free Churches directly to the influence of Calvin's most essential ideas; his idea of a State Church, with its compulsory Christian civilization, they regard as a mediaeval idea, involving mediaeval limitations which it is easy to discard."[19]

Troeltsch, on the other hand, while not denying sectlike elements and a democratizing tendency in primitive Calvinism, sees "the historical starting point of the Free Churches . . . in congregationalism," and the principle of religious toleration as "the fruit of a (Lockean) Liberal view of the relation between Church and State." The influence of the Radical Reformation, Baptist sectarian ecclesiology, is not to be overlooked either. "It is impossible," in his judgment, "to attribute these results [Free Churches] directly to Calvinism itself; they may rather be described as due to the influence of a modified Calvinism affected by Baptist and 'spiritual' influences" (670-72, passim). In its shift to a Free Church concept, "Calvinism has formally drawn closer to the sects." In fact, "Calvinism and the sect-group composed of the Baptists, Methodists, and Salvationists to-day constitute a religious unity which also represents a great sociological collective type of Christian thought" (689). Consequently, the politics of neo-Calvinism is categorically different from that of primitive Calvinism. "In its passage through the Free Church phase the main block of Calvinism became Liberal in politics, and it participates so closely in the tendency of the sects towards an individualistic and purely utilitarian conception of the State that to-day, in this respect, there is scarcely any difference between it and them"

17. Kuyper, *Lectures on Calvinism,* 101, 109. See also Abraham Kuyper, "Calvinism: Source and Stronghold of Our Constitutional Liberties (1874)," in *Abraham Kuyper: A Centennial Reader,* ed. James D. Bratt (Grand Rapids: Eerdmans, 1998), 279-321.

18. Kuyper, *Lectures on Calvinism,* 99, 100.

19. Troeltsch, 660; parenthetical pages references in the following paragraph are to Troeltsch's work.

(670). Not only did neo-Calvinism become liberal in its politics, its association-al "tendency to form societies for ecclesiastical and religious ends, as well as for civic and cultural purposes," so Troeltsch contends, "requires the Christian-Liberal organization of the State and of society, independence and freedom for the individual, equality of opportunity as well as in the eyes of the law, the orga-nization of international peace, and the conquest of the struggle for existence by means of self-discipline and active social help through associated effort" (670, 688). Troeltsch's conclusion follows naturally: "Neo-Calvinism, with its Free Church system, and its accompanying phenomena of democracy and lib-eralism, as well as with the Pietistic Rigorism of a strong self-controlled indi-vidualism, very utilitarian in secular affairs, has moved very far away from the early aristocratic Calvinism of the period of its foundation at Geneva" (688).

Dutch Reformed Protest and Secession

The heart of Troeltsch's critique — Kuyper was more a liberal, modern thinker than a traditional Calvinist — was shared by a number of Kuyper's Dutch Re-formed contemporaries. What is interesting about this critique is that it came simultaneously and apparently independently[20] from opponents on both ex-treme wings of the Dutch Reformed theological and ecclesiastical spectrum. Conservative doctrinalists such as the Christian Reformed minister and theolo-gian F. M. Ten Hoor and self-confessed modernists such as Leiden Old Testa-ment professor B. D. Eerdmans agreed — Kuyper's views were "modernist," not Calvinist or traditional Reformed (Oud Gereformeerd). In order to understand this twin-flanked attack, before we consider the specifics of Ten Hoor's and Eerdmans's critiques, we need to take note of a few important developments in nineteenth-century Dutch Reformed church history.

From 1795 to 1815 the Dutch nation lived under a regime of French revo-lutionary ideology in which a strict separation of church and state was decreed. "The Reformed Church lost its privileged position, its exclusive rights to large portions of ecclesiastical property, and its control over the schools."[21] In the post–Congress of Vienna restoration of the House of Orange, the Reformed church was also restored to a position of privilege, but King William I's ecclesi-astical reorganization was a bitter pill for the pious orthodox Reformed to swal-

20. Although a moderate liberal critic such as C. B. Hylkema — writing in 1911 — was as aware of the conservative, Christian Reformed critiques of Kuyper as he was of the avowedly modernist attack by B. D. Eerdmans. See Hylkema, chap. 1.

21. D. H. Kromminga, The Christian Reformed Tradition (Grand Rapids: Eerdmans, 1943), 72.

low since it shifted the locus of church authority away from the local congregation to a court-appointed national ecclesiastical board. The infamous General
Regulation of 1816 turned the national church into a State Department of Religion, "just another civil institution ruled by a bureaucratic hierarchy."[22] Fueled
by a long-standing tradition of Dutch conventicle pietism,[23] protests against alleged doctrinal, liturgical, and polity deviations from Reformed orthodoxy in
the national church culminated in a significant Secession *(Afscheiding)* in 1834
and the eventual formation of a new denomination, the *Christelijk Gereformeerde Kerk* (Christian Reformed Church).[24]

The Secession of 1834 was not to be the only major defection from the
National Dutch Reformed Church in the nineteenth century. Some fifty years
later, in 1886, another renewal movement, led by Abraham Kuyper and known

22. James D. Bratt, *Dutch Calvinism in Modern America: A History of a Conservative
Subculture* (Grand Rapids: Eerdmans, 1984), 5. For a good discussion of the developments
leading up to the General Regulation and the objections to it, see A. J. Rasker, *De
Nederlandse Hervormde Kerk vanaf 1795*, 2nd ed. (Kampen: Kok, 1981), 19-31.

23. F. Ernest Stoeffler summarizes this tradition thus: "Long traditions of piety were
native to the Netherlands. Here the great Ruysbroek and the brilliant Gerhard Groote had
lived and taught. Here Radewyn had founded the Brethren of the Common Life, a movement fostering a practical type of mystical piety out of which had come *The Imitation of
Christ*. Here, too, the Anabaptists had established their norms of piety and some of them
had dreamed their fanatical dreams and set up their strange theocracies. In all of these
movements the real aid had been some form of piety which to those who practice it held
out the promise both of this life and of the life to come" (*The Rise of Evangelical Pietism*
[Leiden: Brill, 1965], 118). In addition to Stoeffler's work, for discussions of Dutch Re-
formed pietism see H. Heppe, *Geschichte des Pietismus und der Mystik in der Reformierten
Kirche, Namentlich der Niederlande* (Leiden: Brill, 1879); A. Ritschl, *Geschichte des
Pietismus,* vol. 1 (Bonn: Adolph Marchus, 1880); Wilhelm Goeters, *Die Vorbereitung des
Pietismus in der Reformierten Kirche der Niederlande bis zur Labadischten Krisis 1670* (Leip-
zig and Utrecht: Hinrichs & Oosthoek, 1911). For a shorter treatment see S. van der Linde,
"Der Reformierte 'Pietismus' in den Niederlanden," in *Pietismus und Reveil*, ed. J. van den
Berg and J. P. van Dooren (Leiden: Brill, 1978), 102-17.

24. For a succinct but illuminating discussion of the 1834 Secession, see Bratt,
Dutch Calvinism, chap. 1: "Secession and Its Tangents." Also see the commemorative booklet published by the faculty of Mid-America Reformed Seminary, Peter Y. De Jong and
Nelson Kloosterman, eds., *The Reformation of 1834* (Orange City, Iowa: Pluim, 1984). The
substance of Seceder protest is contained in the October 13, 1834, statement, "The Deed of
Secession or Return" ("De Akte van Afscheiding of Wederkeering"), in which Secession
leader H. De Cock and members of his congregation accuse the national church of being a
false church and indicate their intention to return to the Reformed confessional and polity
parameters established by the 1618-19 Synod of Dordt. This statement, along with other
revealing documents of the Secession, can be found in J. N. Bakhuysen van den Brink et al.,
Documenta Reformatoria (Kampen: Kok, 1962), 2:133-34.

as the *Doleantie,* resulted in further division. In many respects the *Doleantie*[25] was a continuation of the long-standing movement of protest against the National Dutch Reformed Church that had led to the Secession of 1834. The *Doleantie* too was a protest against the doctrinal laxity and Erastian polity of the state-controlled church. Like the leaders of the Secession of 1834, Kuyper and others also called for a return to the binding character of the Reformed confessions and the church order of the Synod of Dordt. In both cases concerns about church autonomy from the state played a significant role. In summary, "Both ecclesiastical movements had as their principal goal the maintenance of true doctrine, handed down by the fathers, by means of church government set forth in the Reformed confessions and the church order of Dort."[26]

These important similarities notwithstanding, the Kuyper-led *Doleantie* exhibited some differences from the 1834 Secession, both sociologically and ideologically. The earlier movement was clearly a movement of the "disinherited." "Where the Secession took hold there were significant correlations between social status and ecclesiastical direction. The 'big farmers,' the local aristocracy, the 'progressive' and 'enlightened' elements of society ridiculed the movement; the hired hands, the poorer farmers, and the small tradesmen (but not the destitute) composed almost its entire membership."[27] While it is true that Kuyper's *Doleantie* movement deliberately appealed to and was largely supported by "common folk" (Kuyper's famous *kleine luyden*),[28] it was led by those who were influential in and were attempting to transform the social, cultural, educational, and political leadership of the Dutch nation. Only six years earlier Kuyper had established a new Christian university, and his journalistic and political activity was directed at a national cultural renewal, not church re-

25. The term *Doleantie* comes from the verb *dolerende,* or "mourning." Because it is virtually untranslatable (unlike the term *Afscheiding,* which is readily rendered as "Secession"), the Dutch term will be retained throughout this appendix. For a discussion of the events leading up to and accompanying the *Doleantie,* see Rasker, 171-90.

26. H. De Wilde, *Dr. A Kuyper als Leider van het Volk en als Minister* (The Hague: Nederbragt, 1905), 26.

27. Bratt, *Dutch Calvinism,* 6. Bratt adds: "Official provincial reports for 1836 described Seceder membership as 'for the most part . . . from the lowest ranks,' 'uncultured,' 'the least significant,' having 'no man of name' among them." For a sociological assessment of the Secession, see Lambertus Mulder, *Revolte der Fignen: De Afscheiding van 1834 als Sociaal Conflict en Beweging* (Meppel: Boom, 1973), and J. S. Van Weerden, *Spanningen en Konflicten: Verkenningen Rondom de Afscheiding van 1834* (Groningen: Sasland, 1967).

28. H. Algra's historical overview of the nineteenth century, *Het Wonder van de 19e Eeuw: Van Vrije Kerken en Kleine Luyden* (Franeker: T. Wever, 1966), is an attempt to vindicate the claim for this kind of continuity between the *Afscheiding* of 1834 and the *Doleantie* of 1886.

form alone. For Kuyper, Calvinism was a world-and-life view, a life system, a *Weltanschauung,* not merely an ecclesiastical-confessional or theological system. A summary of Kuyper's own convictions on this matter shows clearly how much further was his reach than that of the seceders:

> One desire has been the ruling passion of my life. One high motive has acted like a spur upon my mind and soul. And sooner than that I should escape from the sacred necessity that is laid upon me, let the breath of life fail me. It is this: That in spite of all worldly opposition, God's holy ordinances shall be established again in the home, in the school and in the State for the good of the people; to carve as it were into the conscience of the nation the ordinances of the Lord, to which Bible and Creation bear witness, until the nation pays homage again to God.[29]

To a large degree, it was Kuyper's very success in implementing this vision, culminating in his prime ministership of 1901-5, that led to the vehement attack on him, particularly from the progressive or modernist side. Before we consider the critique of modernist theologian B. D. Eerdmans, we shall examine the criticism that descended upon him from an articulate spokesman for Reformed orthodoxy, the Secession preacher/theologian F. M. Ten Hoor.[30]

Ten Hoor's Critique of Kuyper

To understand Ten Hoor's antipathy to Kuyper, once again a brief historical note is necessary. Whereas the Secession of 1834 had been a more-or-less spontaneous

29. This is a summary citation of Kuyper's address given on the celebratory anniversary occasion of his editorship of the daily newspaper *De Standaard* (*Gedenkboek* [Amsterdam: Herdes, 1897]). The summary is given by John Hendrick De Vries in the introductory biographical note to his translation of Kuyper's collection of meditations, *To Be Near unto God* (Grand Rapids: Eerdmans, 1925), 7.

30. Foppe Martin Ten Hoor (1855-1934) was a minister in the Secession Christian Reformed Church until 1896 when he emigrated to the United States and served the Christian Reformed Church of North America. He taught systematic theology at Calvin Theological Seminary, Grand Rapids, from 1900 to 1924. His critique of Kuyper's ecclesiology can be found in two publications, *Afscheiding en Doleantie, in Verband met het Kerkbegrip* (1890) and *Afscheiding of Doleantie, Een Woord tot Verdediging en Nadere Toelichting* (1891). These two brochures are republications of series of articles that initially appeared in the Christian Reformed journal *De Vrije Kerk.* For an overview and analysis of Ten Hoor's critique of Kuyper, see Cornelis Pronk, "F. M. Ten Hoor: Defender of Secession Principles against Abraham Kuyper's Doleantie Views" (Th.M. thesis, Calvin Theological Seminary, 1987).

revolt against the National Reformed Church, the *Doleantie* of 1886 proceeded according to a carefully scripted plan of church reform spelled out in Kuyper's 1884 publication, *Tract for the Reformation of the Churches*.[31] In this, as well as in a later treatise entitled *Separation and Doleantie*,[32] Kuyper made a sharp distinction between his own vision of church reform and that of the 1834 Secession. By means of a highly abstract distinction between the church's visible form and its invisible essence,[33] Kuyper insisted upon a separation of true believers from the bureaucratic structure and organization of the national church while retaining a spiritual bond with the Dutch Reformed Church itself through maintained fellowship at the local congregational level. Kuyper thus repudiated the 1834 Secession's categorical separation from the national church because it was judged to be a "false church" according to the description in Articles 28 and 29 of the Belgic Confession. In Kuyper's judgment, though the external structure of a church may be deformed, as long as there are in its midst true believers, it has not lost the essence of church. Thus, "every church still retains the essence of a church, as long as it carries in its womb a circle of living members of Christ, *even though all its institutions are corrupt.*" The corollary of this claim is also true according to Kuyper. "From this it follows that a gathering in which there are no longer members of the body of Christ has lost the essence of church . . . *regardless of how pure it may still be in its institutions* or the administration of the word and sacraments."[34] Seces-

31. Abraham Kuyper, *Tractaat van de Reformatie der Kerken aan de Zonen der Reformatie hier te Lande op Luthers Vierde Eeuwfeest* (Amsterdam: Höveker & Zoon, 1884). A full-length study of Kuyper's ecclesiology can be found in P. A. Van Leeuwen, *Het Kerkbegrip in de Theologie van Abraham Kuyper* (Franeker: T. Wever, 1946). A very useful English summary of Kuyper's ecclesiology is found in Henry Zwaanstra, "Abraham Kuyper's Conception of the Church," *Calvin Theological Journal* 9 (1974): 149-81.

32. Abraham Kuyper, *Separatie en Doleantie* (Amsterdam: Wormser, 1890).

33. "The essence of a visible church is and always remains the invisible church, including therewith the increased impulse of this spiritual and mystical church to manifest itself externally. The invisible church is the body of Christ, that is the organic union of all the elect through the Holy Spirit under Christ as its head. Thus if a certain number of living members of this body of Christ live in a single city or village, then the essence of the church is there and this essence comes to consciousness, as soon as these members, regardless of how broken the manner, exercise the communion of saints, and have the desire and will to bring this fellowship to a fuller and purer churchly manifestation. . . ." Cited and translated from Kuyper's *Tractaat* by Zwaanstra, "Kuyper's Conception," 150-51.

34. Zwaanstra, 151, emphasis added. According to Kuyper, this caution about judging a church so long as it numbers at least some of the elect in its midst extends even to those who are *potentially,* if not *actually,* church members: "Therefore, one ought not to be too hasty in his judgment concerning the church. Without a doubt a group of elect is necessary for the first manifestation of the essence of the church, a group of people who are mature and resolute confessors. Young children, or people who have not yet made confes-

sion was thus viewed as radical separation, while reform by *Doleantie* sought to be renewal from within.

This significant difference in approaches to church reform notwithstanding, when the *Doleantie* took place and did in fact lead to separation from the national church, the response among many leaders of the Secession church was positive, occasionally even euphoric. Important leaders of the Christian Reformed Church, including one of the Secession's "founding fathers," Simon Van Velzen, soon began to call for union between Secession and *Doleantie* churches. Van Velzen, for example, was incredulous that there could be opposition to such union. "I've often been asked," he said, "should we Christian Reformed [believers] be united with [those of] the *Doleantie*? . . . Christian Reformed [believers] and those of the *Doleantie* are already united in everything that ought to unite genuine Reformed believers in one nation. They are united by the bond of faith, a bond by which the Lord himself unites his people. He *has* united them. If the Lord has done and is doing this, the question 'should we unite?' is, to say the least, for Christians wholly inappropriate and unseemly."[35]

It was in this same spirit that the 1888 Synod of the Secession Christian Reformed Church, meeting in Assen, unanimously went on record stating that "union with the *Doleantie* churches was not only desirable but must be considered an obligation commanded by God."[36] Under the mediating leadership of Herman Bavinck,[37] a union was effected in 1892 and a new denomi-

---

sion, even though they belong to God's elect, are incapable of church formation. In an existing church on the other hand, the seed of the church is indeed reckoned a part of it, and the essence of the church has not been lost even though the last of the adult elect have died out and no elect among the youth have come to conversion. . . . The essence of a church can be considered from the viewpoint of her potentiality *(potentia)* or her essence according to her operation *(actus)*. Dynamite is dynamite even though it has not yet exploded, because it carries in itself the potential to explode. Similarly, a gathering possesses the essence of a church even though it may lack every office, because it continues to have the ability to establish the office" (cited and translated from Kuyper's *Tractaat* by Pronk, "F. M. Ten Hoor," 9).

35. As reported by J. S. van der Linden, *Heeft de Christelijke Gereformeerde Kerk Recht van Bestaan?* 2nd ed. (The Hague: Js. Bootsma, 1922), 16. I am indebted for this reference to V. Hepp, *Dr. Herman Bavinck* (Amsterdam: W. Ten Have, 1921), 179.

36. Algra, 334.

37. Bavinck, who was the leading theologian in the Secession community, teaching at the Kampen Theological School, was also a careful but nonetheless committed neo-Calvinist. His crucial role in the process of unification is sketched by his biographers, Hepp, 178-207, and R. H. Bremmer, *Herman Bavinck en zijn Tidgenoten* (Kampen: Kok, 1966), 67-69, 70-74. Appointed by the Christian Reformed Church Synod of Assen in 1888 to draft an invitation to *Doleantie* leaders for a conference on unification, Bavinck penned these classic lines of mediation: "The line by which we walk has been drawn differently

nation formed, the *Gereformeerde Kerken in Nederland*. However, the rejoicing about the union was not unanimous. A small number of Seceders refused to go along with the union, and even among those who did join, significant reservations about Kuyper's neo-Calvinist program remained.[38] Of those critics, Ten Hoor was without question one of the most vigorous and articulate.

Ten Hoor's attack took place on three related fronts — ecclesiology, soteriology, and the nature of theology. In addition to accenting differences about the extent of deformity in the national church and the nature by which reform was to be effected, Ten Hoor also contended — contra Troeltsch's judgment — that Kuyper had not sufficiently broken with the theocratic ideal of a national Reformed state-church *(volkskerk)*.[39] "For all his avowed defense of a free church in a free state, Kuyper could never get rid of the ideal of a Reformed

---

than the one you propose. Nevertheless, the direction we wish to go is none other than the one which leads us to you and all other Reformed people in our nation" (Bremmer, *Tidgenoten,* 56). Bavinck worked tirelessly to clarify the positions of the two groups vis-à-vis one another, and sought constantly to minimize the perceived differences betweeen the two methods of reform. In particular, he wrote extensively in Christian Reformed journals and engaged in personal correspondence with Christian Reformed leaders in an attempt to ameliorate the heavy criticism of Kuyper which existed in his own fellowship. Of note is a lengthy exchange of letters from September through December 1895 between Bavinck and Ten Hoor (published in R. H. Bremmer, *Herman Bavinck als Dogmaticus* [Kampen: Kok, 1961], 378-424) and Bavinck's review article in the Christian Reformed publication *De Bazuin* (November 14, 1890) dealing with Kuyper's treatise *Separatie en Doleantie* and Ten Hoor's *Afscheiding en Doleantie*. Bavinck's conclusion concerning the debate was that differences of principle between the two camps were minimal and that unification was possible provided neither group insisted exclusively upon its own method of reform as the only valid one.

38. For a discussion of the objections to union among the Christian Reformed themselves, see W. Van 't Spijker, "De Strijd om het Voortbestaan," in *En Toch Niet Verteerd,* ed. M. Drayer, W. Van 't Spijker, and J. H. Velema (Kampen: Kok, 1982), 9-27; W. Van 't Spijker, "Enkele Hoofdlijnen van de Geschiedenis van de Christelijke Gereformeerde Kerken sinds 1892," in *Een Eeuw Christelijk Gereformeerd: Aspecten van 100 Jaar Christelijke Gereformeerde Kerken,* ed. W. Van 't Spijker, J. N. Noorlandt, and H. Van der Schaaf (Kampen: Kok, 1992), 9-132. The vehemence of the protest against the union, considering it a Judas-like betrayal, is nicely captured by the author of a pamphlet, Ab. Verheij, *De Christelijke Gereformeerde Kerk Verkocht, Overgelever en Begraven door Middel van de Vereeninging met de Doleantie tot eene Kerk,* 2nd rev. ed. (Delft: C. J. Van Doorne, 1894).

39. This is the burden of Ten Hoor's *Afscheiding of Doleantie.* The full title of this work in the original series of articles as they appeared in the Christian Reformed journal *De Vrije Kerk* in 1890 was "Afscheiding en Doleantie in zake de Verhouding van de Kerk tot de Overheid."

state church."[40] It was rather the Secession, in Ten Hoor's judgment, that truly embodied the ideal expressed in the motto of the Christian Reformed journal *De Vrije Kerk:* "A Free Church in a Free Nation." Kuyper's concern to maintain continuity with the historic Reformed church made it impossible for the *Doleantie* to make the necessary break with the *volkskerk* tradition. In conclusion: "The *Doleantie* is the result of the faulty principle of a state church. The *Doleantie* is the result of an error."[41]

Concerning the remaining two areas of disagreement — soteriology and the nature of theology — we can be more brief. Ten Hoor was a committed infralapsarian and convinced that Kuyper's supralapsarianism and its logical correlate — presumptive and immediate regeneration — was the fruit of speculative-idealistic philosophy rather than scriptural or Reformed confessional teaching.[42] The influence of alien modern philosophy, particularly that of Kant, is also alleged to be the fountain of Kuyper's conviction that theology is but one of the sciences in the organism of science[43] and should, therefore, be studied in

40. Pronk, 72. For a full-length discussion of Kuyper's views on and practice concerning the ideal of a state church, see H. J. Langman, *Kuyper en de Volkskerk* (Kampen: Kok, 1950).

41. Cited and translated from Ten Hoor's *Afscheiding of Doleantie* by Pronk (Pronk, 49). It is interesting to note that Kuyper's critique of the Secession also focuses on the free-church voluntarism of its reform: "By their own decision and act of secession, the seceders voluntarily reduced themselves to the level of simple believers, without any connection to the church as institute and therefore, without any official ecclesiastical status. Then, by another choice of their own free will, they proceeded to establish a new institutional church alongside of and in opposition to the existing church institute. Kuyper insisted that this new church formation, in spite of obvious formal similarities, was not historically continuous with the old Reformed Church" (Zwaanstra, 172. Zwaanstra refers here to Kuyper's *Separatie en Doleantie*, 36-37).

42. For an overview and discussion of this issue, see Pronk, 102-12. Briefly stated, Kuyper held the view that regeneration is an *immediate* act of the Holy Spirit that is brought to the consciousness of the believer through the historically functioning covenant of grace and the institutional church's mediation of grace through preaching and sacraments. It is this objective eternal work of regeneration that is the basis for baptizing children — they are presumed regenerate.

43. The evidence for Ten Hoor's claim is not hard to find. In his *Principles of Sacred Theology,* trans. J. H. De Vries (Grand Rapids: Eerdmans, 1965 [1898]), 293, Kuyper contends that "only when, by and after Kant, the question about the essence and the method of our knowledge, and consequently of the nature of science in general, pressed itself forcefully to the front, in our human consciousness, was there gradually adopted the organic interpretation of Theology as a whole and as one of the sciences in the great unit of the sciences, which is now dominant in the theological faculty, and is being more widely recognized by the other faculties. Formerly a science of theology in that sense was *not necessary,* because the human consciousness in general did not feel the need of such an inter-

the university rather than in a church-related theological school or seminary. For Ten Hoor, maintaining the ecclesiastical character and control of theological education was crucial.[44] Ten Hoor rejects altogether Kuyper's distinction between ecclesiastical and scientific theology with its concern that the latter be truly "academic" and universal. Here Kuyper, in Ten Hoor's judgment, allowed an a priori formal and speculative idea of science[45] rather than Scripture or the Reformed confessional tradition to determine the definition and — eventually but inevitably — the content of Reformed theology. Each of these critiques deserves a full-length study of its own, but for our purposes here it is worth exposing the common thread that runs through them. Essentially, Ten Hoor contends that Kuyper's neo-Calvinist thought is discontinuous with the Reformed or Calvinist tradition[46] on the three fronts mentioned, and that this discontinuity is the fruit of modernist philosophical (speculative-idealist) influences. Abstract notions of the church's "essence," supralapsarianism, and the notion of an organism of science become the famous Reformed "principles" by which Kuyper pushed forward his program for church as well as cultural and political reform. In sum, Kuyper was an innovating modernist, and his neo-Calvinist revival was an aberration from Reformed confessional orthodoxy.

Eerdmans's Critique of Kuyper

We now consider a similar critique of Kuyper from the liberal or modernist wing of the National Dutch Reformed (Hervormd) Church, examining pub-

---

pretation; neither was it *possible*, because the data for such a construction of theology and of all the other sciences, cannot be borrowed from the *knowledge of God*, but from Logic in the higher sense." For a helpful overview of Kuyper's philosophy of science, see Del Ratzsch, "Abraham Kuyper's Philosophy of Science," *Calvin Theological Journal* 27 (1992): 277-303.

44. See, *inter alia*, F. M. Ten Hoor, "'Encyclopaedie der Heilige Godgeleerdheid,' door A. Kuyper," *De Vrije Kerk* 20 (1894): 550-59, 653-74; 21 (1895): 23-43, 95-117; and "Kerkelijke of Universitaire Opleiding," *De Vrije Kerk* 21 (1895): 151-75, 219-44, 257-77, 434-53, 457-76.

45. Cf. Kuyper's definition in *Principles of Sacred Theology*, 292: "The science of theology is that logical action of the general subject of regenerated humanity by which, in the light of the Holy Spirit, it takes up the revealed knowledge of God into its consciousness and from thence reflects it."

46. Ten Hoor even objects to neo-Calvinism's use of the self-designation "Calvinist" rather than the traditional "Reformed" (Gereformeerd). See F. M. Ten Hoor, "De Naam Calvinisme bij Oude Gereformeerden en in Onzen Tijd," *Gereformeerde Amerikaan* 20 (1916): 66-70, 201-8, 313-23, 403-16, 433-42.

lished attacks (in 1909 and 1911) by Leiden University professor B. D. Eerd-mans.[47] Eerdmans's critique of Kuyper was part of what one writer has referred to as a broader "modernist counter-offensive" against neo-Calvinism.[48] This counteroffensive arose at a time when the influence of neo-Calvinism appeared in the ascendancy and the modernist wing of the Dutch Reformed Church itself was in disarray, challenged by a group of "Malcontents" in its own ranks.[49] The "offensive" character of Eerdmans's polemic is clear from the opening sentences of his first treatise on Kuyper's theology. "Reformed theology was dead and, lo, it has come back to life. At least so it seems. But it's only an illusion. Whenever we take a closer look it is clear that what is set before us as living Reformed the-ology, what passes for it and appears to be genuine from a great distance, is in fact something quite different." Eerdmans continues by claiming that the best proof of orthodox Reformed theology's full demise is the fact that Abraham Kuyper is seen by so many to be its great champion. He contends that it is pre-cisely Kuyper "who sought to wed Reformed theology to the spirit of the [mod-ern age] with the result that the small breath of life it [Reformed theology] still enjoyed completely fled the sleeping body."[50]

Eerdmans's critique focused on some of the same issues that concerned Ten Hoor, particularly the centrality of a speculative notion of immediate re-generation in Kuyper's thought. This emphasis, he contends, does not come from Scripture or the confessional tradition but from human experience. Eerd-mans cites passages from Kuyper's writings on common grace[51] which provide copious statistics about infant and child mortality rates, statistics that lead Kuyper to posit a doctrine of immediate regeneration, which occurs apart from

---

47. Bernardus Dirks Eerdmans (1868-1948) was an ordained minister in the Dutch Reformed (Hervormd) Church and taught Old Testament at the University of Leiden from 1898 to 1938. A brief biography is given by P. A. H. De Boer, "In Memoriam," Nederlands Theologisch Tijdschrift 3 (1948): 77-79. The two publications we are considering are De Theologie van Dr. A. Kuyper (Leiden: Van Doesburgh, 1909) and "Moderne" Orthodoxie of "Orthodox" Modernisme (Baarn: Hollandia, 1911).

48. Bremmer, Herman Bavinck als Dogmaticus, 115-22. Bremmer also discusses neo-Calvinist theologian Bavinck's response to the modernist attack in his Free University (of Amsterdam) rectorial address of 1911, Modernisme en Orthodoxie (Kampen: Kok, 1911).

49. On these so-called "Malcontents" in the Dutch Reformed Church, see K. H. Roessingh, Het Modernisme in Nederland (Haarlem: F. Bohn, 1922), 215-23; A. M. Brouwer, De Moderne Richting (Nijmegen: Ten Hoet, n.d.), 128-65. I am indebted to Bremmer, Herman Bavinck als Dogmaticus, 116, for these references.

50. Eerdmans, Theologie, 3.

51. Abraham Kuyper, De Gemeene Gratie, 3 vols. (Amsterdam: Höveker & Wormser, 1902-4).

human agency and human self-consciousness. If such children are to be even potentially among the elect, their regeneration must be immediate and nonself-conscious. According to Kuyper, such immediate regeneration can even take place in the mother's womb. Eerdmans does not even disguise his sarcasm when he observes, "From this citation [of Kuyper's writing] it becomes apparent that the activity of the Bureau of Statistics is of great consequence for the new Reformed theology." The consequence of Kuyper's view is clearly "that churches cannot be institutes of salvation, that conversion unto perseverance is unnecessary and that sanctification is without any real significance."[52]

Eerdmans also insists that Kuyper's views on miracles and the inspiration of Scripture differ significantly from that of traditional Reformed orthodoxy. Kuyper, he contends, is as critical of traditional supernaturalism as any modernist. Kuyper rejects the notion that miracles are an incursion into the world and denies that the Scriptures are wholly the Word of God, substituting the idea of "organic" inspiration in which the Scriptures are seen as a mixture of human and divine. This latter affirmation permits Kuyper to make use of unbelieving critical scholarship on the Bible, including such givens of scholarship as denying the full Mosaic authorship of the Pentateuch. In summary: "In this way contemporary Reformed [theology] employs a two-edged sword in slaying the old [Reformed] doctrine of Scripture. In the first place it teaches that not all of Scripture is divine and that much of it is merely human so that modern critical scholarship in its investigation can discover much that is true and good. Secondly, it teaches that even that which is divine in Scripture is also fully human, that human organisms, human personalities, on their own brought forth the Scriptures."[53]

What is remarkable about Eerdmans's assessment of Kuyper is that he is in fact profoundly sympathetic with the need to bring traditional Reformed theology into rapport with modern consciousness. He is convinced that childlike traditional supernaturalism with its assumption of a direct divine Fatherly care of cosmos and humanity, while spiritually attractive, is untenable in the modern world. When he concludes that Kuyper's "moderate orthodoxy" (*gematigde orthodoxie*) logically expects little more from prayer than "spiritual encouragement" (*geestelijke sterking*), he personally concurs: "That's what we liberals also expect."[54] Eerdmans's protest is against neo-Calvinism's attack on modernism in the name of orthodoxy, an attack that Eerdmans considers both ill-advised and dishonest. Like Ten Hoor, though from the opposite flank, Eerd-

52. Eerdmans, *Theologie*, 10.
53. Eerdmans, *"Moderne" Orthodoxie*, 34.
54. Eerdmans, *"Moderne" Orthodoxie*, 37.

mans is involved in an ecclesiastical battle, and his strategy is to expose the general of the opposing army as vacillating at best or duplicitous at worst. The moderate orthodoxy of neo-Calvinism, he contends, sounds like traditional orthodoxy and uses traditional terminology, especially when engaging its opponents in ecclesiastical warfare, but it means something quite different by it.[55]

Discontinuity and Continuity

From this sketchy overview several conclusions are possible. On the one hand, there is agreement among Troeltsch, Ten Hoor, and Eerdmans that Kuyper's neo-Calvinist vision and program exhibit significant discontinuities with Calvin and the classic Calvinist tradition. There is also agreement that Kuyper's alleged departures from the tradition represent his attempt to press the *universal* claims and concerns of the Christian religion. And finally, there is the striking unanimity about Kuyper's modernism/liberalism, a remarkable conclusion in the face of Kuyper's own consistent and repeated journalistic, ecclesiastical, and political offensive against it.[56] Beyond this level of agreement we run into difficulty. Simply put, all three critiques cannot be correct because there are significant contradictions between them and some internal inconsistencies within them. To begin with, both Troeltsch and Ten Hoor cannot be correct about Kuyper and the state-church/free-church issue. If Troeltsch is correct in asserting that Kuyper is to be distinguished from Calvin by his repudiation of the state-church idea, then Ten Hoor cannot fault Kuyper for allegedly failing to consistently pursue a free-church pattern of reform; and if Ten Hoor is correct, then Eerdmans cannot be correct in his conclusions about Kuyper's ecclesiology. The critique of Kuyper's doctrine of immediate regeneration, which appears to have little need for the church as the means of grace, seems quite at odds with the accusation that Kuyper is still bound to the *volkskerk* ideal where the church is essential as an objective institute of salvation. Kuyper's emphasis on immediate regeneration would seem to be much more consistent with a "free church" ecclesiology.

In addition, this whole discussion illustrates serious problems with the central dogma thesis as propounded, among others, by Troeltsch. If "predestination" is a central dogma in Calvin and the Calvinist tradition, it seems re-

55. Eerdmans, *"Moderne" Orthodoxie,* 17, 42.

56. See, for example, Abraham Kuyper, "Modernism: A Fata Morgana in the Christian Domain (1871)," in *Abraham Kuyper: A Centennial Reader,* 87-124. See also the direct response to Eerdmans's critique by neo-Calvinist Herman Bavinck, *Modernisme en Orthodoxie.*

markable that neo-Calvinism's departure from Calvin on the state-church issue could still appeal to authentic elements within that tradition. This is all the more remarkable since Kuyper, as a good nineteenth-century thinker, regularly used "central dogma" predestinarian language along with that of "principles" (and their consequences) to describe his own Calvinist position. Characteristic also in Kuyper's use of his favorite organic metaphor is the following definition of the "root principle" of Calvinism's political concepts: "This dominating principle [of Calvinism] was not, soteriologically, justification by faith, but, in the widest sense cosmologically, *the Sovereignty of the Triune God over the whole Cosmos,* in all its spheres and kingdoms, visible and invisible."[57] We have here a predestinarian and voluntarist definition that is remarkably similar to Troeltsch's understanding of Calvin and Calvinism.[58] If so, we must ask how the same or, at least, the very similar central dogma in Calvinism and neo-Calvinism could, by Troeltsch's own assessment, yield such decidedly distinct ecclesiologies. What this suggests rather is that we have here further evidence that the central dogma thesis itself needs to be questioned. At any rate, the central dogma appears to be less all-determining than its proponents contend.

This is not the place to explore the precise nature between Calvinism and neo-Calvinism further, but I will offer a suggestion for further study: for all the real differences and even discontinuities between Calvin, the Calvinist tradition, and Dutch neo-Calvinism, there may be (at least) one theme that binds them together — the theme of divine, trinitarian, order.[59] Furthermore, the idea of trinitarian order represents the Calvinist tradition's best efforts — theologically, ethically, and politically — to resolve the problem of unity and diversity, universality and particularity, a particular political concern not only of Abraham Kuyper and Dutch neo-Calvinism but of the modern world itself.

57. Kuyper, *Lectures on Calvinism,* 79.

58. Troeltsch's understanding of Calvin's voluntarist doctrine of God could as easily have been predicated of Kuyper. Behind his doctrine of predestination there lay also that idea of God which was the peculiar element in his own personal piety. In the idea of predestination Calvin is not merely trying to discover and formulate the absolute miracle of salvation, its supernatural character, and the fact that it is a pure gift of free grace (its "givenness"); he is also trying to express the character of God as absolute sovereign will (Troeltsch, 582).

59. The continuity of the theme of order in Calvin and Calvinism is argued by David Little, *Religion, Law, and Order* (New York and Evanston: Harper & Row, 1969). Little's sociological concern is to examine and defend Max Weber's thesis about Calvinism's role in developing a "legal-rational" social order, while the suggestion made here focuses more on the *theological,* trinitarian notion of order in Calvin, Calvinism, and neo-Calvinism. Also see Philip W. Butin, *Revelation, Redemption, and Response: Calvin's Trinitarian Understanding of the Divine-Human Relationship* (New York: Oxford University Press, 1995).

APPENDIX B

Itinerary of Abraham Kuyper's Visit to America in 1898[1]

August 20: Departed from Liverpool, England, on RMS *Lucania*.

August 27: Arrived in New York harbor; stayed at Fifth Avenue Hotel in Madison Square.

Month of September: Vacation in Adirondacks.

Month of October: Delivered the six Stone Lectures on Calvinism at the Miller Chapel, Princeton Theological Seminary, Princeton, N.J., and received an honorary doctorate of law from Princeton University.

October 10: Lecture #1: "Calvinism in History."

October 11: Lecture #2: "Calvinism and Religion."

October 14: Lecture #3: "Calvinism and Politics."

October 19: Lecture #4: "Calvinism and Science."

October 20: Lecture #5: "Calvinism and Art."

October 21: Lecture #6: "Calvinism and the Future."

October 22: Received honorary doctorate of law, Princeton University; Kuyper responded with a brief speech.[2]

October 26: Address to two thousand Dutch Americans in Lockerby Hall, Grand Rapids, Mich. (see app. C).

1. For additional narrative about the Kuyper trip, see Peter Heslam, *Creating a Christian Worldview: Abraham Kuyper's Lectures on Calvinism* (Grand Rapids: Eerdmans, 1998), 57-84. For the details of this itinerary I am particularly indebted to C. A. Admiraal, "De Amerikanse reis van Abraham Kuyper," in *Historicus in het Spanningsveld van Theorie en Praktijk*, ed. C. A. Admiraal et al. (Leiderdorp: Leidse Onderwijsinstellingen, 1985), 110-65. For further bibliography see chap. 3, n. 1.

2. For details see Heslam, 64-66.

October 27: Address to Dutch Americans at Third Reformed Church, Holland, Mich.: "The Future of Calvinism."

October 28: Address to students of Hope College at Winant Chapel, Holland, Mich.

October 29: Kuyper's sixty-first birthday; a banquet in his honor at New City Hotel, Holland, Mich.; Kuyper gave an after-dinner speech.

November 1: Evening address to Dutch Americans; theme unknown.

November 11: Address to Dutch Americans at the First Christian Reformed Church, Pella, Iowa.

November 7: Address to Dutch Americans at the Marlowe Theater, Englewood, Ill.: "The Vocation of Hollanders in America."

November 8: Lecture at McCormick Theological Seminary, Chicago, Ill.: "Calvinism (I)."

November 9: Address to the members of the Holland Society of Chicago at the Chicago Athletic Club, Chicago, Ill.: "The Queen, Her Subjects, Their Ancestors."

November 10: Lecture at McCormick Theological Seminary, Chicago, Ill.: "Calvinism (II)."

November 11: Lecture at McCormick Theological Seminary, Chicago, Ill.: "Calvinism (III)."

November 12: Address to the faculty and students of the Congregational Seminary, Chicago, Ill.; topic unknown.

November 16: Address to Reformed and Presbyterian audience at Old Stone Church, Cleveland, Ohio: "The Political Principles of Calvinism."

November 24: Address to members of the Women's College Club of Rochester, N.Y., at home of Dr. W. R. Taylor: "Holland and Its People."

November 28: Address to faculty and students of New Brunswick Theological Seminary of the Reformed Church in America, New Brunswick, N.J.: "The Antithesis between Symbolism and Revelation."

November 30: Brief meeting with President McKinley at the White House.

December 6: Address to Presbyterian Historical Society in Philadelphia, Pa.: "The Antithesis between Symbolism and Revelation."

December 7: Address to faculty and students of Hartford Theological Seminary, Hartford, Conn.: "Calvinism: A Political Scheme."

December 8: Address to members of Collegiate Church, New York, N.Y.: "A New Development of Calvinism Needed."

December 9: Address at the organizational meeting of the Eastern chapter of the American branch of the Dutch Society "General Dutch Alliance" (Algemeen Nederlandsch Verbond), Fifth Avenue Hotel, New York.

December 10: Left New York for Boulogne on Holland-Amerika liner, SS *Rotterdam*.
December 31: Arrived home in Amsterdam.

Abraham Kuyper's Grand Rapids Address

After delivering the Stone Lectures at Princeton University, Kuyper began a tour of the significant Dutch-American settlements in western Michigan, Chicago, and Iowa. At each stop he was feted and, true to form, gave an inspirational address about the importance of the Reformed, Calvinist faith for social, cultural, and political life. His visit to Grand Rapids is noteworthy not only for the speech he gave (in Dutch) on October 26, 1898, to a gathering of some two thousand Dutch-American Calvinists, but also for the fascinating journalistic tug-of-war that followed by those who sought to claim him and his views for their own political ends and cause. Reading this account is a clear reminder that *plus ça change, de plus la même chose*. We begin with the printed transcribed translation (from memory?) of Kuyper's address in the *Grand Rapids Herald* on Saturday morning, October 29, 1898, even though the public reports and subsequent public controversy over the speech chronologically preceded the publication of the text. The text that follows includes the headlines and other data as printed in the newspapers.

WORDS OF ADVICE

Dr. Kuyper to the Hollanders of Grand Rapids

SYNOPSIS OF HIS LECTURE

Translation From the Dutch Showing Full Outline

Eminent Dutch Statesman Urges His Brethren of the Holland Blood to Be True and Firm for Their Adopted Country and to Be Alive and Progressive

Editor Grand Rapids Herald — I have undertaken to give you from memory a synopsis of Dr. Kuyper's lecture, which was delivered in the Auditorium last Wednesday in the Dutch language. The beauty of expression and words I cannot give; indeed I had hoped to see something in your paper in regard to this from far better heads and pens than mine. If you have no other reports will you kindly give this translation of mine a place in your paper. Respectfully, W. Walker, No. 207 Cass avenue.

Dr. Kuyper spoke as follows:

Men and Brethren — there are times in persons' lives when they live years in a few minutes, such a period I have just passed through, when I stood before you and met with so hearty and unbounded applause. The welcome I have received here and elsewhere since reaching these shores will leave with me memories as long as my life shall last. I am glad my Holland American friends, to meet you this evening, and to stand as I do between these two flags, both the emblem of sturdy liberty (and) loving sentiment. The flag at my left hand is my flag, yours no longer. The stars and stripes on my right hand is your flag. (applause). This is your flag and you should love it and defend it with your life, if called upon, with the same devotion that your Holland ancestors were willing to defend their liberty and their religion. As Hollanders a few centuries ago, we freed ourselves from oppression and brought the proud Spaniard to his knees suing for peace after 80 years of hard fighting. What it took us 80 years to do you accomplished in 80 days and we on the other side rejoice with you and admire your greatness.

I say once more, men and brethren, make this great land your fatherland indeed. You do not want to be Hollanders in America. The Dutch blood and the American blood are so nearly akin that it should mingle without difficulty. America is destined in the providence of God to become the most glorious and noble nation the world has ever seen. Some day its renown will eclipse the renown and splendor of Rome, Greece and the old races.

How do I know this? I will tell you. If I had time I could demonstrate by the past history of the world the fact that whenever and wherever God intended to do something with nations he first stirred them up, ground them together and kneaded them as it were, and thus prepared them for the work in hand. Go back as far as you will in history and you will find this true. There was no progress at all until Cain was driven out of Eden. Then it was that he builded a city. Afterwards, when progress was again stopped with the building of the Babylonian tower, the people were scattered over the face of the earth. Why this disturbance? God intended something great should be done. On the other hand, look at the Chinese, for centuries they lived by themselves, isolated. They are a numerous nation, but they have not done anything. They are of the same color, have the same customs old as their hills, but you never hear from them. The North American Indians are another example. Once they were strong, today they are almost extinct. The Swedes and Norwegians have lived in themselves to a great extent. You never hear much about them. They are a good people enough, but they do not make themselves felt. Isolation and calm is always retrogressive.

What is it that has made England what it is today? Intermingling with other peoples and introduction of new blood makes the Anglo-Saxon land what it is.

I believe that America's greatness is due to a great extent under the providence of God, to the broadening process of all the different nationalities of the world into one great and overwhelming nation.

Men and Brethren: I wish you as your warm friend and brother of the same old stock all the success and prosperity which is at your command in this great country. But, and I hope you will not think me meddlesome when I say this, you should do a little more than simply gather in the American dollar. You should make your presence felt. I am told there are about 25,000 Holland-Americans in this city, and when I visited your high school today I asked your principal, "Is the Dutch taught here?" and he said "No," and I said "That is a shame." I did not mean it was his shame. My friends, it is your shame. Can you not, with your one-fourth population, do this? I know you can, in this free country. If you do not have it, it is your own fault and negligence. From my house on the other side I have been looking for and expecting to see arise from the Holland people to this country poets, painters, artists, writers — poets like Bilderdyk, Da Costa; painters like Rembrandt. You can do this and you owe it to the land of your adoption to give her the best there is in you. Do not only take and absorb, but give something in return. Only in this way can you make your influence felt. So long as you do not do this, you will be only English-speaking Hollanders; something like the Jews in this country and in mine. I do not say this with a purpose of casting a slur on the Jewish nation — only to warn you. For centuries the Jews have lived among us [isolated]. They were very keen and shrewd to make a bargain, and thrifty, and very peaceable and good citizens; but as a people they have given nothing in return.

Men and brethren, you can best serve your country by becoming an integral part of her, and fully intermingling with life. Do not be afraid to marry an American girl if you love her and she is willing. I do not believe in this hard work of trying and fighting and pulling to keep up the Holland language. Preaching can do but little real good, to the child and young man and maidens whose environments are American. Our brethren in the eastern states have tried that to their sorrow too long. They have given that up long ago, and see the result. Roosevelt, Van Wyck, and a legion of prominent novices reveal their Dutch origin and they are proud of it. Some of its greatest men of New York shook hands with me who claimed to have Dutch blood in their veins, but in manner, speech and deportment they were first class American citizens. Now, my friends, I am afraid I am treading on dangerous ground when I talk politics. You will say: "What does this stranger know about politics?" Forgive me this time. We are in a free country, are we not?

When I came here I was told that the greater part of the Hollanders were republicans. I was surprised at this, but after I had asked for and obtained, and read the different platforms, I was no longer surprised. The democrat (platform) stated among other things that they were true to the everlasting principles of Jefferson. Then I was no longer surprised. The educated Hollander who is acquainted with the doctrine and principles of Jefferson cannot be a democrat. If I lived here I should be a republican. I want, however, to qualify this statement by saying that after reading the republican platform, I found that in it there is room for improvement. It should bring out more fully the principles they really advocate.

And now, my dear friends, I wish to say to you in conclusion that the future progress and success of this and in fact, of every other nation, depends in a great measure on what stand you take on religion. I claim that the success of this nation is due to Calvinistic principles and doctrine. I do not mean the repetition of certain forms and creeds, but I mean the living Calvinistic principles which are the life-giving and solid basis of religion. It makes a man know himself and his maker, and fits him for the battles of life.

What would the reformation have been without Calvin? It had really begun before. The Anabaptists laid down their life and bowed their neck before the Spanish executioner to have their heads cut off by the thousand — but the world was made no better. It was not until sturdy John Calvin made himself felt that the world was shaken to its foundations.

How much, think you, does this republic owe to the pilgrim fathers and the Puritans? If there are any of you here who have not read Campbell's work entitled the "Puritans in England, Holland and America," I would advise you, by all means, to procure this and read it — no, take it out of the library for a day or two but purchase it as your own and study it. It will benefit you much more than so many popular books of the day about the good Henry or the gentle Mary.

This country, more than any other is a religious Calvinistic nation. It is born and bred in them. I am told that every session of congress is opened with prayer. This is not so in Holland. I am sorry to say that when parliament was asked by a few of us, to invite the prayers of the churches for our beloved queen, it was not heeded. Here in this country I have read of generals and admirals assembling their crews for prayer on the eve of battle and next month you will be called for thanksgiving. Oh! were it thus on the other side.

Men and brethren, I see a better day dawning for my fatherland. To this end I am working and am meeting with better success than I dared to hope for a few years ago, when I met with only abuse and have received more than one letter threatening my life.

My friends! I once more thank you for the kind reception you have given me. Next Saturday, I reach my sixty-second birthday.[1] My first visit to you will in all human probability be my last one. I wish

1. The transcriber is in error here; in 1898 Kuyper celebrated his sixty-first birthday.

and sincerely hope that our next meeting will be in the better region above. It will be so, if you make the knowledge of yourself and your God, which is the Calvin doctrine in a nutshell, the main concern of your existence. This will make you able and glad to say: "Whom have I in Heaven but Thee? And there is none upon earth that I desire besides Thee."

Live high up among the tops of the mountains, from whom you may now and then catch a glimpse of the Celestial city.

*   *

The next morning the *Grand Rapids Herald* published a fairly objective report of the event. Particular attention should be paid to the paragraph immediately preceding the subhead "In His Lectures" where the report of an interview with Kuyper makes the subtle and appropriate distinction about the word "democrat" that its rival newspaper failed to recognize, and thus generated the controversy that followed.

STORM OF APPLAUSE

GREETED THE REV. DR. ABRAHAM KUYPER OF AMSTERDAM

AT AUDITORIUM LAST NIGHT

TWO HUNDRED HOLLAND-AMERICANS WERE THERE[2]

Itinerary of the Famous Hollander in His Trip Through the United States — Says That He Does Not Advise Hollanders to Vote the Democrat Ticket.

An audience of 2000 Holland-American citizens of Grand Rapids gathered last night in the Auditorium to listen to the eminent Dutch scholar and political leader, Dr. Abraham Kuyper of Amsterdam. Those who had in charge the arrangements for the assembly and the reception were: G. H. Beuker, the Rev. A. B. Buursma, the Revs. DeBey, Voss and Kelser, Messrs. Dosker, Poston, Steketee, Verdler, Benjamin, Exter, Warnshuis and Hulst. These sat upon the stage on either side of the speaker of the evening. A prayer opened the meeting and it was led by the Rev. A. Buursma, of the Fifth Reformed Church.

Two huge flags, one the American and the other the royal flag of Holland, were draped as curtains for the stage, forming very pretty decorations. All of the committee men wore a knot of orange ribbon on the lapels of their coats in honor of the reigning sovereign of the Dutch, who is of the house of Orange.

G. H. Beuker introduced Dr. Kuyper and the utterance of the doctor's name called forth a storm of applause, amid which he arose and stepped to the front of the platform. He spoke on the relations of the American Dutch to their adopted country, urging them to noble citizenship. This followed a brief description of his arrival in this country and his reception. The lecture was delivered in the Holland language.

2. The headline number is in error, as the opening sentence of the article indicates; the number should be two thousand.

Ranks as a Statesman

Dr. Kuyper is a Holland statesman of high rank. He is a member of the second chamber of the states general, a body equivalent to the American house of representatives, and is the leader of what is termed the anti-revolutionary party. He came to the United States on invitation of the faculty of Princeton University to deliver a series of lectures prior to commemoration day on October 22. These lectures finished, the doctor accepted the invitations of numerous friends to appear in many of the large cities of the country, especially where there are thickly settled Holland districts. While at Princeton the doctor was a highly honored guest, and the degree of doctor of laws was conferred upon him. Previous to this his title had been that of doctor of divinity only.

From Grand Rapids Dr. Kuyper will go to Holland, Mich., and from there to Pella, Iowa, and Orange City, Iowa. At Chicago he will deliver four lectures, three at McCormick college, and one in the Holland tongue for the Dutch residents. Cleveland, Rochester, Hartford, New York, Philadelphia. Points in New Brunswick and Patterson, N.J., are also on the lecture tour.

In the course of an interview yesterday Dr. Kuyper said that he does not advise Holland residents of this country to vote the democrat ticket. He says that he is a democrat himself, but that he is one in the Holland sense of the word, not in the sense that it is popularly considered in America.

In His Lectures

In his lectures he speaks upon Calvinistic doctrines and old Calvinistic theories, maintaining that the foundation of the American state is laid upon them from the beginning of its construction. It is not the theological principles that the doctor lauds, but the political and scientific. He claims that they are at the bottom of the great American political institution which he says was taken from Holland, and not from England, as is generally credited. "England had her king," said Dr. Kuyper, "Holland her republic. The United States chose the republic. Holland had her two legislative bodies and after the pattern of these, not after the houses of England, was the American institution organized."

Dr. Kuyper is a professor in the Free University of Amsterdam, and is the chief editor of the Daily Standard, published in Amsterdam. He is connected also with the weekly Heraut, a political paper. At the recent coronation festivities of Wilhelmina, Dr. Kuyper was the president of the committee for the reception of the foreign press, and through his endeavors the American correspondents were especially favored and given detailed accounts of the royal ceremonies.

Dr. Kuyper was shown through the Central High school yesterday and was accompanied by 15 or 20 of the leading Holland citizens of the city. Trustee Verdier and Superintendent Hathaway conducted the party. In some of the rooms Dr. Kuyper spoke to the pupils for a few minutes. On leaving he expressed his pleasure and admiration of what he had seen.

*   *

The *Grand Rapids Democrat,* the same day (October 27), failed to make the appropriate distinction. Kuyper's direct comments in the speech about political parties notwithstanding, the newspaper in reporting the speech claimed Kuyper's vision as its own. In so doing the *Democrat* started a grand Grand Rapids tradition: "A true Calvinist is a Democrat! A Republican!" The joys of a "third way" had not yet been discovered.

HE IS A DEMOCRAT

Dr. Kuyper, the Distinguished Liberal Holland Leader

NOT BIGOTED OR NARROW

Addressed a Large Audience in the Auditorium Wednesday Night with Patriotic Sentiments

When Dr. Abraham Kuyper of Amsterdam, Holland, faced the splendid audience gathered to hear him at the Auditorium last evening he might easily have imagined himself back in his native land. Certainly few if any cities, even in the Netherlands, could have turned out a larger or more intelligent body of Holland-speaking citizens than that which greeted the distinguished gentleman last evening. The meeting was opened with prayer by Rev. A. Bursma and music by a double male quartette. Upon the platform sat the reception committee, consisting of Rev. De Bey, Rev. Buursma, Rev. Warnshuis, Prof. Beuker of the Theological Institute, Rev. Ten Hoor, Rev. Ekster, Rev. Kelser, Rev. J. H. Vos, Sir John Steketee, J. A. S. Verdler, Leonard Benjamin, J. B. Hulst, S. S. Postma, Cornelius Dosker, and Professors Kollen, Winter and Disker, of Hope College. The stage was draped with the American and Holland flags. The proceedings were entirely in the Holland language.

Dr. Abraham Kuyper is chief professor at the Vrije University of Amsterdam, member of the Holland house of representatives, a leader of the Liberal party, editor of the Standaard and the Heraut, and champion of Calvinism. He is considered the most influential Hollander in the world today. He will be 62 years of age next Saturday and though at first bitterly opposed and even threatened by "white-cap" letters, he is now a leader.

He held his audience as if spellbound for three hours last night. He has all the qualities and ideas of a good American citizen. He complimented America for doing in nearly eighty days what took other nations eighty years to accomplish; he believes in immigration, since cross-breeding in man, as well as in animals and plants, gives a new and better offspring and says that if the "survival of the fittest" is the law, Holland will live forever: that Holland is the birthplace of home rule or social autonomy, and referred to Motley's, Campbell's and

Griffith's histories of Holland as authority for the statement that all America's best institutions had their origin in Holland.

Dr. Kuyper, being the Calvinist leader, is a Democrat. In answer to why so many Hollanders were republican in politics he said they should not be. He quoted from the Democratic platform of '96 the following:

"We reaffirm our allegiance to those great principles of justice and liberty upon which our institutions are founded and which the Democratic party has advocated from Jefferson's time to our own freedom of speech, freedom of the press, freedom of conscience and the preservation of personal rights." Also this: "The Democratic party has always been the exponent of political liberty and religious freedom and it renews its obligations and reaffirms its devotion to these fundamental principles of the constitution."

He assured his audience that America was different from France, further advising them not to be too conservative, but more liberal and in favor of home-rule as expounded by the Democratic party, "for these are the genuine and underlying principles of Holland."

"That," said Dr. Kuyper, pointing to the Dutch flag, "is my flag, and this," pointing to the American colors, "is yours." The sentiment was enthusiastically applauded. He urged his auditors to become Americans in everything and not merely expatriated Hollanders.

The use of the English language in daily life, though not to the absolute exclusion of the Holland, he declared necessary to good citizenship. The sturdy virtues of the Dutch should serve their purpose in forming American character as they have in the past; the vices should be left behind.

The similarity of the Dutch and American forms of government was dwelt upon to some length, the speaker declaring that Holland, even more than England, had to a large extent shaped our American institutions.

While in New York Dr. Kuyper said he was struck with the fact that the political banners bore the names of two men of Dutch ancestry, Theodore Roosevelt and Augustus Van Wyck. He was greatly pleased to know that the gallant leader of the Rough Riders bore a Dutch name.

After the speaker had finished Rev. De Bey offered a prayer and the male chorus sang Luther's grand old hymn, "Een Vaste Burg." The meeting closed with the singing of the Doxology by the entire audience standing, after which an impromptu reception was held by Dr. Kuyper upon the stage. He left for Holland City upon a late train.

The singers had intended to render the more modern national hymn of Holland beginning with the words, "Let him in whom true Dutch blood flows untainted, pure, and free," but Dr. Kuyper objected to the restrictive sentiment of the words. The professor has Swiss and German blood himself and believes that a nation becomes strong by intermarriage with other nations.

*   *

Apparently this was too much for the editors of the *Grand Rapids Herald*, which on the next day (October 28) picked up the gauntlet thrown down by its rival to refute the claims made in the *Democrat* headline the previous day.

IS NOT A DEMOCRAT

MISREPRESENTATIONS AS TO
REV. DR. ABRAHAM KUYPER

Hollanders Are Indignant Over the Affair, and it is Branded as an Insult — Vice Consul Steketee's Statement

For some misstatements which were made by one of the Grand Rapids papers a misunderstanding has arisen as to the political belief of Dr. Abraham Kuyper, the Dutch statesman who lectured to a large audience at the Auditorium on Wednesday evening. Such statements Grand Rapids Hollanders brand as absolutely false, and those with whom he is well acquainted say on the contrary the doctor is a thorough republican. In an interview with a reporter, Dr. Kuyper said that he would not advise anyone to vote the democrat ticket, maintaining that the principles of the democrat party, fully lived up to, would deprive the country of its present good government, freedom and prosperity.

Vice Consul Steketee said yesterday: "Dr. Kuyper is not only a republican; he is a protectionist of the strongest sort. He is against free trade of any kind in any country. In Holland he fought free trade. He was the champion of republican principles. In addition to his views on the tariff question he is in harmony with the opinions of republicans on the money question being an advocate of the gold standard, maintaining that the sound money platform is the only plausible position for a well educated man to take. Dr. Kuyper considered it an insult, that he was called a democrat when he had stated his principles so plainly."

*   *

The skirmish was not yet over. The *Grand Rapids Democrat* a day later (October 29) published the following letter with an interpretation that attempted to drive a wedge between Kuyper and those Republicans who had claimed him. Here Kuyper's comment about being a "Holland democrat" gets an interesting twist.

DR. KUYPER'S DEMOCRACY

Appears to Have Been Too Strong
for Consul Steketee

Editor of the Democrat: I notice that *The Herald* this morning publishes an interview with Vice Consul Steketee regarding Dr. Kuyper's politics. He says that he is a Republican on all the issues and planks of the platform. The day before in the report of Dr. Kuyper's lecture *The Herald* said that in an interview with the doctor he stated that he was a Democrat in the Holland sense of the word.

There is no verbatim report of the lecture, but we learn from one who took notes that Dr. Kuyper said that since he was in a free country he would speak freely, meaning that he care not what the majority believed, he would state his views. The doctor spoke of home rule or "local autonomy," as he called it, as being of Dutch origin and named Campbell's history as authority for the statement that all our institutions and form of government had originated in Holland, meaning thereby the principles of freedom, liberty and justice. His manners of speech showed that he was surprised so many of the Hollanders were Republicans and the facial expression of those on the stage gave a similar impression.

He quoted the Democratic platform as containing those principles of freedom, liberty and justice and then advised the people to defend the principles of old Holland and not follow a political party like so many sheep.

He defined Calvinism not as theological principle alone, but as a world principle of general freedom.

There was no applause when the speaker quoted the Democratic platform and it was evident that he did not voice the sentiment of the majority of the audience. He warned them against conservatism and pleaded for more liberality and energy, stating that only a Calvinist had push and energy.

Knickerbocker
October 28, 1898.

*   *

The journalistic battle (Kuyper must truly have felt at home!) came to an end when Kuyper himself tried to clarify the issue by means of a letter to the

Grand Rapids Democrat. The editors in their headlines as well as their editorial "clarification," however, were clearly not prepared to concede defeat. "This settles it!"? Not quite. Once again, Kuyper would have felt at home, and also again, *plus ça change, de plus la même chose.*

THIS SETTLES IT

Dr. Kuyper Tells What He Said Last Week

HE IS A GOOD DEMOCRAT

Believes in Fair Trade and a Double Standard

Opposes Protective Tariffs

Editor of *The Democrat:* In your number of October 27, I have been introduced as "a Democrat," and it has been reported that in my address in the Auditorium, "in answer to why so many Hollanders were Republicans," I should have given as my opinion "that they should not be so."

Owing to my using the Dutch language your reporter evidently misunderstood my statement. Allow me to briefly repeat it here as I gave it in my "free talk."

I insisted upon the duty of every free and, therefore, responsible citizen, and so also of my compatriots, never blindly to follow any political party, but to draw from his own Calvinistic principles his decision why to support the one and to resist the other.

Thereupon I read the preamble of the Democratic platform of Chicago, 1896, and drew the attention of my audience to these words: "We reaffirm our allegiance to those great principles of justice and liberty upon which our institutions are founded, and which the Democratic party has advocated from Jefferson's time." Regarding the mentioning of Jefferson's name, I reminded my hearers that Jefferson, in 1793, took his stand as an advocate of the principles of the French revolution, and that it was Hamilton who declared at that time "that the American revolution was as little akin to the principles of 1789, as a Puritan woman of New England was like the infidel heroine of a French novel." Thence I deduced the conclusion that no true Calvinist could support a political party which thus openly declared its sympathy to Jefferson's principles. On the other hand I pointed to the fact that the same platform "reaffirmed its devotion to the maintenance of local autonomy (local self-government), and this was a point, fully in accordance with our Calvinistic principles.

This brought me to the conclusion perfectly to understand why the Hollanders were inclined to side with the Republicans; not, concealing, however, my regret that the Republican platform of 1896 did not as openly reaffirm Hamilton's Calvinistic principles as their opponents publicly uphold Jefferson's.

I see that another paper of your charming city considers me to be an absolute antagonist of free trade, at every time and in every country, and in addition to this as an advocate of the gold standard. The truth is, that I was always going in for fair trade, and considered protective duties avoidable, as soon as other nations practically closed their markets for our imports; and from what, during my short trip, I have seen of America's social condition, I feel confirmed to this opinion. As to the question of "sound money," I have always pleaded for the "double standard," but under the explicit condition that the value of the silver coin should be regulated by means of an International convention.

Finally I add that in the Netherlands I am known as a Christian democrat, an expression not at all to be confounded with the name "Democrat" in the designation of one of your political parties.

We Christian, or if you please, Calvinistic democrats in the Netherlands, were always considering the principles of the French revolution, which Jefferson advocated, as the very target for our Calvinistic bullets.

I thank you for the obliging insertion of these few lines and remain respectfully,

Dr. A. Kuyper

Member of the States General, Holland.
Holland City, Oct. 28, 1898.
The *Democrat:* Sunday, October 30, 1898.

EDITORIAL: DR. KUYPER AND DEMOCRATS

It is clear from Rev. Abraham Kuyper's letter in regard to his political opinions — which *The Democrat* is glad to publish, as it would not willingly misrepresent so distinguished a visitor — that if he could study American politics for six months he would be the hottest kind of a Democrat. He favors local self-government; a cardinal principal of the Democratic party. He favors a tariff for revenue, seeing as all Democrats see, that tariff duties for revenue are unavoidable, and that tariff laws in one country necessitate the levying of duties more or less retaliatory by other countries. Dr. Kuyper also favors bimetallism and opposes the single gold standard. He favors an international agreement as to the ratio — which the Democratic party has never opposed, although it has not thought it obtainable — but which the present Republican party, in its fidelity to gold alone, has shown itself decidedly opposed to in spite of pledges in its party platform.

*   *

It is fitting here to give the final word to Kuyper himself. In his 1916 definitive exposition of the Antirevolutionary Party's political program, Kuyper advocates the role of diverse political parties in a democratic society and even celebrates multiparty diversity.[3] Nonetheless, where there is basic consensus about the nation's identity, political party formation will fall out along three general orientations depending on whether the present situation is judged positively or negatively and, in the case of the latter, at what pace and rate change is sought. Three answers, generally identifiable under the broad rubrics of *radical, liberal,* or *conservative* (498-501). It is in this connection that Kuyper notes the confusion brought about by the American pattern of allegiance to only two political parties. Furthermore, he mildly laments the fact that party allegiance is often a matter of simple birthright; one is born into a Republican or Democrat family and unthinkingly toes the political party line when voting. Political principles thus vanish into the background; the citizen disappears while the party remains. However, the parties lost their souls in the process (500).

3. Abraham Kuyper, *Antirevolutionaire Staatkunde,* 2 vols. (Kampen: Kok, 1916), 1:486-588; page references that follow in parentheses in the text are to this volume.

Permissions

The author and publisher gratefully acknowledge permission to include the following:

Chapter 1

"Goddess of Democracy," © Peter Turnley/CORBIS.

Frederic E. Church, *Niagara*, 1857, 42½ × 90½, oil on canvas, in the collection of the Corcoran Gallery of Art, Washington, D.C., Museum Purchase, Gallery Fund, 76.15.

George Caleb Bingham, *Daniel Boone Escorting Settlers Through the Cumberland Gap*, 1851-52. Oil on canvas, 36½ × 50¼. Washington University Gallery of Art, St. Louis. Gift of Nathaniel Philips, 1890.

Albert Bierstadt, *Rocky Mountains, Landers Peak,* The Metropolitan Museum of Art, Rogers Fund, 1907 (07.123). All rights reserved, The Metropolitan Museum of Art.

Emanuel Leutze, *Westward the Course of Empire Takes Its Way (Westward Ho!),* courtesy of National Museum of American Art, Washington, D.C./Art Resource, N.Y.

Tompkins Harrison Matteson, *The Last of the Race,* oil on canvas, 1847, 39¾ × 50 inches, accession no. 1931.1. © Collection of the New-York Historical Society.

Cartoon of Kuyper amid cheering crowd, from *Dr. Kuyper in de Caricatur* (Amsterdam: Van Holkema & Warendorf, 1909).

"Cleveland's Welcome. . . ." Appears by permission and with the cooperation of the Historisch Documentatiecentrum voor het Nederlands Protestantisme (1800-heden), Vrije Universiteit, Amsterdam.

Chapter 3

Carl Gutenberg, *The Tea Tax Tempest*, 1778, courtesy of the Library of Congress.

Giovanni Battista Nini, *Benjamin Franklin*, 1777, courtesy of the National Portrait Gallery, Smithsonian Institute/Art Resource, N.Y.

Jean Honoré of Fragonard (1706-32), Franklin being crowned by Liberty, engraving, with Turgot's tribute, "He has Stolen Lightning from the Sky and the Sceptre from Tyrants." Columbia University, New York, N.Y., USA. Courtesy of Art Resource, N.Y.

Painting of the assassination of Coligny by Giorgio Vasari from the series commissioned by Pope Gregory XIII for the *Sala Regia* in the Vatican palace. Courtesy of Alinari/Art Resource, N.Y.

Chapter 6

"Pardon me! It was instinctive!" from *Dr. Kuyper in de Caricatur* (Amsterdam: Van Holkema & Warendorf, 1909).

Chapter 7

"Aanblik van de Tweede Kamer." Appears by permission and with the cooperation of the Historisch Documentatiecentrum voor het Nederlands Protestantisme (1800-heden), Vrije Universiteit, Amsterdam.

Gift presented to Kuyper by the ARP. Appears by permission and with the cooperation of the Historisch Documentatiecentrum voor het Nederlands Protestantisme (1800-heden), Vrije Universiteit, Amsterdam.

Kuyper addressing a crowd of supporters. Appears by permission and with the cooperation of the Historisch Documentatiecentrum voor het Nederlands Protestantisme (1800-heden), Vrije Universiteit, Amsterdam.

Index

abortion, 89, 103, 125, 126, 277n.66, 359, 371, 372, 376, 386, 392, 409, 411, 421, 433
absolutism, 375
Acton, Lord John, xviii, 130, 137, 167-72, 279
  on American civil war, 161-65
  on Calvinism, 158n.86
  on freedom of conscience, 179-80
  on liberty in America, 157
  on religion and freedom, 167-69
  on St. Bartholomew's Day Massacre, 174-77
Acton Institute, 169n.119, 423
Adams, John, 435
aesthetics, 7, 29-30
affirmative action, 125, 359
Afscheiding. See Secession of 1834
Ahlstrom, Sidney, 228, 230
alienation, 293-95
allusion, 29
alternative institutions, 439-40
America, 254
  as Christian nation, 14
  destiny, 42, 122-23, 136
  Evangelical and Catholic common concern for, 390-91
  exceptionalism, 115, 122, 232, 236

experiment in ordered liberty, xxi, 14, 32-33, 157-59, 162, 172, 260
  future linked to Calvinism, 68
  as kingdom of God, 381
  as mosaic, 346
  myth of, 135, 152-53, 157
  as new Israel, 32, 123, 194, 200, 224
  religious activity, 115-20, 159-60, 231-33
  Revolution, 13, 151, 172, 261
  wars of, 122
American Civil Liberties Union, 335, 414n.11, 430
Americans United for Separation of Church and State, 100, 360, 414n.11, 422, 430
Anabaptists, 129, 378, 453n.23
Anema, A., 444n.4
anthropology, 251, 278, 302
anti-Catholicism, 109
Antichrist, 207-8
Anti-Defamation League, 369-72
Antirevolutionary Party, xi n.3, 57, 64, 67, 190n.10, 285-86, 291, 342-43, 396, 423
anti-Semitism, 106-7, 109, 369, 372
antithesis, xvii, 46, 209, 352, 393-94
Apocalypse, 205-12
Aquinas, Thomas, 25n.76, 108, 169, 318